Library of
Davidson College

Readings in
the Economics of
Industrial Organization

Economic Series
Under the Editorship of
Clark W. Reynolds
Stanford University

READINGS IN MICROECONOMICS
edited by
William Breit and Harold M. Hochman
University of Virginia

MODERN POLITICAL ARITHMETIC
Bruce F. Davie and Bruce F. Duncombe
Georgetown University

ECONOMIC ANALYSIS AND INDUSTRIAL STRUCTURE
Douglas Needham
State University of New York, Brockport

READINGS IN THE ECONOMICS OF INDUSTRIAL ORGANIZATION
edited by
Douglas Needham
State University of New York, Brockport

READINGS IN THE HISTORY OF ECONOMIC THEORY
edited by
Ingrid H. Rima
Temple University

Readings in the Economics of Industrial Organization

Edited by

DOUGLAS NEEDHAM

State University of New York, Brockport

HOLT, RINEHART AND WINSTON, INC.
New York, Chicago, San Francisco, Atlanta
Dallas, Montreal, Toronto, London, Sydney

Copyright © 1970 by Holt, Rinehart and Winston, Inc.
All rights reserved
The copyrighted selections in this volume are reprinted
by special permission of their respective copyright holders
and may not be reprinted without similar permission from them.
Library of Congress Catalog Card Number: 70-94890
SBN: 03-078840-4
Printed in the United States of America
9 8 7 6 5 4 3 2 1

Foreword

Professor Needham has made an ingenious selection from among the most topical contributions to the literature on the theory and revealed structure of industry. While designed as a companion to his pioneering volume, *Economic Analysis and Industrial Structure*, this collection of readings stands by itself as a landmark in the field, dealing as it does with the elements of managerial decision-making, economies of scale, growth and firm size, barriers to entry as related to rates of return, product differentiation and advertising as alternatives to price competition, and the place of public policy in a free enterprise system.

Much time has been spent by writers on industry speculating about the relative merits of hypothetical market structures. However, the analysis of the firm and industry as they actually exist; the way in which competition occurs in practice; and the facts about size, structure, and profitability of modern enterprise as they bear on industrial organization theory have been neglected. Much of the material in this volume represents recent quantitative analysis designed to dispel myths and return the theory of industrial organization to a more solid empirical foundation. The fact that these readings disclose a number of unresolved questions about major issues in the field is not an indictment of the subject matter but rather an illustration that in contemporary economics much remains to be done before it will be possible to devise a fully operational theory of industrial enterprise.

A number of standard simplifications in the conventional textbook literature are shattered by the evidence in this volume: (a) firms' objectives often go far beyond simple short-run profit maximization, therefore profit maximization may not always be consistent with the goals of a "rational" industrial decision-maker; (b) technical economies of scale must be set against managerial diseconomies of scale; (c) methods of estimating economies of scale through engineering studies, statistical cost analysis, and the survivor technique look at different problems and therefore provide ambiguous results; (d) there is little factual evidence that the rate of growth of a firm is influenced by its initial size; (e) there is evidence that seller concentration is influenced by barriers to entry and that this results in relatively higher rates of return on capital; (f) seller concentration and research and development activities seem to be positively related, although the direction of causality is indeterminate; (g) advertising expenditure and seller concentration do not appear to be closely correlated, although advertising is positively associated with profits; (h) in cases where firms pursue nonprofit-maximizing objectives or when other sectors of the economy evidence barriers to entry, monopolistic behavior in a particular industry may be compatible with welfare-maximizing resource allocation; (i) information agreements may be more restrictive of competition than are price agreements, and therefore more demanding of public attention; (j) while mergers can act in restraint of trade they may in some cases bring about greater efficiency and welfare than do independent business units; (k) since information is not costless in the real world, advertising expenditures may sometimes provide an equivalent service to consumers; and (l) to the extent that Research and Development provides external economies to society in addition to internal returns to industry, there may be a tendency toward systematic underinvestment in R & D in a purely private enterprise economy. Thus, in referring to the last selection by Harvard economist Kenneth J. Arrow, the editor states: "R & D levels in the economy may in the absence of public policy measures be lower than desirable from the point of view of maximizing the welfare of the community." Architects of future industrial states may well examine these blueprints of the past to assure that their new utopias will be consistent with the actual conditions of technology, individual behavior, and social welfare.

—Clark W. Reynolds

Stanford, California
December 1969

PREFACE

The branch of economic analysis referred to as Industrial Organization is concerned with the structure and behavior of business enterprises and with the implications of this behavior for resource allocation and individual welfare. This volume brings together a number of journal articles in which the interpretative skill, seminal idea, or empirical contributions greatly enhance one's understanding of these matters.

The collection does not pretend to be comprehensive. There are, for example, no papers dealing with the relationship between vertical integration, or diversification, and other dimensions of industrial structure and behavior, even though these relationships are of considerable importance. Such omissions reflect the limitation on the length of the volume and the absence in the professional journals, at the time the list of selections was made, of articles dealing with some aspects of industrial organization in a particularly lucid or illuminating manner. Several articles included in the volume have been reprinted elsewhere since the final list of selections was made. Despite the resulting increase in accessibility, these have been retained in order to preserve the original format of the volume stressing key relationships in industrial organization.

The articles in this collection have been grouped into five sections dealing with the motives underlying firms' behavior, cost conditions, pricing behavior, other features of behavior—including advertising and research and development activities—and public policy aspects of some facets of firms' behavior. Brief introductions to each section comment on the relevance and implications of the articles.

The volume is intended to serve as a supplementary text for courses in Industrial Organization, both at undergraduate and graduate levels. Developments in professional journals tend to be incorporated into basic textbooks only after an often lengthy lapse of time, and in undergraduate courses it is inappropriate to relegate journal articles to the category of advanced reading if they either supersede or greatly simplify the exposition of previous knowledge.

In the preparation of the volume, I have received help from numerous people. Primary acknowledgment is, of course, due to the authors and publishers who gave permission for their material to be reprinted. Specific acknowledgment and complete identification of the original source of each article are found at the beginning of each selection. In addition, I wish to thank the students of Industrial Organization and the colleagues who commented on a preliminary list of selections. The assistance of the publisher, especially Miss Susan Sommers, was invaluable in supplying encouragement and stimulus needed to insure completion of the project without undue delay.

—DOUGLAS NEEDHAM

Brockport, New York
December 1969

CONTENTS

Foreword v
Preface vii

PART I
FIRMS' OBJECTIVES 1

1. *Theories of the Firm: Marginalist, Behavioral, Managerial* 3
Fritz Machlup

2. *The Motives of Managers, Environmental Restraints, and the Theory of Managerial Enterprise* 32
William L. Baldwin

3. *Profit, Growth and Sales Maximization* 48
John Williamson

4. *The Arithmetic of Capital-Budgeting Decisions* 63
Ezra Solomon

PART II
COST CONDITIONS 71

5. *Economies of Scale in Industrial Plants* 74
John Haldi and David Whitcomb

6. *Hierarchical Control and Optimum Firm Size* 89
Oliver E. Williamson

7. *The Economies of Scale* 110
George J. Stigler

8. *What Does the Survivor Technique Show about Economies of Scale?* 129
William G. Shepherd

9. *Firm Size and Rate of Growth* 142
Stephen Hymer and Peter Pashigian

PART III
PRICING BEHAVIOR 161

10. *"Large" and "Small" Numbers in the Theory of the Firm* 164
G. C. Archibald

11. *A Theory of Oligopoly* 171
George J. Stigler

12. *New Developments on the Oligopoly Front* 194
Franco Modigliani

13. *Seller Concentration, Barriers to Entry, and Rates of Return in Thirty Industries 1950–1960* 214
H. Michael Mann

PART IV
PRODUCT DIFFERENTIATION ACTIVITIES 235

14. *Market Structure and the Employment of Scientists and Engineers* 238
F. M. Scherer

15. *Advertising and Competition* 246
Lester G. Telser

16. *Advertising, Market Structure and Performance* 278
William S. Comanor and Thomas A. Wilson

17. *The Firm's Decision Process: An Econometric Investigation* 311
Dennis C. Mueller

18. *A Dissenting View of Duopoly and Spatial Competition* 339
Nicos E. Devletoglou

PART V
FIRMS' BEHAVIOR AND PUBLIC POLICY 359

19. *Information Agreements—A Problem in Search of a Policy* 363
D. P. O'Brien and D. Swann

20. *Mergers and the Market for Corporate Control*   379
Henry G. Manne

21. *The Economics of Information*   392
George J. Stigler

22. *The Economics of Advertising*   410
Harry G. Johnson

23. *Economic Welfare and the Allocation of Resources for Invention*   415
Kenneth J. Arrow

Readings in
the Economics of
Industrial Organization

PART I

FIRMS' OBJECTIVES

The various characteristics of a business enterprise, including the type and level of output, the number of employees and kinds of capital equipment, and the level of advertising and research and development activities have one thing in common. They are the result of decisions made by the people who control the operations of the enterprise. From the numerous alternatives available, a firm's decision-makers will select that combination of characteristics which best achieves their objectives—subject to the constraints imposed upon the decisions by the firm's economic environment. The nature of the decision-makers' objectives is therefore fundamentally important in influencing the characteristics of the firm as a whole.

Traditionally, in economic analysis, the firm's objective was assumed to be profit maximization. In recent years the manner in which the pursuit of alternative goals affect a firm's behavior has increasingly attracted the attention of economists. Part I of this volume consists of four articles dealing with the goals which motivate managers of business firms. Professor Machlup's paper is an instructive survey of different theories of the firm, stressing the multidimensional character of a business enterprise, demonstrating that different concepts of the firm may be appropriate for different purposes, and describing the circumstances in which profit maximization may be adopted as a reasonable approximation of managers' objectives. In "The Motives of Managers, Environmental Restraints, and the Theory of Managerial Enterprise," W. L. Baldwin examines a number of aspects of managerial behavior which are frequently regarded as evidence of the pursuit of objectives other than profit maximization, suggesting that they may be consistent with profit maximization within different environmental constraints. In contrast, in the third article, John Williamson investigates and compares the implications of several different objectives for the output level of a firm confronted by the same set of environmental conditions. The article by E. Solomon contains a particularly lucid exposition of the rationale of the present-value and internal-rate-of-return decision rules frequently applied to decision-making in a multiperiod setting. This is particularly pertinent since student and practitioner alike are sometimes confused by the possibility of multiple internal rates of return for a single investment project, or are insufficiently aware of the assumptions implicit in the use of these rules and the circumstances in which their use is appropriate.

1

Theories of the Firm: Marginalist, Behavioral, Managerial*

Fritz Machlup

Last year, when it was my task to plan the program for the annual meeting of our association, a friend suggested that, with twenty years having passed since the outbreak of the "marginalism controversy," it was appropriate to review what has since happened to the embattled theory of the firm. The topic did not fit the general theme I had chosen for the 1965 meeting, but I reasoned that 1966 would give me a good opportunity to undertake the review myself.

THE BATTLEFIELD REVISITED

So let us recall that literary feud and the warriors, and let us revisit the battlefield. The major battlefield was the *American Economic Review*, with six articles and communications between March 1946 and March 1947 [16] † [43] [21] [17] [22] [44]. There had been earlier gunfire elsewhere, chiefly in the *Oxford Economic Papers* in 1939 [14]. But, since the shooting then was not returned and it takes at least two opponents to join battle, it must be agreed that the real hostilities were the exchanges in the *AER*.

The fight was spirited, even fierce. Thousands of students of economics, voluntary or involuntary readers, have been either shocked or entertained by the violence of some of the blows exchanged and may have thought that the opponents must have become mortal enemies forever. These readers would have been wrong. Even before we came out for the last round of the fight, we exchanged

> Reprinted from *The American Economic Review*, March 1967, pp. 1–33, by permission of the author and publisher.

*Presidential address delivered, in a shorter version, at the Seventy-ninth Annual Meeting of the American Economic Association, San Francisco, December 28, 1966.

† Editor's Note: References in square brackets are listed at the end of the chapter.

friendly letters (December 1946) assuring each other that we would bear no grudges.

We have remained the best of friends; for several years now Richard Lester and I have been colleagues in the same department; and, as a token of our friendship, he has generously accepted my invitation to share this platform with me today as chairman of the session. Thus the veterans of both sides of the War of 1946 are now joined in revisiting the battlefield. This, incidentally, does not mean that either of us has succeeded in converting the other to the "true faith."

What was the outcome of the controversy? Who won? We could not possibly say if we have not first agreed on precisely what the shooting was about. I have heard it said that Machlup won the battle but Lester won the war. What this means, however, cannot be known unless we know what the issues and objectives of the war had been. Was it merely to make economics safe for or from marginalism? Were there not several other issues being fought over?

SOME OF THE MAJOR ISSUES

There were no doubt a good many contentions of all sorts—major, minor, essential, incidental, interpretative, factual, methodological, substantive, and all the rest. To present a complete catalogue of the issues involved would be too ambitious a task for this occasion, but a partial listing might be helpful.

The chief issue, of course, was whether marginal analysis was invalid and ought to be discarded, especially as far as the theory of prices, cost, wages, and employment in manufacturing industry is concerned. This issue, however, implied the question of the correct interpretation of marginal analysis, including the tenets of the marginal-productivity principle. In this connection, differences in the models of the firm customarily used in different kinds of analysis became relevant. Involved here was the question of whether the postulate of maximizing money profits led to conclusions very different from those derivable from assumptions of conduct guided by a variety of largely nonpecuniary considerations.

Underlying all these questions were some issues of general scientific methodology: the legitimacy and usefulness of abstract theorizing on the basis of unrealistic assumptions, or perhaps on the basis of assumptions regarded as "reasonable" though not "universally true." These issues, in particular, were whether an assumption of profit maximization as the effective objective of the firm in the theoretical model may be accepted as a tenable hypothesis only if it can be verified that all or a majority of those who actually run business firms in the real world agree that this is their only or major objective, that they are capable of obtaining all the information and of performing all the calculations needed for the realization of that objective, and are really carrying out the actions found to be optimal in this fashion; or, alternatively, whether all these tests may be dispensed with and the assumption of profit maximization nevertheless accepted as a fruitful postulate from which conclusions can be derived which correspond with what can be observed in the records of prices and quantities.

Concerning the empirical testing of theoretical conclusions, there were issues of the validity of surveys through mailed questionnaires and of the proper interpretation of responses to various types of questions about managerial judgment. In the background of the whole controversy, but undoubtedly of pervasive significance, was the comparative acceptability of empirical findings to the effect that the elasticity of demand for labor was virtually zero and of the conventional theoretical inference that the elasticity was normally above zero.

Realizing how manifold were the issues of the controversy, one can appreciate that no clear decision can be made about its outcome. Some of the issues had been raised decades or centuries before 1946 and were not decided in this confrontation one way or the other. Attacks on the assumption of maximizing behavior and on the lack of realism in price theory have occurred with great regularity ever since "economic man" and similar postulates were introduced. The running battles between the classical and the historical schools were largely on these points. The *Methodenstreit* of 1883–84 dealt essentially with the same issues. And in the United States, institutionalism may be seen as a movement animated by the same spirit of protest against abstract theory.

However, the particular form of explicit marginalism (under the name of "theory of the firm") which became the target of the attacks of 1939 and 1946 had only come into being in the 1930's—if one suppresses the memory of the great master of 1838 [9]. Ironically, some interpreter of recent history of economic thought—I have forgotten who it was—regarded the 1933–34 versions of the theory of the firm [8] [32] [41] as the theorists' concession to institutionalism, as attempts to supplement the neoclassical model of the firm under atomistic competition with some "more realistic" models allowing for a greater variety of conditions. It was this theory of the profit-maximizing firm in all sorts of market positions, in monopolistic and oligopolistic competition as well as in pure and perfect competition, that was attacked by the researchers in Oxford; and it was the marginal-productivity principle in the explanation of the demand for labor on the part of the individual firm that was the prime target of the attack of 1946.

If the chief aim of the attack was to force the abandonment or subversion of marginalism, and if the chief aim of the defense was to turn back the subversive forces and secure the reign of marginalism once and for all, then, to be sure, the war of 1946 ended in a draw. Look at the textbooks and you will find that marginalism has continued to dominate the teaching of microeconomics, perhaps though with occasional reservations and references to current attempts at greater realism. But look at the journals and monographs and you find that research on alternative approaches to the theory of the firm is regularly reported with the implication that a superior theory may eventually replace marginalism. This replacement, however, according to the proponents of the best-known alternatives to marginalism, is expected chiefly with regard to industries where firms are few and competition is ineffective. The marginalist solution of price determination under conditions of heavy competition is not seriously contested.

In pointing this out, I am not trying to claim that marginal analysis is invincible and forever irreplaceable. If I follow the philosophy of science which, instead of pronouncing theories "false" or "true," distinguishes only between those "rejected" and those "still open to criticism" [30, pp. 246–48], the only victory that can be claimed for the cause of marginalism is that it is still open to criticism. I must go beyond this and concede that some anti-marginalist suggestions have led in recent years to a number of revisions in the marginal analysis of the firm which amount to the incorporation of other goals besides money profits into expanded marginalist objective functions.

THE ALTERNATIVE APPROACHES

In their arguments against the profit-maximization model the various alternative approaches to the theory of the firm are very much alike; only their positive programs can distinguish them.

The program of behaviorism is to reject preconceptions and assumptions and to rely only on observation of overt behavior. Thus, behaviorism rejects the assumption of marginal analysis that economic action is directed by the objective to maximize the attainment of ends with given means, and that business action can be deduced from a postulate that firms attempt to maximize money profits. Instead, we are directed to *observe* how businessmen really act and by what processes they reach decisions.

Perhaps it is not entirely fair to suggest here an association between "behaviorism" and the working program of the proponents of a "behavioral theory of the firm" [10]. In any case, behavioral research proposes to observe and study the "real processes," in the sense of a "well-defined sequence of behaviors" by which decisions are reached in "actual business organizations." The hope—faithfully inductive—is to develop a theory "with generality beyond the specific firms studied" [10, p. 2]. Such a theory will be based on "four major sub-theories" regarding "organizational *goals*, organizational *expectations*, organizational *choice*, and organizational *control*" [10, p. 21]. It is assumed that five organizational goals—a production goal, an inventory goal, a sales goal, a market-share goal, and the profit goal—become the subject of bargaining among the various members of the "coalition" which make up the business organization but that the goals are continually adapted and are being pressed with varying force [10, pp. 40–43]. The behavior theory of the firm, with regard to the determination of prices and outputs, will run in terms of a "quasi resolution of conflict" within the organization, of an "adaptively rational, multiple-objective process" with responses to "short-run feedback on performance" and with continuing "organizational learning" [10, pp. 269–70].

This behavioral approach has been characterized as striving for "realism in process," in contrast to approaches aiming at more "realism in motivation" [48, p. 11]. Such realism in motivation is felt to be needed chiefly because of the separation of ownership and control in the modern corporation, whose managements have great power and wide discretion.

In principle, I could expect three different views to be taken regarding the relative independence of corporation management: (1) Whereas owners would run their business chiefly with a view to a maximum of money profits, managers run it with several supplementary and partly competing goals in mind. (2) Whereas owners, especially wealthy ones, would often allow nonprofit considerations to enter their decision-making, managers have a sense of dedication and identification with the business that makes them the more single-minded seekers of profits. (3) Even if managers are inclined to indulge in seeking other goals as long as profits look satisfactory, they are as professionals, trained in the art and science of management, able to make better profits than the owners could ever hope to make running their own show.

What consequences can be drawn from this? One attitude would be to stick with the assumption of profit maximization because it is the simplest and is applicable with much less detailed information to the largest field.[1] Another attitude would be to insist on starkest realism with a complete catalogue of goals and indices of their effectiveness in each firm. A third attitude would be to select two or three of the most important managerial objectives of a type that can be reduced to quantitative analysis and to combine them in a single manageable "objective function." This third approach merges marginalism with managerialism in that it integrates money profits with other managerial goals within one formula of "maximizing behavior."

The question is whether managerial marginalism is prescribed for general application or only for so-called noncompetitive cases. Its most prominent proponents prefer to use the old formula, based on profit maximization, in situations where competition is effective and managerial discretion therefore narrowly circumscribed. In the next sections we shall discuss matters that at first blush may seem unrelated to this issue but on reflection can shed indirect light on it.

THE ANALOGY OF THE THEORETICAL AUTOMOBILE DRIVER

One of the best remembered points in my exposition was the use of an analogy designed to warn against mistaking theoretical variables and their links for realistic descriptions of observable processes. This was the analogy of the "theory of overtaking" automobiles on the highways [21, pp. 534–35].

Analogies are often misleading, but in this particular case it served its main purpose: to show that the theoretical variables need not be estimated and the theoretical equations need not be solved through actual calculation by the actors in the real world whose idealized types are supposed to perform these difficult operations in the models constructed for the explanation of recorded observations.[2] The critics of marginal analysis believed they had refuted it if they could show that the exact numerical calculations of marginal magnitudes—cost, reve-

[1] "To use marginalism in the theory of the firm it is not necessary to assert that firms attempt to maximize money profits only nor to deny that a goodly portion of all business behavior may be nonrational, thoughtless, blindly repetitive, deliberately traditional, or motivated by extra-economic objectives. It merely presupposes that the 'rational-economic' portion of business conduct is by and large sufficiently important to affect what is going on in the world to an extent large enough to warrant analysis; and that the substitution of money profits for a composite of pecuniary and nonpecuniary rewards simplifies the analysis so much that the gain in expediency far exceeds the loss in applicability" [23, pp. 30–31]. A similar view is expressed by Scitovsky: "Empirical studies of businessmen's behavior suggest the need for modifying or qualifying the assumption of profit maximization here and there, rather than scrapping it altogether. Accordingly, . . . we shall retain the assumption that the firm aims at maximizing its profit. But we shall regard this assumption as a working hypothesis rather than as a universal rule" [37, p. 111].

[2] The theoretical automobile driver had to estimate, among other things, the speeds of three vehicles and the distances between them, and to perform calculations involving potential acceleration and a few other things, before he could decide to overtake the truck ahead of him. An actual driver simply "sizes up" the situation and goes ahead.

nue, productivity—were difficult or impossible to perform by real decision-makers.

Yet, my analogy was only partially successful. An implication which should have been obvious has been widely overlooked: that the type of action assumed to be taken by the theoretical actor in the model under specified conditions need not be expected and cannot be predicted actually to be taken by any particular real actor. The empiricist's inclination is to verify the theoretically deduced action by testing individual behavior, although the theory serves only to explain and predict effects of mass behavior.

We may illustrate this again by means of the same analogy, the theory of overtaking. Assume a change of driving conditions occurs, say, that the roads have become wet and slippery and fog has reduced visibility. Theory enables us to predict that traffic will be slower and accidents more frequent, but it does not enable us to predict that any particular driver will drive more slowly or have an accident. The model of the reactions of the individual driver was not designed to explain the actual driving of any particular operator but only to explain the observable consequences of the observed change of conditions by deducing from the model the theoretical reactions of a hypothetical driver.

Our analogy can also show us the limitations of the model: the prediction will hold only if there is a large number of automobiles on the road. If only a very few cars are around, there may be no accident and there need not be a reduction in their speed. Conceivably, the operators may all be good and self-confident drivers. Marginal analysis of hypothetical driver reaction will suffice for explaining and predicting the consequences of a change in driving conditions if the number of automobiles on the highways is large. If the number is small, behavioral research will be needed, though it may or may not be worth the cost.

Still another use can be made of our analogy: to show the vast differences in the scope of questions to which answers can or cannot be expected with the aid of a given theory, for example, from the theory of overtaking as sketched in my article. Compare the following four questions: (1) How fast will traffic move? (2) How fast will the automobile driven by Mr. X move? (3) How will the speed of traffic be affected by fog? (4) How will the speed of Mr. X's driving be affected by fog?

The theory sketched by me offers no answer to the first question, because each of the variables specified may have very different values for different cars and drivers; it has no answer to the second question, and only a suggestion, a rebuttable presumption, for answering the fourth question, because the theory is not really concerned with particular persons or their actions and reactions. The theory is equipped only to answer the third question, regarding the effects of a change in driving conditions on automobile traffic in general, and even this answer will be qualitative only, without good clues to numerical results. It may be interesting to get answers to all four questions, but since Question 3 can be answered with a fraction of the information that would be needed to answer the other questions, it would be foolish to burden the models designed for Question 3 with irrelevant matters, or to reject such models because they cannot do what they are not designed to do.[3]

[3] A behavioral theory of automobile driving would probably study the process by which the decision to pass a truck is arrived at in a sequence of bickering among the

CONFUSION OF PURPOSE

The same sort of confusion about the scope of problems and models for their solution has been fostered in recent writings on the theory of the firm: models have been condemned or rejected because they could not be used for purposes for which they had not been designed, and significant differences in the questions to be answered have been obscured or underemphasized.

Let us again pose four typical questions and see which of them we might expect to answer with the aid of "price theory." (1) What will be the prices of cotton textiles? (2) What prices will the X Corporation charge? (3) How will the prices of cotton textiles be affected by an increase in wage rates? (4) How will the X Corporation change its prices when wage rates are increased?

Conventional price theory is not equipped to answer any but the third question; it may perhaps also suggest a rebuttable answer to the fourth question. But Questions 1 and 2 are out of reach. We could not obtain all the information that would be required for their answers and there is, therefore, no use burdening the models with variables remaining silent and inactive throughout the show.

We ought to guard against an easy misunderstanding of our denial that conventional price theory can predict actual prices of specified goods. Prediction of future prices of a particular commodity may in fact be quite manageable if we know its present price. It should be obvious, however, that this is Question 3, not Question 1. Or, one may be able to predict prices on the basis of good information on production cost. But this presupposes that we know the demand for the commodity and assume it will remain unchanged; which again comes down essentially to evaluations of changes of some variables with others held constant, that is, to Question 3.

If the number of firms producing cotton textiles is large and the X Corporation does not supply a very large part of the aggregate output of the industry, price theory may suggest an answer to Question 4, although this is not the purpose of the theory and there may be a considerable chance for the suggested answer to be wrong. The point is that a model of a theoretical firm in an industry consisting of a large number of firms can do with a much smaller number of assumptions, provided the model is used to predict, not the actual reactions of any one particular firm, but only the effects of the hypothetical reactions of numerous anonymous "reactors" (symbolic firms). If it were to be applied to predictions of reactions of a particular firm, the model would have to be much more richly endowed with variables and functions for which information could be obtained only at considerable effort and with results that may or may not be worth the cost of the required research.

My charge that there is widespread confusion regarding the purposes of the "theory of the firm" as used in traditional price theory refers to this: The model

---

members of the family: Mama and Sis trying to argue against taking an unnecessary risk, Sonny egging on his Dad to speed up and pass the truck "crawling" ahead of them. Moreover, the theory would not be satisfied with "explaining" the decision to overtake but it would also wish to determine the speed of driving, the frequency and length of stops at roadside stands, and all the rest.

of the firm in that theory is not, as so many writers believe, designed to serve to explain and predict the behavior of real firms; instead, it is designed to explain and predict changes in observed prices (quoted, paid, received) as effects of particular changes in conditions (wage rates, interest rates, import duties, excise taxes, technology, etc.). In this causal connection the firm is only a theoretical link, a mental construct helping to explain how one gets from the cause to the effect.[4] This is altogether different from explaining the behavior of a firm. As the philosopher of science warns, we ought not to confuse the *explanans* with the *explanandum*.

MISPLACED CONCRETENESS

To confuse the firm as a theoretical construct with the firm as an empirical concept, that is, to confuse a heuristic fiction with a real organization like General Motors or Atlantic & Pacific, is to commit the "fallacy of misplaced concreteness." This fallacy consists in using theoretic symbols as though they had a direct, observable, concrete meaning.

In some fields, investigators are protected from committing the fallacy, at least with regard to some of their problems, by the fact that a search for any empirical counterpart to the theoretical construct seems hopeless. Thus, some physicists working on particle theory were able to answer the question "Does the Neutrino Really Exist?" [11, pp. 139–41] laconically with "Who cares?" and to explain that any belief in the "real existence" of atoms, electrons, neutrinos, and all the rest, would hold up the progress of our knowledge. Some biologists working in genetics warned, after empirical genes were discovered, that these "operational genes" should not be confused with the "hypothetical genes," which had been useful constructs in explanatory models before the discovery of any empirical

---

[4] The same statement can be made about the household. The "household" in price theory is not an object of study; it serves only as a theoretical link between changes in prices and changes in labor services supplied and in consumer goods demanded. The hypothetical reactions of an imaginary decision-maker on the basis of assumed, internally consistent preference functions serve as the simplest and heuristically satisfactory explanation of empirical relationships between changes in prices and changes in quantities. In other words, the household in price theory is not an object of study.

Behavioral studies of real households are something entirely different. A realistic, behavioral theory of the household might conceivably distinguish the large, children-dominated household from a simpler, father-dominated one. The decisions in the children-dominated household, where mother frequently and father occasionally try to exercise some influence, are probably not consistent, since different preference systems are made explicit at various times, with varying decibels and gestures deployed to make them prevail over the preferences of other members of the family.

One can imagine studies on the behavior of particular households selected at random or in structured samples. If the researcher learns that a spoiled brat in a family wants to eat nothing but beef and throws a tantrum every time his mother tries to feed him other kinds of meat, a reduction in the price of chicken will probably not substantially increase the consumption of chicken in this family. Thus, the weight of the child's taste in the decision process of the family can explain a low elasticity of its demand for chicken. But none of this has much bearing on general price theory.

referents [42, p. 814]. Economists, however, know for sure that firms exist as empirical entities and, hence, they have a hard time keeping the theoretical firm and the empirical firm apart.

For certain economic problems the existence of the firm is of the essence. For example, if we study the size distribution of firms or the growth of the firm, the organization and some of its properties and processes are the very objects of the investigation. In such studies we insist on a high degree of correspondence between the model (the thought-object) and the observed object. For other problems, however, as for problems of competitive-price theory, any likeness between the theoretical construct of the firm and the empirical firm is purely coincidental.

Economists trained in scientific methodology understand this clearly. I might quote a dozen or more writers, but will confine myself to one quotation, which states that "in economic analysis, the business firm is a postulate in a web of logical connections" [15, p. 196]. Let me add the statement of another writer, who however was plaintiff rather than advocate when he wrote that "It is a fascinating paradox that the received theory of the firm, by and large, assumes that the firm does not exist" [45, p. 249].

Here is what I wrote on one of the several occasions when I have discussed this problem:

> ... the firm in the model world of economic micro-theory ought not to call forth any irrelevant associations with firms in the real world. We know, of course, that there are firms in reality and that they have boards of directors and senior and junior executives, who do, with reference to hundreds of different products, a great many things—which are entirely irrelevant for the microtheoretical model. The fictitious firm of the model is a "uni-brain," an individual decision-unit that has nothing to do but adjust the output and the prices of one or two imaginary products to very simple imagined changes in data [26, p. 133].

I went on, of course, to say that this purely fictitious single-minded firm, helpful as it is in competitive-price theory, will not do so much for us in the theory of monopoly and oligopoly. To explain and predict price reactions under monopoly and oligopoly we need more than the construct of a profit-maximizing reactor.[5] I shall come back to this after discussing the demands for "more realistic" assumptions where they are plainly irrelevant and therefore out of place.

---

[5] You may wonder whether I have changed my mind on these matters. Incidentally, I hold that it is important for scholars and scientists to have an open mind, and the only evidence showing that they do are instances in which they have actually changed their minds. On this particular issue, however, I cannot oblige. Whether I am right or wrong, I have been consistent regarding these points. Let me quote from an article I wrote 28 years ago: "The problem of oligopoly is by definition the problem of the effects of the actions of few, giving a greater importance to the behavior of each member of the group. . . . The theory of the oligopoly price involves an interpretation of the significant motives behind the actions of a small number of people. . . . Even the most superficial theory will have to include many more ideal types of behavior in order to handle the problem of *few* sellers than it takes to handle the problem of a *mass* of competitive sellers" [20, p. 235].

On the other hand, I must plead guilty to a charge of the same error of misplaced

REALISTIC MODELS OF THE FIRM UNDER COMPETITION

Many of the proponents and protagonists of a more realistic theory of the firm are quite aware of the fact that the managerial extension and enrichment of the concept of the firm was not needed except where firms in the industry were large and few, and not under the pressure of competition. There are many very quotable statements to this effect.[6]

Too many students, however, want a realistic model of the firm for all purposes. They forget the maxim of Occam's Razor that unnecessary terms in a theory be kept out (or shaved off). These students seem to miss in a simplified model the realistic trimmings of the observable world; they distrust such a model because it is obviously "descriptively false." In view of this sentimental hankering for realism, it may be helpful to survey some of the inclusions which various writers have proposed in order to meet the demands for greater realism in the "theory of the firm," and to examine their relevance to the theory of competitive price. The following considerations are supposed to supplement, qualify, restrict, or replace the objective of maximizing money profits.

(1) Entrepreneurs and managers cannot be expected to have an inelastic demand for leisure; indeed, one must assume that this demand is income-elastic so that higher profit expectations will cause them to sacrifice some income for the sake of more leisure [36, p. 356]. (2) Managers are anxious to avoid resentment on the part of their colleagues and subordinates and will, therefore, not enforce their orders with the sternness required for maximization of profits; similarly, minor functionaries do not want to disturb the routines of their superiors and,

---

concreteness against which I have just warned. It occurred in a sentence in which I spoke of various magnitudes (subjectively) "perceived or fancied by the men whose decisions or actions are to be explained (the business men) . . ." [21, p. 521]. If this sentence referred only to oligopolistic or monopolistic behavior, it would not be so bad for, as I said above, the theoretical constructs of decision-makers in this case have a closer correspondence to real businessmen than the constructs in the theory of competitive prices. But the sentence was supposed to apply to the constructs of the firm in any position whatever. Hence it was a misleading sentence in that (1) it gave the impression that the decision-makers in question were *real* men (real businessmen, whom you could interview) and (2) it said that the actions of these men were to be explained, whereas the purpose of the theory was not to explain observed actions but only observable *results* of imagined (postulated) reactions to observable events.

I apologize for this error. Not that I do not approve of a busy shuttle-traffic between the domain of theoretical construction and the domain of empirical observation, but we must never fail to specify the side of the frontier on which we happen to be. The theoretical terms may have empirical referents (counterparts), but to believe, or allow an impression of belief, that the two are identical is a methodological fallacy.

[6] "When the conditions of competition are relaxed . . . the opportunity set of the firm is expanded. In this case, the behavior of the firm as a distinct operating unit is of separate interest. Both for purposes of interpreting particular behavior within the firm as well as for predicting responses of the industry aggregate, it may be necessary to identify the factors that influence the firm's choices within this expanded opportunity set and embed these in a formal model" [48, pp. 2–3].

hence, they often abstain from suggesting improvements which would maximize profits [31, p. 452]. (3) Managers are more interested in their own salaries, bonuses, and other emoluments, than in the profits of the firm or the income of its owners [27, pp. 226–27]. (4) The realization of certain asset preferences (for example, liquidity as against inventories and fixed assets) may be in conflict with profit maximization [5, p. 99]. (5) The flow and biased screening of information through the various levels of management may cause systematic misinformation resulting in earnings far below the maximum obtainable [27, p. 229]. (6) The objective of maintaining control in the hands of the present control group may require a sacrifice of profit opportunities [31, p. 455]. (7) The preference for security may be so strong that even relatively conservative ways of making higher profits are eschewed [12, pp. 270–71]. (8) The striving for status, power, and prestige may be such that it results in conduct not consistent with a maximum of profit [1, p. 145] [28, p. 207] [13, p. xii] [27, p. 227]. (9) The wish to serve society, be a benefactor, or soothe one's social conscience, may militate against actions or policies that would maximize profits [7, pp. 16–17] [13, pp. 339–40]. (10) The instinct of workmanship [46, p. 187], a desire to show professional excellence [1, p. 146], a pervasive interest in feats of engineering, may lead to performance in conflict with highest possible profits. (11) Compromises among the different goals of executives with different interests—production, sales, personnel relations, finance, research and development, public relations, etc.— are sure to "compromise" the objective of maximum profits [10, p. 29]. (12) A variety of influences may be exerted on management decisions, perhaps pulling in different directions and possibly away from maximum profits, as for example influences from labor organizations, suppliers of materials, customers, bankers, government agencies [13, p. 340] [12, p. 270] [28, pp. 195–205].

I shall not prolong this catalogue even if it is far from complete. Let us admit that each of the possible deviations from maximum profit may be "real" in some circumstances. But how effective and significant are they? If the industry is effectively competitive—and it does not have to be "purely" competitive or "perfectly" competitive—is there much of a chance that the direction in which firms react, through their decisions regarding prices, inputs and output, to a change in conditions would be turned around by any of the "forces" listed? Before we say apodictically no, we should examine a few of the reservations.

SECURITY AND MANAGERIAL COORDINATION

Let us single out two items which have been given especially wide play: the "objective of security" and the question of "managerial coordination."

The demand for the recognition of a separate "security motive" conflicting with the profit motive deserves a good discussion. But when I prepared for it, I reread what I had written on this subject and found that I could not improve on it. Will you do me the favor of reading it [23, pp. 51–53 and 424–28] and, if you like it, make your students read it?

That there are no business profits without risks and that there is not much point in treating the two quite separately; that it would be silly to call a decision one of profit-maximizing if it increased risk and uncertainty so much as to reduce the chance of survival; that the notion of long-run profits comprises all considerations of risks of loss; that, in terms of my automobile-driving analogies, only a fool would assume that maximization of speed means driving 120 miles an hour regardless of curves and bumps; these are some of the things that have to be said in this connection. But the most essential point to be made is that in the economics of *adjustment to change* the issues of security, survival, and maximum profit are merged. How primitive again to confuse new ventures and daring moves with mere responses to stimuli, obvious reactions to change. If a change in conditions calls for a certain reaction in the name of maximum profits, the very same reaction is called for also in the name of security of survival.

The other matter is of a more "behavioral" nature: the coordination of different goals and judgments on the part of different members of the management and the deviations from profit maximization that may be involved in the process. Frankly, I cannot quite see what great difference organizational matters are supposed to make in the firm's price reactions to changes in conditions. Assume, for example, the import duties on foreign products competing with the products of domestic industry are raised, with a resulting increase in the demand for the products of the firm. Why should the clashes and compromises of divergent opinions reverse the direction of the change that would be "dictated" by the simple rule of profit maximization? Perhaps one vice president wants to raise prices without increasing output, while another wants to increase output without (at least at the moment) raising prices. No matter what their compromise will be, it is likely to conform with what the simple rule suggests. But if not, so what? Remember we are talking about industries with more than a few firms and with free entry.[7]

OTHER QUALIFICATIONS TO COMPETITIVE PRICE THEORY

Substitution between income and leisure looks like the strongest reason for a qualification in cases in which the change in conditions is such that not only the locus of maximum profits is shifted but also the amount of profit obtainable is changed. Take again the example of a tariff increase shutting out foreign competition. The firms in the industry will find that given outputs will now fetch higher prices and that increased outputs can be sold at prices higher than those prevailing before tariffs were raised. And profits will be higher in any case, so that managers—even owner-managers—will be inclined to relax their efforts. Yet would anybody seriously argue that the substitution of leisure (coffee breaks, cocktail parties, golf) for potential profits would be such that total output would be reduced instead of increased? It is not a likely story, and where the industry consists of several or many firms, the small probability vanishes quickly. What remains of the argument is that total output would increase, in reaction to the tariff increase, somewhat less than it would if the managers were eager beavers and did not relax in their efforts when profits increased. Thus, the elasticity of

[7] A great champion of more realistic theories of the firm summed up his reflections on their implications for general economics with this statement: "We shall not be far wrong in concluding . . . that the impact of more realistic theories of the firm on static price analysis is likely to be small" [6, p. 42].

supply of the products in question is a little smaller. But since we do not know how much it would be anyhow, the unknown subtraction from an unknown number should not cause the economic theorist any serious anxieties. (And if the politicians who push for the tariff increase decide to push less hard if we tell them that their friends in the industry will enjoy some of the added protection in the form of more leisure and recreation, we would not really mind.)

Even if formal accuracy demanded that we accept the maximization of the decision-maker's total utility as the basic assumption, simplicity and fruitfulness speak for sticking with the postulate of maximization of money profits for situations in which competition is effective. The question is not whether the firms of the real world will *really* maximize money profits, or whether they even *strive* to maximize their money profits, but rather whether the *assumption* that this is the objective of the theoretical firms in the artificial world of our construction will lead to conclusions—"inferred outcomes"—very different from those derived from admittedly more realistic assumptions.

The second qualification in my list—regarding bosses, colleagues and subordinates—is quite irrelevant, except perhaps for questions of welfare economics, where it matters whether firms "really" do all they can to maximize efficiency. For theories concerned with *changes* in prices, inputs, and outputs in response to *changes* to conditions (of production, resource availability, and product demand) the strictness with which efficiency is watched in the firm does not matter. The effects of the tariff increase in our illustration, or the effects of changes in wage rates, interest rates, tax rates, and so forth, are, if there is effective competition, essentially independent of the relations among the various levels in the managerial hierarchy of the firm.

It would take too much time here to go through our entire list of reservations. Anybody who makes the effort will find that some of the "realistic assumptions" proposed for inclusion in the theory can affect (by an unknown amount) the magnitude but not the direction of any change that is likely to result from a specified change in conditions; and that other assumptions will not even do that much. In short, they are all irrelevant for purposes of competitive price theory.

OLIGOPOLY, MONOPOLY, AND MANAGERIAL DISCRETION

I repeat: In the theory of competitive price the "real existence" of firms is irrelevant; imaginary (postulated) agents pursuing a simple (postulated) goal react to assumed changes in conditions and thereby produce (or allow us to infer) changes in prices, inputs, and outputs [24, pp. 13–14]. The correspondence between these inferences (deduced changes) and actual observations (observed changes in prices, inputs, and outputs, following observed changes in conditions) is close for two reasons: (1) The number of firms in the real world is so large that it suffices if some of them react as posited by the theory; and (2) the profits of firms are only about "normal," that is, excess profits are about zero, because of competitive pressures from newcomers (pliopolistic pressures [23, pp. 211–23]), so that profits below the maximum obtainable would in fact be net losses in an economic sense.

These two reasons do not hold in the theories of oligopoly and monopoly price.[8] For these theories the real existence of firms (that is, an empirical counterpart to the theoretical construct) is required, because the explanation of changes in prices, inputs, and outputs is at the same time an explanation of decisions of some particular firms, in the sense of organizations of men acting in particular, sometimes unpredictable, ways. Various attempts have been made to develop patterns of oligopolistic and monopolistic conduct and to correlate these patterns with types of organization or with types of personalities exercising ultimate decision-making power. The success has thus far been small; even if the decision-making (say, pricing) in a particular firm was sometimes satisfactorily modeled (for example, in a simulated computer program), the model has usually not been transferable to other cases, to predict decisions in other firms. I do not recall, moreover, that the behavior patterns in these cases were shown to be inconsistent with the postulate of profit maximization.

Under these circumstances, retreat to simpler, less realistic models of firms in oligopoly and monopoly positions is indicated. The first approach is to apply the polypolistic model, in full awareness that the actual facts are entirely different. In many instances the use of the polypolistic model for situations which in our judgment would merit to be labeled as oligopolistic will still yield satisfactory explanations and predictions. Where this is not so, the analyst will resort to the use of models of oligopolistic or monopolistic firms, postulating the simplest possible pattern of action and reaction, dispensing with all peculiar attitudes and "special" strategies. Only where these simple models of oligopolistic and monopolistic firms yield quite unsatisfactory predictions will the analyst need to go further, to more special types of behavior, provided he finds it worth while. It depends on the research interests and on the problems under examination how much effort one wishes to invest in behavioral research where the findings hold little promise of yielding generalizations of wide applicability.

There are, however, some simple models of oligopolistic behavior which seem

---

[8] The idea that profit maximization is the appropriate hypothesis for the theory of competitive price but not necessarily for the theory of monopoly or oligopoly price has been expressed repeatedly over the last century.

Pareto, for example, said that "pure economics" cannot tell us anything about the continuing shifts of position of competing oligopolists, and we have to turn to "the observation of facts," which would show us the variety of possibilities [29, pp. 601–2].

Schumpeter, in 1928, had this to say about the dichotomy: "We have much less reason to expect that monopolists will . . . charge an equilibrium price than we have in the case of perfect competition; for competing producers *must* charge it as a rule under penalty of economic death, whilst monopolists, although having a *motive* to charge the monopolistic equilibrium price, are not forced to do so, but may be prevented from doing so by other motives" [33, p. 371].

Finally, Scitovsky in 1951 stated that "not only does the monopolist's secure market position enable him to relax his efforts of maximizing profit, but his very position may prevent his aiming at maximum profit. He may regard his immunity from competition as precarious or be afraid of unfavorable publicity and public censure; and for either reason, he may judge it wiser to refrain from making full use of his monopoly position. We conclude, therefore, that although in some cases the monopolist will aim at maximizing his profit . . . in other cases—which may well be the important ones—he will refrain from maximizing profit" [37, p. 377].

to be of sufficiently wide applicability. A model that equips the oligopolistic decision-maker not under heavy competitive pressure with an objective of gross-revenue ("sales") maximization, subject to the constraint of satisfactory net-revenue ("profit") [2, p. 49], succeeds in explaining the lack of response to some cost-increasing events observed in several instances. There are other simple models explaining the same phenomenon, and one may think of good reasons for finding one model or another more satisfactory. If the sales-maximization hypothesis can explain a greater variety of observed responses or nonresponses than other hypotheses can, and if it seems to correspond better with self-interpretations offered by interviewed businessmen, it merits acceptance, at least for the time being.

An alternative to the maximization of sales is the maximization of the growth rate of sales [3, p. 1086]. This hypothesis is especially interesting because it involves an endogenous relation with profits: while some of the growth of gross revenue may encroach on profits, it does so with an automatic limit in that profits are needed to finance the investment required for the growth of sales.

Another extension of the objective function proposed on the basis of behavioral research combines two managerial preferences for specific expenses of the firm with the usual profit motive. The two additional motives are expenditures for staff personnel and expenditures for managerial emoluments; both figure prominently in the utility functions of executives of companies which, sheltered from competitive pressures, make enough profits to allow management to indulge in these personal desires [48, pp. 38–60].

All these "managerial-discretion models" are simple and sufficiently general to allow relatively wide application. We shall have more to say about them later.

EFFECTIVE COMPETITION AND MANAGERIAL DISCRETION

In mapping out the area of applicability for theories of managerial discretion, we have spoken of "oligopoly," "monopoly," and of "firms not under heavy competitive pressure." These are rather vague guideposts, but unfortunately the literature has not been very helpful in ascertaining precisely what it is that allows or restricts the exercise of wide managerial discretion.

Some writers stress the size of the firm, suggesting that it is only in the *large* firm that management can exercise discretion. Others stress the condition of *diffused ownership* as the one that affords management the opportunity of pursuing objectives other than maximization of profits. Those who stress oligopoly as the domain for which objective functions richer than profit maximization are needed are usually not quite specific as to their criterion of an oligopoly position: it may be *fewness of firms* active in the same industry, or the subjective state of awareness of the *interdependence of price making* often characterized as "conjectural variation," or simply the *absence of aggressive competition for increasing shares in the market*. Others again stress *closed entry*, or absence of newcomers' competition, as the essential condition for a profit level sufficiently comfortable to allow managers to indulge in the satisfaction of objectives other than maximization of profits.

To combine all these conditions would probably be far too restrictive; it would confine the application of managerial-discretion models to large firms with diffused ownership, few competitors, full awareness of interdependence in pricing, absence of aggressive efforts by existing competitors to increase their market shares, and little danger of new competitors entering the field. The size of the firm may actually not be relevant, and diffused ownership may not be a necessary condition for some deviations from profit maximization to occur, say, in the interest of larger sales or larger expenditures for staff. Fewness of competitors may be more significant, chiefly because the danger of newcomers' competition is likely to be small where the number of firms has been few and continues to be few; partly also because the few competitors may have learnt that aggressive price competition does not pay. The essential conditions, it seems to me, are these two: that no newcomers are likely to invade the field of the existing firms, and that none of the existing firms tries to expand its sales at such a fast rate that it could succeed only by encroaching on the business of its competitors.

Competition from newcomers, from aggressive expansionists, or from importers is sometimes called "heavy," "vigorous," or "effective." The simplest meaning of these adjectival modifiers is this: a firm is exposed to heavy, vigorous, or effective competition if it is kept under continuing pressure to do something about its sales and its profits position. Under this "competitive pressure" the firm is constantly compelled to react to actual or potential losses in sales and/or reductions in profits, so much so that the firm will not be able to pursue any objectives other than the maximization of profits—for the simple reason that anything less than the highest obtainable profits would be below the rate of return regarded as normal at the time.

I am aware of a defect in this definition: its criterion is lodged in the effect rather than in an independently ascertainable condition. Perhaps, though, "effective" is quite properly defined in this fashion, namely, by whether certain effects are realized: competition is effective if it continually depresses profits to the level regarded as the minimum tolerable. What makes it effective is not part of the definition, but has to be explained by the conditions of entry, aggressive attitudes on the part of existing firms, or imports from abroad.

If my reasoning is accepted, several formulations proposed in the literature will have to be amended. Managerial discretion will be a function, not of the independence of the management from the control of the owners, but chiefly of the independence of the management from urgent worries about the sufficiency of earnings. If one insists, one may still say that all managers are primarily interested in their own incomes. But, since it is clear that their long-term incomes are jeopardized if profits go below the acceptable rate of return, maximization of managerial incomes and maximization of profits come to do the same thing if competition is effective.[9]

There can be no doubt about the fact that competition is not effective in many industries and that many, very many, firms are not exposed to vigorous competition. It follows that managerial discretion can have its way in a large enough number of firms to secure wide applicability of well-designed managerial-discretion models—or to invite the use of managerial total-utility models.

[9] For competition to be effective it is not necessary that competition is either pure or perfect or that all or any of the markets in which the firm buys or sells are perfect.

I was fully aware, when I wrote my 1946 article, that there were many qualifications and exceptions to the principle of profit maximization.[10] But I considered it hopeless for predictive purposes to work with total-utility maximization and I did not see the possibility of combining a few selected managerial goals with the profit motive.

MARGINALISM EXTENDED: TOTAL UTILITY

In order to show how hopeless it is to construct a comprehensive total-utility model and obtain from it definite predictions of the effects of changes in conditions upon the dispositions of the managers, one merely has to visualize the large variety of possible "satisfactions" and the still larger variety of things that may contribute to their attainment. The satisfactions consist not only in receiving money incomes, immediate or deferred, and various incomes in kind, but also in distributing incomes to others and in gaining prestige, power, self-esteem, as well as in enjoying a good conscience and other pleasurable feelings.

What makes things really complicated is that the creation of these satisfactions is related to very different flows of funds into and out of the firm: some to gross revenue (sales volume), others to net revenue; some to profits distributed, others to profits retained; some to investment outlays, others to company expenses. The managers' immediate money incomes and some of the emoluments received in kind are partly at the expense of profits, partly at the expense of corporate income taxes (and every change in tax rates changes the trade-off ratios.) The same is true of several other company expenses which add to the prestige, power, and self-esteem of the managers. Special mention may be made of the provision of stock options for managers, which are either at the expense of the owners' equity (through watering down their stock) or at the expense of potential capital gains on treasury stock earmarked for such stock options, but

---

[10] Several of my statements, if I presented them without source reference, might well be mistaken for quotations from critics of marginalism, including behavioralists and managerialists. Here are samples [21]: ". . . a business man is motivated by considerations other than the maximization of money profits"; "it is preferable to separate the non-pecuniary factors of business conduct from those which are regular items in the formation of money profits" (p. 526); "one may presume that producing larger production volumes [or] paying higher wage rates . . . than would be compatible with a maximum of money profits may involve for the business man a gain in social prestige or a certain measure of inner satisfaction"; "it is not impossible that considerations of this sort substantially weaken the forces believed to be at work on the basis of a strictly pecuniary marginal calculus"; for patriotic reasons during the war "many firms produced far beyond the point of highest money profits"; "the conflict of interests between the hired managers and the owners of the business" may call for "important qualifications" (p. 527); "the interest of the former in inordinately large outlays or investments may be capable of descriptions in terms of a pecuniary calculus, but it is not maximization of the firm's profits which serves here as the standard of conduct" (pp. 527–28); "maximization of salaries and bonuses of professional managers may constitute a standard of business conduct different from that implied in the customary marginal analysis of the firm"; and "the extent to which the two standards would result in sharply different action under otherwise similar conditions is another open question in need of investigation" (p. 528).

which, on the other hand, may be a powerful force aligning the managers' personal interests with the goal of maximizing the net profits of the firm.

The point of it all is that the total utility of managers can be increased by decisions which increase expenses at the expense of profits. (Of course, this is confined to situations where profits are high enough to stand encroachments by avoidable expenses—to situations, that is, where the firm is not hard-pressed by competition.) The question is how various changes in conditions will affect managerial decisions on inputs, outputs, and prices if the objectives of management include the gratification of preferences for certain expenses of the firm that compete with the maximization of profits.[11]

For purposes of illustration let us reproduce in a literary form the utility function of a management (perhaps of its "peak coordinator" [28, pp. 190–91]) in full control and confident that stockholders will not make any fuss as long as the firm makes a "normal" profit and pays out a fair share of it in dividends. Total utility, which the manager by his decisions will try to maximize, will be a function of a large number of variables, by virtue of the contributions they make to his pride, prestige, self-esteem, conscience, comfort, feeling of accomplishment, material consumption, and anticipations of future benefits and pleasures. Among the variables may be total profits of the firm, growth rate of profits, rate of profits to investment, total sales, growth rate of sales, increase in market share, dividends paid out, retained earnings, increase in market value of stock, price-earnings ratio of stock, investment outlay, salary and bonus received, stock options received (capital gains), expense accounts (consumption at company expense), services received (automobile, chauffeur, lovely secretary, theatre tickets, conferences at resorts), size of staff, expenses for public relations and advertising, expenses for research and development, technological and other

---

[11] Instead of cataloguing the various contributions to the "utility" of the management and their relationships to the sources and uses of the firm's funds, one may wish to classify the expenses of the firm with reference to "discretionary" decisions of the management influenced by the decision-makers' preferences. Here is a tentative classification of this sort:

1. Expenses required for the production of (a) current output of unchanged size, (b) additional current output, with marginal cost not exceeding marginal revenue (hence, contributing to higher profits), and (c) additional current output, with marginal cost exceeding marginal revenue (hence, reducing profits).
2. Expenses not required for the production of current output, but increasing the productive capacity or efficiency of the firm for future production.
3. Expenses for managerial personnel in the form of (a) salaries and bonuses, and (b) services rendered to them for their convenience and pleasure.
4. Expenses not required for either current or future production, but (a) expected of a profitable firm as a social service, and only slightly promoting the public image of management, (b) widely recognized as contributing to the social or national benefit and as indicative of the public spirit of the management, (c) contributing chiefly to the gratification of personal desires of supervisory and managerial personnel, and (d) largely wasteful, that is, contributing nothing, and economizing nothing but managerial effort or capability.

This list may be suggestive of the actions that may have to be taken when, after years of ease and growth, the firm finds its profits declining or disappearing.

innovations, leadership in wage increases and good industrial relations, expenses for public or private education and health, other contributions to public interest and patriotic causes, free time for leisure and recreation, and indications of influence over government, industry, and society. This list of variables is, of course, only representative, not exhaustive.[12]

Now what can one do with a utility function of this sort? Will it be of much use in telling us what the firm will do with its freedom of action if it has to respond to a change in conditions?

The answer will depend partly on a simple condition, namely, whether the acceptable trade-off ratios between all the factors contributing to total utility remain unchanged, or approximately the same, if any one of them, say, total profit, increases. If this were the case, we could shout hurrah or sigh a sigh of relief (depending on our temperament). For, if the marginal rates of substitution among all the various "utilifactors" are constant, the distribution of funds among them will remain unchanged with changes in conditions that increase or decrease the total of funds available. Only if the cost of any of the factors changed, say, the cost of staff personnel and, hence, the cost of prestige and other benefits that accrue from having a sizable staff, would the marginal rates of substitution be adapted to the new cost relation. In such a case we might also perhaps be able to tell the kind of response of the decision-makers.

Alas, the condition that the marginal rates of substitution are independent of the total funds available is not likely to be satisfied; in addition, certain types of change in conditions have the bad habit of affecting at the same time funds available and relative costs of utilifactors. For example, an increase in the corporate income tax will change the trade-off ratio between expensable outlays and profits in favor of avoidable expenses.

MARGINALISM EXTENDED: CHOICE OF MAXIMANDA

If we were interested only in a formal solution, and perhaps in a proof of "existence" of an equilibrium position, we might be satisfied with the maximization of total utility by those who effectively run the firm. If, however, we want to predict the direction of the changes which a given change in conditions is likely to bring about, then mere formalism will not be enough. For predictive purposes we need *more* to go by with the help of *fewer* variables. Maximization of money profits is certainly the simplest "objective function," but it works only in the case of firms exposed to vigorous competition. The management of a firm that makes more than enough money need not go all out to maximize profits; it can afford to do a few other things that it likes, such as serving what by its own lights it regards as the national interest or indulging in other luxuries.

Would this imply "giving up" the principle of marginalism in the theory of

---

[12] Perhaps there ought to be a place on the list for some gratifications that are more stable, less subject to quantitative variation, such as the pleasure of being known for honesty and fairness, on the one hand, and for sharpness and shrewdness, on the other, or at least the pleasure of being convinced of having and exercising these qualities. And last, though not least, there is the general feeling of gratification from "running" a large, well-known, profitable, widely respected firm with growing assets and employment.

the profitable firm? This is chiefly a semantic question. I have been inclined to use a more extended definition. In 1946, I called marginalism "the logical process of finding a maximum" [21, p. 519]. I did not say that it had to be maximization of money profits—though I struggled hard to justify the use of profit maximization in all cases. In the meantime several writers have shown that profit maximization may not be a completely unambiguous objective, even where it is used in splendid isolation from all competing goals, in that it may refuse to yield unambiguous conclusions regarding the effects of certain changes, such as the effects of changes in profit taxes. In addition, it has been shown that several workable "objective functions" can be developed that give plausible results with a few relatively simple terms added. Any of these functions that can be maximized, with or without specific constraints, would still be a part of marginal analysis.

The choice of the *maximandum* is of course a pragmatic matter: we should prefer one that yields sufficiently good approximations to what we consider reasonable on the basis of empirical research, with wide applicability and fruitfulness and with great simplicity. The compromise among these goals that we accept is, admittedly, a somewhat "subjective" standard of selection, but perfectly in line with the standard accepted in all scientific fields. Concessions to any one of these desiderata must be at the expense of the others.

Let us list some of the alternative *maximanda* that have been suggested and are available for our choice: Total quasi-rents over a short period of time (But how short? This is good only for a freshman course); total quasi-rents during the service-life of existing fixed assets (But is a replaceable part of a machine a fixed asset? This works only for a one-hoss shay); present value of all profits (after taxes) expected in the future, discounted at a "normal" or "competitive" rate; internal rate of return to equity; equity of controlling stockholders; present values of retained earnings; growth rate of equity; gross rate of total assets; growth rate of gross revenue (sales); gross revenue (sales), if net revenues (profits) are satisfactory (over what period of time?); salaries, bonuses, and other accruals (including services in kind) to management, over their entire lives; all accruals to management plus expenditure for staff personnel, compatible with minimum profits; all accruals to management, consistent with satisfactory profits and gradually rising prices of corporate stock; and, of course, the present values of the various combinations of flows mentioned.

Surely a much longer list could be prepared, but there is no use to this. The point should be clear: profit maximization proper may mean a variety of things —several entries apply to money profits—and in addition there are a few other *maximanda* of possible relevance. Incidentally, if profits or accruals to stockholders are not explicitly included in some of the entries, let no one believe that they are really out of the picture. No management could try to maximize its own accruals in the long run if it completely disregarded the interests of the stockholders. Hence, all *maximanda* are subject to the constraint of some minimum benefits to the owners of the business in the form of dividends, capital gains, or both.[13]

[13] The four "managerial" variables included in the list—sales, growth of sales, expenses for staff, and emoluments to the management—may well be the most important deviations from profit maximization, although I may easily be persuaded of the

SUBJECTIVE INFORMATION
AND THE CHARGE OF TAUTOLOGY

I have a few remaining tasks, and one of them is to lay a ghost, one that has long played tricks on economists and led them astray. He has done this in their discussions of the subject of information, its availability, its uncertainty, and its subjectivity. I mean, of course, information available to the "firm," and this raises the question whether we mean the firm as a purely theoretical construct or the firm as an organization of real people or anything else.

The firm as a theoretical construct has exactly the kind of information the theorist chooses to endow it with in order to design a good, useful theory. The firm as an organization of real people has the information system that it actually happens to have and which, in some instances, the management scientists (operations researchers) have succeeded in developing. For purposes of competitive price and allocation theory, it does not make much difference whether the information which we assume the firm to have concerning the conditions of supply, production, and demand under which it works is correct or incorrect, as long as we may safely assume that any *change* in these conditions is registered correctly. If we want to inquire into the effects of a change in wage rates or tax rates or something of this sort, we must of course take it for granted that the decision-makers who supposedly react to the change have taken notice of it. But whether their "previous" store of information—from which they started when the change occurred—was accurate or not will only in exceptional instances make a qualitative difference to the reactions.

This important difference between information about conditions and information about changes in conditions has eluded several writers, who shouted "tautology" when they confronted my statements about the subjectivity of information. They reasoned like this: If firms act on the basis of information which is entirely subjective, then *anything* they do may be said to follow from whatever they believe they know: hence, the assumption of subjectivism defeats any explanatory purposes. This is a sad confusion. In teaching elementary economics we ought to be able to make our students grasp the difference between the shape and position of a curve, on the one hand, and the shift of a curve, on the other. The direction of the effects which we derive from the shift is usually, though

---

existence of other "extravagances" of management. Among the managements of our large corporations there are so many civic-minded men, bursting with social responsibility and cocksure of their ability to know what is in the national interest, that I incline to the thought that rather serious deviations from the profit motive occur in the area of virtuous striving for the so-called common good. I hope I am not excessively naive if I believe that the excess profits secured through restrictions on competition are to no small extent used for what the discretionary managers believe to be worthy causes. But I see no way of formulating any hypotheses that would enable us to predict either just what the firms' outlays in the public interest will be or how they will affect total output in the long run. I suppose that Boulding's witty question, "do we maximize profit subject to the constraints of morality or do we maximize virtue subject to the constraints of satisfactory profits" [7, p. 17] was not intended to suggest an answer with empirically fertile conclusions.

not always, independent of the shape and position of the original curve. We need not fuss about the curve reflecting "accurate information" if we only want to see what happens when the curve shifts in a certain direction.

Since ghosts are hardy creatures, the laying of this one will probably not constitute a once-and-for-all execution. We shall probably see him again thumbing his nose at us in the next textbook or in the next issue of one of our journals.

IMPERFECT INFORMATION AND THE QUESTION OF "SATISFICING" BEHAVIOR

The same confusion sometimes encumbers the discussions about the alleged "imperfection" of knowledge available to firms for their rational decision-making [39, pp. xxiv–xxvi, 40–41, 81–83, 241–42] and the screens and blockages in "the flow of information through the hierarchies of the organization" [27, pp. 228–29]. But what can be "imperfect" about the information on, say, a tax increase? Why should it take special theories of bureaucracy to explain how the news of a wage increase "flows" through various hierarchical levels up or down or across? Yet this, and this alone, is the information that is essentially involved in the theory of prices and allocation, since it is the *adjustment to such changes* in conditions for which the postulate of maximizing behavior is employed.

One can understand, of course, how the confusion arose. The proponents of managerial analysis have the creditable ambition to reorganize firms in such a way that their managements can really, as a matter of actual fact, maximize the results of their performance, not only in adjusting to changes in conditions, but also in making the most rational arrangements on the basis of the *complete environment* in which they operate.[14] Incidentally, not only "normative microeconomics," as management science has been called [40, p. 279], has this ambition; many propositions of welfare economics are also based on such presuppositions.

As a matter of fact, the interesting distinction made between "satisficing" and "maximizing" or "optimizing" behavior [39, pp. xxiv–xxvi] [40, pp. 262–65] had its origin in precisely the same issue; management, realizing the complexity of the calculations and the imperfection of the data that would have to be employed in any determination of "optimal" decisions, cannot help being satisfied with something less: its behavior will be only "satisficing." What behavior? The mere adjustment to a simple change or the coordinated, integrated whole of its activities? Evidently, only the latter is the overly ambitious aim. The theory of prices and allocation, viewed as a theory of adjustment to change, does not

---

[14] "Economic man deals with the 'real world' in all its complexity," says Herbert Simon [39, p. xxv]. The *homo oeconomicus* I have encountered in the literature was not such a perfectionist. Incidentally, even Simon's "economic man," two years before the ambitious one just quoted, did not have "absolutely complete," but only "impressively clear and voluminous" knowledge of the "relevant aspects of his environment" [38, p. 99]. My point is that we ought to distinguish perfect or imperfect knowledge of (a) the entire environment, (b) the relevant aspects of the entire environment, (c) the relevant changes in environmental conditions.

call for impossible performances.[15] I ask you to remember what I spelled out, twenty years ago, about the difference between exact estimates and calculations, on the one hand, and "sizing up" in nonnumerical terms, on the other [21, pp. 524–25, 534–35]. And I ask you to realize how many more good predictions can be made on the basis of the assumption that firms try to maximize their profits than on the basis of the assumption that they want no more than satisfactory profits. Take one illustration: if an easy-money policy is introduced, we expect that some firms will increase their borrowings, some firms will increase their purchases, some firms will sell at higher prices, and some firms will increase their output. But if everybody was satisfied before the change, we cannot infer any of these things. On the other hand, if we assume the firms prefer a larger profit to a smaller one, all the mentioned consequences follow from the simple model.

THE TWENTY-ONE CONCEPTS OF THE FIRM

Several times in this paper I have spoken of the fallacy of misplaced concreteness, committed by mistaking a thought-object for an object of sense perception, that is, for anything in the real, empirical world. My warnings might have given rise to another confusion, namely, that there are only two concepts of the firm. There are many more, and I do not wish to suppress altogether my strong taxonomic propensities. I shall offer a list of ten different contexts calling for even more different concepts, some theoretical, some more empirical.

One of my favorite philosophers, who was a past-master of the art of making fine distinctions, enumerated 13 concepts of "pragmatism" [18], 66 concepts of "nature" [19, pp. 447–56], and "a great number" of concepts of "God."[16] I am sure there are at least 21 concepts of the firm employed in the literature of business and economics, but I shall exercise great forbearance and confine myself to a selection. Everyone may join in the game and fill in what I leave out. I shall first state the context, then delimit the concept, and finally add a few words of explanation.

[15] Suppose the government imposes a 15 per cent surcharge on all import duties. The theory of the profit-maximizing firm will without hesitation tell us that imports will decline. What will the theory of the satisficing firm tell us? "Models of satisficing behavior are richer than models of maximizing behavior, because they treat not only of equilibrium but of the method of reaching it as well. Psychological studies of the formation and change of aspiration levels support propositions of the following kinds. (a) When performance falls short of the level of aspiration, search behavior (particularly search for new alternatives of action) is induced. (b) At the same time, the level of aspiration begins to adjust itself downward until goals reach levels that are practically attainable. (c) If the two mechanisms just listed operate too slowly to adapt aspirations to performance, emotional behavior—apathy or aggression, for example—will replace rational adaptive behavior" [40, p. 263]. I admit that this is an unfair use of the theory of satisficing, but I wanted to show that everything has its place and no theory can be suitable to all problems. I suspect, however, that Simon's theory of satisficing behavior will yield neither quantitative nor qualitative predictions.

[16] "Lovejoy Denied Approval by Senate Group," *The Baltimore Sun*, April 1, 1951.

1. In the theory of competitive prices and allocation, the firm is *an imaginary reactor to environmental changes*. By "imaginary" I mean to stress that this is a pure construct for which there need not exist an empirical counterpart. By "reactor" I mean to deny that this robot or puppet can ever have a will of his own: he is the theorist's creature, programmed to respond in the predetermined way.
2. In the theory of innovation and growth, the firm is *an imaginary or a typical reactor or initiator*. Depending on which theory one has in mind, we see that several combinations are possible. In the theory of "entrepreneurial innovation" by men of very special qualities [34, pp. 78–94] the entrepreneur is neither imaginary nor a mere reactor; he is a typical initiator. By "typical" I do not refer to the ideal type of German sociology [47, p. 44] [35, pp. 20–63, 81] [25, pp. 21–57], but rather to the common-sense kind of person that many of us have met in person or, at least, have heard about. On the other hand, there are also theories of "induced invention"—assuming latent inventiveness (though an invention can never be a mere reaction)—and theories of "induced growth," employing the construct of the imaginary reactor.
3. In welfare economics, the firm is *an imaginary or a typical reactor or initiator with accurate knowledge of his opportunities*. Depending on the proposition in question, all combinations are again possible, but in any case a new requirement is introduced: accurate knowledge of the environmental conditions on the part of all reactors and initiators. For, in contrast to the theory of price and allocation, the welfare theorist wants to ascertain, not only in which direction price, input, and output will move in response to a change, but also whether this move will increase or reduce welfare. For such an exercise it is no longer irrelevant whether the subjective information of the firms is correct or false.
4. In the theory of oligopoly and monopoly, the firm is *a typical reactor and initiator in a small (or zero) interacting group*. I have explained earlier why a theory of oligopoly with nothing but imaginary reactors may not be widely applicable.
5. In the theory of organization (or bureaucracy), the firm is *a typical cooperative system with authoritative coordination*. I have accepted this formulation from one of the authorities [28, p. 187] and thus may disclaim responsibility for it.
6. In management science (or the art of business management), the firm is *a functional information system and decision-making system for typical business operations*. The normative nature of management science should be stressed. Several management scientists include operations research among the agenda of management science. I take this to mean that the principal techniques of operations research of such matters as inventory problems, replacement problems, search problems, queueing problems, and routing problems have to be mastered by the management scientist. He should, however, make a distinction between the science and its application: the science deals with typical systems, but is applied to particular cases.
7. In operations research and consultation, the firm is *an actual or potential client for advice on optimal performance*. In this context the reference

is not to the techniques and principles of operations research but rather to the particular projects planned or undertaken.

8. In accounting theory, the firm is *a collection of assets and liabilities*. It should be clear how different this concept is from most of the others.

9. In legal theory and practice, the firm is *a juridical person with property, claims, and obligations*. This may be a very deficient formulation; I defer to the experts, who will surely correct it.

10. In statistical description (such as the Census of Manufactures) the firm is *a business organization under a single management or a self-employed person with one or more employees or with an established place of business*. I have adopted here the definition used by the U.S. Census.

This exercise should have succeeded in showing how ludicrous the efforts of some writers are to attempt *one* definition of *the* firm as used in economic analysis, or to make statements supposedly true of "the" firm, or of "its" behavior, or what not. Scholars ought to be aware of equivocations and should not be snared by them.

A SENSE OF PROPORTION

I hope there will be no argument about which concept of the firm is the most important or the most useful. Since they serve different purposes, such an argument would be pointless. It would degenerate into childish claims about one area of study being more useful than another.

I also hope the specialist who uses one concept of the firm will desist from trying to persuade others to accept his own tried and trusted concept for entirely different purposes. The concept of the firm in organization theory, for example, need not at all be suitable for accounting theory or legal theory; and I know it is not suitable for either competitive price theory or for oligopoly theory.

Most of the controversies about the "firm" have been due to misunderstandings about what the other specialist was doing. Many people cannot understand that others may be talking about altogether different things when they use the same words.

I am not happy about the practice of calling any study just because it deals with or employs a concept of the firm "economics" or "microeconomics." But we cannot issue licenses for the use of such terms and, hence, must put up with their rather free use. My own prejudices balk at designating organization theory as economics—but other people's prejudices are probably different from mine, and we gain little or nothing from arguing about the correct scope of our field.

Now what conclusions from all our reviewing may we draw on the conflicts between marginal analysis, behavioral theory, and managerial theory of the firm? Fortunately, not much time is being wasted on descriptive studies of a narrowly behaviorist kind, in the sense of recording observed behavior without any prior theoretical design. Most proponents of behavioral studies of the firm are too competent theorists for that. As far as the proponents of managerial theories are concerned, they have never claimed to be anything but marginalists, and the behavior goals they have selected as worthy for incorporation into behavior equations, along with the goal of making profits, were given a differentiable form so that they could become part of marginal analysis.[17] Thus, instead of a heated contest between marginalism and managerialism in the theory of the firm, a marriage between the two has come about.

Not all marriages, these days, are permanent; divorces are frequent. Whether this marriage will last or end in divorce will depend chiefly on what offspring it will produce. If the match of the profit hypothesis with the various managerial hypotheses proves fertile of sufficiently interesting deductions, the prospects of a lasting marriage are good.

It is not easy to judge the future sterility or fertility of this marriage between marginalism and managerialism, because most of us are inclined to underrate the kinds of problem on which we have never worked: we have a bias in favor of our own research experience. Most of the researchers on behavioral versions of the theory of the firm look for their problems to the records of selected large corporations. They take it for granted that their theory must be designed to explain and predict the behavior of these firms. This, however, is less so in the case of economists engaged in the analysis of relative prices, inputs, and outputs. They look for their problems to the records of entire industries or industrial sectors. To be sure, some industries are dominated by large corporations, yet the accent of the analysis is not on the behavior of these firms but at best on some of the results of that behavior. Where the focus is not on the behavior of the firm, a theory that requires information on particular firms to be "plugged in" seems to them less serviceable than a more general theory, at least as long as only qualitative, not numerical, results are sought. Hence, even if the "partial-equilibrium analyst" knows full well that the actual situation is not a really competitive one, he probably will still make a first try using the competitive model with good old-fashioned profit maximization. And if the results appear too odd, appropriate qualifications may still be able to take care of them more simply than if he had started with a cumbersome managerial model. (In saying this, I am showing my bias.)

It is revealing to ask what kind of theory we would apply, at least in a first approximation, if we were called upon to predict the results of various kinds of public-policy measures. For questions regarding short-run effects of changes in the corporation income tax (or an excess-profits tax) I believe a strong case

---

[17] While under profit maximization $MR - MC = 0$, sales maximization requires that $MR = 0$; hence, for some of the output sold marginal revenue is less than marginal cost, which cuts into profits. A minimum-profit constraint sets a limit to this.

In the case of maximization of the growth rate of sales the limit on nonremunerative selling is built into the objective itself because a growth of productive assets is required to support the growth of sales, and the acquisition of these assets presupposes a sufficiency of profits, either for internal financing or as a basis for outside finance [3, pp. 1086–87]. If at any time sales were pushed too hard at the expense of profits, there would arise a shortage of funds for acquiring the productive assets needed for producing more output. Thus no separate minimum-profit constraint has to be imposed, since it is inherent in the objective of maximization of the growth of sales. It should be understood, however, that the growth rate of assets under this objective is still less than it could be under straight profit maximization. (This shows why we should never speak of the "growth of the firm" without specifying by what criterion we measure it.)

can be made in favor of a model of the firm with some managerial variables. If the problem is whether an increase in cigarette taxes is likely to be fully shifted onto the consumer or what portion of it may be absorbed by the producers, I may feel safer with a model that includes managerial objectives. If, however, the problem is what qualitative effects an increase in the import duty on a material used in several industries will have on its imports and on the prices and outputs of the various products of the industries in question, I would be inclined to work with the simple hypothesis of profit maximization. I would find it far too cumbersome in this case to go down to the level of the "real" firms; I could probably not obtain the necessary data and, even if I did, I might not be able to rely on the composite results obtained from a firm-by-firm analysis. The old theory of the firm, where all firms are pure fictions, may give me—in this case—most of the answers, in a rough and ready way, not with any numerical precision, but with sufficient reliability regarding the directions of change.

I conclude that the choice of the theory has to depend on the problem we have to solve.[18] Three conditions seem to be decisive in assigning the type of approach to the type of problem. The simple marginal formula based on profit maximization is suitable where (1) *large groups* of firms are involved and nothing has to be predicted about particular firms, (2) the effects of a *specified change* in conditions upon prices, inputs, and outputs are to be explained or predicted rather than the values of these magnitudes before or after the change, and nothing has to be said about the "total situation" or general developments, and (3) only *qualitative answers*, that is, answers about directions of change, are sought rather than precise numerical results. Managerial marginalism is more suitable to problems concerning particular firms and calling for numerical answers. And, I am sure, there are also some problems to which behavioral theory may be the most helpful approach. My impression is that it will be entirely concerned with particular firms and perhaps designed to give answers of a normative, that is, advisory nature.

It looks as if I had prepared the ground for a love feast: I have made polite bows in all directions and have tuned up for a hymn in praise of peaceful coexistence of allegedly antagonistic positions. But I cannot help raising a question which may tear open some of the wounds of the battle of 1946. The question is whether the effects of an effective increase in minimum wages upon the employment of labor of low productivity can, at our present state of knowledge, be fruitfully analyzed with any other model than that of simple marginalism based on unadulterated profit maximization.

If I answer in the negative, does this mean that we are back at the old quarrel and have not learned anything? It does not mean this. Deficiencies in marginal analysis have been shown and recognized; and a great deal of good empirical as well as theoretical work has been accomplished. But the deficiencies dealt with were not just those which the critics twenty years ago attacked. That attack questioned the applicability of marginal analysis to the employment effects of wage increases in industries with many firms presumably under heavy competition

---

[18] As a matter of fact, it will also depend on the research techniques which the appointed analyst has learned to master; we can eliminate this bias by assuming an ideal analyst equally adept in all techniques.

[16, pp. 64, 75–77]. In such circumstances the managerial theories of the firm, according to their proponents, do not apply. On this narrow issue, therefore, the old-type marginalist cannot retreat.

REFERENCES

1. C. I. Barnard, *Functions of the Executive*. Cambridge, Mass. 1938.
2. W. J. Baumol, *Business Behavior, Value and Growth*. New York 1959.
3. "On the Theory of the Expansion of the Firm," *Am. Econ. Rev.*, Dec. 1962, *52*, 1078–87.
4. *Economic Theory and Operations Analysis*, 2nd ed. Englewood Cliffs, N.J. 1965.
5. K. E. Boulding, *A Reconstruction of Economics*. New York 1950.
6. "Implications for General Economics of More Realistic Theories of the Firm," *Am. Econ. Rev.*, Proc., May 1952, *42*, 35–44.
7. "Present Position of the Theory of the Firm," in K. E. Boulding and W. A. Spivey, *Linear Programming and the Theory of the Firm*, New York 1960, pp. 1–17.
8. E. H. Chamberlin, *The Theory of Monopolistic Competition; A Reorientation of the Theory of Value*. Cambridge, Mass. 1933.
9. A. A. Cournot, *Recherches sur les principes mathématiques de la théorie des richesses*, Paris 1838. English transl. by N. T. Bacon under the title *Researches into the Mathematical Principles of the Theory of Wealth*, New York 1897, reprinted 1927.
10. R. M. Cyert and J. G. March, *Behavioral Theory of the Firm*. Englewood Cliffs, N.J. 1963.
11. S. M. Dancoff, "Does the Neutrino Really Exist?" *Bull. Atomic Scientists*, June 1952, *8*, 139–41.
12. R. A. Gordon, "Short-Period Price Determination in Theory and Practice," *Am. Econ. Rev.*, June 1948, *38*, 265–88.
13. *Business Leadership in the Large Corporation*, 2nd ed. with a new preface, Berkeley 1961.
14. R. L. Hall and C. J. Hitch, "Price Theory and Business Behaviour," *Oxford Econ. Papers*, May 1939, *2*, 12–45. Reprinted in T. Wilson, ed., *Oxford Studies in the Price Mechanism*, Oxford 1951, pp. 107–38.
15. S. R. Krupp, "Theoretical Explanation and the Nature of the Firm," *Western Econ. Jour.*, Summer 1963, *1*, 191–204.
16. R. A. Lester, "Shortcomings of Marginal Analysis for Wage-Employment Problems," *Am. Econ. Rev.*, March 1946, *36*, 63–82.
17. "Marginalism, Minimum Wages, and Labor Markets," *Am. Econ. Rev.*, March 1947, *37*, 135–48.
18. A. O. Lovejoy, "The Thirteen Pragmatisms," *Jour. Philosophy*, Jan. 2, 1908, *8*, 5–12, 29–39. Reprinted in *The Thirteen Pragmatisms and Other Essays*, Baltimore 1963.
19. A. O. Lovejoy and G. Boas, *Primitivism and Related Ideas in Antiquity*. Baltimore 1935.
20. F. Machlup, "Evaluation of the Practical Significance of the Theory of Monopolistic Competition," *Am. Econ. Rev.*, June 1939, *29*, 277–36.

21. "Marginal Analysis and Empirical Research," *Am. Econ. Rev.*, Sept. 1946, *36*, 519–54.
22. "Rejoinder to an Antimarginalist," *Am. Econ. Rev.*, March 1947, *37*, 148–54.
23. *The Economics of Sellers' Competition.* Baltimore 1952.
24. "The Problem of Verification in Economics," *So. Econ. Jour.*, July 1955, *22*, 1–21.
25. "Idealtypus, Wirklichkeit, und Konstruktion," *Ordo*, 1960–1961, 21–57.
26. *Essays on Economic Semantics.* Englewood Cliffs, N.J. 1963.
27. R. J. Monsen and A. Downs, "A Theory of Large Managerial Firms," *Jour. Pol. Econ.*, June 1965, *73*, 221–36.
28. A. G. Papandreou, "Some Basic Problems in the Theory of the Firm," in B. F. Haley, ed., *A Survey of Contemporary Economics*, Vol. II, Homewood, Ill. 1952, pp. 183–219.
29. V. Pareto, *Manuel d'économie politique*, 2nd ed. Paris 1927.
30. K. R. Popper, *Conjectures and refutations.* New York and London 1962.
31. M. Reder, "A Reconsideration of the Marginal Productivity Theory," *Jour. Pol. Econ.*, Oct. 1947, *55*, 450–58.
32. J. Robinson, *The Economics of Imperfect Competition.* London 1933.
33. J. A. Schumpeter, "The Instability of Capitalism," *Econ. Jour.*, Sept. 1928, *38*, 361–86.
34. *The Theory of Economic Development.* Cambridge, Mass. 1934.
35. A. Schutz, *Collected Papers*, Vol. II. The Hague 1964.
36. T. Scitovsky, "A Note on Profit Maximisation and Its Implications," *Rev. Econ. Stud.*, Winter 1943, *11*, 57–60. Reprinted in AEA, *Readings in Price Theory*, Homewood, Ill. 1952, pp. 352–58.
37. *Welfare and Competition.* Chicago 1951.
38. H. A. Simon, "A Behavioral Model of Rational Choice," *Quart. Jour. Econ.*, Feb. 1955, *69*, 99–118.
39. *Administrative Behavior*, 2nd ed. New York 1957.
40. "Theories of Decision-Making in Economics and Behavioral Science," *Am. Econ. Rev.*, June 1959, *49*, 253–83.
41. H. von Stackelberg, *Marktform und Gleichgewicht.* Vienna 1934.
42. L. J. Stadler, "The Gene," *Science*, Nov. 19, 1954, *120*, 811–19.
43. G. J. Stigler, "The Economics of Minimum Wage Legislation," *Am. Econ. Rev.*, June 1946, *36*, 358–65.
44. "Professor Lester and the Marginalists," *Am. Econ. Rev.*, March 1947, *37*, 154–57.
45. H. B. Thorelli, "The Political Economy of the Firm: Basis for a New Theory of Competition?" *Schweiz Zeitscher. Volkswirtschaft und Stat.*, 1965, *101*, 248–62.
46. T. Veblen, *The Instinct of Workmanship and the State of the Industrial Arts.* New York 1914.
47. M. Weber, *On the Methodology of the Social Sciences*, transl. and ed. by E. A. Shils and H. A. Finch, Glencoe, Ill. 1949.
48. O. E. Williamson, *Economics of Discretionary Behavior: Managerial Objectives in a Theory of the Firm.* Englewood Cliffs, N.J. 1964.

2

The Motives of Managers, Environmental Restraints, and the Theory of Managerial Enterprise

William L. Baldwin

INTRODUCTION

Recent additions to the large and rapidly growing body of literature analyzing the modern corporation reject, almost without exception, earlier concepts of the business firm in which the firm was treated as an organization designed to implement the economic objectives of an individual or group who were both its owners and managers. Yet in spite of this obvious common source of dissatisfaction among students of the business firm, as well as widespread agreement on the conceptual challenge posed by today's giant corporation, critical reactions to the owner-entrepreneur as an abstraction have led to distinct and not entirely harmonious lines of investigation.

One major line, which may be described as attempts to develop a theory of managerial enterprise, assumes the separation of ownership and control in large, widely owned corporations and recognizes the fact that most of these corporations operate in oligopolistic markets where their managers are free enough from the pressures of competition to choose among alternative courses of action. Theories of managerial enterprise deal primarily with the objectives of professional managers, the external restraints under which these objectives are carried out in oligopolistic markets, and the business behavior which results from the assumed managerial objectives and restraints. The common assumptions underlying this line of work are that management, emancipated from control by owners, for-

Reprinted by permission of the publisher from William L. Baldwin, *The Quarterly Journal of Economics,* Cambridge, Mass.: Harvard University Press, Copyright 1964, by the President and Fellows of Harvard College.

mulates the objectives of the firm and that managerial goals may differ from those of the stockholders.

It would be a caricature of the theories of managerial enterprise, and grossly unfair to a number of discerning writers, to state that the theories assume that managers' objectives alone motivate the market behavior of giant corporations. Certainly, the literature recognizes restraints on managers other than the actions of oligopolistic rivals. Yet I consider it a fair criticism to observe that there is a distinguishable body of work in which attention has been directed almost exclusively to management as the group which impresses its goals on the corporation in the process of both making and carrying out basic corporate decisions. This emphasis leads to assumptions that frequently ignore and are occasionally inconsistent with the findings of recent studies which deal with the corporate organization, its environment, and the nature of power in the modern business world. Some of these studies threaten to make models based on managerial autonomy appear nearly as simplistic and inapplicable to modern corporate reality as are earlier models based on the owner-entrepreneur.

The purpose of this paper is to argue that further development of the theory of managerial enterprise, if it is to become of increasing value for descriptive, normative and policy-formulating purposes, must place greater emphasis on the varied types of nonmarket as well as market restraints within which managerial functions are performed. I maintain that only after examining a number of significant contributions to our understanding of managerial goals and functions and placing these contributions within an appropriate framework of restraints, is it possible to assess the effect of the elimination of the owner-entrepreneur on the usefulness of a revised theory of the firm. The restraints appear to be of such nature that it is inadvisable to substitute managerial goals for the traditionally assumed business orientation towards profits.

BEHAVIORAL ASSUMPTIONS UNDERLYING THEORIES OF MANAGERIAL ENTERPRISE

The most important distinguishing assumptions behind the concept of managerial enterprise are the central role of managers in determining the purposes for which the large, widely owned corporation is operated, and the relatively unhindered power of managers to make the decisions necessary to carry out these purposes.[1] In the late 1940's and early 1950's, works concerned with various aspects of managerialism typically treated a high degree of managerial control over business property as a phenomenon to be discussed but as one whose exis-

---

[1] The pioneering work is, of course, A. A. Berle and G. C. Means, *The Modern Corporation and Private Property* (New York: Macmillan, 1932). For further attempts at assessing the extent and importance of separation of ownership and control, see the following: M. E. Dimock and H. K. Hyde, T.N.E.C. Monograph, No. 11, *Bureaucracy and Trusteeship in Large Corporations* (Washington: Government Printing Office, 1940); James Burnham, *The Managerial Revolution: What Is Happening in the World* (New York: John Day, 1941); and R. A. Gordon, *Business Leadership in the Large Corporation* (Washington: Brookings Institution, 1945).

tence could be assumed to have been demonstrated by earlier writers.[2] It was further recognized that the motives of managers would differ from those of the profit-maximizing owner-entrepreneur. Motives such as personal vanity, desire to control the largest possible industrial empire, maximization of personal remuneration, and recognition of widespread professional responsibilities have not only been attributed to management but also treated as the forces which underlie and explain corporate behavior.[3]

Theories of managerial enterprise, explicitly or tacitly accepting the dominance of managers, have focused on the formulation of managerial objectives which can be treated as the motivational forces in various descriptive and predictive models. It should be noted that the essence of a theory and of a broadly applicable model is abstraction. Thus, it is no valid criticism of a motivational assumption to provide one or a few scattered counterexamples from the real world. Yet in a theory of the firm which claims current relevance we can hope for simplifying assumptions which in description or effect approximate important aspects of modern corporate reality. The most significant among assumptions in recent literature which appear to meet reasonable standards of realism and relevance can be grouped into three general types: target rate of return, maximization of sales or growth subject to a profit constraint, and managerial mediation of the claims made by various groups on what has been called the "Responsible Corporation." All three types have two things in common. They are supported by logic or by respectable evidence based on observation or testimony, and they reject profits maximization as a useful or realistic abstraction.

Pricing to yield a predetermined target rate of return on investment might be viewed as a behavioral assumption developing with some logic out of earlier studies of full-cost pricing, or out of the organizational theory concept of "satisficing" which March and Simon describe as looking for a sharp enough needle in the haystack, rather than the sharpest. Cyert and March apply the concept to the business firm by assuming the firm's objective is an acceptable level of profit rather than the maximum attainable. Satisficing has been tested in experimental goal-seeking and problem-solving situations and appears to be a verifiable type of human behavior.[4]

However, the most important recent contribution which stresses target rate of return pricing is the 1958 study made under the auspices of the Brookings Institution by Kaplan, Dirlam and Lanzillotti, which relies primarily on the direct evidence of actual pricing practices of large firms as reported in interviews with

[2] See, e.g., the following: Peter Drucker, *Concept of the Corporation* (New York: John Day, 1946); Oswald Knauth, *Managerial Enterprise: Its Growth and Methods of Operation* (New York: Norton, 1948); David Lilienthal, *Big Business: A New Era* (New York: Harper, 1952); A. A. Berle, *The 20th Century Capitalist Revolution* (New York: Harcourt, Brace, 1954); Herrymon Maurer, *Great Enterprise: Growth and Behavior of the Big Corporation* (New York: Macmillan, 1955).

[3] The leading work is C. I. Barnard, *The Functions of the Executive* (Cambridge: Harvard University Press, 1938). Similar ideas are expressed in the works of Drucker, Knauth, Lilienthal, Berle, and Maurer cited above.

[4] J. C. March and H. A. Simon, *Organizations* (New York: Wiley, 1958), pp. 140-41. See also R. M. Cyert and J. G. March, "Organizational Factors in the Theory of Oligopoly," *The Quarterly Journal of Economics*, LXX (Feb. 1956), 44-64.

business executives.[5] The Brookings researchers carefully qualified their findings, noting difficulties inherent in the interview technique and warning readers that their findings should not be interpreted as contradictory to the assumption of profits maximization. They regard profits maximization as of little if any operational usefulness, rather than as incorrect. "For the most part," they observed, "the companies doubted that by changing their pricing policies they could raise their profits in the long run." [6] Kaplan, Dirlam and Lanzillotti concluded, "There has been, as already noted, some clustering around a norm of target return pricing. But the discussions of policy also disclosed that among those that could be characterized in general as following an administered, stabilized, cost-plus system of pricing, the degree of precision and of compliance ranged too widely to make target return a master key to pricing." [7]

Both target rate of return and satisficing models treat some form of profits as an objective. Thus Lanzillotti, referring to the Brookings findings, states, "The foregoing data, above all, make it clear that management's approach to pricing is based upon *planned* profits." [8] Cyert and March argue for the use of an "acceptable-level profit norm" in place of profits maximization as a motivational assumption warranted by current knowledge of both individual and organizational behavior.[9]

In contrast to target rate of return and satisficing, recent models presented by Baumol and Marris make a more fundamental break with traditional assumptions by treating the need for profits as a restraint on managers who are maximizing other variables.[10] Although rejection of the role of profits as an objective is a basic change in *assumptions*, the *methods* employed by Baumol and Marris are in accord with traditional economic analysis of maximization or minimization, unlike theories assuming some given level of profits as a goal. In *Business Behavior, Value and Growth*, Baumol offers the hypothesis that oligopolistic firms seek to maximize sales revenue subject to a restraint in the form of a minimum necessary rate of profit. Baumol argues that the hypothesis is more realistic than profits maximization and that it can be used to explain certain aspects of observed behavior that are inconsistent with the older assumption. In defending the greater realism of his assumption, Baumol draws convincingly on his personal experiences as a business consultant. In his later article, Baumol suggests

[5] A. D. H. Kaplan, J. B. Dirlam and R. F. Lanzillotti, *Pricing in Big Business: A Case Approach* (Washington: Brookings Institution, 1958).

[6] *Ibid.*, p. 130.

[7] *Ibid.*, p. 284. See also R. F. Lanzillotti, "Pricing Objectives in Large Companies," *American Economic Review*, XLVIII (Dec. 1958), 921–40. Lanzillotti's statement on the uselessness of profits maximization as a motivational hypothesis is stronger than that in the Brookings study.

[8] *Op. cit.*, p. 938. Italics in original.

[9] *Op. cit.*, pp. 47–49.

[10] W. J. Baumol, *Business Behavior, Value and Growth* (New York: Macmillan, 1959); idem, "The Theory of Expansion of the Firm," *American Economic Review*, LII (Dec. 1962), 1078–87. Robin Marris, "A Model of the 'Managerial' Enterprise," *The Quarterly Journal of Economics*, LXXVII (May 1963), 185–209. Marris explicitly notes the restraining role of profits as a feature distinguishing his and Baumol's models from prior satisficing models of organizational theorists.

that maximization of the rate of growth of sales, which implies an optimum rather than a maximum profit rate, is an appropriate motivational assumption for a dynamic model of an oligopolistic firm.[11] Marris, who assumes maximization of the rate of growth of corporate capital limited by a desire for security against bankruptcy and take-over raids, does not regard his model as contradictory to Baumol's. He notes in respect to indicia of size of the firm that "maximizing the long-run growth rate of any one indicator can reasonably be assumed equivalent to maximizing the growth rate of most others." [12]

Some defenders of giant firms and of the resulting concentration of industry have drawn support from the separation of ownership and control. Management, it is claimed, is becoming a profession; and professional managers tend to regard themselves as trustees of corporate property, exercising their powers for the benefit of virtually all those who come into contact with the corporation and adjudicating conflicting claims of such beneficiaries as stockholders, employees, customers, suppliers, communities and the general public. This concept of managerial motivation may be described by Herrymon Maurer's phrase, "the Responsible Corporation." [13] Pronouncements by corporate executives and their public relations department indicating firm and undeviating adherence to corporate responsibility may be regarded with deep skepticism, but we cannot dismiss as merely naïve the acceptance of the importance of these goals by several students of the corporation. Berle, for example, sees corporate recognition of public responsibilities as a response to an observed need for justifying or giving legitimacy to managerial power.[14] Legitimacy may well be recognized as a necessary condition for continued possession of power. Further, if the doctrine of the Responsible Corporation is repeated frequently and fervently enough, executives who expound it, and more importantly their successors, may come to believe in or at least live by what was originally a mere rationalization. It is almost as hard to believe that all claims of recognition of public responsibility are examples of self-seeking hypocrisy as it is to believe in the absolute truth of all. At least some of the verbiage ought to be accepted as a genuine search for a *raison d'être* among business executives.

Thus, managerial enterprise has been described as driven by at least three fundamental motivational forces. Behavioral hypotheses based on all three can be justified on grounds of both a priori logic and substantial degrees of empirical evidence. However, those wishing to develop or apply a theory of managerial enterprise are not necessarily forced into a difficult or arbitrary selection and rejection of motivational assumptions. Two other alternatives are open. First, one could argue that among a diverse business population motivational forces would differ with size of the firm, form of organization, nature of product, various

---

[11] *Op. cit.*, pp. 1085–86.

[12] *Op. cit.*, p. 192.

[13] *Op. cit.*, pp. 68–71. Recognition of some or all of these responsibilities is also attributed to management in the works of Berle, Drucker, Knauth, and Lilienthal previously cited.

[14] *Op. cit.* For further discussion of the concept of "legitimacy" see Berle, *Power Without Property: A New Development in American Political Economy* (New York: Harcourt, Brace, 1959), and Richard Eels, *The Government of Corporations* (New York: The Glencoe Free Press, 1962).

aspects of market structure and other environmental influences. Lanzillotti, who found target rate of return pricing the most frequently stated objective, but only one among several within the firms interviewed, advocates such an approach.[15] Baumol defends the realism of his sales maximization hypothesis only in application to models of oligopolistic firms. Cyert and March state, in presenting a model of an oligopolistic decision-making process, "It is believed that decision rules must have an empirical basis and that they cannot be derived by deduction." Therefore they refrain from positing any general method for determining an acceptable profit level.[16] But this alternative appears to be a counsel of despair, threatening to reduce the theory of managerial enterprise to a chaotic state in which each firm is examined as a unique entity and in which theorizing about oligopolistic markets involving a number of dissimilar firms with various objectives seems nearly hopeless.[17] Before accepting such a sacrifice of simplicity, neatness and generality of the theory as inevitable, a second alternative should be explored. The three types of behavioral assumptions mentioned above may be examined for consistency among themselves and for the extent of their inconsistency with profits maximization. Hopefully they can be fitted into a single meaningful motivational framework. The remainder of this paper is primarily devoted to this task.

TARGET RATE OF RETURN PRICING AS A MANAGERIAL TOOL

There is no question but that prices are frequently calculated on the basis of a predetermined rate of return on business assets.[18] Yet if the objective of management is viewed as earning a certain percentage yield on total invested capital, whether supplied by stock purchases, borrowing or retained earnings, obvious elements of indeterminacy arise. A specified target rate might be achieved by setting prices to yield that rate on a given volume of assets, or additional capital might be invested until the target rate is earned with a given set of prices, or both prices and the level of investment might be varied with numerous combinations leading to the target rate. In order to yield determinate prices and levels

---

[15] *Op. cit.*, pp. 938–39.

[16] *Op. cit.*, pp. 46, 61.

[17] The chaos may possibly be made manageable by further developments in the theory of interfirm organization, as suggested by Almarin Phillips, "A Theory of Interfirm Organization," *The Quarterly Journal of Economics*, LXXIV (Nov. 1960), 602–13. See also by the same author, *Market Structure, Organization and Performance* (Cambridge: Harvard University Press, 1962), chap. 1.

[18] In addition to the survey by Kaplan, Dirlam and Lanzillotti, the prevalence of target rate of return pricing or its equivalent is indicated in N. W. Chamberlain, *The Firm: Micro-economic Planning and Action* (New York: McGraw-Hill, 1962), chap. 4. Target rate of return and full-cost pricing are consistent with each other, since a predetermined rate of return on total assets may be converted into a standard percentage mark-up on full costs by dividing the target rate of return on assets by the asset turnover ratio $\left(\dfrac{\text{cost of goods sold}}{\text{average total assets}} \right)$, assuming standard costs at a given percentage of capacity output.

of investment, additional assumptions are necessary. One might, for example, assume that managers desire the largest possible volume of sales or of assets under their control consistent with the target rate.

Another use of target rate of return is as a device for determining increments of investment. Under this test, a potential project is undertaken only if the estimated yield on the required investment is equal to or exceeds a predetermined rate.[19] But a yield on investment can be computed only after prices and associated outputs are estimated. One cannot use a predetermined yield to set prices and evaluate an investment proposal simultaneously. Also, it should be noted that target rate of return as a criterion for limiting investment is fundamentally inconsistent with pricing to yield a target rate of return, as the former is an incremental or marginal concept implying an average rate of return above the target, whereas the latter implies an average rate of return equal to the target rate.

A final objection to target rate of return pricing as an objective is that simply assuming a target rate avoids the question which is most important both in the decision-making process and in any attempt to use the theory of managerial enterprise for normative purposes: i.e., what determines or limits the target rate?

It would appear that although a target rate of return is in fact frequently utilized in corporate planning and decision-making, it cannot be regarded as a true goal of management. Rather, it seems far more reasonable to assume that a target rate of return is a tool, used to assist in the attainment of other goals. Chamberlain, on the basis of an extensive review of managerial and accounting literature and a questionnaire survey of his own, concludes that both standard mark-up on fully allocated costs and pricing to yield a target rate of return on investment are "simply useful instruments in its [management's] objective of making a profit."[20] The observation of Kaplan, Dirlam and Lanzillotti, that most of the firms they interviewed did not believe they could increase their long-run profits by changing their pricing procedures, is consistent with Chamberlain's conclusion.[21] A. E. Kahn, in a perceptive comment on Lanzillotti's article, emphasizes the significance of the firms' belief. "The misconstruction," he noted, "is in confusing *procedures* with *'goals.'* Actually, the target return seems above all to reflect what the executives think the company can get; and to the extent actual earnings diverge from the target, it is because the market turns out to allow more or less."[22]

[19] This is a highly simplified statement. In Chamberlain, *op. cit.*, chap. 12, and in Joel Dean, *Capital Budgeting* (New York: Columbia University Press, 1951), investment criteria involving alternative methods of discounting and deciding upon cut-off points are discussed.

[20] *Op. cit.*, p. 207. To avoid misinterpretation, it should be noted that Chamberlain further maintains that the profit sought is not a predetermined theoretical maximum, but rather "as good a performance as management can expect in its effort to secure certain rather specific primary and anterior goals."

[21] An outstanding apparent exception is the United States Steel Corporation, one of whose officials stated, "U.S. Steel has never tried to price to maximum profit not only in the short run but even in the long run." Kaplan, Dirlam and Lanzillotti, *op. cit.*, p. 23.

[22] "Pricing Objectives in Large Companies: Comment," *American Economic Review*, XLIX (Sept. 1959), 670–78, at p. 671. Italics in original.

One of the most interesting possibilities relates target rate of return pricing to barriers to entry. Means has suggested that if a firm is concerned with maintaining a level of profit above the competitive rate, "the price-maker starts with an estimate of the highest rate of profits which will not induce new entrants and then works back to determine the prices which will just yield this rate of profit when operating at a reasonable proportion of capacity. This procedure has come to be known as pricing for a target rate of return on investment or, more simply, as *target pricing*." [23]

Bain has developed a classification of barriers to entry based on the influence of potential entrants on price policy. Bain describes entry as "blockaded" when the price that would attract new entrants is above the profit-maximizing price of the most favored firms now in the industry and is hence irrelevant. Entry is "effectively impeded" if the entry-forestalling price is lower than the price which would exist in the absence of concern over possible entrants but is far enough above the competitive price to make the present value of profits associated with the entry-forestalling price greater than the present value of those which could be gained by charging higher prices and attracting entrants. Entry is "ineffectively impeded" when the entry-forestalling price is so slightly above the competitive level that it is more profitable to charge higher, entry-inducing prices.[24] Bain's second case, of "effectively impeded" entry would appear to coincide with the conditions described by Means.

In addition, Bain classified twenty industries in terms of the height of barriers to entry rather than degree of impedance. A comparison of this latter classification with Lanzillotti's list of primary pricing objectives of twenty firms yields results suggesting consistency with Means' statement.[25] Very crudely, we should expect to find a positive correlation between the height of barriers to entry and use of target rate of return pricing unless entry is blockaded. For each of his industries, Bain lists the four largest firms; and nine of Lanzillotti's firms appear on these lists. Of the nine, four indicated target rate of return as their primary pricing objective. One of these four is in an industry classified by Bain as having very high entry barriers, and the other three are in industries whose barriers are classified as substantial. Of the five firms reporting other primary objectives (maintenance of market share, stabilization of price and meeting competitors), three are in industries with substantial barriers to entry and the remaining two are in industries classified as having moderate to low entry barriers.[26]

Thus, use of a target rate of return is consistent with a profit motivation, with or without the restraining condition of potential entry. If the objective is assumed to be profits and the target rate determined either by the maximum rate

---

[23] G. C. Means, *Pricing Power and the Public Interest* (New York: Harper, 1962), p. 236. Italics in original.

[24] J. S. Bain, *Barriers to New Competition: Their Character and Consequences in Manufacturing Industries* (Cambridge: Harvard University Press, 1956), pp. 21–23.

[25] The comparison is of such a small sample and is so unsystematic that it is definitely not to be regarded as independent verification. Further, Bain warns that the height of absolute barriers to entry is only roughly comparable to his classification of the degrees of impedance.

[26] Bain, *op. cit.*, pp. 192–194. Lanzillotti, *op. cit.*, pp. 924–27.

attainable or the highest rate which will not attract entrants,[27] the outcome is determinate and the target rate becomes a workable planning device.

The use of a target rate of return is also consistent with objectives other than profit. Baumol's minimum necessary rate of return, which acts as a constraint on the maximization of sales revenue, may be viewed as a target, determined in his model by the prices set for securities in a competitive capital market and by a firm's need for capital. Similarly, Marris regards the rate of profit necessary to ensure an adequate degree of security against bankruptcy and take-over raids as a constraint on the growth rate when the profit rate associated with maximum growth is deemed too low to furnish such security. But in the models of Baumol and Marris, as in those treating profits as an objective, a determinate result is obtained only when the determinants of the target rate are specified and a variable to be maximized is posited.

Finally, a "just," "fair" or "traditional" target rate of return might be assumed by the proponents of the Responsible Corporation as a necessary but not sufficient condition to balance management's responsibilities to stockholders against responsibilities to other groups.

Target rate of return pricing, in summary, should be viewed as a tool rather than as an objective. As such, it is in no way inconsistent with the hypothesized objectives still to be discussed.

MANAGEMENT GOALS AND RESTRAINTS ON MANAGERIAL AUTONOMY

Theories of managerial enterprise such as those of Baumol and Marris and the literature of the Responsible Corporation have two things in common. First, they deny that profits maximization is a reasonable assumption to make about managerial goals; and second, they focus on managerial goals they regard as more plausible, assuming that since management controls the business property these goals best explain the motive force behind the actions of the firm. In order to assess the import of these critical modifications of the traditional theory of the firm, while granting that an attempt to resurrect the owner-entrepreneur would be retrogressive, it is necessary to consider the extent of the conflict between profits and the assumed goals of managers and to examine the actual amount of freedom managers have to impose their goals on the firm.

[27] In my book, *Antitrust and the Changing Corporation* (Durham: Duke University Press, 1961), I argued that existing oligopolistic firms need not actually hold price down to the entry-barring level if potential entrants consider predicted rather than existing prices as relevant to their decision to enter, at pp. 201–3. Where economies of scale are such that potential entrants must be large, it seemed reasonable to attribute to them the same sort of oligopolistic rationale usually attributed to firms already in a market of few sellers. I still maintain that it is not always reasonable for the potential entrant to assume that the worst thing that can happen to him will be that existing firms will maintain their output so that the industry's price drops by enough to absorb his output. Price may drop much further if existing degrees of tacit or overt collusion are upset by the entrant. But I now suspect that I made too much of an issue over a logical possibility, as a result of underestimating the preference of oligopolistic firms for price stability and therefore overestimating the likelihood of firms deliberately cutting price as a defensive or retaliatory tactic after entry had occurred.

Managers, taken as individuals engaged in an organizational activity, clearly have numerous goals of their own such as personal financial rewards, security, power and prestige within the organization, desire to be liked, human sympathy, the urge to create and perhaps occasionally the desire for an easy life. But all employees bring a complex of personal objectives to the organizations in which they participate. Indeed, one central concern of modern organization theory is with the methods by which organizations induce members to join and to participate in achieving the goals of the organization and in the process resolve conflicts between personal and organizational goals.[28] Thus it is recognized that organizations have goals of their own and that a certain degree of fulfillment of participants' personal goals is a necessary cost incurred in channeling individual actions towards achievement of the organization's purpose. In this respect, individual managers are no different from other employees. The use of committees as decision-making units, requirements that proposals be justified by estimated rates of return, decentralization of authority and responsibility, salary and promotion boards, the inability of any one man to comprehend all aspects of a giant firm, and the philosophy and traditions embodied in the "corporate personality,"[29] to say nothing of the much-publicized pressures towards conformity among "organization men," all serve to prevent any individual from imposing his will on the corporate organization. The managerial motives which should concern us, therefore, are those which are common to management as a group or suborganization. Sales revenue and growth maximization can both be defended on the ground that the salaries and very probably prestige of the entire managerial group are more dependent on the scale of operation than on profit.[30] Acceptance of social corporate responsibility has been regarded as a necessary defense of the position and perquisites of management as a whole.

To some extent, achievement of the goals ascribed to managers enhances profitability. Baumol notes that maximizing sales revenue helps long-run profits in several ways. Consumers may favor products they consider growing in use, credit may be positively related to sales volume, a firm's market power may decline if it loses distributors or market share, and employee relations are better in firms which are hiring than in those which are firing.[31] In Marris' model, once the financial policy dealing with retention of earnings, dividends and reinvestment is given, maximizing the rate of growth implies maximization of the rate of profit.[32] Virtually all of the writers who emphasize management's responsibilities to various groups note that the corporate property must be managed efficiently in order to carry out the responsibilities properly.[33] But the meaning of efficiency is elusive. Mason has raised a crucial question as to what criteria managers are

---

[28] March and Simon, *op. cit.*, chaps. 3, 4, 5.

[29] For an extended discussion of corporate philosophy, tradition and personality see Maurer, *op. cit.*, chaps. 8, 9, 10.

[30] Baumol, *Business Behavior, Value and Growth, op. cit.*, p. 46. See also D. R. Roberts, "A General Theory of Executive Compensation Based on Statistically Tested Propositions," *The Quarterly Journal of Economics*, LXX (May, 1956), 270-94.

[31] *Business Behavior, Value and Growth, op. cit.*, p. 46.

[32] *Op. cit.*, p. 204.

[33] Drucker, *op. cit.*, pp. 39-40, 119, 122, 231, has perhaps the most comprehensive and forceful discussion of the importance of internal efficiency.

supposed to use in setting prices and remunerating factors when they are trying to do the best they can for society, laborers, customers and owners. "I can find no reasoned answer," he notes, "in the managerial literature."[34] One partial answer, and as Mason observes it is only partial, is that efficiency implies the most profitable price and resource use. The profits might then be distributed among various claimants in accordance with some concept of social justice or fairness, perhaps using rebates to reimburse customers.

The managerial motives under discussion are not fully consistent with profits maximization. In the absence of a profit restraint Baumol's sales revenue maximizer will aim for the price and output combination at which the demand curve facing it is of unitary elasticity and its marginal revenue is zero, implying a price below and an output above that of a profits maximizer with positive marginal costs. Marris notes that when the financial policy assumed in his model is permitted to vary, the associated maximum growth and profit rates vary in opposite directions from each other. Maximizing the profit which then may be distributed is not an appropriate strategy for managers concerned with "fairness" to groups who cannot be identified or reimbursed. If managers with the motives assumed by Baumol or Marris or a group managing a Responsible Corporation were free to run a firm as they saw fit, the results would not be those of a profit-maximizing firm.

Nevertheless, the same decisions would often be made under profits maximization and some other criterion; and it would appear that if managers were under certain types of constraints their motives could be utilized as incentives in directing their activities towards an organizational goal of profits. For example, a non-management group such as an outside board of directors or dominant stockholders could impose some form of profit-maximizing financial policy on a firm and then leave a group of Marris' managers free to maximize the growth rate subject to that policy. Profits maximization, alone, is not sufficient to determine the precise financial policy which should be adopted. The policy, of course, will also depend on the extent of the controlling group's preference for present over future income and the degree of their aversion to risk.

Lilienthal [35] and Kaplan,[36] in 1952 and 1954 respectively, noted the rise of important institutional investors as alert and knowledgeable stockholder groups. In the decade since they wrote, institutional investment has continued to grow. In 1959 books, both Berle and Father P. P. Harbrecht explored the extent and significance of the phenomenon.[37] Harbrecht found that financial institutions controlled the voting rights of 27 to 30 per cent of all corporate stocks outstanding and found ample reason to believe that these institutions will continue their net stock purchases. Although many pension and trust funds have policies against acquiring a controlling interest in any one firm, the funds are concentrated in a few major New York banks who, as trustees, vote the stocks of funds they are

---

[34] E. S. Mason, "The Apologetics of 'Managerialism,'" *Journal of Business of the University of Chicago*, XXXI (Jan. 1958), 1–11, at p. 7.

[35] *Op. cit.*, p. 135.

[36] A. D. H. Kaplan, *Big Enterprise in a Competitive System* (Washington: Brookings Institution, 1954), p. 179.

[37] Berle, *Power Without Property, op. cit.*; Paul P. Harbrecht, S.J., *Pension Funds and Economic Power* (New York: Twentieth Century Fund, 1959).

managing and who may be unable to avoid positions of control. Further, institutional purchases are concentrated in "blue chip" securities which are predominantly those of giant corporations. Harbrecht's conclusions deserve to be quoted at some length:

> It may not be too much to say that the center of influence in our economy, having left the Wall Street of the 1920s and migrated in the 1930s and 1940s to the provincial centers of corporate power, has now returned to New York financial circles. What is more, the financial strength now building up in the New York banks is of a different character. The power position that was consolidated in the 1920s was deliberately sought by the financiers and had no stable institutional character. But, as we have already noted, the present concentration of financial power is not so much the result of a drive for power as it is of (1) social demands which require the aggregation of great wealth to provide security, and (2) the fortunate presence of the financial institutions as apt media for administering this wealth. The alignment of forces now taking shape is of an institutional and permanent character which will be part of our economic and social structure for some time to come. What we are witnessing is a genuine evolutionary development rather than a temporary consolidation of power resulting from personal acquisitiveness.[38]

Harbrecht's findings strongly imply that the managerial literature of the 1930's, 1940's and early 1950's may have been valid at the time of writing, but of only transitory importance. The group which predominates in shaping the objectives of giant corporations may prove to be managers of banks, mutual funds and insurance companies rather than those managing the actual corporate property. The institutional investors, like other stockholders, should be primarily interested in profits; and unlike many small individual investors, however sophisticated, the institutions should find it a rational allocation of staff and executive time to devote much observation and study to the policies and prospects of firms in which they have invested or may invest. It may be argued that institutional trust officers have individual and group objectives similar to those of corporate management, but even if this contention is granted their attitudes towards corporations whose securities they acquire should be as objective and profit-oriented as the attitudes of corporate managers towards specific machines or tools.[39]

Harbrecht and others have pointed out that even if institutions refrain from exercising their control through voting power or support existing management as a matter of policy, their investment decisions will have an important influence on security prices and the availability of capital. Scattered small shareholders

---

[38] *Op. cit.*, pp. 249–50.

[39] There is one significant qualification to the assumption that fund managers should seek to maximize profits. Traditionally and under present law, trustees are expected to manage the *corpus* of a trust in the best interests of the beneficiaries. But where, as in a pension fund, beneficiaries are entitled to fixed, contractual incomes, increasing the rate of return on the fund can only redound to the benefit of the creator of the fund, whose periodic payments may be reduced as a result. Harbrecht, *op. cit.*, p. 101.

have, as a group, a similar power to influence management by sale of their holdings when they are dissatisfied, since the sale of a small fraction of an outstanding security issue may depress the price severely.

Other restraints on management which tend to direct their activities towards profits maximization may be mentioned. First, there is the threat of a proxy fight. Corporate raiding has become almost a profession, or more accurately a full-time highly skilled occupation. In all probability the very largest corporations are quite immune from raids—at least I find it difficult to imagine a successful attack on General Motors or U.S. Steel—but those most invulnerable to the raider are those Harbrecht finds most attractive to the institutional investor. And it seems clear from the work of Karr and others that in the firms which we might call middle-sized giants, perhaps among the nation's largest 500 but below the top 50, the position of inefficient or self-serving management is far from secure against proxy attacks.[40] Second, the law still presumes that directors have a fiduciary relation to stockholders and are trustees for them. Stockholders' derivative suits, as difficult as they may be to win, possess a substantial nuisance value. Finally, Earley's studies of accounting and budgeting practices show increasing adoption of managerial techniques utilizing marginal principles. In one article Earley concludes, "Undoubtedly the new techniques of business management make it advisable to change somewhat the simpler models of the business firm and its behavior. But the postulate that the typical firm searches vigorously for larger profits and has impressive means to conduct this search should be retained."[41] Use of sophisticated and profit-oriented methods of financial reporting and control should be regarded, in part, as a managerial response to external pressures but also as an additional organizational restraint imposed on the present management.

In summary, we have reviewed only those motives ascribed to management which appear logically reasonable and in accord with available evidence. These motives are apparently such that, under appropriate external and organizational restraints, the activities of a managerial group can be directed towards an organizational goal of profits without undue conflict. None of the writers cited in this paper assumes that managers have absolute autonomy in their control of corporate property. But it does appear that the managerial literature, taken as a whole, has failed to recognize the full range and significance of internal and external restraints in limiting the ability of managers to translate their objectives into organizational purposes. The cumulative effect of these restraints would appear to be such as to cast grave doubts on the wisdom of substituting managerial goals for profits.

[40] David Karr, *Fight for Control* (New York: Ballantine Books, 1956). Marris, *op. cit.*, p. 19 notes a "dramatic crop" of raids in the United Kingdom, citing George Bull and Anthony Vice, *Bid for Power* (London: Elek, 1958) and several articles in *Fortune* and the *London Observer*.

[41] James S. Earley, "Business Budgeting and the Theory of the Firm," *Journal of Industrial Economics* (Nov. 1960), 23–42, at p. 39. See also, by the same author, "Recent Developments in Cost Accounting and the 'Marginal Analysis,'" *Journal of Political Economy*, LXIII (June 1955), 227–42, and "Marginal Policies of 'Excellently Managed' Companies," *American Economic Review*, XLVI (March 1956), 44–70.

IMPLICATIONS FOR THE THEORY OF THE FIRM

We have noted two arguments in support of throwing profits maximization onto the same scrap pile of obsolete tools where the owner-entrepreneur now rests in order to develop a realistic theory of managerial enterprise. First, the assumption is said to be unrealistic for the modern giant corporation with which the theory is concerned; and second, even if some form of long-run profits maximization is regarded as the ultimate objective, the concept is considered too vague to be useful.

It is not contended here that the external and organizational restraints just reviewed are sufficient to compel all corporate managers to make all of their decisions exclusively on the basis of maximization of organizational profits. But if we want a theory of managerial enterprise which assumes a single organizational objective subject to maximization or minimization, profit does appear to be more realistic than any of the alternatives offered. The advantages of such a unified theory are substantial if we want to apply theoretical analysis to markets involving a number of firms, to prediction and evaluation of industrial performance, and to problems of public policy. The findings reviewed in this paper strongly suggest, although the contention is in no way definitely proven, that profit maximization is a fairly close approximation to actual motives of the typical large corporation and that any losses suffered by abstracting from the complexity of interplay among real-world motives will be relatively minor.

The fact remains that the theory of the firm is in an inadequate state. Even if profits maximization is the most accurate single motivational assumption we can make in dealing with the modern corporation, it may be virtually useless as a basis for determination of a single most rational solution to many problems. The core of the difficulty lies in the fact that often a course of action which could not be predicted can be explained in terms of long-run profits maximization after the fact, if and only if certain *ex post* assumptions are made about the internal organization of the firm and about how its environment affected its views on risk aversion, the probabilities of future developments, and the appropriate rate at which to discount future earnings.[42] It is a valid criticism that the concept of

[42] There is a semantic trap to be avoided in dealing with profit as an ultimate objective. Saying that the firm maximizes long-run rather than short-run profits implies that the income stream whose present value is being maximized is based on estimates extending several years or even decades into the future and the discount rate used is low enough so that events rather distant in the future have an appreciable effect on the present value of the stream. In the traditional static partial equilibrium theory of the firm, short run and long run have completely different meanings. To determine short-run equilibrium certain costs are held fixed, so that the associated marginal costs are zero; while to determine long-run equilibrium all costs are permitted to vary. Calendar time, strictly speaking, has nothing to do with the distinction. A firm maximizing long-run profits may still be viewed as equating short-run marginal cost and marginal revenue in making certain decisions. Both Chamberlain, *op. cit.*, and Earley, especially in "Recent Developments in Cost Accounting and the 'Marginal Analysis,'" *op. cit.*, emphasize the crucial importance modern managerial accounting techniques put on determining the precise costs which should be taken into account in making a certain decision. Thus, assuming that managerial firms aim at maximizing long-run profits should not be equated with denying the value of short-run analysis in the theory of managerial enterprise.

long-run profits maximization is vague. Individuals and presumably organizations differ in their time preferences and degrees of aversion to risk. Even if the rate for discounting future income is assumed, there is no generally accepted formulation of rational behavior under conditions of uncertainty.[43] Modigliani and Miller have recently made effective use of maximization of the present market value of the firm's outstanding shares as the criterion for investment and financing decisions under conditions of uncertainty, thus throwing the ascertainment of appropriate risk and time preference functions back to a market-determined consensus of present and potential investors.[44] In the absence of a refined and undoubtedly complex theory of securities market behavior, profits maximization will continue to yield ambiguous results in many cases. But this empty box should not preclude us from assuming, in the numerous problems where relative profitabilities can be compared, that the most profitable course of action will be chosen.

The defense of profits maximization embodied in this paper amounts only to an argument that the trouble with the existing body of theory is inadequacy instead of error. But it also implies that the remedy lies in further exploration of the relevant characteristics of modern giant corporations and of their environments, rather than new motivational assumptions. Baumol, for example, notes as an advantage of and justification for his assumption of sales revenue maximization that the resulting model can be used to explain observed patterns of behavior which are inexplicable in traditional theory, such as price changes in response to changes in fixed overhead costs and the actual shifting of taxes which have been regarded as unshiftable. But these and similar shortcomings of traditional theory need not be blamed on the assumption of profit-maximizing behavior. Rather, the error may lie in neglect of the constraints to which such behavior is subject. In Bain's analysis, for one, changes in such items as fixed costs and lump-sum or percentage-of-profit taxes will influence even the short-run equilibrium of a profit-maximizing firm if the changes affect conditions of potential entry and thus the entry-barring price.

The literature already includes valuable pioneering contributions to greater understanding of crucial characteristics of the corporate world. Managerial decisions are made and profits earned in an environment which includes the market for corporate securities, conditions of entry such as noted by Bain, the external

---

[43] For a brief but excellent summary of alternative decision rules under uncertainty, see W. J. Baumol, *Economic Theory and Operations Analysis* (Englewood Cliffs: Prentice-Hall, 1961), chap. 19.

[44] Franco Modigliani and M. H. Miller, "The Cost of Capital, Corporation Finance and the Theory of Investment," *American Economic Review*, XLVIII (June 1958), 261–97, at p. 264. F. A. and Vera Lutz have shown that, under conditions of certainty, maximizing present value leads to the same investment decisions as maximizing profit, in *The Theory of Investment of the Firm* (Princeton: Princeton University Press, 1951). Miller and Modigliani, assuming maximization of present value, have used the assumption in analysis which includes uncertainty. See also M. J. Gordon, "The Savings Investment and Valuation of a Corporation," *Review of Economics and Statistics*, XLIV (Feb. 1962), 37–51. Gordon demonstrates the complexity inherent in a comprehensive theory of the securities market by emphasizing the dependence of stock prices on dividends as well as earnings.

institutional influences analyzed by Harbrecht, accounting and budgetary checks and guides described by Chamberlain and Early, and aspects of organizational and communications systems being developed into a meaningful theory by students such as Simon, March and Cyert.[45] If the argument of this paper is correct, the descriptive and predictive value of the theory of the firm will be enhanced and more relevant models will be developed as a result of further such work on the conditions under which decisions that may be assumed to be profit-maximizing are made in today's giant, widely owned and professionally managed corporations.

[45] In addition to the contributions already discussed or cited in this paper, mention should be made of Edith T. Penrose, *The Theory of the Growth of the Firm* (New York: Wiley, 1959), a perceptive study of factors underlying the growth of the firm and illustrative of the approach argued for here. While assuming profits maximization, Mrs. Penrose deals with organizational and managerial features, as well as with aspects of market structure, which tend to stimulate or limit expansion; and as a result she derives conclusions consistent with maximizing behavior, not predictable from traditional theory, and of particular relevance to large, diversified corporations with specialized departmental managerial functions.

3
Profit, Growth and Sales Maximization[1]

John Williamson

INTRODUCTION

One of the more discredited concepts in the theory of the firm is that of an "optimum size" of firm. Empirical evidence has provided no substantiation for the thesis of a long-run U-shaped cost curve and, since firms are not restricted to the sale of a single product or even a particular range of products, there is no more reason to expect profitability to decline with size than there is evidence to suggest that it does. This raises the question as to what does limit the size of a firm. The answer that has been given is that there are important costs entailed in *expanding* the size of a firm and that these expansion costs tend to increase with the firm's rate of growth. This view was first advanced by Edith Penrose [7],[2] has been most fully developed by Robin Marris [5], and has received its most elegant formulation in a paper by Professor Baumol [2].

The development of a theory of growth of the firm was a necessary prerequisite to another feature of the last two analyses just cited—the consideration of alternative assumptions about managerial objectives. Only static profit-maximization and Baumol's static sales maximization hypothesis [1] (with its seemingly arbitrary minimum profit constraint) can be analyzed other than in a growth context. Many economists, the author included, would judge that these are less realistic

Reprinted from *Economica*, February 1966, pp. 1–16, by permission of the author and publisher.

[1] The author is indebted to William Baumol, Keith Hartley, Alan Peacock and Alan Williams for useful comments on an earlier draft. Responsibility for any errors and opinions expressed is that of the author alone.
[2] References in square brackets are listed at the end of the chapter.

assumptions than that management wishes to maximize growth or a discounted sum of future sales. Whether they in fact are is an empirical question whose resolution demands a technique for elucidating the alternative implications of different objectives. The principal purpose of this paper is to construct a model which will permit one to derive the differences in behaviour that would follow from the objectives of maximizing profits, maximizing growth and maximizing (discounted) sales.

The framework in which this is accomplished is that of a permanent growth model of the firm. The model is based upon that presented by Baumol [2], but has been considerably extended. It is developed in the next section, simplified in the section after and solved in the section following that. The basic assumption of a permanent growth model is that unit costs and revenues are independent of the absolute scale involved, although they depend in the traditional ways on the level of the firm's operations relative to its present size. It therefore follows that, if prices and technology are unchanging or altering in appropriately offsetting ways, management is able to make a once-for-all selection of the values of its policy variables. (Where these are not expressed in ratio form, the appropriate value of the variable will increase at a constant proportionate rate over time.) Of course, if at some future date (contrary to the expectations presently held with certainty) there were a change in external circumstances, or a change in management's objectives, or a change in management (perhaps as a result of take-over) with a consequential change in objectives, then the values of these variables would change to new "permanent" levels.

The (economic) policy variables on which any firm has to reach decisions may conveniently be classified into four categories, though the firm actually has only three degrees of freedom in selecting them. First, there are the decisions on input levels required to satisfy the efficiency conditions—the selection of least-cost input combinations, the optimal distribution of given investment funds among alternative projects, and the optimal distribution of sales effort.[3] Second, there is the other decision that is analyzed in traditional price theory, that of the output, price or sales[4] level in the current period; this will be referred to as the output decision. Third, there are the financial decisions embracing the division of profits between dividends and retained earnings, the flotation of new equity and the raising of new capital by bond finance. Fourth, there is the decision as to how much should be spent on expanding the size of the firm—the investment decision.

The present paper is largely confined to a consideration of the output decision, the retention ratio and the flotation of new equity. The reasons for this restriction are as follows. The efficiency conditions are irrelevant to our aims since they will be satisfied by a firm successfully pursuing any of the objectives under investigation (or, for that matter, virtually any other consistent aim apart from an easy life). If the firm sells bonds, it will not be able to increase the ratio of debt to assets (i.e. its "gearing" or "leverage") indefinitely because of the added risk involved ([5], p. 206). The extra investment funds that accrue from this source will therefore bear a constant ratio to the funds obtainable from the

---

[3] This is intended to include the decision as to whether to raise price in order to finance, say, extra advertising, given whatever constraint is imposed by the "output decision."

[4] The existence of a demand curve implies that these are equivalent.

other two sources, so that inclusion of this complication would not add any qualitatively different conclusions. Finally, the investment decision need not be considered explicitly as it is implied by the net revenue and the financial decisions of the firm—this is the missing degree of freedom.

Given the framework outlined, and in particular the basic assumption of rather stationary external circumstances that is necessary to construct a permanent growth model, only weak additional assumptions are necessary to prove the following results:

A. The growth rate of the firm cannot be increased by resort to additional equity finance.
B. Growth is never limited by lack of finance as such, as postulated by Baumol [2] and Downie [3], but by the fear of takeover, as postulated by Marris [5].
C. A profit or growth maximizer will grow at a positive rate if it is a profitable firm; a sales maximizer need not.
D. It is not possible, as Baumol has claimed [2], to derive the static sales maximization model from the assumption of growth maximization. (It can, however, be derived from a long-run sales maximization assumption.)
E. A profit and growth maximizer would reach the same output decision, but a sales maximizer would, except in a limiting case, produce more.
F. A profit maximizer would, except in a limiting case, distribute more of its profits than a growth maximizer.

DEVELOPMENT OF THE MODEL

We define the following variables, where lower-case letters denote ratios and capitals denote other variables. Where no time subscript appears, that variable is to be interpreted as applying to time zero. (The time subscript for period zero is included in those equations where variables for other periods appear as well.) Since the rate of interest is assumed constant and the permanent growth context implies that retention ratio and rate of new issue are maintained constant, the variables i, r, and f never carry a time subscript.

(a) Policy variables:
$S =$ value of sales or total revenue; $r =$ retention ratio; $f =$ (permanent) growth rate of equity.
(b) Exogenous variables:
$$k = \frac{\text{value of firm at which it would be taken over}}{\text{potential maximum value of firm}};$$
$i =$ rate of interest.
(c) Variables which are exogenous at time zero but endogenous thereafter:
$K =$ capital; $F =$ equity.
(d) Endogenous variables:
$R =$ net revenue (profits), which consists of total revenue less those costs which the firm would incur to maintain current output if it were not growing; $X \equiv C + I =$ expansion costs (i.e., all other costs incurred by the firm); $I =$ (net) investment, i.e. addition to capital;

C = non-investment expansion costs; M = market value of firm; g = future (permanent) growth rate of S_t, R_t, K_t, X_t, I_t, C_t; $m \equiv M/F$ = value of share.

Most of these definitions are self-explanatory. The exceptions are k, which will be explained in the section "A Comparison of Profit, Growth and Sales Maximization" and g, the future permanent growth rate of the firm. This, it should be noted, is an endogenous variable whose value is determined by the particular decisions made regarding the firm's policy variables. In order to assess the generality of the model, it is necessary to investigate briefly the plausibility of the assumption that the six variables listed will all grow at the same rate.

Consider a perfectly competitive firm with an unchanging linear homogenous production function facing constant prices, and assume that the increasing costs of growth arise because the process of expanding management requires existing managers to spend some of their time training new managers and integrating them into the managerial team. Then increasing output by a certain proportion, g, over its present level would increase total revenue, costs and hence net revenue in this same proportion. Moreover, the output expansion would require an equal proportionate increase in the capital stock, since with unchanging technology the firm would wish to maintain the ratio of capital to output found optimal in the present period. A growth of g in the present period requires a certain level of spending on management training, C; an equal proportionate increase in the next period requires an expenditure of $(1+g)C$, since the unit cost of training managers is maintained constant by the increased stock of existing managers to do the training, but the number needing to be trained increases by the proportion g. In this simple case, therefore, it is easy to show that total revenue, net revenue, the capital stock and the various forms of expansion costs all increase at the same rate g.

Although it cannot be demonstrated in an equally rigorous manner, the implication of recent discussion is that much the same conclusion is likely to apply to a diversified, oligopolistic firm. Suppose that the general level of output prices is constant; then total revenue will expand at the same rate as output provided that the firm is not forced to cut its prices in order to move down existing demand curves. But the virtually unlimited opportunities for diversification remove any such necessity. Net revenue will also expand at this rate, not only if factor prices and technology are constant, but also if they offset one another; this would occur if wages increased at the same rate as productivity rose due to neutral technical progress. It is well known that with neutral technical progress the capital-output ratio is constant, so that the capital stock and therefore investment will also increase at the same rate. No modification of the argument in the previous paragraph is required so far as C is concerned. Consequently, it is not unreasonable to postulate that S, R, K, X, I and C will all increase at the same rate as output if the price level is constant. (If prices were increasing at a constant rate, these variables would all increase at the same rate in real terms but an appropriately magnified rate in money terms.)

The first relationship we shall derive, that between sales and net revenue, comes from the standard theory of the firm. As output expands (in the current period), net and total revenue both increase initially but eventually both reach maxima. Net revenue reaches a maximum first due to positive marginal costs, and the position of maximum total revenue marks the end of the economically interesting output range. The relationship may therefore be summarized as

$$R = R(S) \qquad R'' < 0. \tag{3.1}$$

Second, let us analyze expansion costs. By definition, these consist of the cost of adding to the capital stock to keep it in line with the planned greater sales in the following period plus such other costs as the firm must incur in the process of expansion. Assuming a constant capital-output ratio and constant prices, it is evident that $I = gK$. More interesting are the other expansion costs, which were the principal interest in Mrs. Penrose's enquiry [7] and have been extensively discussed by Marris [5]. They consist largely of the managerial- diseconomies involved in growing fast and the costs of research, development and sales promotion entailed in diversification. The literature on this point may conveniently be summarized for our purposes by the assumptions made about $C(g)$ below, although the last one—that the marginal cost of growth is negligible for very small growth rates—is less firmly founded than the others.

$$X \equiv I + C = gK + C(g) \qquad \begin{array}{l} C' > 0 \\ C'' > 0 \\ C(0) \equiv 0 \\ C'(0) \approx 0. \end{array} \tag{3.2}$$

Taking the inverse function of equation (3.2), one derives

$$g = g(X) \qquad g' > 0, g'' < 0. \tag{3.3}$$

The statement that growth depends on the amount spent on expansion, but that there are decreasing returns to such expenditure, is actually weaker than the assumptions from which it was derived. As a matter of fact, the latter are needed only in the proof of result C.

The sources from which expansion funds may be obtained are retained earnings and the proceeds of new equity issues. Retained earnings are defined as the product of the retention ratio and net revenue. (Of course, insofar as the tax laws permit some expansion costs to be counted as current costs, the conceptual retention ratio differs from the published ratio of a firm.) The amount raised by floating new equity is the product of the price for which the shares are sold and the number that are sold. The number sold in period 0 is the product of the proportionate increase in the number of shares and the number outstanding at the start of the period, or fF. Their price is computed on the assumption that dividends are paid on existing shares prior to selling the new shares, so that the amount that investors will be willing to pay for the new shares is the price of a share in period 1, m_1, discounted to the present period. It follows that

$$X_0 = rR_0 + \frac{m_1}{1+i} \cdot fF_0 = rR_0 + \frac{fM_1}{(1+i)(1+f)}. \tag{3.4}$$

The market value of the firm is given by the discounted future earnings of the shares at present outstanding.[5] In period t, the firm will earn a net revenue of

---

[5] This is only one of several possible ways in which the stock-market value of the firm may be computed. It is what Miller and Modigliani [6] term the "stream of

$(1+g)^t R$, but it will only pay out $(1-r)(1+g)^t R$. Moreover, some of this will accrue to those who purchase new securities issued between time zero and t; only $F/(1+f)^t F$ will accrue to those who own shares at the beginning. Discounting these future earnings and summing yields the market value of the firm as

$$M = \sum_{t=0}^{\infty} \left[\frac{1+g}{(1+f)(1+i)}\right]^t (1-r)R \tag{3.5}$$

$$= \left[\frac{1}{1 - \frac{1+g}{(1+f)(1+i)}}\right](1-r)R = \frac{(1-r)(1+f)(1+i)R}{i-g+f+if}$$

provided that $(1+f)(1+i) > 1+g$ so that the geometric series converges. A sufficient condition for this is $i > g$. Although we have listed i as an exogenous variable, there is an overwhelming economic reason for believing that $i > g(R)$; since otherwise a firm which invested slightly less than R would have an infinite valuation by the stock market, the interest rate would be revised upwards by the stock market till this ceased to be true. And it will be shown in the next section that $i > g(R)$ is a sufficient condition to ensure that $i > g$. It may also be noted that, since $R_1 = (1+g)R_0$ and all other factors in equation (3.5) are invariant over time, one has

$$M_1 = (1+g)M_0. \tag{3.6}$$

SIMPLIFICATION OF THE MODEL

It is interesting to analyze a frequent assumption to the effect that there is an absolute limit to the amount of finance a firm can obtain for expenditure on expansion.[6] The reasoning is that with low pay-out rates any increase in dividends is so effective in raising share prices as to permit a greater augmentation of external finance than the loss of internal finance; and *vice versa* when pay-out rates are high. Consequently there is a trade-off between external and internal finance and some optimum financial policy which maximizes access to total funds. At this point expansion funds reach an absolute maximum.

To investigate this proposition, one substitutes equations (3.5) and (3.6) into (3.4) to yield

$$X = rR + \frac{(1-r)(1+g)fR}{i-g+f+if}. \tag{3.7}$$

To find that combination of the firm's financial policy variables which maximizes the finance available for expansion (and therefore its growth rate), one differentiates (3.7) with respect to r and f.

---

dividends approach" to valuation, and is the simplest one to apply in the present model. The other approaches are logically equivalent since we are implicitly assuming absence of transactions costs, taxes and uncertainty. It may be noted that the permanent growth context permits one to dispense with consideration of undistributed profits or capital stocks.

[6] See, for example, Baumol [2] pp. 1085–86, Downie [3] p. 66.

$$\frac{\partial X}{\partial r} = R$$
$$+ \frac{fR}{(i - g + f + if)^2} [(1 - r)(1 + i)(1 + f) \, \partial g/\partial r - (1 + g)(i - g + f + if)]. \tag{3.8}$$

At $r = 1$, this simplifies to $\dfrac{\partial X}{\partial r} = \dfrac{(1 + f)(i - g)R}{i - g + f + if} > 0$, provided that $i > g$. Since the first term in the square brackets in (3.8) is positive when $r < 1$, it follows that $\partial X/\partial r > 0$ throughout the feasible range of r and irrespective of the value of f.

$$\frac{\partial X}{\partial f} = \frac{(1 - r)R}{(i - g + f + if)^2} [(1 + g)(i - g) + f(1 + i)(1 + f) \, \partial g/\partial f] > 0.$$

Assuming that as $f \to \infty$ the growth rate approaches a finite limiting value g_0, one has, however,

$$\lim_{f \to \infty} X = rR + (1 - r)(1 + g_0)R/(1 + i). \tag{3.9}$$

One concludes that there is no optimum retention ratio and rate of equity creation which maximize the availability of new finance. An increase in the rate of selling shares will always increase the funds available, though these funds will approach a finite limiting value. Similarly, any increase in the retention ratio will increase the availability of funds.

The maximum funds that would be available through retentions are R. This exceeds the maximum available if new equity is issued, since the value of equation (3.7) is always less than R provided $r < 1$; and if $r = 1$ then $X = R$ and all funds are raised internally. But when the retention ratio is unity the value of the firm is zero by equation (3.5). Marris has argued that this is not an economically significant solution ([5], chapter 1), since when a potentially profitable firm is depressed to a low market value it creates the risk of provoking a take-over raid.[7] This indeed seems by far the most powerful reason for believing that firms will be constrained at some determinate point in their desire to grow.

Result A of the first section was proved in the last paragraph; growth can never be increased by resort to additional equity finance. The significance of this conclusion may be assessed by supposing that the firm has made its investment decision, so that X and therefore g are determined, and its output decision, so that R is specified. Then from equation (3.7) the rate of equity creation, f, needed to finance X will depend on r by the formula

$$f = \frac{(i - g)(X/R - r)}{(i - g)r + (1 + g) - X/R(1 + i)}.$$ Substituting in (3.5) and simplifying yields[8] $M = (1 + i)(R - X)/(i - g)$. In other words, we are living in a Miller and

[7] Analytically, take-over means that new values of the policy variables are selected, presumably with the aim of raising M. The raiders will make a profit provided that the new value of M exceeds that which existed under the policies of the previous management. (We assume a perfect capital market.)

[8] It may be noted that this bears a close similarity to Baumol's equation (3) ([2], p. 1081), except that we have provided, by breaking down his $C(g)$ into $\Sigma \left(\dfrac{1 + g}{1 + i}\right)^t X$, a rather convincing reason for expecting his second-order conditions to be fulfilled.

Modigliani [6] type of world where, because there are no transactions cost, taxes or uncertainty, the purely financial decisions of the firm have no impact on its value or on the rate of return enjoyed by investors. There is therefore no compelling reason for a firm to choose any particular method of raising finance. However, it is a familiar fact that management prefers to raise finance internally and that new equity issues are comparatively unusual occurrences, and this is presumably explicable in terms of the frictions involved in equity flotation that are ignored in our model. The analysis therefore suggests that the essential rôle of new issues is to finance occasional bursts of abnormal expansion where increasing returns are present rather than permanent, steady growth. In view of the above, it is possible to simplify the analysis of the next section very considerably by assuming that all finance is raised internally with no loss of generality.

Result B was that the restraint on growth always consists of a fear of takeover rather than that there exists some absolute maximum on the amount of funds the firm could obtain; this proposition was also established above. Although not immediately obvious, this conclusion is intuitively plausible. Essentially, a firm could always increase its expansion funds at the cost of its present shareholders, either by reducing its dividends or by promising a higher proportion of future dividends to new shareholders, were it not for the power of present shareholders to sell out to a new management which would engage in fewer expansion activities which are so costly as to earn a return below the current rate of interest.

Finally, it may be noted that we have also established that $i > g(R)$ is sufficient to ensure $i > g$. By definition, X cannot exceed R when $f = 0$. And we also established that $r < 1$ implies $X < R$. Consequently, expansion funds cannot exceed net revenue,[9] so that the assumption that the stock market behaves in such a way as to give the firm a finite value ensures that no firm can ever (i.e. even with the aid of new issues) achieve a permanent growth rate as large as the interest rate.

A COMPARISON OF PROFIT, GROWTH AND SALES MAXIMIZATION

Profit maximization is, of course, interpreted as the desire to maximize the present value of the firm, M. Neither is there any difficulty in interpreting the meaning of growth maximization in the context of a permanent growth model, since total revenue, net revenue, and assets all expand permanently at the same rate g. Slightly less obvious is the appropriate definition of sales maximization, since the total sales of a firm between now and infinity are obviously infinite. But so, of course, are total profits over this period: they are reduced to a well-defined value by the technique of discounting. It seems quite plausible to suppose that managements which derive utility from the size of the undertaking they control will similarly discount future sales. After all, most managers must anticipate retirement or coronary thrombosis in the less than infinitely far distant future, so that it is reasonable to suppose that they will prefer an increase in sales in the

---

[9] It should be noted that, if we were to take account of bond finance, the maximum funds available to the firm could exceed R. Consequently, the condition $i > g(R)$ would require strengthening.

present to an equal increase in the future. We therefore assume that management applies a discount rate s to future sales, and therefore seeks to maximize a function H of the form

$$H = \sum_{t=0}^{\infty} \left(\frac{1+g}{1+s}\right)^t S = \frac{1+s}{s-g} S, \qquad (3.10)$$

provided that $s > g$ so that the geometric series converges. It must be admitted that there is no particularly convincing reason for believing that $s > g$ analogous to that for assuming $i > g$; if the condition does not hold, presumably management is in a state of bliss. Or perhaps it just satisfices.

Profit Maximization

It was shown in the last section that it is possible to assume that all finance is raised internally without loss of generality. One may therefore set $f = 0$ in equation (3.5), so that the problem of the profit-maximizing firm is to select S and r so as to maximize

$$M = (1-r)(1+i)R/(i-g), \qquad (3.11)$$

subject to
$$g = g(rR) \qquad g' > 0, \ g'' < 0$$
$$R = R(S) \qquad R'' < 0.$$

Now
$$\frac{\partial M}{\partial R} = \frac{(i-g)(1-r)(1+i) + (1-r)(1+i)R \, \partial g/\partial R}{(i-g)^2} > 0$$

so that the profit-maximizing firm will select that output level S^* that maximizes net revenue (R^*).

One also has

$$\frac{\partial M}{\partial r} = \frac{-(i-g)(1+i)R + (1-r)(1+i)R \, \partial g/\partial r}{(i-g)^2} = 0, \text{ or } 1 - r = \frac{i-g}{\partial g/\partial r} \qquad (3.12)$$

as the first-order condition for a profit-maximizing retention ratio.

This result is most easily interpreted diagrammatically. By substituting R^* into $g = g(rR)$, one obtains a unique relationship between the retention ratio and the growth rate that this permits, and from the signs on the derivatives of g this has the shape shown by $g(rR^*)$ in Figure 3.1. Intuitively, for a given level of net revenue—which happens to be the maximum possible level since the firm desires to maximize profits—the amount of finance available for expansion is a linear function of the retention ratio, but the assumption of increasing costs of expansion leads to a situation in which the permitted rate of growth increases less than in proportion to the retention ratio.

One may also plot on this diagram a series of curves which reflect the extent to which the objective function of the firm is met, i.e. a set of curves which show all those combinations of r and g at which the value of the firm would be equal to some particular level of M. We shall borrow the term "iso-valuation line" from Marris ([5], p. 252) to describe these loci of points at which the value of M is constant. Each one is labelled with the value of M that it represents when R has the value specified after M. The iso-valuation lines show a relationship between g and r and may therefore be derived by rearranging equation (3.11) to yield

$$g = i - \frac{(1+i)R}{M} + \frac{(1+i)R}{M}r.$$

Hence all of the iso-valuation lines converge on the point A at which $r = 1$ and $g = i$, although they do not do anything quite as embarrassing as meet at this point since M is undefined when $g = i$. They are all upward-sloping straight lines: higher growth is needed to compensate for reduced dividends if the value of the firm is to remain unchanged. Finally, the less steep is the line—i.e., the higher it appears—the greater is the value of M that it represents.

The object of the profit-maximizing firm is therefore to reach the highest possible iso-valuation line. This occurs in the diagram at B, the point of tangency to $g(rR^*)$. We shall denote the value of the firm at this point by M^*. At B it is evident that $BC = AC/\tan \alpha$, i.e., $1 - r = \dfrac{i-g}{\partial g/\partial r}$ which is the first-order condition (3.12) for a profit maximizing retention ratio. It is apparent that the assumption of decreasing returns to expansion expenditure reflected in the shape of $g(rR^*)$ ensures that the second-order condition will be satisfied.

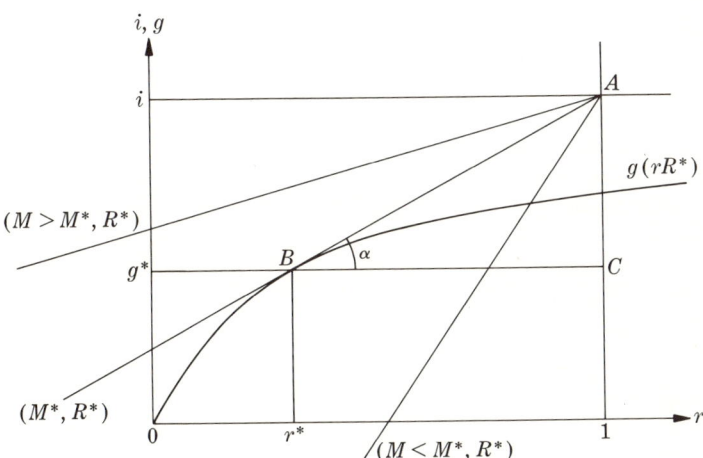

Figure 3.1

There is nothing in the diagram to show that this tangency condition need occur at a positive g. However, the assumptions made about $C(g)$ in equation (3.2) imply that in the neighborhood of $g = 0$, we have $gK \approx X = Rr$, so that $\partial g/\partial r \approx R/K$. Now the definition of a profitable firm is one that earns a rate of return on capital employed greater than the rate of interest, so that, if the firm is profitable, $R/K > i$, which implies $\partial g/\partial r > i$ at $g = 0$. At this point, therefore, the left-hand side of (3.12) exceeds the right-hand side, and reducing this inequality requires a higher r and g. Since it is by definition true that a growth-maximizing firm will grow at least as fast as a profit-maximizing one, this establishes that (profitable) profit and growth maximizers will grow at a positive rate, which was the first part of Proposition C.

Growth Maximization

It was shown in the last section that the constraint on a growth-maximizer arises from the danger of being taken over. A firm is likely to be taken over when its market value sinks to a low level in comparison with what the new owners could expect to make out of it.[10] The measure that Marris adopts as an indicator of the value of the firm to a take-over raider is the value of its net assets which, in our model, are represented by K. However, a more appropriate norm would seem to be M^*, since it is in general reasonable to expect that a new management would not change the total nature of the trading activities in which the firm engages. It will therefore be assumed that management wishes to prevent the stock market value of the firm falling below a specified proportion, k, of its potential maximum value, in order to safeguard its job security. This proportion k will vary inversely with the efficiency of existing management relative to that which would be provided by the potential raiders; it will tend to vary directly with the extent to which these raiders are themselves "profit-motivated." Without some sort of general equilibrium analysis beyond the scope of the present paper, it is necessary to take k as exogenous.

The problem of the growth-maximizer is therefore to select S and r so as to maximize
$$g = g(rR)$$
subject to
$$M \geqq kM^* \qquad 0 < k \leqq 1$$
$$R = R(S).$$

Since $\partial g/\partial R > 0$, the growth-maximizer will select the same output level S^* as the profit-maximizer; both will seek the highest possible level of current net revenue.[11] This is the first part of result E; it has the (happy?) consequence that the voluminous literature on pricing policy may be applied without modification to growth-maximizing firms. It also establishes that it is not possible to derive the static sales maximization model from the postulate of growth-maximization, as was stated in proposition D.[12]

---

[10] For his development of a theory of take-over, on which the present remarks are largely based, see Marris [5] chapter 1.

[11] Intuitively, one might have expected a growth-maximizer to keep his initial sales down so as to "keep the base small." While this factor would operate in any finite period model (and this constitutes an additional reason for believing that the sales-maximization hypothesis may be fruitful), it is inoperative in a permanent growth context since it would involve keeping subsequent sales down correspondingly as well.

[12] Baumol's error arose from a confusion between the firm's current net revenue, R, and what one may term its profitability (the excess of revenue over *all* costs), $R - X$. Specifically, he argued that since faster growth involves lower profits (meaning profitability), the sales level needed to maximize growth would be determined as a compromise between the desire to earn profits to finance expansion and the reduction in profits (here equated to net revenue) caused by this faster growth. But it is clear that a growth-maximizer will never be prepared to forego current net revenue, unless one introduces some quite different postulate such as that future expansion costs will be less if sales are pushed further in the present. (A rationale for this might be the creation of consumer goodwill.) In other words, the unprofitable activities that a growth-maximizer engages in are those involved in pushing g beyond g^* and not those arising from pushing S beyond S^*. See [2] section III.

Since $\partial g/\partial r > 0$ and $\partial M/\partial r < 0$ for values of $r > r^*$, it is obvious that the constraint will be exactly satisfied and r_g, the growth-maximizing retention ratio, will be given by a corner solution. The diagrammatic solution to the problem is shown in Figure 3.2. If one draws any horizontal from AB to the iso-valu-

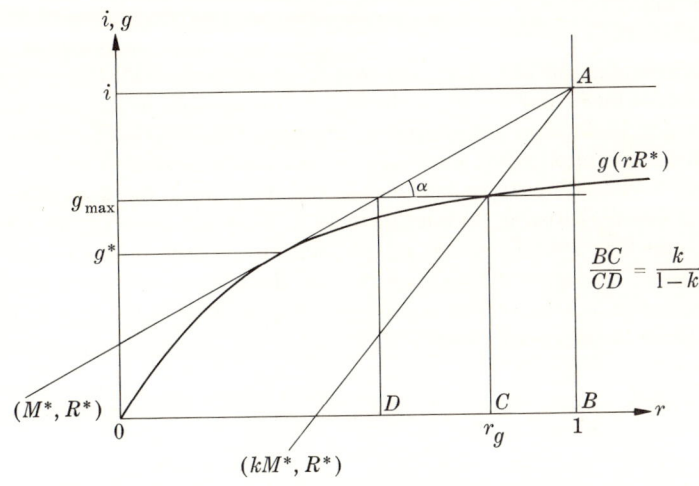

Figure 3.2

ation line (M^*, R^*), and then divides this horizontal in the ratio $1 - k : k$, the iso-valuation line passing through the resulting point is (kM^*, R^*). The intersection of this iso-valuation line with $g(rR^*)$ yields the maximum possible growth rate, $g_{\max}$ which is clearly greater than the profit-maximizing growth rate g^* unless $k = 1$.

Formally, one derives $M = \dfrac{(1 - r)(1 + i)R^*}{i - g} = \dfrac{k(1 - r^*)(1 + i)R^*}{i - g^*} = kM^*,$

or $\dfrac{1 - r}{k} = \dfrac{1 - r^*}{i - g^*}(i - g) = \dfrac{(i - g)}{\tan \alpha}$

which is satisfied at $g_{\max}$ since $(i - g)/\tan \alpha = BC + CD = BC/k = (1 - r)/k$.

It may be noted that the only case in which the growth-maximizer and profit-maximizer would distribute the same proportion of their profits is that in which they stand in imminent danger of take-over, i.e. when $k = 1$. This is the result asserted in proposition F.

Sales Maximization

At the beginning of this section we concluded that the problem of the sales-maximizer is to select r and S so as to maximize

$$H = \frac{1 + s}{s - g} S \qquad \text{(provided } s > g\text{)} \qquad (3.10)$$

subject to $M \geq kM^*$, $g = g(rR)$, $R = R(S)$.

Now $\partial H/\partial g > 0$, $\partial g/\partial r > 0$ and $\partial M/\partial r < 0$ imply that the sales-maximizer will also exhaust such slack as may be provided by $k < 1$ and exactly satisfy the constraint. It follows that $1 - r = \dfrac{kR^*}{R} \dfrac{1 - r^*}{i - g^*} (i - g)$, so that one could construct the relevant iso-valuation line on Figure 3.2 by making $\dfrac{BC}{CD} = \dfrac{kR^*/R_s}{1 - kR^*/R_s}$ if one knew R_s, the sales maximizing value of R. There is, however, no way of determining R_s from this diagram. If we assume that R_s is known and is less than R^*, then the optimal iso-valuation line (kM^*, R_s) would lie between (kM^*, R^*) and (M^*, R^*). The equilibrium r would occur at the highest intersection of this line with $g(rR_s)$, which would lie to the right of $g(rR^*)$. However, this diagram does not yield any very interesting information for the sales-maximizing case.

Consider instead the way in which g will vary with S, given that the constraint is exactly satisfied. As sales increase to S^*, g will rise to reach a maximum of $g_{\max}$ and then start to decline as the "surplus" is used to finance unprofitable sales rather than unprofitable growth. One therefore obtains a curve with the properties of $g = h(S)$ in Figure 3.3. An increase in k would reduce the height of this curve throughout its length.

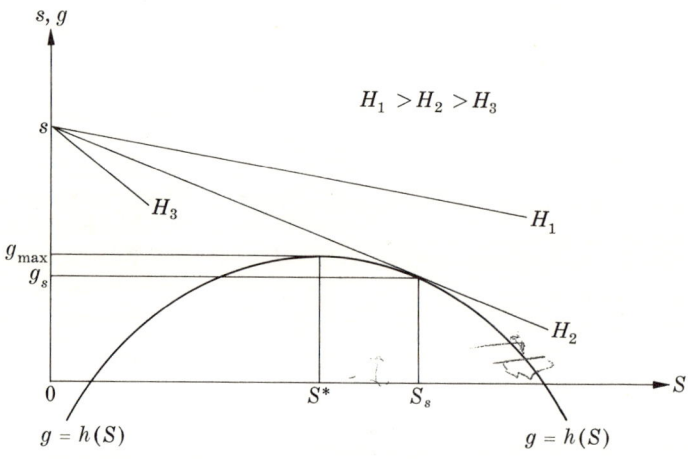

Figure 3.3

One may also derive a series of iso-H curves by rearranging (3.10) to read

$$g = s - \dfrac{1 + s}{H} S.$$

The iso-H curves therefore all approach the point $(S = 0, g = s)$, though they do not actually reach it since H is undefined at this point. They are all downward-sloping straight lines. Higher curves represent larger values of H.

It is obvious that the highest attainable value of H is H_2, where the iso-H curve is tangential to $h(S)$. It is easy to confirm that this is the maximum by differentiating (3.10) with respect to S to get the first-order condition for the sales-maximizing level of sales S_s, and it is apparent from the diagram that the second-order condition will also be satisfied provided the demand curve is monotonic:

$$\frac{\partial H}{\partial S} = \frac{(s-g)(1+s) + (1+s)S\,\partial g/\partial S}{(s-g)^2} = 0, \quad \text{or } s - g + S\frac{\partial g}{\partial S} = 0.$$

It is obvious that this condition is satisfied at $S = S_s$, $g = g_s$. If management's time preference is sufficiently high, i.e. if s is large enough (and k is small enough), it is evident that the sales-maximizer, unlike the profit and growth-maximizers, will not in fact grow, as is asserted in the second part of result C. It is also evident that $s > g_{\max}$ ensures that $S_s > S^*$ unless $k = 1$, when the curve $g = h(S)$ (which is defined to include the stock-market constraint) is compressed to the single point $S = S^*$, $g = g^*$. This was the second part of result E.

Finally, suppose that the sales-maximizer were considering its output decision subject to the constraints that it wished to avoid being taken over and that it wished to grow at g_s. This is logically equivalent to the problem maximize S, subject to $R \geqq R_s$.

This demonstrates that Baumol's static hypothesis, that firms try to maximize sales subject to a minimum profit constraint, can be derived from the long-run sales-maximization hypothesis, as asserted in result D.

CONCLUSION

In a paper such as this one cannot delve into the vast body of theory underlying many of the relationships assumed. For example, a large part of the books by Edith Penrose and Robin Marris are devoted to investigating the theory behind the restrictions that we have placed on the shape of $g(X)$. Similarly, we have joined Joan Robinson [8] in sweeping aside all the complications of oligopolistic interdependence by assuming that the output decision is taken on the basis of well-defined demand curves. What a permanent growth model of the type developed in this paper is capable of providing, however, is a means of linking such problems as these together in a simple and systematic way.

We have demonstrated that doing this enables one to establish a number of interesting results, some of which are far from trivial. The most interesting were listed in the Introduction, so that there is no point in repeating them here. The most general conclusion is one that one would hesitate to state explicitly were it not for the suspicion it still seems to engender in certain quarters: that in all cases except where profitability is at best the minimum sum necessary to prevent take-over,[13] the policies the firm pursues will depend on the form of its objectives. Profit, growth and sales-maximizers will act differently.

One could easily extend the above analysis to include more general managerial utility functions such as $U(g, M)$ or $U(g, S)$. The former would yield indifference curves tangential to $g(rR^*)$ above r^* in Figure 3.1, the latter indifference curves tangential to some point on the downward-sloping part of $h(S)$ in Figure 3.3. But no very interesting insights seem to emerge from such a generalization.

Of more interest is the observation that any one of the three objectives is capable of yielding a set of comparative-statics theorems. For example, inspec-

---

[13] Baumol's conclusion in [1] that a sales-maximizer who could only just satisfy his minimum-profit constraint would act in the same way as a profit-maximizer is, of course, a special case of this result.

tion of Figures 3.1 and 3.2 makes it clear that an increase in the rate of interest would reduce the growth rate and the retention ratio for both profit and growth-maximizing firms. Changes in the efficiency of the firm or the prices of its factors would have straightforward implications for the position of such curves as $g(rR^*)$ and $h(S)$, which could similarly lead to comparative static predictions. It does not seem to be possible to predict the effect of a proportional profits tax on the retention ratio without making assumptions additional to those contained in the paper; I suspect that one requires some condition such as $g''' = $ constant to get a definite solution.

Finally, it is interesting to draw attention to an empirical finding which has caused a certain amount of discomfort in the past but for which we are able to offer a superior explanation to "systematic irrationality on the part of the investigating public" (Miller and Modigliani, [6], p. 432), or discount rates that vary with the futurity of the return (Marris [5], p. 221). This is the finding that "when stock prices are related to current dividends and retained earnings, higher dividend payout is usually associated with higher price-earnings ratios" (Friend and Puckett [4], p. 657). The reason that this has caused dismay is that "investors should be indifferent if the present value of the additional future returns resulting from earnings retention equals the amount of dividends foregone" (*idem.*), whereas apparently they are not. But, of course, investors are irrational in preferring dividends only if the present value of the additional future returns actually *does* equal the amount of dividends foregone, and if the firm is a growth (or for that matter a sales) maximizer then it is obvious from Figure 3.2 that they do not, for the retention ratio is pushed beyond the point at which the value of the firm is maximized. With a great deal of ingenuity Friend and Puckett manage to cast a certain amount of doubt on the conventional findings, but the bulk of the empirical evidence would still seem to indicate that dividends are more highly valued. Since this is consistent with the view that shareholders are rational in seeking to maximize their wealth, and that management rationally seeks objectives other than profit-maximization, while any other interpretation assumes that at least one of these parties acts irrationally, one may conclude that there is substantial empirical evidence favouring abandonment of the time-honoured profit-maximization assumption.

REFERENCES

1. Baumol, W. J., *Business Behavior, Value and Growth* (New York, 1959).
2. "On the Theory of Expansion of the Firm," *American Economic Review*, December 1962.
3. Downie, J., *The Competitive Process* (1958).
4. Friend, I. and Puckett, M., "Dividends and Stock Prices," *American Economic Review*, September 1964.
5. Marris, R., *The Economic Theory of "Managerial" Capitalism* (1964).
6. Miller, M. H. and Modigliani, F., "Dividend Policy, Growth, and the Valuation of Shares," *Journal of Business*, October 1961.
7. Penrose, E., *The Theory of the Growth of the Firm* (Oxford, 1959).
8. Robinson, J., *The Economics of Imperfect Competition* (1933).

4
The Arithmetic of Capital-Budgeting Decisions

Ezra Solomon

In order to make correct capital-expenditure decisions, corporate management needs at least three sets of information. Estimates must be made of net capital outlays required and future cash earnings promised by each proposed project. This is a problem in engineering valuation and market forecasting. Estimates must also be made of the availability and cost of capital to the company. This is a problem in financial analysis. Finally, management needs a correct set of standards by which to select projects for execution so that long-run economic benefits to present owners will be maximized. This is a problem in logic and arithmetic. This paper is concerned exclusively with the last of these three problems.[1]

With respect to the question "Should this investment proposal be accepted or rejected?" the problem of arriving at a correct decision is uncomplicated. Either one of two approaches to measuring the investment worth of a proposal will provide a correct answer.[2] In the usual form in which these approaches are used as capital-rationing criteria, they are:

Reprinted from *The Journal of Business*, April 1956, pp. 124-129, by permission of the author and publisher.

[1] For a discussion of the first two problems see Joel Dean, *Capital Budgeting* (New York: Columbia University Press, 1951), and Ezra Solomon, "Measuring a Company's Cost of Capital," *Journal of Business*, XXVIII (October, 1955), 240-52.

[2] There are other criteria in use, e.g., determining capital budgets by size of department, by pay-out periods, or by the postponability of projects. It has already been shown that these are at best crude approximations to a correct solution (see Dean, *op. cit.*, chap. ii, and M. J. Gordon, "The Payoff Period and the Rate of Profit," *Journal of Business*, XXVIII [October, 1955], 253-60).

The Rate-of-Return Approach

This approach expresses each project's estimated value as a single over-all "rate of return per annum." This rate is equal to the rate of interest at which the present value of expected capital outlays is exactly equal to the present value of expected cash earnings on that project. The concept is identical with the "effective yield to maturity" on a bond that is purchased at some price other than its par value. It has also been called the "internal rate of profit" [3] or the "marginal efficiency of capital." [4]

If the rate of return on a project is greater than the company's cost of capital (also expressed as a percentage per annum rate), then the project should be accepted.

The Present-Value Approach

For each project, find the present value of the expected capital outlays, using the cost of capital as a discount rate. Likewise, find the present value of the expected cash earnings. If the present value of earnings is greater than the present value of outlays, the project should be accepted.

These two approaches give the same results for "accept or reject" decisions. This is so because the computed rate of return on a project will be higher than the cost of capital in all cases for which the present value of earnings, discounted at the cost of capital, is greater than the present value of outlays. Or, conversely, if a project promises a rate of return greater than the company's cost of capital, then the present value of its earnings, discounted at the cost of capital, will be greater than the present value of its outlays.

For problems which involve more than a simple "accept or reject" decision, the application of these two criteria, as they are generally defined, often yield contradictory or ambiguous results. The purpose of this paper is to explore the reasons for these contradictions or ambiguities and to reformulate this general approach to measuring investment worth so that it always provides a unique and correct basis for decision making.

MUTUALLY EXCLUSIVE PROPOSALS

It is often necessary for management to ask not only "Is this project worth undertaking?" but also "which of two projects is the better one?" This latter question is crucial whenever two or more projects or proposals are mutually exclusive. For example, the proposals may be alternative ways of doing the same thing. Both might be profitable in an absolute sense. But since only one of the two can be undertaken, the problem is to decide which alternative is the better one.

When the relative merit of alternative proposals is at issue, the rate-of-return criterion, as defined earlier, and the present-value criterion, as defined, can yield contradictory results. With the increased interest in applying rational approaches to the solution of capital-investment decisions, this possible conflict between the

---

[3] See Kenneth L. Boulding, *Economic Analysis* (rev. ed.; New York: Harper & Bros., 1948), chaps. xxxv and xxxvi.

[4] See J. M. Keynes, *The General Theory of Employment, Interest, and Money* (New York: Macmillan Co., 1936), pp. 140 ff.

two generally acceptable criteria has received renewed attention. Several recent papers have shown that when projects are ranked by the rate-of-return standard, the results may differ from a ranking of the same projects based on the present-value standard.[5] For analytical purposes, the simplest example of such a conflict will suffice: Assume that there are two investment opportunities available. Both are profitable in an absolute sense, but only one can be undertaken because the two are mutually exclusive.

Project X requires an outlay of $100 now, at time t_0, and promises to return $120 exactly 1 year hence at time t_1. Project Y also requires an outlay of $100 now and promises to return $174.90 exactly 4 years hence at time t_4. Assume also that the degree of certainty attaching to each project is identical and that the investor's present "cost of capital" is 10 per cent.

The "rate of return" on project X is 20 per cent, and on project Y it is 15 per cent. The present value of project X, discounted at the cost of capital, is $109.09. For project Y, the present value, discounted at the cost of capital, is $119.46. If the two projects are ranked by their rate of return, project X is the better one. If, on the other hand, they ranked in terms of present value, project Y is the better one. Which should the investor choose?

In order to resolve the problem correctly, it is necessary to isolate the source of the conflict between the two approaches. The easiest way to do this is to compare the two investment proposals in terms of their relative value as of the terminal date (t_4) of the longer-lived project.[6]

According to the data given, proposal Y will provide the investor with $174.90 at time t_4. All we know about proposal X is that it provides $120.00 at time t_1. What happens to these funds between time t_1 and t_4 is obviously an important piece of necessary information. Neither the rate-of-return approach nor the present-value approach answers this question *explicitly*. But they both answer it *implicitly* and in different ways. This is the source of the conflicting results that they yield.

Those who use the rate-of-return approach, as it is usually defined, would choose project X over project Y. Hence they must assume that this choice will yield a larger terminal value than that promised by project Y, i.e., $174.90. This, in turn, implies that the $120 obtained from project X at time t_1 can be reinvested between time t_1 and t_4 at a rate lucrative enough to accumulate to more than $174.90 by time t_4. *In general*, the implicit assumption made by the rate-of-return approach is that the reinvestment rate is at least equal to the rate promised by the longer-lived of the two projects, in this case, 15 per cent.[7]

[5] See James H. Lorie and Leonard J. Savage, "Three Problems in Rationing Capital," *Journal of Business*, XXVIII (October, 1955), 229–39; George Terborgh, "Some Comments on the Dean-Smith Article on the MAPI Formula," *Journal of Business*, XXIX (April, 1956), 138–40; and A. A. Alchian, "The Rate of Interest, Fisher's Rate of Return over Costs, and Keynes' Internal Rate of Return," *American Economic Review*, XLV (December, 1955), 938–42.

[6] The "terminal date" refers to the date at which cash earnings from the longer-lived of the two competing projects cease.

[7] For example, if project Z, a third alternative, yielded 15 per cent in perpetuity and project X yielded 20 per cent, the rate-of-return approach would choose project X over project Z. Hence the approach must assume that funds received from project X can be reinvested at least at 15 per cent.

The present-value approach, as usually defined, assumes that the funds obtained from either project can be reinvested at a rate equal to the company's present cost of capital, i.e., 10 per cent. Using this assumption, the investor will end up at time t_4 with only $159.72 if he chooses project X. With project Y, he would have $174.90. Thus, according to this approach, project Y is the better choice.

The question of which assumption is likely to be the more justified one is important, but it is not relevant to the argument being made in this paper, namely, that the apparent conflict between the two approaches results only from differing assumptions that each makes about the future. If a common assumption is adopted, both approaches will always rank projects identically.

Let us assume, for example, that the investor can put money to use between time t_1 and time t_4 at an average return of 12 per cent. The following computations and results would ensue:

Terminal Value

For project Y this is $174.90. For project X we have $120 at time t_1, plus interest at 12 per cent per annum for 3 years. This would accumulate to $168.47.

Rate of Return

For project Y this averages 15 per cent up to the terminal date at time t_4. For project X the rate would be 20 per cent for 1 year and 12 per cent for 3 years—an over-all rate equal to 13.9 per cent.

Present Value

For project Y this would be $174.90, discounted from time t_4 back to time t_1 at 12 per cent[8] and back from time t_1 to t_0 at 10 per cent. This gives $113.17. For project X the present value would be $120 discounted from time t_1 to time t_0 at 10 per cent, or $109.09.

All three criteria rank the two projects in the same order. With the particular assumption we used, project Y is the better one by any standard. Using some other assumption, the ranking might be reversed, but the alternative approaches would still yield identical results.

Our conclusion is that correct and consistent ranking of the investment worth of competing proposals can be obtained only if the following factors are taken into account:

1. The valid comparison is not simply between two projects but between two alternative courses of action. The ultimate criterion is the total wealth that the investor can expect from each alternative by the terminal date of the longer-lived project. In order to make a fair comparison, an explicit and common assumption must be made regarding the rate at which funds released by either project can be reinvested up to the terminal date.
2. If the rate of return is to be used as an index of relative profitability, then the relevant rate is the per annum yield promised by each alternative

---

[8] This is the relevant rate because we are assuming that the investor can earn 12 per cent on his funds between time t_1 and time t_4.

course of action from its inception to a common terminal date in the future (usually the terminal date of the longer-lived project).

3. If the present value is to be used as an index of relative profitability, the expected reinvestment rate or set of rates should be used as the discounting factor. These rates will be equal to the company's present cost of capital only by coincidence. When comparing two projects requiring different outlays, it is necessary to compare "present value per dollar of outlay" rather than the absolute present value of the projects.

THE PROBLEM OF "DUAL RATES OF RETURN"

In a recent paper Lorie and Savage[9] have drawn attention to a second problem involving the arithmetic of capital budgeting. In this paper the authors attempt to show that certain rare and complex investment situations exist which cannot be expressed in terms of a single, unique "rate of return." In such situations the application of the usual prescription for finding *the* rate of return yields two solutions, and thus "the rate-of-return criterion for judging the acceptability of investment proposals, as it has been presented in published works, is ambiguous or anomalous." [10]

In order to understand the problem involved, it is helpful to recognize two basic types of investment situation, classified according to the pattern of estimated cash flows that are projected. In the usual type of situation, which we will call "pattern A," the stream of net cash inflows promised by a project ends either before or when it reaches that point in time beyond which the value of *net future flows* is negative. In other words, the project is assumed to terminate before the stage beyond which its continuation yields a net loss to the investor. The second situation, which we call "pattern B," is a much rarer one. Projects which fall into this category continue beyond the point defined previously, i.e., the terminal section contains a net cash outflow (a net loss). Such a pattern obviously exists only if there are contractual or other compelling reasons which make it impossible for the investor to avoid the terminal losses.

As far as pattern A projects are concerned, it is always possible to express the investment worth of the project as a single, meaningful "rate of return" and hence to make a clear-cut decision on the basis of such a criterion. For pattern B projects the application of the usually prescribed method of finding the appropriate "rate of return" can yield more than one answer.[11]

Let us take a specific example of a pattern B investment project. The proposal being considered is the installation of a larger oil pump that would get a fixed quantity of oil out of the ground more rapidly than the pump that is already in use. Let us assume that, by operating the existing pump, the investor can expect $10,000 a year hence and $10,000 two years hence. Let us assume that, by installing the larger pump at a net cost of $1,600 now, he can expect $20,000 a year hence and nothing the second year. The installation of the larger pump can be viewed as a project having the cash-flow characteristics shown in Table 4.1.

---

[9] *Op. cit.*
[10] *Ibid.*, p. 237.
[11] Lorie and Savage explain the general basis for dual rates (*ibid.*, p. 237).

Table 4.1

TIME PERIOD	INCREMENTAL CASH FLOW DUE TO INVESTMENT
t_0	− $ 1,600
t_1	+ 10,000
t_2	− 10,000

The usual prescription for finding the rate of return of a project is to find that rate which makes the discounted value of net cash flows equal to the discounted value of capital outlays. Alternatively—and this amounts to the same thing—find that rate which makes the algebraic sum of the discounted cash outflows and inflows equal to zero. The application of this method to our example will yield two answers, namely, 25 and 400 per cent. In other words, using a 25 per cent rate, the discounted value of the cash flows is exactly equal to the outlay of $1,600. However, a rate of 400 per cent also equates cash flows with capital outlay. Which of the two "rates" is the correct measure of the investment worth of the project, 25 or 400 per cent?

The answer is that neither of these rates is a measure of investment worth, neither has relevance to the profitability of the project under consideration, and neither, therefore, is correct. The fault lies in the incorrect application of the "usual prescription" for finding the rate of return. A closer look at the implications of defining the rate of return in this context as that rate (or rates) which reduce the discounted cash flows to zero reveals the gross error that such a process entails. In order to find this error, let us vary the net outlay required to install the larger pump (keeping all other cash flows constant) and solve for the "rate of return," using the usual prescription. We get the following absurd results:

1. If the larger pump costs nothing, then the project is worth 0 per cent, i.e., at at 0 per cent, the discounted value of the net cash flows is equal to the value of the outlay.[12]
2. If the larger pump costs $827, the project, according to this method, suddenly becomes quite profitable and is rated at 10 per cent, i.e., at a rate of 10 per cent, the discounted value of the net cash flows is equal to $827.
3. The more the pump costs, the more "profitable" the project becomes! At a cost of $1,600 the rate of return is 25 per cent; at a cost of $2,500 it yields 100 per cent. The method would have us believe that the engineer who first thought of the idea of installing the larger pump could have a gold mine if only he could persuade the pump manufacturer to charge him enough for the installation![13]

Needless to say, any definition of "profitability" that leads to these absurd results must itself be in error.

The correct solution for the investment worth of the project is simple and

---

[12] Alternatively, one could say that the rate is infinitely large.
[13] This increase in the "rate," as the cost of the pump increases, reaches a maximum level, after which the relationship is reversed.

straightforward. But it requires an explicit answer to a relevant question: "What is it worth to the investor to receive $10,000 one year earlier than he would have otherwise received it?" This is actually all that the installation of the larger pump achieves. If the investor expects to be able to put the $10,000 to work at a yield of x per cent per annum, then getting the money a year earlier is worth $100x$. If x is 23 per cent, for example, getting $10,000 a year earlier is worth $2,300. In other words, if he spent $1,600 on the larger pump now (at time t_0), he would end up at time t_2 having $2,300 more than he otherwise would have had. This can be stated as an equivalent "rate of return," which in this case would be about 20 per cent ($1,600 at 20 per cent per annum would amount to $2,304 at the end of two years). Using this approach, a unique and meaningful rate of return can always be found for any set of cash inflows and outflows.

SUMMARY

The rate of return is a useful concept that enables us to express the profitability of an investment proposal as a single explicit value. This value automatically adjusts for differences in the time pattern of expected cash outflows and inflows. It is also independent of the absolute size of the project. Thus it provides a useful standard by which all types of projects—large and small, long-run and short-run—can be ranked against each other in relative terms and also against the company's cost of capital, in order to judge their absolute worth. The arithmetic involved in rate-of-return computations is generally straightforward. However, there are two situations in which such computations require a careful consideration of the logic that is involved.

    1. When mutually exclusive proposals are being compared, it is necessary to compute the rate on each alternative course of action up to the terminal date of the longer-lived alternative. This requires an explicit estimate of the yield to be derived from the cash flows generated by each of the alternatives being considered.

    2. When a rate is being computed for complex proposals that have negative terminal values, the usual mechanistic prescription for solving for rates does not apply. This situation also requires an explicit estimate of the yield to be derived from incremental cash flows generated by a project. Given this estimate, the equivalent dollar value of the incremental cash flows can be computed explicitly. A comparison of this value with the outlays required for the project will give a correct and unambiguous measure of the project's rate of return.

If these concepts and methods are used in defining and computing rates of return, this criterion will always provide an unambiguous investment standard, the use of which will lead to a maximization of the investor's net present worth, in so far as the estimates used are accurate.

PART II

COST CONDITIONS

The term "cost conditions" is generally used to refer to the relationship between the minimum cost of producing a firm's product and each rate of output. Cost conditions influence the behavior of decision-makers and affect other features of industrial structure. Given the demand conditions anticipated by a firm's decision-makers, and their objectives, cost conditions determine how much output the firm will produce per period. The demand conditions associated with a firm's product depend on the firm's anticipations regarding the policies of other firms already producing the product and the policies of potential entrants into the industry. The height of entry barriers, which affect the behavior of potential entrants, depends to a large extent on cost conditions associated with the industry's product. Cost conditions will also influence the degree of seller concentration existing in particular industries; while decisions about diversification depend on cost conditions associated with the combination of products being considered. As a final example of the significance of cost conditions the question of whether the long-run unit cost of producing a firm's product increases if the scale of the firm's output is expanded beyond a certain level is intimately bound up with the question of whether a limit exists to the size of individual firms.

The articles comprising Part II are a mixture of theory and empirical verification. The paper by J. Haldi and D. Whitcomb describes the principles underlying economies of scale more clearly than do most existing texts, and attempts to estimate the practical importance of scale economies in industrial plants. The distinction made in the article between static and dynamic sources of economies of scale illuminates the often-neglected distinction between the rate of a firm's output and the total planned volume of output.

In the second selection, O. E. Williamson explains the logic of managerial diseconomies of scale in industrial firms more clearly and convincingly than does earlier literature dealing with this aspect of industrial organization. The author focuses attention on the cumulative loss of control experienced by the peak coordinator of a firm, when information and instructions are transmitted across successive hierarchical levels, as the factor responsible for diseconomies of scale in a given state of knowledge concerning techniques of communication. In an appendix he attempts to reconcile his analysis with the fact that empirical evidence generally fails to reveal any diseconomies of scale. The evidence may, for example, simply reflect the fact that developments in techniques of processing and disseminating information are continually expanding the scale of operations at which unit costs increase as a result of the control-loss phenomenon.

The two traditional methods of estimating cost conditions existing in firms and plants are the engineering studies method and statistical cost analysis. The former, used by Haldi and Whitcomb, considers a set of hypothetical plants or firms, each producing the same product with the same technology available and differing only in the scale of output produced. In contrast, statistical cost analysis employs cost data originating in firms actually producing different scales of output of a particular product. The last three papers in Part II deal with two other approaches to the estimation of cost conditions,—both of relatively recent origin. Professor Stigler's paper is the seminal article on the survivor technique. In this approach the firms in an industry are grouped into size classes, and the share of industry output accounted for by each size class, at two or more points in time, is compared. The shape of the cost curve is inferred by assuming that changes in the share of industry output of different-size classes are related to differences in the average cost of production in these size classes.

W. G. Shepherd's article contains a critical appraisal of the survivor technique, including a discussion of several recent studies employing this method. In one section of the paper the author assesses the analytical strengths and weaknesses of the technique, and in another section considers the statistical difficulties associated with survivor estimates. The fundamental weaknesses of the survivor technique stem from the fact that the share of industry output accounted for by a firm depends on factors other than the height of the static long-run average cost curve associated with the product in question. For example, a firm may have the same average cost as other firms whose share of industry output is growing faster, but may have a lower growth-rate objective. Alternatively, growth-rate objectives may be similar but decision-makers' expectations about the profitability of expansion in other industries may differ, resulting in differences in the share of output contributed to a particular industry. The fact that the survivor technique embraces dynamic elements, sometimes claimed to be a major advantage, limits its usefulness as a method of estimating the shape of static long-run average cost curves to situations where technology has remained unchanged.

The final article in Part II, by S. Hymer and P. Pashigian, is a prominent example of much recent research into the implications of firms' growth rates for cost conditions existing in the firms concerned. The authors argue that empirical evidence on growth rates is consistent with continually declining long-run average cost curves. This view contrasts markedly with the conclusions of the majority of studies employing the other three methods of estimating cost curves, which suggest the existence of L-shaped long-run average cost curves. The article is an excellent illustration of the way in which hypotheses concerning cost conditions can be tested by ingenious use of available statistical evidence.

5

Economies of Scale in Industrial Plants

*John Haldi and David Whitcomb**

This paper presents evidence derived from engineering data on economies of scale in manufacturing and processing plants. The evidence presented here relates solely to production cost. Costs associated with factors such as marketing, general overhead, transportation, dispersal of market, and raw materials are excluded from this study. The chief purpose underlying this research was to provide some empirical justification for investigations into the nature and extent of investment barriers created by economies of scale in less developed countries.[1] In light of this purpose, certain dynamic phenomena (such as learning curves) that have a scale effect will also be discussed briefly.

Our main conclusion is that in many basic industries, such as petroleum refining, primary metals, and electric power, economies of scale are found up to very large plant sizes (often the largest built or contemplated). These economies occur mostly in the initial investment cost and in operating labor cost, with no significant economies observed in raw material cost. Scale economies can also result from learning curve effects, spreading of set-up costs, and certain stochastic processes associated with inventories. With some reservations, we feel that these general results based on data from Western countries can also be applied to less

Reprinted from *Journal of Political Economy* (August 1967), by permission of The University of Chicago Press. Copyright, 1967, pp. 373–385.

* The authors wish to thank Hollis Chenery and Donald Keesing for helpful comments and criticisms. Part of this research was supported by the Ford Foundation and by the Stanford Project for Quantitative Research in Economic Development.

[1] The implication of economies of scale for industrialization strategies is the subject of two similar models by Chenery (1959) and Haldi (1960).

developed countries, where limited demand and the resulting inability to realize potential economies of scale can present a barrier to investment.

Evidence that there are economies of scale in plant production cost is not inconsistent with the observation that in the United States most industries have at least several plants, often differing in size. This is explained both by historical development and by the other elements of total cost which we have excluded. Average transportation cost rises with the output of a single plant, since average distance to market rises, *ceteris paribus*. Furthermore, product differentiation may place an ultimate demand constraint on expansion, with market diseconomies appearing as that constraint is approached.

ECONOMIES OF SCALE IN STATIC COST CURVES

The traditional long-run envelope cost curve assumes that all considerations like technology and price structure are fixed. Although the envelope curve is easily defined, its actual shape is difficult to determine even under the best conditions because it reflects only a small portion of the cost schedules of many plants of different sizes.

Sources and Scope of the Data

In determining short-run cost curves for entire plants, one can use either engineering studies or historical accounting data. We prefer engineering studies.

Data from Accounting Records

It is difficult to obtain actual data on the construction and operating costs of industrial plants because these data are usually closely held. If actual cost records were available, we still could not necessarily derive reliable estimates of economies of scale.[2] Even with complete historical cost data on any particular industry, one would have a major problem identifying cost changes due to differences in scale from those cost changes caused by other variables. Observed cost variation between two plants in an industry can result not only from differences in size but also from (1) unstable demand, so that existing capacity is used differently; (2) non-homogeneous output; (3) age differences, with the newer plant embodying technological improvements unrelated to scale and unavailable to the older plant; (4) different locations, with the cost of preparing the construction site having little relationship to scale; and (5) other factors, such as different technology induced by differences in relative factor prices.

Besides the statistical identification problems inherent in the use of historical cost records, Milton Friedman (1955) has noted that another serious conceptual problem may also arise with accounting data. If a firm has made a mistake and is either larger or smaller than the optimal size, the loss from that mistake will have become capitalized either by accounting practice or by changes in the ownership of the firm. Thus there is good reason to expect that accounting data may not yield reliable estimates of scale economies. In fact, in a perfect capital market, an estimating process based on market valuation of equity would always yield constant returns.

[2] For a rather thorough treatment of the shortcomings of actual cost records, see Caleb Smith (1955).

Engineering Studies

Engineers' cost estimates are especially useful to a study on economies of scale because they embody assumptions consistent with those underlying the envelope curve. That is, an engineering study generally varies capacity while keeping constant relative factor prices, supply conditions, product homogeneity, location, and so forth. Engineering studies do admit changes in technique but only within the limits of the technology available at a given time and optimal for each plant size. Such adjustments are, of course, not only admissible but are assumed in the construction of the envelope curve.

Engineering studies can, on the other hand, be rather unreliable. Sometimes engineers forecast cost rather accurately, and sometimes they err considerably. But it is the slope and not the height of the envelope curve that reflects economies of scale. Because those unforeseen factors that cause engineering estimates to err can shift the entire curve without seriously affecting the slope, engineering studies may successfully reflect the extent of economies of scale even when they are wrong about the absolute level of costs. Sometimes the usefulness of engineering studies is also limited by the fact that they estimate costs for only a few plant sizes in a relatively narrow capacity range. The range of sizes covered can often be much smaller than an economist would like. Fortunately, though, our data generally covered a wide range of sizes.

The bulk of our evidence on economies of scale as revealed through static cost curves is derived from the engineering literature. The information is mostly from the 1950's and 1960's and comes entirely from North American and European sources. The data are limited chiefly to manufacturing plants in certain industries, and omitted are other components of total "system" cost, such as transportation and selling costs. We have thus adopted a sort of input-output approach to analyze manufacturing value added as a separate, distinguishable sector of the economy.[3] To isolate technological economies of scale in the manufacturing portion of total product cost, we have assumed that (1) all labor and raw material inputs are available in unlimited quantities at constant prices, and (2) cost estimates for larger plants do not reflect demand conditions for output which might limit plant size. Under these assumptions, production costs do not reflect any increasing or decreasing returns in other sectors of the economy; for example, any quantity discounts, or diseconomies in the gathering together of inputs or dispersion of outputs are assumed to be reflected in the production functions of other sectors.[4] To make inferences about total system cost one must, of course, aggregate over all relevant sectors.

To isolate better the various sources of scale economies within a single plant,

---

[3] For applications of such input-output type models, see Chenery (1959) and Haldi (1960).

[4] These other sectors remain to be studied. For example, quantity discounts received by a firm may reflect production economies in other firms, marketing economies, reaction by sellers to uncertain demand conditions, or excessive bargaining power possessed by a buyer in an imperfect market. In a competitive market, economies of scale in the production of larger equipment sizes are passed on to buyers of the equipment via the price mechanism.

we collected data on (1) the cost of individual units of industrial equipment, (2) the initial investment in plant and equipment, and (3) operating costs (namely, labor, raw materials, and utilities). These three groups of data are discussed below.

Cost of Basic Industrial Equipment

Equipment cost constitutes a major portion of the total investment in new plants. In this section we therefore present data on scale economies in numerous items of basic industrial equipment, along with a brief rationale for these observed economies. An outstanding virtue of equipment cost data is the almost total lack of problems caused by non-homogeneous product mixes, construction specially designed for expansion to avoid future bottlenecks, and so forth, which are so troublesome when dealing with complete plant data.

Technological Scale Economies

For many items of equipment and machinery, an increase in capacity and output does not require a proportionate increase in material and labor. This arises from two phenomena: (1) indivisibilities of machinery and individual workers, which have been discussed at length in the literature; and (2) a family of geometric relationships which relate the material required for the building of equipment to the equipment's capacity.[5] The amount of material required for containers (tanks, furnaces, kettles, pipes, and so on) depends principally on the surface area, whereas capacity depends on the volume inclosed. Thus for a pipe of a given length, for example, circumference will be the chief determinant of material requirements, whereas capacity depends on the cross-sectional area of the pipe.

We can express all these geometric relationships by a generalized exponential function of the form

$$C = aX^b, \qquad (5.1)$$

where C represents cost, X output capacity, and a is a constant; the exponent b may be called the "scale coefficient." A value of $b < 1$ implies increasing returns to scale, $b = 1$ shows constant returns, and $b > 1$ implies decreasing returns.[6] Geometric relationships apply to many basic industrial processes. An exponential function therefore provides an appropriate basis for fitting a least-squares line to cost-capacity data, and all data reported on in this paper have been fitted to equation (5.1).

---

[5] These and other technological relationships are discussed at some length by Chenery (1949). Note also that labor cost often varies with the amount of material being worked, rather than with capacity. Thus, these geometric relationships often save labor as well as material cost.

[6] For a numerical example, consider two spherical containers. The above relationship can be expressed mathematically, letting $r =$ radius, as

$$\frac{\text{Surface area of } 1 (= 4r_1^2)}{\text{Surface area of } 2 (= 4r_2^2)} = \frac{(\text{Volume of } 1)^b}{(\text{Volume of } 2)} = \frac{(\frac{4}{3}r_1^3)^b}{(\frac{4}{3}r_2^3)}$$

from which it can be derived that the exponent b equals 2.

Empirical Results

Table 5.1 summarizes estimates of the scale coefficient for a large assortment of common industrial equipment. In most instances, the exponential or linear log function fits the data well through the observed range of capacities.[7]

Table 5.1

SUMMARY DISTRIBUTION OF ECONOMIES OF SCALE
IN BASIC INDUSTRIAL EQUIPMENT

VALUE OF THE SCALE COEFFICIENT, b*	INSTALLED PLANT EQUIPMENT†		OTHER EQUIPMENT‡		TOTAL	
	NUMBER OF ESTIMATES OF b	PERCENTAGE	NUMBER OF ESTIMATES OF b	PERCENTAGE	NUMBER OF ESTIMATES OF b	PERCENTAGE
	(1)	(2)	(3)	(4)	(5)	(6)
Under .30	22	3.3	5	20.0	27	3.9
.30– .39	44	6.6	3	12.0	47	6.8
.40– .49	96	14.5	6	24.0	102	14.9
.50– .59	143	21.6	0	0	143	20.8
.60– .69	142	21.5	5	20.0	147	21.4
.70– .79	90	13.7	2	8.0	92	13.4
.80– .89	60	9.0	0	0	60	8.7
.90– .99	29	4.4	1	4.0	30	4.4
1.00–1.09	18	2.7	2	8.0	20	2.9
Over 1.10	18	2.7	1	4.0	19	2.8
Totals	662	100.0	25	100.0	687	100.0

* Estimate of b in $C = aX^b$.
† Much of the equipment in this column directly embodies the technological relationships discussed in the text. Included here are containers, pipes, reaction vessels, kilns, and so forth.
‡ This category includes equipment like construction and mining machinery.
Source: Table 4 of an Appendix available from the authors upon request.

Most of the underlying cost-size observations came from catalogues of industrial equipment. The bulk of these raw data was collected by industrial cost

---

[7] Of the 687 estimates of the scale coefficient, 188 indicated some deviation from equation (5.1). In 87 per cent of these 188 cases, the equipment tended toward smaller scale economies in the larger size ranges. However, not all of the studies applied goodness-of-fit measures, and some reported deviations may not have been statistically significant. In a significant study by Bauman (1962), 92 of his 173 estimates (that is, 53 per cent) showed some curvilinearity in logs. Seventy-two of these showed smaller scale economies in the larger size ranges. Of these seventy-two, though, only ten ever reached constant returns at their largest sizes, and only three reached decreasing returns. Thus it is fair to say that our data support the conclusion that there are increasing returns in equipment up to and including the largest sizes built.

estimators and published in engineering journals.[8] A small amount of raw data was collected by the present authors, and in several instances we had to estimate the scale coefficient from the data given by other authors. Most of the equipment items are used in the chemical and other process industries; the choice of items was probably dictated by the various interests of the cost analysts. Frequently, an estimated installation cost was added to the basic equipment price. In these particular observations, the basic equipment price is not subject to estimation error, but the installation cost is. The articles from which these estimates are taken generally do not give enough information to permit us to apply standard statistical tests. To allow for sampling error, therefore, let us arbitrarily classify scale coefficients where b is between 0.90 and 1.10 as not significantly different from 1.0. With this adjustment, out of a total of 687 scale coefficients, 618 (90.0 per cent) show increasing returns, and 50 (7.3 per cent) show constant returns. Only 19 (2.8 per cent) observed scale coefficients reflect decreasing returns, which is not surprising. We should expect to observe few values of b greater than 1.0 because, when decreasing returns set in, large units usually are not built, and prices for these sizes are simply not available. Instead, multiple units are used (multiple pot lines in alumina reduction plants, for example).[9]

Possible Bias

The scale coefficients summarized in Table 5.1 were derived from quoted market prices. If all sizes of a particular type of equipment were sold in perfectly competitive markets, prices would everywhere reflect true social cost. However, entry is generally easier for manufacturers of small equipment items, so there are usually more producers of an item of small equipment, and both the market and the profit rate for small items of equipment are at least as competitive as the market and the profit rate for large equipment. Hence our estimated scale coefficients may slightly overestimate social costs for the larger units, thereby understating the "real" economies of scale.

For broad long-range planning, it would be desirable to know something about attainable social cost as well as actual cost under existing conditions. To evaluate our data under such a requirement, we would have to know the extent to which potential economies of scale are realized in the manufacture of various sizes of equipment. Unfortunately, available information did not allow us to make quantitative estimates of potential cost reduction from unexploited economies of scale. But we note that as a rule many small units of equipment are manufac-

---

[8] These sources are given in the bibliography to Table 4 of an Appendix which is available upon request from the authors and which gives more detail on the tables here. Whenever one of our sources gave data that also appeared in another source, we dropped the redundant estimate. Thus, to the best of our knowledge, the estimates of the scale coefficient here and in the other tables in this paper are independent. Also, we dropped any items of equipment for which the physical capacity measure did not relate directly to economic capacity.

[9] Multiple units may not always be feasible, and some plants may, therefore, use equipment that seems to provide decreasing returns because on an over-all basis it is economic. Stamping presses offer a possible example. Since two 50,000-ton presses cannot perform certain tasks that a 100,000-ton press can, this larger press may be purchased even if it costs more than twice what two 50,000-ton presses would cost.

tured for each large unit produced. For example, many more small electric motors are made than large ones. Thus, manufacturers of smaller equipment probably come closer to achieving maximum potential economies of scale (and reflecting them in equipment prices) than do manufacturers of larger equipment.[10] Hence, any unexploited economies of scale in equipment manufacturing probably lie more with larger equipment, with resulting understatement of the potential scale economies in manufacturing and processing plant investment.

Construction Cost of Plants and Process Areas

Inferences from Equipment Cost Data

Although Table 5.1 shows increasing returns for most equipment, it does not immediately follow that the investment cost of entire plants will exhibit a similar pattern. Nevertheless, the data encourage such an inference, and its basis is examined briefly here.

Engineers can design larger plants by (1) expanding all equipment uniformly, (2) breaking design bottlenecks, (3) changing technique, or (4) using multiple units. The first three methods generally lead to some economies of scale in total construction cost.

1. *Expand all equipment uniformly.* Let the installed cost of equipment be given by

$$C_i = a_i X_i^{b_i}, \quad (5.2)$$

where the terms are defined as in equation (5.1). Then total equipment cost, C^*, is equal to the sum of the equipment cost,

$$C^* = \Sigma\, a_i X_i^{b_i}. \quad (5.3)$$

If all b_i are less than one, cost will not increase proportionately with capacity.[11]

2. *Break bottlenecks.* When bottlenecks are caused by indivisibilities in the size of some equipment, parts of the plant may possess unutilized capacity. In this case, we need enlarge only certain critical areas to increase total capacity. When it is possible to expand design capacity by breaking bottlenecks, any scale economy in the equipment or processes expanded will result in even larger economies for the whole plant. Even if the expanded units exhibit diseconomies, the total plant may still achieve increasing returns until all major bottlenecks have been overcome. The economic

---

[10] Unexploited scale economies probably arise from spreading of set-up costs, described in detail in the second part of this article. When a job-lot manufacturer doubles the number of units to be produced, his unit set-up cost should decrease, and *ceteris paribus*, he will be closer to achieving maximum potential economies of scale than a manufacturer producing half that number of units.

[11] Note that $\log \Sigma\, X_i$ is not equal to $\Sigma \log X_i$. As capacity increases, therefore, those items of equipment with the greatest increasing returns (the smallest b_i) decline as a percentage of the total cost. If capacity could increase without bound, the rate of increase of C^* would asymptotically approach the largest b_i.

literature frequently describes this situation as one in which economies of scale exist up to "the point of the least common denominator."

3. *Change technique.* When engineers change technique, they intend to accomplish the same end result by a different method (for example, pure capital substitution or capital-labor substitution). Since engineers can always duplicate smaller units of equipment and smaller plants, they will use different techniques in large plants only when these techniques are more economical. Thus when different techniques are observed in the design of larger plants they will generally reflect economies of scale.

4. *Use multiple units.* Multiple units are normally used when equipment scale economies have been exhausted. Barring economies in peripheral equipment, expansion by this method alone should not be expected to give further plant economies of scale.

We know of no method for directly estimating scale economies in plant investment cost by aggregating equipment data. However, this discussion of how engineers design larger plants helps show the relevance of the equipment cost data to our basic purpose: exploring the nature and extent of plant economies of scale. Cost-capacity figures for equipment are not subject to statistical confounding problems, and the scale coefficients are usually derived from actual price quotations rather than from engineers' estimates. For these reasons they tend to be the most accurate data available, and they considerably increase our confidence in the scale coefficients given in Table 5.2 for the investment cost of entire plants.

Data on Actual Plant Costs

The engineering studies presented here usually represent a set of hypothetical plants, each producing the same product with the same technology available (although optimum technique may vary), and differing only in size. A few of the estimates are not for hypothetical plants but come instead from carefully selected historical data on actual plants.[12] Table 5.2 summarizes estimates of the scale coefficient for 221 long-run cost curves.[13] All estimates of plant cost and many of the scale coefficients were calculated by cost engineers and were reported in the journal articles given in the bibliography to the Appendix noted above. When only cost-capacity figures were available, scale coefficients were computed by the present authors. As with the equipment data, redundant estimates were eliminated. Building, equipment, and installation labor make up the investment costs. Site preparation costs are sometimes included, but always on the basis of a "standard site." Interest on funds expended before the plant begins operating is not included. For these reasons, economies of scale may be overstated slightly, since larger plants may have longer gestation periods.

Virtually all of the plants reported on here produce fairly homogeneous stand-

[12] See n. *a* to Table 6 in the Appendix available from the authors.
[13] The linear logarithmic form of the exponential function in equation (5.1) was used. In eleven out of the 221 observations, however, a curvilinear log function would have been more appropriate. For six of these eleven cases, an average slope was used in Table 5.2. For further details, see n. *d* to Table 6 in the Appendix.

82 COST CONDITIONS

Table 5.2

SUMMARY DISTRIBUTION OF ECONOMIES OF SCALE IN PLANT INVESTMENT COSTS*
(NUMBER OF ESTIMATES OF SCALE COEFFICIENT b IN $C = aX^b$)

INDUSTRY	UNDER .40	.40–.49	.50–.59	.60–.69	.70–.79	.80–.89	.90–.99	1.00–1.09	1.10 AND UP	TOTALS
	(1)	(2)	(3)	(4)	(5)	(6)	(7)	(8)	(9)	(10)
Cement				1	1			1		3
Chemicals, excluding petroleum:										
Fertilizer		3		2					1	6
Gases	4		6	9	15	9			2	45
Industrial chemicals		2	3	10	11	9	6	1		42
Plastics				1	1		1			3
Rubber				2	1	2	1	1		8
Miscellaneous chemicals	3			2	1	2			2	8
Desalination					4	1	1			6
Electric power		1	7	1	2	2	2			15
Petroleum refining and by-products		5	6	15	15	13	2		1	57
Aluminum				2	3	3	4	1	2	15
Pulp and paper					2	2	1		1	6
Shipping					1					1
Miscellaneous	2	1			2	1				6
Totals	9	12	22	45	61	37	20	6	9	221
Percentage	4.1	5.4	10.0	20.4	27.6	16.7	9.0	2.7	4.1	100.0

* Number of individual plant studies classified by industry and by extent of scale economies.
Source: Table 6 of an Appendix available from the authors upon request.

ardized products (where non-homogeneous products are made, a standard product mix was used for all sizes). However, the "industries" in Table 5.2 are not strictly homogeneous (we found a number of different scale coefficients for each industry), and industry-wide generalizations are limited. For the aluminum industry, where larger plants use multiple production units (pot lines), the scale coefficients are high, with seven of fifteen estimates at or above the 0.90 level (approximately constant returns). This result coincides with the a priori reasoning given above. Among various types of plants in the industry—bauxite, alumina, ingots, and extrusions—there seemed to be no uniformly consistent pattern. Another standardized product is sulfuric acid, but it is made by several processes. Table 5.2 contains eleven scale factors for sulfuric acid, and, despite the variety of processes, all scale coefficients fall within a narrower range than that exhibited by many other products with multiple estimates. This was also true for acetylene and hydrogen, but not for oxygen (all classed under "Gases").

Sample size and goodness-of-fit information were often unavailable for many of the original estimates because they were presented in summary form. However, the size range covered was usually available. The ratio of the largest to the smallest capacity varies from 1.33 to 1,500, but most ratios fall between 4 and 20.[14] Because we know so little about most of the original estimates and what errors they may embody, we were not able to apply standard tests of statistical significance to the estimated scale coefficients. In the absence of better confidence limits, we again arbitrarily classify estimates of b between 0.90 and 1.10 as not significantly different from 1.0. By this criterion, 186 of 221 estimates of the scale coefficient show increasing returns, 26 show constant returns, and only 9 show decreasing returns. The median scale coefficient is 0.73. On this basis, we conclude that economies of scale in production cost are significant and widespread for the types of plants surveyed here.

Operating Cost

We defined operating cost as in-plant production cost less taxes and payments to capital (including depreciation). We relied exclusively on engineering estimates of operating cost. As with equipment and plant investment costs, we eliminated non-independent estimates. Multiple estimates appear in the same "industry" because industries are not homogeneous and because there are often several processes for making the same product. The results, given in Table 5.3, show clearly that many plants exhibit substantial economies of scale in total operating costs.

In an independent study, Isard and Schooler (1955) derived thirty-five estimates of scale coefficients for operating labor cost in the petrochemical industry. These are shown in column (4) of Table 5.3. They differ considerably from our seventeen labor scale coefficients for several industries, shown in column (3) of Table 5.3. Their scale coefficients were mostly smaller than the ten we were able to obtain for the petrochemical industry. Possible explanations may be that (a) the petrochemical industry is not very homogeneous, and the types of plants

[14] Extrapolation of the scale coefficient beyond the highest observed capacity would be dangerous. However, the highest observations were usually large by standards of industrial countries.

Table 5.3

SUMMARY DISTRIBUTION OF ECONOMIES OF SCALE IN PLANT OPERATING COSTS

VALUE OF THE SCALE COEFFICIENT, b*	TOTAL OPERATING COST		LABOR COST ONLY			
	NO. OF ESTIMATES	PERCENTAGE	OUR RESULTS: NO. OF ESTIMATES	ISARD AND SCHOOLER† NO. OF ESTIMATES	TOTAL NO. OF ESTIMATES	PERCENTAGE
	(1)	(2)	(3)	(4)	(5)	(6)
Under .40	4	12.5	8	29	37	71.2
.40– .49	1	3.1	1	4	5	9.6
.50– .59	5	15.6	6	2	8	15.4
.60– .69	3	9.4	1	0	1	1.9
.70– .79	10	31.3	1	0	1	1.9
.80– .89	9	28.1	0	0	0	0
.90– .99	0	0	0	0	0	0
1.00–1.09	0	0	0	0	0	0
1.10 and up	0	0	0	0	0	0
Totals	32	100.0	17	35	52	100.0

* Estimates of b in $C = aX^b$.
† W. Isard and E. W. Schooler (1955).
Source: Table 7 of an Appendix available from the authors upon request.

surveyed vary from one study to the other; or (b) most of our observations are for process units—plants within a petrochemical complex—whereas their estimates were for complete plants.

Many of the studies summarized in Table 5.3 did not break operating labor into individual components; for example, operating labor, supervision, raw material, and so on. Cost data that were available are summarized in Table 7 of the Appendix, and following is a brief summary of what these data show.

1. *Raw materials.* There appear to be no great scale economies attainable in the consumption of primary raw materials.
2. *Utilities.* Unit costs for utilities sometimes decline slightly with size increases because larger furnaces, motors, and other such equipment units perform more efficiently than smaller ones.
3. *Labor.* What data we could obtain showed that large economies of scale in labor costs are possible for process-type plants. Labor's chief function in process plants is to watch gauges, adjust valves, and perform maintenance tasks. Consequently, large increases in capacity often require few extra workers.[15]

---

[15] For a discussion of how labor costs may fit a hyperbolic curve, see Bruni (1964).

4. *Supervision and management.* The data indicate substantial economies of scale in supervisory and management costs, about on the order of economies of scale for operating labor.[16] We found no direct evidence for the familiar proposition that diseconomies of scale arise through exhaustion of managerial capability as plant scale increases. This source of diseconomies is usually thought to operate indirectly, however, and most estimates would not be expected to measure it.

5. *Maintenance.* The evidence in Table 7 of the Appendix indicates substantial economies of scale in maintenance costs. These arise from several sources: (*a*) Some repair and janitorial costs have a geometric cost-capacity relationship similar to construction costs; (*b*) there are indivisibilities in some labor costs for equipment repair; and (*c*) costs of spare parts inventories often exhibit stochastic scale economies (discussed in the second section).

A few engineering studies on industries other than the ones considered here are available; their results generally coincide with ours. For example, Chenery (1957) studied scale economies in the metalworking industry by applying linear programming techniques to data on metalworking processes developed by the RAND Corporation. He found that significant economies can be realized by substituting capital for labor as the desired output of an item increases. Along the same lines, Bain (1956) found significant economies of scale in auto production, also due in part to the big manufacturers' substitution of capital for labor.

Manufacturing and Processing Cost: Conclusions

Determining the optimum plant size for a particular supply-demand situation requires more information than is outlined here. However, the data obtained in this study support the opinion of engineers who feel that unit processing and manufacturing costs decline as plants increase in size, up to very large plant sizes. More specifically:

1. We can generally expect initial investment cost (and, therefore, the amortization portion of total cost) in most types of plants and equipment to exhibit economies of scale up to the largest plants observed in industrial countries. In the more capital-intensive industries, savings in capital cost are an important source of scale economies.
2. In process plants, operating expenses for labor, supervision, and maintenance also show significant economies of scale.
3. Consumption of utility services shows slight economies of scale, and consumption of raw materials generally shows none.

DYNAMIC AND STOCHASTIC SOURCES OF INCREASING RETURNS

The envelope curve shows only how cost varies with changes in plant size and the average rate of output. Larger firms may also derive cost advantages from

---

[16] An interesting theoretical analysis of the direct cost of supervision and management is given by Beckmann (1960).

certain dynamic and stochastic processes. Like the more traditional economies of scale, these also give rise to some of the external economies so widely discussed in the development literature.[17]

Manufacturing Progress Functions and Set-Up Costs

Within limits, workers become more efficient as they repeat the same task. For this reason, the length of production run can be an important factor in scale economies. Manufacturing progress functions, frequently called "labor learning curves," introduce the length of production run as an explicit variable and depict growth in worker efficiency with repetition.[18]

Cost reduction from learning curves has consequences similar to those of other scale economies. Firms with the largest share of a given market can, in the absence of diseconomies elsewhere, achieve longer production runs than smaller firms. Verdoorn (1960), in assessing the importance of this source of increasing returns, estimates that between the United States and Europe, differences in production run length may affect costs more than differences in plant sizes. This source of cost reduction is probably somewhat more important in assembly-line or job-order type plants than in continuous-process plants like oil refineries.

Longer production runs can cause other and even more obvious economies. Job-order shops must frequently incur a substantial set-up cost for each production run; the more units to which these costs can be allocated, the smaller will be the set-up cost per unit. Further, longer production runs often make it possible to reduce cost significantly by automating production and substituting capital for labor. As with other economies of scale, market size determines whether the potential economies from long production runs are in fact realizable.[19]

Stochastic Increasing Returns

The traditional theory of the firm does not consider ordinary day-to-day uncertainty from random variations in a firm's operations. But in many commonplace situations random variations may be a factor in reducing costs in large plants. We might call the cause of such reductions "stochastic economies of scale." There are many stochastic models that cover differing sets of circumstances and that reflect prevailing cost-size relationships. Although describing such a model in detail is beyond the scope of this discussion, we can outline the principle behind it.

Plants always keep spare parts on hand to take care of possible machinery breakdowns. Let one such part be a "widget," and assume X widgets are in regular operation throughout the plant. Assume further that one widget failure

---

[17] See Scitovsky (1954) for a good discussion of external economies.

[18] The extent to which "learning" can reduce cost has been studied by Asher (1956), Hirsch (1956), and Alchian (1963) and has been treated in a broader economic setting by Arrow (1962).

[19] Countries or regions with small internal markets and with little access to export markets will have a distinct disadvantage in manufacturing products requiring substantial set-up costs (of course, as an economy grows, these disadvantages diminish). Since set-up costs represent social as well as private cost, less developed countries should take these costs into account in deciding which industries to encourage.

is independent of other such failures. By constructing a model that embodies (1) the probability function describing widget failures, (2) the time necessary to replenish the inventory of widgets, (3) the cost of down-time, and other pertinent factors, we can determine the optimum inventory of spare widgets. If the number of widgets in regular operation increases as the plant grows (through duplication of machinery), the optimum inventory of spares per unit of capacity will decrease. This is because the variance of the number of expected breakdowns does not increase proportionately to increases in the number of widgets used (due to the law of large numbers).[20]

In conclusion, we point out that a great deal of additional empirical research needs to be done in order to develop a broader base of understanding about economies of scale. We need to know more about economies in transportation relative to volume carried and diseconomies relative to length of haul; about economies in marketing, finance, and administration of multiplant firms; and about the effect of technological change on efficient scale.

REFERENCES

1. Alchian, Armen. "Reliability of Progress Curves in Airframe Production," *Econometrica*, XXXI, No. 4 (October, 1963), 679–93.
2. Arrow, Kenneth J. "The Economic Implications of Learning by Doing," *Rev. Econ. Studies*, XXIX (June, 1962), 155–73.
3. Asher, Harold. *Cost Quantity Relationships in the Airframe Industry.* (No. R-291.) RAND Corporation, July 1, 1956.
4. Bain, Joe S. *Barriers to New Competition.* Cambridge, Mass.: Harvard Univ. Press, 1956.
5. Bauman, H. R. "Up-to-Date Equipment Costs," *Industrial and Engineering Chemistry*, LIV, No. 1 (January, 1962), 49–60.
6. Beckmann, M. J. "Some Aspects of Returns to Scale in Business Administration," *Q.J.E.*, LXXIV (August, 1960), 464–71.
7. Bruni, L. "Internal Economies of Scale with a Given Technique," *J. Industrial Econ.*, XII (July, 1964), 175–90.
8. Chenery, H. B. "Engineering Bases of Economic Analysis." Ph.D. dissertation, Harvard Univ., 1949.
9. "Capital Labor Substitution in Metalworking Processes." (Memorandum No. C-3 of the Stanford Project for Quantitative Research in Economic Development.) Stanford, Calif.: Department of Economics, Stanford Univ., February, 1957 (mimeographed).

[20] In the economic-lot-size problem, with known uniform demand plus known order costs and holding costs, the familiar "square root rule" determines the optimum order size plus the average inventory. In this elementary but widely applied model, total inventory cost (exclusive of purchase cost) varies with the square root of demand. In terms of the exponential equation (1) used throughout the first section, this implies a scale factor (b) of 0.50. Increasing stochastic returns can also apply to the size of the labor force needed to repair periodic breakdowns. Large textile mills, for example, are said to require proportionately less standby labor than smaller mills.

10. "The Interdependence of Investment Decisions," in M. Abramovitz (ed.). *The Allocation of Economic Resources.* Stanford, Calif.: Stanford Univ. Press, 1959.
11. Friedman, Milton. "Comment" on Caleb Smith, "A Survey of the Empirical Evidence on Economies of Scale," in *Business Concentration and Price Policy.* Princeton, N.J.: Princeton Univ. Press, 1955, pp. 230–38.
12. Haldi, John. "Economies of Scale in Economic Development." Ph.D. dissertation, Stanford Univ., 1960.
13. Hirsch, Werner Z. "Firm Progress Ratios," *Econometrica,* XXIV (April, 1956), 136–43.
14. Isard, W., and Schooler, E. W. *Location Factors in the Petrochemical Industry.* (PB-111640.) Washington: U.S. Dept. of Commerce, July, 1955.
15. Scitovsky, Tibor. "Two Concepts of External Economies," *J.P.E.,* LXII (April, 1954), 143–51.
16. Smith, Caleb. "A Survey of the Empirical Evidence on Economies of Scale," *Business Concentration and Price Policy.* Princeton, N.J.: Princeton Univ. Press, 1955.
17. Verdoorn, P. J. "Debate" in E. A. G. Robinson (ed.). *Economic Consequences of the Size of Nations.* New York: St. Martins Press, 1960.

6
Hierarchical Control and Optimum Firm Size

Oliver E. Williamson*

There is a great deal of evidence that almost all organizational structures tend to produce false images in the decision-maker, and that the larger and more authoritarian the organization, the better the chance that its top decision-makers will be operating in purely imaginary worlds. This perhaps is the most fundamental reason for supposing that there are ultimately diminishing returns to scale.[1]

Although we are quite in agreement with Professor Boulding's judgment that problems of transmitting accurate images across successive levels in a hierarchical organization are fundamentally responsible for diminishing returns to scale, there is less than unanimity on this issue. Indeed, it has long been disputed whether or in what ways the management factor is responsible for a limitation to firm size. Although descriptive treatments of this question have been numerous, these have generally been too imprecise to permit testable implications to be derived. The present analysis attempts a partial remedy for this condition by embedding in a formal model the control-loss features of hierarchical organization that have recently been advanced in the bureaucratic-theory literature. The background

Reprinted from *Journal of Political Economy* (April 1967), by permission of The University of Chicago Press. Copyright, 1967, pp. 123–138.

* The views expressed are not necessarily those of the Justice Department. Research on this paper was supported by a grant to the author from the National Science Foundation and from the Lilly Foundation grant to the University of California, Los Angeles, for the study of the economics of property rights.
[1] Kenneth E. Boulding, Richard T. Ely Lecture, 78th Annual Meeting of the American Economic Association.

to this discussion of control loss as a limitation to firm size is reviewed in the first section. A simple model possessing basic control-loss attributes is developed and its properties derived in the following section. In the next section, we extend and elaborate the model, developing additional implications and indicating some of the problems to expect in empirical testing. The conclusions are given in the last section.

BACKGROUND TO THE ANALYSIS

That the question of the optimum size firm presented a serious dilemma for the theory of the firm was noted by Knight in 1933. Thus, he observed:

> The relation between efficiency and size is one of the most serious problems of theory, being in contrast with the relation for a plant, largely a matter of personality and historical accident rather than of intelligible general principles. But this question is peculiarly vital because the possibility of monopoly gain offers a powerful incentive to *continuous and unlimited* expansion of the firm, which force must be offset by some equally powerful one making for decreased efficiency (in the production of money income) with growth in size, if even boundary competition is to exist [Knight, 1965, p. xxiii].

Within a year, Robinson (1934, 1962) proposed what we believe to be a substantially correct answer, namely, that problems of coordination imposed a static limitation to firm size; and Coase in his classic 1937 article on "The Nature of the Firm" generally supports this position (1952, pp. 340–41). Kaldor (1934), however, argued that problems of coordination vanished under truly static conditions, and hence only declining product-demand curves or rising factor-supply curves could be responsible for a static limitation to firm size. Only in the context of firm dynamics did coordination problems, in his view, constitute a genuine limitation to firm size. But as Robinson was quick to point out, Kaldor's argument rested on his peculiar specification of the static condition as one in which the control problem is defined to be absent. This approach to the economics of the firm he found quite uninstructive for, as he pungently noted, "In Mr. Kaldor's long period we shall not only be dead but in Nirvana, and the economics of Nirvana . . . is surely the most fruitless of sciences" (Robinson, 1934, p. 250).

The argument remained there[2] until Ross (1952–53, p. 148), in a sweeping attack on the economic treatments of this question, took the position that this whole literature bordered on the irrelevant for its failure to incorporate "certain aspects of the theory of organization and management." Recasting the problem in what he regarded as suitable organizational terms, he concluded that "by appropriate measures of decentralization and control the firm may expand without incurring increasing costs of coordination over a range sufficiently wide to cover all possible cases within the limits imposed by scarcity of resources" (Ross,

---

[2] Chamberlin (1948, pp. 249–50) objected to some aspects of the argument in his treatment of the divisibility question, but nevertheless acknowledged that problems of coordination arising from increasing complexity eventually were responsible for increasing unit costs.

1952–53, p. 154). Starbuck imputes similar views to Andrews, albeit incorrectly,[3] and, in apparent sympathy with Ross, likewise regards the treatment by economists of these issues as entirely too narrow and probably self-serving (Starbuck, 1964, p. 343).

Mrs. Penrose also finds this literature unsatisfactory, observing that "whether managerial diseconomies will cause long-run increasing costs [requires that] management . . . be treated as a 'fixed factor' and the nature of the 'fixity' must be identified with respect to the nature of the managerial task of 'coordination.' *This identification has never been satisfactorily accomplished*" (Penrose, 1959, p. 12; italics added). She continues to regard the issue as a vital one, however, but argues with Kaldor that it is the dynamics, not the statics of coordination, that give rise to a limitation to firm size. In their view, expansion is contingent on knowledgeable planning and skilful coordination where these are a function of internal experience. Since experience is available in restricted supply, the rate of growth is thereby necessarily restricted. Variations on this argument have since been developed, and some have come to regard the growth rate as the only limitation to firm size.[4]

It is unfortunate (although understandable) that the static limitation argument should continue to be misunderstood in this way. The difficulty is probably traceable to the distinction between truly static and quasi-static conditions. Those who reject the static-limitation argument tend to adopt the former position, while those who advocate it take the latter. This is implicit in the Kaldor-Robinson dispute cited above. Differences of this sort are especially difficult to resolve, but an effort to explicate the quasi-static position may nevertheless be useful.

The problem can be stated in terms of deterministic versus stochastic equilibrium. A steady state is reached in each. But whereas in the former the data are unchanging, in the latter the firm is required to adapt to circumstances which are predictable in the sense that although they occur with stochastic regularity, precise advance knowledge of them is unavailable. Although the deterministic condition provides circumstances in which the usual management functions can be progressively eliminated through the refinement of operations, this is the world of Kaldor's Nirvana and has limited relevance for an understanding of business behavior. Instead, customers come and go, manufacturing operations break down, distribution systems malfunction, labor and materials procurement are subject to the usual vagaries, all with stochastic regularity, not to mention minor shifts in demand and similar disturbing influences of a transitory nature. Throughout all of this, the management of the firm is required to adapt to the

[3] According to Starbuck, Andrews takes the position that "it is impossible to conceive of any human organization too vast for organized efficiency." Andrews (1949, pp. 134–35), however, is quite specific in stating otherwise.

[4] Thus, John Williamson takes the position that: "One of the more discredited concepts in the theory of the firm is that of an 'optimum size' firm . . . [S]ince firms are not restricted to the sale of a single product or even a particular range of products, there is no more reason to expect profitability to decline with size than there is evidence to suggest that it does. This raises the question as to what does limit the size of a firm. The answer . . . is that there are important costs entailed in *expanding* the size of a firm, and that these expansion costs tend to increase with the firm's growth rate" [Williamson, 1966, p. 1].

new circumstances: request the relevant data, process the information supplied, and provide the appropriate instructions. Coordination in these circumstances is thus essential. If, simultaneously, a general expansion of operations accompanies these quasi-static adjustments, additional direction would be required. But in no sense is growth a necessary condition for the coordinating function to exist. We, therefore, take the position that bounded rationality[5] imposes a (quasi)-static limitation to firm size through the mechanism of control loss and that growth considerations act mainly to intensify this underlying condition.

In resorting to the notion of bounded rationality, we ally ourselves with Ross in his claim that economic arguments regarding a static limitation to firm size have not taken adequately into account the contributions which organization theory has made to this problem. But rather than resort to the normative literature of administrative management theory as Ross does, we turn instead to the positive theories of bureaucratic behavior. The former, as March and Simon (1958, pp. 22–32) have aptly observed, is a generally vacuous literature in which most of the interesting problems of organizational behavior are defined away. Although Ross' instincts were correct, his preference for a normative rather than a positive theory put him onto the wrong trail and inevitably led to untestable conclusions of the sort cited above.

The aspect of bureaucratic theory that we regard as particularly relevant for studying the question of a static limitation to firm size is what we will refer to as the "control-loss" phenomenon. It is illustrated daily in the rumor-transmission process and has been studied intensively by Bartlett in his experimental studies of serial reproduction. His experiments involved the oral transmission of descriptive and argumentative passages through a chain of serially linked individuals. Bartlett concludes from a number of such studies that:

> It is now perfectly clear that serial reproduction normally brings about startling and radical alterations in the material dealt with. Epithets are changed into their opposites; incidents and events are transposed; names and numbers rarely survive intact for more than a few reproductions; opinions and conclusions are reversed—nearly every possible variation seems as if it can take place, even in a relatively short series. At the same time the subjects may be very well satisfied with their efforts, believing themselves to have passed on all important features with little or no change, and merely, perhaps, to have omitted unessential matters [Bartlett, 1932, p. 175].

Bartlett (1932, pp. 180–81) illustrates this graphically with a line drawing of an

[5] Robinson (1934, p. 254) came very close to stating it in these terms, but he failed to formalize the argument and lacked an explanation for the control-loss phenomenon. Hence, Mrs. Penrose's discontent with his argument as expressed above. For a modern discussion of the notion of bounded rationality, see March and Simon (1958, chap. vi). Simon (1957a, p. xxiv) observes that "it is precisely in the realm where human behavior is *intendedly* rational, but only *limitedly* so, that there is room for a genuine theory of organization and administration." The theory advanced here attempts to make explicit the way in which intended but limited rationality operates as a limitation to firm size.

owl which—when redrawn successively by eighteen individuals, each sketch based on its immediate predecessor—ended up as a recognizable cat; and the further from the initial drawing one moved, the greater the distortion experienced. The reliance of hierarchical organizations on serial reproduction for their functioning thus exposes them to what may become serious distortions in transmission.

Although this phenomenon is widely experienced, it was not generally regarded as having special theoretical significance until Tullock (1965, pp. 142–93) argued that not only was authority leakage possible in a large government bureau, but it was predictable and could be expressed as an increasing function of size. Downs has since elaborated the argument and summarized it in his "Law of Diminishing Control: *The larger any organization becomes, the weaker is the control over its actions exercised by those at the top"* (1966, p. 109). The cumulative loss of control as instructions and information are transmitted across successive hierarchical levels is responsible for this result.

Thus, assuming that economies of specialization have been exhausted and that superiors are normally more competent than subordinates, a quality-quantity trade-off necessarily exists in every decision to expand. It arises for two reasons, both of which are related to the distance of the top executive from the locus of productive activity. First, expansion of the organization (adding an additional hierarchical level) removes the superior further from the basic data that affect operating conditions; information regarding those conditions must now be transmitted across an additional hierarchical level which exposes the data to an additional serial reproduction operation with its attendant losses. Furthermore, the top executive or peak coordinator (to use Papandreou's term [1952, p. 204]) cannot have all the information that he had before the expansion plus the information now generated by the new parts (assuming that he was fully employed initially). Thus, he can acquire additional information only by sacrificing some of the detail provided to him previously. Put differently, he trades off breadth for depth in undertaking the expansion; he has more resources under his control, but the quality (serial reproduction loss) and the quantity (bounded capacity constraint) of his information are both less with respect to the deployment of each resource unit. In a similar way, being further removed from the operating situation and having more subordinates means that his instructions to each are less detailed and are passed across an additional hierarchical level. For precisely the same reasons, therefore, the behavior of the operating units will scarcely correspond as closely to his objectives as it did prior to the expansion. Taken together, this loss in the quality of the data provided to the peak coordinator and in the quality of the instructions supplied to the operating units made necessary by the expansion will be referred to as "control loss." It will exist even if the objectives of the subordinates are perfectly consonant with those of their superiors and, a fortiori, when subordinate objectives are dissonant.

There are, of course, anti-distortion control devices that the leadership has access to, and Downs (1966, pp. 78–90) has examined a number of them. These include redundancy, external data checks, creation of overlapping areas of responsibility, counterbiases, reorganization so as to keep the hierarchy flat, coding, and so on. The problem with all of these is that they are rarely available at zero cost and invariably experience diminishing returns. Hence, eventually, increasing size encounters control loss. Our objective here is to show how this argument, initially developed in the context of the behavior of government bureaus, has relevance for the static limitation to firm size issue.[6]

THE BASIC MODEL

Consider a hierarchically organized business firm with the following characteristics: (1) only employees at the lowest hierarchical level do manual labor; the work done by employees at higher levels is entirely administrative (planning, forecasting, supervising, accounting, and so on); (2) output is a constant proportion of productive input; (3) the wage paid to employees at the lowest level is w_0; (4) each superior is paid β ($\beta > 1$) times as much as each of his immediate subordinates; (5) the span of control (the number of employees a supervisor can handle effectively) is a constant s ($s > 1$) across every hierarchical level; (6) product and factor prices are parameters; (7) all non-wage variable costs are a constant proportion of output; (8) only the fraction $\bar{\alpha}$ ($0 < \bar{\alpha} < 1$) of the intentions of a superior are effectively satisfied by a subordinate; (9) control loss is strictly cumulative (there is no systematic compensation) across successive hierarchical levels.

The first assumption can be restated as: there are no working foremen.[7] This seems quite reasonable and permits us to simplify the analysis of the relation of output to input. Taken together with assumption (2) which assures that there are no economies of specialization in production (in the relevant range), we are able to express output as a constant proportion of productive input. The distinction between direct labor input and productive labor input should be emphasized. The former refers to the total labor input at the lowest hierarchical level. The latter is that part of the direct labor input which yields productive results. The latter is smaller than the former not by reason of labor inefficiencies but because of the cumulative control loss in the transmission of data and instructions across successive hierarchical levels.

Assumption (3) is innocuous; assumption (4) is plausible and appears to correspond with the facts. This is Simon's conclusion in his study (1957b) of the theory and practices of executive compensation. The constant β condition is also reported by a recent U.S. Department of Labor study (1964, p. 8) of salary structures in the large firm, which found that "the relationship maintained between salary rates for successive grades was more commonly *a uniform percentage spread* between grades than a widening percentage spread" (italics added). An independent check of this hypothesis is also possible from the data on executive compensation included in the Annual Reports of the General Motors Corporation from 1934 to 1942. This is developed in Appendix I.

Assumption (5), that the span of control is constant across levels, is also employed in the wage model tested in Appendix I, although the cumulative distribu-

[6] Monsen and Downs (1965) have used the argument that control loss varies directly with firm size to examine the self-interest seeking behavior of management in the large business firm. However, their analysis is entirely descriptive, and they pass over the optimum firm-size issue and focus instead on the implications of control loss for bureaucratic decision-making within the firm.

[7] This assumption has been expressed in this way by Mayer (1960).

tion relation tested does not uniquely imply this relation.[8] Taken in conjunction with the Department of Labor findings on β, however, the fits reported in Appendix I also lend support to the constant span of control assumption. We nevertheless show in the next section where this assumption can be relaxed somewhat and the basic results preserved.

Assumption (6) permits us to treat prices in the product and factor markets as parameters. As we will show, this can also be relaxed without affecting the qualitative character of our results. Assumption (7) is not critical, but permits us a modest simplification. Assumptions (8) and (9) are merely restatements of the earlier argument. They are responsible for the control-loss attributes of the model. Since much of the exposition in subsequent parts of the paper will be explicitly concerned with them, we will say no more about them here.

For purposes of developing a model around these assumptions, let:

s = span of control
$\bar{\alpha}$ = fraction of work done by a subordinate that contributes to objectives of his superior $(0 < \bar{\alpha} < 1)$; it is thus a compliance parameter.
N_i = number of employees at the ith hierarchical level = s^{i-1}
n = number of hierarchical levels (the decision variable)
P = price of output
w_0 = wage of production workers
w_i = wage of employees at ith hierarchical level
      = $w_0 \beta^{n-i}$ ($\beta > 1$)
r = non-wage variable cost per unit output
Q = output
    = $\theta (\bar{\alpha} s)^{n-1}$
R = total revenue
    = PQ
C = total variable cost
    = $\Sigma_{i=1}^{n} w_i N_i + rQ$

Without loss of generality, we assume that $\theta = 1$. The objective is to find the value of n (the number of hierarchical levels, and hence the size of the firm) so as to maximize net revenue. This is given by:

$$R - C = PQ - \sum_{i=1}^{n} w_i N_i - rQ = P(\bar{\alpha}s)^{n-1} - \Sigma_{i=1}^{n} w_0 \beta^{n-i} s^{i-1} - r(\bar{\alpha}s)^{n-1} \quad (6.1)$$

now

$$\Sigma_{i=1}^{n} w_0 \beta^{n-i} s^{i-1} = w_0 \left(\frac{\beta^n}{s}\right) \sum_{i=1}^{n} \left(\frac{s}{\beta}\right)^i$$

[8] Strictly speaking, the empirical results reported in Table 6.2 support the proposition that the ratio log s/log β is constant across successive hierarchical levels, not that s and β are identical across levels. Letting log s/log $\beta = \gamma$, where γ is a constant, implies that $\beta = s^{1/\gamma}$ at every level. Thus, changes in the span control would be accompanied by changes in the wage multiple according to the relation $\beta_i = s_i^{1/\gamma}$. That β and s are related in this way seems at least as special as to assume that they are constant across levels. Moreover, in view of the Department of Labor report that β is indeed constant across levels, the constant s condition is implied by our results.

where

$$\Sigma_{i=1}^{n}\left(\frac{s}{\beta}\right)^{i} = \frac{\left(\frac{s}{\beta}\right)^{n+1} - \left(\frac{s}{\beta}\right)}{\frac{s}{\beta} - 1} \simeq \frac{s^{n+1}}{(s-\beta)\beta^{n}}.$$

Thus, we have

$$R - C = P(\bar{\alpha} s)^{n-1} - w_0 \frac{s^n}{s - \beta} - r(\bar{\alpha} s)^{n-1}. \tag{6.1'}$$

Differentiating this expression with respect to n and setting equal to zero (and letting ln denote natural logarithm), we obtain as the optimal value for n:

$$n^* = 1 + \frac{1}{ln\ \bar{\alpha}}\left[ln\ \frac{w_0}{P-r} + ln\ \frac{s}{s-\beta} + ln\left(\frac{ln\ s}{ln\ (\bar{\alpha} s)}\right)\right]. \tag{6.2}$$

The values of $\bar{\alpha}$ and $w_0/P - r$ in this expression are both between zero and unity, while $\beta < s$ and $\alpha s > 1$. The condition $\beta < s$ must hold for the approximating relation to apply and is supported by the data.[9] The condition $\bar{\alpha} s > 1$ must hold if there is to be any incentive to hire employees. Not merely diminishing but negative returns would exist were $\bar{\alpha} s < 1$. Since $ln\bar{\alpha} < 0$, the expression in brackets must be negative, a condition which is virtually assured by the stipulation that the firm earn positive profits.[10] Assuming that the appropriate bounds and inequality conditions are satisfied, the following *ceteris paribus* conditions are obtained from the model:

a) Optimal n increases as the degree of compliance with supervisor objectives ($\bar{\alpha}$) increases.

b) Optimal n is infinite if there is no loss of intention ($\bar{\alpha} = 1$) between successive hierarchical levels. Only a declining product-demand curve or rising labor-supply curve could impose a (static) limit on firm size in such circumstances.

c) Optimal n decreases as the ratio of the basic wage to the net price over non-wage variable costs ($w_0/P - r$) increases. Thus, the optimum size for an organization will be relatively small and the optimum shape relatively flat in labor intensive industries.

d) Optimal n increases as the span of control (s) increases. Intuition

[9] If $\beta > s$, then $(\log s/\log \beta) < 1$ and $\alpha_1 = -(\log s/\log \beta) + 1 > 0$. But as the results in Table 6.2 show, α_1 is clearly negative, which requires that $s > \beta$, as assumed.

[10] The condition that the firm earn positive profits implies that

$$(P - r)(\bar{\alpha} s)^{n-1} - \frac{s^n}{s - \beta} w_0 > 0,$$

or

$$\frac{w_0}{P - r} \cdot \frac{s}{s - \beta} \cdot \frac{1}{\bar{\alpha}^{(n-1)}} < 1.$$

This requires that

$$\left[ln\ \frac{w_0}{P-r} + ln\ \frac{s}{s-\beta} + ln\ \frac{1}{\bar{\alpha}^{(n-1)}}\right] < 0.$$

Since $ln\ [1/\bar{\alpha}^{(n-1)}]$ is approximately of the same magnitude as $ln\ [ln\ s/ln(\bar{\alpha} s)]$, or if anything is likely to exceed it, the condition that the firm earn positive profits is tantamount to requiring the bracketed term in equation (2) to be negative.

would have led us to expect that flatter organizations (fewer hierarchical levels) would be associated with wider spans of control, but obviously this is not the case.[11]

e) Optimal n decreases as the wage multiple between levels (β) increases.

Plausible values for $\bar{\alpha}$ can be obtained by substituting estimated values for each of the parameters into equation (6.2). This is done below. In addition, propositions (c), (d), and (e) can be tested empirically by observing that total employment is given by

$$N^* = \Sigma_{i=1}^{n^*} N_i = \Sigma_{i=1}^{n^*} s^{i-1}. \tag{6.3}$$

The sum of this series is given by

$$N^* = \frac{s^{n^*} - 1}{s - 1} \simeq \frac{s^{n^*}}{s - 1}. \tag{6.4}$$

Taking the natural logarithm and substituting the value of optimal n^* given by equation (6.2), we have:

$$ln\, N^* \simeq ln\left(\frac{1}{s-1}\right) + ln\, s \left\{1 + \frac{1}{ln\, \bar{\alpha}}\left[ln\, \frac{w_0}{P-r} + ln\, \frac{s}{s-\beta} + ln\left(\frac{ln\, s}{ln\,(\bar{\alpha}\, s)}\right)\right]\right\}. \tag{6.5}$$

Expressing the optimal size firm in this way avoids the necessity of collecting data by hierarchical levels.

Employment among the five hundred largest industrials in the United States runs generally between one thousand and one hundred thousand employees. For values of s between 5 and 10, which is the normal range (Koontz and O'Donnell, 1955, p. 88), this implies an optimal n of between 4 and 7. If all of our assumptions were satisfied, if there were no additional factors (risk, growth, and so on) acting as limitations to firm size, and for values of β in the range 1.3 to 1.6 and $w_0/P - r$ in the range ⅓ to ⅔, the implied value of $\bar{\alpha}$ is in the neighborhood of 0.90. Since other factors are likely to act as limitations to some extent, the true value of $\bar{\alpha}$ may generally be higher than this. It is our contention, however, for the reasons given above, that values of $\bar{\alpha}$ less than unity are typical and that the cumulative effects of control loss are fundamentally responsible for limitations to firm size.

EXTENSIONS

Although the basic model developed in the preceding section makes evident the critical importance of control loss as a static limitation to firm size in a way which is more precise than was heretofore available and thus both clarifies the issues and expresses them in a potentially testable form, it is obviously a highly special model and may be properly regarded with scepticism for that reason. We

[11] This result should be interpreted with some care. It assumes that $\bar{\alpha}$ is unaffected by increasing the span of control. Within any given firm, this is possible only if the increase in the span of control results from a management or technical innovation. Otherwise, increasing the span of control would lead to an increase in control loss. With this caveat in mind, the result indicated in the text is less counterintuitive. See "Compliance and Span of Control Interaction" in the next section.

attempt in this section to generalize the analysis in such a way as to make clear its wider applicability. First, the possibility of introducing economies of scale, either through the specialization of labor or in the non-labor inputs, to offset diseconomies due to control loss is examined. Second, we develop the properties of a model in which the utility function of the firm includes both profits and hierarchical expense. Next, imperfections in the product market are permitted. Fourth, we allow for the possibility of variations in the span of control at the production level. Finally, the compliance parameter ($\bar{\alpha}$) is expressed as a function of the span of control.

Economies of Scale

We assume above that economies of scale due to specialization of labor or in the non-labor inputs have been exhausted so that diseconomies of scale due to control loss give rise to increasing average cost conditions in the range of output under consideration. These assumptions can be made more precise here. For this purpose, we express the parameter θ which converts input to output as a function of n. Over the range where economies of specialization exist $\partial \theta / \partial n > 0$, whereas when these have been exhausted $\partial \theta / \partial n = 0$. Thus, average cost can be expressed as:

$$AC = w_0 \frac{s}{s - \beta} \cdot \frac{1}{\theta \bar{\alpha}^{n-1}} - r \tag{6.6}$$

and AC will decrease so long as $\partial \theta / \partial n > \theta \ln \bar{\alpha}$. When these two are in balance, constant returns to the labor input will prevail, but as $\partial \theta / \partial n$ declines (and eventually goes to zero), diminishing returns due to control loss will set in.

In a similar way, the non-wage variable cost per unit output parameter, r, can be expressed as a function of output, where $\partial r / \partial Q < 0$ initially, but eventually $\partial r / \partial Q = 0$. Thus, average costs will at first decline for this reason as well, but the cumulative effects of control loss will ultimately dominate and the average cost curve will rise. Implicitly, the model in the second section assumes that both $\partial \theta / \partial n$ and $\partial r / \partial Q$ are zero, so that economies with respect to both labor and non-labor inputs are assumed to be exhausted in the relevant range. Actually, this is somewhat stronger than is necessary for control loss to impose a limitation to firm size; this result would obtain under the assumptions that $\partial^2 \theta / \partial n^2 < 0$ and $\partial^2 r / \partial Q^2 > 0$. This latter, however, would lead only to changes in degree and not in kind from those derived above.

A Utility-Maximizing Version

As we have argued elsewhere, a shift from a profit-maximizing to a utility-maximizing assumption seems appropriate where large firm size is involved, since the characteristics of the opportunity set that the management has access to progressively favor non-profit objectives as size increases. In addition, the bureaucratic operations of a large firm may be less attractive to strictly profit-oriented managers than to managers who have broader objectives. Alternatively, if profit-directed managers are typically less adept politicians, they may simply be outmaneuvered and displaced in circumstances which encourage or permit the pursuit of non-profit goals. In any case, only modest changes in the above model are necessary to transform it to a utility-maximizing form of the sort that we have investigated previously (Williamson, 1964). For this purpose, we assume that the management has a utility function that includes both staff (or hierarchical expense) and profits as principal components. Designating staff expense as H and treating this as all wage expense above the operating level, we have

$$H = \sum_{i=1}^{n-1} w_0 \beta^{n-1} s^{i-1} \simeq w_0 \frac{\beta \, s^{n-1}}{s - \beta}. \tag{6.7}$$

We represent the utility function by U and, given our assumption that staff and profits are the principal components, the objective becomes: maximize

$$U = U(H, R - C) = U\left[w_0 \frac{\beta \, s^{n-1}}{s - \beta}, P(\bar{\alpha} s)^{n-1} - w_0 \frac{s^n}{s - \beta} - r(\bar{\alpha} s)^{n-1}\right]. \tag{6.8}$$

Treating n as the only decision variable and all other variables in this expression as parameters, optimal n is now given by:

$$n^* = 1 + \frac{1}{\ln \bar{\alpha}} \left[\ln \frac{w_0}{P - r} + \ln \frac{s - (U_1/U_2)\beta}{s - \beta} + \ln\left(\frac{\ln s}{\ln \bar{\alpha} s}\right)\right]. \tag{6.9}$$

Comparing this expression with that obtained in equation (6.2), we observe that the only difference is the presence of a $(U_1/U_2)\beta$ term in the brackets of equation (6.9), where U_1 is the first partial of the utility function with respect to staff, and U_2 is the first partial with respect to profits. Obviously, if staff is valued objectively only for the contribution that it makes to profits, U_1 is zero and (6.9) becomes identical with (6.2). If, however, the management displays a positive preference for hierarchical expense so that the ratio U_1/U_2 is not zero, the optimal value of n^* in the utility-maximizing organization will be larger than in the corresponding profit-maximizing organization with identical parameters.[12]

The response of n^* to an increase in each of the parameters is identical with that given previously with the exception of β. Whether n^* will increase or decrease in response to an increase in β depends on whether U_1/U_2 is greater than or less than unity respectively.

Imperfection in the Product Market

If product price is not treated as a parameter but instead $P = P(Q)$, $\partial P/\partial Q < 0$, we obtain the following expression for optimal n:

$$n^* = 1 + \frac{1}{\ln \bar{\alpha}} \left\{\ln \frac{w_0}{P\left(1 - \frac{1}{\eta}\right) - r} + \ln \frac{s}{s - \beta} + \ln \frac{\ln s}{\ln (\bar{\alpha} s)}\right\}, \tag{6.10}$$

where η is the elasticity of demand.

Obviously, in a perfect product market, where $\eta = \infty$, (6.10) is identical with (6.2). As is to be expected, the value of optimal n decreases as demand becomes more inelastic.

Variation in the Span of Control Over Operators

It is assumed in the model developed in the second section that the span of control is uniform throughout the organization. Although variations in the span

---

[12] As we argue below, it seems plausible to suppose that $\bar{\alpha}$ will be larger in utility-maximizing organizations in which the goal of the firm represents a consensus among those managers whose preferences count.

of control among the administrative levels of the organization are generally small, this is frequently untrue between the foremen and operatives. Typically, the span of control is larger here and the reasons are quite obvious: Tasks tend to be more highly routinized, and thus the need for supervision and coordination are correspondingly attenuated. Letting σ be the span of control between foremen and operatives, total employment of operatives is now given by the product of σ and the number of foremen, where this latter is s^{n-2}. Productive output is thus the product of control loss, $(\bar{\alpha})^{n-1}$, times σs^{n-2}, or $\bar{\alpha}\sigma(\bar{\alpha}s)^{n-2}$. The value of optimal n derived from this version of the model is:

$$n^* = 1 + \frac{1}{\ln \bar{\alpha}} \left\{ \ln \frac{w_0}{P-r} + \ln \left(\frac{\sigma + \beta s/s - \beta}{\sigma} \right) + \ln \left[\frac{\ln s}{\ln (\bar{\alpha} s)} \right] \right\}. \quad (6.11)$$

Again, it is obvious by comparing this expression with equation (6.2) that when $\sigma = s$ they are identical and that qualitatively the properties are the same. The additional implication that obtains from this model is that as σ increases, optimal n increases. That is, for $\bar{\alpha}$ unchanged, increasing the span of control between the foremen and operatives leads to a general increase in the number of levels and, consequently, number of employees in the hierarchical organization, a result which is completely in accord with our intuition.

Compliance and Span of Control Interaction

The difficulties associated with the selection of an optimum span of control have been noted by Simon as follows:

> The dilemma is this: in a large organization with interrelations between members, a restricted span of control produces excessive red tape. . . . The alternative is to increase the number of persons who are under the command of an officer. . . . But this, too, leads to difficulty, for if an officer is required to supervise too many employees, his control over them is weakened.
>
> Granted, then, that both the increase and the decrease in span of control have some undesirable consequences, what is the optimum point [Simon, 1957a, p. 28]?

More precisely, the dilemma can be stated in terms of compliance ($\bar{\alpha}$) and span of control (s) interaction. Whereas the preceding analysis treats the level of compliance ($\bar{\alpha}$) and the span of control (s) independently, in fact they are intimately related. Increasing the span of control means that while each supervisor has more productive capability responsive to him he has less time to devote to the supervision of each, and hence a loss of control results. For purposes of examining this behavior, we let

$$\bar{\alpha} = f(s), \qquad \partial f/\partial s < 0. \qquad (6.12)$$

Given that $\bar{\alpha}$ is a declining function of s as indicated, the question next arises: What is the optimum value of s and how is this related to size of firm? Now output is given by $Q = (\bar{\alpha}s)^{n-1}$, so that for any particular level of output, say $\bar{Q}$, choice of n implies a value for s (and, hence, through [12], α) and conversely.[13]

[13] Actually, two values of s and $\bar{\alpha}$ are consistent with each feasible choice of n: a high $\bar{\alpha}$, low s pair and a low $\bar{\alpha}$, high s pair. Of these two, the high $\bar{\alpha}$, low s position

To determine the relation between optimum s and $\overline{Q}$, we observe that since gross revenue is fixed given the level of output, the optimization problem can be expressed as one of minimizing labor costs subject to constraint. Thus, the objective is:

Minimize $\qquad C_L = w_0 \dfrac{s^n}{s - \beta}$

subject to $\qquad (i) \quad (\overline{\alpha}s)^{n-1} = \overline{Q}$ $\qquad\qquad\qquad$ (6.13)
$\qquad\qquad\quad (ii) \quad \overline{\alpha} = f(s).$

The standard technique for studying the behavior of this system is to formulate it as a Lagrangian and perturbate the first order conditions with respect to $\overline{Q}$.

Table 6.1

COMPARATIVE STATICS RESPONSES

DECISION VARIABLE	SHIFT PARAMETER	
	OUTPUT ($d\overline{Q}$)	GOAL INCONSISTENCY (dk)
Hierarchical level (dn)	+	+
Span of control (ds)	−	−
Control effectiveness ($d\overline{\alpha}$)	+	?

Unfortunately, the resulting expressions cannot be signed on the basis of the general functional relation $\overline{\alpha} = f(s)$. Assuming, however, that the function is bell-shaped on the right (which intuitively is the correct general configuration), we can replace (6.12) and, hence, the second constraint, by

$$\overline{\alpha} = e^{-ks^2}. \qquad (6.12')$$

The value of the exponent k in this expression can be interpreted as a goal-consistency parameter. As goal consistency increases, the value of k decreases and $\overline{\alpha}$ increases at every value of s.

The comparative statics responses of n and s (and hence $\overline{\alpha}$) to changes in firm size (as measured by output) and goal inconsistency (k) are shown in Table 6.1. The direction of adjustment of any particular decision variable to a displacement from equilibrium by an increase in either of those parameters is found by referring to the row and column entry corresponding to the decision variable-parameter pair.[14]

is always preferred since, with output fixed, gross revenues are unaffected by choice of s (and the associated value of $\overline{\alpha}$), while increasing s for a given n leads to higher employment and hence costs increase. More precisely, costs vary roughly in proportion to s^{n-1}, and the lower the value of s the lower the associated labor costs.

[14] The responses to changes in k are unambiguous. Those for changes in $\overline{Q}$ hold over all relevant values of $\overline{\alpha}$ ($\geq .7$) and s (≥ 2).

That the number of hierarchical levels should increase as output increases is not surprising. That the span of control should decrease, however, is less obvious. Moreover, it contradicts what little data there are on this question. Thus, Starbuck (1964, p. 375) concludes his systematic survey of the relevant literature bearing on this issue with the observation that the "administrative span of control . . . probably increases with organizational size." Unless our model can be somehow extended to explain this condition, it calls seriously into question the validity of the control-loss approach to organizational behavior. Thus, one of the merits of formalizing this argument as we have is that we can go beyond mere plausibility arguments to discover the less obvious properties of the model and address the relevant evidence to them. Appendix II concerns itself with this dilemma.

That an increase in k (goal inconsistency) leads to a decrease in the span of control and hence increase in n for a fixed size organization is entirely in accord with our intuition. Indeed, given that control loss is cumulative across hierarchical levels, we would expect that consistency is relatively high (k is low) and thus the span of control large in large organizations. That organizations such as the Catholic Church successfully operate with relatively flat hierarchical structures is surely partly attributable to the high degree of goal consistency that the organization possesses. Selection and training procedures obviously contribute to this result.

High goal consistency is probably also more likely in business firms that are operated as utility-maximizing rather than profit-maximizing concerns, where the utility function of the former results from the goal consensus among the management, whereas the latter represents a constraint that is rarely identical with underlying managerial objectives (Williamson, 1964, pp. 32–37, 153–60). It does not follow, therefore, that requiring strict adherence to a profit goal necessarily leads to maximum profits. Contentious discord can be expected to develop in such circumstances which implies high k and may yield low profits. We thus have the paradox that (within limits) the permissive pursuit of nonprofit goals may actually lead to the realization of higher profits.

CONCLUSIONS

The proposition that the management factor is responsible for a limitation to firm size has appeared recurrently in the literature. But the arguments have tended to be imprecise, lacked predictive content, and consequently failed to be convincing. The present paper attempts to overcome some of these shortcomings by developing a formal model in which the control-loss phenomenon is made central to the analysis. The importance of control loss to an understanding of bureaucratic behavior in non-market organizations has been noted previously. Our use of this proposition here is based on one of the fundamental tenets of organization theory: namely, virtually all of the interesting bureaucratic behavior observed to exist in large government bureaucracies finds its counterpart in large nongovernment bureaucracies as well, and this is particularly true where the phenomenon in question is a result of the bounded rationality attributes of decision-makers. We, therefore, borrow from the bureaucracy literature the proposition that control loss occurs between successive hierarchical levels (and that this tends to be cumulative) and introduce it into a theory of the firm in which neither declining product-demand curves nor rising factor-supply curves are permitted to impose a static limit on firm size.

For any given span of control (together with a specification of the state of technology, internal experience, etc.) an irreducible minimum degree of control loss results from the simple serial reproduction distortion that occurs in communicating across successive hierarchical levels. If, in addition, goals differ between hierarchical levels, the loss in control can be more extensive.

The strategy of borrowing behavioral assumptions from the organization-theory literature and developing the implications of the behavior observed within the framework of economic analysis would seem to be one which might find application quite generally. Thus, the organization-theory approach to problems tends frequently to be rich in behavioral insights but weak analytically, while economics generally and the theory of the firm literature in particular has a highly developed modeling apparatus but has evidenced less resourcefulness in its use of interesting behavioral assumptions. Combining these two research areas so as to secure access to the strengths of each would thus appear to be quite promising. In any case, it is the strategy followed in this paper and, to the extent we have had any success, suggests itself for possible use elsewhere.

Appendix I to Reading 6

TEST OF THE WAGE MODEL

Our basic wage hypothesis is that $w_i = W_0 \beta^{n-i}$, where w_0 is the base level salary, n is the number of hierarchical levels, i is the particular level in question, and β is the wage multiple. Unfortunately, the General Motors data are reported by wage ranges of unequal size rather than by hierarchical levels. It can nevertheless be used to test our hypothesis by developing the cumulative distribution counterpart of our model.

Taking logarithms of this wage relation, we have $\log w_i = \log w_0 + (n-i) \log \beta$. By assumption (6.5), the total number of employees at level i is $N_i = s^{i-1}$, where s is the span of control. Taking this logarithm, we obtain $\log N_i = (i-1) \log s$. Solving for i in this second logarithmic expression and substituting into the first we obtain:[15]

$$\log N_i = \log b_0 - \left(\frac{\log s}{\log \beta}\right) \log w_i, \tag{6.14}$$

or

$$N_i = b_0 w_i^{-b_1}$$

[15] The derivation of equation (6.14) is similar to Simon (1957b). Simon does not, however, go on to derive the cumulative relationship given by equation (6.15), which is ordinarily the only testable version of the model. A similar derivation to ours can, however, be found in Davis (1941, chap. ix).

where
$$\log b_0 = (\log s/\log \beta) \cdot [\log w_0 + (n-1) \log \beta]$$
and
$$b_1 = (\log s/\log \beta).$$

We denote by $N(\bar{w})$ the total number of individuals having a wage greater than $\bar{w}$. This is given by

$$N(\bar{w}) = \int_{\bar{w}}^{\infty} b_0 w^{-b_1} \, dw = \left(\frac{b_0}{b_1}\right) \bar{w}^{(-b_1+1)} \quad (6.15)$$

or
$$N(\bar{w}) = \alpha_0 \bar{w}^{-\alpha_1}$$

where
$$\alpha_0 = b_0/b_1$$

and
$$\alpha_1 = -b_1 + 1.$$

This cumulative form does not require either information about the hierarchical levels or uniform size classes and, hence, can be applied to the General Motors (or any similar class of) wage data. Being derived from our wage-employment hypotheses, it should produce a good fit to the data if these hypotheses are substantially close approximations. The results are reported in Table 6.2.

Table 6.2

WAGE MODEL FIT TO GENERAL MOTORS SALARY DATA, 1934–42*

	1934	1936	1938	1940	1942
No. Observations	10	11	6	6	6
$\bar{R}^2$	.940	.970	.956	.907	.944
Log $\hat{\alpha}_0$	10.022	10.828	10.688	11.859	10.822
	(0.733)	(0.523)	(0.882)	(1.400)	(1.077)
$\hat{\alpha}_1$	−1.904	−2.067	−2.037	−2.297	−2.045
	(0.160)	(0.116)	(0.193)	(0.306)	(0.236)

* Standard errors are shown in parentheses.

As is quickly apparent from inspecting the Table 6.2 results, the wage model given by (6.15) provides an excellent fit to the data. The coefficients of determination adjusted for degrees of freedom all exceed .90, and the estimates of the coefficients are both stable over the entire interval and significantly different from zero in every year. Assuming that General Motors salary schedules are not atypical (and since General Motors is frequently regarded as a model of better management practices we might expect imitation from other firms in this respect), we have some confidence that the assumptions underlying our wage model are correct at least for the class of large corporations that we are principally concerned with.

Appendix II to Reading 6

A DIGRESSION OF DYNAMICS

The analysis in the text has at least two disturbing implications. First, not only does control loss impose a limit to firm size, but once this limit is reached the firm will stabilize at this level. Since continuing expansion of large firms is common, the model appears to be at variance with reality in this aspect. Second, the model predicts that the span of control decreases with firm size, while the evidence points to the contrary. Either the control-loss argument must be fundamentally incorrect, or the model must be amended in one or more respects.

We propose an extension, one that mainly involves allowance for dynamic conditions ignored in our static analysis. At least three factors are operative. First, increases in experience lead to refinements, shortcuts, and routinization, all of which permit increasing the span of control for a fixed level of control loss. And experience is obviously positively related to firm size. Second, although most of the economies of scale resulting from specialization and indivisibilities are ordinarily exhausted at a relatively modest firm size (Bain, 1956, chap. iii), the economies that result from a large data-processing capability may well extend considerably beyond this size. Since for a given level of control loss increases in information-processing capability permit the span of control to be expanded, the association of an increasing span of control and large firm size may be due in part to this information processing and firm size relation. Third, the rate of change of firm size may have an important influence. Penrose (1959, pp. 44–48) has argued persuasively that the dynamics of growth require additional hierarchical personnel than are needed when the expansion is completed. Presumably this is because problems of coordination and control are more serious during periods of expansion. Expressing this argument in span of control terms, an inverse relation is to be expected between span of control and the growth rate. The remaining question then is what, if any, association between growth rate and size is to be expected. The data here are scant, but the results from the stochastic, serial correlation, growth models of Ijiri and Simon (1964, pp. 86–87) are at least suggestive, namely, that "firms which grow large experience most of their growth [early in their history] . . . , then reach a plateau." Assuming that this is generally valid, growth rates will tend to be inversely related to firm size. Thus here again we have a dynamic, size-related condition that helps to explain the apparent contradiction between the data relating span of control to firm size and our static analysis.

Taking these dynamic or age-related characteristics into account suggests that, given the value of $\bar{\alpha}$, the optimum span of control be expressed as:

$$s = \varphi(Q, k, t, d, dQ/dt, \ldots) \tag{6.16}$$

where

$Q =$ output: $\varphi_Q < 0$
$k =$ goal inconsistency parameter; $\varphi_k < 0$
$t =$ chronological age (a proxy for experience); $\varphi_t > 0$
$d =$ data processing capability; $\varphi_t > 0$
$dQ/dt =$ rate of change of output; $\varphi(dQ/dt) < 0$.

Among the advantages of this formulation is that it permits us to accommodate parts of Mrs. Penrose's theory as a part of our own. Thus, if increases in dQ/dt reduce the span of control, additional hierarchical levels will be required to sustain the level of output. But for fixed $\bar{\alpha}$, cumulative control loss which is given by $(1 - \bar{\alpha}^n)$ now increases. Hence, costs increase as dQ/dt increases, and the optimum growth rate is therefore restricted. Although Mrs. Penrose's emphasis is on internal experience and no attention is given to notions such as the span of control, the existence of control loss is implicit in her discussion and our model helps make this clear. Similarly, she observes that "as plans are completed and put into operation, managerial services absorbed in the planning processes will be gradually released" (Penrose, 1959, p. 49). Plan realization here implies that dQ/dt decreases, hence the span of control increases and the release of managerial services follows necessarily.

The above formulation also points up the very real dangers of performing simple correlations between s and Q. For the reasons given above, Q is positively related to t and d and negatively related to dQ/dt. Inasmuch as φ_t and φ_d are positive while $\varphi dQ/dt$ is negative, the combined effect of these three factors could easily swamp the true effect of Q on s (as predicted by our static model) if simple bivariate analysis were attempted.

REFERENCES

1. Andrews, P. W. S. *Manufacturing Business.* New York: Macmillan Co., 1949.
2. Bain, J. S. *Barriers to New Competition.* Cambridge, Mass.: Harvard Univ. Press, 1956.
3. Bartlett, F. C. *Remembering.* New York: Cambridge Univ. Press, 1932.
4. Chamberlin, E. H. "Proportionality, Divisibility and Economies of Scale," *Q.J.E.,* LXII (February, 1948), 229–62.
5. Coase, R. H. "The Nature of the Firm," *Economica,* N.S., IV (1937), 386–405. Reprinted in George J. Stigler and Kenneth E. Boulding (eds.). *Readings in Price Theory.* Homewood, Ill.: Richard D. Irwin, Inc., 1952.
6. Davis, H. T. *The Analysis of Economic Time Series.* Granville, Ohio: Principia Press, 1941.
7. Downs, Anthony. *Bureaucratic Structure and Decisionmaking* (RM-4646-PR). Santa Monica, Calif.: RAND, March, 1966.
8. Ijiri, Yuji, and Simon, H. A. "Business Firm Growth and Size," *A.E.R.,* LIV (March, 1964), 77–89.
9. Kaldor, Nicholas. "The Equilibrium of the Firm," *Econ. J.,* XLIV (March, 1934), 70–71.
10. Knight, F. H., *Risk, Uncertainty and Profit.* New York: Harper & Row, 1965.
11. Koontz, H., and O'Donnell, C. *Principles of Management.* New York: McGraw-Hill Book Co., 1955.
12. March, J. G., and Simon, H. A. *Organizations.* New York: John Wiley & Sons, Inc., 1958.
13. Mayer, Thomas. "The Distribution of Ability and Earnings," *Rev. Econ. and Statis.,* XLII (May, 1960), 189–98.
14. Monsen, R. J., Jr., and Downs, Anthony. "A Theory of Large Managerial Firms," *J.P.E.,* LXXIII (June, 1965), 221–36.
15. Papandreou, A. G. "Some Basic Issues in the Theory of the Firm," in B. F. Haley (ed.). *A Survey of Contemporary Economics.* Homewood, Ill.: Richard D. Irwin, Inc., 1952.
16. Penrose, Edith. *The Theory of the Growth of the Firm.* New York: John Wiley & Sons, Inc., 1959.
17. Robinson, E. A. G. "The Problem of Management and the Size of Firms," *Econ. J.,* XLIV (June, 1934), 240–54.
18. *The Structure of Competitive Industry.* Chicago: Univ. of Chicago Press, 1962.
19. Ross, N. S. "Management and the Size of the Firm," *Rev. Econ. Studies,* XIX (1952–53), 148–54.
20. Simon, H. A. *Administrative Behavior.* 2d ed. New York: Macmillan Co., 1957 (*a*).
21. "The Compensation of Executives," *Sociometry* (March, 1957), 32–35 (*b*).
22. Starbuck, W. H. "Organizational Growth and Development," in J. G. March (ed.). *Handbook of Organizations.* Chicago: Rand McNally & Co., 1964.
23. Tullock, Gordon. *The Politics of Bureaucracy.* Washington: Public Affairs Press, 1965.

24. U.S. Department of Labor. *Salary Structure Characteristics in Large Firms* (1963). (Bull. No. 1417.) Washington, August, 1964.
25. Williamson, John. "Profit, Growth and Sales Maximization," *Economica,* XXXIII (February, 1966), 1–16.
26. Williamson, O. E. *The Economics of Discretionary Behavior: Managerial Objectives in a Theory of the Firm.* Englewood Cliffs, N.J.: Prentice-Hall, Inc., 1964.

7
The Economies of Scale*

George J. Stigler

The theory of the economies of scale is the theory of the relationship between the scale of use of a properly chosen combination of all productive services and the rate of output of the enterprise. In its broadest formulation this theory is a crucial element of the economic theory of social organization, for it underlies every question of market organization and the role (and locus) of governmental control over economic life. Let one ask himself how an economy would be organized if every economic activity were prohibitively inefficient upon alternately a small scale and a large scale, and the answer will convince him that here lies a basic element of the theory of economic organization.

The theory has limped along for a century, collecting large pieces of good reasoning and small chunks of empirical evidence but never achieving scientific prosperity. A large cause of its poverty is that the central concept of the theory —the firm of optimum size—has eluded confident measurement. We have been dangerously close to denying Lincoln, for all economists have been ignorant of the optimum size of firm in almost every industry all of the time, and this ignorance has been an insurmountable barrier between us and the understanding of the forces which govern optimum size. It is almost as if one were trying to measure the nutritive values of goods without knowing whether the consumers who ate them continued to live.

The central thesis of this paper is that the determination of the optimum size

Reprinted from *The Journal of Law and Economics*, vol. 1, 1958, pp. 54-71 by permission of the author and publisher.

* This paper was prepared at the National Bureau of Economic Research. I must thank Nester Terleckyj for performing most of the statistical work.

is not difficult if one formalizes the logic that sensible men have always employed to judge efficient size. This technique, which I am old-fashioned enough to call the survivor technique, reveals the optimum size in terms of private costs—that is, in terms of the environment in which the enterprise finds itself. After discussing the technique, we turn to the question of how the forces governing optimum size may be isolated.

THE SURVIVOR PRINCIPLE

The optimum size (or range of sizes) of enterprises in an industry is now ascertained empirically by one of three methods. The first is that of direct comparison of actual costs of firms of different sizes; the second is the comparison of rates of return on investment; and the third is the calculation of probable costs of enterprises of different sizes in the light of technological information. All three methods are practically objectionable in demanding data which are usually unobtainable and seldom up-to-date. But this cannot be the root of their difficulties, for there is up-to-date information on many economic concepts which are complex and even basically incapable of precise measurement (such as income). The plain fact is that we have not demanded the data because we have been unable to specify what we wanted.

The comparisons of both actual costs and rates of return are strongly influenced by the valuations which are put on productive services, so that an enterprise which over- or undervalues important productive services, will under- or overstate its efficiency. Historical cost valuations of resources, which are most commonly available, are in principle irrelevant under changed conditions. Valuations based upon expected earnings yield no information on the efficiency of an enterprise—in the limiting case where all resources are so valued, all firms would be of equal efficiency judged by either average costs or rates of return. The ascertainment on any scale of the maximum value of each resource in alternative uses is a task which only the unsophisticated would assume and only the omniscient would discharge. The host of valuation problems are accentuated by the variable role of the capital markets in effecting revaluations and the variable attitudes of the accountants toward the revaluations.[1]

The technological studies of costs of different sizes of plant encounter equally formidable obstacles. These studies are compounded of some fairly precise (although not necessarily very relevant) technical information and some crude guesses on nontechnological aspects such as marketing costs, transportation rate changes, labor relations, etc.—that is, much of the problem is solved only in the unhappy sense of being delegated to a technologist. Even ideal results, moreover, do not tell us the optimum size of firm in industry A in 1958, but rather the optimum size of new plants in the industry, on the assumption that the industry starts *de novo* or that only a small increment of investment is being made.

The survivor technique avoids both the problems of valuation of resources and the hypothetical nature of the technological studies. Its fundamental postulate is that the competition of different sizes of firms sifts out the more efficient enterprises. In the words of Mill, who long ago proposed the technique:

[1] These problems are discussed by Milton Friedman in *Business Concentration and Price Policy*, pp. 230 ff. (1955).

Whether or not the advantages obtained by operating on a large-scale preponderate in any particular case over the more watchful attention, and greater regard to minor gains and losses usually found in small establishments, can be ascertained, in a state of free competition, by an unfailing test. . . . Wherever there are large and small establishments in the same business, that one of the two which in existing circumstances carries on the production at the greater advantage will be able to undersell the other.[2]

Mill was wrong only in suggesting that the technique was inapplicable under oligopoly, for even under oligopoly the drive of maximum profits will lead to the disappearance of relatively inefficient sizes of firms.

The survivor technique proceeds to solve the problem of determining the optimum firm size as follows: Classify the firms in an industry by size, and calculate the share of industry output coming from each class over time. If the share of a given class falls, it is relatively inefficient, and in general is more inefficient the more rapidly the share falls.

An efficient size of firm, on this argument, is one that meets any and all problems the entrepreneur actually faces: strained labor relations, rapid innovation, government regulation, unstable foreign markets, and what not. This is, of course, the decisive meaning of efficiency from the viewpoint of the enterprise. Of course, social efficiency may be a very different thing: the most efficient firm size may arise from possession of monopoly power, undesirable labor practices, discriminatory legislation, etc. The survivor technique is not directly applicable to the determination of the socially optimum size of enterprise, and we do not enter into this question. The socially optimum firm is fundamentally an ethical concept, and we question neither its importance nor its elusiveness.

Not only is the survivor technique more direct and simpler than the alternative techniques for the determination of the optimum size of firm, it is also more authoritative. Suppose that the cost, rate of return, and technological studies all find that in a given industry the optimum size of firm is one which produces 500 to 600 units per day, and that costs per unit are much higher if one goes far outside this range. Suppose also that most of the firms in the industry are three times as large, and that those firms which are in the 500 to 600 unit class are rapidly failing or growing to a larger size. Would we believe that the optimum size was 500 to 600 units? Clearly not: an optimum size that cannot survive in rivalry with other sizes is a contradiction, and some error, we would all say, has been made in the traditional studies. Implicitly all judgments on economies of scale have always been based directly upon, or at least verified by recourse to, the experience of survivorship.

This is not to say that the findings of the survivor technique are unequivocal. Entrepreneurs may make mistakes in their choice of firm size, and we must seek to eliminate the effects of such errors either by invoking large numbers

[2] *Principles of Political Economy*, p. 134 (Ashley ed.). Marshall states the same argument in Darwinian language: "For as a general rule the law of substitution— which is nothing more than a special and limited application of the law of survival of the fittest—tends to make one method of industrial organization supplant another when it offers a direct and immediate service at a lower price." *Principles of Economics*, p. 597 (8th ed., 1920).

of firms so errors tend to cancel or by utilizing time periods such that errors are revealed and corrected. Or the optimum size may be changing because of changes in factor prices or technology, so that perhaps the optimum size rises in one period and falls in another. This problem too calls for a close examination of the time periods which should be employed. We face these problems in our statistical work below.

We must also recognize that a single optimum size of firm will exist in an industry only if all firms have (access to) identical resources. Since various firms employ different kinds or qualities of resources, there will tend to develop a frequency distribution of optimum firm sizes. The survivor technique may allow us to estimate this distribution; in the application below we restrict ourselves to the range of optimum sizes.

The measure of the optimum size is only a first step toward the construction of a theory of economies of scale with substantive content, but it is the indispensable first step. We turn in later sections of this paper to the examination of the methods by which hypotheses concerning the determinants of optimum size may be tested.

ILLUSTRATIVE SURVIVORSHIP MEASURES

The survivor principle is very general in scope and very flexible in application, and these advantages can best be brought out by making concrete applications of the principle to individual industries. These applications will also serve to display a number of problems of data and interpretation which are encountered in the use of the survivor technique. We begin with the American steel industry.

In order that survivorship of firms of a given size be evidence of comparative efficiency, these firms must compete with firms of other sizes—all of the firms must sell in a common market. We have therefore restricted the analysis to firms making steel ingots by open-hearth or Bessemer processes.[3] Size has perforce been measured by capacity, for production is not reported by individual companies, and capacity is expressed as a percentage of the industry total to eliminate the influence of the secular growth of industry and company size.[4] The geographical extent of the market is especially difficult to determine in steel, for the shifting geographical pattern of consumption has created a linkage between the various regional markets. We treat the market as national, which exaggerates its extent, but probably does less violence to the facts than a sharp regional classification of firms. The basic data are given in Table 7.1.

Over two decades covered by Table 7.1 (and, for that matter, over the last half century) there has been a persistent and fairly rapid decline in the share of the industry's capacity in firms with less than half a per cent of the total, so that we may infer that this size of firm is subject to substantial diseconomies

[3] Crucible steel, which is made by smaller companies on average, is viewed as a separate, but closely related, industry.
[4] Capacity is least objectionable as a measure of firm size in an industry where production is continuous round the clock and the upward trend of output confers relevance on capacity. Both steel and our later example of petroleum refining meet these conditions.

of scale.[5] The firms with one-half to two-and-one-half per cent of industry capacity showed a moderate decline, and hence were subject to smaller diseconomies of scale. The one firm with more than one-fourth of industry capacity declined moderately, so it too had diseconomies of scale. The intervening sizes,

Table 7.1

DISTRIBUTION OF OUTPUT OF STEEL INGOT CAPACITY
BY RELATIVE SIZE OF COMPANY

COMPANY SIZE (PER CENT OF INDUSTRY TOTAL)	1930	1938	1951
1. PER CENT OF INDUSTRY CAPACITY			
Under ½	7.16	6.11	4.65
½ to 1	5.94	5.08	5.37
1 to 2½	13.17	8.30	9.07
2½ to 5	10.64	16.59	22.21
5 to 10	11.18	14.03	8.12
10 to 25	13.24	13.99	16.10
25 and over	38.67	35.91	34.50
2. NUMBER OF COMPANIES			
Under ½	39	29	22
½ to 1	9	7	7
1 to 2½	9	6	6
2½ to 5	3	4	5
5 to 10	2	2	1
10 to 25	1	1	1
25 and over	1	1	1

Sources: Directory of Iron and Steel Works of the United States and Canada, 1930, 1938; *Iron Age*, January 3, 1952.

from two-and-one-half to twenty-five per cent of industry capacity, grew or held their share so they constituted the range of optimum size.

The more rapid the rate at which a firm loses its share of the industry's output (or, here, capacity), the higher is its private cost of production relative to the cost of production of firms of the most efficient size.[6] This interpretation should not be reversed, however, to infer that the size class whose share is growing more rapidly is more efficient than other classes whose shares are growing more slowly; the difference can merely represent differences in the quantities of various

[5] In 1930 the firm with one-half per cent of the industry capacity had a capacity of 364,000 net tons; in 1951, 485,000 net tons. Of course, we could have employed absolute firm size classes, but they are less appropriate to many uses.

[6] How shall we assess the efficiency of a size of firm which merely holds its share of industry output or capacity? Although more subtle interpretations are possible, it seems simplest to view this size class as one whose trend of industry share is imperfectly estimated from the data, and that with fuller data (i.e., for more firms or a longer period), all firm sizes would display rising or falling industry shares.

qualities of resources.[7] In the light of these considerations we translate the data of Table 7.1 into a long run average cost curve for the production of steel ingots and display this curve in Figure 7.1. Over a wide range of outputs there is no evidence of net economies or diseconomies of scale.

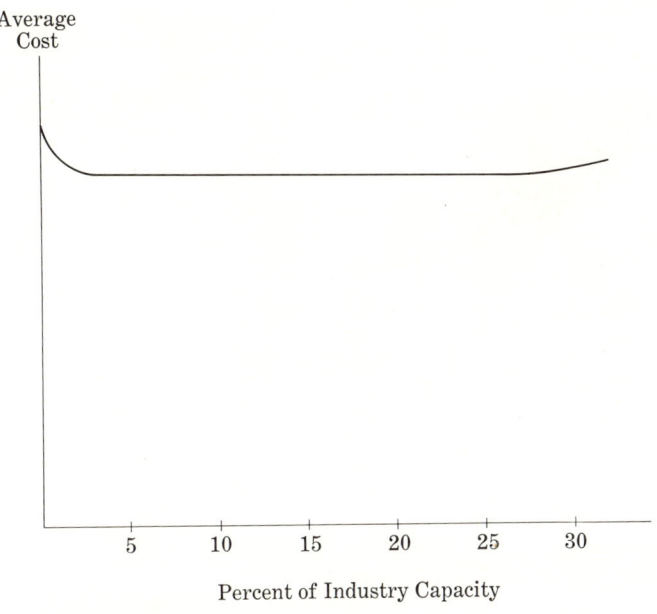

Figure 7.1

Although the survivor test yields an estimate of the shape of the long run cost curve, it does not allow an estimate of how much higher than the minimum are the costs of the firm sizes whose shares of industry output are declining. Costs are higher the more rapid the rate at which the firm size loses its share of industry output, but the rate at which a firm size loses a share of industry output will also vary with numerous other factors. This rate of loss of output will be larger, the less durable and specialized the productive resources of the firm, for then exit from the industry is easier. The rate of loss will also be larger, the more nearly perfect the capital and labor markets, so that resources can be obtained to grow quickly to more efficient size. The rate of loss will be smaller, given the degree of inefficiency, the more profitable the industry is, for then the rate of return of all sizes of firms is larger relative to other industries.

By a simple extension of this argument, we may also estimate the most efficient size of *plant* in the steel ingot industry during the same period (Table 7.2).

[7] For example, one firm size within the optimum range may utilize superior salesmen, another firm size inferior salesmen (at suitably lower rates of pay), and the relative numbers of the two types will influence the relative growth in the industry shares of the two sizes.

Table 7.2

DISTRIBUTION OF OUTPUT OF STEEL INGOT CAPACITY

PLANT SIZE (PER CENT OF INDUSTRY TOTAL)	1930	1938	1951
1. PER CENT OF INDUSTRY CAPACITY			
Under $\frac{1}{4}$	3.74	3.81	3.25
$\frac{1}{4}$ to $\frac{1}{2}$	6.39	5.81	7.20
$\frac{1}{2}$ to $\frac{3}{4}$	6.39	4.18	3.82
$\frac{3}{4}$ to 1	9.42	12.29	10.93
1 to $1\frac{3}{4}$	21.78	15.56	20.67
$1\frac{3}{4}$ to $2\frac{1}{2}$	13.13	16.73	17.01
$2\frac{1}{2}$ to $3\frac{3}{4}$	23.49	17.18	8.10
$3\frac{3}{4}$ to 5	8.82	12.07	12.46
5 to 10	6.82	12.37	16.56
2. NUMBER OF PLANTS			
Under $\frac{1}{4}$	40	29	23
$\frac{1}{4}$ to $\frac{1}{2}$	20	16	18
$\frac{1}{2}$ to $\frac{3}{4}$	11	7	6
$\frac{3}{4}$ to 1	11	14	12
1 to $1\frac{3}{4}$	18	13	15
$1\frac{3}{4}$ to $2\frac{1}{2}$	6	8	8
$2\frac{1}{2}$ to $3\frac{3}{4}$	8	6	3
$3\frac{3}{4}$ to 5	2	3	3
5 to 10	1	2	3

Source: Same as Table 7.1.

We again find that the smallest plants have a tendency to decline relative to the industry, and indeed this is implied by the company data. There is no systematic tendency toward decline in shares held by plants between ¾ per cent and 10 per cent of the industry size. We may therefore infer that the tendency of very small plants and companies to decline relative to the industry is due to the diseconomy of a small plant, and the tendency of the largest company (U.S. Steel) to decline has been due to diseconomies of multi-plant operation beyond a certain scale.

An equally important and interesting industry, passenger automobiles, uncovers different problems. Here we can use production data instead of capacity, and have no compunctions in treating the market as national in scope. The basic data for the individual firms are given in Table 7.3.

A striking feature of the automobile industry is the small number of firms, and this poses a statistical problem we have glossed over in our discussion of steel: what confidence can be attached to changes in the share of industry output coming from a firm size when that size contains very few firms? For the automobile industry (unlike steel) we possess annual data, and can therefore take into account the steadiness of direction or magnitude of changes in shares of

Table 7.3

PERCENTAGES OF PASSENGER AUTOMOBILES PRODUCED IN UNITED STATES BY VARIOUS COMPANIES, 1936–41 AND 1946–55

YEAR	GENERAL MOTORS	CHRYSLER	FORD	HUDSON	NASH	KAISER	WILLYS OVERLAND	PACKARD	STUDE-BAKER	OTHER
1936	42.9	23.6	22.6	3.3	1.5	—	0.7	2.2	2.4	0.8
1937	40.9	24.2	22.6	2.7	2.2	—	2.0	2.8	2.1	0.5
1938	43.9	23.8	22.3	2.5	1.6	—	0.8	2.5	2.3	0.3
1939	43.0	22.7	21.8	2.8	2.3	—	0.9	2.6	3.7	0.3
1940	45.9	25.1	19.0	2.3	1.7	—	0.7	2.1	3.1	0.1
1941	48.3	23.3	18.3	2.1	2.1	—	0.8	1.8	3.2	0.1
1946	38.4	25.0	21.2	4.2	4.6	0.6	0.3	1.9	3.6	0.2
1947	40.4	21.7	21.3	2.8	3.2	4.1	0.9	1.6	3.5	0.5
1948	40.1	21.2	19.1	3.6	3.1	4.6	0.8	2.5	4.2	0.7
1949	43.0	21.9	21.0	2.8	2.8	1.2	0.6	2.0	4.5	0.2
1950	45.7	18.0	23.3	2.1	2.8	2.2	0.6	1.1	4.0	0.1
1951	42.2	23.1	21.8	1.8	3.0	1.9	0.5	1.4	4.2	0.1
1952	41.5	22.0	23.2	1.8	3.5	1.7	1.1	1.4	3.7	—
1953	45.7	20.3	25.2	1.2	2.2	1.0		1.3	3.0	—
1954	52.2	13.1	30.6	1.7		0.3		0.5	1.6	—
1955	50.2	17.2	28.2	2.0		0.1			2.3	—

Source: *Ward's Automotive Yearbook* 1951, 1955, 1956.

various firm sizes, and to this extent increase our confidence in the estimates. We may also extend the period which is surveyed, although at the risk of combining periods with different sizes of optimum firms. Aside from recourse to related data (the survivorship pattern of the industry in other countries, for example), there is no other method of reducing the uncertainty of findings for small number industries.

The survivorship record in automobiles (summarized in Table 7.4) is more complicated than that for steel. In the immediate pre-war years there was already a tendency for the largest company to produce a rising share and for the 2½ to 5 per cent class to produce a sharply declining share; the smallest and next to largest sizes showed no clear tendency. In a longer span of time, however, the smallest companies reveal a fairly consistently declining share.[8] In the immediate postwar period, the 2½ to 5 per cent size class was strongly

Table 7.4

PERCENTAGE OF PASSENGER AUTOMOBILES PRODUCED
BY VARIOUS COMPANY-SIZES

YEAR	COMPANY SIZE (AS PER CENT OF INDUSTRY)				NUMBER OF COMPANIES	
	OVER 35%	10–35%	2½–5%	UNDER 2½%	2½–5%	UNDER 2½%
1936	42.9	46.2	3.3	7.6	1	5*
1937	40.9	46.8	5.5	6.8	2	4*
1938	43.9	46.1	5.0	5.0	2	4*
1939	43.0	44.4	9.1	3.5	3	4*
1940	45.9	44.1	3.1	6.9	1	6*
1941	48.4	41.6	3.2	6.8	1	5
1946	38.4	46.2	12.4	3.0	3	4
1947	40.4	43.0	13.6	3.0	4	3
1948	40.1	40.3	18.0	1.5	5	2
1949	43.0	42.9	10.0	4.0	3	4
1950	45.7	41.3	6.8	6.1	2	5
1951	42.2	44.9	7.2	5.7	2	5
1952	41.5	45.2	7.2	6.1	2	5
1953	45.6	45.5	3.0	5.8	1	4
1954	52.2	43.7	0	4.1	0	4
1955	50.2	45.4	0	4.4	0	3

* Or more.
Source: Table 7.3.

favored by the larger companies' need to practice price control in a sensitive political atmosphere, and the same phenomenon reappeared less strongly in the first two years after the outbreak of Korean hostilities. From this record we would infer that there have been diseconomies of large size, at least for the

[8] See Federal Trade Commission, *Report on Motor Vehicle Industry*, p. 29 (1939).

largest size of firm, in inflationary periods with private or public price control, but substantial economies of large scale at other times. The long run average cost curve is saucer-shaped in inflationary times, but shows no tendency to rise at the largest outputs in other times.

The automobile example suggests the method by which we determine whether changing technology, factor prices, or consumer demands lead to a change in the optimum firm size. We infer an underlying stability in the optimum size in those periods in which the survivorship trends are stable. Indeed it is hard to conceive of an alternative test; one can judge the economic importance, in contrast to technological originality, of an innovation only by the impact it has upon the size distribution of firms.

Before we leave these applications of the survivorship technique we should indicate its flexibility in dealing with other problems which seem inappropriate to our particular examples. For example, a Marshallian may object that firms must begin small and grow to optimum size through time, so that the size structure of the industry in a given period will reflect this historical life pattern as well as the optimum size influences. In an industry such as retail trade this interpretation would be quite plausible. It can be met by studying the survivor experience of firm sizes in the light of the age or rate of growth of the firms. Again, one may argue that firms of different sizes have different comparative advantages at different stages of the business cycle. Such a hypothesis could be dealt with by comparing average survivorship patterns in given cycle stages with those calculated for full cycles.

Let us now turn to the methods by which one may test hypotheses on the determinants of optimum size.

INTER-INDUSTRY ANALYSES OF THE DETERMINANTS OF OPTIMUM SIZE

Once the optimum firm size has been ascertained for a variety of industries, the relationship between size and other variables can be explored. This is in fact the customary procedure for economists to employ, and the present investigation differs, aside from the method of determining optimum size, only in being more systematic than most such investigations. For example, numerous economists have asserted that advertising is a force making for large firms, and they usually illustrate this relationship by the cigarette industry. Will the relationship still hold when it is tested against a list of industries which has not been chosen to illustrate it? This is essentially the type of inquiry we make here.

Although the survivor method makes lesser demands of data than other methods to determine optimum firm size, it has equally exacting requirements of information on any other variable whose influence is to be studied. In the subsequent investigation of some 48 ("three-digit") manufacturing industries, whose optimum firm size is calculated from data in *Statistics of Income*, we have therefore been compelled to exclude some variables for lack of data and to measure others in a most imperfect manner. The industries we study, and the measures we contrive, are given in Table 7.5; we describe their derivation below.

Size of Firm

The optimum size of firm in each industry is determined by comparing the percentage of the industry's assets possessed by firms in each asset class in 1948 and 1951.[9] Those classes in which the share of the industry's assets was stable or rising were identified, and the average assets of the firms within these sizes were calculated.[10] The range of optimum sizes is also given in Table 7.5. An industry was excluded if it had a very large noncorporate sector (for which we could not measure firm size) or gave strong evidence of heterogeneity by having two widely separated optimum sizes (as, for example, in "aircraft and parts").

Advertising Expenditures

We have already remarked that extensive advertising is often mentioned as an explanation for the growth of large firms, especially in consumer goods industries such as cigarettes, liquor, and cosmetics. The argument supporting this view can take one of three directions. First, national advertising may be viewed as more efficient than local advertising, in terms of sales per dollar of advertising at a given price. Second, long continued advertising may have a cumulative impact. Finally, and closely related to the preceding point, the joint advertising of a series of related products may be more efficient than advertising them individually. We measure the variable by the ratio of advertising expenditures to sales, both taken from *Statistics of Income*.

Technology and Research

A host of explanations of firm size are related to technological characteristics and research. Complicated production processes may require large companies, or at least large plants. The economies of research are held to be substantial; the outcome of individual projects is uncertain, so small programs are more risky; a balanced research team may be fairly large; and much capital may be required to bring a new process to a commercial stage and to wait for a return upon the outlay.

At present there is no direct measure available for either the importance of research or the intricacy of technology.[11] We use an index, chemists and engineers as a ratio to all employees, that may reflect both influences, but probably very imperfectly. When it becomes possible to make a division of these personnel between research and routine operation, a division which would be very valuable for other purposes also, the interpretation of an index of technical personnel will be less ambiguous.

---

[9] These particular dates were dictated by the data; there were large changes in industry classification in 1948, and no minor industry data were tabulated for 1952. A better, but more laborious, determination of optimum size could have been made if the data for intervening years were utilized.

[10] A rough allowance for sampling fluctuations was made by comparing three-asset class moving averages.

[11] In earlier experiments with two-digit manufacturing industries, capital-sales ratios were found to be uncorrelated with optimum firm size.

Plant Size

Plant size normally sets a minimum to company size, and therefore exerts an obvious influence on the differences among industries in company size. We are compelled to resort to a measure of plant size—value added per establishment in 1947—which is not directly comparable to company size because the 1947 Census of Manufactures did not report corporate establishments at the requisite level of detail.[12]

Preliminary analysis revealed that there is no significant relationship between firm size and advertising expenditures, so this variable was omitted from the statistical calculations. The average ratio of advertising expenditures to sales was 1.97 per cent in consumer goods industries and 0.57 per cent in producer goods industries, but in neither group was there a significant relationship between the ratio and firm size.[13]

A regression analysis confirms the impression one gets from Table 7.5 that the other variables we examine are positively related to optimum firm size:

$$X_1 = -5.092 + 34.6 X_2 + 42.7 X_3,$$
$$(10.8) \quad (12.2)$$

where X_1 is firm size, in millions of dollars of assets,
X_2 is plant size, in millions of dollars of value added,
X_3 is engineers and chemists per 100 employees.

The standard errors of the regression coefficients are given below the coefficients.[14]

An examination of Table 7.5 suggests that the correlation would be higher if the data were somewhat more precise. The size of plant is unduly low in motor vehicles, because of the inclusion of suppliers of parts. Moreover the plant sizes have not been estimated by the survivor technique. Technological personnel are exaggerated in nonferrous foundries because we are compelled to use the ratio for a broader class, and the same is true of concrete products. The relatively small size of company in footwear, as compared to plant size, is at least partially due to the fact that the machinery was usually leased, and hence not included in assets. Industries which are "out of line" have not been omitted, however, for similar considerations may have caused other industries to be "in line." Yet the general impression is that the correlation would rise substantially with improved measurements of the variables.

The range of optimum sizes is generally wide, although the width is exaggerated, and our measurements impaired, because the largest asset class (over $100 million) embraces numerous firms of very different sizes—growth and inflation are outmoding the size classes used in *Statistics of Income*. In ten industries

---

[12] But even if plants were measured by assets there would be some incomparability arising out of the fact that many large firms operate in many industries but are classified according to their dominant activity.

[13] The respective rank correlation coefficients were $-.187$ and $-.059$.

[14] The correlation coefficients are:

$r_{12} = .460$ $\quad r_{12.3} = .400$
$r_{13} = .471$ $\quad r_{13.2} = .413$
$r_{23} = .252$ $\quad r_{23.1} = .046$

Table 7.5

BASIC DATA ON FORTY-EIGHT MANUFACTURING INDUSTRIES

INDUSTRY	OPTIMUM COMPANY SIZE (IN THOUSAND DOLLARS OF TOTAL ASSETS) (1948–51)	OPTIMUM RANGE CLASS LIMITS (IN THOUSAND DOLLARS) FROM	TO	AVERAGE ESTABLISHMENT SIZE (IN THOUSAND DOLLARS OF VALUE ADDED) (1947)	NUMBER OF CHEMISTS AND ENGINEERS PER 100 EMPLOYED (1950)	ADVERTISING EXPENDITURE AS PER CENT OF GROSS SALES (1950)
Motor vehicles, incl. bodies and truck trailers	$827,828	$100,000	$open	$ 3,715	1.5879	0.4395
Petroleum refining	765,716	100,000	open	3,420	6.9171	0.4562
Blast furnaces, steel works and rolling mills	525,485	100,000	open	8,310	2.0956	0.1321
Dairy products	446,483	100,000	open	110	0.7865	1.5221
Distilled, rectified and blended liquors	248,424	100,000	open	2,090	0.9041	1.3674
Pulp, paper, and paperboard	203,794	100,000	open	1,645	1.4927	0.3357
Paints, varnishes, lacquers, etc.	175,404	100,000	open	394	6.0431	1.3539
Railroad equipment, incl. locomotives and streetcars	150,217	100,000	open	3,407	2.7171	0.3611
Tires and tubes	141,600	10,000	open	11,406	2.0974*	0.9453
Grain mill products ex. cereals preparations	128,363	100,000	open	210	1.0344	1.2492
Drugs and medicines	123,662	100,000	open	552	6.2599	8.3858
Smelting, refining, rolling, drawing and alloying of nonferrous metals	100,398	10,000	open	1,658	2.9845†	0.4088
Office and store machines	65,914	10,000	open	1,411	2.5860	1.5812
Bakery products	58,960	50,000	100,000	192	0.2359	2.1335
Yarn and thread	44,375	10,000	open	687	0.4461	0.3238
Carpets and other floor coverings	37,337	10,000	100,000	1,119	1.2391	1.7295
Broadwoven fabrics (wool)	31,265	10,000	open	1,211	0.4461	0.3400
Watches, clocks, and clock work operated devices	31,025	10,000	50,000	705	1.2027	5.3238
Cement	29,554	10,000	100,000	1,600	2.1277‡	0.2726
Malt liquors and malt	28,922	10,000	open	1,750	0.9041	4.7962

THE ECONOMIES OF SCALE

Industry					
Agricultural machinery and tractors	$ 28,291	$ 1,000	open	$ 684	2.1816	0.8956
Structural clay products	24,001	10,000	100,000	253	1.6292	0.4552
Newspapers	23,428	10,000	$100,000	168	0.1348§	0.1948
Knit goods	17,918	10,000	100,000	273	0.1244	0.8522
Confectionery	13,524	5,000	50,000	335	0.5950	2.6281
Commercial printing including lithographing	11,939	5,000	50,000	97	0.1348§	0.6474
Furniture—household, office, public building, and professional	11,378	5,000	50,000	209	0.3990‖	0.9152
Men's clothing	10,077	5,000	50,000	247	0.0456#	0.8795
Dyeing and finishing textiles, excl. knit goods	9,625	5,000	50,000	545	1.1223	0.3472
Canning fruit, vegetables and seafood	6,536	1,000	open	240	0.9144	1.8462
Broadwoven fabrics (cotton)	5,847	50	open	2,595	0.4461**	0.2822
Footwear, exc. rubber	4,359	1,000	100,000	524	0.1474	1.1619
Paperbags, and paperboard containers and boxes	4,127	1,000	100,000	428	0.6939	0.1854
Cigars	3,753	250	50,000	174	0.2274††	2.3188
Meat products	2,665	500	100,000	322	0.5983	0.4264
Nonferrous foundries	2,365	500	50,000	172	2.9845†	0.2793
Fur goods	1,966	1,000	5,000	55	0.0456#	0.4119
Partitions, shelving, lockers, etc.	1,545	500	50,000	121	0.3990‖	0.8678
Narrow fabrics and other small wares	1,382	500	5,000	226	0.4461**	0.3212
Wines	1,304	500	5,000	227	0.9041‡‡	3.5854
Women's clothing	1,304	500	50,000	150	0.0456#	0.9150
Books	1,137	50	50,000	399	0.1348§	2.8796
Periodicals	1,117	250	10,000	307	0.1348§	0.5245
Leather—tanning, curring and finishing	764	0	10,000	720	0.8140	0.1813
Concrete, gypsum and plaster products	762	250	10,000	53	2.1277‡	0.6855
Window and door screens, shades and venetian blinds	667	100	10,000	110	0.3990‖	1.0581
Non-alcoholic beverages	546	100	50,000	75	0.9041‡‡	4.0740
Millinery	468	250	5,000	108	0.0456#	0.4438

* Rubber products.
† Primary nonferrous.
‡ Cement, and concrete, gypsum and plaster products.
§ Printing, publishing and allied industries.
‖ Furniture and fixtures.
†† Tobacco manufactures.
‡‡ Beverage industries.
# Apparel and accessories.
** Yarn, thread, and fabric mills.

only this largest size has had a rising share of industry assets, and in another nine industries it is included in the range of sizes with rising shares. When the upper limit of optimum sizes is known, the range of optimum sizes is typically three or four times the average size of the firms in these sizes.

The results of this exploratory inter-industry study are at least suggestive—not only in their specific content but also in pointing out a line of attack on the economies of scale that escapes that confession of failure, the case method. The chief qualifications that attach to the findings are due to the imperfections of the data: the industry categories are rather wide; and the measure of technical personnel is seriously ambiguous. At least one finding—a wide range of optimum firm sizes in each industry—is so general as to deserve to be taken as the standard model in the theory of production.

INTRA-INDUSTRY ANALYSIS OF THE DETERMINANTS OF OPTIMUM SIZE

One may also examine the varying fates of individual firms within an industry in the search for explanations of optimum size. If, for example, firms moving to optimum size were vertically integrated and those moving to or remaining in nonoptimum size were not so integrated, we could infer that vertical integration was a requisite of the optimum firm in the industry. This approach has the advantage over the inter-industry approach of not requiring the assumption that a determinant such as advertising or integration works similarly in all industries.

The intra-industry analysis, however, has a heavy disadvantage; it can be applied only to those variables for which we can obtain information on each firm and in industries with numerous firms hardly any interesting variables survive this requirement. Because we could examine so few influences, and because the results were so consistently negative, we shall be very brief in describing our results in the industry—petroleum refining—in which this approach was tried.

The basic survivor experience for companies and plants in petroleum refining is given in Tables 7.6 and 7.7, for the postwar period 1947–1954. In each case only operating plants are included, and asphalt plants and companies are excluded. Capacities are measured in terms of crude oil; as in the case of steel plants, actual outputs cannot be obtained for all companies.[15]

There is a family resemblance between the data for petroleum and steel companies: in each case there has been a substantial reduction in the share of the largest company. In the petroleum refining industry, the size range from ½ of one per cent to 10 per cent has contained all the size classes which have stable or rising shares of industry capacity.

The plant survivor data suggest that the disappearance of the smaller companies has been due to the relative inefficiency of the smaller plants, for all plant size classes with less than one-half of one per cent of the industry's capacity

---

[15] One per cent of industry capacity was 52,508 barrels per day in 1947, and 76,811 barrels in 1954. Tentative calculations for regional markets indicate that the results are not greatly affected by using a national base.

Table 7.6

DISTRIBUTION OF PETROLEUM REFINING CAPACITY BY RELATIVE SIZE OF COMPANY

COMPANY SIZE (PER CENT OF INDUSTRY CAPACITY)	1947	1950	1954
1. PER CENT OF INDUSTRY CAPACITY			
Under 0.1	5.30	4.57	3.89
0.1 to 0.2	4.86	3.57	3.00
0.2 to 0.3	2.67	2.16	2.74
0.3 to 0.4	2.95	2.92	1.65
0.4 to 0.5	2.20	0	.89
0.5 to 0.75	3.04	4.66	5.05
0.75 to 1.00	.94	0	1.58
1.0 to 2.5	11.70	12.17	10.53
2.5 to 5	9.57	16.70	14.26
5 to 10	45.11	42.15	45.69
10 to 15	11.65	11.06	10.72
2. NUMBER OF COMPANIES			
Under 0.1	130	108	92
0.1 to 0.2	34	24	22
0.2 to 0.3	11	9	11
0.3 to 0.4	8	8	5
0.4 to 0.5	5	0	2
0.5 to 0.75	5	8	8
0.75 to 1.00	1	0	2
1.0 to 2.5	6	7	6
2.5 to 5.0	3	5	5
5.0 to 10.0	7	6	7
10.0 to 15.0	1	1	1
Total	211	176	161

Source: Bureau of Mines, Petroleum Refineries, including Cracking Plants in the United States, January 1, 1947, January 1, 1950, January 1, 1954, Information Circulars 7455 (March 1948), 7578 (August 1950), and 7963 (July 1954).

have also declined substantially. The sizes between one-half of one per cent and 2.5 per cent of industry capacity have all grown relatively, and the top plant size has declined moderately, so that the growth of company sizes beyond 2.5 per cent of industry capacity has presumably been due to the economies of multiple plant operation.

It has been claimed that backward integration into crude oil pipe lines was necessary to successful operation of a petroleum refinery. We tabulate some of the material bearing on this hypothesis in Table 7.8. There does not appear to be any large difference between the changes in market shares of firms with and without pipe lines. Since all firms with more than 0.75 per cent of industry

Table 7.7

DISTRIBUTION OF PETROLEUM REFINING CAPACITY
BY RELATIVE SIZE OF PLANT

PLANT SIZE	1947	1950	1954
1. PER CENT OF INDUSTRY CAPACITY			
Under 0.1	8.22	7.39	6.06
0.1 to 0.2	9.06	7.60	7.13
0.2 to 0.3	6.86	4.95	3.95
0.3 to 0.4	5.45	4.99	7.28
0.4 to 0.5	4.53	6.56	4.06
0.5 to 0.75	9.95	10.47	11.82
0.75 to 1.0	5.35	7.07	8.33
1.0 to 1.5	12.11	10.36	13.38
1.5 to 2.5	17.39	23.64	22.45
2.5 to 4.0	21.08	16.96	15.54
2. NUMBER OF PLANTS			
Under 0.1	184	158	138
0.1 to 0.2	64	53	51
0.2 to 0.3	27	19	16
0.3 to 0.4	15	14	21
0.4 to 0.5	10	15	9
0.5 to 0.75	17	16	19
0.75 to 1.0	6	8	10
1.0 to 1.5	10	8	11
1.5 to 2.5	9	12	12
2.5 to 4.0	7	5	5
Total	349	308	292

Source: Same as Table 7.6.

refining capacity have some pipe lines, a comparison (not reproduced here) was made between changes in their market shares and crude pipe line mileage per 1,000 barrels of daily refining capacity. There was no relationship between the two variables.[16]

The intra-industry analysis has its chief role, one may conjecture, in providing a systematic framework for the analysis of the data commonly employed in industry studies. A complete analysis of the plausible determinants of firm size requires such extensive information on the individual firms in the industry as to make this an unattractive method of attack on the general theory.

---

[16] A corresponding investigation was made for research laboratories, which are reported in the Directory of Research Laboratories of the National Research Council. That the results showed no relationship between firm size and size of laboratories is not surprising, for the work of the research laboratories would influence only the firm's long-term growth.

Table 7.8

INDUSTRY SHARES OF PETROLEUM REFINING COMPANIES WITH AND WITHOUT CRUDE PIPE LINES IN 1950

COMPANY SIZE (AVERAGE OF 1947, 1950, AND 1954 PERCENTAGE OF INDUSTRY CAPACITY)	COMPANIES WITH PIPE LINES			COMPANIES WITHOUT PIPE LINES		
	NUMBER 1950	SHARE 1947	SHARE 1954	NUMBER 1950	SHARE 1947	SHARE 1954
Under 0.1	25	1.40	1.12	60	2.87	2.18
0.1 to 0.2	17	2.19	2.50	5	0.77	0.77
0.2 to 0.3	6	1.48	1.63	2	0.34	0.50
0.3 to 0.4	5	1.90	1.63	0	—	—
0.4 to 0.5	1	0.40	0.55	2	0.54	1.22
0.5 to 0.75	7	3.59	4.72	1	0.38	0.61
0.75 to 1.0	0	—	—	0	—	—
1.0 to 2.5	7	11.54	13.10	0	—	—
2.5 to 5.0	4	11.11	11.69	0	—	—
5.0 to 10.0	7	45.11	45.69	0	—	—
10.0 to 15.0	1	11.65	10.72	0	—	—
Not in existence all years	16	2.30	0.05	79	2.43	1.33
Total	96	92.67	93.40	149	7.33	6.60

Source: *International Petroleum Register.*

CONCLUSION

The survivor technique for determining the range of optimum sizes of a firm seems well adapted to lift the theory of economies of scale to a higher level of substantive content. Although it is prey to the usual frustrations of inadequate information, the determination of optimum sizes avoids the enormously difficult problem of valuing resources properly that is encountered by alternative methods.

Perhaps the most striking finding in our exploratory studies is that there is customarily a fairly wide range of optimum sizes—the long run marginal and average cost curves of the firm are customarily horizontal over a long range of sizes. This finding could be corroborated, I suspect, by a related investigation: if there were a unique optimum size in an industry, increases in demand would normally be met primarily by near proportional increases in the number of firms, but it appears that much of the increase is usually met by expansion of the existing firms.

The survivor method can be used to test the numerous hypotheses on the factors determining the size of firm which abound in the literature. Our exploratory study suggests that advertising expenditures have no general tendency to lead to large firms, and another experiment (which is not reported above) indicates that fixed capital-sales ratios are also unrelated to the size of firms. The size of plant proves to be an important variable, as is to be expected, and the survivor method should be employed to determine the factors governing plant size. A rather ambiguous variable, the relative share of engineers and chemists in the labor force, also proves to be fairly important, and further data and work is necessary to disentangle research and routine technical operations. The determination of optimum size permits the investigator to examine any possible determinants which his imagination nominates and his data illuminate.

8

What Does the Survivor Technique Show about Economies of Scale?

William G. Shepherd*

There have been three main approaches, each with different concepts and data techniques, employed to measure economies of scale in individual industries. First, since the 1930's there have been numerous estimates of industry average-cost functions, using mainly cross-sectional data.[1] The second approach, taken by Bain, has canvassed managerial estimates of "optimum" scale of plants and inter-plant scale economies. Bain's measures for 20 major industries have become fixed points of reference for other estimates.[2]

Since 1958 the field has been entered in depth by a third approach, the survivor technique.[3] It has been applied by Thomas Saving and Leonard Weiss to

Reprinted from *The Southern Economic Journal*, July 1967, pp. 113–122 by permission of the author and publisher.

* I am indebted to John B. Lansing, Joe S. Bain, Thomas Saving and especially to Shorey Peterson for constructive comments on several points in this paper. Generous research assistance has been provided by the Institute of Public Administration at the University of Michigan.

[1] Reviews of these studies include: *Cost Behavior and Price Policy*, National Bureau of Economic Research, 1943; C. A. Smith, "Survey of the Empirical Evidence on Economies of Scale," in George J. Stigler, ed., *Business Concentration and Price Policy*, National Bureau of Economic Research, Princeton University Press, 1955; and J. Johnston, *Statistical Cost Analysis*, McGraw-Hill, 1960.

[2] Bain, *Barriers to New Competition*, Harvard University Press, 1956.

[3] Though John Stuart Mill and Willard Thorp have been claimed as originators, the modern originator is George J. Stigler; see "Monopoly and Oligopoly by Merger," *American Economic Review*, May 1950, pp. 23–34. See also Milton Friedman's "Comment" in *Business Concentration and Price Policy, op. cit.*, pp. 230–38. Stigler gave it the first full-dress exposition and trial, applying it to entire firms, in "The Economies of Scale," *Journal of Law and Economics*, 1958, pp. 54–71.

no less than 137 of the approximately 450 Census 4-digit manufacturing industries.[4] These estimates have already been incorporated in related research, and other extensions and variations of the technique have been made and are in prospect.[5]

In view of both the widening activity and ambitious nature of the technique itself, it is appropriate now to take an inventory of the survivor technique and its contribution. The evaluation will proceed on two levels. First the analytical strengths and limits of the technique will be set forth (in the first section). Then the quality of the actual survivor estimates (including new estimates by myself for 117 industries) will be reviewed (in the second section). A concluding section will summarize the appraisal.

THE TECHNIQUE IN PRINCIPLE

The mechanics of survivor technique are relatively simple. For illustration, consider S.I.C. 4-digit industry 2522, Metal Office Furniture. The distribution of value added in plants of different employment sizes (from 1–4 employees to 2500-plus) is shown in Table 8.1 for 1947, 1954 and 1958, the available Census years.[6] Plants from 50 to 499 employees are increasing their share of industry value-added, while larger and smaller plants are not keeping up.[7] Assuming this trend to continue, or at least not reverse, the plants in the 50–499 range will "survive." Therefore the size range of 50–499 employees is designated as "the range of optimal plant size."[8]

The survivor technique offers three main advantages. First, it finesses the

---

[4] Saving, "Estimation of Optimum Size of Plant by the Survivor Technique," *Quarterly Journal of Economics*, 1961, pp. 569–607 gives estimates for 91 industries; Weiss, "The Survival Technique and the Extent of Suboptimal Capacity," *Journal of Political Economy*, 1964, pp. 246–261, offers 65 more (some overlapping). See also Weiss, "The Extent of Suboptimal Capacity: A Correction," *Journal of Political Economy*, 1965, pp. 300–301.

[5] Weiss, "The Survival Technique and the Extent of Suboptimal Capacity," *op. cit.*, pp. 257–260; Weiss, "An Evaluation of Merges in Six Industries," *Review of Economics and Statistics*, 1965, pp. 172–181; "T. R. Saving, The Four Parameter Lognormal, Diseconomies of Scale, and the Size Distribution of Manufacturing Establishments," *International Economic Review*, 1965, pp. 105–114.

[6] The use of an input (employment) rather than output for measuring "size" is dictated by necessity; value-added or other output size distributions of plants are not published by the Census, though they could be compiled. This may, and probably does, bias the estimates of "optimum size," as will be noted below.

Saving and Weiss used only 1947 and 1954, not the three-year sequence shown here.

[7] Some slight erratic movements (as in the 50–99, 100–249, and 250–499 classes) are overlooked. The frequency of such erratic shifts is discussed below.

[8] A variety of assumptions about transition probabilities and terminal states can be chosen from; see also Saving, *op. cit.* Evidently it is hazardous to assume, as the users have, that the most recent configuration represents a long-run equilibrium or final size-distribution. Though the problem lends itself to Markov chain treatment, it may be doubted that the available data justify extended experiments in that direction. Nonetheless the results might be of interest.

Table 8.1

ILLUSTRATION OF THE SURVIVOR TECHNIQUE: CHANGES IN THE SHARE OF VALUE-ADDED IN DIFFERENT SIZE PLANTS DURING 1947 TO 1958 IN S.I.C. 2522, METAL OFFICE FURNITURE

	PERCENT OF INDUSTRY VALUE-ADDED IN PLANTS WITH EMPLOYEES NUMBERING:								
	1–4	5–9	10–19	20–49	50–99	100–249	250–499	500–999*	1000–2499*	2500*
1947	0.2	0.5	1.0	4.9	4.7	10.3	18.1		60.4	
1954	0.3	0.4	1.0	4.3	4.5	23.5	16.6		49.4	
1958	0.3	0.3	1.7	4.2	6.8	19.1	25.2		42.5	

"Optimal Size Range"

* Sizes 500–2500+ are grouped together because Census disclosure requirements prevented publication of figures for each class.

problem of the capitalization of rents into costs, a process which drives disparate measured average costs toward equality.[9] This long-recognized problem has plagued and seriously undermined the cross-section and time-series cost studies; the apparent flatness of cost functions over large ranges of size may be, in large part, an economic illusion.

Second, survivor estimates deal directly with plant size. Difficulties in defining the unit of output of allocating joint costs correctly therefore do not pose some of the major problems which have boxed in the earlier studies. Also, the required data (the distribution of plants by number of workers) are among the more consistent and reliable information in the Census of Manufactures.

Finally, the technique reflects trends and adaptive processes in industries, rather than dealing only with single periods. Therefore it embraces dynamic elements which could tie its results in with an analysis of industrial behavior which tries to go beyond traditional static-equilibrium assumptions. One step in this direction has already been made by Weiss, in studying the differential rates at which "sub-optimal" capacity is eliminated.[10]

The technique also suffers from a number of serious disadvantages and limitations. The following remarks will assume away the statistical difficulties of survivor estimates (such as the section will cover), in order to assess the purely conceptual limits of the technique.

The primary limitation is that the technique gives *descriptive*, not *normative*, estimates of "optimality": it tells what *is*, not necessarily what is *optimum* or *efficient* in terms of net social costs. Though this has been recognized, the temptation to endow the estimates with normative virtues verges on the irresistible. The term "optimal" is applicable only in a specialized, even subtle, sense; the surviving size ranges are in fact simply "the surviving size ranges." The predictive, technical uses of survivor estimates may be important, as Stigler, Saving and Weiss have, to some degree, shown. But there are many reasons besides social efficiency why plants—in small, medium or large size classes—may survive, too many in fact to permit normative interpretations without extreme caution.

Unfortunately, this problem is severe in precisely those industries (where market imperfections are greatest) for which normative estimates of scale economies are most needed, for purposes of public policy. Thus, survivor estimates for firm sizes are likely to be more valid for atomistic industries (including farming) than for highly concentrated ones (such as steel, chemicals, drugs, and autos).

Recognizing this, Saving and Weiss have shifted from estimating optimal *firm* sizes, settling instead for *plant* estimates. Weiss, especially cautious, has focused his estimates only on the *minimum* efficient size of plant ("efficient" is used by Weiss largely as a synonym for "optimal"). Clearly these two reductions leave the survivor technique as a ghost of the original intent and main policy use, namely to measure the range and degree of scale economies for firms in important industries. Even so, these strategic withdrawals do not eliminate the prob-

[9] See Friedman, *op. cit.*, and Donald Dewey, "The Ambiguous Notion of Average Cost," *Journal of Industrial Economics,* 1962, pp. 231–37.

[10] In "The Survival Technique and the Extent of Suboptimal Capacity," *op. cit.*

lem, because even the estimates of *minimum* efficient scale may fail to measure the lower range of socially efficient size. This is especially so in heterogeneous and fragmented industries, where small (and large) units may survive owing to special advantages not generally available in the industry. That is, the "economies" may be inherent in the unique situation, not in the size. In such situations, the estimated range of optimal size will be too wide. Moreover, estimates of *maximum* optimal scale are also important, for antitrust and other policy purposes. In settling for what it may do relatively well, the users of the survivor technique have withdrawn from much of the main field of interest.

Survivor trends usually will reflect more than costs internal to the plant, in contrast to the cross-section or questionnaire approach. A fall in transport costs or other external changes may shift the distribution of plants from centralized to localized, as in meat packing.[11] For certain descriptive purposes, especially in predicting future trends or summarizing past ones, this extra sensitivity to influences outside the plant may be a decided advantage. But for other purposes, including some policy judgments, this inclusiveness (which reflects *everything* affecting plant size) will not be wanted. Analysis of why size patterns have changed (including the basic distinction between technical and pecuniary gains) must go entirely beyond the survivor technique itself.

Survivor estimates also lack an indication of the *degree* of scale economies (or diseconomies); instead they only indicate the borders of a range. Yet for anti-trust purposes, to take one example, it is the trade-offs between the firm's scale economies and other objectives (such as the probability of preventing collusive action) which are in question. For many nonnormative purposes, too, this would reduce the utility of the survivor technique.

The users of the survivor technique have translated the "range of optimal size" into a "range of constant costs." [12] Yet no such saucer-shaped cost function (relating unit cost and output) can be inferred from survivor estimates alone (which relate industry output shares and employment size of plant). For one thing, survival may reflect higher revenues rather than lower costs. And within the "optimal range," costs may vary with size, rather than be constant.

As noted earlier, the use of an employment size dimension, rather than output, introduces the possibility of bias caused by innovation. Only if innovation is absent or maintains labor-output ratios unchanged at all size-levels of plants will the employment-based estimates be unbiased. The strong trend toward higher output-employment ratios (with different incidence over the size range of plants) in postwar years therefore introduces strong biases—probably downward in most but not necessarily all cases—in the survivor estimates. Some discussion of this is given in the next section.

Also the technique treats alike all plants, whether operated by one-plant or multi-plant firms. Accordingly the differences in this factor, which may be important for survival, are not removed from the determination of "optimal" size.

---

[11] Again, differences in input prices and other local peculiarities—fatal to a normative interpretation of the "optimum scale" estimates—are not factored out by the survivor technique.

[12] See especially Stigler, "The Economies of Scale," *op. cit.,* p. 59.

The distinct tendency for large firms to have relatively large plants further complicates the interpretation of the all-inclusive survivor findings.[13] Further, the survival quality of small plants may be exaggerated if new plants, especially of new firms, tend to be smaller than old, in part because they apply newer technology. Also, the use of specific census-year data may disturb the results if (as in 1954 and 1958) many plants have temporarily low output and employment.

Finally, the technique ignores the static distribution of plants.[14] Therefore when the distribution is constant over the years, the technique can only conclude that *every* plant is of optimal size, a condition which requires much explaining on other grounds. And freakish estimates can and do result. A size group accounting for a mere trace of industry capacity can be designated "optimal," while another class embracing nearly all of industry capacity can—because of barely perceptible, perhaps transitory, declines—be declared non-optimal. The application of the technique is unavoidably an art, not a purely objective, scientific process.

Apart from its other limitations, therefore, the survivor technique cannot safely be used on its own. Its estimates need to be screened against other evidence, such as the static size distribution and an analysis of the influences at work on plant sizes. The survivor technique may, under favorable conditions, yield preliminary or supplementary indications of certain ranges in industry cost functions. But as an estimator of scale economies its applicability is limited, even when its numerical results are perfectly clear.

THE TECHNIQUE APPLIED

Published survivor estimates are Stigler's measures of the range of optimal firm size, Saving's measures of the range of optimal plant size, and Weiss' estimates of the minimum efficient plant size. To judge the technique on its strongest points, only the plant estimates (Saving, Weiss) will be considered here. Saving gives estimates for 91 4-digit industries and Weiss estimates for 65 industries; in both cases the measures were based on 1947 and 1954 size distributions. To these the present study adds the results of estimates for 117 industries, using data for 1958 as well as for 1947 and 1954. All three sets of estimates (Saving, Weiss and Shepherd) were picked on different bases, but there is enough overlap in their coverage to permit some comparisons of different estimates for the same industries.

Criteria for appraising these results would include:

1) is the choice of the estimating procedure a clear-cut one?
2) are data readily available?
3) does the procedure give clear and reliable results for all or most industries for which data are available?
4) do estimates made by different researchers agree?

[13] On plant and firm sizes, see R. L. Nelson, *Concentration in the Manufacturing Industries of the United States* (New Haven, Conn.: Yale University Press, 1963), pp. 59–77; and R. Evely and I. M. D. Little, *Concentration in British Industry* (Cambridge: Cambridge University Press, 1960), pp. 83–114 and 296–312.

[14] For a survey based on distributions, rather than *changes* in the distributions, see Bain, *Barriers to New Competition, op. cit.*, pp. 227–262.

First, procedure. Survival may be relative (holding one's share in the industry) or absolute. *Relative* survival could be shown by the shares of the industry's value-added, value of shipments, employment, or numbers of plants in each size class. Saving and Weiss have used relative survival, usually as shown by shares of value-added. Yet a strong case can also be made for using *absolute* survival as the criterion; for example, has the value-added, employment or *number* of plants in each size class risen or fallen? There is no conclusive way to choose between these procedures, each of which may give different estimates.

Next, data. For Census years there is an array of plant data by number of employees per plant for every 4-digit manufacturing industry. The 1957 revision of the classification system has, however, nearly halved the number of industries which can be estimated and checked with data more recently than 1954. This has seriously hampered Weiss' more recent estimates, as well as my own. For a number of fairly obvious reasons, S.I.C. revisions were required precisely in many industries which—from their growth, diversification and policy importance —are of the greatest interest; and this fact of life will continue.

Third, clearness and reliability. Unfortunately it seems possible to generate clear and reliable results for only a fraction of the industries one sets out to estimate. Saving began with a random sample of 200, but finally presented estimates for only 91.[15] Of these, many (such as Hatter's Fur, Embroideries, Watchcases, and Dolls, among others) are of slight interest. Also, in 57 of the 91 estimated industries, Census disclosure rules suppressed data in at least one size class (in many cases, several or more), thereby weakening the estimates.

Weiss first made detailed estimates for five major industries (autos, steel, petroleum refining, flour and cement) using trade data for a series of years since 1924. Encouraged by these results, he then tackled 101 large industries. Of these 101, 36 were dropped for technical reasons, including 8 whose patterns showed erratic shifts. For the remaining 65 industries which yielded survivor industry output coming from plants smaller than this minimum. In no less than 18 of the 65, this "suboptimal capacity" accounted for more than 40 per cent. Weiss' attempts to explain these high proportions are imaginative and informative, and concentration may, as he suggests, influence the rate of adjustment. But the high proportions are in themselves so improbable as to cast doubt on the reliability of these (and the other) estimates.

Weiss' more recent attempt to extend his estimates with the 1958 Census (comparing 1954 and 1958 patterns) for the same industries is hardly reassuring.[16] Meaningful estimates were possible for only 23 of the 65 industries; S.I.C. definitions changed for 24 industries, and in 18 industries the shifts did not yield interpretable survivor estimates (in some, for example, large size classes shrank and *all* small size classes expanded).

[15] Some 43 were dropped because Census disclosure rules suppressed data for one or more size classes. Another 25 came out because of heterogeneity of products and unsuitable market definitions. Of the remaining industries, 43 more showed erratic, bimodal or other irregular patterns; their rejection left 91 industries for which optimal-size estimates were finally presented. Though Saving's Appendix Table 1 has "89" in its title, there are actually 91 industries in it.

[16] Weiss, "A Correction," *op. cit.*

Of the 23 estimates for 1954–58, 13 were substantially (50 per cent or more) different from the 1947–54 estimates. Thus, the estimate of "minimum efficient plant size" in Pharmaceutical Preparations changed from 1000 workers in 1947–54 to 100 in 1954–58. Although such large changes in "optimal size" are possible, they surely call for independent confirmation. In any case, Weiss was able to supply numerically consistent estimates for 1947 through 1958 for only somewhere between 10 and 23 of the original 101 large industries.

In my own estimates the results were even more slender. The intention was to derive estimates using the three years (1947, 1954 and 1958) for all of those 4-digit industries which may be considered to be "important or interesting." Antitrust importance (such as Steel, Aluminum and Switchgear), previous studies of scale economies, high concentration and changing concentration, and other

Table 8.2

SUMMARY OF RESULTS OF SURVIVOR TESTS (1947–54–58)
FOR 117 INDUSTRIES

RESULT	NUMBER OF INDUSTRIES	SHARE OF TOTAL (%)	VALUE ADDED IN 1962 ($ MILL)	SHARE OF TOTAL (%)
Clear	17	14.5	7,999	12.4
Partially clear	27	23.1	16,316	25.2
Unclear	37	31.6	19,382	30.0
Disclosure problems	21	18.0	5,614	8.7
Incompatible	15	12.8	15,263	23.7
Totals	117	100.0	64,574	100.0
Subtotals				
At least partially clear	44	37.6	24,315	37.6
Unclear or worse	73	62.4	40,259	62.4

Clear: a surviving range emerged with upper and lower borders.
Partially clear: only one border could be detected.
Unclear: shifts were erratic, with no borders evident.
Disclosure problems: enough (in many cases most) data classes were suppressed for disclosure reasons to make any estimation impossible.
Incompatible: the results were incompatible with the assumptions of the survivor technique, because the middle size ranges were shrinking.

bases for inclusion were used.[17] Although the selection was partly subjective, it did provide the survivor technique a broad change to show how well it could do with industries which, in a general sense, "really matter." [18]

Of the 162 industries chosen in this subjective way, 45 were reclassified in

---

[17] A detailed listing of the industries and the survivor results has been omitted here. I shall be happy to provide the enumeration on request.

[18] This would be a more direct way of appraising what the technique can contribute, compared with selections based on random samples or industry size alone. The reader is invited, of course, to draw up his own list.

1957 enough to make an estimate for 1947–54–58 unsafe.[19] The results for the remaining 117 industries are summed up in Table 8.2 with the categories defined at the foot of the table. The estimating process was tolerant; many marginally erratic shifts were overlooked in the attempt to discern general patterns.[20] A mechanical procedure would have yielded much fewer Clear and Partially Clear cases.

Even from this indulgent view only about three-eighths of the 117 industries (one-quarter of the original 162) yielded any meaningful estimates at all. Only 17 industries showed tolerably Clear ranges. Almost as many results (15) were fundamentally in conflict with the survivor approach, because the bottom and top size ranges were surviving (implying a humpbacked "average cost curve") In no less than 72 per cent of the original 161 industries, the estimates were Impossible (to make), Unclear, or Incompatible. This is not a rich harvest.

Nonetheless it is a harvest of sorts, and so we turn to test the comparability of the estimates from the three sources. First, there are 19 industries which both Saving and Weiss estimated, applying the same technique to identical 1947–54 data. Table 8.3 summarizes their estimates of the minimum boundary of optimal plant size; my own results for these industries are given in column 4. Note that this tests the survivor technique at its strongest point: *minimum* scale for *plants* (not the *range* or *upper* limit, not for firms, not an estimate of the degree of scale economies).

The estimates by Saving and Weiss agree for 11 of the 19 industries, as shown by columns 1 and 2. For the other 8, the estimates differ, some of them spectacularly (2033, 2751, 3571, and 3615 all differ by a factor of at least 5). Of the entire 19 industries, I was able to make 1947–54–58 estimates for only 9, the others having been significantly regrouped in the new S.I.C. system. Of these 9, 4 showed Unclear patterns, and 1 showed Incompatible (spreading) size changes. Minimum estimates were possible for 4 industries, and these all agreed with the Saving-Weiss estimates for 1947–54.[21] But in 3 of 4 cases (Flour and Meal, Distilled Liquors, and Newspapers), Weiss' later 1954–58 estimates differ from my 1947–54–58 estimates, which were made by basically the same procedure.

One concludes that the stock of confirmed, numerically consistent survivor estimates now totals between 1 and 11 industries. If one insists on estimates more recent than 1954, the total is closer to 1 than to 11, even including the 5 more detailed studies made by Weiss. Also the Census size intervals (100, 250, 500, 1000, and so forth) force the estimates to be rather crude, especially in the higher ranges.

[19] The pre-1947 4-digit codes for these industries were: 2023, 2271, 2562, 2563, 2613, 2661, 2811, 2825, 2841, 2893, 3011, 3231, 3275, 3312, 3316, 3352, 3392, 3393, 3431, 3441, 3443, 3461, 3491, 3521, 3522, 3531, 3542, 3567, 3582, 3585, 3611, 3613, 3616, 3621, 3661, 3662, 3716, 3717, 3742, 3811, 3821, 3841, 3842, 3931, and 3951. Evidently this group includes many of the really interesting industries.

[20] In fact, the industry used in Table 8.1 as an illustration had *the* clearest patterns of the entire 117, even though there are some odd shifts for it too.

[21] However, in 2 of these 4 cases (Women's and children's underwear, and Newspapers) Saving's upper-bound estimates were not borne out by my estimates, which showed no pattern at all.

Table 8.3

SAVING'S, WEISS' AND SHEPHERD'S ESTIMATE OF MINIMUM SURVIVING SIZE IN 19 INDUSTRIES USING 1947–54 DATA

INDUSTRY CODE	NAME	MINIMUM SURVIVING PLANT SIZE* (WORKERS PER PLANT)			
		SAVING (VALUE-ADDED BASIS) (1)	WEISS (VALUE-ADDED BASIS) (2)	WEISS (EMPLOYMENT BASIS) (3)	SHEPHERD† (1947–58) (VALUE-ADDED BASIS) (4)
2033	Canned fruits & vegetables	500	100	50	Regrouped
2041	Flour and meal	100	100	100	100
2085	Distilled liquors	100	100	250	100
2092	Shortening & cooking oil	50	100	100	Regrouped
2234	Synthetic broad woven fabrics	250	100	100	Unclear
2341	Women's & children's underwear	250	250	100	250
2432	Plywood plants	100	(not made)	100	Regrouped
2711	Newspapers	250	250	250	250
2751	Commercial printing	100	1000	1000	Regrouped
2834	Pharmaceuticals	1000	1000	1000	Unclear
2911	Petroleum refining	100	500	500	Unclear
3271	Concrete products	20	20	20	Regrouped
3312	Steel works and rolling mills	500	500	500	Regrouped
3441	Structural & ornamental work	100	100	100	Regrouped
3542	Metal working machines	500	500	500	Regrouped
3571	Computing equipment	100	2500	2500	Unclear
3611	Wiring devices	50	50	100	Regrouped
3615	Transformers	100	1000	1000	Incompatible
3662	Electronic tubes	1000	1000	1000	Regrouped

* Weiss used both the share of value-added in each size class and the share of employment, in making alternative estimates, as shown in columns 2 and 3. See Table 8.2 for an explanation of the terms in column 4. "Regrouped" means that a change in S.I.C. definition made estimation impossible.

Bain gives estimates of optimal plant scale (in 1950 or so) for 5 of the 19 industries in Table 8.3. For three of them (2033, 2041 and 2085) the estimates are tolerably close. But for the more important two (Petroleum Refining and Steel), the survivor estimates are so far below Bain's estimates as to suggest that they may significantly understate "optimal" size.

By way of further check, the 17 Clear and "important" industries were estimated again, using changes in absolute numbers of plants rather than in shares of industry value-added. In four industries (3141, 3494, 3559, and 3642), the new estimated range was tolerably similar to the value-added results. In 7 industries, *one* boundary of the range was similar. No similarity was found for the remaining 6 industries.

In the same vein the 15 Incompatible industries were redone using numbers of plants, this time with rather more luck. In 8 cases (2721, 2823, 2831, 2872, 2896, 3494, 3615 and 3617) the same spreading pattern was found as before, and in 4 others the spreading appeared to be over a somewhat wider range than shown by the first estimates. Spreading of this sort may simply reflect excessively broad S.I.C. industry definitions, but it is a difficult problem to overcome. In any case, the results vary significantly with the specific technique used, casting further doubt on their reliability.

One unexpected, but possibly significant, result was the high frequency of decline in the largest size categories. Of the 133 industries tested, 78 showed declines in the share of the largest plants.[22] Apparently there are strong pressures in many industries toward smaller employment-size of plants, including changes in transportation and information handling, both of which encourage greater decentralization. Also the bias introduced by innovation is undoubtedly at work. Even so, these downward shifts justify further comment here.

A closer look at the whole range of twenty two-digit industries shows that the largest-size plants declined in eleven, rose in seven, and showed no clear change in two, as Table 8.4 shows. The declines in the heavy industry groups S.I.C. 34, 35, and 36 (Fabricated Metal Products and Machinery) are unexpected. By contrast, the rises in 28 (Chemicals), 33 (Primary Metals) and 37 (Transportation Equipment) conform to the prevailing impressions.

Actually the rises are dominated by a handful of the larger 4-digit industries. These are shown in Table 8.5, along with their concentration ratios. Especially in Cigarettes, Pharmaceutical Preparations, Aircraft, and Scientific Instruments, there were shifts toward larger plants (as measured by employment size). When the eight industries in Table 8.5 (plus two new defense industries, 1925, Guided Missiles, and 1941, Sighting and Fire-control Equipment) are removed, the share of the largest-size plants in *all* other industries declined from 14.2 to 13.2 per cent of value-added.

This handful of industries forms a fairly special group. Their value-added grew much more rapidly (183 per cent) during 1947–58 than did that of the rest of the industries (81 per cent). And, directly and indirectly, most of them

---

[22] In 41 of these 78 cases, the rest of the distribution shifted so erratically as to place it in the Unclear category, or disclosure problems put it in the Disclosure category. Therefore only 37 of these 78 industries are found in the Clear and Partially Clear groups.

Table 8.4

CHANGES IN THE SHARE OF THE LARGEST-SIZE PLANTS: 2-DIGIT INDUSTRY GROUPS

GROUP NUMBER	NAME	PERCENT OF INDUSTRY VALUE ADDED IN THE LARGEST-SIZE PLANTS		CHANGE, 1947 TO 1958
		1947	1958	
20	Food and kindred products	27.5	25.5	−2.0
21	Tobacco products	61.0	78.8	+17.8
22	Textile mill products	32.5	19.2	−13.3
23	Apparel and related products	42.2	42.2	0
24	Lumber and wood products	49.7	43.0	−6.8
25	Furniture and fixtures	23.3	19.1	−4.2
26	Paper and allied products	28.7	42.5	+13.8
27	Printing and publishing	23.8	22.3	−1.5
28	Chemicals and allied products	60.5	69.0	+18.5
29	Petroleum and coal products	22.7	25.5	+2.8
30	Rubber and plastics products	49.5	22.3	−27.2
31	Leather and leather products	25.5	17.5	−8.0
32	Stone, clay and glass products	36.4	27.3	−9.1
33	Primary metal industries	32.8	42.6	+9.8
34	Fabricated metal products	38.4	31.0	−7.4
35	Machinery, except electrical	69.9	62.8	−7.1
36	Electrical machinery	34.2	27.4	−6.8
37	Transportation equipment	57.4	60.5	+3.1
38	Instruments and related products	22.9	34.8	+11.9
39	Miscellaneous manufacturing	*	*	*

* Industries in group 19 (ordnance) were included in the 1958 Census data, and so the patterns for 1947 and 1958 are not meaningfully comparable.

are heavily involved with defense procurement. Despite their shift toward larger plants, concentration declined in four of the six industries for which the data are available. To put it at its mildest, rising relative plant size did not lead to increased concentration in the largest companies.

Altogether, one concludes that there has been no widespread shift at all toward larger plants (as measured by number of employees). The relatively few upward shifts have been focused in a few industries, and most of these are involved in defense production. Even in these cases, the upward shift has not usually led to rises in concentration.

ON FURTHER ESTIMATES

Taken altogether, these results fall short of the early promise of the survivor technique: the failures are many, the proven successes few. Most of the numerically reliable measurements are for relatively trivial industries, leaving unilluminated most of the really interesting cases. In any event the technique is only

Table 8.5

THE MAIN INDUSTRIES WITH SHIFTS TOWARD LARGER PLANT SIZES

INDUS-TRY NUMBER	NAME	PER CENT OF INDUSTRY VALUE-ADDED IN LARGEST-SIZE PLANTS:		FOUR-FIRM CONCENTRATION RATIOS:		
		1947	1958	1947	1954	1958
2111	Cigarettes	(61.0)	(78.8)	90	82	79
2834	Pharmaceutical preparations	22.7	33.1	28	25	27
2911	Petroleum refining	(22.7)	(25.5)	37	33	32
3312	Blast furnaces and steel mills	71.2	76.4	50	55	53
3721	Aircraft	88.7	96.5	—	—	59
3722	Aircraft engines	80.5	83.7	72	62	56
3811	Scientific instruments	30.2	56.3	—	51	45
3861	Photographic equipment	65.0	72.6	61	—	65

Figures in parentheses are estimated from the patterns in the two-digit industry groups.

faintly normative, and it is weakest where good measurements are most badly needed.

Yet the technique has made some contribution, and it can do more, especially when applied intensively to a few industries at a time. Stigler's estimates and Weiss' five-industry results show that concentrated excavation can turn up estimates which are at least statistically consistent. The research effort is, however, not much less than for the alternative approaches.

The rapid-fire, hundreds-of-industries surveys using two or three Census years will still be worth doing. But their results will probably continue to be of limited use, suitable at best as preliminary indicators for more careful work. The survivor technique has, in short, gone through the usual cycle of an innovation: a novel idea, a group of applications, and a re-appraisal. Although the net contribution of the technique so far is but a fraction of the first hopes, it is not negative.

Yet, there remains the inability of the survivor technique to provide normative estimates of scale economies above the plant level. These other levels—distribution, research, sales promotion, factor purchasing, and others—often are precisely the point at issue, especially in antitrust actions.[23] Although other methods of estimating inter-plant, intra-firm returns to scale are still primitive, the survivor technique is, almost by definition, inappropriate. What is, is not necessarily what ought to be.

[23] And especially in assessing conglomerate diversification and merges.

9
Firm Size and Rate of Growth[1]

Stephen Hymer and Peter Pashigian

INTRODUCTION

Two recent articles—one published in the United States by Simon and Bonini and the other in England by Hart and Prais[2]—have advanced several important and interesting hypotheses about the firm. In this paper we submit these hypotheses to further testing and clarification, using data we have collected on the growth rates of the one thousand largest manufacturing firms in the United States in the decade between 1946 and 1955. The two articles do not cover exactly the same ground, so it is unfair to treat them as one; but for purposes of our investigation their results may be summarized as follows:

1. In a large number of industries, the size distribution of firms is J-shaped: there are a few large firms and a large number of small firms.
2. Statistical distributions of this type are generated by processes in which

Reprinted from *Journal of Political Economy* (December 1962), by permission of The University of Chicago Press. Copyright, 1962, pp. 556–569.

[1] This study was conducted when the authors were graduate students in the Department of Economics at the Massachusetts Institute of Technology. The analysis was greatly aided by a grant from the Department and by helpful comments by Professor M. A. Adelman and other members of the faculty. The computations were conducted at the Harvard Computational Center. An earlier draft was presented at the Econometrics Society meetings, December, 1958.

[2] H. A. Simon and C. P. Bonini, "The Size Distribution of Business Firms," *American Economic Review*, XLVIII (September, 1958), 607–17; P. E. Hart and S. J. Prais, "The Analysis of Business Concentration," *Journal of the Royal Statistical Society*, Part 2 (1956), pp. 150–91.

the "law of proportionate effect" holds. In this context the "law of proportionate effect" implies that the probability of a firm growing x per cent is independent of its size. The observed size distributions of firms in the American and British economies are consistent with the operation of this law; that is, there have been, in fact, no differences between the growth rates of large and small firms.[3]

3. The law of proportionate effect is more in keeping with an assumption that unit cost curves are horizontal (at least beyond some minimum size) than with the more usual assumption that unit cost curves are U-shaped.

In this paper we are interested in testing the validity of these findings, particularly the second and third. In the second part we test the law of proportionate effect by computing and comparing the distribution of growth rates for different size classes of firms in our sample of the one thousand largest manufacturing firms. We find that the average growth rates do not differ for firms of different sizes. However, the law of proportionate effect implies that the entire distribution of growth rates is the same for large and small firms; and although we find the means similar, we find the variances of the growth rates different. There is a systematic tendency for the variance to be larger for small firms than it is for large firms.

This pattern of distribution of growth rates contradicts the Simon-Bonini-Hart-Prais model and raises the question whether the implication drawn by Simon and Bonini—that cost curves are horizontal—is valid. In the fifth part we argue that the pattern we find of equal average growth rates for different size classes, but of declining standard deviation with increasing size, is inconsistent with constant costs and implies instead that either unit costs decrease with size, or that large firms are more monopolistic than are small ones.

We have not attempted to complete our analysis by explaining how the growth pattern we observe results in a J-shaped size distribution of firms (point 1). This is partly because we are not completely convinced that the size distribution of firms is in fact J-shaped.[4] Consequently, we conclude instead with the suggestion that the fact that many industries have a few large firms and many small ones may after all be explained by economies of scale, not merely by time and chance.

EMPIRICAL PATTERN OF GROWTH RATES: FIRST TESTS

The law of proportionate effect states that the probability distribution of growth rates is independent of firm size. We tested this hypothesis by comparing the means and standard deviations of distributions of growth rates of firms in different size classes. The sample consists of the one thousand largest manufac-

[3] More accurately, Simon and Bonini claim that there is no difference in the growth rates of firms above a critical minimum size. They studied the growth rates of the five hundred largest firms for 1954–56 and consequently said nothing about the growth rates of smaller firms.

[4] Several tests we performed on the data suggested that the assumption of a lognormal size distribution of firms is not valid.

turing firms as of December, 1946.[5] The size of a firm was measured by its assets in 1946;[6] its growth rate was measured by the percentage change in these assets between 1946 and 1955.[7]

The one thousand firms were divided into twenty S.I.C. two-digit industries. Ten of these industries had too few firms for the type of study we wished to do, so, we were left with only ten industries. In each of these industries we ranked the firms in order of size and divided them into quartiles. The number of firms and the average size of firm in each quartile and each industry are presented in Table 9.1. Our problem then was to compare for each industry the distributions of growth rates for the various size classes. If the law of proportionate effect applies, each size class should have the same distribution.

The mean and the standard deviation for each size class in each industry are presented in Tables 9.2 and 9.3. Table 9.2 shows no relationship between the mean growth rate and size of firm. Mean growth rates are higher in the second quartile than in the first in four industries, and lower in six. Between the second

---

[5] The list was obtained from the United States Federal Trade Commission, *Report of the Federal Trade Commission on Interlocking Directorates* (Washington: Government Printing Office, 1951), Appendix A. A few errors and omissions in this list were corrected by reference to a later publication: United States Federal Trade Commission, *A List of the 1,000 Largest Manufacturing Firms and Their Subsidiaries and Affiliates 1948* (Washington: Government Printing Office, 1951). It is important to note that neither of these lists refers to the one thousand largest firms but only to the one thousand largest of those firms that *publish* financial data. Omissions from the list are more numerous for small firms than they are for large firms. The one thousand largest firms account for only a tiny fraction of all firms, but they do account for a large share of value added. For purposes of evaluating industry behavior, the share of output seems more important in judging the sample than does the number of firms.

[6] For a defense of the use of assets rather than some other measure of size see M. A. Adelman, "The Measurement of Industrial Concentration," *Review of Economics and Statistics*, XXXIII (November, 1951), 272-74.

The growth rates can be calculated by a relatively straightforward procedure except where mergers or dissolutions occurred. Since there is no good theoretical guide for handling these cases, the following arbitrary procedures were used. Firms that were dissolved during the period were given a growth rate of minus 100 per cent. For merged firms, the calculated assets of the merged firm in 1955 were allocated to each partner in proportion to its relative size at the time of the merger, and growth rates computed as if there had been no merger. The only defenses we can offer for this procedure are that we know of no better one, and that the other methods we devised gave essentially the same results when they were tried in some of the tests.

These methods were (1) to exclude mergers and dissolutions from the sample; (2) to assume that in any merger the largest firm simply buys out the smallest one. On the latter method, all the assets of the merged firms were allocated to the firm that was larger at the time of merger. The smaller firm was recorded as dissolved and given the growth rate of minus 100 per cent.

[7] In order to conduct some of our tests, we classified the one thousand firms into the finer three-digit industries. In some cases there were only a few firms in each industry. When we used the three-digit industries, we used seventy-three of them, and the median industry contained nine firms.

FIRM SIZE AND RATE OF GROWTH

Table 9.1

NUMBER OF FIRMS IN INDUSTRY AND AVERAGE SIZE OF FIRM IN 1946, BY QUARTILE

S.I.C. CODE NO. AND INDUSTRY*		AVERAGE SIZE OF FIRM ($ MILLIONS)				NO. OF FIRMS IN INDUSTRY
		1ST QUARTILE	2D QUARTILE	3D QUARTILE	4TH QUARTILE	
20	Food and kindred products	126.0	31.9	16.7	9.6	132
22	Textile mill products	69.4	24.0	12.4	8.5	83
26	Paper and allied products	75.4	28.6	12.2	8.7	59
28	Chemicals and allied products	167.1	32.6	16.9	9.1	91
29	Products of petroleum and coal	887.2	240.4	41.0	12.4	41
33	Primary metals industries	357.5	42.0	16.6	8.9	80
34	Fabricated metal products	74.2	19.1	10.5	7.9	59
35	Machinery (except electrical)	84.3	20.7	12.1	8.5	134
37	Transportation equipment	246.0	48.5	19.8	9.9	90

* Electrical machinery excluded because of a computational error.
Source: Firms obtained from United States Federal Trade Commission, *Report on Interlocking Directorates, op. cit.*, Appendix A, pp. 481–97.

Table 9.2

ARITHMETIC AVERAGE OF FIRM GROWTH RATES,* BY QUARTILE, FOR SELECTED TWO-DIGIT INDUSTRIES†

S.I.C. CODE NO. AND INDUSTRY		1ST QUARTILE	2D QUARTILE	3D QUARTILE	4TH QUARTILE
20	Food and kindred products	63	71‡	48	35§
22	Textile mill products	82‡	50	59	37§
26	Paper and allied products	135	151	187‡	116§
28	Chemicals and allied products	106	135‡	127	105§
29	Products of petroleum and coal	154	139	124§	197‡
33	Primary metals industries	117	83§	156	168‡
34	Fabricated metal products	101	73§	107	146‡
35	Machinery (except electrical)	115	122‡	99	68§
36	Electrical machinery	132	120	233‡	117§
37	Transportation equipment	111	92	71§	139‡
	Average of index numbers in quartile (1st quartile = 100)†	100	93	106	98

* Growth rate = (1955 Size/1946 Size) − 100.
† Each quartile mean was expressed as a percentage of the mean of the 1st quartile. An average of the index numbers in each quartile was computed.
‡ Maximum quartile average in industry.
§ Minimum quartile average in industry.
Source: See Table 9.1.

and the third quartiles the pattern is reversed: the mean growth rate increases in six industries and falls in four. Between the third and the fourth quartiles there is again a reversal: the mean growth rate rises in four industries and falls in six. In total, the mean growth rate increases in fourteen cases and decreases in sixteen, suggesting a virtually equal probability of an increase or a decrease. In contrast, Table 9.3 shows that the standard deviation usually increases as we

Table 9.3

STANDARD DEVIATION OF FIRM GROWTH RATES, BY QUARTILE, FOR SELECTED TWO-DIGIT INDUSTRIES*
(Per Cent)

S.I.C. CODE NO. AND INDUSTRY		1ST QUARTILE	2D QUARTILE	3D QUARTILE	4TH QUARTILE
20	Food and kindred products	45†	54	63	86‡
22	Textile mill products	98‡	72	75	68†
26	Paper and allied products	69†	92	135‡	93
28	Chemicals and allied products	71†	94	101	181*
29	Products of petroleum and coal	47†	57	117	221*
33	Primary metals industries	57†	68	184	186*
34	Fabricated metal industries	86	58†	93	135*
35	Machinery (except electrical)	75†	109*	91	90
36	Electrical machinery	99†	183	189‡	146
37	Transportation equipment	83†	111	142	208‡
	Average of index numbers in quartile (1st quartile = 100)*	100	123	172	212

* Each quartile standard deviation was expressed as a percentage of the quartile standard deviation of the first quartile. An average of the index numbers in each quartile was computed.
† Minimum quartile standard deviation in industry.
‡ Maximum quartile standard deviation in industry.
Source: See Table 9.1.

move from the first quartile to the second, from the second to the third, and from the third to the fourth. In all, the standard deviation increases in twenty-three cases and decreases in seven.[8]

It appears that the mean growth rate is not related to the size of firm while the standard deviation of the distribution of growth rates is inversely related to the size of the firm. Our conclusion is a tentative one. There are many objections to the data and our procedures which can be answered only by further tests. We present some further results in the next section. Needless to say, these results have not caused us to reject completely the conclusions we have just presented. Thus, the reader may wish, on first reading, to skip to the section entitled "Theoretical Implication" where we draw some implications from these results.

[8] One might apply an analysis of variance to test for significant differences in the quartile means. But the assumption of equality of quartile variances needed for analysis of variance is not valid.

FURTHER TESTS

The Problem

One of the main drawbacks of our test procedure is that the two-digit classification may be too broad: the aggregation of three-digit industries into the two-digit industries may itself be responsible for our findings. This could happen in a number of ways.

(a) There could be a positive relation between the size of firm and firm growth rate in each three-digit industry. If three-digit industries with predominantly small firms grew more rapidly than did three-digit industries with predominantly large firms, aggregation of these three-digit industries into a two-digit industry could lead to errors. Aggregation could result in there being no relation between size of firm and firm growth rate and an inverse relation between size of firm and the standard deviation of growth rates in the two-digit industry.

(b) There could be no relation between size of firm and firm growth rate in each three-digit industry and no differences between the growth rates of three-digit industries. However, if the variability among firm growth rates were greater in industries with small firms than in industries with large firms, aggregation would generate the observed growth rates of the two-digit industries.

(c) There could be a positive relation between size of firm and firm growth rate in some three-digit industries and an inverse relation in other three-digit industries. Aggregation could obscure these relations and result in there being no relation between size of firm and firm growth rate and an inverse relation between size of firm and the standard deviation of growth rates in the two-digit industry.

(d) There could be no relation between size of firm and firm growth rate in each three-digit industry and no difference between the *mean* of industry growth rates of three-digit industries with small firms and the *mean* of industry growth rates of three-digit industries with large firms. However, if the variability of industry growth rates is greater among industries with small firms than it is among industries with large firms, aggregation could generate the observed distributions of the two-digit industries.

While aggregation may lead to errors, disaggregation can also lead to errors. One serious problem arises from the technical difficulty of separating firms into three-digit industries; this difficulty is quite independent of the inherent theoretical difficulties of defining industries.[9] While some data on the product mixes of firms exist, they are too limited to assure reliable groupings of firms into industries.[10] Because classification is difficult and uncertain, we divided the

---

[9] There is little theoretical guidance on how to define an industry. The theoretical definitions that do exist are all in terms of *products* while the units of study in this paper are firms that produce many products.

[10] We canvassed government publications, annual reports, and registration statements before we classified the firms into three-digit industries.

three-digit industries into two groups according to the degree of confidence we had in the homogeneity of the industry and then ran separate tests on the two groups. Industries were classified as *pure* industries if we were confident of the homogeneity of the product structure of member firms; other industries were classified as *mixed* industries.

We carried out certain tests on the three-digit industry data. The limited number of firms in the three-digit industries forced us to rely on a regression analysis of the relation between the firm growth rate and size of firm and prevented us from studying the relation between size of firm and the standard deviation of growth rates. The form of the regression equation was

$$G_F = a + bS_F + cR_F + dG_I, \quad (9.1)$$

where G_F denotes the growth rate of the firm, and S_F denotes its 1946 assets.[11] R_F is the ratio of the firm's size to the size of the largest firm in the industry and G_I is the industry growth rate.[12]

The industry rate of growth is included to account for differences in rates of growth of three-digit industries and to eliminate the error described in (a). R_F is included to permit comparison of a relatively large firm in an industry typified by small firms with a relatively large firm in an industry typified by large firms. This variable standardizes for differences between industries in the absolute size of firm.

As described in (c), aggregation of three-digit industries could result in the cancellation of a positive relation between size of firm and rate of growth in some industries against an inverse relation in some other industries. To guard against this possibility, industries with a positive relation were separated from industries with an inverse relation. This separation was made by comparing the simple average of the growth rates of firms in the industry and the weighted average growth rate for each industry.[13]

[11] Errors of measurement of initial assets will introduce a downward bias in the coefficients of the size variables.

[12] Common elements in the growth rate of firm and the growth rate of industry will introduce an upward bias in the coefficients of the industry growth rate variable.

We ran this test on the two-digit data as well. For two-digit industries, data on the assets of *all* firms in the industry were available and the industry growth rate was computed from these data (see Federal Trade Commission, Securities and Exchange Commission, *Quarterly Financial Report of All Manufacturing Firms in the United States* [Washington: Government Printing Office], 1st quarter, 1947, and 1st quarter, 1956). When we began this study, reliable estimates of total industry assets of three-digit industries were not available. For each three-digit industry, we summed the assets in 1946 and in 1955 of the firms in our sample, calculated the growth rate of this total, and used it as an estimate of the growth rate of the industry. This is an imperfect measure of the growth rate of the industry. Stigler has recently estimated total assets of three-digit industries throughout the postwar period. It may be possible to rerun some of our tests with these data.

[13] Let A_i represent the ith firm's assets in 1946 and $\overline{A}_i$ represent the ith firm's assets in 1955. The firm growth rate is defined as

$$\left(\frac{\overline{A}_i}{A_i} - 1\right) 100.$$

For an industry, the mean growth rate is defined as

Results

The results of the regression and correlation analyses are presented in Tables 9.4 and 9.5. Separate results are presented for (1) pure and mixed industries, (2) industries in which large firms have grown more rapidly than small firms and industries in which large firms have grown more slowly than small firms, and (3) two-digit and three-digit industries.

The industry growth-rate variable has more explanatory power in the three-digit industry analysis than in the two-digit industry analysis. This shows that it was in fact important to adjust for the growth rate of the three-digit industry.[14]

The regression coefficients of the absolute size variable are usually positive but never statistically significant.[15] The evidence suggests that there have not been significant differences in the growth rates of large and small firms. The regression coefficient of R_F is statistically significant in two of the regressions. But, this variable is not of statistical significance when industries are combined.

We still have to consider the possibility that the inverse relation between the variance of firm growth rates and size of firm disclosed by our two-digit industry analysis is spurious—the result of the aggregation errors. The relation might arise because the variability of *industry growth rates* is greater among industries with small firms than it is among industries with large firms (described above in subsection [d]), or because the variability of *firm growth rates* is greater in industries with small firms than it is in industries with large firms (described above in subsection [b]).

We were able to test only the second possibility. If there is greater variability among firm growth rates in industries with small firms than in industries with large firms, there will be a negative relation between the industry standard deviation and the average size of firm in the industry. Our test consisted of regressing the standard deviation of the three-digit industry on the average size of firm in the three-digit industry. Two other variables were included in the regression equation—the industry concentration ratio and the industry growth rate. We tested the hypothesis that the higher the level of concentration the

$$\frac{\sum_{i}^{N}\left(\frac{\overline{A}_i}{A_i} - 1\right)100}{N}. \tag{9.2}$$

The weighted average growth rate of the industry is defined as

$$\left(\frac{\sum \overline{A}_i}{\sum A_i} - 1\right)100. \tag{9.3}$$

If the weighted average is greater than (9.3), the large firms have grown faster than small firms and vice versa.

[14] The industry growth rate appears to be of little use to an investor who might want to select firms by first determining the industry growth rate. Deciding that the electronics industry will grow more rapidly than another industry still leaves plenty of room for errors in selecting firms within the electronics industry.

[15] Application of conventional tests of significance is not strictly warranted because of the inverse relationship between size of firm and variance of firm growth rates.

Table 9.4

DETERMINANTS OF FIRM GROWTH RATE: CORRELATION ANALYSIS

	SIMPLE* AND PARTIAL CORRELATION† COEFFICIENTS: INDEPENDENT VARIABLES			MULTIPLE CORRELATION COEFFICIENT
	ABSOLUTE SIZE	RELATIVE SIZE	INDUSTRY GROWTH RATE	
Two-digit industries	.049	N.i.‡	.247§	.249§
	.028	N.i.	.244§	
Three-digit industries:				
Industries where small firms grew faster than large firms:				
Pure industries	−.012	−.201§	.473§	.494§
	−.047	−.127	.457§	
Mixed industries	−.061	−.184§	.274§	.301§
	−.055	−.116	.242§	
Industries where small firms grew slower than large firms:				
Pure industries	.230§	.181§	.310§	.399§
	.090	.207§	.314§	
Mixed industries	.136	.210§	.335§	.380§
	.043	.164‖	.317§	
Pure industries combined	.072	−.092	.399§	.400§
	.007	−.032	.380§	
Mixed industries combined	.019	−.026	.266§	.267§
	.015	−.018	.264§	
All three-digit industries combined	.047	−.065	.350§	.351§
	.013	−.026	.339§	

* Top row.
† Bottom row.
‡ "N.i." denotes variable not included.
§ Significant at .05 probability level.
‖ Significant at .01 probability level.
Source: See Table 9.1.

Table 9.5
DETERMINANTS OF FIRM GROWTH RATE: REGRESSION ANALYSIS

	REGRESSION COEFFICIENT* AND STANDARD ERROR†				AVERAGE* AND STANDARD DEVIATION		
	INTERCEPT	ABSOLUTE SIZE	RELATIVE SIZE	INDUSTRY GROWTH RATE	ABSOLUTE SIZE	RELATIVE SIZE	INDUSTRY GROWTH RATE
Two-digit industry	14.59	.00001815 .00002054	— N.i.‡	.8002§ .1008	59,388 165,500	— N.i.	106.1 33.7
Three-digit industry:							
Industries where small firms grew faster than large firms:							
Pure industries	25.17	−.00002193 .00003341	−57.39 32.18	1.1943§ .1672	121,183 292,932	.257 .303	94.4 55.6
Mixed industries	35.55	−.00000517 .00007458	−42.35 24.08	.9267§ .2463	47,621 100,550	.283 .319	97.3 28.2
Industries where small firms grew slower than large firms:							
Pure industries	3.77	.00004837 .00003989	56.70§ 20.02	.4951§ .1115	57,408 166,822	.396 .327	89.6 57.9
Mixed industries	3.08	.00004679 .00007708	56.73‖ 24.33	.6940§ .1482	39,110 87,278	.277 .276	125.1 43.1
Pure industries combined	23.24	.00000366 .00002547	−11.72 19.06	.8466§ .1061	90,383 242,537	.324 .322	92.1 56.8
Mixed industries combined	34.84	.00001674 .00005447	−6.57 17.20	.6986§ .1235	43,681 94,732	.280 .300	110.1 38.5
All industries combined	26.34	.00000766 .00001521	−9.35 8.85	.7924§ .0545	65,567 181,325	.301 .311	101.7 48.8

* Top row.
† Bottom row.
‡ "N.i." denotes variable not included.
§ Significant at .05 probability level.
‖ Significant at .01 probability level.
Source: See Table 9.1.

greater the probability of a market sharing agreement and hence the more probable the equality of firm growth rates. If the hypothesis is correct, we expect to find a negative relation between the concentration ratio and the standard deviation of firm growth rates. We included the industry growth rate to determine if there is greater variability among firm growth rates in more rapidly growing industries.

Table 9.6

DETERMINANTS OF STANDARD DEVIATION OF FIRM GROWTH RATES

A. CORRELATION COEFFICIENTS

	SIMPLE* AND PARTIAL† CORRELATION COEFFICIENTS			MULTIPLE CORRELATION COEFFICIENTS
	INDUSTRY GROWTH RATE	CONCENTRATION RATIO	AVERAGE SIZE OF FIRM	
Two-digit industries	.667‡	N.i.§	N.i.	.667‡
Three-digit industries:				
Pure industries	.441‡	−.035	.171	.491‡
	.456‡	−.238	.114	—
Pure and mixed industries combined	.400‡	−.040	.107	.425‡
	.403‡	−.147	.111	—

B. SIMPLE CORRELATION MATRICES, THREE-DIGIT INDUSTRY

VARIABLE	INDUSTRY GROWTH RATE	CONCENTRATION RATIO	AVERAGE SIZE OF FIRM
Industry growth rate:			
Pure industries	1	.331‖	.324‖
Mixed industries	1	.073	−.053
Pure and mixed industries combined	1	.147	.158
Concentration ratio:			
Pure industries	—	1	.409‡
Mixed industries	—	1	.625‡
Pure and mixed industries combined	—	1	.472‡
Average size of firm:			
Pure industries	—	—	1
Mixed industries	—	—	1
Pure and mixed industries combined	—	—	1

* Top row.
† Bottom row.
‡ Significant at .01 probability level.
§ "N.i." denotes variable not included.
‖ Significant at .05 probability level.
Source: United States Federal Trade Commission, *Report on Interlocking Directorates, op. cit.*, Appendix A, pp. 481–97, and *Concentration in American Industry*, Report of the Subcommittee on Antitrust and Monopoly of the Committee on the Judiciary, U.S. Senate, 85th Cong., 1st sess., pursuant to Sen. Res. 57, pp. 41–62.

Table 9.7

DETERMINANTS OF STANDARD DEVIATION OF FIRM GROWTH RATES: REGRESSION ANALYSIS

	REGRESSION COEFFICIENTS* AND STANDARD ERROR†				AVERAGE* AND STANDARD DEVIATION†		
	INTERCEPT	INDUSTRY GROWTH RATE	CONCEN-TRATION RATIO	AVERAGE SIZE OF FIRM	INDUSTRY GROWTH RATE	CONCEN-TRATION RATIO	AVERAGE SIZE OF FIRM (THOUSANDS)
Two-digit industries	37.04	.598§ .021	N.i.‡ —	N.i. —	106.07 33.72	N.i. —	N.i. —
Three-digit industries:							
Pure industries	60.60	.431§ .139	−46.42 31.10	.00006573 .00009385	89.39 51.78	.484 .239	64,707 79,093
Pure and mixed	59.67	.339§ .092	−30.66 24.59	.00007963 .00008499	100.85 52.80	.426 .221	53,446 64,188

* Top row.
† Bottom row.
‡ "N.i." denotes variable not included.
§ Significant at .01 probability level.

The form of the regression equation was:

$$D = a + b\bar{S} + cG_I + dC, \qquad (9.4)$$

where D is the standard deviation of firm growth rates in the industry, $\bar{S}$ is the *average* size of firm in the industry, G_I is the industry growth rate, and C is the concentration ratio. Separate regressions were run for pure and mixed industries and for two-digit industries. The results are presented in Tables 9.6 and 9.7. These results are interesting for several reasons. The average size of firm is *not* negatively related to the standard deviation of the three-digit industry. Thus, it does not appear that the variability among firm growth rates is greater in three-digit industries with small firms than in three-digit industries with large firms. Second, the standard deviation of firm growth rates seems to be positively related to the industry rate of growth. Also, we can be reasonably sure that the greater variability among the growth rates of small firms in the two-digit industries does not come about because they are in rapidly growing three-digit industries. Inspection of the simple correlation coefficients between the three-digit industry growth rate and the *average size* of firm reveals little association. Consequently, it appears that the greater variability of the growth rates of small firms in the two-digit industries does not arise because small firms are located in three-digit industries with greater risks or because they are in more rapidly growing industries, but simply because of their small size.

The regression coefficient of the concentration ratio has the expected sign but is not statistically significant. This suggests that the reason why the standard deviations are smaller in some of the three-digit industries is not that there are effective market-sharing agreements in these industries.

It is puzzling that the correlation coefficient of the pure industries is only slightly higher than the correlation coefficient of the pure and mixed industries combined, and both are considerably lower than the correlation coefficient of the two-digit industries.[16]

We have not tested to determine whether the inverse relation between size and standard deviation is caused by the greater variability of industry growth rates of industries with small firms than of industries with large firms.

A SUMMARY OF THE RESULTS OF PREVIOUS STUDIES

The results of our tests suggest that no relation existed between size of firm and mean growth rate from 1946 to 1955 and that an inverse relation existed between the size of firm and the standard deviation of firm growth rates.

These results may be compared with the results of some other studies.

1. Simon and Bonini found no relation between the size of firm and the mean rate of growth or between the size of firm and the standard deviation of firm growth rates.[17] The sample included the five hundred largest manufacturing firms (according to sales) and the period of analysis was 1954–56.

---

[16] This result may be due to the use of the "estimated" three-digit industry growth rate rather than the actual (but unobtainable) three-digit industry growth rate.
[17] *Op. cit.*, pp. 607–17.

2. Hart and Prais found no relation between size of firm and mean rate of growth or between the size of firm and the standard deviation of firm growth rates.[18] The sample included firms listed on the London Stock Exchange. The growth rates from 1885 to 1950 were studied.

3. Meyer and Kuh found a negative relation between the size of firm and mean rate of growth and a negative relation between size of firm and variability in growth rates of firms.[19]

4. Adelman found that industrial concentration changes "at the pace of a glacial drift."[20] Since there are usually few changes among the ranks of large firms, and since concentration ratios are stable, it is implied that there is an over-all equality of the growth rates of large and small firms.

5. In separate studies Alexander[21] and McConnell[22] found no relation between mean rate of return and size of firm and an inverse relation between the variability of rate of return and size of firm.

THEORETICAL IMPLICATIONS: INTRODUCTION

We have found that average growth rates are not related to size and that standard deviations of growth rate are inversely related to size. The evidence, limited as it is, warrants further consideration: we now proceed to explore its implications. We believe that the evidence implies falling costs and that the J-shaped distributions of firm sizes of high concentration may well be the result not of chance but of the presence of economies of scale. Our argument rests largely on the rate of decline of the standard deviation. But first we discuss average growth rates.

IMPLICATION OF MEAN GROWTH RATE FOR COST CURVES

Suppose there were internal diseconomies of scale in an industry. Then further expansion of the firm beyond a certain size would lead to higher unit costs and declining profit margins. Ultimately, market forces would curtail the expansion of the large firms in the industry. The large firms would grow more slowly than the industry, and market concentration would decline. The available evidence indicates that, while some such force may be at work in a number of industries, it is not strong enough or pervasive enough for us to accept the frequent existence of important diseconomies.

Suppose that unit costs were constant. There would then be no reason to

---

[18] *Op. cit.*, pp. 150–91.

[19] J. R. Meyer and E. Kuh, *The Investment Decision* (Cambridge, Mass.: Harvard University Press, 1957), pp. 163–65.

[20] Adelman, *op. cit.*, p. 295.

[21] Sidney Alexander, "The Effect of Size of Manufacturing Corporation on the Distribution of the Rate of Return," *Review of Economics and Statistics*, XXXI (August, 1949), 229–35.

[22] Joseph McConnell, "1942 Corporate Profits by Size of Firm," *Survey of Current Business*, January 1946, pp. 10–16.

expect large firms to grow slower or faster on average than small firms. Our data are consistent with constant costs, so we accept this tentatively as a possibility.

For reasons of symmetry, it is tempting to assume that, if cost curves are decreasing, large firms will grow faster than small firms. We believe that this is not necessarily so. Falling unit costs might very well lead to constant growth rates. If growth rates are independent of size one cannot infer whether cost curves are falling or constant. The test does not discriminate, and we must use other means (namely, standard deviations) to tell the difference.

Suppose cost curves are falling and we compare the growth experience of a group of small (high-cost) firms with a group of large (low-cost) firms. Because of their higher unit costs, the small firms would have lower profits. Their survival value would be lower. There would be a tendency for them to be driven out of the industry. Economists would generally explain the size distribution in these terms, and superficially this analysis might suggest that small firms would grow more slowly than large firms. However, this conclusion ignores some offsetting effects. Small firms with high unit costs will have an incentive to expand and to realize further economies of scale, that is, to become one of the large, low-cost firms. If we compare the forces affecting growth rates, we reach the following conclusion. The small firm has a greater probability of decline (because of high unit costs) than does the large firm and at the same time a greater probability of faster growth (because of the incentive to realize cost savings through increased size). The dispersion in growth rates should be higher for the small firm than for the large one, but there is no reason to expect that the average growth rates would differ. They could differ, depending on how these effects balance out, but they need not. One cannot say that the lack of a relation between size and growth rates eliminates the possibility of declining costs. It is consistent with declining costs as well as with constant costs.

This argument does not differ substantially from the usual one. If costs are falling, the industry will soon be dominated by a large firm or a few large firms. But as long as the adjustment to changing equilibrium positions is slow and growth is not dominated completely by costs—that is, as long as there is uncertainty, product differentiation, oligopoly—we can conceive of firms of different costs existing side by side in the industry during a period of adjustment. The large firms with their lower unit costs will withstand adverse conditions better and will have a higher survivor value. A few, through bad judgment or misjudgment, will decline and drop out of the industry. But most of the large firms will do as well as the industry. Among the small, high-cost firms, some will succeed and become large, and others will fail. Average growth rates need not differ; however, standard deviations should differ. This is our version of the trees in the forest analogy when the representative firm has falling costs.[23]

---

[23] We have decided the implications of the case of declining variance but constant average. What if we had found declining variance combined with large firms growing faster than small firms? Our hunch is that this would strengthen the case of economies of scale. But what if we had found declining variance and large firms growing more slowly than small firms? We would be at a loss to explain this in any simple fashion.

IMPLICATIONS OF DECREASING STANDARD DEVIATIONS

We have concluded that the observed equality of average growth rates rules out the possibility of increasing unit costs but does not discriminate completely between constant and decreasing unit costs.

Suppose that average costs are constant *no matter how small the firm*. The average growth rates should not then be different for large and small firms. What about the standard deviations? The argument for differing standard deviations presented above—namely, that small firms have a greater inclination for either extreme growth or extreme decline—does not apply here because costs are the same. There is, however, another reason why standard deviations might decline. The larger firm may be large because it operates in more markets than does the small firm. It may then be more diversified: its bad fortunes in one market may be offset by its good fortunes in another and it may be more stable than a small firm. If this were true, standard deviations would decline with increasing size.

While this argument is plausible, it does not apply in this case because of the extreme assumption we have made about costs. We have assumed that unit costs are constant, no matter how small the firm. This means that a small firm can achieve the same diversification as a large firm, for it can divide into as many parts as it wants without incurring any cost disadvantage. It can therefore enter as many markets and achieve as much diversification as it wants. Standard deviations would then be the same for firms in all size classes, including the largest size classes. Our results suggest that the standard deviations decline in the largest size classes, so we reject the assumption of constant costs. This is not a very important conclusion because few would ever assume that costs were constant, no matter how small the firm. It would be usual instead to assume a critical minimum size, after which unit costs are constant. We argue that the declining standard deviations pattern we observe suggests not a *falling and eventually leveling out* cost curve but a *continuously falling* curve.

Let us assume there is a certain critical minimum size after which unit costs are constant. And let us make a second crucial assumption: we suppose a large firm to be merely a collection of *independent* small firms of the critical minimum size. In other words, we assume that a large firm is essentially a holding company operating independent divisions. We now show that these two assumptions lead to conclusions inconsistent with the empirical results we have obtained and therefore that at least one of them must be wrong.

A large firm has the same average costs as a small firm, but it is able to achieve more diversification than a small firm. A small firm is prevented from diversifying because of the requirement of a critical minimum size. Because large firms are able to diversify, their growth rates will have less variability (smaller standard deviations) than do the growth rates of small firms. Not only can we conclude this, but by an elementary theorem in statistics we can predict *exactly* the decline in standard deviation that will result. The large firm is now a large sample of small firms. The standard deviation of the mean of large samples is $1/\sqrt{n}$ times the standard deviation of the population where n is the size of sample. In this problem the critical minimum size of firm is the unit of the population, while n, the size of the sample, is the number of small firms needed to make one large firm.[24]

We can now test to see whether the *actual* standard deviations decline in accordance with the $1/\sqrt{n}$ rule (which we will call the *predicted* standard deviation). If it does not, then one of our two assumptions—critical minimum size or independence—is not valid. Table 9.8 presents the ratio of the actual standard

Table 9.8

RATIO OF ACTUAL STANDARD DEVIATION TO PREDICTED STANDARD DEVIATION FOR SELECTED TWO-DIGIT INDUSTRIES

INDUSTRY	1ST QUARTILE	2D QUARTILE	3D QUARTILE	4TH QUARTILE
Food	1.83	1.09	.92	1.00
Textiles	4.12	1.77	1.33	1.00
Paper	2.17	1.59	1.74	1.00
Chemicals	1.68	.98	.78	1.00
Petroleum	1.76	1.10	.96	1.00
Primary metals	1.96	.81	1.35	1.00
Fabricated metals	1.95	.66	.76	1.00
Machinery (except electrical)	2.57	1.87	1.20	1.00
Electrical machinery	3.27	1.83	1.48	1.00
Transportation	1.97	1.16	.95	1.00
Average	2.33	1.29	1.15	1.00

Source: Actual standard deviations, Table 9.5.

Predicted standard deviation of qth quartile = $\dfrac{\text{Standard deviation of 4th quartile}}{\sqrt{n}}$.

$n = \dfrac{\text{Average size of firm in } q\text{th quartile}}{\text{Average size of firm in 4th quartile}}$.

deviation of the predicted standard deviation for each quartile.[25] The ratios are usually greater than 1.00. This means that the actual standard deviations are greater than the predicted standard deviations.[26] Therefore, the large firms in our sample are in one sense *more* risky than the small firms in the sample. This, in turn, implies that they are not collections of independent firms but that their divisions are related. They may be related in two separate ways.

[24] While these firms are called small, they are only small relative to other firms in the industry. The average asset size of firm in the fourth quartile *in 1946* was about eight million dollars and in the third quartile about fifteen million dollars.

[25] The selection of the critical minimum size is not a troublesome problem. The theory maintains that the standard deviation of any two sets of samples will be in inverse proportion to the square root of the sample size. For convenience of presentation we use the small firms of the fourth quartile.

[26] What is particularly puzzling is the increase in the ratio. While we would expect the ratio to be greater than one, we would expect the ratio to be smaller the larger the size of firm, if further economies from increasing size became smaller and smaller.

1. They may be related through economies of scale: the firm cannot be subdivided into units because unit costs would rise. Then, assumption 1—that cost curves decline at first and become flat at the critical minimum size—must be rejected and the assumption that costs decline *continually* for firms above the critical minimum size must be accepted.
2. The other possibility is that the units are not independent for reasons other than economies of scale. If so, an investor, by picking a random sample of small firms instead of one large firm, can obtain the same average performance and lower variability. Unless individuals are unconcerned about variance, the large firm would be less likely to survive under these conditions. It would have to be more profitable in order to survive. We have by hypothesis ruled out lower costs (economies of scale); hence, the profits must come from some imperfection of the demand side. It may arise from some temporary or permanent monopoly position of the larger firms which offsets the relatively greater variability in the growth rates of large firms. This is a possibility and, if accepted, would indicate that our conclusion of continuing economies of scale is unjustified.

CONCLUSIONS

This analysis leads to the following conclusion: either there are continual economies of scale with increasing size; or large firms are able to secure temporary or permanent monopoly returns but small firms are not. This conclusion is at variance with the conclusions reached in other studies. We recognize, however, that our conclusion is necessarily tentative. Our theory, though intuitively appealing, is open to several criticisms, and the empirical results on which it rests are limited.[27]

The Simon-Bonini model could be modified to conform with the 1946–55 results. This modified Simon-Bonini model could be used to generate predictions of the size distribution of firms and to determine whether they fit the actual distribution more closely than do the predictions of the Simon-Bonini model.

[27] Some further tests can be conducted. We have argued that the large firms are "inefficient" in the sense that the variability of the growth rates of the large firms was greater than the variability of the growth rates of a sample of small firms. We would expect the market to place a higher value on the shares of small firms per dollar of earnings than it places on the shares of large firms.

PART III

PRICING BEHAVIOR

The four papers comprising Part III illuminate some of the main determinants of firms' pricing behavior, apart from cost conditions and firms' objectives. G. C. Archibald emphasizes that the different equilibrium price-marginal cost relationships associated with the market types of conventional price theory do not depend on differences in the number of firms in each market situation. They depend instead on the belief about the policy of its rivals attributed to an individual firm in each market situation. Price behavior which equates the price and marginal cost of a product, usually associated with the analytical model of pure competition, is quite compatible with a small number of competing firms. Similarly, monopoly pricing can arise in an industry composed of a large number of firms despite the absence of collusion, provided that each individual firm makes the appropriate assumption about its rivals' reactions.

There are persuasive a priori reasons why the number of firms in an industry might influence the nature of each firm's expectations about the reactions of other firms to its own policies and therefore affect the firm's behavior. A firm's rivals will react to its policies only if they are aware of its actions. Information about a firm's actions may be transmitted to other firms by the resulting variations in the sales of those firms. Other things being equal, the larger the number of firms operating in the same industry, the smaller the sales variation experienced by an individual firm as a result of another firm's actions. If the detection of rivals' actions become more difficult with increases in the number of firms in an industry, this may affect the expectations, and therefore the behavior, of individual firms in the industry. However, as G. J. Stigler's paper emphasizes, the ability of firms to detect rivals' moves depends on other variables in addition to the number of firms selling in the same market.

The review article by Modigliani analyzes the relationship between entry barriers and industry pricing. Entry barriers are obstacles confronting a firm which is considering whether or not to produce a particular product or service. Conventional price theory indicates that the price charged for the product of an industry characterized by absence of entry barriers cannot, in the long run, exceed the unit cost of production (including normal profits). If entry barriers exist, it is argued that price cannot in the long run exceed unit cost by more than the "height" of these barriers. More recently a number of economists have argued that the threat of potential entry may affect the price charged by firms already established in an industry and preserve the aforementioned relationship even in the short run and despite the absence of actual entry. If valid, this line of reasoning elevates entry barriers, and in particular their height, to a position of great importance in determining price and output patterns in the economy as a whole.

The article by Modigliani is particularly useful in focusing attention on the behavioral assumptions, which must be attributed to potential entrants and established firms in order to validate the preceding propositions, and in emphasizing that in order to derive any conclusions concerning the behavior of potential entrants or established firms, it is necessary to make some assumptions about the reactions anticipated by the firms when formulating their policies. The behavior of potential entrants, for example, depends on their expectations regarding the post-entry behavior of established firms, because the anticipated reaction of established firms to entry determines the anticipated post-entry demand conditions facing the potential entrant. These demand conditions, together with the entrant's cost conditions, determine the anticipated profitability of entry from the entrant's point of view and therefore determine whether or not he will enter the industry. Again, the behavior of firms already established in a particular industry depends on their expectations regarding the reactions of potential entrants to established firms' policies, while the effect of actual entry on industry price and output levels depends on individual firms' anticipations concerning rivals' behavior after entry has occurred.

Entry theory can be viewed as a special case of the analysis of oligopoly in conventional price theory. Oligopoly deals with situations in which a firm's behavior is influenced by its expectations regarding the behavior of other firms already producing the same product. Similarly, the behavior of potential entrants depends on their expectations about the reaction of firms already producing the product to entry. As for the effect of potential entry on the behavior of established firms, entry theory merely extends the number of firms considered by established firms in their policy-making and includes firms not already in the industry who may react to the established firms' policies by entering the industry. However, whereas the behavior of potential entrants depends on how they expect established firms to react to entry, the behavior of established firms depends on how established firms *think* potential entrants expect them to react to entry.

Although theoretical considerations suggest that firms' pricing behavior will be influenced by entry barriers and the number and size distribution of firms selling a particular product, whether this is the case in practice can only be determined by empirical investigation of the relationship between pricing and the various possible operational measures of the relevant variables. The task of empirical verification is complicated by the fact that a priori analysis indicates that entry barriers and seller concentration are each capable of influencing industry pricing independently. The paper by H. M. Mann is an empirical study of the relationship between seller concentration, entry barriers, and rates of return in thirty industries in the United States for the period 1950–1960. Mann points out that although the evidence is consistent with the predictions of a priori analysis, rates of return may be inadequate indicators of price-cost margins, and the results of the study are entirely dependent on the particular operational measures chosen to represent the variables being investigated.

10
"Large" and "Small" Numbers in the Theory of the Firm[1]

G. C. Archibald

The problem of group or industry equilibrium is commonly divided into a "large numbers" case and a "small numbers" case. The large numbers case is again subdivided into two: perfect competition and the large numbers case of Chamberlin. It is argued here that what matters to the analysis is not the (arithmetic) number of firms, but the beliefs about the policy of the rival(s) attributed to the individual firm. Number may be relevant as a test of the appropriateness of the beliefs attributed, but number itself is analytically irrelevant, and the distinction in terms of number alone is misleading. To illustrate this we shall consider first the analysis of Cournot and Chamberlin, and then the case of perfect competition. It will be shown that there is no *analytical* distinction between the Cournot solution in the case of two firms and the Chamberlin solution in the case of "many" firms because the same beliefs about the reaction of the rival(s), and hence the same behaviour, are attributed to the individual firm in each case. Not only the analytical tools but also *the equilibrium conditions* are identical. The argument is simply that, if the individual firm is assumed to believe that the price or output of its rival(s) remains constant, its behavior is independent of whether its rival is supposed to be one firm or many. We then go on to

Reprinted from *The Manchester School of Economics and Social Studies*, 1959, pp. 104–109 by permission of the author and publisher.

[1] The proposition discussed here appears rather obvious, and is mainly of scholastic interest. I discovered it while endeavouring to simplify the analysis for presentation in lectures, and offer it now merely because it does not appear to be generally known. I am indebted to Professor H. G. Johnson, Mr. K. Klappholz, and Dr. R. G. Lipsey for their comments and criticisms.

show that the distinction between a "large numbers" group and a perfectly competitive group similarly depends, not on numbers, but on the beliefs attributed to the firms.

There is a subsidiary problem to clear up: the definition of a Chamberlin group in the large numbers case, which is well-known to be difficult if the product is differentiated. In the case of non-homogeneity, the concept of an "equal price change" is ambiguous, and so, therefore, is the "share-of-the-market" demand curve, the DD' of Chamberlin's analysis. Non-homogeneity also makes the concept of "equal costs" ambiguous or even meaningless. And non-homogeneity, of course, makes it difficult, or even impossible, to mark off analytically the boundaries of the group. Hence, in order to make Chamberlin's analytical apparatus *work* in the large numbers case, and to obtain the tangency solution with the aid of the "share-of-the-market" and "particular" demand curves, it is necessary to assume a homogeneous product.[2] It is now also necessary to assume that firms adjust quantity rather than price. If this is not done, then in the large number case the demand for the product of each firm is infinitely elastic up to the total quantity which will be taken by the market at each price, and, for further individual price cutting, coincides with the total market demand curve. Thus in order to obtain the "share-of-the-market" and "particular" demand curves of Chamberlin, we must assume that the product is homogeneous, and that each firm adjusts quantity, accepting the new price, instead of quoting a new price itself.

Given, then, that these assumptions are necessary in order to make Chamberlin's analysis of the "large numbers" case work, we can show that it does not differ from Cournot's analysis of the "small numbers" case. In the Cournot case, illustrated in Figure 10.1, we have two firms and a homogeneous product. We assume for simplicity a linear total market demand curve, D_T, and constant marginal costs, identical for each firm. If the two firms charge the same price, sales are equally divided between them.[3] Suppose that each firm is producing OM and that price is MQ. If both increase output by MN, total output increases to $OL\ (=2ON)$, and the price that clears the market is OB. But each firm is to assume the output of the other constant at OM. If firm 'A' increases output to ON, it expects total output to be $OZ\ (=OM+ON)$, and price to be OE. Hence each expects to reach the position P, each increases output by MN, and each actually reaches the position C. Q, C, are, of course, points on the curve $\frac{1}{2}D_T$: QC is thus the "share-of-the-market" demand curve or DD', of Chamberlin. Q, P, are points on the curve $D_T - OM$, expected sales on the assumption that the other's output is constant: QP is thus the "particular" demand curve, or dd', of Chamberlin. And, as in Chamberlin's analysis, dd' "slides down" DD': both firms increase output, hoping to reach P, and in fact reach C; through C there passes a dd' curve CV, so that both now expect to reach V, and in fact reach G on DD' with total output OT. If each firm endeavors to maximize profits on the

[2] The group we obtain is not the group assumed by Chamberlin; but it is the group we require for Chamberlin's analysis.

[3] If the product is homogeneous and the market perfect, demand is presumably divided between sellers at random. Analytical convenience requires that we assume the division of sales to be exactly fifty-fifty.

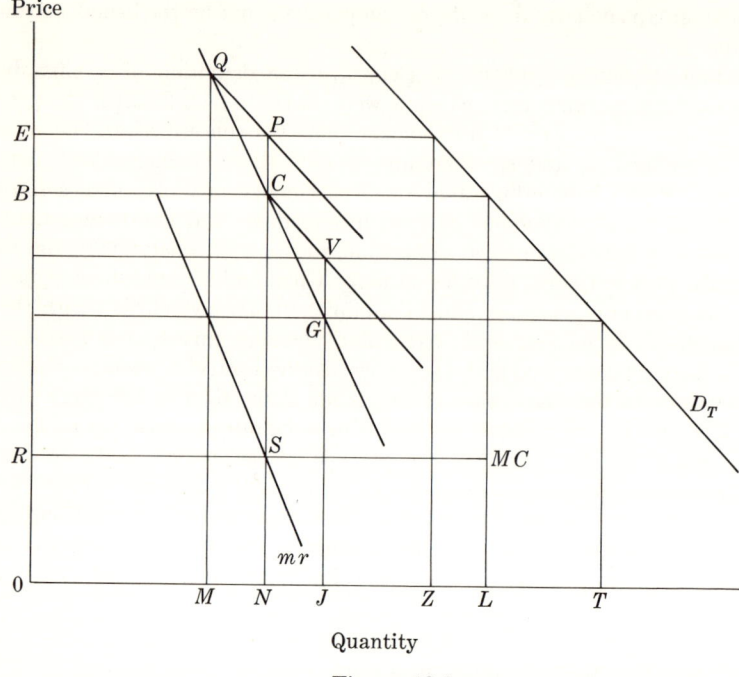

Figure 10.1

assumption that rival's output is constant, each firm continues to increase output from any position such as Q or C so long as the marginal revenue to the dd' curve through that point exceeds marginal cost. Thus if, in Figure 10.1, marginal cost is constant at OR, and mr is the marginal revenue curve to CV, cutting mc in S at output ON, C is a position of equilibrium, obviously consistent with any level of (positive or negative) profits. This equilibrium is given by the cost curves, the "share-of-the-market" demand curve QCG, and the particular assumption about behavior. It is the short-run equilibrium of Chamberlin's group. In the long run we may alter QCG by changing the number of firms as easily in the case in which there are originally "two" as in the case in which there are originally "many." And, if we choose normal profits as a long-run equilibrium condition, we can obtain a tangency solution for *any* original number of firms.[4]

Thus there is no analytical difference between the Cournot duopoly case and Chamberlin's large numbers. The results are in both cases obtained by attributing to the individual firm the same belief about the behavior of the other(s), and so deriving the same policy, and the same equilibrium conditions. Given homogeneity, and the Cournot-Chamberlin assumption that each firm assumes the other(s) to be paralysed, the number of others makes no difference to the analysis.

[4] There is the difficulty that, if the original number of firms is "small," DD' will move in "large" discontinuous jumps when their number alters.

We have been considering groups of firms producing a homogeneous product, and selling in a perfect market. An obvious question is how, if at all, a "large" group is to be distinguished from a perfectly competitive group. The answer once again depends, not upon members, but upon the beliefs attributed to the firms. We cannot, that is, proceed from a Cournot-Chamberlin group to perfect competition merely by increasing the number of firms. We shall now see how the assumptions must be changed to obtain perfect competition.

Consider the linear-demand duopoly case analysed above. If the market demand function is $p = a - nx$, the particular demand for the product of firm 'A' is $p = a - nx_a - nx_b$, which, when nx_b is assumed constant,[5] can be written $p = k - nx_a$. It is obviously immaterial what number of firms is deemed to contribute its output to k; and the slope of the particular demand curve is n whatever the size of k. Thus we cannot obtain the horizontal demand curve of perfect competition by altering the size of k or the number of firms sharing it. So long as the firm's particular demand curve is constructed by assuming the output of the rivals' constant, and subtracting that constant from the market demand, the slope of the particular curve is necessarily that of the market curve. While the slope of the particular demand curve cannot be altered by changing numbers, however, its elasticity can be, and can be made to approach infinity. This apparent paradox is easily shown and easily resolved.[6] The elasticity of the market demand curve is

$$\eta = \frac{a - nx}{nx};$$

and the elasticity of 'A' 's particular demand curve is

$$\eta_a = \frac{a - nx}{nx_a}.$$

Define 'A' 's share of the market as $S_a = \frac{x_a}{x}$, and

$$\eta_a \cdot S_a = \frac{a - nx}{nx_a} \cdot \frac{x_a}{x} = \frac{a - nx}{nx} = \eta.$$

Thus $\eta_a = \frac{\eta}{S_a}$, and, as the number of firms increases, S_a ('A' 's share) approaches zero, so η_a (the elasticity of 'A' 's particular demand curve) approaches infinity. Thus we have, in the limit, the infinite elasticity of perfect competition, but not the horizontal slope.

The explanation of this apparent paradox is simply that the elasticity is the product of (the reciprocal of) the slope and the ratio of price to quantity, and that we can get it to infinity as easily by altering the latter as the former. When we change the number of firms without altering the construction of the particular

---

[5] We may complete the usual solution of the Cournot case as follows: assuming x_b to be a constant, total revenue for firm 'A' is $px_a = ax_a - nx^2_a - nx_ax_b$, and expected marginal revenue is $a - 2nx_a - nx_b$, which may be put equal to marginal cost. Expected marginal revenue for firm 'B' is analogously $a - 2nx_b - nx_a$.

[6] On this point I am particularly indebted to Professor H. G. Johnson.

demand curve, this is all we do: we move the curve bodily without altering its slope. In the limit the intercept of the curve with the vertical axis takes place at the price at which elasticity is measured, and elasticity is consequently infinity (if S_a is to approach zero without total output approaching infinity, 'A' 's output must approach zero).

It follows, then, that so long as the group is selling a homogeneous product in a perfect market, no alteration in the size of the group alters the analysis. To obtain the horizontal demand curve of perfect competition we must drop the Cournot-Chamberlin assumption. We require instead the explicit assumption that the firm believes that changes in its output do not alter price. Between the limits of a single firm and an infinite number of firms, changes in number alone mark off no divisions or subdivisions for separate analysis.

ADDENDUM [7]

In this note it will be argued that the theory of duopoly presented in Archibald's Figure 10.1 is a variant of Cournot's, that in any case its exposition stands in need of correction at some points, and, finally, that Archibald's purpose could, perhaps, have been better served by comparing a price-variation version of duopoly with Chamberlin's large group. It should be stressed, however, that these observations in no way qualify Archibald's contention that "number itself is analytically irrelevant."

Identification of the Model

In Archibald's Figure 10.1 the firms are assumed to make their moves simultaneously. Thus, in the first period both increase their output by MN, and in the second period by NJ, and so on, in what appears as a Chamberlinian "slide." Simultaneous "plays" are also a feature of Chamberlin's dynamic adjustment process in his large group analysis. Cournot, however, assumed alternating moves, as is apparent in the adjustment process demonstrated in his "reaction curve" diagram.[8]

The assumption of simultaneous moves combined with the assumption of a homogeneous product makes it necessary to make a further assumption about the division of the market between the two firms in a situation where both set the same price and either could supply the whole market at that price. Archibald opts, reasonably enough, for equal shares. This combination of assumptions gives a starting point somewhere on the $QCG = \frac{1}{2}D_T$ curve in his diagram. The ex post position of each firm remains on this curve after each move. In contrast, in Cournot's model the firms produce different outputs in each period (except in equilibrium).

[7] The inclusion of this addendum follows an enjoyable correspondence with Professor Archibald and his generous suggestion that my points be summarized in this form rather than in footnotes to his reprinted article. I am grateful to Professor F. G. Davidson for helpful comments.

[8] A. Cournot, *Researches into the Mathematical Principles of the Theory of Wealth*, translated from the original French by Nathaniel T. Bacon (1897).

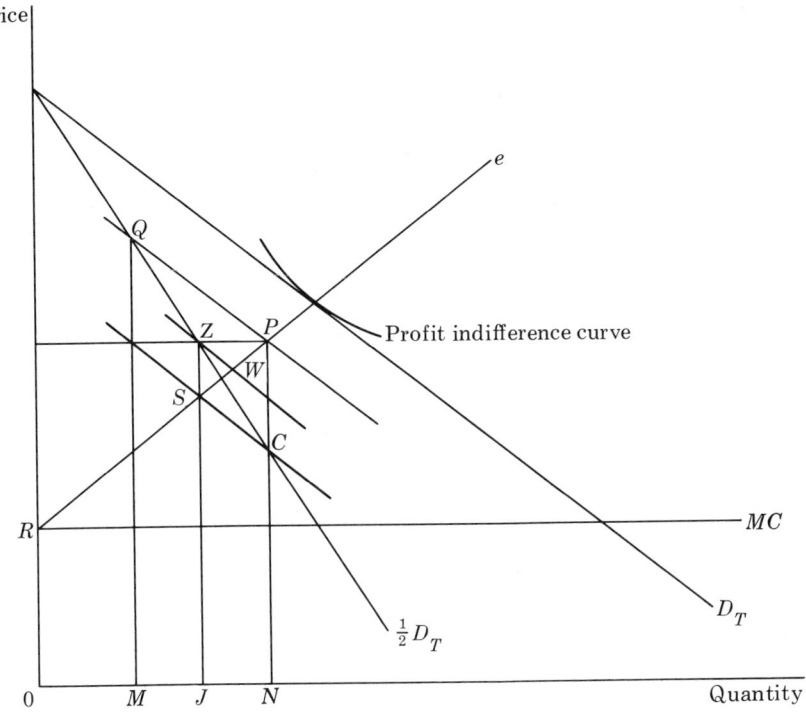

Figure 10.2

The Workings of the Model

In Archibald's model a downward price slide occurs; in Cournot's, a damped oscillation of price. In Archibald's model the (identical) outputs of the firms "slide" upward to the equilibrium level; in Cournot's the output of the firm having the first move will approach the equilibrium level asymptotically from above, and that of the second firm asymptotically from below.[9] When the Archibald-Cournot model is correctly analysed, the Chamberlin-style price slide disappears here also. The simplest way of demonstrating this is to introduce into

[9] For a clear exposition of these properties of the Cournot model see Cliff Lloyd, *Microeconomic Analysis* (1967), p. 201 ff.

Archibald's diagram, here reconstructed as Figure 10.2, a set of isoprofit contours. Because of the assumption that marginal cost is constant, these will be rectangular hyperboles asymptotic to MC and the vertical axis and with origin R. The profit expansion path for the set of all straight-line "particular" demand curves with the slope of D_T is the ray R_e. This must be so if P is to be the maximum ex ante profit point on the particular demand curve QP. But if both firms, in trying to reach P, actually reach C, their next move must involve not an expansion of output and a slide down $\frac{1}{2}D_T$ but a *contraction* of output. For, from vantage point C, both firms see their ex ante profits maximized by the move to S. The effect of their identical reductions in output by JN is to shift their ex post position upward along $\frac{1}{2}D_T$ to Z, vertically above S. From Z the desired point for both firms is W, which involves an expansion of output, and so on. Equilibrium will be reached at the intersection of $\frac{1}{2}D_T$ and R_e. The dynamic adjustment process involves damped oscillations of firm and industry outputs, and also damped price oscillations.

An Alternative Approach

If we wish to compare Chamberlin's analysis with a theory of duopoly which *does* produce a "Chamberlinian slide," we can use Bertrand's price-variation version of Cournot.[10] In a situation where each firm sells the same product, and each sets his price on the assumption that his rival's price will not be changed in response to a change in his own, we can, with alternating moves, produce a competitive price war with each rival successively undercutting the other. With the further assumptions of simultaneous moves and 50/50 percentage market shares, we can turn the process for each firm into an identical slide of a horizontal particular demand curve down a share-of-the-market demand curve. In each period each firm's actual sales will be given by the share-of-the-market demand curve.

To obtain Chamberlin's large group model from this simultaneous version of the Bertrand price-war model all we have to do is introduce product differentiation (which tilts the particular demand curve), relabel the share-of-the-market demand curve $\frac{1}{n}D_T$, where n is "large," and, for the tangency result, insert a U-shaped average cost curve. Clearly, if $n = 2$, no essential analytical features of Chamberlin's model are affected.

La Trobe University, Victoria, Australia —L. Roy Webb
School of Social Sciences

[10] J. Bertrand, in a review of Cournot in *Journal des Savants,* 1883, p. 503. For a discussion of Bertrand-style "competitive bidding" see E. H. Chamberlin, *The Theory of Monopolistic Competition* (Cambridge, Mass., 1932 and later editions), chap. 3, section 3.

11
A Theory of Oligopoly

George J. Stigler[1]

No one has the right, and few the ability, to lure economists into reading another article on oligopoly theory without some advance indication of its alleged contribution. The present paper accepts the hypothesis that oligopolists wish to collude to maximize joint profits. It seeks to reconcile this wish with facts, such as that collusion is impossible for many firms and collusion is much more effective in some circumstances than in others. The reconciliation is found in the problem of policing a collusive agreement, which proves to be a problem in the theory of information. A considerable number of implications of the theory are discussed, and a modest amount of empirical evidence is presented.

THE TASK OF COLLUSION

A satisfactory theory of oligopoly cannot begin with assumptions concerning the way in which each firm views its interdependence with its rivals. If we adhere to the traditional theory of profit-maximizing enterprises, then behavior is no longer something to be assumed but rather something to be deduced. The firms in an industry will behave in such a way, given the demand-and-supply functions (including those of rivals), that their profits will be maximized.

The combined profits of the entire set of firms in an industry are maximized when they act together as a monopolist. At least in the traditional formulation of

Reprinted from *Journal of Political Economy* (February 1964), by permission of The University of Chicago Press. Copyright, 1964, pp. 44-61.

[1] I am indebted to Claire Friedland for the statistical work and to Harry Johnson for helpful criticisms.

the oligopoly problem, in which there are no major uncertainties as to the profit-maximizing output and price at any time, this familiar conclusion seems inescapable. Moreover, the result holds for any number of firms.

Our modification of this theory consists simply in presenting a systematic account of the factors governing the feasibility of collusion, which like most things in this world is not free. Before we do so, it is desirable to look somewhat critically at the concept of homogeneity of products, and what it implies for profit-maximizing. We shall show that collusion normally involves much more than "the" price.

Homogeneity is commonly defined in terms of identity of products or of (what is presumed to be equivalent) pairs of products between which the elasticity of substitution is infinite. On either definition it is the behavior of buyers that is decisive. Yet it should be obvious that products may be identical to any or every buyer while buyers may be quite different from the viewpoint of sellers.

This fact that every transaction involves two parties is something that economists do not easily forget. One would therefore expect a definition of homogeneity also to be two-sided: if the products are what sellers offer, and the purchase commitments are what the buyers offer, full homogeneity clearly involves infinite elasticities of substitution between both products and purchase commitments. In other words, two products are homogeneous to a buyer if he is indifferent between all combinations of x of one and (say) $20 - x$ of the other, at a common price. Two purchase commitments are homogeneous to a seller if he is indifferent between all combinations of y of one and (say) $20 - y$ of the other, at a common price. Full homogeneity is then defined as homogeneity both in products (sellers) and purchase commitments (buyers).

The heterogeneity of purchase commitments (buyers), however, is surely often at least as large as that of products within an industry, and sometimes vastly larger. There is the same sort of personal differentia of buyers as of sellers—ease in making sales, promptness of payment, penchant for returning goods, likelihood of buying again (or buying other products). In addition there are two differences among buyers which are pervasive and well recognized in economics:

1. The size of purchase, with large differences in costs of providing lots of different size.
2. The urgency of purchase, with possibly sufficient differences in elasticity of demand to invite price discrimination.

It is one thing to assert that no important market has homogeneous transactions, and quite another to measure the extent of the heterogeneity. In a regime of perfect knowledge, it would be possible to measure heterogeneity by the variance of prices in transactions; in a regime of imperfect knowledge, there will be dispersion of prices even with transaction homogeneity.[2]

The relevance of heterogeneity to collusion is this: It is part of the task of maximizing industry profits to employ a price structure that takes account of the larger differences in the costs of various classes of transactions. Even with a

---

[2] Unless one defines heterogeneity of transactions to include also differences in luck in finding low price sellers; see my "Economics of Information," *Journal of Political Economy,* June, 1961.

single, physically homogeneous product the profits will be reduced if differences among buyers are ignored. A simple illustration of this fact is given in the Appendix; disregard of differences among buyers proves to be equivalent to imposing an excise tax upon them, but one which is not collected by the monopolist. A price structure of some complexity will usually be the goal of collusive oligopolists.

THE METHODS OF COLLUSION

Collusion of firms can take many forms, of which the most comprehensive is outright merger. Often merger will be inappropriate, however, because of diseconomies of scale,[3] and at certain times and places it may be forbidden by law. Only less comprehensive is the cartel with a joint sales agency, which again has economic limitations—it is ill suited to custom work and creates serious administrative costs in achieving quality standards, cost reductions, product innovations, etc. In deference to American antitrust policy, we shall assume that the collusion takes the form of joint determination of outputs and prices by ostensibly independent firms, but we shall not take account of the effects of the legal prohibitions until later. Oligopoly existed before 1890, and has existed in countries that have never had an antitrust policy.

The colluding firms must agree upon the price structure appropriate to the transaction classes which they are prepared to recognize. A complete profit-maximizing price structure may have almost infinitely numerous price classes: the firms will have to decide upon the number of price classes in the light of the costs and returns from tailoring prices to the diversity of transactions. We have already indicated by hypothetical example (see Appendix I) that there are net profits to be obtained by catering to differences in transactions. The level of collusive prices will also depend upon the conditions of entry into the industry as well as upon the elasticities of demand.

Let us assume that the collusion has been effected, and a price structure agreed upon. It is a well-established proposition that if any member of the agreement can secretly violate it, he will gain larger profits than by conforming to it.[4] It is, moreover, surely one of the axioms of human behavior that all agreements whose violation would be profitable to the violator must be enforced. The literature of collusive agreements, ranging from the pools of the 1880's to the electrical conspiracies of recent times, is replete with instances of the collapse of conspiracies because of "secret" price-cutting. This literature is biased: conspiracies that are successful in avoiding an amount of price-cutting which leads to collapse of the agreement are less likely to be reported or detected. But no conspiracy can neglect the problem of enforcement.

Enforcement consists basically of detecting significant deviations from the agreed-upon prices. Once detected, the deviations will tend to disappear because they are no longer secret and will be matched by fellow conspirators if they are

---

[3] If the firms are multiproduct, with different product structures, the diseconomies of merger are not strictly those of scale (in any output) but of firm size measured either absolutely or in terms of variety of products.

[4] If price is above marginal cost, marginal revenue will be only slightly less than price (and hence above marginal cost) for price cuts by this one seller.

not withdrawn. If the enforcement is weak, however—if price-cutting is detected only slowly and incompletely—the conspiracy must recognize its weakness: it must set prices not much above the competitive level so the inducements to price-cutting are small, or it must restrict the conspiracy to areas in which enforcement can be made efficient.

Fixing market shares is probably the most efficient of all methods of combating secret price reductions. No one can profit from price-cutting if he is moving along the industry demand curve,[5] once a maximum profit price has been chosen. With inspection of output and an appropriate formula for redistribution of gains and losses from departures from quotas, the incentive to secret price-cutting is eliminated. Unless inspection of output is costly or ineffective (as with services), this is the ideal method of enforcement, and is widely used by legal cartels. Unfortunately for oligopolists, it is usually an easy form of collusion to detect, for it may require side payments among firms and it leaves indelible traces in the output records.

Almost as efficient a method of eliminating secret price-cutting is to assign each buyer to a single seller. If this can be done for all buyers, short-run price-cutting no longer has any purpose. Long-run price-cutting will still be a serious possibility if the buyers are in competition: lower prices to one's own customers can then lead to an expansion of their share of their market, so the price-cutter's long-run demand curve will be more elastic than that of the industry. Long-run price-cutting is likely to be important, however, only where sellers are providing a major cost component to the buyer.

There are real difficulties of other sorts to the sellers in the assignment of buyers. In general the fortunes of the various sellers will differ greatly over time: one seller's customers may grow threefold, while another seller's customers shrink by half. If the customers have uncorrelated fluctuations in demand, the various sellers will experience large changes in relative outputs in the short run.[6] Where the turnover of buyers is large, the method is simply impracticable.

Nevertheless, the conditions appropriate to the assignment of customers will exist in certain industries, and in particular the geographical division of the market has often been employed. Since an allocation of buyers is an obvious and easily detectible violation of the Sherman Act, we may again infer that an efficient method of enforcing a price agreement is excluded by the anti-trust laws. We therefore turn to other techniques of enforcement, but we shall find that the analysis returns to allocation of buyers.

In general the policing of a price agreement involves an audit of the transactions prices. In the absence or violation of antitrust laws, actual inspection of the accounting records of sellers has been employed by some colluding groups, but even this inspection gives only limited assurance that the price agreement is

---

[5] More precisely, he is moving along a demand curve which is a fixed share of the industry demand, and hence has the same elasticity as the industry curve at every price.

[6] When the relative outputs of the firms change, the minimum cost condition of equal marginal costs for all sellers is likely to be violated. Hence industry profits are not maximized.

adhered to.[7] Ultimately there is no substitute for obtaining the transaction prices from the buyers.

An oligopolist will not consider making secret price cuts to buyers whose purchases fall below a certain size relative to his aggregate sales. The ease with which price-cutting is detected by rivals is decisive in this case. If p is the probability that some rival will hear of one such price reduction, $1 - (1 - p)^n$ is the probability that a rival will learn of at least one reduction if it is given to n customers. Even if p is as small as 0.01, when n equals 100 the probability of detection is .634, and when n equals 1000 it is .99996. No one has yet invented a way to advertise price reductions which brings them to the attention of numerous customers but not to that of any rival.[8]

It follows that oligopolistic collusion will often be effective against small buyers even when it is ineffective against large buyers. When the oligopolists sell to numerous small retailers, for example, they will adhere to the agreed-upon price, even though they are cutting prices to larger chain stores and industrial buyers. This is a first empirical implication of our theory. Let us henceforth exclude small buyers from consideration.

The detection of secret price-cutting will of course be as difficult as interested people can make it. The price-cutter will certainly protest his innocence, or, if this would tax credulity beyond its taxable capacity, blame a disobedient subordinate. The price cut will often take the indirect form of modifying some non-price dimension of the transaction. The customer may, and often will, divulge price reductions, in order to have them matched by others, but he will learn from experience if each disclosure is followed by the withdrawal of the lower price offer. Indeed the buyer will frequently fabricate wholly fictitious price offers to test the rivals. Policing the collusion sounds very much like the subtle and complex problem presented in a good detective story.

There is a difference: In our case the man who murders the collusive price will receive the bequest of patronage. The basic method of detection of a price-cutter must be the fact that he is getting business he would otherwise not obtain. No promises of lower prices that fail to shift some business can be really effective—either the promised price is still too high or it is simply not believed.

Our definition of perfect collusion, indeed, must be that no buyer changes sellers voluntarily. There is no competitive price-cutting if there are no shifts of buyers among sellers.

To this rule that price-cutting must be inferred from shifts of buyers there is one partial exception, but that an important one. There is one type of buyer who usually reveals the price he pays, and does not accept secret benefices: the government. The system of sealed bids, publicly opened with full identification of

---

[7] The literature and cases on "open-price associations" contain numerous references to the collection of prices from sellers (see Federal Trade Commission, *Open-Price Trade Associations* [Washington, 1929], and cases cited).

[8] This argument applies to size of buyer relative to the individual seller. One can also explain the absence of higgling in small transactions because of the costs of bargaining, but this latter argument turns on the absolute size of the typical transaction, not its size relative to the seller.

each bidder's price and specifications, is the ideal instrument for the detection of price-cutting. There exists no alternative method of secretly cutting prices (bribery of purchasing agents aside). Our second empirical prediction, then, is that collusion will always be more effective against buyers who report correctly and fully the prices tendered to them.[9]

It follows from the test of the absence of price competition by buyer loyalty—and this is our third major empirical prediction—that collusion is severely limited (under present assumptions excluding market-sharing) when the significant buyers constantly change identity. There exist important markets in which the (substantial) buyers do change identity continuously, namely, in the construction industries. The building of a plant or an office building, for example, is an essentially non-repetitive event, and rivals cannot determine whether the successful bidder has been a price-cutter unless there is open bidding to specification.

The normal market, however, contains both stability and change. There may be a small rate of entry of new buyers. There will be some shifting of customers even in a regime of effective collusion, for a variety of minor reasons we can lump together as "random factors." There will often be some sharing of buyers by several sellers—a device commending itself to buyers to increase the difficulty of policing price agreements. We move then to the world of circumstantial evidence, or, as it is sometimes called, of probability.

THE CONDITIONS FOR DETECTING SECRET PRICE REDUCTIONS

We shall investigate the problem of detecting secret price-cutting with a simplified model, in which all buyers and all sellers are initially of equal size. The number of buyers per seller—recalling that we exclude from consideration all buyers who take less than (say) 0.33 per cent of a seller's output—will range from 300 down to perhaps 10 or 20 (since we wish to avoid the horrors of full bilateral oligopoly). A few of these buyers are new, but over moderate periods of time most are "old," although some of these old customers will shift among suppliers. A potential secret price-cutter has then three groups of customers who would increase their patronage if given secret price cuts: the old customers of rivals; the old customers who would normally leave him; and new customers.

Most old buyers will deal regularly with one or a few sellers, in the absence of secret price-cutting. There may be no secret price-cutting because a collusive price is adhered to, or because only an essentially competitive price can be obtained. We shall show that the loyalty of customers is a crucial variable in determining which price is approached. We need to know the probability that an old customer will buy again from his regular supplier at the collusive price, in the absence of secret price-cutting.

The buyer will set the economies of repetitive purchase (which include smaller transaction costs and less product-testing) against the increased probability of secret price-cutting that comes from shifting among suppliers. From the view-

---

[9] The problem implicitly raised by these remarks is why all sales to the government are not at collusive prices. Part of the answer is that the government is usually not a sufficiently large buyer of a commodity to remunerate the costs of collusion.

point of any one buyer, this gain will be larger the larger the number of sellers and the smaller the number of buyers, as we shall show below. The costs of shifting among suppliers will be smaller the more homogeneous the goods and the larger the purchases of the buyer (again an inverse function of his size). Let us label this probability of repeat purchases p. We shall indicate later how this probability could be determined in a more general approach.

The second component of sales of a firm will be its sales to new buyers and to the floating old customers of rivals. Here we assume that each seller is equally likely to make a sale, in the absence of price competition.

Let us proceed to the analysis. There are n_0 "old" buyers and n_n new customers, with $n_n = \lambda n_0$ and n_s sellers. A firm may look to three kinds of evidence on secret price-cutting, and therefore by symmetry to three potential areas to practice secret price-cutting.

The Behavior of Its Own Old Customers

It has, on average, n_0/n_s such customers, and expects to sell to $m_1 = p n_0/n_s$ of them in a given round of transactions, in the absence of price cutting. The variance of this number of customers is

$$\sigma_1^2 = \frac{(1-p)pn_0}{n_s}.$$

The probability of the firm losing more old customers than

$$\frac{(1-p)n_0}{n_s} + k\sigma_1$$

is given by the probability of values greater than k. The expected number of these old customers who will shift to any one rival is, say,

$$m_2 = \frac{1}{n_s - 1}\left[\frac{(1-p)n_0}{n_s} + k\sigma_1\right],$$

with a variance

$$\sigma_2^2 = \frac{n_s - 2}{(n_s - 1)^2}\left[\frac{(1-p)n_0}{n_s} + k\sigma_1\right].$$

The probability that any rival will obtain more than $m_2 + r\sigma_2$ of these customers is determined by r. We could now choose those combinations of k and r that fix a level of probability for the loss of a given number of old customers to any one rival beyond which secret price-cutting by this rival will be inferred. This is heavy arithmetic, however, so we proceed along a less elegant route.

Let us assume that the firm's critical value for the loss of old customers, beyond which it infers secret price-cutting, is

$$\frac{(1-p)n_0}{n_s} + \sigma_1 = \frac{(1-p)n_0}{n_s}\left[1 + \sqrt{\left(\frac{p}{1-p}\frac{n_s}{n_0}\right)}\right] = \frac{(1-p)n_0}{n_s}(1 + \theta),$$

that is, one standard deviation above the mean. Any one rival will on average attract

$$m_2 = \frac{1}{n_s - 1}\left[\frac{(1-p)n_0}{n_s} + \sigma_1\right]$$

of these customers, with a variance of

$$\sigma_2{}^2 = \frac{n_s - 2}{(n_s - 1)^2}\left[\frac{(1 - p)n_0}{n_s} + \sigma_1\right].$$

Let the rival be suspected of price-cutting if he obtains more than $(m_2 + \sigma_2)$ customers, that is, if the probability of any larger number is less than about 30 per cent. The joint probability of losing one standard deviation more than the average number of old customers and a rival obtaining one standard deviation more than his average share is about 10 per cent. The average sales of a rival are n_0/n_s, ignoring new customers. The maximum number of buyers any seller can obtain from one rival without exciting suspicion, minus the number he will on average get without price-cutting ($[1 - p]n_0/n_s$ $[n_s - 1]$), expressed as a ratio to his average sales, is

$$\frac{[\theta(1 - p)n_0/(n_s - 1)n_s + \sigma_2]}{n_0/n_s}.$$

This criterion is tabulated in Table 11.1.

The entries in Table 11.1 are measures of the maximum additional sales obtainable by secret price-cutting (expressed as a percentage of average sales) from any one rival beyond which that rival will infer that the price-cutting is taking place. Since the profitability of secret price-cutting depends upon the amount of business one can obtain (as well as upon the excess of price over marginal cost), we may also view these numbers as the measures of the incentive to engage in secret price-cutting. Three features of the tabulation are noteworthy:

> *a*) The gain in sales from any one rival by secret price-cutting is not very sensitive to the number of rivals, given the number of customers and the probability of repeat sales. The aggregate gain in sales of a firm from price-cutting—its total incentive to secret price-cutting—is the sum of the gains from each rival and therefore increases roughly in proportion to the number of rivals.
>
> *b*) The incentive to secret price-cutting falls as the number of customers per seller increases—and falls roughly in inverse proportion to the square root of the number of buyers.
>
> *c*) The incentive to secret price-cutting rises as the probability of repeat purchases falls, but at a decreasing rate.

We have said that the gain to old buyers from shifting their patronage among sellers will be that it encourages secret price-cutting by making it more difficult to detect. Table 11.1 indicates that there are diminishing returns to increased shifting: The entries increase at a decreasing rate as p falls. In a fuller model we could introduce the costs of shifting among suppliers and determine p to maximize expected buyer gains. The larger the purchases of a buyer, when buyers are of unequal size, however, the greater is the prospect that his shifts will induce price-cutting.

In addition it is clear that, when the number of sellers exceeds two, it is possible for two or more firms to pool information and thus to detect less extreme cases of price-cutting. For example, at the given probability levels, the number

Table 11.1

PERCENTAGE GAINS IN SALES FROM UNDETECTED PRICE-CUTTING BY A FIRM

$$\text{Criterion I: } \frac{1}{(n_s - 1)}\left[\theta(1 - p) + \sqrt{\frac{n_s(n_s - 2)(1 - p)(1 + \theta)}{n_0}}\right] \quad \theta = \sqrt{\frac{p}{1 - p}\frac{n_s}{n_0}}$$

PROBABILITY OF REPEAT SALES (p)	NUMBER OF BUYERS (n_0)	NUMBER OF SELLERS					
		2	3	4	5	10	20
$p = 0.95$	20	6.9	11.3	11.3	11.4	11.8	12.7
	30	5.6	8.9	8.8	8.8	9.0	9.6
	40	4.9	7.5	7.4	7.4	7.5	7.9
	50	4.4	6.6	6.5	6.4	6.5	6.8
	100	3.1	4.4	4.3	4.3	4.2	4.4
	200	2.2	3.0	2.9	2.8	2.8	2.8
	400	1.5	2.1	2.0	1.9	1.8	1.8
$p = 0.90$	20	9.5	14.8	14.7	14.6	14.8	15.7
	30	7.8	11.7	11.5	11.4	11.4	12.0
	40	6.7	10.0	9.7	9.6	9.5	9.9
	50	6.0	8.8	8.6	8.4	8.3	8.6
	100	4.2	6.0	5.8	5.6	5.4	5.5
	200	3.0	4.1	3.9	3.8	3.6	3.6
	400	2.1	2.8	2.7	2.6	2.4	2.4
$p = 0.80$	20	12.6	19.3	18.9	18.7	18.6	19.4
	30	10.3	15.4	15.0	14.7	14.5	15.0
	40	8.9	13.1	12.7	12.5	12.2	12.5
	50	8.0	11.6	11.2	11.0	10.6	10.8
	100	5.7	8.0	7.7	7.4	7.1	7.1
	200	4.0	5.5	5.3	5.1	4.8	4.7
	400	2.8	3.8	3.6	3.5	3.2	3.2
$p = 0.70$	20	14.5	22.3	21.8	21.5	21.2	21.9
	30	11.8	17.8	17.3	17.0	16.6	16.9
	40	10.2	15.2	14.8	14.5	14.0	14.2
	50	9.2	13.5	13.1	12.8	12.3	12.4
	100	6.5	9.3	9.0	8.7	8.2	8.2
	200	4.6	6.5	6.2	6.0	5.6	5.5
	400	3.2	4.5	4.3	4.2	3.8	3.7

of old customers that any one rival should be able to take from a firm was shown to be at most

$$(1 - p)\frac{n_0(1 + \theta)}{n_s - 1},$$

with variance

$$\frac{(n_s - 2)(1 - p)(1 + \theta)}{(n_s - 1)^2} n_0.$$

At the same probability level, the average number of old customers that one rival should be able to take from T firms is at most

$$\frac{T(1-p)n_0}{n_s - T}\left(1 + \frac{\theta}{\sqrt{T}}\right),$$

with the variance

$$\frac{(n_s - T - 1)}{(n_s - T)^2}(1-p)\left(1 + \frac{\theta}{\sqrt{T}}\right)n_0 T.$$

Each of these is smaller than the corresponding expression for one seller when expressed as a fraction of the customers lost by each of the firms pooling information.

There are of course limits to such pooling of information: not only does it become expensive as the number of firms increases, but also it produces less reliable information, since one of the members of the pool may himself be secretly cutting prices. Some numbers illustrative of the effect of pooling will be given at a later point.

The Attraction of Old Customers of Other Firms Is a Second Source of Evidence of Price-Cutting

If a given rival has not cut prices, he will on average lose $(1-p)(n_0/n_s)$ customers, with a variance of σ_1^2. The number of customers he will retain with secret price-cutting cannot exceed a level at which the rivals suspect the price-cutting. Any one rival will have little basis for judging whether he is getting a fair share of this firm's old customers, but they can pool their information and then in the aggregate they will expect the firm to lose at least $(1-p)(n_0/n_s) -$

Table 11.2

OLD CUSTOMERS THAT A SECRET PRICE-CUTTER CAN RETAIN, AS A PERCENTAGE OF AVERAGE SALES

$$\text{Criterion II:} \quad 2\sqrt{\frac{p(1-p)}{2}\frac{n_s}{n_0}}$$

PROBABILITY THAT OLD CUSTOMER WILL REMAIN LOYAL (p)	NUMBER OF OLD CUSTOMERS PER SELLER (n_0/n_s)			
	10	20	50	100
0.95	13.8	9.7	6.2	4.4
.90	19.0	13.4	8.5	6.0
.85	22.6	16.0	10.1	7.1
.80	25.3	17.9	11.3	8.0
.75	27.4	19.4	12.2	8.7
.70	29.0	20.5	13.0	9.2
.65	30.2	21.3	13.5	9.5
.60	31.0	21.9	13.9	9.8
.55	31.5	22.2	14.1	10.0
0.50	31.6	22.4	14.1	10.0

$2\sigma_1$ customers, at the 5 per cent probability level. Hence the secret price-cutter can retain at most $2\sigma_1$ of his old customers (beyond his average number), which as a fraction of his average sales (ignoring new customers) is

$$\frac{2\sigma_1}{n_0/n_s} = 2\sqrt{\frac{(1-p)pn_s}{n_0}}.$$

This is tabulated as Table 11.2.

If the entries in Table 11.2 are compared with those in Table 11.1,[10] it is found that a price-cutter is easier to detect by his gains at the expense of any one rival than by his unusual proportion of repeat sales. This second criterion will therefore seldom be useful.

The Behavior of New Customers Is a Third Source of Information on Price-Cutting

There are n_n new customers per period,[11] equal to λn_0. A firm expects, in the absence of price-cutting, to sell to

$$m_3 = \frac{1}{n_s}\lambda n_0$$

of these customers, with a variance of

$$\sigma_3^2 = \left(1 - \frac{1}{n_s}\right)\frac{\lambda n_0}{n_s}.$$

If the rivals pool information (without pooling, this area could not be policed effectively), this firm cannot obtain more than $m_3 + 2\sigma_3$ customers without being deemed a price-cutter, using again a 5 per cent probability criterion. As a percentage of the firm's total sales, the maximum sales above the expected number in the absence of price-cutting are then

$$\frac{2\sigma_3}{n_0(1+\lambda)/n_s} = \frac{2}{1+\lambda}\sqrt{\frac{(n_s-1)\lambda}{n_0}}.$$

We tabulate this criterion as Table 11.3.

Two aspects of the incentive to cut prices (or equivalently the difficulty of detecting price cuts) to new customers are apparent: the incentive increases rapidly with the number of sellers[12] and the incentive increases with the rate of

---

[10] For example, take $p = .95$. The entry for 10 customers per seller is 13.8 in Table 11.2—this is the maximum percentage of average sales that can be obtained by price reductions to old customers. The corresponding entries in Table 11.1 are 6.9 (2 sellers, 20 buyers), 8.9 (3 and 30), 7.4 (4 and 40), 6.4 (5 and 50), 42 (10 and 100), etc. Multiplying each entry in Table 11.1 by $(n_s - 1)$, we get the maximum gain in sales (without detection) by attracting customers of rivals, and beyond 2 sellers the gains are larger by this latter route. Since Table 11.1 is based upon a 10 per cent probability level, strict comparability requires that we use 1.6 σ, instead of 2 σ, in Table 11.2, which would reduce the entries by one-fifth.

[11] Unlike old customers, whose behavior is better studied in a round of transactions, the new customers are a flow whose magnitude depends much more crucially on the time period considered. The annual flow of new customers is here taken (relative to the number of old customers) as the unit.

[12] And slowly with the number of sellers if customers per seller are held constant.

182 PRICING BEHAVIOR

entry of new customers. As usual the incentive falls as the absolute number of customers per seller rises. If the rate of entry of new buyers is 10 per cent or more, price-cutting to new customers allows larger sales increases without detection that can be obtained by attracting customers of rivals (compare Tables 11.1 and 11.3).

Table 11.3

MAXIMUM ADDITIONAL NEW CUSTOMERS (AS A PERCENTAGE OF AVERAGE SALES) OBTAINABLE BY SECRET PRICE-CUTTING

$$\text{Criterion III: } \frac{2}{1+\lambda} \sqrt{\frac{\lambda(n_s - 1)}{n_0}}$$

RATE OF APPEARANCE OF NEW BUYERS (λ)	NUMBER OF OLD BUYERS (n_0)	NUMBER OF SELLERS					
		2	3	4	5	10	20
1/100	20	4.4	6.3	7.7	8.9	13.3	19.3
	30	3.6	5.1	6.3	7.2	10.8	15.8
	40	3.1	4.4	5.4	6.3	9.4	13.6
	50	2.8	4.0	4.8	5.6	8.4	12.2
	100	2.0	2.8	3.4	4.0	5.9	8.6
	200	1.4	2.0	2.4	2.8	4.2	6.1
	400	1.0	1.4	1.7	2.0	3.0	4.3
1/10	20	12.9	18.2	22.3	25.7	38.6	56.0
	30	10.5	14.8	18.2	21.0	31.5	45.8
	40	9.1	12.9	15.8	18.2	27.3	39.6
	50	8.1	11.5	14.1	16.3	24.4	35.4
	100	5.8	8.1	10.0	11.5	17.2	25.1
	200	4.1	5.8	7.0	8.1	12.2	17.7
	400	2.9	4.1	5.0	5.8	8.6	12.5
1/5	20	16.7	23.6	28.9	33.3	50.0	72.6
	30	13.6	19.2	23.6	27.2	40.8	59.3
	40	11.8	16.7	20.4	23.6	35.4	51.4
	50	10.5	14.9	18.3	21.1	31.6	46.0
	100	7.4	10.5	12.9	14.9	22.4	32.5
	200	5.3	7.4	9.1	10.5	15.8	23.0
	400	3.7	5.3	6.4	7.4	11.2	16.2
1/4	20	17.9	25.3	31.0	35.8	53.7	78.0
	30	14.6	20.7	25.3	29.2	43.8	63.7
	40	12.6	17.9	21.9	25.3	38.0	55.1
	50	11.3	16.0	19.6	22.6	33.9	49.3
	100	8.0	11.3	13.9	16.0	24.0	34.9
	200	5.7	8.0	9.8	11.3	17.0	24.7
	400	4.0	5.7	6.9	8.0	12.0	17.4

Of the considerable number of directions in which this model could be enlarged, two will be presented briefly.

The first is inequality in the size of firms. In effect this complication has already been introduced by the equivalent device of pooling information. If we tabulate the effects of pooling of information by K firms, the results are equivalent to having a firm K times as large as the other firms. The number of old customers this large firm can lose to any one small rival (all of whom are equal in size) is given, in Table 11.4, as a percentage of the average number of old cus-

Table 11.4

PERCENTAGE GAINS IN SALES FROM UNDETECTED PRICE-CUTTING BY A SMALL FIRM

Criterion IV:

$$\frac{1}{n_s - K}\left[\theta(1-p)\sqrt{K} + \sqrt{\frac{n_s K(1-p)(n_s - K - 1)(1 + \theta/\sqrt{K})}{n_0}}\right]$$

$$\theta = \sqrt{\frac{p}{1-p}\frac{n_s}{n_0}}$$

PROBABILITY OF REPEAT SALES (p)	NUMBER OF FIRMS ($n_s - K + 1$)	BUYERS PER SMALL SELLER (n_0/n_s)	SIZE OF LARGE FIRM (K)			
			1	2	5	9
$p = 0.9$	2	10	9.5	13.4	21.2	28.5
		30	5.5	7.7	12.2	16.4
		50	4.2	6.0	9.5	12.7
	3	10	11.7	15.8	23.9	31.4
		30	6.3	8.7	13.3	17.6
		50	4.8	6.6	10.2	13.5
	4	10	9.7	13.1	19.7	25.7
		30	5.2	7.1	10.9	14.4
		50	4.0	5.4	8.3	11.0
	10	10	5.4	7.2	10.7	14.0
		30	2.9	3.9	5.9	7.7
		50	2.2	2.9	4.5	5.9
$p = 0.8$	2	10	12.6	17.9	28.3	37.9
		30	7.3	10.3	16.3	21.9
		50	5.7	8.0	12.6	17.0
	3	10	15.4	21.0	32.1	42.3
		30	8.4	11.6	18.0	23.9
		50	6.4	8.9	13.8	18.4
	4	10	12.7	17.3	26.3	34.7
		30	6.9	9.5	14.7	19.5
		50	5.3	7.3	11.3	15.0
	10	10	7.1	9.5	14.4	18.9
		30	3.8	5.2	8.0	10.6
		50	2.9	4.0	6.1	8.1

tomers of the small firm; the column labeled $K = 1$ is of course the case analyzed in Table 11.1.

The effects of pooling on the detection of price-cutting are best analyzed by comparing Table 11.4 with Table 11.1. If there are 100 customers and 10 firms (and $p = 0.9$), a single firm can increase sales by 5.4 per cent by poaching on one rival, or about 50 per cent against all rivals (Table 11.1). If 9 firms combine, the maximum amount the single firm can gain by secret price-cutting is 28.9 per cent (Table 11.4). With 20 firms and 200 customers, a single firm can gain 3.6 per cent from each rival, or about 30 per cent from 9 rivals; if these rivals merge, the corresponding figure falls to 14.0 per cent. The pooling of information therefore reduces substantially the scope for secret price-cutting.

This table exaggerates the effect of inequality of firm size because it fails to take account of the fact that the number of customers varies with firm size, on our argument that only customers above a certain size relative to the seller are a feasible group for secret price-cutting. The small firm can find it attractive to cut prices to buyers which are not large enough to be potential customers by price-cutting for the large seller.

The temporal pattern of buyers' behavior provides another kind of information: What is possibly due to random fluctuation in the short run cannot with equal probability be due to chance if repeated. Thus the maximum expected loss of old customers to a rival in one round of transactions is (at the 1σ level)

$$\frac{n_0}{(n_s - 1)n_s}(1 - p)(1 + \theta),$$

but for T consecutive periods the maximum expected loss is (over T periods)

$$\frac{T}{n_s - 1}(1 - p)\frac{n_0}{n_s}[1 + \theta\sqrt{T}],$$

with a variance of

$$\sigma_5^2 = \frac{(n_s - 2)}{(n_s - 1)^2}T(1 - p)\frac{n_0}{n_s}[1 + \theta\sqrt{T}].$$

This source of information is of minor efficacy in detecting price-cutting unless the rounds of successive transactions are numerous—that is, unless buyers purchase (enter contracts) frequently.

Our approach has certain implications for the measurement of concentration, if we wish concentration to measure likelihood of effective collusion. In the case of new customers, for example, let the probability of attracting a customer be proportional to the firm's share of industry output (s). Then the variance of the firm's share of sales to new customers will be $n_n s(1 - s)$, and the aggregate for the industry will be

$$C = n_n \sum_1^r s(1 - s)$$

for r firms. This expression equals $n_n(1 - H)$, where

$$H = \Sigma s^2$$

is the Herfindahl index of concentration. The same index holds, as an approximation, for potential price-cutting to attract old customers.[13]

The foregoing analysis can be extended to non-price variables, subject to two modifications. The first modification is that there be a definite joint profit-maximizing policy upon which the rivals can agree. Here we may expect to encounter a spectrum of possibilities, ranging from a clearly defined optimum policy (say, on favorable legislation) to a nebulous set of alternatives (say, directions of research).[14] Collusion is less feasible, the less clear the basis on which it should proceed. The second modification is that the competitive moves of any one firm will differ widely among non-price variables in their detectability by rivals. Some forms of non-price competition will be easier to detect than price-cutting because they leave visible traces (advertising, product quality, servicing, etc.) but some variants will be elusive (reciprocity in purchasing, patent licensing arrangements). The common belief that nonprice competition is more common than price competition is therefore not wholly in keeping with the present theory. Those forms that are suitable areas for collusion will have less competition; those which are not suitable will have more competition.

SOME FRAGMENTS OF EVIDENCE

Before we seek empirical evidence on our theory, it is useful to report two investigations of the influence of numbers of sellers on price. These investigations have an intrinsic interest because, so far as I know, no systematic analysis of the effect of numbers has hitherto been made.

The first investigation was of newspaper advertising rates, as a function of the number of evening newspapers in a city. Advertising rates on a milline basis

[13] A similar argument leads to a measure of concentration appropriate to potential price-cutting for old customers. Firm i will lose

$$(1 - p)n_0 s_i$$

old customers, and firm j will gain

$$(1 - p)n_0 \frac{s_i s_j}{1 - s_i}$$

of them, with a variance

$$(1 - p)n_0 \frac{s_i s_j}{1 - s_i}\left(1 - \frac{s_j}{1 - s_i}\right).$$

If we sum over all i ($\neq j$), we obtain the variance of firm j's sales to old customers of rivals

$$(1 - p)n_0 s_j(1 + H - 2s_j),$$

to an approximation, and summing over all j, we have the concentration measure,

$$(1 - p)n_0(1 - H).$$

The agreement of this measure with that for new customers is superficial: that for new customers implicitly assumes pooling of information and that for old customers does not.

[14] Of course, price itself usually falls somewhere in this range rather than at the pole. The traditional assumption of stationary conditions conceals this fact.

Table 11.5

RESIDUALS FROM REGRESSION OF ADVERTISING RATES ON CIRCULATION*

NUMBER OF EVENING PAPERS	n	MEAN RESIDUAL (LOGARITHM)	STANDARD DEVIATION OF MEAN
One	23	0.0211	0.0210
With morning paper	10	−.0174	.0324
Without morning paper	13	.0507	.0233
Two	30	−0.0213	0.0135

* The regression equation is

$$\log R = 5.194 - 1.688 \log c + .139 (\log c)^2,$$
$$\quad\quad\quad\quad (.620) \quad\quad (.063)$$

where R is the 5 M milline rate and c is circulation.
Source: American Association of Advertising Agencies, *Market and Newspaper Statistics*, vol. VIIIa (1939).

are closely (and negatively) related to circulation, so a regression of rates on circulation was made for fifty-three cities in 1939. The residuals (in logarithmic form) from this regression equation are tabulated in Table 11.5. It will be observed that rates are 5 per cent above the average in one-newspaper towns and 5 per cent below the average in two-newspaper towns, and the towns with one evening paper but also an independent morning paper fall nearly midway between these points. Unfortunately there were too few cities with more than two evening newspapers to yield results for larger numbers of firms.

The second investigation is of spot commercial rates on AM radio stations in the four states of Ohio, Indiana, Michigan, and Illinois. The basic equation

Table 11.6

REGRESSION OF AM SPOT COMMERCIAL RATES (26 TIMES) AND STATION CHARACTERISTICS, 1961
($n = 345$)

INDEPENDENT VARIABLES*	REGRESSION COEFFICIENT	STANDARD ERROR
1. Logarithm of population of county, 1960	.238	0.026
2. Logarithm of kilowatt power of station	.206	.015
3. Dummy variables of period of broadcasting:		
a) Sunrise to sunset	−.114	.025
b) More than (a), less than 18 hours	−.086	.027
c) 18–21 hours	−.053	.028
4. Logarithm of number of stations in county	−.074	0.046
$R^2 = .743$		

* Dependent variable: logarithm of average rate, May 1, 1961 (dollars).
Source: "Spot Radio Rates and Data," *Standard Rate and Data Service, Inc.*, vol. XLIII, no. 5 (May 1961).

introduces, along with number of rivals, a series of other factors (power of station, population of the county in which the station is located, etc.). Unfortunately the number of stations is rather closely correlated with population ($r^2 = .796$ in the logarithms). The general result, shown in Table 11.6, is similar to that for newspapers: the elasticity of price with respect to number of rivals is quite small ($-.07$). Here the range of stations in a county was from 1 to 13.

Both studies suggest that the level of prices is not very responsive to the actual number of rivals. This is in keeping with the expectations based upon our model, for that model argues that the number of buyers, the proportion of new buyers, and the relative sizes of firms are as important as the number of rivals.

To turn to the present theory, the only test covering numerous industries so far devised has been one based upon profitability. This necessarily rests upon company data, and it has led to the exclusion of a large number of industries for which the companies do not operate in a well-defined industry. For example, the larger steel and chemical firms operate in a series of markets in which their

Table 11.7

PROFITABILITY AND CONCENTRATION DATA

INDUSTRY*	CONCENTRATION (1954)		AVERAGE RATE OF RETURN (1953–57)		RATIO OF MARKET VALUE TO BOOK VALUE (1953–57)
	SHARE OF TOP 4	H†	ALL ASSETS	NET WORTH	
Sulfur mining (4)	98	0.407	19.03	23.85	3.02
Automobiles (3)	98	.369	11.71	20.26	2.30
Flat glass (3)	90	.296	11.79	16.17	2.22
Gypsum products (2)	90	.280	12.16	20.26	1.83
Primary aluminum (4)	98	.277	6.87	13.46	2.48
Metal cans (4)	80	.260	7.27	13.90	1.60
Chewing gum (2)	86	.254	13.50	17.06	2.46
Hard-surface floor coverings (3)	87	.233	6.56	7.59	0.98
Cigarettes (5)	83	.213	7.23	11.18	1.29
Industrial gases (3)	84	.202	8.25	11.53	1.33
Corn wet milling (3)	75	.201	9.17	11.55	1.48
Typewriters (3)	83	.198	3.55	5.39	0.84
Domestic laundry equipment (2)	68	.174	9.97	17.76	1.66
Rubber tires (9)	79	.171	7.86	14.02	1.70
Rayon fiber (4)	76	.169	5.64	6.62	0.84
Carbon black (2)	73	.152	8.29	9.97	1.40
Distilled liquors (6)	64	0.118	6.94	7.55	0.77

* The number of firms is given in parentheses after the industry title. Only those industries are included for which a substantial share (35 per cent or more) of the industry's sales is accounted for by the firms in the sample, and these firms derive their chief revenues (50 per cent or more) from the industry in question.
† H is Herfindahl index.

position ranges from monopolistic to competitive. We have required of each industry that the earnings of a substantial fraction of the companies in the industry (measured by output) be determined by the profitability of that industry's products, that is, that we have a fair share of the industry and the industry's product is the dominant product of the firms.

Three measures of profitability are given in Table 11.7: (1) the rate of return on all capital (including debt); (2) the rate of return on net worth (stockholders' equity); (3) the ratio of market value to book value of the common stock.

In addition, two measures of concentration are presented: (1) the conventional measure, the share of output produced by the four leading firms; and (2) the Herfindahl index, H.

The various rank correlations are given in Table 11.8. The various concentra-

Table 11.8

RANK CORRELATIONS OF MEASURES OF PROFITABILITY
AND MEASURES OF CONCENTRATION

MEASURE OF CONCENTRATION	MEASURE OF PROFITABILITY		
	RATE OF RETURN ON ALL ASSETS	RATE OF RETURN ON NET WORTH	RATIO OF MARKET VALUE TO BOOK VALUE
Share of output produced by four largest firms	.322	.507	.642
Herfindahl index (H)	.524	.692	.730

tion measures, on the one hand, and the various measures of profitability, on the other hand, are tolerably well correlated.[15] All show the expected positive relationship. In general the data suggest that there is no relationship between profitability and concentration if H is less than 0.250 or the share of the four largest firms is less than about 80 per cent. These data, like those on advertising rates, confirm our theory only in the sense that they support theories which assert that competition increases with number of firms.

Our last evidence is a study of the prices paid by buyers of steel products in 1939, measured relative to the quoted prices (Table 11.9). The figure of 8.3 for

[15] The concentration measures have a rank correlation of .903. The profitability measures have the following rank correlations:

	RETURN ON ALL ASSETS	RATIO OF MARKET TO BOOK VALUE
Return on net worth	.866	.872
Ratio of market to book value	.733	—

Table 11.9

PRICES OF STEEL PRODUCTS, 1939, AND INDUSTRY STRUCTURE, 1938

PRODUCT CLASS	PRICES, 2D QUARTER, 1939 (PER CENT)		HERFINDAHL INDEX	OUTPUT IN 1939 RELATIVE TO 1937
	AVERAGE DISCOUNT FROM LIST PRICE	STANDARD DEVIATION		
Hot-rolled sheets	8.3	7.3	0.0902	1.14
Merchant bars	1.2	4.5	.1517	0.84
Hot-rolled strip	8.5	8.3	.1069	0.56
Plates	2.6	4.8	.1740	0.85
Structural shapes	3.2	4.3	.3280	0.92
Cold-rolled strip	8.8	9.8	.0549	0.88
Cold-rolled sheets	5.8	5.0	.0963	1.14
Cold-finished bars	0.9	3.4	0.0964	0.83

Source: Prices: "Labor Department Examines Consumers' Prices of Steel Products," *Iron Age*, April 25, 1946; industry structure: 1938 capacity data from *Directory of Iron and Steel Works of the United States and Canada*; output: *Annual Statistical Report*, American Iron and Steel Institute (New York, 1938, 1942).

hot-rolled sheets, for example, represents an average of 8.3 per cent reduction from quoted prices, *paid by buyers*, with a standard deviation of 7.3 per cent of quoted prices. The rate of price-cutting is almost perfectly correlated with the standard deviation of transaction prices, as we should expect: the less perfect the market knowledge, the more extensive the price-cutting.

In general, the more concentrated the industry structure (measured by the Herfindahl index), the larger were the price reductions. Although there were no extreme departures from this relationship, structural shapes and hot-rolled strip had prices somewhat lower than the average relationship, and cold finished bars prices somewhat higher than expected, and the deviations are not accounted for by the level of demand (measured by 1939 sales relative to 1937 sales). The number of buyers could not be taken into account, but the BLS study states:

> The extent of price concessions shown by this study is probably understated because certain very large consumers in the automobile and container industries were excluded from the survey. This omission was at the request of the OPA which contemplated obtaining this information in connection with other studies. Since a small percentage of steel consumers, including these companies, accounts for a large percentage of steel purchased, prices paid by a relatively few large consumers have an important influence upon the entire steel price structure. Very large steel consumers get greater reductions from published prices than smaller consumers, often the result of competitive bidding by the mills for the large volume of steel involved. One very large steel consumer, a firm that purchased over 2 pct of the total consumption of hot and cold-rolled sheets in 1940, refused to give purchase prices. This firm wished to protect its suppliers, fearing that "certain trans-

actions might be revealed which would break confidence" with the steel mills. However, this company did furnish percent changes of prices paid for several steel products which showed that for some products prices advanced markedly, and in one case, nearly 50 pct. The great price advances for this company indicate that it was receiving much larger concessions than smaller buyers.[16]

These various bits of evidence are fairly favorable to the theory, but they do not constitute strong support. More powerful tests will be feasible when the electrical equipment triple-damage suits are tried.[17] The great merit of our theory, in fact, is that it has numerous testable hypotheses, unlike the immortal theories that have been traditional in this area.

[16] See "Labor Department Examines Consumers' Prices of Steel Products," *op. cit.*, p. 133.

[17] For example, it will be possible to test the prediction that prices will be higher and less dispersed in sales on public bids than in privately negotiated sales, and the prediction that price-cutting increases as the number of buyers diminishes.

Appendix I to Reading 11

The importance of product heterogeneity for profit-maximizing behavior cannot well be established by an a priori argument. Nevertheless, the following simple exposition of the implications for profitability of disregarding heterogeneity may have some heuristic value. The analysis, it will be observed, is formally equivalent to that of the effects of an excise tax on a monopolist.

Assume that a monopolist makes men's suits, and that he makes only one size of suit. This is absurd behavior, but the picture of the sadistic monopolist who disregards consumer desires has often made fugitive appearances in the literature so the problem has some interest of its own. The demand curve of a consumer for suits that fit, $f(p)$, would now be reduced because he would have to incur some alteration cost a in order to wear the suit. His effective demand would therefore decline to $f(p + a)$. Assume further that the marginal cost of suits is constant (m), and that it would be the same if the monopolist were to make suits of various sizes.

The effect on profits of a uniform product—uniform is an especially appropriate word here—can be shown graphically (Figure 11.1). The decrease in quantity sold, with a linear demand curve, is

$$MB = \tfrac{1}{2} a f'(p).$$

The decrease in the price received by the monopolist is

$$DN = \frac{MB}{f'(p)} - a = -\frac{a}{2},$$

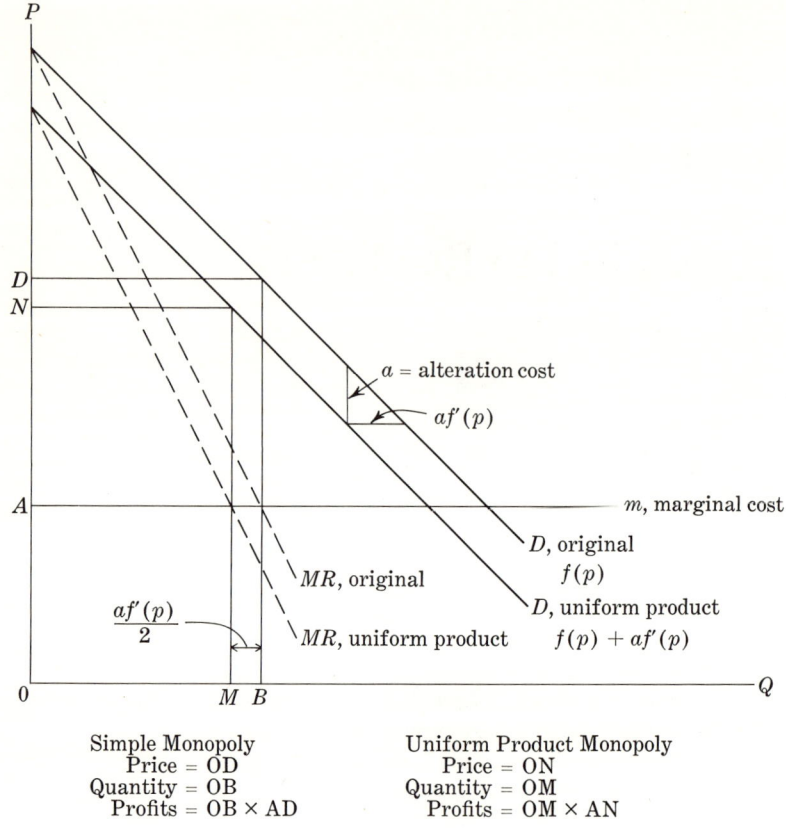

Figure 11.1

so if π is profit per unit, and q is output, the relative decline in total profit is approximately

$$\frac{\Delta \pi}{\pi} + \frac{\Delta q}{q},$$

or

$$\frac{MB}{OB} + \frac{ND}{AD}.$$

Since

$$OB = \frac{f(m)}{2}$$

$$AD = -\frac{p}{\eta},$$

where η is the elasticity of demand, the relative decline of profits with a uniform product is

$$\frac{af'(p)}{f(m)} + \frac{a\eta}{2p} = \frac{a\eta}{2p} + \frac{a\eta}{2p}$$

$$= \frac{a\eta}{p}.$$

The loss from imposed uniformity is therefore proportional to the ratio of alteration costs to price.

Our example is sufficiently unrealistic to make any quantitative estimate uninteresting. In general one would expect an upper limit to the ratio a/p, because it becomes cheaper to resort to other goods (custom tailoring in our example), or to abandon the attempt to find appropriate goods. The loss of profits of the monopolist will be proportional to the average value of a/p, and this will be smaller, the smaller the variation in buyers' circumstances.

Still, monopolists are lucky if their long-run demand curves have an elasticity only as large as -5, and then even a ratio of a to p of 1/40 will reduce their profits by 12 per cent. The general conclusion I wish to draw is that a monopolist who does not cater to the diversities of his buyers' desires will suffer a substantial decline in his profits.

12
New Developments on the Oligopoly Front[1]

Franco Modigliani

In my opinion the two books reviewed in this article represent a welcome major breakthrough on the oligopoly front. These two contributions, which appeared almost simultaneously, though clearly quite independently, have much in common in their basic models and method of approach to the problem. But, fortunately, they do not significantly repeat each other; for, having started from the same point of departure, the authors have followed divergent paths, exploring different implications of the same basic model.

Sylos deals almost exclusively with *homogeneous oligopoly* defined as a situation in which all producers, actual and potential, are able to supply the identical commodity (more generally, commodities that are perfect substitutes for each other) and have access to the very same long-run cost function. He thus focuses on barriers to entry resulting from economies of scale. Bain, on the other hand, also analyzes the effect of competitors being altogether unable to produce perfect substitutes—that is, product-differentiation barriers—or being able to do so only at higher costs—absolute cost-advantage barriers. Furthermore, Bain's book is greatly enriched by fascinating empirical data, painstakingly collected through a variety of means, and by a courageous attempt at an empirical verification of the

Reprinted from *Journal of Political Economy* (June 1958), by permission of The University of Chicago Press. Copyright, 1958, pp. 215–232.

[1] A review article of Paolo Sylos Labini, *Oligopolio e progresso tecnico* ("Oligopoly and Technical Progress"). Milan: Giuffrè, 1957. Pp. 207. L. 1,000. Joe S. Bain, *Barriers to New Competition*. Cambridge, Mass.: Harvard University Press, 1956. Pp. xi + 329. $5.50. A preliminary edition of Sylos' book was published in 1956 for limited circulation. References in this article are to the final edition.

implications of his model. However, Bain is concerned primarily with the analysis of long-run market equilibrium, while Sylos devotes more than half of his book to examining the implications of his model for many other issues, such as (1) the effect of short-run or cyclical variations in demand and costs, (2) the validity of the so-called full-cost pricing model, (3) the effect of technological progress, and (4) the impact of oligopolistic structures on the formation and reabsorption of unemployment. His analysis is primarily theoretical and does not purport to provide new empirical evidence, with one rather significant exception. In an appendix to the introductory chapter Sylos presents indexes of concentration for various sectors of the American economy, based on the Gini coefficient.[2] Sylos finds that, according to this measure, concentration has tended to increase appreciably over the period considered—generally from the first decade of the century to the end of the 1940's—for all but one of the distributions analyzed. These include the distribution of plants by value added and by value of sales for manufacturing as a whole and by size of labor force for all manufacturing and for selected industries[3] and the distribution of corporations by size of assets. These findings are rather striking, since they run counter to widely accepted views based on well-known studies of the share of the market of the four or eight largest firms. They will undoubtedly deserve close scrutiny by the experts on the subject.

It would be impossible within the scope of a review article to summarize adequately the content of both books and take a good look at the promising new horizons they open. Under these conditions it appears wise to devote primary attention to Sylos' work. The reader can do full justice to Bain's contribution by reading the original, while in the case of Sylos this possibility is open only to the "happy few." With respect to Bain's book, therefore, my only goal will be to whet the reader's appetite.

Until quite recently little systematic attention has been paid in the analysis of monopoly and oligopoly to the role of entry, that is, to the behavior of potential competitors. This neglect is justified for monopoly, which is generally defined as the case of a single actual as well as potential producer whose demand curve is not significantly influenced, either in the short or in the long run, by his price policy. Oligopoly could also be defined to exclude entry, fewness being then the result of the impossibility, for firms not now in the group, of producing the commodity—whether for physical or legal reasons. And, undoubtedly, the impossibility of entry is frequently at least implicitly assumed in the analysis of oligopoly, following the venerable example of Cournot, with his owners of mineral wells. But such a narrow definition leaves out the far more interesting case where fewness is the result of purely economic forces, entry being prevented

[2] The Gini coefficient is a measure of the area lying between the actual Lorenz curve and the equidistribution Lorenz curve.

[3] The individual industries, chosen on the ground that their definition has remained reasonably stable over time, are: (1) steel works and rolling mills; (2) electrical machinery; (3) petroleum refining; (4) lumber and timber products; and (5) shipbuilding and iron and steel. For these industries indexes are given for 1914 and 1947. The distribution for lumber is the single instance in which concentration has decreased.

by—and within the limits of—certain price-output policies of existing producers. This is precisely the essence of homogeneous oligopoly analyzed by both Sylos and Bain.

One might suppose that, as long as potential entrants have access to a long-run cost function identical in all respects to that of existing firms, entry must tend to occur whenever the market price is higher than the minimum long-run average cost. (Cost is used hereafter in the sense of opportunity cost, including therefore an appropriate allowance for "normal" profits.) But then long-run market equilibrium would have to involve a price equal to minimum average cost and a corresponding output[4] and would be undistinguishable from perfectly competitive equilibrium. This supposition is, however, invalid whenever the output of an optimum size firm represents a "non-insignificant" fraction of pre-entry output. The price that is relevant to the potential entrant is the price *after* entry. Even if the pre-entry price is above the lowest achievable cost, the additional output he proposes to sell may drive the price below cost, making the entry unprofitable.

Unfortunately for the theorist, the exact anticipated effect of the entry on price is not independent of the (anticipated) reaction of existing producers. The more they are willing to contract their output in response to the entry, the smaller will be the fall in price; in the limiting case the price may even be completely unaffected. Both authors have wisely refused to be stopped by this difficulty. They have instead proceeded to explore systematically the implications of the following well-defined assumption: that potential entrants behave as though they expected existing firms to adopt the policy most unfavorable to them, namely, the policy of maintaining output while reducing the price (or accepting reductions) to the extent required to enforce such an output policy. I shall refer to this assumption as "Sylos' postulate" because it underlies, more or less explicitly, most of his analysis, whereas Bain has also paid some attention to the possibility of potential entrants, assuming a less belligerent behavior on the part of existing firms.

The significance of Sylos' postulate lies in the fact that it enables us to find a definite solution to the problem of long-run equilibrium price and output under homogeneous oligopoly, or at least a definite upper limit to the price, to be denoted by P_0 and a corresponding lower limit to aggregate output, say, X_0. Both authors have essentially reached this conclusion, though through somewhat different routes.

I shall not attempt to reproduce faithfully their respective arguments, but shall instead concentrate on developing the logical essence of their approach. To this end, let $X = D(P)$ denote the market demand curve for the product and let P' denote the pre-entry price, $X' = D(P')$ being then the corresponding aggregate output. Under Sylos' postulate the prospective entrant is confronted not by an infinitely elastic demand at the price P' but by a sloping

[4] This is, in fact, the conclusion reached by H. R. Edwards, "Price Formation in Manufacturing Industry and Excess Capacity," *Oxford Economic Papers,* VII, no. 1 (February, 1955), 194–218, sec. 4.2, which is, in turn, an elaboration of the model developed by P. W. S. Andrews in *Manufacturing Business* (London: Macmillan & Co., 1949). In other respects Edwards' stimulating analysis anticipates many of the conclusions of Sylos and Bain.

demand curve which is simply *the segment of the demand curve to the right of P'*. I shall refer to this segment as the marginal demand curve. Note that it is uniquely determined by the original demand curve and the pre-entry price P'. Suppose P' to be such that the corresponding marginal demand curve is *everywhere* below *the* long-run average cost function. Clearly, under these conditions, entry will not be profitable; that is, such a P' is an *entry-preventing price*. The critical price P_0 is then simply the *highest* entry-preventing price, and the critical output X_0 is the corresponding aggregate demand, $D(P_0)$. Under perfect competition, where the output of an optimum size firm is negligible relative to market demand, the marginal demand curve is itself infinitely elastic *in the relevant range*; hence the familiar conclusion that the long-run equilibrium price cannot exceed minimum average cost. But, where the output of an optimum plant is not negligible, P_0 will exceed minimum cost to an extent which depends on the nature of the demand and the long-run cost function.

In order to explore the factors controlling P_0, let us denote by $\bar{x}$ the optimum scale of output, that is, the scale corresponding to the lowest point of the long-run average cost curve. (If this scale is not unique, $\bar{x}$ will mean the smallest scale consistent with minimum cost.) If k denotes the corresponding minimum average cost, then the perfectly competitive equilibrium price is $P_c = k$, and the corresponding equilibrium output is $X_c = D(P_c) = D(k)$. Finally, let us define the size of the market, S, as the ratio of the competitive output to the optimum scale; $S = X_c/\bar{x}$. (This definition is not the same as that of either Sylos or Bain; it appears, however, to be the most convenient for theoretical purposes, even though it may have drawbacks for empirical investigations.)

Now, following Bain, consider first the simplest case in which the technology of the industry is such that, at a scale less than $\bar{x}$, costs are prohibitively high, so that an entrant can come in only at a scale $\bar{x}$ or larger. In this case the entry-preventing output X_0 is readily found to be

$$X_0 = X_c - \bar{x} = X_c\left(1 - \frac{\bar{x}}{X_c}\right) = X_c\left(1 - \frac{1}{S}\right), \qquad (12.1)$$

or $(100/S)$ per cent below the competitive output. Suppose in fact that aggregate output were smaller; it would then be profitable for a firm of scale $\bar{x}$ to enter. Indeed, the post-entry output would then still be smaller than X_c, and hence the post-entry price would be larger than P_c, which is in turn equal to the entrant's average cost. By the same reasoning an output X_0 (or larger) would make entry unattractive. The critical price P_0 corresponding to X_0 can be read from the demand curve or found by solving for P the equation $X_0 = D(P)$. The relation between P_0 and the competitive equilibrium price P_c can be stated (approximately) in terms of the elasticity of demand in the neighborhood of P_c; if we denote this elasticity by η, we have

$$P_0 \simeq P_c\left(1 + \frac{1}{\eta S}\right),$$

or $100/\eta S$ per cent above P_c.[5]

[5] This approximation will not be very satisfactory for small values of S. In particular, if the demand curve has constant elasticity, then, for small values of S, the extent of price rise will be significantly underestimated.

We can now replace the very special cost function assumed so far with the more conventional one, falling, more or less gradually, at least up to $\bar{x}$. In this general case the critical output may be somewhat larger, and the critical price may be lower, than indicated in the previous paragraph. Indeed, while at the output X_0 is given by (12.1) it is not profitable to enter at the scale $\bar{x}$, it *may* still be profitable to come in at a *smaller* scale.

This possibility and its implications can be conveniently analyzed by means of the graphical apparatus presented in Figure 12.1. (This graphical device is

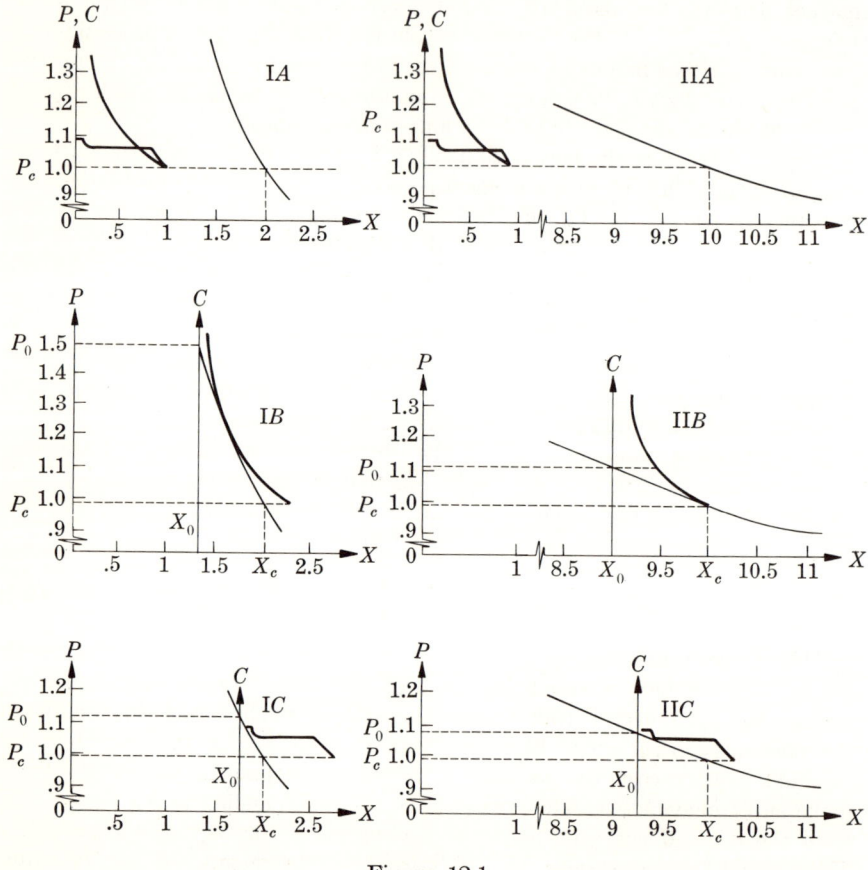

Figure 12.1

not to be found in either of the books under review, but I believe that it is quite helpful in bringing out the essence of the authors' arguments.)[6] In panels IA and IIA, the light lines falling from left to right are the (relevant portions of the) market demand curve. For the sake of generality it is convenient to take $\bar{x}$ (the optimum scale) as the unit of measurement for output X and to take k

---

[6] In the case of Sylos, I am less sure of my ground, since his argument rests almost entirely on a detailed analysis of two numerical examples.

(the corresponding minimum cost) as the unit of measurement for price, P. It follows that the competitive equilibrium price is, by definition, unity, while the corresponding output is precisely the size of the market S. Thus panel IA of Figure 12.1 relates to an industry of size 2 and panel IIA to an industry of size 10. The two demand curves have constant unit elasticity in the range shown, but, as will become apparent, the effect of different assumptions about the elasticity of demand can readily be handled.

The two heavy lines in each of the two panels represent alternative cost curves, graphed on the same scale as the demand curve, for outputs up to $\bar{x}$ (that is, for values of X up to 1). Because of the choice of units, each curve shows the behavior of costs, in percentage of minimum cost, as a function of plant scale, expressed in percentage of optimum scale. The steeper of the two curves is the kind of traditional, well-behaved cost function that underlies Bain's analysis and involves marked economies of scale. It is, in fact, based on the information reported by him for the cement industry, which appears to have more marked economies of scale than any other of the twenty industries analyzed in his book. It is obtained by joining with a smooth curve the data provided there for discrete scale sizes. The other cost curve, involving less pronounced economies of scale, depicts the kind of cost function that underlies Sylos' numerical examples. Sylos explicitly assumes, on grounds of presumed realism, the existence of very pronounced discontinuities in the available technologies. Plants can thus have only sizes that are very specific and far apart—only three sizes in his examples and in my graph. The rounded portions of the curve result from the fact that, beyond certain critical outputs, it pays to shift to a plant of a larger size, even though such a plant could not be utilized to capacity.[7]

The critical price and output, P_0 and X_0, for a given cost curve can now be readily located by means of the following simple device. Slide the cost curve to the right parallel to itself, together with its co-ordinate axis, until no point of this curve lies inside the demand curve. This step is illustrated in panels IB and IIB for the steeper cost curve and in panels IC and IIC for the flatter one. The point at which the Y-axis so displaced cuts the demand curve represents P_0; the point at which it cuts the X-axis is X_0. For, clearly, the portion of the demand curve to the right of the displaced axis is precisely the marginal demand curve when the aggregate output of the existing firms is X_0. If the cost curve is nowhere below this marginal demand curve, there is no possibility of profits for a new entrant.

As can be seen from Figure 12.1, the cost curve in its terminal position may be either tangent to the demand curve, as in IB, or may touch it at a "corner," as in IC and IIC, or, finally, may touch it at its lower extreme, as in IIB.[8] The X co-ordinate of the point where the two curves touch, referred to the axis of the cost curve, indicates the size of firm which represents the most immediate threat of entry. Where this immediate threat comes from an optimum size plant, as in IIB, X_0 is precisely that given by formula 12.1 above; it is now seen that

[7] If Sylos' assumption is taken literally, the portions of the curves shown as straight lines parallel to the X-axis should really have a scalloped shape. This refinement can, however, be ignored, since it does not affect the results.

[8] It may, of course, also have several discrete points of contact with the demand curve or overlap a portion of it.

this possibility represents a limiting case—and that, in general, the formula provides only a lower bound to X_0.

With the help of Figure 12.1 we can also establish several interesting propositions in comparative statics. First, by comparing panel IB with IC and IIB with IIC, we see that, for given market size, P_0 will tend to be higher the steeper the cost curve, that is, the greater the economies of scale. The common sense of this result is apparent: when economies of scale are important, the effective threat will tend to come from large-scale plants, which must widen the gap between X_0 and X_c. Similarly, by comparing IB with IIB and IC with IIC, it appears that, for a given cost curve and elasticity of demand, P_0 will tend to fall with the size of the market; it will, in fact, approach unity (the competitive price) as the size of the market approaches infinity. Furthermore, since, for given size S, a higher elasticity of demand implies a rotation of the cost curve in a counterclockwise direction around the competitive point, it is apparent that a higher elasticity will act in the same direction as a larger size with given elasticity; that is, it will tend to lower P_0.

In summary, under Sylos' postulate there is a well-defined, maximum premium that the oligopolists can command over the competitive price, and this premium tends to increase with the importance of economies of scale and to decrease with the size of market and the elasticity of demand.[9]

I have now laid down the basic long-run equilibrium model common to both Bain and Sylos. Hereafter, their roads part, and I shall first follow Sylos in his explorations of some of the fascinating implications of the model.

The first of these implications refers to the size distribution of firms (or, more precisely, of plants) within the group—its *internal structure*, as I shall call it. If we look, for example, at panel IC, we see that the price P_0 is considerably above the average cost of the medium-size firms and even slightly above that of the smallest. If then any such firm *happened* to be a member of the group—Sylos here, in good Walrasian tradition, speaks of the initial structure as "criée par hasard"—it could survive and even prosper.

But would it not be profitable for the larger firms to expand, eliminating the smaller ones and securing for themselves the small firms' share of the market? In Sylos' model this possibility can be largely dismissed, thanks to his assumption of sharp technological discontinuities. Suppose, for instance, that there are only two possible scales: (a) large plants, producing 10,000 units, and (b) small plants, producing 500 units. Suppose further that X_0 is 15,000 and that this output is initially produced by one large firm and ten small ones. There is, then, no real incentive for the large firm to drive the small ones out of the market, for, in order to produce the extra 5,000 units, it would, in fact, have to operate ten small plants (at least as long as the average cost of a small plant is less than the average incremental cost of producing an extra 5,000 units by operating two large plants at 75 per cent of capacity). But the cost of a small firm must be such as to yield very little, if any, abnormal profit at the price P_0. In fact,

---

[9] As Bain points out, it is conceivable, though not likely, that P_0 will be higher than the price that "maximizes the profit" of the existing firms, in which case it will have no bearing on long-run equilibrium. See the last section of this article.

this price must be such as not to give an inducement to enter the market with a small plant. Hence there will generally be no incentive for the large firm to undertake the price war necessary to eliminate the smaller firms.

If there existed a technology of intermediate size, say, size 5,000, the situation might look somewhat different, since at price P_0 such a plant would make some profits. However, even in this case the elimination of small firms would involve a costly price war. The price would have to be kept below prime cost of the small firms for a time long enough to induce them to fold up or below their average cost until their fixed plant wears out. Sylos suggests that usually the war will not be worth the prize and that it will be preferable for the larger firms not to disturb the delicate balance that always prevails in a homogeneous oligopoly structure.

Are we then to conclude that any structure, "criée par hasard," will tend to perpetuate itself as long as it is consistent with a price not higher than P_0? Sylos does not investigate this issue systematically, confining himself to illustrating various possibilities on the basis of his specific numerical examples. I suggest, however, that with the help of Sylos' model it is possible to throw some interesting light on this question. To this end I shall first introduce a definition. Consider any two structures A and B consistent with no inducement to entry: let us say that A is more rational than B if the total profits accruing to the members of the group are larger under structure A than under B.[10] It follows from this definition and our previous analysis that there exists a *most rational* structure, namely, that structure (not necessarily unique) which produces at the smallest total cost the output X_0 that can be sold at price P_0.[11] This most rational structure has two features worth mentioning. (1) From a welfare point of view, it has certain optimal properties in that X_0 is being produced at the smallest (social) cost; but it still involves a departure from the usual conditions of Pareto optimality in that the output X_0 is, generally, too small and P_0 too high. (2) From a technological point of view, it has the property that the total capacity of the plants of a given size must necessarily be no larger than the capacity of one plant of the next larger size.

It seems reasonable to suppose that, if a structure B is less rational than a structure A, it will be less likely to be observed. For there is some incentive to a shift from B to A, since such a shift is accompanied by a net gain; that is, losses, if any, are more than compensated by gains. But there will be no corresponding incentive to move back from A to B. It does not follow, however, that structures other than the most rational have no chance at all of ever existing or surviving. As Sylos rightly points out, moving from one structure to another generally involves costs—at best, the cost of reaching an agreement; at worst, that of war—and the potential gain may not be worth the cost, espe-

[10] It is apparent that this notion bears a close affinity to that of *dominance* in the theory of games.

[11] This statement is valid only to a first approximation. It is possible that the output X_0 cannot be produced with an integral number of plants of various sizes working at capacity, in which case profit maximization may involve an output somewhat above X_0. However, the departure from X_0 will tend to be negligible, at least as long as the output of the smallest size consistent with P_0 represents a minor fraction of X_0.

cially when the gain, and even more the cost, may be problematic and uncertain.

The conclusions to which we are led are therefore, as it were, of a probabilistic nature. Less rational structures are less likely to be observed than more rational ones, and very irrational structures are unlikely to maintain themselves for any length of time. But certainly structures other than the most rational can exist and survive, especially in a world that is moving and in which the most rational structure is itself continuously changing. Similar considerations apply to the price; while we should not expect prices higher than P_0 to be long maintainable, lower prices may have a certain degree of permanence. But, again, a gap between P and P_0 will provide a stimulus to reorganization of the structure, and this stimulus will be more powerful, and hence more likely to produce a response, the greater the gap.

By drawing together the analysis of market equilibrium and that of internal structure, we may venture some tentative conclusions about the factors which, according to Sylos' model, tend to control the degree of scatter in the size distributions of firms. We already know that only those sizes can survive whose average cost is no larger than P_0. From an analysis of the figure it can therefore be inferred that the possible range of the scatter of sizes will tend to be greater the smaller (a) the economies of scale, (b) the size of the markets, and (c) the elasticity of demand.

These implications, as well as those relating to P_0, are in principle testable. Indeed, it is to both Bain's and Sylos' credit that, by moving us away from conjectural variations and similar subjective notions and focusing instead on objective market and technological data, they have provided us with theories rich in empirical content and capable of being disproved by the evidence. To be sure, such tests may not be easy to carry out, especially with the information presently available, as is amply attested by Bain's gallant efforts in this direction. But, with a clear theoretical framework available as a guide in the collection of data, one may hope that more reliable and abundant evidence will sooner or later accumulate.

Even at this stage, ingenuity can do much to remedy inadequacies of the data. For instance, in order to compute the actual value of P for a given industry, one would need to know not only the market price but also the minimum average cost of an optimal plant. Bain ingeniously suggests that, even in the absence of precise information on this point, some notion of the relative height of P for various industries may be gotten by ranking them in terms of the rate of profits of the largest firms in each industry, since the average cost of such firms will presumably tend to be reasonably close to the minimum.[12] It should be

---

[12] In his book and in earlier contributions Bain measures the rate of profit as the rate of return, net of taxes, on the book value of equity. It would seem preferable to use the rate of return before taxes and interest on the book value of assets, since such a measure is not affected by financial structure. Perhaps a still more relevant measure, for the purpose of testing the model, could be derived from the rate of profit on sales. In fact, letting p denote the market price, we have

$$P = \frac{p}{k} = \frac{px}{kx} = \frac{\text{Sales}}{\text{Sales} - \text{Profit}} = \frac{1}{1 - \frac{\text{Profit}}{\text{Sales}}}.$$

By profit I mean here earnings over and above a "normal" rate of return on the

noted, however, that, contrary to what Bain seems to imply in some of his empirical tests, there is no reason to expect any simple association between P_0 (or its proxy, the rate of profit) and the degree of scatter in plant sizes, at least within Sylos' model. While it is true that a large scatter is not to be expected when P_0 is very close to unity—for then only firms of near-optimum size can survive—it does not follow that there is a positive association between P_0 and scatter. The only safe statement we can make is that, for given P_0, the scatter should tend to be smaller the steeper the cost curve and that, for given cost curve, the association between P_0 and scatter should be positive, both variables tending to decline as the size of the market and the elasticity of demand increase. A cursory examination of Bain's data for those industries in which product-differentiation and absolute-cost advantages are not supposed to be dominant does not seem to contradict this inference conspicuously. Unfortunately, the data in question provide no information on the elasticity of demand and, what is more serious, leave too much room for personal judgment in ranking industries in terms of any variable.

It is tempting to explore the extent to which the implications we have derived from Sylos' model would be affected if we relaxed some of his very rigid assumptions. This question is especially pressing with respect to his assumption of technological discontinuities. Indeed, Bain has emerged from his empirical investigation with a strong conviction that, although there exists a fairly definite scale $\bar{x}$ at which average cost reaches its minimum, costs do not generally tend to rise for scales larger than $\bar{x}$. This possibility in no way affects our analysis of long-run equilibrium price and output but has considerable bearing on the conclusions concerning the size structure. Clearly, under a Bain-type cost function, the "most rational structure" must be such that all the output X_0 is produced by plants of size $\bar{x}$ or larger. It would follow that structures involving smaller plant sizes would tend to be unstable, especially where the cost function is steep in the range of (relative) costs from 1 to P_0.

The reader can decide for himself just how serious this conclusion is for Sylos' construction.[13] I shall limit myself to suggesting that Sylos' case may be considerably strengthened when we recognize the existence of product differentiation of a type not altogether inconsistent with the notion of homogeneous oligopoly, such as spatial differentiation or modifications in product design to meet customers' specifications. Under these conditions the area of the market supplied by smaller

---

book value of assets, which may not be easy to estimate in practice. One may also have some reservations about the assumption that minimum long-run average cost can be approximated from the actual average cost of the dominant firms in the industry. Franklyn Fisher has suggested that a better approximation may be obtained by utilizing, at least as supplementary evidence, the rate of profit on sales of the most profitable firms.

[13] Rosenstein-Rodan has pointed out to me that Bain's long-run cost function may not be too relevant where plant is very long lived. For, even though it may be possible to design a plant having cost k at sizes larger than $\bar{x}$, nonetheless an existing firm wishing to undertake a moderate expansion may have to utilize a smaller-scale technique with higher costs.

firms may be such that the dominant firms would have little to gain by capturing it, either because they have no cost advantage or because this would require an unprofitable price policy on other lines of product.

Consider, for example, the case of spatial differentiation. Suppose the large firm has a cost of 10 and the cost of transportation to a given distant market is 1. Suppose further that the highest f.o.b. price preventing entry that the large firm can charge is 12. The delivered price in the given market is then 13, and it may well be that, at this price, the market can be profitably supplied by a small local firm at, say, a cost of 12.5. In order to capture that relatively small market, the large firm would have to keep the price well below 11.5 for some considerable length of time and then keep it no higher than 11.5 indefinitely —a policy which may well be unprofitable.[14] There is thus room for smaller firms in the industry, but this room is generated by market "exploitation" on the part of the large firm, and all customers are paying a higher price (by 2 per unit) than under competitive equilibrium.

Consider next the case of product modifications. It may well be that a class of customers is willing to pay an extra premium of 1 for a specific variation of the standard product. If the large firm charges 12 for the standard line, even though it has a cost of 10, these customers are therefore willing to pay 13. Now, suppose that, given the size of the market for the specialty, the average cost of the product is again, say, 12.5, whether it is produced by the larger firm or by a smaller one specializing in that line. If such a smaller firm exists, it is not worthwhile for the large firm to try to capture the market. But note once more that the existence of the smaller firm is made possible by the larger firm's oligopoly power. Under competitive conditions the small firm could not exist, since, if customers could get the standard product for 10, they would not be willing to pay enough for the specialty to cover its production cost of 12.5.

In short, in many situations the presence of a variety of sizes may be rendered reasonably stable by the fact that the larger firms find it advantageous to skim the fattest segment of the market, leaving it for smaller firms to supply less profitable pockets. Nor should one forget altogether, even within the realm of pure theory, the public relations advantages that tend to accrue to the large firms from the coexistence of smaller and weaker partners. The argument that prices cannot be lowered without playing havoc with large numbers of honest and industrious small enterprises is always one of great public appeal. And, where antitrust laws are a potential threat, the advantages of having smaller competitors is even more evident.[15]

---

[14] It is assumed that the alternative, and more profitable, course of quoting a delivered price of 12.5 is not available. It is interesting to note in this connection that the prohibition of freight absorption as an antitrust measure will have a desirable effect if it induces the producer to choose a lower price in order not to lose distant markets to smaller local firms but that it will have an undesirable outcome if the producer finds it more advantageous to abandon those markets, in which case the demand will be supplied at a higher social cost.

[15] The considerations of this section clearly point to the importance of factors other than those discussed in the previous section in controlling the scatter of the size distribution of firms and plants. In particular, under a Bain-type cost function, the model has nothing to say about the size distribution of firms above the optimum

Before closing the subject of long-run static analysis, I must report one more observation on which Sylos lays a great deal of stress and which has to do with the effects of technological progress. While improvements in technology that are applicable to all scales must necessarily tend to depress price and expand output, he argues that improvements applicable only at, or near, the largest scale will not affect the critical price and hence will tend to result in higher profits for the larger firms. Furthermore, Sylos seems to feel that technological changes are very commonly of this type, and he is inclined to account in this fashion for a presumed tendency of the profit margin of large firms to grow over time. Here, however, I cannot avoid feeling that Sylos is going too far. For, in the first place, even a change that affects only the largest scale may well lower P_0 when the immediate threat is, in fact, from firms of size $\bar{x}$; and, in the second place, any innovation that affects only plants of suboptimal size (and such innovations are by no means inconceivable) will also result in a fall in the critical price and thus will reduce the profit of the largest firms whose costs have remained unchanged. There is therefore serious doubt whether Sylos' argument can account for a long-run relative rise in large firms' profits, not to mention the equally serious doubt whether such a relative rise has in fact occurred. The model does suggest, however, that changes in technology may cause radical changes in the most rational structure and thus eventually may lead to pervasive changes in the actual structure, including the possible elimination of whole layers of small-scale plants.

I now proceed to consider with Sylos some implications of the model for the effect of short-run changes in demand and cost conditions. Note, first, that in the analysis of market equilibrium I have made no mention of the standard categories of monopolistic competition theories, namely, marginal cost and marginal revenue. To be sure, with sufficient ingenuity, the analysis could be forced into that cast,[16] but such an undertaking would be merely an exercise in semantics and formal logic and would in no way increase our understanding of what is involved. On the other hand, our result can readily be recast in the framework of the so-called full-cost pricing principle. According to this principle, prices are determined by adding to prime cost a markup to cover overhead per unit and by adding further an "appropriate" profit margin. So far, however, it has never been convincingly explained just at what level of output the overhead charge is computed or what determines the "appropriate" profit margin. Sylos' and Bain's models do provide answers to both questions. The large firms, which

---

size $\bar{x}$. Here one may have to fall back on stochastic models of the type advanced, for example, by H. Simon in *Models of Man* (New York: John Wiley & Sons, 1957), chap. ix. In any event the analysis presented casts most serious doubts on the argument advanced by some authors and well exemplified by the following quotation: "Actually, we find that in most industries firms of very different sizes survive, and we may infer that commonly there is no large advantage or disadvantage to size over a very considerable range of outputs" (George Stigler, *The Theory of Price* [New York: Macmillan Co., 1952], p. 144).

[16] For such an attempt see, for example, J. R. Hicks, "The Process of Imperfect Competition." *Oxford Economic Papers*, VI (February, 1954), 41–54.

typically set the pace in the market, must base their price on long-run average cost (so that the overhead must normally be computed at capacity operation, with due allowance for normal seasonal and cyclical variations in the rate of utilization) and apply to this cost the largest profit markup that "the traffic will bear," namely, the markup P_0—for P_0, it will be recalled, is precisely the ratio of the highest possible price to average cost.

The usefulness of translating the result of the static analysis into the language of full-cost pricing becomes fully apparent when we proceed to examine the effects of a variation, say, an increase, in some element of prime cost. Such a change will generally affect all firms and hence will raise the long-run cost curve more or less uniformly. This development in turn will raise the level of the critical price and make it profitable to raise the actual price to this new level. Now it can be verified that, at least for moderate variations in costs and well-behaved demand functions, a good approximation of the new critical price can be obtained precisely by adding to the new average cost the very same profit margin that prevailed before the change; and nearly as good an approximation can be obtained by applying to the new prime cost the original total percentage markup. Thus full-cost pricing may well represent a very useful rule of thumb in reacting to cost changes affecting the entire industry, at least as long as such changes are not too drastic.

Now that we have a solid rationale for the full-cost principle, we need not have qualms about acknowledging two other sets of factors that tend to give it further sanction. (1) In an oligopolistic situation, with its precarious internal equilibrium, there is much to be gained from simple and widely understood rules of thumb, which minimize the danger of behavior intended to be peaceful and cooperative being misunderstood as predatory or retaliatory.[17] (2) The experience of those who, like myself, have conducted extensive personal interviews with executives suggests that these respondents have a strong propensity to explain their behavior in terms of simple mechanical principles, especially when they feel that these principles are blessed by general respectability.

So much about the effect of variations in cost. Let us now turn to the effect of cyclical variations in demand. For the sake of concreteness, let us start out from the prosperity phase, in which plants are being operated at, or near, capacity rates. If the demand curve now shifts to the left as a result of a fall in aggregate income, our model suggests that the optimum markup may have a slight tendency to increase. There are two main reasons for this contention: (1) the critical price P_0 tends to rise when the size of the market falls and (2), with substantial idle capacity and sharply reduced profits, or even losses, prevailing in the industry, even a price somewhat higher than P_0 is not likely to encourage entry, especially where the effective threat is from plants large enough to require a substantial investment. This tendency for the critical markup to rise may partly be offset or even more than offset if, as the demand shifts, its elasticity increases; it will be reinforced if the elasticity falls—a case

[17] See, for example, A. Henderson, "The Theory of Duopoly," *Quarterly Journal of Economics*, LXVIII (November, 1954), 576–79, sec. VII, and T. C. Schelling "Bargaining, Communication, and Limited War," *Conflict Resolution*, I (March, 1957), 19–36.

which Sylos regards as more typical, though, in our view, not very convincingly.
On the whole, then, the critical price P_0 may have some mild tendency to rise; but this does not mean that the actual markup will necessarily rise, for, with much idle capacity, the temptation for individual members of the oligopolistic group to secure a larger share of the shrunken business is very strong. Thus the self-discipline of the group may well tend to break down, with a resultant fall in the effective price if not in the officially quoted one.

In the course of the recovery the markup will of course tend to retrace the path followed in the contraction. But here some new interesting possibilities arise which Sylos himself has not considered. In an expanding economy the recovery will tend to push demand to levels higher than previous peaks. As a result of a rise in demand that is rapid and larger than expected, or as a result of circumstances beyond its control, such as war, the industry may be caught with capacity inadequate to satisfy the demand at the critical price P_0. In terms of traditional patterns of thinking, one would expect firms in the industry to be eager to exploit the situation by charging higher prices. But such a price policy may not be so appealing to the larger firms whose long-run interest is to secure for themselves as much as possible of the additional demand at the profitable price P_0. A higher price may tend to encourage entry, which would not only reduce their share but possibly also threaten the maintenance of self-discipline in periods of depressed demand. Thus the dominant firms may have an incentive to "hold the price line" by such devices as lengthening delivery schedules and informal rationing (even at the risk of gray markets), while at the same time expanding capacity—but only to an extent that seems warranted by the anticipated long-run demand at the price P_0. These considerations may help to explain the otherwise rather puzzling behavior of certain important sectors of the economy in the early postwar period.[18]

On the whole it would appear that no very definite general conclusion can be reached about the cyclical behavior of the markup, although the model may have a good deal to say for well-defined classes of situations. One might, however, go along with Sylos on the following two tentative generalizations: (1) on the average, the markup is not likely to change much in the course of the cycle, but one should expect some scatter around this central tendency, and (2) prices should tend on the average to fluctuate more in relation to prime cost where there is more chance for the discipline of the group to break down, and this chance presumably should tend to increase with the size of the group and decrease with degree of concentration (in Sylos' sense). These generalizations appear to be consistent with the evidence assembled by Stigler in his well-

[18] A similar explanation is advanced in Edwards, *op. cit.*, and in Kuh and Meyer, *The Investment Decision* (Cambridge, Mass.: Harvard University Press, 1957), esp. chap. xii. It has also been suggested that the price policies in question may be explained by the concern that higher prices and consequent higher profits would have led to irresistible pressure for wage concessions, difficult to reverse. By contrast, the abnormally high profits of dealers or gray-market operators could be counted on to disappear automatically as the supply gradually caught up with demand. I am indebted to Albert G. Hart and Richard Cyert for stimulating discussions on the relevance of Sylos' model to the explanation of the postwar experience.

known criticism of the kinky demand curve,[19] though they may be less easy to reconcile with certain empirical studies of price flexibility.[20]

Sylos attempts to dispose of the latter evidence by an ingenious argument which is not entirely convincing in this context but which is of interest on its own merit. Specifically, he suggests that, where the full-cost principle is widely adhered to, it may be in the interest of the larger firms to sustain the prices of factors entering into prime cost; in fact, provided that the shifted demand curve has a sufficiently low elasticity, such a policy will increase the over-all profit of the industry. Where the large firms are themselves important producers of some critical raw materials, they may best achieve this purpose by sustaining these particular prices; where this is not possible, they may acquiesce to an increase in real wages.[21] However, the advantage of an increase in prime costs is realized only where full-cost pricing is adhered to in spite of widespread excess capacity. Hence this policy can be sensible only where discipline is maintained, which, as suggested earlier, may be related to small number and heavy concentration. Sylos suggests that these considerations may help to explain certain empirical results indicating a positive association between cyclical wage rigidity and degree of concentration.[22]

The last two parts of Sylos' book expound the thesis that monopolistic and oligopolistic market structures are an important factor contributing to the development of unemployment, especially technological unemployment. In spite of the importance of the subject, this part will be reviewed in very sketchy form, both for lack of space and because Sylos' argument is not so convincing as his partial equilibrium analysis.

The main thread of his argument in Part II seems to run as follows. Starting from a stationary situation with full employment, a labor-saving innovation initially displaces labor. The reabsorption of this unemployment requires some net saving to be invested in the equipment necessary to outfit the displaced workers. (The alternative possibility of a fall in real wages leading to an appropriate change in capital coefficients is excluded by assumption.) Under perfectly

---

[19] George Stigler, "The Kinky Oligopoly Demand Curve and Rigid Prices," *Journal of Political Economy*, LV (October, 1947), 432–49.

[20] Richard Ruggles, "The Nature of Price Flexibility and Determinants of Relative Price Changes in the Economy," in *Business Concentration and Price Policy* (A Conference of the Universities-National Bureau Committee for Economic Research [Princeton, N.J.: Princeton University Press, 1955]), pp. 441–505.

[21] Note that this argument is applicable even to long-run equilibrium analysis. That is, when the market demand is sufficiently inelastic, an increase in wage rates may increase the total excess of receipts over (opportunity) costs accruing to the group. It may then be profitable for existing firms to tolerate high wages, as long as these are enforced by a trade union strong enough to impose the same wage scale on any potential entrant.

[22] The major piece of evidence quoted in this connection is J. W. Garbarino, "A Theory of Interindustry Wage Structure Variation," *Quarterly Journal of Economics*, LXIV (May, 1950), 282–305.

competitive market structures, the fall in cost would lead to higher real income for all those who have not lost their employment, and this rise in real income, especially profits, supposedly produces the saving and investment necessary for the reabsorption. On the other hand, under oligopolistic structures, the fall in cost will frequently not be accompanied by a proportionate fall in prices and will thus result in an increase in the value added of the sector where costs have fallen. (I have already expressed some doubt about the validity of this conclusion in the fifth section above.) To the extent that the increase in value added is absorbed by higher wages, the necessary saving will not be forthcoming, since, by an assumption which is particularly unpalatable to me, workers have a marginal propensity to consume equal to 1. To the extent that the increase in value added results in higher profits—and even if these profits give rise to savings—there may still be difficulties. Sylos suggests in fact that the entrepreneurs to whom the profits accrue will be disinclined to invest outside their own industry, whereas the investment required should be spread throughout the economy.

The conclusion Sylos draws is that, with widespread oligopolistic market structures, the forces making for reabsorption, though not entirely absent, will be lagging and weak. In a world of continuous technological change this weakness is sufficient, in his view, to account for a substantial permanent pool of unemployment, whose continuing existence is therefore an essentially dynamic phenomenon. He further argues that the kind of innovations the larger firms in the oligopolistic group will be inclined to adopt are likely to aggravate the technological displacement of labor. He maintains in fact that, though these firms will tend to be quite progressive in searching for, and adopting, innovations that cut costs at current level of output, they will nonetheless shun improvements that would cut costs only at a large scale of operation. But this argument is not quite consistent with his own model, since the new, larger-scale, and cheaper technique may itself become the immediate threat to entry. Nor is it clearly relevant—for it does not per se establish a bias in favor of labor-saving innovations.

Part III purports to explore the implications of the previous analysis for the standard Keynesian theory of effective demand. This part again contains many interesting observations but also has its shortcomings. In particular, the author does not seem to be sufficiently aware that the implications of the analysis of Part III are profoundly different for an economy poor in capital and savings like the Italian economy and for one in which the main threat to unemployment springs from a lack of effective demand. In the former case, labor-saving innovations may indeed tend to aggravate the problem of unemployment, especially when coupled with powerful unions and downward wage rigidity. But, in the latter case, such innovations are, as it were, a blessing, since they increase the required stock of capital and thus make possible the absorption of full-employment saving.

This sketch of Parts III and IV may well fail to do justice to Sylos' argument. But such a failure would serve to confirm the earlier statement that these final chapters do not quite match the high level of performance that characterizes the rest of this remarkable book.

Let us now look briefly at that part of Bain's analysis that does not overlap Sylos'.

Still with respect to barriers from economies of scale, Bain makes a halfhearted attempt to explore the consequences of dropping Sylos' postulate (see the second section). Unfortunately, as long as we are dealing with homogeneous oligopoly, it is hard to find a well-defined sensible alternative. Certainly, the diametrically opposite assumption that existing firms will adopt a policy of maintaining price, by contracting their output, would generally be a rather foolish one for the entrant to make. It implies that established firms will graciously allow the entrant to carve out for himself whatever slice of the market he pleases, while suffering losses on two accounts: (1) by losing sales and (2) by incurring a higher average cost, at least in the short run and possibly even in the long run, if their original plant was of no more than optimal size. Furthermore, such a policy, if consistently followed, would unavoidably result in the original members' being gradually squeezed out of the market.

The only alternative systematically explored by Bain is for the entrant to assume that price will be maintained but only provided he is contented with a share of the market no larger than that of the existing firms—which are conveniently assumed, for this purpose, to be all of equal size. There is, then, in general, a well-defined critical price (and corresponding output) such that entry is unprofitable even if a prospective entrant proceeds on the stated "optimistic" assumption.[23]

As Bain is well aware, this alternative assumption is but one of a large class of assumptions that could be constructed and explored. But he has wisely refrained from following this line, which is rather unpromising at this stage. For the moment, at least, we must be satisfied with the conclusion that there exists a well-defined upper limit to the price that can be maintained under oligopoly in the long run, and this upper limit is P_0, obtained under Sylos' postulate. It is the upper limit because, at a price higher than this, entry will be profitable even if the existing firms are bent on doing the entrant as much damage as they possibly can.[24] But a price lower than P_0 cannot be excluded a priori, even in the long

---

[23] It is easy to verify that the stated critical price, say, p_0, and corresponding output are given by the simultaneous solution of the following two equations:

$$X = D(p) \qquad (12.2)$$

$$p = c\frac{X}{(n+1)}, \qquad (12.3)$$

where $c(q)$ denotes the minimum long-run average cost of producing the quantity q, and n is the number of plants. In general, p_0 is an increasing function of n and is larger than the competitive price, at least as long as n is larger than S. Furthermore, for sufficiently large n, each firm is of less than optimal size, and the equilibrium bears a close resemblance to that described by Chamberlin in *Monopolistic Competition*, chap. v, sec. 5.

[24] A somewhat higher price could conceivably be maintained if the industry produced an output smaller than X_0, but had enough capacity to produce X_0 or more and a record of readiness to exploit the extra capacity to *expand* output in the face of entry. Such behavior would presumably require more or less open collusion, of a nature likely only with a very small and well-disciplined group.

run, especially where P_0 would cover the cost at a scale of output which represents a small fraction of X_0 and where a plant of such scale would require a relatively small investment. But, broadly speaking, these are precisely the conditions under which P_0 is close to 1, and the classical competitive model may provide a reasonable approximation. Conversely, Sylos' postulate may well provide a reasonable approximation precisely where it makes a real difference—where it implies a value of P_0 appreciably above unity.

Dropping the assumption that all producers, actual and potential, have access to identical cost functions enables us to analyze another set of forces which can account for a long-run excess of price over cost, and which Bain labels "absolute cost advantages." Such differential costs, arising from factors like control of scarce resources, patents and trade secrets, and generally superior technical and managerial know-how, have already been extensively analyzed and understood in the received body of theory. They underlie the traditional theory of monopoly, oligopoly without entry, and rents. Of course, with cost differential in the picture, there is no longer a specific entry-forestalling price, even under Sylos' postulate. Rather the critical price depends on the cost of the most efficient potential entrant and, hence, on just which firms are already in the group. It may then not be in the interest of existing firms to try to prevent the entry of very efficient producers, since this might require an unprofitably low price. When the price-output policy of existing firms is not intended to discourage potential entrants, Bain speaks of "ineffectively impeded" entry, in contrast to "effectively impeded" entry, in which price and output policy is designed to make entry unprofitable, and to "blockaded entry," in which the price and output policy that is most advantageous to the group, without regard to entry, happens to make entry unattractive.

But Bain's most significant finding about absolute cost barriers is probably at the empirical level. He finds in fact that, at least for his sample of twenty industries, such barriers are generally not important. Natural scarcity appears to be a significant factor in at most two industries—copper and possibly steel. In only three other cases do patents and/or technical know-how possibly play some role and apparently not a major one.

Bain also provides a valuable tabulation of available information on the size of the investment required by a new entrant (with an optimum scale plant). These capital requirements represent a somewhat special type of barrier to entry whose possible significance has been repeatedly mentioned earlier.

The remaining barrier to entry—resulting from the inability of potential competitors to produce a commodity that is a perfect substitute for the product of existing firms—is again one that has received considerable attention in the past. Bain's new contribution in this area consists of a penetrating empirical investigation of the specific barriers that impede the production of perfect or near-perfect substitutes for each industry and their consequences. The main factors may be classified roughly as follows: (1) Allegiance to brands, supported by large advertising outlays, and possibly also, by a long record of reliability; this factor is found to provide the main barrier, and a significant one, almost only in the case of inexpensive durable or non-durable consumers' goods such as cigarettes, liquor, and soap. (2) Control by the manufacturer of an extensive and exclusive dealers' organization attending to the sale and the servicing of the product; as one might expect, this phenomenon is of major importance for expensive durable goods, such as automobiles, typewriters, and tractors and other farm machinery, but it is apparently also of some significance for other commodities, such as petroleum and rubber tires. (3) Patents protecting some feature of the product or related auxiliary services. (4) Special services provided to customers. These last two factors are rarely mentioned and generally do not seem to offer very effective protection.

It is worth noting that factors (2) and (3), and in part also factor (1), could be largely treated as economies of scale in marketing. Both Bain and Sylos are aware of this possibility; in fact, the latter—though he pays only passing attention to product differentiation fostered by advertising—hints that the effect of this type of barrier could be analyzed along lines similar to those utilized in the homogeneous oligopoly model. That is, a new entrant could hope to match the profit performance of the successful large firms only by securing a market of the same absolute size. But, given the over-all size of the market, even if the entrant succeeded in capturing a share comparable to that of existing firms, each member would be left with too small a market, so that the final result of the entry would be to make the business unattractive for all.

After evaluating for his twenty industries the over-all barriers to entry resulting from the joint effect of economies of scale, absolute cost advantages, and product differentiation and after summarizing the effects that these over-all barriers should have on various aspects of market performance on the basis of his theoretical analysis, Bain proceeds to check his deductions against available evidence on actual performance. To be sure, the present evidence on barriers to entry as well as on market performance is frequently far from adequate, and one may have reservations about the details of some of the test procedures. Nonetheless, Bain's courageous attempt at systematic testing and his candid admission of occasional failures of his predictions is a highly welcome novelty and one whose importance can hardly be overestimated.

Finally, the implications of the analysis for public policy designed to foster workable competition are set forth in a very cautious and restrained spirit in the concluding chapter viii. On the whole, the outlook for effective public policy is not too optimistic, although it is by no means as gloomy as that of Sylos. But, then, Sylos' gloom is understandable. His inspiration comes from the Italian economy, where markets are naturally small and are made still smaller by tariffs and other artificial restrictions. According to his own model, the tendency to oligopolistic structures, and their power of market exploitation, will tend to be greater the smaller the size of the market.

I hope I have succeeded in justifying the glowing statement with which this review begins and in showing how well the two books complement each other. To be sure, much work still remains to be done in the area of oligopolistic market structures. In particular, the analysis of both authors is still largely limited to a static framework, and there is reason to believe that certain aspects of oligopolistic behavior can be adequately accounted for only by explicitly introducing dynamic elements into the analysis.[25] In my view, the real significance of Bain's

---

[25] Some promising beginnings in this direction are already to be found in Sylos and, even more, in Bain. The latter's notion of ineffectively impeded entry, for example,

and Sylos' contributions lies not merely in the results that they have already reached but at least as much in their having provided us with a framework capable of promising further developments and leading to operationally testable propositions. In addition, Bain deserves high credit for having led the way on the path of empirical testing.

---

is an essentially dynamic one. Similarly, Sylos hints that, where demand is growing, existing firms, to discourage entry, may have to keep their capacity somewhat larger than X_0 and their markup somewhat below P_0. Needless to say, the mere emphasis on the problem of entry is, per se, a significant movement in the direction of a dynamic analysis.

13

Seller Concentration, Barriers to Entry, and Rates of Return in Thirty Industries, 1950–1960*

H. Michael Mann

Conventional price theory predicts that industries in which output is produced by a few dominant firms may, in the long run, earn higher rates of return on the owners' investment than the opportunity cost of the equity capital, commonly called the normal or competitive rate of return. The emphasis on the long run recognizes that actual profit rates may differ from normal in the short run for reasons independent of the number of sellers, e.g., changes in demand or cost which raise or lower profits until the reallocation of resources pushes the industry toward long-run equilibrium.

The word "may" indicates that seller concentration is a necessary, but not sufficient, condition. For instance, if the few sellers fail to cooperate with regard to price and output, profits may well turn out to be normal. Or, if entry is relatively easy, the oligopolists may set a price close to the competitive level in order to discourage potential entrants. A price policy so designed is called limit pricing, the "limit" being that price above which entry would be attracted.[1]

Joe Bain has examined the latter possibility by measuring the influence of barriers to entry, classified as very high, substantial, and moderate-to-low, on the

Reprinted from *Review of Economics and Statistics*, August 1966, pp. 296–307 by permission of the author and publisher.

*The author is indebted to Joe Bain for very helpful comments on an earlier draft. Valuable research assistance was received from John Walgreen and James Meehan.

[1] This argument is advanced by Joe Bain in "A Note on Pricing in Monopoly and Oligopoly," *American Economic Review* (1949), 448–464, reprinted in Richard B. Heflebower and George W. Stocking, ed., *Readings in Industrial Organization and Public Policy* (Homewood, Illinois: Richard D. Irwin, 1958).

profit rates of the leading firms in a sample of oligopolistic industries for the periods 1936–1940 and 1947–1951.[2] He expected that the limit price and the monopoly price would probably coincide in the very high barrier class while oligopolists in markets with substantial or moderate barriers might find it profitable to set an entry-forestalling price below the monopoly level, a price which approaches the competitive price as entry barriers decrease. Therefore, profit rates should decline as barriers to entry decrease. Bain found a distinct difference between the average profit rates of those industries in the very high barrier category and those in the other classes. No such clear difference appeared between the substantial and the moderate-to-low barrier classes. He further found ". . . that seller concentration alone is not an adequate indicator of the probable incidence of extremes of excess profits and monopolistic output restriction. The concurrent influence of the condition of entry should clearly be taken into account." [3]

The purpose of this paper is to present the results of research into the relationship between seller concentration, barriers to entry, and profit rates for 1950 to 1960 to determine whether the pattern Bain found holds for a period of time that was not part of the Great Depression or of rapid postwar inflation. The findings support Bain's results, suggesting that a beginning has been made toward the accumulation of some evidence regarding the influence of two major aspects of market structure on rates of return.

CHARACTERISTICS OF THE SAMPLE

Thirty industries were assigned to three classes which denote the difficulty of entry. These categories were: very high barriers to entry; substantial barriers to entry; and moderate-to-low barriers to entry.

Very high barriers to entry result from one or some combination of the following four situations. (1) Economies of scale are so important that an entrant would have to supply a substantial fraction of industry output in order to operate at the minimum optimal scale of plant or of firm. Entry at this scale would lead to excess capacity and either higher costs or a price war. The reduction of profits due to either of these eventualities discourages the entrant. (2) The established firms have built up product differentiation advantages which necessitate very large sales promotion outlays on the part of entrants in order to overcome the preferences for the leading firms' products. (3) The established firms may control scarce raw materials forcing entrants to use inferior supplies or to buy at prices above the competitive level from the going firms, have patent protection on superior production techniques which entrants can only obtain for royalty charges, or have access to factors of production at lower prices than entrants. Any or all of these advantages of established firms mean that the entrant will operate at higher costs even if his scale of production realizes optimal efficiency. (4) The entrant may have to raise large amounts of capital, not only to build efficient

---

[2] The lowest concentration ratio in Bain's sample was 27 per cent for the top four sellers. Joe Bain, *Barriers to New Competition* (Cambridge, Mass.: Harvard University Press, 1956), 45.

[3] *Ibid.,* 201.

plants or to acquire its own supplies of raw materials, but also to compensate for losses, possibly for a number of years, until profits are made.[4]

Industries which have substantial barriers are characterized by one or a combination of the entry barriers just described, but the disadvantage to the potential entrant is not so great. Industries with moderate or low barriers can be entered rather easily.

Of the 30 industries, 17 were listed in Bain's work. (See Table 13.6, Appendix II.) All but one were classified identically to Bain's designations.

The one exception was the cement industry, which Bain put into the moderate-to-low barrier class. This study places cement in the substantial barrier category because some tentative evidence suggests that economies of scale may be an important barrier to entry into the cement industry.

Between 1952 and 1962, the modal plant size increased from between one and two million barrels to between two and three million barrels per year. The number of plants in the former category was 58 in 1962 or 18.7 per cent of the total number of plants, down from 88 in 1952 or 56 per cent of the total number of plants. The "survivor technique," a method of estimating minimum optimal plant size by comparing frequency distributions of plant sizes between two or more points in time, suggests that a plant of between two and three million barrels capacity per year has become the minimum optimal size, because the number and importance of plants in the one-to-two million barrel category has declined.[5]

Since cement is a regional industry,[6] estimates of the importance of minimum efficient scale should be made in terms of regional capacity. If we assume that the minimum optimal scale is about 2.5 million barrels per year and examine those producing districts listed by the Bureau of Mines which approximate meaningful markets, i.e., 11 districts in which the local cement producers could be identified as accounting for a significant fraction of the shipments to destinations within the district, we find that the lowest percentage of a district's total capacity represented by a 2.5 million barrel plant is about six per cent. The highest is over 22 per cent. These percentages are approximately consistent with Bain's estimates for two regional market categories: the proportion of capacity contained in a plant of minimally efficient scale for the largest region was four to five per cent and for the smallest major region, 27 to 33 per cent.

These estimates, along with Bain's finding that average costs rise rather sharply at less than optimal plant-scale in the cement industry, indicate that economies

---

[4] This is a brief summary of Bain's careful and detailed analysis. See Joe Bain, *Barriers to New Competition,* chaps. 3–6.

[5] The distribution of plants according to size intervals is contained in Oliver S. North and Esther V. Baker, "Cement," in Bureau of Mines, Department of the Interior, *Minerals Yearbook,* I (Washington, 1953), 255; and J. M. West and Cordell H. Lindquist, "Cement," *Ibid.* (Washington, 1963), 372.

For a discussion of the background of the survivor technique and its application to a sample of industries, see T. R. Saving, "Estimation of Optimum Size of Plant by the Survivor Technique," *The Quarterly Journal of Economics* (Nov. 1961), 569–607. For a more recent article see L. W. Weiss, "The Survival Technique and the Extent of Suboptimal Capacity," *Journal of Political Economy* (June, 1964), 246–261.

[6] According to one source ". . . the economic shipping range is 350 miles." "Ready-Mixed Competition," *Business Week* (May 23, 1964), 62.

SELLER CONCENTRATION, BARRIERS TO ENTRY, AND RATES OF RETURN 217

of plant size may be a very important barrier to entry and that cement may properly belong in the substantial barrier class.[7]

The 13 industries which were added to Bain's group were placed in one of the three barriers-to-entry categories for the reasons set out in Appendix I. The 30 industries contain eight in the very high barrier class, nine in the substantial barrier class, and 13 in the moderate-to-low barrier class.

The sample is more or less oligopolistic. The lowest concentration ratio is that of bituminous coal, where the ten largest firms in 1955 had 29.1 per cent of the total output.[8] Highly concentrated industries, those having a concentration ratio of above 70 per cent for the top eight firms, make up the very high barrier class, account for all but one of the substantial barrier class, and also account for five of the 13 industries in the moderate-to-low barrier group.

Profit rates were computed in the following way. The average rate of return (net income to average net worth)[9] for the leading firms in each industry over the period 1950–1960 was recorded.[10] The industry average rate of return is the average of the dominant firms' rates of return. (See Table 13.6, Appendix II.)

In order to minimize the effect of diversification by firms, an attempt was made to select firms which received at least 50 per cent of their sales revenue from the product of the industry in which they were placed. For most of the firms in the sample, there was no problem. However, there were a few, notably the tire and tube companies, which barely met the criterion. The results should, therefore, be interpreted with this limitation in mind.

[7] The producing district for which a 2.5 million barrel plant is six per cent of the district's total capacity is Texas where approximately 90 per cent of the shipments within the state are made by producers within Texas. The higher percentage, 22 per cent, is for Illinois where 78 per cent of the shipments within the state are made by producers within Illinois. F. F. Netzeband, Thomas R. Early, and Roselle M. Girard, "Texas," and Matthew G. Sikich and L. G. Marshall, "Illinois," Bureau of Mines, Department of the Interior, *Area Reports 1962*, vol. 3 (Washington, 1963), Table 14, p. 1015 and p. 368, respectively.

Bain's submarket estimates are from *Barriers to New Competition*, Table V, p. 76. His finding on the shape of the cost curve below optimal size is contained in Table VII, p. 80 of the same work. The importance of this finding is that a relatively shallow plant-scale curve permits suboptimal entry without any serious disadvantage with respect to efficiency.

[8] Simon Whitney, *Antitrust Policies*, vol. 1 (New York: the Twentieth Century Fund, 1958), Table 46, 413.

[9] As explained in footnote †, Table 13.6, Appendix II, a better measure of the rate of return for the leading firms in the aluminum industry was net income plus interest to the average of net worth plus long-term debt.

[10] For a large part of the sample, the returns for the years 1954–1960 were taken from Federal Trade Commission, *Rates of Return (after Taxes) for Identical Companies in Selected Manufacturing Industries*. For the rest of the industries and for the years not reported by the FTC, the source was Moody's Investors Service, *Moody's Industrial Manual*.

The net income used was that derived from operations. All special credits, such as nonrecurring capital gains, were excluded. Net worth was the sum of capital stock outstanding, paid-up or other capital surplus, earned surplus, minority interest in capital stock and surplus and surplus reserves.

Table 13.1

AVERAGE PROFIT RATES FOR THIRTY INDUSTRIES, 1950–1960, CLASSIFIED INTO TWO GROUPS: THOSE INDUSTRIES WITH A CONCENTRATION RATIO EQUAL TO OR ABOVE SEVENTY PER CENT FOR THE TOP EIGHT FIRMS AND THOSE WITH A CONCENTRATION RATIO BELOW SEVENTY PER CENT FOR THE TOP EIGHT FIRMS*

INDUSTRY	AVERAGE PROFIT RATES 1950–1960	INDUSTRY	AVERAGE PROFIT RATES 1950–1960
Above 70%.		Rayon	8.5
Automobiles	15.5	Gypsum Products	14.4
Chewing Gum	17.5	Metal Containers	9.9
Cigarettes	11.6	Cement	15.7
Ethical Drugs	17.9	Average	13.3
Flat Glass	18.8		
Liquor	9.0	*Below 70%.*	
Nickel	18.9		
Shoe Machinery	7.4	Petroleum Refining	12.2
Sulphur	21.6	Shoes (Diversified)	9.6
Aluminum Reduction	10.2	Canned Fruits and Vegetables	7.7
Biscuits	11.4	Meat Packing	5.3
Steel	10.8	Flour	8.6
Soap	13.3	Beer	10.9
Farm Machinery and Tractors	8.8	Baking	11.0
Copper	11.5	Bituminous Coal	8.8
Glass Containers	13.3	Textile Mill Products†	6.9
Tires and Tubes	13.2	Average	9.0

Source: Subcommittee on Antitrust and Monopoly, United States Senate, *Concentration Ratios in Manufacturing 1958*, Table 2, pp. 14–15.

* The general criterion for separation was the 1958 concentration ratio for the top eight firms as reported in Subcommittee on Antitrust and Monopoly, United States Senate, *Concentration Ratios in Manufacturing 1958*, Part I (Washington, 1962), Table 2. This criterion was not used for five industries which were assigned to the above 70 per cent group.

In three, shoe machinery, nickel, and sulphur, the Bureau of the Census does not record a four-digit industry classification. These industries were assigned on the basis of information contained in the sources cited in Appendix A. The cement industry, as indicated in the text, is a regional industry. Concentration ratios on a regional basis suggest that cement may properly belong in the above 70 per cent group. *Ibid.*, Part II (Washington, 1962), 505.

The four-digit industry classification that might have been used for ethical drugs is too broad. Therefore, the five-digit product classes which correspond to ethical drugs were employed. These classes had concentration ratios above 70 per cent. *Ibid.*, (Part I), 132.

† Textile mill products embrace nine product lines. Eight-firm concentration ratios are published for eight of these:

INDUSTRY	PER CENT OF VALUE OF SHIPMENTS ACCOUNTED FOR BY EIGHT LARGEST COMPANIES, 1958
Cotton system yarn mills	36
Cotton broad woven fabrics	40
Yarn throwing mills	48
Synthetic broad woven fabrics	44
Yarn mills, wool except carpet	34
Woolen and worsted fabrics	46
Finished textiles except wool‡	36
Finished woolen textiles‡	85
Converters	—

‡ "Shipments of finished textiles do not include custom work for converters except for the commissions earned by finishers. Realistically, the converters' shipments and the finished goods shipments (but not commissions) should be taken together. If they were, the concentration ratio for finished textiles might well be lower." Leonard W. Weiss, *Economics and American Industry* (New York: John Wiley and Sons, 1961), 130.

The reason for the selection of the dominant firms has best been stated by Bain:

> In regard to the appearance of the predicted association of the condition of entry to profit rates, it would be expected to be evident most definitely for the largest or dominant established firms in an industry, which will in general have the maximum aggregate advantage over potential entrants, and are most likely to be operating with minimal or close to minimal average costs. The profit rates of smaller firms, with inefficiently small plants or firm scales or with smaller product differentiation advantages over entrants, might be expected to show a less certain or distinct relationship to a condition of entry calculated primarily with reference to positions of the dominant firms.[11]

PRESENTATION OF THE RESULTS

Bain found that seller concentration and barriers to entry each had an independent influence on rates of return. Tables 13.1 to 13.3 present this present study's findings regarding the respective influence of seller concentration and barriers to entry.

The three tables indicate the following kinds of relationships. Table 13.1 shows that there is a distinct cleavage between the average profit rates of two groups of industries, divided according to whether the concentration ratio for the top eight firms is greater or less than 70 per cent. This finding is consistent with Bain's study. It also confirms[12] the results of earlier work by Bain in which he found that, for a sample of 42 industries, divided into two groups, those with a concentration ratio above 70 per cent for the top eight firms and those with a concentration ratio below 70 per cent, there was a statistically significant difference in the average profit rates of the two classes.[13]

Table 13.2 shows that there is a distinct difference between the average profit rates of the very high barrier group and the other two classes. A difference occurred between the substantial and moderate-to-low barrier classes, but it was less than one-half of the difference between the very high and the substantial barrier categories. This outcome is similar to that found by Bain.

The failure to find a sharp difference between the average profit rates of the substantial and moderate-to-low barrier classes may reflect incorrect identification of the industries within each category. Or, as Bain suggests, the leading firms in the latter group may view

> ... the barriers as low enough to encourage them to strive for relatively high, entry-attracting prices rather than to set prices sufficiently low to forestall entry. This could lead at least periodically to profit rates roughly

---

[11] Joe Bain, *Barriers to New Competition*, 191.
[12] The difference between average rates of return is statistically significant at the .01 level.
[13] Joe Bain, "Relation of Profit Rate to Industry Concentration, 1936–40," *Quarterly Journal of Economics* (Aug. 1951), 293–324.

Table 13.2

AVERAGE PROFIT RATES FOR THIRTY INDUSTRIES, 1950–1960, CLASSIFIED BY BARRIERS TO ENTRY

INDUSTRY	AVERAGE PROFIT RATE 1950–1960
Very High Barriers	
Automobiles	15.5
Chewing Gum	17.5
Cigarettes	11.6
Ethical Drugs	17.9
Flat Glass	18.8
Liquor	9.0
Nickel	18.9
Sulphur	21.6
Class Average	16.4
Substantial Barriers	
Aluminum Reduction	10.2
Biscuits	11.4
Petroleum Refining	12.2
Steel	10.8
Soap	13.3
Farm Machinery and Tractors	8.8
Copper	11.5
Cement	15.7
Shoe Machinery	7.4
Class Average	11.3
Moderate-to-Low Barriers	
Glass Containers	13.3
Tires and Tubes	13.2
Shoes (Diversified)	9.6
Rayon	8.5
Gypsum Products	14.4
Canned Fruits and Vegetables	7.7
Meat Packing	5.3
Flour	8.6
Metal Containers	9.9
Beer	10.9
Baking	11.0
Bituminous Coal	8.8
Textile Mill Products	6.9
Class Average	9.9

as high as those resulting from the entry-forestalling limit prices anticipated in industries with "substantial" entry barriers . . . .[14]

The limit price hypothesis, then, remains neither confirmed nor rejected.

Table 13.3 shows that barriers to entry apparently exert an independent influence in that highly concentrated industries with very high barriers to entry earned a distinctly higher average return than highly concentrated industries in other categories.

Table 13.3

AVERAGE PROFIT RATES FOR TWENTY-ONE INDUSTRIES, ALL OF HIGH SELLER CONCENTRATION,* CLASSIFIED ACCORDING TO BARRIERS TO ENTRY, 1950-1960

INDUSTRY	AVERAGE PROFIT RATES
Very High Barriers	
Automobiles	15.5
Chewing Gum	17.5
Cigarettes	11.6
Ethical Drugs	17.9
Flat Glass	18.8
Liquor	9.0
Nickel	18.9
Sulphur	21.6
Class Average	16.4
Substantial Barriers	
Aluminum Reduction	10.2
Biscuits	11.4
Steel	10.8
Soap	13.3
Farm Machinery and Tractors	8.8
Copper	11.5
Cement	15.7
Shoe Machinery	7.4
Class Average	11.1
Moderate-to-Low Barriers	
Glass Containers	13.3
Tires and Tubes	13.2
Rayon	8.5
Gypsum Products	14.4
Metal Containers	9.9
Class Average	11.9

* High seller concentration means a concentration ratio above 70 per cent for the top eight firms.

[14] Joe Bain, *Barriers to New Competition*, 198-199.

One clear outcome of Bain's work and of this study is that the "monopoly problem" appears to exist most noticeably in those industries which are highly concentrated and have high barriers to entry. If public policy seeks to improve resource allocation, industries with these structural characteristics seem to be a good place to start.

CONCLUSIONS

This investigation into the impact of seller concentration and barriers to entry on rates of return found that Bain's results were confirmed. This study employed a larger sample and an eleven-year period which was not part of two of the most severe economic fluctuations of modern times in the United States.

The confirmation of Bain's findings has one negative and one positive aspect. The former is that the limit price hypothesis remains neither proved nor disproved. More research into this question is called for.

The latter is that industries with high concentration ratios and high barriers to entry appear to be at the core of any resource misallocation due to monopolistic pricing. It is these industries which might be called to the attention of antitrust authorities.

Finally, it should be pointed out that more research is needed on the relationship between market structure and rates of return. This study, in confirming Bain, adds to the body of evidence. But rates of return may be inadequate indicators of price-cost margins, the particular barrier-to-entry classification into which an industry was placed may be incorrect, the period 1950–1960 may be a short run for some of the industries in the sample, and some important sufficient conditions for the exercise of monopolistic pricing may not be fulfilled. More research would help to provide firmer conclusions.

Appendix I to Reading 13

CLASSIFICATION OF INDUSTRIES WITH RESPECT TO BARRIERS TO ENTRY

The classification of 16 of the industries comes from Bain, *Barriers to New Competition*, Table XVI, pp. 192–194. The derivation of the classification is from the designation of the height of specific entry barriers. *Ibid.*, Table XIV, p. 169. The 16 are denoted in Table 13.6, Appendix II. Cement was classified differently from Bain's classification for reasons explained in the text.

The remaining 13 were classified according to the significance of specific entry barriers, indicated in Table 13.4 below by the notations "I," "II," and "III." These designations represent unimportant, moderately important, and very important entry barriers, respectively.

The particular rankings for each specific entry barrier were used to estimate the over-all barrier to entry for each industry. This estimate was based on intuitive judgment, not on any addition or averaging of specific barrier ranks. The lack of data or information by which to give ranks to specific entry barriers for some industries, the fact that economies of scale estimates are for plant only, and the difficulty in interpreting some of the information available precluded reliance on any procedure which did not involve use of judgment.

The information on which Table 13.4 depends follows. Each industry is grouped according to the judgment made about its over-all barrier-to-entry ranking.

VERY HIGH BARRIERS TO ENTRY

The most important barrier to entry into the sulphur industry is the control of the natural raw material by the dominant firms. Of the 12 salt domes from which

Table 13.4

RELATIVE HEIGHTS OF SPECIFIC ENTRY BARRIERS IN THIRTEEN INDUSTRIES
(HIGHER NUMBERS DENOTE HIGHER ENTRY BARRIERS)

INDUSTRY	SCALE-ECONOMY BARRIER	PRODUCT-DIFFERENTIATION BARRIER	ABSOLUTE-COST BARRIER	CAPITAL-REQUIREMENT BARRIER
Sulphur	n.a.	II	III	II
Nickel	n.a.	II	III	n.a.
Ethical Drugs	I	III	n.a.	II
Flat Glass	III	I	n.a.	II
Chewing Gum	n.a.	III	II	II
Aluminum Reduction	II	I	II	II
Shoe Machinery	I	I	III	n.a.
Biscuits	I	II	n.a.	I
Glass Containers	I	I	I	n.a.
Baking*	I to III	I to III	I	I
Bituminous Coal	I	I	II	II
Beer	I	I	n.a.	n.a.
Textile Mill Products	I	I	I	I

* The alternative rankings refer to entry by an independent baker or by a grocery store chain. The former faces high barriers compared to the latter.

elemental sulphur (sulphur which is not combined with any other substance) was mined in the United States in 1960, Texas Gulf Sulphur and Freeport Sulphur controlled nine. The sulphur obtained from these domes is Frasch sulphur[15] and is superior to that obtained from pyrites (metal sulphides which are roasted to obtain sulphur dioxide), the major alternative source[16] because the major consumers of sulphur (sulphuric acid manufacturers) can derive about 30 per cent more acid from a given weight of elemental sulphur than from pyrite sulphur.

The only other source of Frasch sulphur is Mexico. Pan American Sulphur, which mined 82 per cent of Mexico's supply in 1960, entered the American Market through price cutting during the years 1956 to 1958. Since that time, Pan American has behaved as an oligopolist interested in group control of price.

[15] Frasch sulphur is so named because Dr. Herman Frasch discovered the process which extracts sulphur from its underground deposits. A description of the process is contained in Federal Trade Commission, *Report on the Sulphur Industry and International Cartels* (Washington, 1947), 20.

[16] In the early 1960's, sulphur recovered from the hydrogen sulfide obtained during the sweetening of sour natural gas has become more important than pyrites as an alternative to Frasch sulphur. Furthermore, recovered sulphur is as good, if not better, in quality as Frasch sulphur.

However, the major source of sour natural gas is in Canada and the predictions are that recovered sulphur from Canada will only constitute about ten per cent of United States consumption of sulphur.

Sulphuric acid manufacturers prefer to receive their sulphur in a molten, rather than solid, state because the former saves the expense of melting the sulphur for pumping to the burners of the acid plants. The dominant sulphur producers have established local distribution terminals which supply either molten or solid sulphur. "When a user becomes accustomed to using a convenient local supply of molten sulphur, an effective tie between supplier and customer is established." [17] This suggests that a moderate degree of product differentiation exists.

The facilities which provide molten sulphur are expensive.[18] W. G. Brese estimated that Freeport Sulphur's outlays to establish the requisite facilities exceed $20,000,000, a "large" capital requirement.[19]

Like the sulphur industry, the major barrier to entry into the nickel industry is the control of the natural raw material by the dominant firms.[20] International Nickel (Inco) and Falconbridge account for over 90 per cent of the proved ore reserves of virtually the sole supplier of the United States market, Canada. Buyers have little recourse to alternative supplies because nickel has certain unique properties, particularly its toughness and noncorrosiveness, which isolate it from the competition of substitutes in many uses, notably in the production of stainless steel. Supplies of nickel recovered from scrap are a very minor portion of the market.

Although nickel is a homogeneous good, Inco apparently has a research and marketing organization which represents a formidable obstacle to a new entrant. *Business Week* states that "Inco is vulnerable on neither product nor services" and that Falconbridge has found it quite difficult to make inroads into Inco's near complete dominance of the United States market.

The first difficulty facing a potential newcomer into the ethical drug industry is the patent protection on existing drugs.[21] Entry can occur only by being

[17] W. G. Brese, *An Analysis of the Sulphur Industry in Alberta* (Edmonton, Alberta, 1962), 45 and 47.

[18] W. G. Brese, *An Analysis of the Sulphur Industry in Alberta* (Edmonton, Alberta, 1962); Federal Trade Commission, *Report on the Sulphur Industry and International Cartels* (Washington, 1947); "Sulfur," *Chemical Week* (Sept. 12, 1964); and Robert Sheehan, "The 'Little Mothers' and Pan American Sulphur," *Fortune* (July, 1960).

[19] Bain has four classes with respect to capital requirements: Very large (generally above 100 million dollars), large (generally 10 to 50 million dollars), moderate (generally 2.5 to 10 million dollars), and small (generally under 2 million dollars). Joe Bain, *Barriers to New Competition,* Table XIII, 158–159.

[20] Ore reserves were estimated by taking the figures of the two dominant firms as a percentage of all Canadian firms, as found in Moody's Investors Service, *Moody's Industrial Manual*; I. V. Cobleigh, "Canadian Nickel: Investor Slanted Notes on This Strategic Metal," *Commercial and Financial Chronicle* (Aug. 9, 1956); and "Mining New Markets for Nickel," *Business Week* (Sept. 5, 1964).

[21] William S. Comanor, "Research and Competitive Product Differentiation in the Pharmaceutical Industry in the United States," *Economica* (Nov. 1964), 372–384; Henry Steele, "Patent Restrictions and Price Competition in the Ethical Drugs Industry," *The Journal of Industrial Economics* (July, 1964), 198–223; Federal Trade Commission, *Economic Report on Antibiotics Manufacture* (Washington, 1958); and Subcommittee on Antitrust and Monopoly, United States Senate, *Administered Prices, Drugs, Report* (Washington, 1961).

granted a license or by making some technical advance in the form of a new drug or an improvement in an existing drug. Entry by technical advance introduces the costs and risks associated with research outlays. And even if a new or improved drug is discovered, the entrant must be ready to spend large sums to promote it.[22]

The capital necessary to build an efficient plant is difficult to estimate, but probably falls into Bain's moderate capital-requirement category.[23]

It is not clear how important economies of scale are, but, on balance, they do not appear to be significant. It is true that the average plant size in one major ethical drug category, antibiotics, is large relative to the industry output. However, the costs of production seem to be constant over a wide range of output.[24]

The evidence indicates that the technological transformation in the early 1900's from hand to machine manufacture in the flat glass industry necessitated large-scale plants for efficiency.[25] The following table shows the change in the number of plants producing plate and sheet glass, which account for most of the flat glass output, between 1899 and 1935.

The average plant size is still very large. In 1960, Pittsburgh Plate operated four sheet and four plate glass plants. Libby-Owens-Ford operated one sheet and three plate glass plants and one which produced both plate and sheet glass. Since these firms account for about 90 per cent of the value of plate glass production and 65 per cent of the value of sheet glass output, each of their plants accounts for about ten per cent of the value of the industry output. This information doesn't tell us what the shape of the plant-scale curve is, but Table 13.5 suggests

---

[22] One estimate indicates that, for a single drug, it requires about one million dollars to reach one-half of the physicians with one visit by a salesman. More intensive efforts, say, through additional visits, begin to be very costly. Subcommittee on Antitrust and Monopoly, United States Senate, *Administered Prices, Drugs, Report* (Washington, 1961), 78.

The emphasis on promotional activities can be indicated by the fact that the five companies included in this study spent, on the average, in 1958, 26 per cent of their sales revenue on advertising, the distribution of samples, and calls by salesmen upon physicians and pharmacists. The outcome of such efforts has been to emphasize brand names, which virtually insures that physicians will not treat the drugs of different companies, even if generically identical, as homogeneous commodities. *Ibid.*, Table 9, p. 31.

[23] One small drug manufacturer indicated that an investment of five million dollars would allow him to enter the production, assuming the research was done, of prednisone and prednisolone, two corticosteroids. On the other hand, penicillin plants cost as much as 16 million dollars to build in the early 1950's.

[24] In 1956, 3,081,373 pounds of antibiotics were produced by 19 plants. Efficient size of plant, though, appears to be variable over a range of output. Federal Trade Commission, *Economic Report on Antibiotics Manufacture* (Washington, 1958), Table 9, 74–75, Table 21, pp. 98 and 118.

[25] David A. Loehwing, "The Glass Makers," *Barron's* (March 11, 1963); Select Committee on Small Business, United States Senate, *Studies of Dual Distribution: The Flat Glass Industry, Report* (Washington, 1960); and United States Tariff Commission, *Flat Glass and Related Products*, Report No. 123, 2nd Series (Washington, 1937).

Table 13.5

NUMBER OF PLANTS AND TOTAL PRODUCTION OF PLATE
AND SHEET GLASS, SELECTED YEARS, 1899 TO 1935

YEAR	PLANTS (NUMBER)		PRODUCTION	
	PLATE GLASS	SHEET GLASS	PLATE GLASS (SQUARE FEET)	SHEET GLASS BOXES (50 SQUARE FEET)
1899	16	100	16,884,000	4,341,000
1925	16	42	117,369,000	11,343,000
1929	8	—	118,670,136	—
1935	6	13	180,383,801	8,135,108

Source: United States Tariff Commission, *Flat Glass and Related Products*, Report No. 123, 2nd Series (Washington, 1937), Table 12, p. 49 and Table 37, p. 96.

that it is probably steep enough to make the minimum optimal plant size very large relative to the industry output.[26]

Since plate glass and sheet glass are largely sold to manufacturers, there is little scope for much product differentiation.

The capital required for a plate glass plant is estimated to run $45 to $50 million dollars, while for a sheet glass plant, the amount runs $12 to $15 million dollars. These are "large" capital requirements.

The major barrier to entry into chewing gum appears to be product differentiation.[27] Wrigley spent, on the average, better than eight per cent of its sales revenue on advertising from 1952 to 1960. American Chicle, between 1954 and 1960, averaged about seven per cent of its sales revenue on advertising expenditures. Both of these percentages exceed the proportion of sales revenue spent by the dominant cigarette firms, a market where product differentiation is very important.

---

[26] Bain classifies scale economies as very important if the minimum optimal size plant or firm supplies ten per cent or more of the market's output and if unit costs rise significantly at less than optimal scale. Moderately important scale economies occur if four or five per cent of the market's output is required for optimal size and if unit costs rise significantly at less than optimal scale. Scale economies are unimportant if only one or two per cent of the market's output is produced at minimum optimal scale and the scale-curve is relatively flat below minimum optimal size. Joe Bain, *Barriers to New Competition*, 103–104.

[27] Faye Henle, "Snap in Chewing Gum," *Barron's* (May 28, 1956), 13–15; and William S. Jackson, "American Chicle Co.," *Banker's Monthly* (Mar. 15, 1961), 46–49. The advertising expenditures come from the following issues of *Printers' Ink, Advertisers' Guide to Marketing*: 1957, p. 73; 1959, p. 158; 1961, p. 343, and 1963, p. 386. The figures for advertising are understated to some degree because they include only national space and time and do not include all media in some years. Sales revenue figures are from *Moody's Industrials*.

In addition to product differentiation, one source suggests that technical know-how and the cost of machinery also block the way of the potential entrant. Since no quantitative magnitude could be attached to the capital requirement for machinery or the degree of technical know-how involved, the absolute-cost and capital-requirement barriers were given a moderate ranking.

SUBSTANTIAL BARRIERS TO ENTRY

The ranking of aluminum reduction as having substantial barriers to entry presumes that vertical integration is not required for entry.[28] If it is, then aluminum reduction belongs in the very high barrier class.[29]

Efficient plant size obtains at about three per cent of the industry's capacity. Although no estimate was made of the cost curve's shape below minimum optimal scale, this percentage borders on the moderately important category of scale economies. Production differentiation is unimportant in this industry.

The capital necessary to build an efficient plant is large, running about 63 million dollars. In addition, the established firms have lower costs because new capacity is more expensive than older capacity and the latter has cheap hydropower to use.

The major cause of United Shoe Machinery's almost complete domination of the shoe machinery industry until 1954 was the employment of certain market practices which made it very difficult for any competitor, actual or potential, to win business.[30] Only if a competitive machine were much better or much cheaper than a United machine would a shoe manufacturer find it worthwhile to pay the substantial costs of "untying" from United. Therefore, the absolute-cost barrier was given the highest notation.

Economies of scale and product differentiation appear to be relatively unimportant.[31]

An antitrust case in 1954 resulted in the prohibition of many of the entry-inhibiting practices and, therefore, considerably reduced the importance of the absolute-cost barrier ranking. Before the antitrust case, then, shoe machinery might have belonged in the very high barrier group, whereas, after the case, the

---

[28] Merton J. Peck, *Competition in the Aluminum Industry, 1945–1958* (Cambridge, Mass.: Harvard University Press, 1961), chap. X.

[29] Aluminum reduction probably ranks near the top of the substantial barrier-to-entry class because, if vertical integration is necessary, the scale-economy and capital-requirement barriers would be raised to a "III" rating. The major study of this industry in the postwar period does not reach a conclusion on the necessity of vertical integration.

[30] Carl Kaysen, *op. cit.*

[31] The evidence is thin, but Carl Kaysen's examination of economies in production, distribution, service, and research do not indicate very important scale economies. United enjoys some product differentiation by virtue of its full line of machines and its marketing of supplies which are used with the machines. Apparently these advantages do not give United much edge over potential competitors. Carl Kaysen, *United States v. United Shoe Machinery Corporation* (Cambridge, Mass.: Harvard University Press, 1956), 92–98 and 229–232.

moderate-to-low barrier class would be appropriate. A compromise was made and shoe machinery was placed in the substantial barrier category.

Bureau of the Census data on the distribution of plant sizes in the biscuit industry, according to the number of employees, show no tendency for the smallest classes to disappear between 1947 and 1958.[32] Since the plants in these classes account, on the average, for less than one per cent of the industry value added in 1958, economies of scale appear to be unimportant.

Between 1951 and 1959, National Biscuit and Sunshine Biscuits spent about 2.3 per cent and 1.4 per cent of their sales revenue on advertising, respectively. These percentages understate their promotional efforts, however, since they do not take into account the expenditure on store displays and other kinds of promotional activity. *Barron's* reports that National Biscuit and Sunshine Biscuits invest closer to five per cent and three per cent of their sales revenue on advertising and promotion, respectively.

No precise estimate of capital requirements is possible. *Business Week* cites United Biscuit's new plant in Denver, Colorado as being modern and efficient and as having cost 9.5 million dollars, a moderate capital requirement.

The biscuit industry appears to rank near the top of the substantial barrier class. It does not make the very high barrier class, in the author's judgment, because its expenditure on sales promotion does not quite reach the proportion of sales revenue characteristic of industries with significant product differentiation.

MODERATE-TO-LOW BARRIERS TO ENTRY

Economies of scale do not seem to be important in the glass container industry.[33] Bureau of the Census data on the distribution of establishments by number of employees show no tendency for smaller plants to disappear.[34]

[32] David Loehwing, "The Biscuit Makers," *Barron's* (Dec. 16, 1957); and "Baking an Assortment in One Cake," *Business Week* (Dec. 29, 1962). The distribution of establishments by employee-size comes from Bureau of the Census, Department of Commerce, *Census of Manufacturers,* vol. II (1947), Table 4, p. 115; vol. II, part I (1954), Table 4, p. 20E–11; vol. II, part I (1958), Table 4, p. 20E–12. The source for advertising expenditures come from the following issues of *Printers' Ink, Advertisers' Guide to Marketing: 1957,* pp. 91, 97; *1959,* pp. 178, 187; *1960,* pp. 328, 337; and *1961,* pp. 360, 367. The figures for advertising are understated to some degree because they include only national space and time and do not include all media in some years. Sales revenue figures are from *Moody's Industrials.*

[33] R. L. Bishop, "The Glass Container Industry," in Walter Adams, ed., *The Structure of American Industry* (New York: Macmillan, 1950). The distribution of establishments by employee-size classes come from Bureau of the Census, Department of Commerce, *Census of Manufacturers,* vol. II (1947), Table 4, p. 494; vol. II, part II (1954), Table 4, p. 32A–7; and vol. II, part II (1958), Table 4, p. 32A–10.

[34] Between 1954 and 1958, there was an increase of 15 establishments in the industry. The largest increase, seven, occurred in the 250–499 employee range. The average plant size in this class accounted for slightly less than one per cent of the industry value added in 1958. This suggests that the minimum optimal plant size is quite small.

The increase in establishments did not occur because of the reclassification of

Glass containers are principally producers goods. This permits little room for product differentiation.

The absolute-cost barrier, although once important, is so no longer.[35]

The discussion of specific barriers to entry into the baking industry refers to the white bread segment of the industry, its most important branch.[36] For entrants other than grocery chains, economies of scale are a very important barrier to entry, largely because the relevant markets are small relative to the optimal size plant.[37] The reason why grocery chains do not face such a high scale-economy barrier is that they can efficiently serve market areas much larger than independent bakers—400 to 500 miles versus 150 miles.[38]

The leading firms spend about four per cent of their sales revenue on advertising, which apparently influences preferences.[39] The dominant firms also seem to have established preferential agreements with many grocery stores regarding shelf space and prominent positions for their displays. The advantages gained in these respects do not seriously hinder grocery chains since they control the shelf and the display space in their own outlets and typically charge prices for their private brands which are lower than those of established brands, thus offsetting some of the effectiveness of the large independent bakers' advertising.

Inputs and technical know-how are easily available to all potential newcomers.

---

establishments from some other industry into the glass container industry. Both the primary product specialization and coverage ratios, which measure the degree of homogeneity of the industry's output, were nearly equal to 1.00 in 1954 and 1958. For a discussion of the measures of homogeneity, see Subcommittee on Antitrust and Monopoly, United States Senate, *Concentration Ratios in Manufacturing 1958* (Washington, 1962), 1–6.

[35] From World War I until 1946, two firms, Owens-Illinois and Hartford-Empire, controlled, through patents, the technology of the industry. An antitrust suit ended this control, thereby removing a major barrier to entry into the industry.

[36] Charles C. Slater, *Baking in America: Market Organization and Competition*, Vol. II (Evanston, Illinois: Northwestern University Press 1956); and Richard G. Walsh and Bert M. Evans, *op. cit.*

[37] "For example, in the Omaha market with 400,000 to 500,000 people, the required market share for entry at optimum levels of efficiency would be roughly 70–90 per cent. Given the further condition that five operating plants share the bulk of that market and operate at varying levels of under-capacity such that any two of them with nearly full plant utilization could supply the entire market, the height of the entry barrier is further raised. . . . For markets with higher or increasing population, the barrier may be somewhat less, but it is still a significant deterrent to entry at optimum levels of efficiency." Richard G. Walsh and Bert M. Evans, *Economics of Change in Market Structure, Conduct, and Performance: The Baking Industry 1947–58* (Lincoln, Nebraska, 1963), 43.

[38] This is due to economies in distribution which permit full exploitation of production economies. The independent bakers' method of distribution runs into decreasing returns before the increasing returns in production are exhausted. These decreasing returns outweigh the gains from the continued expansion of production.

[39] According to one consumer survey, advertising was the principal reason given for brand preferences. Richard G. Walsh and Bert M. Evans, *op. cit.*, 37.

The capital requirement for an efficient plant appears to be small, between one and two million dollars.

A study of the midwestern coal region finds that an underground mine exhausts economies of scale at around 500,000 tons.[40] In 1959, this region produced over 90 million tons, of which approximately 37 million tons came from underground mines. The optimally efficient underground mine size, then, is a little over one per cent of the underground output.

The strip mine has a larger optimal scale, estimated to be around five per cent of the strip mine output, about 53 million tons in the midwestern region in 1959. For both kinds of mines, the cost curve seems to be fairly flat for some distance.

Established firms enjoy little advantage from product differentiation since coal is an industrial good. The established firms do enjoy a moderate advantage in the absolute-cost category. Although only seven per cent of midwestern reserves are controlled by the top 20 firms, these firms control virtually all of the highest quality reserves. This is particularly true of strip reserves, an important consideration because strip mines operate at lower average costs than underground mines. Nevertheless, the absolute-cost category did not get the highest barrier ranking because there exists a strong possibility that the poorer reserves may become very valuable under the impact of the electric utilities' changing locational requirements.

A one million ton per year mine, which is larger than necessary for an efficient underground mine, requires an investment of eight million dollars. However, the optimal strip mine (about four million tons a year) would require around 30 million dollars.

Bureau of the Census data on establishments in the beer and ale industry, distributed according to the number of employees, show a decline in the number of breweries with less than 500–999 employees between 1947 and 1958.[41] The survivor technique suggests that this size has become the minimum optimal size. The average value-added of plants within this category in 1958 was one per cent of the industry value-added. This percentage is sufficiently low to suggest that economies of scale are unimportant.[42]

[40] Reed Moyer, *Competition in the Midwestern Coal Industry* (Cambridge, Mass.: Harvard University Press, 1964), especially chaps. V and VI.

[41] I. U. Cobleigh, "Brewing Earning Power," *Commercial and Financial Chronicle* (Dec. 15, 1960); S. A. Grayser, "Case of the Befuddled Brewers," *Harvard Business Review* (March 1961), 136–141. This reference contains the results of the consumer survey. The distribution of establishments by employee-size come from Department of Commerce, Bureau of the Census, *Census of Manufactures*, vol. II (1947), Table 4, p. 132; vol. II, part I (1954), Table 4, p. 20G–7; and vol. II, part I (1958), Table 4, p. 20G–11.

[42] A recent study concludes that the minimum optimal size brewery produces about 1,500,000 barrels per year. In 1961, 95 million barrels were produced, meaning that the size of brewery obtaining the lowest unit costs accounted for approximately 1.5 per cent of the annual production in that year. Ira Horowitz and Ann R. Horowitz, "Firms in a Declining Market: The Brewing Case," *The Journal of Industrial Economics* (March 1965), 129–153.

Product differentiation does not appear to be significant. One consumer survey indicates that beer-drinkers do not show a marked preference for nationally advertised beers.

Two estimates of the percentage of industry capacity accounted for by optimally efficient mills in coarse yarn and in fine cotton woven goods suggest that economies of scale are quite unimportant in the textile mill products industry.[43] In coarse yarn, the minimum optimal size occurs at around 0.04 per cent of industry capacity. In fine cotton woven goods, the percentage is about 0.3 per cent. More generally, small plants dominate the distribution of plants by employee-size categories and there seems to be no tendency for the small plants to disappear in favor of larger plants.

Textile mill products in finished form are sold to retailers who are experts regarding the quality of the product which they are buying, permitting little opportunity for product differentiation.

Neither important patents covering the industry's technology nor tight control over raw materials exist. One economist, while making no quantitative estimate, indicates that the capital requirement is low.[44]

[43] Leonard W. Weiss, *Economics and American Industry* (New York: John Wiley & Sons, 1961), chap. 4; and Simon Whitney, *Antitrust Policies*, vol. I (New York: The Twentieth Century Fund, 1958). The distribution of plants by the number of employees was compared for all the four-digit groups used in this study between 1947 and 1954, except for synthetic broad woven fabrics and converters. Department of Commerce, Bureau of the Census, *Census of Manufactures* (1947), Table 4, p. 159 and Table 4, p. 173; vol. II, part I (1954), Table 4, p. 22B–10 and Table 4, p. 22A–6.

[44] Simon Whitney, *op. cit.*, 535.

Appendix II to Reading 13

Table 13.6

AVERAGE RATE OF RETURN (NET INCOME TO AVERAGE NET WORTH) FOR THE DOMINANT FIRMS IN THIRTY INDUSTRIES, CLASSIFIED BY ENTRY BARRIERS, 1950 TO 1960

INDUSTRY AND FIRM	AVERAGE ANNUAL PROFIT RATE (UNWEIGHTED) 1950–1960	INDUSTRY AND FIRM	AVERAGE ANNUAL PROFIT RATE (UNWEIGHTED) 1950–1960
Industries with very high barriers:		Schenley	5.7
Automobiles*		Hiram Walker	12.8
General Motors	21.5	Nickel	
Ford	14.5	International Nickel	17.5
Chrysler	10.5	Falconbridge	20.2
Chewing Gum		Sulphur	
Wrigley (Wm., Jr. Co.)	15.3	Texas Gulf-Sulphur	27.4
American Chicle	19.7	Freeport Sulphur	16.4
Cigarettes*		Industries with Substantial Barriers:	
Reynolds	14.6	Aluminum†	
American Tobacco	11.7	Alcoa	8.7
Liggett & Meyers	10.0	Reynolds Metals	10.0
Phillip Morris	10.2	Kaiser	11.9
Ethical Drugs		Biscuits	
Merck & Co.	14.4	National Biscuit	12.2
Pfizer (Charles)	17.1	Sunshine Biscuits	13.4
Schering Corp.	23.1	United Biscuits	8.6
Parke, Davis & Co.	20.7	Petroleum Refining*	
Abbott Laboratories	14.4	Standard Oil (N.J.)	14.6
Flat Glass		Texaco	15.2
Pittsburgh	14.5	Socony Mobil	10.3
Libby-Owens-Ford	23.1	Standard Oil (Ind.)	8.5
Liquor*		Steel*	
Seagram	9.3	U.S. Steel	10.7
National Distillers	8.0	Bethlehem	11.8

234 PRICING BEHAVIOR

INDUSTRY AND FIRM	AVERAGE ANNUAL PROFIT RATE (UNWEIGHTED) 1950–1960	INDUSTRY AND FIRM	AVERAGE ANNUAL PROFIT RATE (UNWEIGHTED) 1950–1960
Steel (Continued)		Genesco	12.1
Republic	12.0	Endicott Johnson	3.2
Jones & Laughlin	8.7	*Rayon**	
Soaps*		American Viscose	7.8
Proctor & Gamble	15.9	Celanese	8.2
Colgate-Palmolive Co.	10.7	Beaunit Corp.	8.9
Farm Machinery and Tractors*		*Gypsum Products*·‡*	
International Harvester	7.5	U.S. Gypsum	15.9
Allis-Chambers	8.8	National Gypsum	12.9
Deere	10.2	*Canned Fruits and Vegetables**	
Copper*		California Packing Co.	8.6
Kennecott	13.8	Libby-McNeil	6.8
Anaconda	7.2	Stokely-Van Camp	7.6
Phelps Dodge	15.3	*Meat Packing**	
American Smelting & Refining	9.6	Swift	5.1
Cement*		Armour	5.2
Ideal Cement Co.	17.8	Wilson	5.6
Lone Star	14.3	*Flour**	
Lehigh Portland	10.4	General Mills	10.0
General Portland	20.2	Pillsbury	7.2
Shoe Machinery		*Metal Containers*·‡*	
United States Shoe Machinery Corp.	7.4	American Can	10.3
Compo Shoe Machinery Corp.	7.4	Continental Can	9.6
		Beer	
		Anheuser-Busch	10.7
Industries with Moderate-to-Low Barriers:		Pabst Brewing Co.	4.8
		Falstaff Brewing	16.3
Glass Containers		*Baking*	
Owens-Illinois	13.6	Continental Baking Co.	13.2
Anchor-Hocking	13.4	American Bakeries Co.	12.7
Thatcher Glass Manufacturing Co.	12.5	General Baking Co.	7.1
Tires and Tubes*		*Bituminous Coal*	
Goodyear	13.5	Consolidation Coal Co.	8.2
Firestone	14.6	Peabody Coal Co.	7.8
U.S. Rubber	12.3	Island Creek Coal Co.	10.4
Goodrich	12.5	*Textile Mill Products*	
Shoes*		Burlington Industries	7.9
International Shoe	9.6	J. P. Stevens	6.7
Brown Shoe	13.4	Cone Mills Corp.	6.3
		Dan River Mills, Inc.	6.7

* These are the 17 industries taken from Bain. In seven of the 17 industries, the sample of dominant firms differs. In six of these, the difference involves only one firm. In cement, two firms differ. Ideal Cement Co., and General Portland were, on the basis of 1960 capacity, dominant firms. Bain used Alpha Portland and Penn Dixie.

† The rates of return for the three aluminum companies are measured by the ratio of net income plus interest to the average of net worth plus long term debt. These companies have very high debt to equity ratios which inflates their rates of return on net worth considerably. Thus, capital structure obscures the influence of market structure. Except for aluminum, leverage did not seriously distort returns and make invalid comparisons of the affects of market structure.

‡ Gypsum products and metal containers were classified in the substantial barrier category by Bain. However, he argued that this was valid only for the period prior to 1950. After that year, the moderate-to-low barrier classification was appropriate. Joe Bain, *Barriers to New Competition*, 170.

PART IV

PRODUCT DIFFERENTIATION ACTIVITIES

The price and level of output of a firm's product are only two of the many facets of a firm's behavior. Other features include the level of the firm's expenditure on advertising and sales promotion activities, or on research and development. These activities, which influence the cost and demand conditions associated with the firm's products, are sometimes referred to as product differentiation activities. Product differentiation exists whenever the products of different firms in the same industry are not perfect substitutes for each other from the point of view of buyers of the industry's products. The efforts of an individual firm to differentiate its product from those of other firms are often just as important in contributing to the firm's objectives as the price charged for the firm's products.

Conventional price theory says virtually nothing about the determinants of the level or characteristics of a firm's product differentiation activities. In price theory product differentiation is simply assumed to exist in certain market situations, notably monopolistic competition and oligopoly with differentiated products, and is shown to have certain implications for pricing behavior. The main implication is that the price of a firm's product will exceed the marginal cost of producing and distributing the product. A particular price-cost relationship is compatible, however, with numerous different levels of expenditure on product differentiation activities, while any particular level of expenditure on this type of activity can be allocated in many different ways. Price theory omits consideration of these other aspects of a firm's behavior almost entirely.

Expectations about rivals' reactions may be just as important in determining the magnitude and character of product differentiation activities as they are in influencing pricing behavior. Although these expectations may be related to the number and size distribution of firms selling in the same market, the relationship is probably much more complex than in the case of pricing behavior, and a priori theorizing on this point is inconclusive. Other factors which may affect the magnitude and character of a firm's product differentiation activities are technological opportunity and certain features of buyers' information in the market in which the firm operates, because these factors influence the returns anticipated from Research & Development and advertising activities.

Part IV consists of five papers which deal with nonprice aspects of firms' behavior and the relationship between these aspects and pricing. F. M. Scherer's article is one of many recent studies of the empirical relationship between seller concentration and research and development inputs. It was chosen in preference to other papers analyzing this aspect of industrial organization because it attempts to take into account the influence of interindustry differences in scientific and technological opportunity on the observed relationship between R&D inputs and seller concentration. The article also emphasizes that even if a causal relationship exists between these two variables, it is possible that high levels of R&D activity cause high seller concentration by creating patent and know-how entry barriers, instead of the reverse chain of causality more frequently assumed to exist.

In the second article L. Telser considers the relationship between advertising and seller concentration. He finds little empirical association between these two variables and concludes that advertising is quite compatible with a competitive structure. In the empirical study by W. S. Comanor and T. A. Wilson the authors point out that the weak correlation between concentration and advertising observed by Telser may simply indicate that these two variables affect industry pricing independently of one another. Attention is focused on the empirical relationship between advertising and industry profits, and statistical evidence is shown to be consistent with the hypothesis that advertising affects industry pricing by influencing the height of entry barriers into the relevant industry. The direction in which the conclusions point contrasts markedly with that of Telser's study.

The interdependence of pricing and product differentiation activities receives further emphasis in the econometric study by D. Mueller. His evidence, which indicates that policies directed at one aspect of a firm's behavior may also affect other features of the firm's behavior, has important implications both for a study of the firm and for public policy measures designed to affect individual characteristics of firms' behavior. A close relationship between different aspects of a firm's behavior may be attributable to the fact that the funds available to a firm are limited at any particular point in time. Decisions concerning the level of the firm's spending on current production, advertising, and R&D activities may be made by weighing the anticipated effects of spending funds on one activity rather than another, and by comparing the anticipated contribution of each activity to the achievement of the decision-maker's objectives. A change in the firm's economic environment which changes the return anticipated from one type of activity will, in these circumstances, often lead to a change in the allocation of funds among different activities and affect all activities undertaken by the firm. If different policy-variables are related in this way, simultaneous consideration of the effect of changes in the firm's environment on all policy-variables may be necessary for purposes of predicting the firm's behavior and formulating logically consistent public policy measures designed to affect business conduct. In addition to pricing, other aspects of economic performance, including advertising and R&D activities, also influence resource allocation and the welfare of the community. Public policy measures imposed without regard to their effect on all aspects of firms' behavior may have side-effects on some facets of behavior which, on balance, render the measures undesirable.

The final paper in Part IV, by N. E. Devletoglou, is the seminal article on a subject of increasing interest to some economists. Conventional price theory indicates that the nature of a firm's pricing behavior is influenced by the firm's expectations about its rivals' pricing behavior. In the case of product differentiation activities, an early article by Hotelling[1] argued that the optimal strategy for a firm in a situation of duopoly is to imitate its rival in dimensions of product policy. This conclusion is based upon a number of assumptions about the firms' environment. If these assumptions are altered by postulating more than two competing firms, or by assuming the existence of imperfect information on the part of buyers or sellers, the conclusion may be changed. Devletoglou focuses attention on another condition required to validate the Hotelling thesis; namely, the assumption that buyers act in a hypersensitive manner and respond to the slightest difference in terms offered by different sellers. The article demonstrates that even when buyers possess full information about sellers' terms, the "optimum degree of imitation" in the spatial location of sellers is different from the Hotelling conclusion if threshold-sensitive behavior on the part of buyers is introduced into the analysis. This may have important implications for other dimensions of a firm's product differentiation activities, in addition to spatial characteristics.

[1] H. Hotelling, "Stability in Competition," *Economic Journal*, March 1929.

14
Market Structure and the Employment of Scientists and Engineers

F. M. Scherer

In the December 1965 *American Economic Review,* I reported results unfavorable to Professor Schumpeter's conjectures regarding the relationship between monopoly power and technological innovation [4, pp. 1117–21]*. An analysis of 48 narrowly defined manufacturing industries revealed no significant tendency for the output of the industry leaders' 1954 patented inventions to increase with the industries' 1950 four-firm concentration ratios, *ceteris paribus.* Here I shall extend the analysis, utilizing data from a new and more comprehensive sample.

THE DATA

The hypothesis tested is that industrial inventive and innovative effort, measured by the employment of technical engineers and scientists, increases with the concentration of market power, other relevant variables such as total industry employment, technological opportunity, and product characteristics being held constant. Three dependent variables were used. One is the number of technical engineers E_i plus natural scientists S_i employed in 56 manufacturing industry groups during 1960. The second is the number of natural scientists S_i only (averaging 14 per cent of total technical employment $E_i + S_i$). Estimates of both E_i and S_i were obtained from a five per cent sample of the 1960 Census of Population [6].[1]

Reprinted from *The American Economic Review,* June 1967, pp. 524–531 by permission of the author and publisher.

* Editor's note: References in square brackets are listed at the end of the chapter.
[1] The engineering employment variable excludes sales engineers, while the scientific employment variable includes mathematicians. Three "not specified" catchall groups

The third dependent variable requires more explanation. Although production engineers, quality control mathematicians, and similar personnel are undoubtedly responsible for some inventions and innovations [1] [5], the prime source of new industrial technology is presumably the formally organized research and development laboratory. But only 45 per cent of U.S. manufacturing industry's scientific and engineering employees during 1960 were engaged in formal R&D work [8, p. 25]. Furthermore, only 57 per cent of (nonaircraft) industry's R&D effort was supported with private funds, and hence subject to the market incentives to which Schumpeter's market structure hypotheses are solely applicable [7, p. 65]. Consequently, a third estimated private research and development employment variable $RD_i = (F_i)(P_i)(E_i + S_i)$ was defined, where F_i is the proportion of the ith industry's scientific and engineering work force engaged in formal R&D and P_i is the fraction of the industry's R&D financed privately.[2]

The definitions of the 56 industry groups sampled (covering nearly all of U.S. manufacturing industry for 1960) were governed by the availability of data. Classification problems forced the Census Bureau to use a heterogeneous system in aggregating the occupational data by industry. The industry groups ranged from narrow clusters of one or a few four-digit S.I.C. industries (i.e., synthetic fibers) to quite broad two-digit sectors (i.e., electrical machinery, equipment, and supplies), although most were at the three-digit level of aggregation. It was therefore necessary to use a weighted average index of concentration as the independent variable of primary relevance to the hypothesis tested. The concentration index C_i of the ith industry group is the average (weighted by value of shipments) of the 1958 four-firm concentration ratios for all four-digit S.I.C. industries included in that group [9, pp. 11–42].

To take into account interindustry differences in scientific and technological opportunity, dummy variables are defined for four broad classes: general and mechanical (G&M), electrical, chemical, and traditional. Each industry group was assigned to one of these classes after analysis of the group's product technology characteristics.[3] Choices involving the electrical and chemical classifications were straightforward, but it was difficult to avoid some arbitrary judgments in distinguishing between industries with G&M as opposed to traditional product technologies. In borderline cases, the G&M classification (used as the intercept class in all regressions) was favored.

Three additional dummy variables were used to distinguish durable from nondurable goods industries, consumer from producer goods industries, and industries

---

were excluded from the sample. In addition, the aircraft and shipbuilding industries were left out because their technical activities lie for the most part outside the private market sector, and newspaper publishing was excluded because of its peculiar product and market characteristics.

[2] Data on F_i and P_i were obtained for 13 and 19 broader industry groups respectively from [8] and [7]. These ratios were applied, after a few adjustments based upon supplemental knowledge, to the 56 narrower industry groups. The resulting estimates are crude, although there is no reason to suppose that the estimation errors are systematic.

[3] The classifications conform closely to those found significant in [4, pp. 1103 and 1107]. A table giving the industry classifications and other raw data used in the study is available upon request from the author.

characterized by local or regional markets from those essentially nationwide in scope.

THE MODEL AND TESTS

If Schumpeter's conjectures are correct, one would expect the absolute differences in technical employment associated with concentration to be greater for large industries than for small. Past experience with similar data has shown that the error terms of untransformed linear regressions on the industry size variable are heteroscedastic, and that observations from extremely large industries can dominate the regression estimates. These theoretical and statistical considerations call for either a multiplicative or ratio specification of the model. In my 1965 article a multiplicative model was chosen to test the concentration hypothesis. With the present sample variables, the model can be written:

$$(E_i + S_i) = aN_i^\alpha C_i^\beta \left(\prod_j 10^{\delta_j D_{ij}} \right) u_i; \qquad (14.1)$$

where N_i is total 1960 employment of the *ith* industry (scaled in thousands), D_{ij} is a dummy variable with the value of 1 if the *ith* industry is in the *jth* technology or product characteristic class and zero otherwise; and u_i is the error term. The dummy variables in this model relate to the slope of the regression hyperplane with respect to both industry size N_i and concentration C_i. This specification implies that as C_i tends to zero, $(E_i + S_i)$ also tends to zero, no matter how high δ_j and N_i are—that is, no matter how large the industry is and how favorable the technological opportunities confronting the industry are. But it seems more reasonable that, in a field as enriched as, say, the electronics industries are with opportunities opened up by the advance of science, many scientists and engineers would be employed even if the industry structure were atomistic. While the specification of equation (14.1) might serve adequately over the range of concentration values actually observed (the lowest was 10 per cent), the use of an alternative ratio model appears preferable on a priori grounds:

$$\frac{(E_i + S_i)}{N_i} = c + \sum_j d_j D_{ij} + gC_i + v_i. \qquad (14.2)$$

In this form, the influence of interindustry differences operates independently of the concentration level. From when the industry is atomistic ($C_1 \to 0$) it can have a significant fraction of its work force assigned to scientific and engineering tasks.

Because it appears more consistent with a priori knowledge, I am inclined to favor model (14.2) over model (14.1). But since the case for model (14.2) is not ironclad, and since the conclusions depend to some extent upon the choice of models, I shall first summarize the tests of model (14.1). Regressions were run in logarithmic form for the three dependent variables on N_i alone; on N_i with C_i; and on N_i with all dummy variables, with and without C_i. When the concentration variable was introduced into regressions of log $(E_i + S_i)$, log S_i, and log RD_i on log N_i without dummy variables, its regression coefficients were in all cases positive and highly significant, and it made an incremental contribution to the percentage of variance explained (100 R^2) of 25.5, 15.9, and 22.4 percentage points respectively.

The concentration regression coefficients remained positive and significant when all dummy variables (and also subgroups of the dummies) were introduced, as shown in the following equations, where $Elec_i$ is the electrical class dummy, $Chem_i$ the chemical class dummy, $Trad_i$ the traditional product technology class dummy, Reg_i the regional market dummy, Dur_i the durable goods dummy, and $Cons_i$ the consumer goods dummy. Standard errors are given in parentheses under the coefficients.

$$\log (E_i + S_i) = -.03 + .95 \log N_i + .94 \log C_i + .30\ Elec_i \qquad (14.3)$$
$$ (.11) \qquad (.24) \qquad (.24)$$
$$+ .44\ Chem_i - .47\ Trad_i - .05\ Reg_i + .05\ Dur_i$$
$$(.17) \qquad (.11) \qquad (.13) \qquad (.10)$$
$$- .14\ Cons_i; \qquad R^2 = .830.$$
$$(.09)$$

$$\log S_i = 1.09 + .95 \log N_i + 1.34 \log C_i + .10\ Elec_i \qquad (14.4)$$
$$ (.22) \qquad (.48) \qquad (.49)$$
$$+ .63\ Chem_i - .54\ Trad_i + .14\ Reg_i - .67\ Dur_i$$
$$(.34) \qquad (.22) \qquad (.26) \qquad (.21)$$
$$- .37\ Cons_i; \qquad R^2 = .600.$$
$$(.18)$$

$$\log RD_i = -.36 + .93 \log N_i + .80 \log C_i + .27\ Elec_i \qquad (14.5)$$
$$ (.11) \qquad (.24) \qquad (.24)$$
$$+ .51\ Chem_i - .41\ Trad_i - .01\ Reg_i + .10\ Dur_i$$
$$(.17) \qquad (.11) \qquad (.13) \qquad (.10)$$
$$- .09\ Cons_i; \qquad R^2 = .805.$$
$$(.09)$$

When equations (14.3) through (14.5) were computed with the concentration variable deleted, the amount of variance explained (100 R^2) fell by 5.5, 6.6, and 4.5 percentage points respectively. Thus, the incremental explanatory power of concentration is much less when dummy variables are included than when the concentration variable is used with industry employment N_i alone. Still all of the incremental variance gains due to including C_i in equations (14.3) through (14.5) are significant in F-ratio tests at the 1 per cent level. These results therefore tend to support Schumpeter's hypothesis that inventive and innovative activity increases with market concentration.

Turning now to the ratio model, the simple correlations involving only technical employment, total employment, and concentration also supported the hypothesis, although not as consistently. The r^2's were .21 between $(E_i + S_i)/N_i$ and C_i; .19 between RD_i/N_i and C_i; but only .027 between S_i/N_i and C_i. Introduction of the six dummy variables led to much sharper declines in the explanatory power of concentration than in the multiplicative model. The equations were as follows (with the dependent variables scaled in technical personnel per 1,000 total employees):

$$\frac{E_i + S_i}{N_i} = 16.4 + .155C_i + 38.1\ Elec_i + 35.7\ Chem_i - 14.3\ Trad_i \quad (14.6)$$
$$\phantom{\frac{E_i + S_i}{N_i} = 16.4 + }(.109) \quad\ \ (9.0) \qquad\quad (6.6) \qquad\quad\ \ (4.1)$$
$$\phantom{\frac{E_i + S_i}{N_i} =}- 4.6\ Reg_i + 4.9\ Dur_i - 1.3\ Cons_i; \qquad R^2 = .728.$$
$$\phantom{\frac{E_i + S_i}{N_i} =\ \ }(5.0) \qquad\ \ (4.0) \qquad\ \ (3.5)$$

$$\frac{S_i}{N_i} = 5.0 + .01C_i + .36\ Elec_i + 25.4\ Chem_i - 2.2\ Trad_i \quad (14.7)$$
$$\phantom{\frac{S_i}{N_i} = 5.0 +\ }(.05) \quad\ (4.16) \qquad\ (3.0) \qquad\quad (1.9)$$
$$\phantom{\frac{S_i}{N_i} =}- 1.0\ Reg_i - 2.3\ Dur_i - .45\ Cons_i; \qquad R^2 = .715.$$
$$\phantom{\frac{S_i}{N_i} =\ }(2.3) \qquad\ \ (1.8) \qquad\ \ (1.61)$$

$$\frac{RD_i}{N_i} = 4.3 + .054C_i + 8.4\ Elec_i + 11.9\ Chem_i - 4.0\ Trad_i \quad (14.8)$$
$$\phantom{\frac{RD_i}{N_i} = 4.3 + }(.036) \quad\ (3.0) \qquad\ \ (2.2) \qquad\quad (1.4)$$
$$\phantom{\frac{RD_i}{N_i} =}- 1.1\ Reg_i + 1.5\ Dur_i + .3\ Cons_i; \qquad R^2 = .669.$$
$$\phantom{\frac{RD_i}{N_i} =\ }(1.7) \qquad\ \ (1.3) \qquad\ \ (1.2)$$

In equations (14.6) and (14.8) the concentration coefficient is barely significant at the 10 per cent level in a one-tail test; in equation (14.7) is it clearly not significant. Deletion of the concentration variable from equations (14.6) and (14.8) causes reductions in the amount of variance explained of 1.1 and 1.6 percentage points respectively—increments significant only at the 20 per cent level in F-ratio tests.

To determine whether the regression relationship between intensity of technical employment and concentration was consistent within individual technology classes, separate linear regressions (omitting product characteristic dummy variables) were computed for the classes on which a reasonably large number of observations was available. For the 25 industries classified in the traditional product technology category, the fitted equations were:

$$\frac{E_i + S_i}{N_i} = 1.20 + .176C_i; \qquad r^2 = .223. \qquad (14.9)$$
$$\phantom{\frac{E_i + S_i}{N_i} =\ \ }(2.17)\ (.063)$$

$$\frac{S_i}{N_i} = -.18 + .079C_i; \qquad r^2 = .134. \qquad (14.10)$$
$$\phantom{\frac{S_i}{N_i} =\ }(1.33)\ (.042)$$

For the 24 industries classified as having general and mechanical product technologies, the following estimates resulted:

$$\frac{E_i + S_i}{N_i} = 13.36 + .291C_i; \qquad r^2 = .091. \qquad (14.11)$$
$$\phantom{\frac{E_i + S_i}{N_i} =\ \ }(8.68)\ (.197)$$

$$\frac{S_i}{N_i} = .71 + .070C_i; \qquad r^2 = .091. \qquad (14.12)$$
$$\phantom{\frac{S_i}{N_i} =\ }(2.07)\ (.047)$$

In all four cases the concentration coefficients are positive. All pass statistical significance tests at the 10 per cent level or higher, with the traditional group showing a somewhat more consistent tendency for the intensity of technical employment to increase with concentration.[4]

---

[4] For the $(E_i + S_i)/N_i$ regressions, a test of the hypothesis that the traditional class intercept is greater than or equal to the G&M class intercept was rejected at

INTERPRETATION

We find then divergent results. Using one specification of the model, Schumpeter's hypothesis is sustained with flying colors. Using the alternative and theoretically preferred specification, the support is weaker but not entirely absent. Differences in the role of the dummy variables, and especially the technology class dummies, underlie this divergence. Still one important result is common to both models. When the dummy variables are introduced, the incremental explanatory power of concentration falls sharply.

Further analysis shows that the technology class dummies compete with concentration for explanatory power because they are positively correlated. The technically vigorous electrical and chemical groups had average and minimum concentration indices well above the full sample means. Average concentration in the electrical subsample (with only two observations) was 58, with a minimum value of 48. For the five chemical observations the average was 44, with a minimum of 31. The G&M group had an average C_i index of 41, with a range of from 18 to 70. In distinct contrast, the least progressive traditional class had an average of 29, with a minimum of 10 and only one observation (tobacco products) exceeding 50. Two alternative causal chains are compatible with this interdependence. The electrical and chemical classes might be more progressive on the average because they are more concentrated, or they may be more concentrated because in the past they have been more progressive.

Neither possibility can be rejected conclusively. It is clear, however, that the greater apparent progressiveness of the chemical and electrical groups is not due solely to higher concentration, for science has obviously been exceptionally generous to these groups during the past century. More support can be mustered for the contention that technological innovation associated with opportunity has led to concentration.[5] The high concentration of market power in such fields as synthetic fibers, plastics materials, electric lamps, telephone equipment, and computing equipment was built at least partly upon patent and know-how barriers to entry and (in an earlier era) restrictive patent cross-licensing agreements. The successful exploitation of favorable opportunities may also have permitted especially rapid market share growth for innovating firms, contributing to above-average concentration. On the other hand, the undramatic pace of technological advance in such product areas as sawmill products, furniture, bakery products, shoes, and canned vegetables afforded little opportunity for the erection of strong patent and know-how entry barriers. It seems reasonable to conclude tentatively

---

the 10 per cent level, but a similar hypothesis regarding the slopes can be rejected only at the 35 per cent level. This lends support for regression model (14.2), which assumes different intercepts but equal slopes, over model (14.1), which assumes identical (zero) intercepts but unequal slopes. For the S_i/N_i regressions, there is no indication of significant differences in either the slopes or intercepts.

Simple linear regressions for industries in the chemical technology class revealed a *negative* correlation between both $(E_i + S_i)/N_i$ and S_i/N_i and concentration. However, the regression coefficients had t-ratios of only .61 and 1.24 respectively, and only five observations were involved.

[5] See also Almarin Phillips' analysis [3], which stresses this possibility.

that the electrical and chemical technology class dummy variables have not captured explanatory power more appropriately attributable causally to concentration, although the possibility of a reverse flow from past opportunity to present concentration cannot be excluded.

Once interindustry opportunity differences are taken into account, the tendency for technical employment to increase with concentration is most persistent for the traditional industries, which are least concentrated on the average. This suggests a possible threshold effect: increases in concentration are conducive to technical vigor only in relatively atomistic industries, becoming an unimportant stimulus once a certain broad threshold is crossed [2]. To explore this possibility, an additional variable C_i^2 was introduced into regressions otherwise identical to equations (14.9) through (14.12). This test for nonlinearities yielded modest support for the hypothesis. In all four regressions, a relationship concave to the concentration axis was found, although only in the nonlinear analogue of equation (14.9) was the squared term's (negative) coefficient significant at the 5 per cent level. In all four cases technological employment per 1,000 employees reached a predicted maximum at concentration levels between 50 and 55 per cent—values exceeded only by the tobacco products industry in the traditional class, but by five to eight industries in the G&M class. The four regression equations predicted a zero ratio of technical to total employment at concentration levels between 10 and 14 per cent, suggesting that the threshold lies somewhere above this low range.

These results appear consistent with the neo-Schumpeterian hypothesis that oligopolists display a special affinity toward nonprice competition. Some degree of concentration is required before firms eschew price-cutting and grapple for market position through more complex innovative strategies. But in industries with high concentration—e.g., when the four-firm ratio exceeds 55 per cent—pricing interdependence is fully recognized, and group discipline may even be sufficiently strong to permit a "live and let live" attitude toward technological innovation.

CONCLUSION

Three tentative conclusions emerge. First, the relationship between industrial inventive and innovative effort and concentration is a complex one, since high concentration and rich technological opportunity tend to coincide. Naive tests of the Schumpeterian market power hypotheses are not apt to add much to our understanding. Second, even after interindustry differences in technological opportunity are taken into account crudely, there remains evidence of a modest positive correlation between the employment of scientists and engineers and concentration. This correlation is stronger than the results of my 1965 analysis suggested—undoubtedly because industries with traditional product technologies were deliberately excluded from the sample. And third, technological vigor appears to increase with concentration mainly at relatively low levels of concentration. When the four-firm concentration ratio exceeds 50 or 55 per cent, additional market power is probably not conducive to more vigorous technological efforts and may be downright stultifying.

REFERENCES

1. S. Hollander, *The Sources of Increased Efficiency: A Study of du Pont Rayon Plants*. Cambridge, Mass., 1965.
2. J. W. Markham, "Market Structure, Business Conduct, and Innovation," *Am. Econ. Rev., Proc.*, May 1965, *55*, 323–32.
3. Almarin Phillips, "Patents, Potential Competition, and Technical Progress," *Am. Econ. Rev., Proc.*, May 1966, *56*, 301–10.
4. F. M. Scherer, "Firm Size, Market Structure, Opportunity, and the Output of Patented Inventions," *Am. Econ. Rev.*, Dec. 1965, *55*, 1097–1125.
5. J. Schmookler, "Inventors Past and Present," *Rev. Econ. Stat.*, Aug. 1957, *39*, 321–33.
6. U.S. Department of Commerce, Bureau of the Census, *Census of Population: 1960*, "Occupation by Industry," PC(2) 7C. Washington, 1963.
7. U.S. National Science Foundation, *Research and Development in Industry: 1961*. Washington, 1964.
8. *Scientific and Technical Personnel in Industry: 1960*. Washington, 1961.
9. U.S. Senate, Committee on the Judiciary, Subcommittee on Antitrust and Monopoly, *Concentration Ratios in Manufacturing Industry: 1958*. Washington, 1962.

15
Advertising and Competition[1]

Lester G. Telser

INTRODUCTION

Hardly any business practice causes economists greater uneasiness than advertising. Among the many reasons for this feeling is the opinion held by some economists that competition and advertising are incompatible. Henry Simons, perhaps one of the most outspoken critics of advertising, summed it up neatly when he wrote that "a major barrier to really competitive enterprise and efficient service to consumers is to be found in advertising—in national advertising especially, and in sales organizations which cover great national or regional areas."[2] Many other distinguished economists share this view. My main purpose in this article is the investigation of the charge that advertising and competition are incongruous.

At the outset, consideration of the effects of advertising encounters the problem of fitting advertising into a competitive model. Certain kinds of advertising which provide buyers with useful information—identify sellers, give terms of sale,

Reprinted from *Journal of Political Economy* (December 1964), by permission of The University of Chicago Press. Copyright, 1964, pp. 537–562.

[1] I wish to acknowledge helpful comments and suggestions by Aaron Director, Zvi Griliches, Harry Johnson, Peter Pashigian, George Stigler, and Stanislaw Wellisz. I am grateful to the Walgreen Foundation for helping support this research. I assume responsibility for all errors and defects.

[2] Henry C. Simons, *Economic Policy for a Free Society* (Chicago: University of Chicago Press, 1948), p. 95. Cf. Nicholas Kaldor, "The Economic Aspects of Advertising," *Review of Economic Studies*, XVIII (1950–51), 1–27; Richard Caves, *American Industry: Structure, Conduct, Performance* (Englewood Cliffs, N.J.: Prentice-Hall, 1964), pp. 17–20.

and describe products—facilitate competition. Although much advertising is informative, not even its staunchest defender claims this of all advertising. Moreover, in a competitive industry certain forces work against many kinds of advertising because a sponsor of advertising would expect to obtain only a fraction of the fruits of his advertising. This by itself suggests that advertising may be less prevalent in competitive industries, although it does not imply that the advertising itself may impair competition. Whether advertising is theoretically compatible with competition is the topic of the first section; it is shown that a clearcut theoretical case cannot be brought and that it is necessary to turn to the empirical evidence.

The next section considers certain implications of the proposition that there is an inverse association between the intensity of competition and the intensity of advertising. First, I look at the relation between concentration of output among the four leading firms by industry and the percentage of sales allocated to advertising by industry. Next, I examine the stability of market shares for three broad classes of consumer goods—foods, soaps, and toiletries—which differ greatly in the intensity of advertising. If advertising does inhibit competition, the most advertised goods should have the most stable market shares. Finally, I examine the life-cycles of leading brands in these three classes to see whether the more advertised products exhibit a pattern consistent with the view that advertising is a means of product differentiation.

In the last part of the article I consider the effects of advertising on the size of firms. The core of the problem is the nature of the returns to advertising. This requires a close look at the advertising mechanism and the effects of advertising messages on sales. With the help of this analysis I show that the nature of the product, the structure of the market, and the characteristics of the advertising audiences serve to explain why some products are much advertised whereas others are little advertised. The same analysis explains the allocation of promotional outlays between advertising and personal selling. I find it necessary to separate the physical amount of advertising as measured by advertising messages from the dollar amount because the relation between each of these and sales effectiveness is by no means the same. Finally I use the analysis of the advertising mechanism to examine the effects of advertising on scale.

IS ADVERTISING THEORETICALLY COMPATIBLE WITH PERFECT COMPETITION?

The traditional advertising model begins by assuming that the sales of a given firm depend on its advertising outlay and its price. In effect this presumes that advertising and competition are theoretically incompatible because the price the firm can charge depends on its rate of sales. Surely this is an unsatisfactory way to begin an analysis of advertising because it should not be taken for granted that there cannot be advertising in a perfectly competitive industry. Therefore, instead of starting at the outset with the premise that the firm which advertises must possess monopoly power, I propose to assume that the firm operates in a perfectly competitive market and that it offers advertising together with the physical product.

I begin with a simple sketch of a competitive market in which goods of various qualities are offered for sale by a number of competing firms operating under conditions of perfect competition. The generic commodity is a composite of many characteristics, and the specification of a particular model consists of the input per unit of each of the characteristics it is important to consider. For example, horsepower is one characteristic of a car and a particular model has an engine of a certain horsepower. Generally, a model may be described by a list of numbers, $v_1, v_2, \ldots, v_n$, such that v_j is the input of characteristic j per unit of the commodity.

Each firm takes as given a price that is a function of the particular product it chooses to make and sell. Thus there is a price schedule for every possible model as follows:

$$p = f(v_1, \ldots, v_n). \qquad (15.1)$$

Every firm faces the same price schedule and can make any kind of product or model as specified by a list of v's. Once it decides on the product or model within the generic commodity class, the price it receives is given by equation (15.1). The assumption of perfect competition means that the price firm i charges for its product is independent of $x(i)$, the amount it sells. I assume that the total cost to firm i of producing $x(i)$ units of a certain product or model is given by

$$c = g[x(i), s_1(i), \ldots, s_n(i)] \qquad (15.2)$$

$$s_j(i) = v_j x(i) = \text{input of the } i\text{th characteristic.}$$

Since to make a given model the firm chooses how much of the various quality specifications it offers per unit, $s_j(i)$ gives the total amount of the quality factor j needed to produce $x(i)$ units of the finished product. I assume all firms are alike in the sense that all have access to the same technology and can produce a given output of a certain model at the same total cost.

The net revenue of firm i is given by

$$r(i) = px(i) - g[x(i), s_1(i), \ldots, s_n(i)]. \qquad (15.3)$$

The firm chooses an output rate $x(i)$ and selects a set of specifications v_j to maximize net revenue. Therefore, at the optimal output, price equals marginal cost, where marginal cost is

$$\frac{dg}{dx(i)} = \frac{\partial g}{\partial x(i)} + \sum_{j=1}^{n} \frac{\partial g}{\partial s_j(i)} v_j. \qquad (15.4)$$

The optimal set of specifications for firm i satisfies $\partial r(i)/\partial v_j = 0$. This gives

$$x(i) \frac{\partial p}{\partial v_j} = \frac{\partial g}{\partial s_j} \frac{\partial s_j}{\partial v_j} = \frac{\partial g}{\partial s_j} x(i)$$

so that

$$\frac{\partial p}{\partial v_j} = \frac{\partial f}{\partial v_j} = \frac{\partial g}{\partial s_j} \qquad j = 1, \ldots, n. \qquad (15.5)$$

Since $\partial p/\partial v_j$ is independent of each firm's output, consumers face a price schedule such that price differentials among the various models reflect the marginal costs of the different specifications. Moreover, no firm can obtain more than the normal rate of return no matter what quality of product it decides to make. In long-run equilibrium the net revenue of every firm is zero, and every model is produced at minimum long-run average cost. The analysis so far is merely a straightforward extension of the classical theory to take into account the variety of models within a product class offered to consumers.

Insofar as nothing has been said about the nature of the specifications v_j, the analysis is abstract. Clearly if the v_j's are physical characteristics of the product so that each unit sold is literally a combination of v's, then the analysis requires only the well-known qualifications of perfectly competitive models. Whether it is valid to allow one of the v's to be advertising per unit remains to be seen.

There are several reasons for treating advertising as an input supplied together with the physical product. First, the advertising may give certain kinds of information about the product that consumers value. Second, advertising may signal a certain level of quality. A well-known article, one that has been advertised and on the market for a long time, is more likely to yield satisfactory service than one about which little is known or one with which consumers must experiment. Therefore consumers may justifiably regard the risk of using the advertised product to be less than the risk of using the non-advertised product. However, this kind of advertising, since it stands for the seller's reputation, is not physically tied to the product. Third, certain kinds of informative advertising are required to identify sellers. For example, a seller may display his goods, exhibit signs, and be listed in a directory. Fourth, in some cases the advertising is itself a part of the product. Thus in the treatment of certain psychosomatic disorders, an advertised proprietary remedy may be more effective than the same product sold under its chemical name at a fraction of the price of the advertised article. Fifth, a product that is advertised on a radio or television program supplies entertainment which the sponsor of the advertising pays for out of sales of the product.

The advertising that supplies information about the seller or the product is not necessarily incompatible with a purely competitive market. If sellers must identify themselves in order to remain in business, then formally unless they spend a certain minimum amount on advertising their rate of sales will be zero. Regardless of price, buyers would not know of sellers' existence unless the sellers make themselves known by incurring these advertising outlays. Each seller may have no power to affect the price of the product and yet find it necessary to display a sign or be listed in a directory. Such advertising costs are an overhead item, and the price of the product must be high enough to cover this expense.

Describing the product or giving instructions for use is surely compatible with competition. Since all sellers may give the same information, none gains any advantage by so doing. Although labeling obviously destroys anonymity this may well be a necessary condition of sale in order to guarantee good performance and build up a reputation for quality. These do not impair competition.

Although advertising per se need not weaken competition, the copyright and patent laws prevent sellers from making literal copies of each other's wares. Nevertheless the law may have no effect if buyers recognize that several sellers offer substantially the same good despite the efforts of sellers to differentiate their products by means of advertising. Therefore it is an empirical and not a theoretical question to determine whether buyers consider similar goods as being close substitutes in spite of the sellers' efforts to the contrary.

If consumers regarded one seller's product as a close substitute for that of another and the individual sellers are small relative to the market, then the commodity will not be much advertised. For example, let the proverbial wheat farmers organize an advertising campaign to persuade people to buy more bread. Each farmer individually has a strong incentive not to contribute to the campaign, and by so doing benefit at the expense of all other wheat farmers. Basically, this is possible because each farmer's wheat is a nearly perfect substitute for any other farmer's wheat, each farmer contributes a very small part of total wheat production, and each can expect to share in the greater sales due the advertising regardless of his own contribution to its cost. However, if individual firms are large relative to the market, it may pay for them to advertise even if buyers regard their product as a close substitute for their rivals' wares. Under these conditions, because the advertising firm is large relative to the market, it gets enough increased profits to justify its expense although its advertising also benefits its competitors.

Advertisers indirectly supply entertainment by sponsoring television and radio programs. Obviously a consumer may enjoy the entertainment without buying the product. Therefore the jointness between the physical product and the advertising is impaired. Moreover, consumers have no direct incentive to buy a product merely because they happen to like the entertainment that the advertising pays for. To the extent that consumers feel obligated to buy the product because they like the entertainment, the advertising is differentiating. Whether this impairs competition depends on the availability of enough rival products that offer similar entertainment.

Although the advertising-sponsored entertainment and the product itself are physically separable, it may nevertheless be true that the advertising stimulates enough additional sales under certain conditions to pay for itself. First, and most obvious, the advertising may serve to differentiate the firm's product. Second, the firm may advertise because it is large relative to the market or because its product is differentiated from its rivals for reasons that have nothing to do with its advertising. Under these conditions, an advertiser has good reason to sponsor popular entertainment in order to attract a large audience, thereby maximizing exposure to the advertising. The entertainment might be valued enough by the audience for them to be willing to pay for it separately without going through the intermediate step of buying the product. However, it may be cheaper to supply entertainment jointly with advertising and collect the cost from the sponsor instead of directly from the audience.

Thus there are some kinds of advertising that are compatible with, and indeed essential to, competition—information on seller identity and reliability, price and terms of sale, and instruction on the use of the product. There are other kinds that only pay if the selling firm has some monopoly power, for example, if it is large relative to the total supply so that it benefits from increases in total demand. There are other kinds that themselves create monopoly power that otherwise would not exist. A priori reasoning cannot reveal to what extent advertising is associated with reduced competition. Therefore it is necessary to turn to empirical evidence on the compatibility of advertising and competition.

ADVERTISING—A SOURCE OF MONOPOLY?

In this section I consider three kinds of evidence bearing on the question of whether advertising is a source of monopoly power. First, I consider the relevance

Table 15.1

CONCENTRATION RATIOS AND ADVERTISING OUTLAYS PER DOLLAR OF SALES BY SELECTED THREE-DIGIT INDUSTRIES

INDUSTRY	CONCENTRATION RATIOS (PER CENT)			ADVERTISING OUTLAYS ÷ SALES* (PER CENT)		
	1947	1954	1958	1948	1954	1957
Beer and malt	23.1	27.9	29.0	3.488	6.766	6.872
Wines	26.4	38.0	35.0	3.746	4.839	4.395
Distilled liquor	74.6	64.0	60.0	1.113	1.950	2.408
Meats	38.6	32.7	28.4	0.379	0.545	0.610
Dairy products	38.8	37.6	36.4	1.119	1.956	1.885
Canning	28.9	32.3	31.0	1.867	2.655	2.658
Grain-mill products	24.9	32.7	32.0	1.018	1.783	1.695
Bakery	27.1	30.5	30.3	1.683	2.352	2.803
Sugar	66.5	65.0	65.1	0.121	0.200	0.280
Confectionery	32.4	36.4	37.2	2.500	2.899	3.543
Cereals	74.9	88.0	83.0	6.202	4.727	4.845
Miscellaneous foods	43.5	43.6	41.2	2.393	3.495	4.073
Cigars	40.6	44.0	54.0	1.988	2.386	2.370
Other tobacco	86.7	79.4	77.0	2.605	4.194	5.429
Knit goods	15.8	17.3	18.9	0.763	1.072	1.075
Carpets	56.4	55.7	51.4	1.675	2.203	2.052
Hats	52.9	54.2	63.2	1.830	1.825	2.124
Men's clothing	13.9	14.3	14.6	0.867	0.995	0.928
Women's clothing	7.4	9.0	9.6	0.787	1.102	1.263
Millinery	7.0	7.0	6.0	0.391	0.302	0.326
Furs	2.6	4.0	5.0	0.415	0.398	0.916
Miscellaneous apparel	25.5	23.4	23.6	0.764	1.155	1.269
Furniture	20.0	19.5	18.4	0.906	1.383	1.451
Periodicals	34.3	29.0	31.0	0.333	0.277	0.304
Books	20.5	21.0	16.0	2.904	2.255	2.702
Drugs	35.0	30.5	30.4	8.480	8.583	10.280
Soaps	65.1	65.1	63.0	9.206	9.123	7.938
Paints and varnish	33.5	36.4	35.4	1.330	1.525	1.450
Perfumes	23.8	25.0	29.0	12.605	14.358	14.723
Petroleum refining	37.3	33.0	32.0	0.388	0.471	0.507
Tires and tubes	76.6	79.0	74.0	1.109	1.258	1.885
Footwear	27.8	29.5	26.5	1.107	1.416	1.326
Miscellaneous leather goods	21.3	24.3	25.3	0.855	1.274	1.204
Hand tools	32.0	38.5	33.3	1.912	3.891	3.791
Household and service	44.6	44.8	49.5	1.501	1.732	1.901
Appliances	35.8	50.0	43.0	2.448	3.266	3.296
Communications	52.2	41.3	44.3	1.960	1.928	2.034
Motorcycles and bicycles	42.3	50.0	58.0	1.383	0.905	1.078
Motor vehicles	72.1	88.1	n.a.	0.525	0.566	0.907
Parts and accessories	28.3	33.3	n.a.	0.754	0.985	0.700

INDUSTRY	CONCENTRATION RATIOS (PER CENT)			ADVERTISING OUTLAYS ÷ SALES* (PER CENT)		
	1947	1954	1958	1948	1954	1957
Professional and scientific instruments	46.3	47.8	47.8	1.939	1.759	2.086
Clocks and watches	40.7	43.6	48.9	5.171	4.534	5.629
Jewelry (except costume)	35.2	35.2	32.4	2.561	3.018	2.202
Costume jewelry	23.8	14.0	12.0	0.963	1.222	2.498

* It should be noted that these figures are considerably lower than those reported in two other studies. Cf. U.S. Federal Trade Commission, *Distribution Methods and Costs*. Part V, *Advertising as a Factor in Distribution* (Washington: Government Printing Office, 1944); Nicholas Kaldor and Rodney Silverman, *A Statistical Analysis of Advertising Expenditure and of the Revenue of the Press* (Cambridge: Cambridge University Press, 1948). However, the figures for classes of retail establishments also given in the Source Book of Income agree very well with an independent source. See U.S. Federal Trade Commission, *Chain Stores: Chain Store Advertising* (Washington: Government Printing Office, 1934). I have not thought it worthwhile to reconcile these differences.
Sources: 1947 and 1954 concentration ratios from George J. Stigler, *Capital and Rates of Return in Manufacturing Industries* (Princeton, N.J.: Princeton University Press, 1963). 1958 concentration ratios from the 1958 Census of Business computed by the author using Stigler's procedure. Advertising outlay-to-sales ratio computed from the Source Book of Income, U.S. Internal Revenue Service.

of a comparison between the prices of advertised and of unadvertised goods. Is it a legitimate conclusion from the fact that advertised goods are often more expensive than non-advertised goods that the advertising is a source of monopoly profit? Second, I examine the relation between concentration of sales among the leading firms by industry and advertising intensities for forty-two broadly defined consumer products. If advertising is a source of monopoly profit, we should find a positive association between concentration and advertising intensity. Third, I examine the stability of market shares for three classes of consumer goods which differ markedly in their advertising intensities. If advertising is a source of monopoly, the more heavily advertised class should also contain the products with the more stable market shares.

To see whether advertising could differentiate a firm's product from its rivals, we may compare the prices of more- and less-advertised goods by product class. Available data seem to show that advertised goods are generally more expensive than non-advertised goods.[3] This finding, however, does not permit the conclu-

[3] Frequently cited data on the difference between the prices of branded and unbranded drug items are contained in U.S. Temporary National Economic Committee, *Price Behavior and Business Policy* (Monograph No. 1 [Washington: Government Printing Office, 1940]), Table 6. Extensive comparisons are also presented in U.S. Federal Trade Commission, *Chain Store Private Brands* (Washington: Government Printing Office, 1933). Another valuable source of data is Neil H. Borden, *The Economic Effects of Advertising* (Chicago: Richard D. Irwin, Inc., 1942), Part IV. A more recent comparison for canned fruits and vegetables is Robert H. Cole et al., *Manufacturer and Distributor Brands: Some Facts and Issues* (Urbana: University of Illinois, 1955). This study compares three main types of brands: (1) packer brands, (2) chain-store brands, and (3) wholesale brands. Roughly speaking, the packer brands are the most advertised and the chain-store brands are the least advertised. In most cases packer brands have higher prices than chain-store brands, in those chains where both are available.

sion that advertising is a source of monopoly profit. First, the prices of the more advertised goods might be higher than the prices of less advertised goods because of the higher average quality of the advertised goods. Second, even if the average qualities are the same for both classes, it may be that the advertised goods vary less in quality. Thus the higher price of the more advertised goods may be explained by the stricter quality control exercised over these goods. If one were to choose at random an item from the class of non-advertised goods, the risk of unsatisfactory performance would be greater than if the choice were restricted to a random selection from the class of advertised goods. The risk is reduced still more if the choice is confined to a class of long-established and advertised products. The evidence of some studies supports this view.[4] Third, it is clear from the joint-supply theory of advertising given in the preceding section that even under a competitive regime advertised goods would be more expensive. Equation (15.5) is especially pertinent, since it explains why this would be so. Appendix I analyzes the conditions under which price evidence can show whether advertising differentiates the firm's product.

Because price comparisons are ambiguous, it appears simpler to estimate directly the relation between monopoly power and advertising intensity. Concentration of sales among the four leading firms in an industry is a widely accepted measure of monopoly. The ratio of advertising outlays to dollar sales is a measure of advertising intensity. If advertising fosters monopoly, then concentration and advertising should be positively correlated.[5]

Table 15.2 contains the regressions of concentration on advertising intensity calculated from the figures shown in Table 15.1. Although the correlations are positive for all three census years 1947, 1954, and 1958, the R^2 is only about 3 per cent in all three years. In addition, a 1 per cent increase in the ratio of advertising to sales is associated with only a 0.08 per cent increase in concentration. Thus for the forty-two broadly defined consumer product industries at the three-digit level, the correlation between concentration and advertising is unimpressive.

[4] The most direct evidence I know of that bears on the question of quality differences is U.S. Federal Trade Commission, *Chain Stores: Quality of Canned Vegetables and Fruits* (Washington: Government Printing Office, 1933). Table 3 of this publication gives figures on the chance of getting a high grade of canned goods by selecting at random from a class of advertised versus a class of non-advertised brands. There is an attempt to replicate this FTC study in the University of Illinois publication referred to in the previous footnote. Unfortunately the Illinois study is not comparable to the FTC report because the Illinois researchers confined their sample of brands to the fancy class for the vegetables and either the fancy or the choice grades for fruits. Therefore, unlike the FTC study, the Illinois findings cannot be used to determine the risk to a consumer who would choose at random among the three classes of brands, fancy, choice, and standard, without knowing how the brands are classified and possessing only the knowledge of which brands are advertised and which are not.

[5] Nicholas Kaldor expects a positive association between concentration and advertising intensity (*op. cit.*, pp. 13 ff.). A witty article in the *Business Review* of the Federal Reserve Bank of Philadelphia reports no association between concentration and advertising intensity—results that are in accord with my findings in the text (Lawrence C. Murdoch, Jr., "Advertising and Charlie Brown," *Business Review*, June, 1962).

Table 15.2

REGRESSIONS OF CONCENTRATION RATIOS y AND ADVERTISING OUTLAYS AS PERCENTAGE OF SALES r, FOR FORTY-TWO THREE-DIGIT INDUSTRIES*

YEAR	REGRESSIONS OF y ON r	REGRESSION COEFFICIENTS OF r ON y	MULTIPLE CORRELATIONS	MEANS y	r
1947	$y = 34.19 + 1.247r$	.0214	.163	37.06	2.304
	(1.190)	(.0204)		(19.54)	(2.562)
1954	$y = 34.82 + 1.162r$	.0233	.165	37.96	2.714
	(1.101)	(.0221)		(19.36)	(2.743)
1958	$y = 34.32 + 1.150r$	.0250	.169	37.67	2.907
	(1.057)	(.0230)		(19.17)	(2.824)

* y = concentration ratio in per cent; r = advertising outlay ÷ sales in per cent.

Perhaps the poor showing of the regressions is due to faultiness in the data. It is undeniable that the data are far from ideal, and Table 15.3 gives a glimpse of some of the problems. Since the advertising data are obtained from the Internal Revenue Service, which classifies companies into a three-digit class, the concentration figures have to be calculated on a comparable basis. The Census, however, gives concentration for only the more refined four- and five-digit industry

Table 15.3

METHOD OF CALCULATING CONCENTRATION RATIOS FOR THREE-DIGIT INDUSTRIES, ILLUSTRATED FOR HAND TOOLS, 1954*

PRODUCT CLASS	CONCENTRATION OF SHIPMENTS AMONG FOUR LEADING FIRMS (PER CENT)	MILLION DOLLARS	
		VALUE OF SHIPMENTS	VALUE ADDED
Cutlery	49	170	122
Cutlery, scissors, shears	24	85†	n.a.
Razors, razor blades	97	68	n.a.
Edge tools	25	70	48
Hand tools, n.e.c.	20	257	162
Files	94	27	19
Hand saws and saw blades	56	84	53
Hardware, n.e.c.	39	1,111	640
Hand tools	38.5	1,718	1,044

* For a detailed discussion of the method of calculating the concentration ratios for three-digit classes see George J. Stigler, *Capital and Rates of Return in Manufacturing Industries* (Princeton, N.J.: Princeton University Press, 1963), Appendix C.
† The cutlery total is based on company shipments; the figures for the two components come from product class data.

classes, and it is necessary to estimate three-digit concentration from a weighted average of the four-digit figures. Table 15.3 shows the details for one three-digit class, hand tools. The final concentration ratio, 38.5 per cent, is a weighted average of the four-digit figures using as weights the value added of the four-digit constituents (see the last column of Table 15.3). Most of the advertising of hand tools is accounted for by a single five-digit category, razors and razor blades, that is part of the four-digit industry, cutlery. Although concentration in cutlery is 49 per cent, in razors concentration is 97 per cent. The weighted average concentration figure for hand tools, a three-digit IRS class, is only slightly above the mean of the forty-two industries, whereas the advertising ratio is about one-half a standard deviation unit above the forty-two-industry mean.

In general the standard deviation of variables on a three-digit basis is less than on a more detailed four- or five-digit basis whenever the four-digit constituents of the respective three-digit industries are heterogeneous. However, this does not necessarily mean that the relation between concentration and advertising is attenuated by measurement error. Such attenuation depends partly on whether aggregation reduces the dispersion of one variable more than another. Although this cannot be verified, at least the coefficients of variation of the two variables, concentration and advertising intensity, are about the same. There is another way of loking at attenuation that I shall discuss below.[6]

I excluded three consumer product industries because the relevant variables were difficult to measure objectively and because their inclusion would have reduced the correlation between advertising and concentration. Had I included non-alcoholic beverages, motor vehicles, and motor vehicle parts and accessories, the correlations would have been still closer to zero.

The ratio of advertising to sales of non-alcoholic beverages varies between 4 and 5 per cent during the sample period. This is a separate three-digit IRS class and a separate four-digit Census industry with a concentration level of about 10 per cent in 1954. Bottlers are generally confined to particular localities by the terms of their franchise with syrup manufacturers. This accounts for the low concentration in bottling. However, concentration in the five-digit class, syrup manufacture, is 89 per cent, which is a better reflection of the state of competition in the industry. Syrup manufacture is within the four-digit class, flavorings, which is classified in the three-digit IRS category, miscellaneous foods. The regressions include miscellaneous foods and exclude non-alcoholic beverages.

Motor vehicles pose the same problem as non-alcoholic beverages. The concentration ratio is high and the advertising ratio is low, so that the observation is an outlier which would lower the correlation were it included in the regression. Retail dealers account for a substantial part of auto advertising, and these outlays should be combined with the manufacturers' expenditures. The ratio of the combined figure to retail sales of automobiles is a measure of advertising intensity in automobile manufacturing. It is biased upward since it includes retail advertising on used cars. I calculated the regressions for the first two Census years, using the adjusted measure of advertising intensity, and found the results to

[6] For an excellent discussion of attenuation see G. Udny Yule and M. G. Kendall, *An Introduction to the Theory of Statistics* (14th ed.; London: Charles Griffen & Co., Ltd., 1950), pp. 313–15.

differ very little from the regressions that exclude both automobile categories. Motor vehicles and parts are combined into a single category by the Census because of the difficulty of correcting for different degrees of vertical integration of the auto manufacturers. The concentration figures for the two separate categories were calculated by Stigler for the years 1947 and 1954.[7] Since the results obtained by including these observations for 1947 and 1954 differed so little from the regressions excluding them, it was not worth the trouble to estimate concentration for 1958. Hence the regressions exclude motor vehicles and parts for all three years.

The last difficulty is due to the fact that the years do not coincide exactly for concentration and advertising intensity. 1948 is the first year for which the advertising data are available, whereas the concentration ratio is based on the 1947 Census. The last advertising ratio is for 1957 and the concentration ratio is for 1958. Both sets of data coincide in 1958. Manifestly, the empirical results are little affected by this difficulty.

There is another way of testing for the presence of attenuation based on change in the sample means between census years. Measurement error has the effect of biasing the cross-sectional regression coefficients toward zero. If measurement error is not a serious problem, then the slope as estimated from the change in sample means over the census years should be approximately the same as the regression coefficients calculated from the cross-section data. From 1947 to 1958 the advertising ratio increased on average from 2.3 to 2.9 per cent, which is 0.6 percentage points, while concentration increased by the same amount. This gives an estimated slope of 1, which is in close agreement with the regression slopes based on the cross-sections. The same technique applied to the adjacent census years does not work as well, since for 1947–54 the slope is about 2, and for 1954–58 it is actually negative. This is consistent with the plausible reasoning that measurement error is less for the change between the more widely separated years.

These results suggest a regression between the change in the concentration ratio and the change in the advertising intensity over the period 1947–58. If the levels of the two variables are positively correlated, the first differences should also be positively correlated, particularly in view of the fact that the three regression coefficients are so nearly alike. First differencing gives the additional benefit of correcting for possible industry effects since those industry-specific factors that change slowly over time are subtracted out. The results are presented in Table 15.4. The correlation between the change in concentration and the change in advertising intensity between 1947 and 1958 is negative and is larger than the correlations using first differences for the adjacent census years. Thus for the two most widely separated years, which indicated the least measurement error according to the preceding test by changes in sample means, there is actually an inverse relation between concentration ratios and the ratio of advertising outlays to dollar sales.

If advertising succeeds in sheltering a firm's products from competitive

---

[7] See George J. Stigler, *Capital and Rates of Return in Manufacturing Industries* (Princeton, N.J.: Princeton University Press, 1963), Table C-2.

Table 15.4

REGRESSIONS RELATING CHANGE IN CONCENTRATION TO CHANGE IN ADVERTISING INTENSITY

PERIOD	REGRESSIONS		CORRELA-TIONS	MEANS	
				Δy	Δr
1958–47	$\Delta y =$	$1.238 - 1.047 \Delta r$	.146	.607	.603
		(1.217) (1.124)		(6.538)	(.909)
1954–47	$\Delta y =$	$.818 + .205 \Delta r$	.029	.902	.410
		(.977) (1.127)		(5.517)	(.773)
1958–54	$\Delta y =$	$-.445 + .773 \Delta r$	.104	$-.295$	.193
		(.629) (1.174)		(3.778)	(.506)

inroads, this should be reflected in more stable market shares of the more advertised goods. According to Table 15.1, the three most intensively advertised commodity classes are drugs, perfumes, and soaps. A much less intensively advertised class is food. If advertising is a source of monopoly, the market shares of food products should be lower and less stable than the market shares of soap products, and the latter in turn should have less stable market shares than a group of cosmetic and proprietary goods. Since I use somewhat unconventional data to test this hypothesis, some explanation of these data is necessary.

Instead of using market shares based on sales, I use share data based on consumer interviews that were compiled by the *Milwaukee Journal* from its annual surveys of households in the Milwaukee area. These surveys report the percentages of "users" who name the various brands they typically buy. Such a percentage is best described as the recalled-brand share, in contrast to market shares derived from actual sales data.

The recalled-brand shares, although highly correlated with the market-brand shares, are biased estimates. First, and perhaps most important, recalled shares of the advertised brands tend to overstate actual market shares. This has been established by a comparison of the recalled shares with the market shares of the same brands obtained from consumer-panel data. The latter give close estimates of actual market shares based on sales figures. In addition, the recalled shares of the private and other less-advertised brands tend to be biased downwards. It is reasonable to conclude from these findings that advertising leads consumers to respond to the interviews by overstating their purchases of the well-known advertised brands and understating their purchases of chain-store and other private brands.[8]

There is a test of my interpretation of the interviews. If the interpretation is correct, recalled shares should be more stable than actual market shares. This is

---

[8] For a detailed study comparing recalled-brand shares with those based on consumer-panel estimates, see Seymour Sudman, "On the Accuracy of Recording of Consumer Panels" (unpublished Ph.D. Dissertation, Graduate School of Business, University of Chicago, 1962), chap. iv.

indeed the case. Estimates of brand shares derived from what consumers tell the interviewers change less rapidly over time than the actual market shares.[9]

These biases of recalled shares tend to overstate the level and stability of the shares of more advertised goods relative to less-advertised goods. Therefore the recalled shares of the cosmetics-proprietary group should be even higher and more stable compared to food than would be the case with actual market share data—provided advertising inhibits competition.

The average recalled share of the leading brands is lower for the more heavily advertised group, toiletries, than for the less heavily advertised group, soaps, and the latter is lower than that for the least intensively advertised group, food products.[10] These results agree with the previous findings of no relation between concentration and advertising intensity. For the three broad product classes I computed the mean recalled share for each of the four leading brands in the three years 1948, 1953, and 1959. For thirty food products, the mean recalled share of the leading brand was 44 per cent in 1948. It was 39 per cent for the leading brand in the nine soap products and 35 per cent for the 15 cosmetics and toiletries. In 1959 the average recalled shares of the leading brands were 40, 39, and 30 per cent, respectively, for the thirty-nine food items, fifteen soaps, and seventeen toiletries. Note that the leading brand in 1948 was not necessarily the leading brand in 1959 and that the 1959 sample includes a larger number of products within each commodity class.

By tracing the time path of the shares of a given group of brands, it is possible to see how stable the shares are and to measure the life-cycle of the brands. To estimate share stability, consider the four leading brands in a product class at a certain point in time. At either earlier or later points in time these four brands should have lower shares. The change in share from a certain time to the time when the brand was among the four leaders measures stability. According to the hypothesis that advertising is a source of monopoly, the most heavily advertised group of commodities should show the smallest change in share. Therefore, food

---

[9] To test whether the recalled shares are more stable than estimates of market shares, I calculated the autocorrelation of recalled shares and market shares, respectively. If recalled shares are more stable than market shares, the autocorrelation of recalled shares should exceed the autocorrelation of market shares. The *Chicago Sun-Times* obtained recalled-brand share data for several years by using the same methods as the *Milwaukee Journal*. In addition the *Chicago Tribune* collects market-share data from its consumer panel. The panel data are much closer to the actual sales shares than is the case for the recalled-brand shares. For twenty-one consumer products I calculated the share of the leading brand in 1956 and the share of the same brand in 1960 using the two different sets of data. Let x_{it} denote the consumer panel market share for product i at time t and let y_{it} denote the recalled-brand share. The regression results are as follows:

(a) $x_{it} = 2.05 + 0.80\, x_{i,\, t-5}$,
$R^2 = 0.563,\ n = 21$;

(b) $y_{it} = 1.84 + 1.04 y_{i,\, t-5}$,
$R^2 = 0.771$.

Clearly, the recalled shares are much more stable than the market shares. This is confirmed by comparing the means: $\bar{x}_t = .87 \bar{x}_{t-5}$, and $\bar{y}_t = .996\ \bar{y}_{t-5}$.

[10] Appendix II lists the products studied.

products should have the largest share change and cosmetics-toiletries the smallest share change. A glance at Table 15.5 shows the opposite. Cosmetic-product shares are less stable than food-product shares and, albeit with some exceptions, soap-product shares are less stable than food-product shares and more stable than cosmetic-product shares.

In addition to measuring share stability, we can exploit the same data to study part of the life-cycle of the leading brand alone and of the four leading brands combined. Consider the average share of a group of leading brands in 1948 and the average share of the same brands in 1953 and 1959. The leading brands in 1948 should have lower shares on the two subsequent dates. Similarly, consider the average share of the leading brands in 1959 and the average shares of the same brands in 1953 and 1948. The leading brands in 1959 should have lower shares in both of the earlier years. If growth occurs in a regular fashion, the average share of the leading brands in 1959 should exceed the average share of the same brands in 1953, and the latter should be bigger than the average share of the same brand in 1948. By looking at a given group of products within the broadly defined classes, it is possible to trace part of the life-cycle during a twenty-four-year period for a group of brands that were leaders in the twelfth year. The trajectory of the leading brands in 1948 for the following twelve years shows the descending phase, and the average share of the leading brands in 1959 traced backward to 1948 shows the ascending phase. Putting both phases together gives an estimate of the trajectory for a twenty-four-year period.

On the hypothesis that a stable process generates the life-cycle, the average share of leading brands in 1948 and the average share of the brands that were leading in 1959 should be approximately equal. In the food category (see Table 15.5), the mean share per brand of the four leaders in 1948 was 21 per cent, whereas in 1959 the leading four brands had a mean share of 20 per cent. The results for toiletries are about the same, but there are somewhat larger differences for soaps, waxes, and polishes. For the leading brand alone, instead of the mean share of the four leading brands combined, there is remarkable stability for food products (see Table 15.6). There is less stability for the other two categories.

To correct for a possible bias in the mean share attainable by leading brands because of changes in underlying conditions, the life-cycle estimates are adjusted to a 1948 base. Thus the 1959 mean share is multiplied by the ratio of the average share of the 1948 leaders to the average share of the 1959 leaders and the result shown in the rows labeled "adjusted" in Tables 15.5 and 15.6.

Table 15.5 leaves no doubt that the food products are the most stable and the toiletries the least stable category. The rise to the peak is greater for the latter and so is the decline. The soaps are intermediate and have a less clear cut pattern. Table 15.6, which gives the same data for the leading brand instead of the mean share of the four leading brands, shows a similar pattern. Hardly surprising, the rises and falls for the leading brands alone are larger than for the four leaders combined.

Since the recalled shares are more stable than the actual market shares, these results show that the market shares of the more advertised products—cosmetics and toiletries—are probably much less stable than the market shares of food products—a much less advertised category. These results refute the view that advertising stabilizes market shares. I explain these findings on the ground that

Table 15.5

RECALLED-BRAND SHARES OF FOUR LEADING BRANDS AND MEASURES OF SHARE STABILITY

YEAR BRANDS WERE LEADING	AVERAGE SHARE OF FOUR LEADING BRANDS AT PEAK YEAR AND AT TWO OTHER SELECTED YEARS*				
	−12 YEARS	−6 YEARS	LEADING YEAR	+6 YEARS	+12 YEARS
28 food products:					
1959	17.64	19.46	20.07	—	—
1948	—	—	20.69	18.98	16.43
Adjusted†	18.18	20.06	20.69	18.98	16.43
	(87.87)	(96.95)	(100.00)	(91.73)	(79.14)
Change of adjusted figures	+1.88	+0.63	−1.71	−2.55	
9 soaps, waxes, polishes, etc.:					
1959	13.42	17.46	18.16	—	—
1948	—	—	16.76	15.09	11.44
Adjusted†	12.38	16.11	16.76	15.09	11.44
	(73.87)	(96.12)	(100.00)	(90.04)	(68.26)
Change of adjusted figures	+3.73	+0.65	−1.67	−3.65	
15 toiletries, cosmetics, etc.:					
1959	13.97	15.09	17.04	—	—
1948	—	—	17.82	14.75	12.33
Adjusted†	14.61	15.78	17.82	14.75	12.33
	(81.99)	(88.55)	(100.00)	(82.77)	(69.19)
Change of adjusted figures	+1.17	+2.04	−3.07	−2.42	

* Figures represent the share per brand; the combined share of the four leading brands is four times the number shown.
† Adjusted figures (in per cent) are obtained by choosing the 1948 share of the leading brands for the base.

there is more frequent introduction of new toiletries and cosmetics than of new food items. Despite heavier advertising, brands of cosmetics and toiletries are unable to maintain consumer acceptance for as long a time as branded food products.

According to this interpretation the relatively intensive advertising of certain goods is associated with high turnover of brands within the product class. Although this does not imply a correspondingly high turnover of the firms that sell these brands, there is probably some association between the two. Contrary to popular belief, there may well be more entry and competition among the firms that produce heavily advertised goods.

Although this evidence suggests that intensive advertising is associated with a high turnover of brands within a product class, it does not rule out the possibility

Table 15.6

RECALLED-BRAND SHARE OF LEADING BRANDS AND MEASURES OF SHARE STABILITY

YEAR BRANDS WERE LEADING	AVERAGE SHARE OF LEADING BRANDS AT PEAK YEAR AND AT TWO OTHER SELECTED YEARS				
	−12 YEARS	−6 YEARS	LEADING YEAR	+6 YEARS	+12 YEARS
28 food products:					
1959	36.67	41.66	42.21	—	—
1948	—	—	42.62	38.15	34.06
Adjusted*	37.03	42.06	42.62	38.15	34.06
	(86.88)	(98.69)	(100.00)	(89.51)	(79.91)
Change of adjusted figures	+5.03	+0.56		−4.47	−4.09
9 soaps, waxes, polishes, etc.:					
1959	27.18	33.17	40.34	—	—
1948	—	—	38.93	35.31	29.92
Adjusted*	26.23	32.01	38.93	35.31	29.92
	(67.38)	(82.22)	(100.00)	(90.70)	(76.86)
Change of adjusted figures	+5.78	+6.92		−3.62	−5.39
15 toiletries, cosmetics, etc.:					
1959	29.75	27.62	30.13	—	—
1948	—	—	35.54	29.93	25.39
Adjusted*	35.09	32.58	35.54	29.93	25.39
	(98.73)	(91.67)	(100.00)	(84.21)	(71.44)
Change of adjusted figures	−2.51	+2.96		−5.61	−4.54

* Adjusted figures in per cent.

that turnover would be even greater without advertising. To the extent that advertising reminds consumers, it may stabilize the market share of firms that make established products. Cigarette evidence supports this. By increasing advertising relative to competing brands, a given brand was able to raise repeat purchases and lower the propensity of buyers to switch to other brands. The cigarette data also strongly support the view that one of advertising's main funtions is to introduce new products. A large increase in advertising relative to sales occurred during the postwar period as a result of the cancer scare and the introduction of many new brands.[11]

Although it is theoretically possible that advertising could diminish competition for the reasons set out in the second section, this view receives little empirical support from the evidence presented in this section.

[11] See my "Advertising and Cigarettes," *Journal of Political Economy,* LXX (1962), 471–99.

ADVERTISING MESSAGES

An inverse association between advertising and competition is expected on two theoretical grounds. First, firms that have some monopoly power are more likely to advertise because they can obtain most of the increased sales stimulated by their advertising. Under highly competitive conditions some of the benefits of the advertising spill over to firms that may not have borne any of the advertising expense. Second, advertising may be a source of monopoly by means of product differentiation. Regardless of the logical merit of these points, the evidence of the preceding section does not support the contention that advertising impairs competition. This evidence, however, does not directly apply to another prevalent view about the effects of advertising on industrial structure. According to this view advertising tends to increase the minimum optimum size of firms. This size effect impedes entry and thereby weakens competition. The validity of this argument that advertising is a barrier to entry depends on the nature of the returns to advertising, which cannot be analyzed without clearly understanding the advertising mechanism. In this section I develop a model of the mechanism in terms of advertising messages. With the help of this model it becomes possible to comprehend why different products are not advertised to the same extent. In the next section this model of the advertising mechanism is used to examine the effects of advertising on the size of firms.

The main advertising media are television, newspapers, magazines, radio, direct mail, and outdoor advertising. The advertiser conveys messages via these media to potential customers while fully recognizing that some of these messages will go unheeded. The firm decides whether to promote sales by means of these media and "writes" messages that maximize sales effectiveness for a given advertising expenditure. The firm determines its promotional strategy on the basis of the product characteristics, the nature of the potential market, and the type of media audiences.

Direct mail provides a convenient model of the advertising mechanism. To a list of potential customers the firm mails letters containing an advertising message. The firm conveys a number of messages equal to the number of recipients on its list. Since some recipients ignore the letters, the number of messages received falls short of the number conveyed. Finally, the advertising messages themselves can have only a limited influence on the recipient's decision to buy the product. Hence the number of buyers who are persuaded to purchase the item by the advertising is below the number who receive the message. Obviously, regardless of price, some products have no interest to some members of the mailing list. Thus the advertiser tries to select lists relevant to the product he wishes to sell.

For the other advertising media the audience is the counterpart to the direct-mailing list. The advertiser chooses among the various media on the basis of the cost of advertising messages, the proportion of the audience that consists of potential customers, and the size of the audience. It is no easy task to ascertain the size and nature of an audience relevant to a particular advertiser.

For some media, audience size estimates are especially prone to error. This is obviously true of television and radio partly because listeners and viewers do not pay for their entertainment. Even media which have a paid circulation such as newspapers and magazines pose problems of audience estimation. Readership generally exceeds circulation, is more relevant to the advertiser than circulation, and is harder to estimate.

The kind of media audience is also important to the advertiser since this determines his market potential in the audience. Analyzing the character of the audience can be a costly and hazardous undertaking. To some extent the research is avoidable because the advertiser can control the composition of the audience by his choice of entertainment and media. Thus the choice of entertainment and media attracts an audience of a predictable kind that is most valuable to certain classes of advertisers. Certain magazines and newspapers owe their existence in large part to the fact that they provide advertisers with common interests an appropriate audience. Trade and professional newspapers and magazines, women's magazines, literary journals, hobbyists' magazines, and certain radio stations are ready examples.

Technical media characteristics determine the content of advertising messages. Products that can be demonstrated on television can only be described or illustrated in print. A reader can consult a magazine or newspaper repeatedly to verify the details of an advertising message without imposing additional costs on the publisher. This makes printed media somewhat better suited for providing information on price, terms of sale, location and identity of sellers.

The allocation of promotional outlays between personal selling and advertising is determined by the same factors as the allocation of the advertising expenditure among the various media. Since the firm cannot have precise information about the audience of the advertising media, it composes an advertising message appropriate to its knowledge of the audience. In personal selling more precise information can be provided. A salesman calling on a customer or a retail clerk responding to the inquiry of a potential customer can give information that is tailored to the specific occasion. This is more expensive than advertising but more effective in stimulating sales. Personal promotion and advertising differ in another important respect. The audience of a salesman in a store is self-selected. In this audience the proportion of potential customers is high and generally higher than in the audience of an advertising medium. Hence the firm wastes less promotional outlay in dealing with a self-selected clientele. When there are relatively few potential customers in the audience of the advertising medium or these are difficult to identify, we may expect personal selling to be the more important means of promotion. In this respect advertising and personal promotion are substitutes. Thus certain products with a specialized appeal are not advertised in the general media. Sellers are listed in a directory, may advertise in special printed media, and may use direct mail. Tombstones and glass eyeballs are extreme examples of such products.[12]

[12] The Federal Trade Commission study, *Distribution Methods and Costs* (see footnote to Table 15.1), presents data on selling expense and on advertising as percentages of sales. These percentages tend to vary inversely, thus giving the appearance of substitutability between advertising and selling expense. Obviously there would be a perfect inverse correlation between the two proportions if the sum of the two percentages were constant over all products. The more nearly constant the sum of the two percentages, the stronger the inverse correlation between the constituents. Thus

Advertising and personal selling may also complement each other. Because some products are complex, it is important to allow potential customers to request and receive particular kinds of information. Drug companies hire detail men who call on physicians and tell them about drugs. In 1958, the drug companies are estimated to have spent $3,200 per physician on promotion, of which 43 per cent was allocated to advertising and the remainder to detail men. The annual cost to the medical schools per medical student in 1957 was $6,800, a figure that is 2.1 times larger than the annual amount spent on drug promotion per practicing physician.[13] It is interesting to speculate whether physicians receive one-third as much information per year from drug companies as they did as medical students. For drugs, soaps, cosmetics, and toiletries both advertising

a more appropriate test of substitutability might be the variation of the sum of the two percentages and not the correlation between them. Unfortunately it is difficult to determine the degree of substitutability in this way because there is no criterion for judging whether the variation of the combined percentage is high or low.

Some Census data provide another way of looking at the substitutability between selling expense and advertising. In U.S. Bureau of the Census, *Enterprise Statistics: 1958*, Part I: *General Report* (Washington: Government Printing Office, 1963), Table 7 gives the employees of multi-unit manufacturing firms (those with more than one establishment) in manufacturers' sales branches and offices together with the number of employees in the manufacturing establishments by industry. The ratio of the two is a rough measure of the number of salesmen per production worker. Comparing this with advertising as a percentage of sales by industry, one gets a very loose positive association. For two industries, drugs, and perfumes and soaps, both salesmen as a percentage of manufacturing employees and advertising as a percentage of sales are very high.

Unfortunately, these Census data do not allow a consistent allocation of employees between sales branches owned by the manufacturer and wholesale establishments owned by the same manufacturer. Thus, if some manufacturing concerns engage in wholesaling and retailing on a large scale, whereas others confine their activities to manufacturing, the industries are not comparable. The problem is most obvious in the case of petroleum refining, where there is one production employee for nearly every company-employed salesman, a category that excludes both self-employed service-station operators and their employees.

[13] Charles D. May estimates at $200 million the total funds available to all medical schools in the United States in 1957 ("Selling Drugs by 'Educating' Physicians," *Journal of Medical Education*, XXXVI [1961], 1–23, esp. 7 and 15). In 1957–58 there were 29,473 students in medical schools, a record number (see "Medicine," *The Americana Annual, 1959* [New York: Americana Corp., 1959]). This gives a figure of $6,800 per medical student. According to the Kefauver Report on drugs, the total promotional outlay by the drug industry was approximately $750 million in 1958 (*Administered Prices, Drugs* [Report of the Committee on the Judiciary, U.S. Senate (Washington: Government Printing Office, 1960)], Table 84). Hence the promotional outlay per physician is about $3,200. On p. 158 the Kefauver Report erroneously states the number of physicians at 150,000, which is much too low. The Kefauver Report states that the promotional outlay of twenty-two companies was $580 million in 1958, of which $330 million was allocated to detail men and related expenses. The remainder, $250 million, is advertising, a figure in reasonably close agreement with the amount of advertising reported in 1957 to the Internal Revenue Service by drug and medicine manufacturers ($225 million).

and personal selling expenditures are large, which suggests a complementary relation between personal and impersonal promotion for these products.

Firms which sell industrial products tend to rely more heavily on personal selling than on advertising. This is easily comprehensible according to the above analysis of advertising. It would be obviously wasteful to advertise certain industrial products by national media because the audience contains a negligible fraction of the potential buyers. Instead there is considerable reliance on advertising in the trade journals because of the larger proportion of potential buyers in their audience. The personal selling of certain industrial products is the most economic means of promotion because there are few potential buyers, and these readily identified and easily contacted. Industrial products that do not meet these conditions are promoted in the same way as consumer goods. Although it is sometimes argued that there is less advertising of industrial products because the buyers are better informed and more rational than household consumers, it is equally plausible to explain the difference in sales methods by the relative costs of reaching different kinds of customers.

The difference in advertising intensity between consumer and industrial products is particularly important because it is evidence against the view that advertising is a means to monopoly. By and large, competition is at least as vigorous among makers of industrial products as among producers in the consumer product industries. The difference in promotional methods is largely explained by the cost of contacting customers using different methods. For the most part advertising is the more economic method for consumer products and personal promotion for the industrial products.

Another implication of the above analysis is that advertising outlays per dollar of sales are not always an appropriate measure of advertising intensity. A better measure is the advertising outlay per potential customer. This point is well illustrated by the automobile industry. According to Internal Revenue Service figures, the ratio of advertising outlays to sales by automobile manufacturers is about 0.5 per cent. However, the absolute advertising outlay by manufacturers was $100 million in 1954, and incorporated retail dealers spent $192 million advertising both new and used cars. In 1954, there were approximately 47 million households so that automobile advertising came to about $6 per household. By 1957, automobile advertising had risen to $390 million, including both retail and manufacturing outlays, and the number of households had risen to 50 million. Thus advertising per household was nearly $8. Nevertheless, some products are intensively advertised by any measure. About 14 per cent of perfume, cosmetics, and toiletries sales are alloted to advertising; and the absolute expenditure by manufacturers was $75 million in 1954 and well over $100 million in 1957.[14]

[14] Many businessmen and even some economists think that a constant proportion of sales revenue is spent on advertising particular products. Although they must admit that the proportion varies among products, within a product class they claim that the proportion remains stable over time. Such stability is generally inconsistent with profit-maximizing behavior. The appearance of a stable ratio between sales and advertising is easily explained. A mature product that has gained consumer acceptance requires continuous advertising because there is a turnover of clientele or because of growth in the market so that some new customers are uninformed. For

ADVERTISING AND THE SIZE OF FIRMS

The analysis of the advertising mechanism in terms of messages implies that eventually the marginal sales effectiveness of advertising a given product must decrease. Although the number of advertising messages conveyed might vary proportionately with the advertising outlay, sooner or later most of the potential buyers will have received messages more than once. Though repetition does effect some increase in sales, there comes a point when additional messages are ignored. Finally, even without the fatigue of repetition, there is generally a limit to the amount of a given product consumers are willing or able to buy. On these a priori grounds there should be decreasing marginal sales effectiveness of advertising messages beyond some point. It is important to note that the effectiveness of the advertising is calculated with respect to a physical measure—the number of messages conveyed.

At low levels of the advertising input there could be increasing marginal sales effectiveness for two different reasons—a threshold effect and word-of-mouth advertising.

There might be a threshold of awareness such that consumers fail to notice a product unless they have received at least a certain number of messages. Perhaps the threshold results from inertia. Consumers may not be willing to try a new product until the sustained advertising of the product has signaled to the more cautious that it has obtained a sufficient degree of acceptance.

Word-of-mouth advertising stimulated in the first instance by ordinary advertising that had induced initial sales could also produce increasing marginal sales effectiveness of advertising messages. Since it is not uncommon for consumers to exchange information about products among themselves, a given injection of advertising could trigger a sequence of responses that give the appearance of increasing marginal sales effectiveness. For example, suppose that the proportion of buyers increases at a rate that varies directly with the probability of a buyer meeting a non-buyer because a certain fraction of such contacts results in an exchange of information about the product which persuades the non-buyer

---

either of these reasons, the firm finds it advantageous to transmit advertising messages continuously in order to remind the old customers and inform the new customers just entering the market. However, when a product reaches a steady state, its sales and advertising both approach certain time paths, and this explains why the ratio of advertising to sales becomes stable. New products are more advertised than old products according to this explanation, and we do observe that the ratio of advertising to sales of new products declines as they become established. Similarly, established products experience a rise in the ratio of advertising to sales whenever they are modified so that it becomes necessary to inform potential buyers of the changes. There is a related discussion of these issues in S. A. Ozga, "Imperfect Markets through Lack of Knowledge," *Quarterly Journal of Economics*, LXXIV (1960), 29–52; George J. Stigler, "The Economics of Information," *Journal of Political Economy*, LXIX (1961), 213–25, esp. 220–21; and my "How Much Does It Pay Whom to Advertise?" *American Economic Review*, LI (1961), 194–205.

For a rather abstract explanation of a constant ratio of advertising to sales see Marc Nerlove and Kenneth J. Arrow, "Optimal Advertising Policy under Dynamic Conditions," *Economica*, XXIX (1962), 140, and the references cited therein.

to purchase the product. Let the probability of contact between buyers and non-buyers be measured by the proportion of buyers multiplied by the proportion of non-buyers. It follows that the proportion of buyers as a fraction of the population changes over time according to a logistic trend. For a logistic the proportion of buyers rises at an increasing rate during its early stages; this can be interpreted as increasing marginal sales effectiveness of advertising messages.[15]

The direct sales effect of the physical quantity of advertising messages should not be confused with the indirect effects of the dollar advertising outlays. It is generally true that advertising rates rise as audience rises but less rapidly. Therefore, an increase in advertising outlay buys a proportionately greater increase in the number of advertising messages.[16] This by itself may cause increasing marginal effectiveness of advertising with respect to dollar outlays. There need not, however, be increasing marginal sales effectiveness with respect to advertising messages. The nature of the returns to dollar advertising outlay depends both on the terms of sale that apply to the purchases of the services of the advertising media and on the consumer response to advertising messages. It is convenient to examine the nature of the returns to advertising separately with respect to these two factors.

Three arguments are usually given in defense of the assertion that advertising benefits the larger firm. First, if a successful advertising campaign requires a large capital, then credit rationing confers an advantage on the larger firm. Second, if advertising increases the minimum optimal scale of firms in an industry, given the size of market, it reduces the number of firms that can remain viable. Third, a large firm may have access to certain national advertising media unavailable to the small local firm; this impedes entry and inhibits competition.[17]

If a successful advertising campaign does require a large capital, then, given the phenomenon of credit rationing, it may be impossible for the small firm to borrow the wherewithal necessary to advertise at the requisite scale. No one disputes that, as the amount borrowed rises relative to the borrower's equity, the lender demands a higher interest rate. Moreover, for a given equity there is an absolute limit to the amount anyone can borrow no matter how much interest he may offer to pay. It does not follow, however, that profitable advertising opportunities are thereby overlooked. To establish advertising as a capital barrier to entry, one must show that despite reasonable profit expectations the required capital, equity or borrowed, is so large as to be out of the reach of most firms.

Increased advertising, far from signifying an obstacle to entry, is very often symptomatic of the reverse. It is the high turnover of brands and sometimes of

[15] For a fuller discussion of this type of model see S. A. Ozga, *op. cit.*
[16] For data on newspaper advertising rates see James M. Ferguson, *The Advertising Rate Structure in the Daily Newspaper Industry* (Englewood Cliffs, N.J.: Prentice-Hall, 1963), Appendix 2. Magazine advertising rates show the same general tendencies as do newspaper rates. Although there is little reliable evidence on television and radio rates, there is every reason to believe the same general pattern applies to them.
[17] Stigler found no significant relation between the minimum viable size of firm and the ratio of advertising to sales ("The Economies of Scale," *Journal of Law and Economics*, I [1958], 63–66).

firms that accounts for the large advertising outlays on some products. The most frequently cited example of advertising blocking entry is the cigarette industry, where advertising is intense and concentration is high. In fact, in the cigarette industry the sharpest increase in advertising as a percentage of sales occurred after the cancer alarms when many new brands were introduced. That new firms did not enter the industry then (1952) is probably the result not of credit rationing but of considerable doubt about the long-term prospects of the industry. There was a sales drop and a decline in profits immediately following the announcement of a link between smoking and lung cancer. The risk created by the subsequent news connecting smoking with sundry ailments could hardly attract even a mildly prudent businessman. In the 1920's when sales and profits grew rapidly, entry into cigarette manufacturing did occur.[18]

Advertising is used to illustrate the general proposition that, in an industry which requires firms to invest a large capital, entry is deterred. Credit rationing per se, however, will be of little practical importance if there is an adequate supply of venturesome entrepreneurs who possess equity capital. Moreover, an advertiser might campaign intensively in one region at the proper scale without a large absolute capital. To this point I shall return.

According to the second argument, advertising tends to increase the viable minimum scale, and this reduces the number of firms that may operate successfully in a given market. This argument tacitly assumes a type of market and product for which advertising is an economic method of promotion. Conditions favorable to advertising are a mass market, so that the number of potential buyers is large, and a marginal production cost that does not rise steeply with output. Even under these conditions small firms can be successful. Some consumers are willing to experiment with various goods and to seek the lower-priced, non-advertised items. The small firm can thrive on this clientele just as handily as the large firm that caters to the mass market. The validity of the proposition that advertising raises minimum viable scale depends more on the nature of production costs than on advertising. Given declining marginal cost of production, it is to the firm's advantage to increase sales. This can be done by lowering the price. But advertising is an efficient means of disseminating information about the product and terms of sale, thereby facilitating the growth of firms to an efficient size.

The third argument asserts the superiority of national over local media. It is undeniable that certain kinds of advertising cannot be undertaken in a local market. Until recently there were no regional editions of any national magazines, and it is still true that local firms cannot sponsor network radio or television programs. Nevertheless, many advertising media cater primarily to the local market, particularly newspapers and the spot television announcements. Technological constraints do not prevent a local firm from undertaking an inexpensive and intensive advertising campaign in one region. Indeed many large firms began by advertising heavily in local markets. Meeting with success in the local market, such firms were encouraged to enter other markets and gradually expand to a large size. Even large established firms introduce new products in small areas

---

[18] Telser, "Advertising and Cigarettes."

before embarking on national distribution, since it would be foolish to do otherwise.

The main source of advertising scale economies thus comes from the advertising rate structure and not from the response to the physical quantity of the advertising messages. The data clearly show a decline in the average cost of advertising messages as the number purchased rises. Taken by itself, this fact does not confer scale economies in the manufacture and sale of a given product. To the advertiser there is an incentive to combine in a single firm a complex of products that can be advertised together on a scale large enough to benefit from the economies offered by the structure of advertising rates. Certain large firms, such as General Foods, American Home Products, Procter and Gamble, make and sell a variety of consumer goods and owe their size in part to marketing economies of which advertising is one of the more important. These large companies own establishments classified in various industries, but concentration levels in these industries are neither very high nor very low. Although advertising economies may partly explain the size and diversity of these concerns, it is still apparently true that smaller firms manage to survive in competition with them. Suppose that by selling a variety of products a firm could reduce its overhead marketing expense by taking advantage of the quantity discounts of the advertising rate structure. Such a firm could undersell its competitors who fail to organize themselves so as to benefit from the same over-all economies. One possible result could be a rise in concentration levels in those industries which contain establishments owned by diversified companies. The empirical evidence of the third section, however, shows little, if any, positive correlation between concentration and advertising intensity.

There is another possible effect of these marketing economies. It may be that large companies account for a rising share of total sales or value added because savings in advertising impel them to a larger absolute size. Even if this is true, it does not imply impairment of competition in any industry. The larger scale can permit more efficient distribution of goods if it results from genuine savings inherent in the technology of the advertising media.

CONCLUSIONS

There is little empirical support for an inverse association between advertising and competition, despite some plausible theorizing to the contrary. I examined four pieces of evidence. First, for three cross-sections of manufacturing industries that make consumer products, concentration and advertising intensity are virtually independent. Second, there is a negative correlation between the change in concentration and the change in advertising intensity from 1947 to 1958. In some industries a rise in advertising accompanied a fall in concentration. Third, brand shares of food products are markedly more stable than brand shares of toiletries, although the latter are more heavily advertised than the former. Fourth, brands of toiletries have a shorter expected life than branded food items. This is shown by the larger changes around the levels reached by a group of leading brands and the lower levels attained by leading brands of toiletries as compared to branded food items. Advertising is frequently a means of entry and a sign of competition. This agrees with the view that advertising is an important source of information.

Simple figures confirm the latter point. According to the Internal Revenue Service data, in 1959 total advertising outlays were $8.7 billion of which about $5 billion were spent by all manufacturers, $2.5 billion by wholesalers and retailers, and the balance by concerns in finance and services. Almost all advertising by wholesalers, retailers, and financial firms is informative in a narrow sense because of the prominent place given to prices and terms of sale in the advertising messages. Obviously some part of manufacturer advertising is also informative. For another check on the relative importance of informative advertising, note that radio, television, and magazine advertising, the three categories which can be said to be least informative by the strictest definition, account for only 27 per cent of all advertising. Moreover, this figure includes spot and local advertising in these media, which is informative. Newspapers, primarily a medium of informational advertising, are the largest single advertising medium and account for 31 per cent of the total advertising expenditure.

Appendix I to Reading 15

CAN ADVERTISING DIFFERENTIATE THE PRODUCT?

A recurrent problem in the economic analysis of advertising is how to tell whether advertising can change the price elasticity of demand, or, in other words, differentiate the product. This problem can be approached directly by estimating the demand function. There is also an indirect method which draws inferences about the price elasticity from a study of the effects of changes in production and advertising costs on the price of the product and the number of advertising messages transmitted. This indirect method is formally equivalent to looking at a set of reduced-form equations and asking what can be learned about the structural equations from the signs of the reduced-form coefficients.

Consider first the direct method. The firm's demand equation is

$$x = D(p, y, v), \qquad (15.6)$$

where y is real income, p is the deflated price, v is the quantity of advertising messages, and x is the rate of sales. A direct estimate of equation (15.6) could show whether increased advertising reduces the price elasticity. The demand function takes on a special form if the price elasticity is independent of the level of advertising. In this case the demand function can be written as follows:

$$x = F(p, y)G(v). \qquad (15.6')$$

Equation (15.6′) shows that the total rate of sales can be regarded as a product of two functions, one of which depends on the price and the other on advertising.

The function F could be considered the demand for the representative consumer, and G then shows how advertising can increase the number of buyers.

Although at first one might think the only reasonable alternative to equation (15.6′) is a demand schedule that implies that more advertising reduces the price elasticity, this is not true. Nothing a priori rules out the possibility that more advertising results in a larger price elasticity as well as in additional sales. Suppose, for instance, the increased advertising attracts a more price-sensitive clientele than the present customers of the farm. The firm thereby faces a more elastic demand as a result of its increased advertising.

The direct estimates of the demand schedule proved inconclusive in the case of cigarettes. Four types of demand equations were estimated. The first was linear in all of the variables—quantity, real price, real income, and advertising outlays; the second was linear in quantity and linear in the logs of all other variables. The third was linear in the logs of all variables. The fourth was linear in the logs of quantity and linear in all other variables. The third and fourth types satisfy equation (15.6′) so that their price elasticities are independent of the advertising outlays. Both of these gave distinctly poorer fits. Unfortunately, the estimated price elasticities of all four types are unreliable so that, although the first two forms give much better fits, it cannot be concluded that advertising does affect the price elasticity.[19]

Now consider the indirect method. The problem is to discover from the signs of the coefficients of the reduced-form equations whether advertising can affect the price elasticity. There are two kinds of structural equations; first, the cost and demand equations of the firm and, second, the behavioral equations derived from the hypothesis of profit maximization. The two endogenous variables are price and the number of advertising messages. These are chosen by the firm so as to maximize profits. There are, therefore, two reduced-form equations, one for each of the endogenous variables. These reduced form equations are the firm's price and advertising policies, respectively, since they relate its price and advertising to the underlying cost and demand parameters. Is it possible to tell from the signs of the partial derivatives of price and advertising messages with respect to certain underlying parameters whether the price elasticity varies inversely with the quantity of advertising messages? To answer this question requires the use of comparative statics to do econometrics without numbers. It will come as no surprise to discover that without knowledge of the size of the coefficients not much can be learned except in special cases.

The total cost function is

$$c = H(x, v) + bv + mx. \tag{15.7}$$

The two terms bv and mx represent, respectively, that part of total cost that is linear in output and advertising messages. A change in b can be interpreted as a change in the average cost of advertising messages and a change in m as a change in the level of marginal production cost. The function $H(x, v)$ is the non-linear part of total cost with respect to its arguments, and it allows for interaction between production costs and the advertising. For example, if more

[19] *Ibid.*, pp. 478–80.

advertising requires stricter quality control, this will raise marginal production costs ($H_{xv} > 0$).

Net revenue, R, is defined by

$$R = pD(p, v) - c. \tag{15.8}$$

Note that real income is not displayed explicitly; the reason for ignoring real income is that to do otherwise does not help determine the effects of advertising on the price elasticity. To maximize R with respect to p and v it is necessary that

$$R_p = x + (p - H_x)D_p - m\,D_p = 0, \tag{15.9}$$
$$R_v = -H_v + (p - H_x)D_v - b - mD_v = 0.$$

It is sufficient for maximum R that the Hesseian B is negative definite where B is defined as follows:

$$B = \begin{pmatrix} R_{pp} & R_{vp} \\ R_{vp} & R_{vv} \end{pmatrix}. \tag{15.10}$$

Since the rate of sales x is a function of p and v, the two equations in (15.9) implicitly define two reduced-form equations for p and v. Our goal is the calculation of the slopes of these two reduced-form equations with respect to b and m. The slopes of the reduced-form equations with respect to b satisfy

$$B \begin{bmatrix} \dfrac{\partial p}{\partial b} \\ \dfrac{\partial v}{\partial b} \end{bmatrix} = - \begin{bmatrix} R_{bp} \\ R_{bv} \end{bmatrix} = \begin{bmatrix} 0 \\ 1 \end{bmatrix}. \tag{15.11}$$

Similarly, the slopes with respect to m satisfy

$$B \begin{bmatrix} \dfrac{\partial p}{\partial m} \\ \dfrac{\partial v}{\partial m} \end{bmatrix} = - \begin{bmatrix} R_{mp} \\ R_{mv} \end{bmatrix} = \begin{bmatrix} D_p \\ D_v \end{bmatrix}. \tag{15.12}$$

Therefore,

$$\frac{\partial p}{\partial b} = -\frac{R_{vb}}{\det B}, \quad \frac{\partial v}{\partial b} = \frac{R_{pp}}{\det B} < 0. \tag{15.13}$$

$$\frac{\partial p}{\partial m} = \frac{D_p R_{vv} - D_v R_{vp}}{\det B},$$

$$\frac{\partial v}{\partial m} = \frac{D_v R_{pp} - D_p R_{vp}}{\det B}. \tag{15.14}$$

By hypothesis the signs of the partial derivatives are as follows:

$$D_p < 0, \quad D_v > 0, \tag{15.15}$$
$$R_{vv} < 0, \text{ and } R_{pp} < 0.$$

The latter two inequalities are required for profit maximization. On the basis of equation (15.15) it follows that

$$R_{vp} \leq 0$$

implies

$$\frac{\partial p}{\partial b} \geq 0, \qquad \frac{\partial p}{\partial m} > 0, \qquad \frac{\partial v}{\partial m} < 0. \qquad (15.16)$$

Since $\partial v/\partial b$ is always negative, only the partial derivatives of price with respect to b, and the partials of p and v with respect to m can reveal information about the sign of R_{vp}, which is important in discovering the effect of advertising on the price elasticity. Table 15.7 shows the pattern of signs of the three slopes of interest when $R_{vp} \leq 0$. Therefore, if the slopes of p and v, which are the coefficients of p and v with respect to the two exogenous variables b and m in the reduced-form equations, have signs given by equation (15.16), then it must be true that R_{vp} is non-positive.

R_{vp} can be positive but it cannot be too large. To see why, consider

$$0 < R_{vp} < \frac{D_p}{D_v} R_{vv} = J_1. \qquad (15.17)$$

$$0 < R_{vp} < \frac{D_v}{D_p} R_{pp} = J_2. \qquad (15.18)$$

It must be true that

$$R_{vp} < \max(J_1, J_2), \qquad (15.19)$$

for to suppose the contrary would violate the negative definiteness of B. Therefore, either both inequalities (15.17) and (15.18) are satisfied, so that R_{vp} is positive and small, or

$$0 < \min(J_1, J_2) < R_{vp} < \max(J_1, J_2). \qquad (15.20)$$

In the event that equations (15.17) and (15.18) both hold, Table 15.7 shows the pattern of signs for the three partials. For $0 < R_{vp} < \min(J_1, J_2)$, a rise in marginal production cost raises price and reduces the number of advertising messages transmitted, whereas a rise in the cost of advertising lowers the price of the product. Thus the difference between a non-positive R_{vp} and a small positive R_{vp} can be seen only from the sign of $\partial p/\partial b$. When R_{vp} is large and positive so that equation (15.20) applies, then there are two distinct cases depending on which of the two, J_1 or J_2, is larger. So long as R_{vp} is positive, $\partial p/\partial b$ must be negative, as is evident from equation (15.13). It is, therefore, possible to distinguish the two cases $J_1 < J_2$ or $J_2 < J_1$ solely on the basis of the effect of a change in m on the price of the product and the quantity of advertising. Table 15.7 shows the signs of the coefficients when J_1 is the larger, and the pattern when J_2 is the larger. In the latter case it is of interest to note that a rise in cost reduces the price and the quantity of advertising messages. It is now possible to examine the connection between the sign of R_{vp} and the effect of advertising on the price of elasticity.

From equation (15.9)

$$R_{vp} = -D_p(H_{xx}D_v + H_{xv}) + D_v + (p - H_x - m)D_{vp}. \qquad (15.21)$$

Since by definition the price elasticity of demand η is $(p/x)D_p$, the partial of η with respect to v is

$$\frac{\partial \eta}{\partial v} = \frac{p}{x}\left(D_{pv} - \frac{D_p D_v}{x}\right). \qquad (15.22)$$

Using equation (15.9) which gives $p - H_x - m = -x/D_p$, equation (15.21) reduces to

$$R_{vp} = -D_p[H_{xx}D_v + H_{xv}] + D_v - x\frac{D_{vp}}{D_p}$$

$$= -D_p[H_{xx}D_v + H_{xv}] - \frac{x}{D_p}\left[D_{vp} - \frac{D_v D_p}{x}\right].$$

Finally from equation (15.22),

$$R_{vp} = -D_p(H_{xx}D_v + H_{xv}) - \frac{x}{\eta}\frac{\partial \eta}{\partial v}. \qquad (15.23)$$

This gives the sought-for connection between R_{vp} and the slope of the price elasticity with respect to v.

Assume that the two reduced-form equations are available and that the slope of p with respect to b is positive. As shown in Table 15.7 and as given by equa-

Table 15.7

			Either		
				J_1 is max	
$\frac{\partial p}{\partial m} > 0,$	$\frac{\partial v}{\partial m} < 0$	$\frac{\partial p}{\partial m} > 0$	$\frac{\partial p}{\partial m} > 0$	and	$\frac{\partial v}{\partial m} > 0,$
			or		
				J_2 is max	
$\frac{\partial p}{\partial b} > 0$		$\frac{\partial v}{\partial b} < 0$	$\frac{\partial p}{\partial m} < 0$	and	$\frac{\partial v}{\partial m} < 0.$
			In either case		
			$\frac{\partial p}{\partial b} > 0$	$\frac{\partial p}{\partial b} < 0$	
0		min (J_1, J_2)		max (J_1, J_2)	R_{vp}

tion (15.13), R_{vp} must be negative. Assume in addition that $H_{xx} > 0$, which means that marginal production costs are rising, that $H_{xv} > 0$ so that increased advertising requires a higher marginal production cost, and that $D_v > 0$. These imply

$$(H_{xx}D_v + H_{xv}) > 0. \qquad (15.24)$$

Since sales vary inversely with price, equation (15.24) plus the assumption of a negative R_{vp} can only mean that the price elasticity increases in size as v increases ($\partial \eta/\partial v < 0$, keeping in mind that $\eta < 0$). In other words the empirical observation that the slope of p with respect to b is positive in the reduced-form equation for p plus assumption (15.24) establishes that increased advertising makes the price elasticity a bigger number.

Now what can be learned from finding that $\partial p/\partial b < 0$, which means that the price of the product varies inversely with the cost of advertising? In this case R_{vp} is positive, which might result entirely from the cost conditions as shown in equation (15.24). Thus an inverse relation between the price of the product and the average cost of advertising messages is consistent with either a positive or a negative sign of $\partial \eta/\partial v$. Since a rise in the level of b reduces v, this means that even though the product is less advertised and the price falls, it is incorrect to conclude that the reduction in the advertising raised the price elasticity in magnitude.

In this case it is clear from Table 15.7 that knowledge of the effects of changes in m on v and p give no assistance. Even if the signs of both $\partial p/\partial m$ and $\partial v/\partial m$ were known, one could not be sure of how much of the effect on price to attribute to advertising's effect on the price elasticity.[20]

[20] There is a related discussion of these matters in G. C. Archibald, "Chamberlin versus Chicago," *Review of Economic Studies*, XXIX (1962), 2–28. In this interesting article Archibald uses a less general cost function than is given in eq. (2) and fails to point out the connection between his exercises in comparative statics and the problem of identifying a set of structural parameters, given only the signs of the reduced-form parameters.

Appendix II to Reading 15

LISTS OF PRODUCTS INCLUDED IN MEASURES
OF RECALLED-SHARE STABILITY*

1. Food products (28):
   White bread
   Rye bread
   Potato chips
   Coffee, regular
   Coffee, instant
   Tea bags
   Peanut butter
   Flour, regular
   Pancake or waffle
     mix
   Pie-crust mix
   Cake mix
   Baby cereals
   Junior baby foods
   Strained baby
     foods
   Fresh milk
   Soda crackers
   Shortening
   Wieners
   Canned peas
   Fruit cocktails
   Frozen vegetables
   Tomato juice
   Rice, packaged
   Ice cream
   Dry soup mixes
   Catsup
   Luncheon meat,
     canned
   Corned beef hash
2. Soaps, waxes, and
   polishes (9):
   Bleach, liquid
   Scouring cleanser
   Self-polishing floor
     wax
   Paste floor wax
   Water softener
   Soaps for fine
     fabric
   Wall and woodwork
     cleanser
   Household laundry
     soap
   Dish soap
3. Cosmetics, toiletries,
   etc. (15):
   Lipstick
   Toothpaste
   Brushless shaving
     cream
   Headache remedies
   Cream shampoo
   Liquid shampoo
   Hair tonic for men
   Nail polish
   Facial cream
   Facial tissues
   Home permanents
   Deodorant (men)
   Deodorant (women)
   Toilet soap (bath)
   Toilet soap (hands
     and face)

* The data on brand shares are taken from the *Milwaukee Journal Consumer Analysis*, 1948, 1953, and 1959.

16

Advertising, Market Structure and Performance

William S. Comanor and Thomas A. Wilson*

This paper presents an empirical analysis of the role of advertising in consumer goods industries. The primary finding is that advertising has a statistically significant and quantitatively important impact upon profit rates which provide a measure of market performance as well as indicate the existence of market power. This result is robust, and the estimated multivariate equations account for half of the inter-industry variance of profit rates.

This finding has implications which are precisely the opposite of the conclusions reached by Telser in a recent important article.[1] This contradiction is a reflection primarily of differences in the conceptual and statistical approaches adopted rather than differences in data or sample, for with minor exceptions, we used the same set of industries, and drew upon the same basic data for advertising outlays.

We shall therefore proceed as follows. First, we shall describe the conceptual framework used. Then we shall examine the relationships which are likely to

Reprinted from *The Review of Economics and Statistics,* November 1967, pp. 423–440 by permission of the authors and publisher.

* A preliminary version of this paper was presented at the December 1965 meetings of the Econometric Society. The authors thank Frank Edwards for his discussion of the paper at that time, and William Hughes and Lester Taylor for their comments on a subsequent draft. Special thanks are due Richard Caves and R. B. Heflebower, both of whom provided us with extensive and constructively critical comments.

The authors are grateful for financial assistance provided by the small grant program of the Ford Foundation and a grant from the Alfred P. Sloan Foundation.

[1] Lester Telser, "Advertising and Competition," *Journal of Political Economy* (Dec. 1964).

exist between product differentiation, advertising and entry barriers. Finally, we shall present the empirical results which are the core of this paper.

FRAMEWORK OF ANALYSIS

The analytical approach is to examine the joint effect of various dimensions of market structure upon profit rates. Not only do profit rates provide some indication of market performance in terms of the normal criteria of allocative efficiency, but also high returns signal the possible existence of market power.[2] If exercised in the direction of profit maximization, market power should lead to rates of return which exceed those in competitive industries that are comparable in terms of risk and growth of demand.

In this framework, concentration is simply one dimension of market structure and is not of itself a measure of monopoly or market power. Another major dimension is the height of entry barriers, which is determined in part by technical factors such as the extent of production economies of scale relative to the size of the market, the absolute amount of capital required to operate a plant of minimum efficient scale, and other absolute production cost disadvantages of new entrants.

Product differentiation, a third major dimension of market structure, plays a dual role. Not only does it directly influence the character of competition among established firms, but it also raises the height of entry barriers.[3] In this study, however, we do not deal directly with product differentiation, but focus instead upon advertising expenditures, which are both a symptom and a source of differentiation. Not only are advertising budgets influenced by product and market characteristics, but also they depend on the policies pursued by individual firms. In addition, past advertising outlays appear to be an important determinant of the extent of product differentiation. Differences in advertising, therefore, reflect both structural and behavioral differences between industries.

On these grounds, the empirical analysis which follows takes the form of multivariate regression equations which explain the interindustry variation in profit rates as a function of different combinations of the following variables:

Seller concentration,
The rate of growth of demand,
Economies of scale in production in relation to the size of the market,
Absolute capital requirements for a plant of minimum efficient scale,[4] and
Advertising.

[2] Low or average profit rates do not necessarily indicate that market power is absent. Firms may become lax in minimizing costs when the discipline of competition is weak. For a discussion of such behavior, see Carl Kaysen, *U.S. vs. United Shoe Machinery Corporation* (Cambridge: Harvard University Press, 1956), 114–116.

[3] Joe Bain, *Barriers to New Competition* (Cambridge: Harvard University Press, 1956), 21.

[4] No attempt was made to measure any other absolute cost disadvantages of new entrants. Bain found that only in those industries in which established firms controlled scarce natural resources were these important. Bain, *op. cit.*, 155–156. In addition, no attempt was made to measure risk. The sources of the data and various technical adjustments are described in Appendix I.

The specific variables used, the alternative functional forms, and other specifications of the estimated equations are described below. The conceptual relationship between advertising, product differentiation, and the height of entry barriers is discussed in the next two sections.

Before proceeding, however, it is useful to contrast the framework adopted here with that used by Telser. One of his major empirical findings is that the simple correlation between advertising outlays as a percentage of sales and the level of seller concentration is statistically insignificant. In each of the years studied, he finds that this coefficient is about 0.16, and from this, concludes that "There is little empirical support for an inverse association between advertising and competition."[5]

This approach raises the problem of whether concentration ratios are an adequate measure of the extent of competition. Telser justifies their use by stating that "Concentration of sales among the four leading firms is a widely accepted measure of monopoly."[6] While this statement is unfortunately correct, it ignores the fact that the concentration ratio measures only one dimension of market structure, and is therefore an inadequate indicator of market power, which depends on additional structural variables as well as on established behavior patterns. The significance of advertising expenditures depends on whether they represent an additional factor affecting the achievement of market power. The weak correlation between concentration and advertising simply indicates that these are independent rather than collinear variables.

ADVERTISING AND PRODUCT DIFFERENTIATION

The relationship between advertising outlays and product differentiation is important for an evaluation of the competitive effects of advertising because the former reflects the policies adopted by individual firms, while the latter is a dimension of market structure.

The degree of product differentiation in a market is measured by the cross elasticities of demand and supply which exist among competing products. Low cross elasticities of demand between these products indicate that buyers prefer the products or brands of particular sellers and will not switch in significant numbers in response to small differences in price. Low cross elasticities of supply, on the other hand, signify that firms are unable to imitate the products of their rivals sufficiently well to eliminate these consumer preferences. While cross elasticities between the products of existing producers affect the character of the rivalry which exists between them, cross elasticities between the products of established firms and potential entrants influence the height of entry barriers posed by product differentiation.[7]

Product differentiation reflects two sets of factors: the basic characteristics

[5] Telser, *op. cit.*, 544 and 558.
[6] *Ibid.*, 542.
[7] It is important to distinguish product differentiation from product variety. The steel industry, for example, produces a great variety of products which are sold to knowledgeable buyers, but product differentiation is minimal. In contrast, the cigarette industry offers a smaller variety of products, but product differentiation—based largely on extensive advertising—is great. Bain, *op. cit.*, 127–129.

of products within the market, and the present and past policies of established firms with respect to advertising, product design, servicing, and distribution. On the demand side, products are more likely to be differentiable when buyers are relatively uninformed about the relative merits of existing products. This is particularly important for differentiation achieved via advertising. On the supply side, differentiation is more likely where the products of rivals cannot easily be imitated and where new entrants have difficulties in producing products which are similar to those sold by successfully established firms. In producer goods industries, successful imitation requires investment in product design and adequate service facilities. In consumer goods industries, successful imitation may require investment in advertising as well.

It is noteworthy that Bain, in his authoritative examination of product differentiation in 20 manufacturing industries, found advertising to be the most important source of product differentiation in the consumer goods industries in his sample. Distribution policies are also important where forward integration is prevalent, while customer services and product design play contributing but relatively minor roles.

For typical consumer goods industries, then, a persistently high level of advertising expenditures can be viewed in two ways:

a) If firms behave reasonably, high levels of advertising indicate that the product is differentiable. In this sense, advertising is a symptom of differentiation.

b) The high level of advertising is itself an important determinant of the level of differentiation which is realized by established firms vis-à-vis potential entrants. In this sense, advertising is a source of product differentiation.

Provided that firms act reasonably, observed advertising expenditures provide a useful measure of the extent of product differentiation. We write reasonably rather than rationally since, in an oligopolistic market, rational policies are not unambiguous. What is rational policy for the group acting in concert is not rational policy for the individual firm expecting to gain a march on its rivals. It is quite possible, moreover, that rivalry via advertising among established firms is carried to the point of diminishing returns in terms of group profit rates. However, even in this case, the result of extensive advertising rivalry may be to permit the achievement of higher future profits for the group by raising entry barriers.

THE EFFECT OF ADVERTISING ON ENTRY BARRIERS

Although advertising is only one source of product differentiation, it is especially important in a number of consumer goods industries where it has a strong direct impact on entry barriers.[8] In these industries, new entrants generally are forced to sell at a price below the established brands or else incur heavy selling costs. This explains the phenomenon of unbranded products selling at prices substantially below those of highly advertised products even where there is little

[8] *Ibid.*, 114–143.

"real" difference between them. On this account, established firms can set prices above existing cost levels, including advertising and other selling expenses, without inducing entry.

Product differentiation via advertising affects entry barriers in three ways, each of which is analogous to the other determinants of overall entry barriers. First, high prevailing levels of advertising create additional costs for new entrants which exist at all levels of output. Because of buyer inertia and loyalty, more advertising messages per prospective customer must be supplied to induce brand switching as compared with repeat buying. Since the market which prospective entrants must penetrate is made up largely of consumers who have purchased existing products, advertising costs per customer for new entrants will be higher than those of existing firms who are maintaining existing market positions. Moreover, the costs of penetration are likely to increase as output expands and customers more inert or loyal need to be reached.[9] This effect of advertising creates an absolute cost advantage for established producers, since they need not incur penetration costs.

In addition, the effect of advertising on firm revenues is subject to economies of scale which result from the increasing effectiveness of advertising messages per unit of output as well as from decreasing costs for each advertising message purchased. The first source of economies will exist whenever the effect of advertising on consumer decisions is sufficiently important that a threshold level of advertising is required for a firm to stay in the market and maintain its current market share. In such a situation, larger firms have the advantage of being able to spread this cost over more units of output and thereby spend less per unit sold. This advantage creates economies of scale at the firm level, since an established firm does not have to spend twice as much on advertising to maintain a market share which is twice that of a rival. Higher output levels are associated with lower unit costs.[10] As a result, smaller firms, including most entrants, are placed at a strong disadvantage.[11]

Economies of scale in advertising also result when the cost per advertising message declines as the number of messages supplied increases. An increased use

---

[9] These penetration costs depend on past as well as current advertising outlays by established firms. The importance of past outlays is examined by Kristian S. Palda who concludes that "distributed lag models both give a better fit to the Pinkham data and forecast better than the models which do not incorporate lagged effects." *The Measurement of Cumulative Advertising Effects* (Prentice-Hall, 1964), 94.

[10] In the automobile industry, for example, the two smaller firms during the 1950's were forced to spend more than twice as much on advertising per car sold as did either Ford or General Motors. Between 1954 and 1957 Studebaker and American Motors spent annually on national advertising approximately $64.04 and $57.89, respectively, per automobile sold while G.M. spent $26.56 per unit and Ford spent $27.22 per unit. Chrysler was in an intermediate position, spending $47.76 per unit. Leonard W. Weiss, *Economics and American Industry* (New York: John Wiley and Sons, 1961), 342.

[11] This result occurs *within* the relevant market. When a firm in a regionally segmented market expands its national market share by moving into new geographic areas, unit advertising costs do not decline.

of some forms of advertising leads to a lower cost per message, and available evidence suggests that this is very important for advertising on national television and in national magazines.[12]

If advertising in a particular industry is characterized by economies of scale for either of these reasons, an entrant will suffer an additional cost disadvantage if he enters at a relatively small scale. If he enters at a scale sufficient to realize available economies of scale in advertising, however, his actions are likely to influence the price or advertising policies of the established firms. The possible reactions of established firms increase the costs and risks of entry.

Finally, if economies of scale exist either in production or in advertising, the need to obtain funds for advertising will give rise to capital requirements over and above those needed for physical plant and equipment. Furthermore, this investment in market penetration will involve a particularly risky use of funds since it does not generally create tangible assets which can be resold in the event of failure. The required rate of return on such capital will therefore be high.

These various effects are illustrated diagrammatically in Figure 16.1. Curve APC

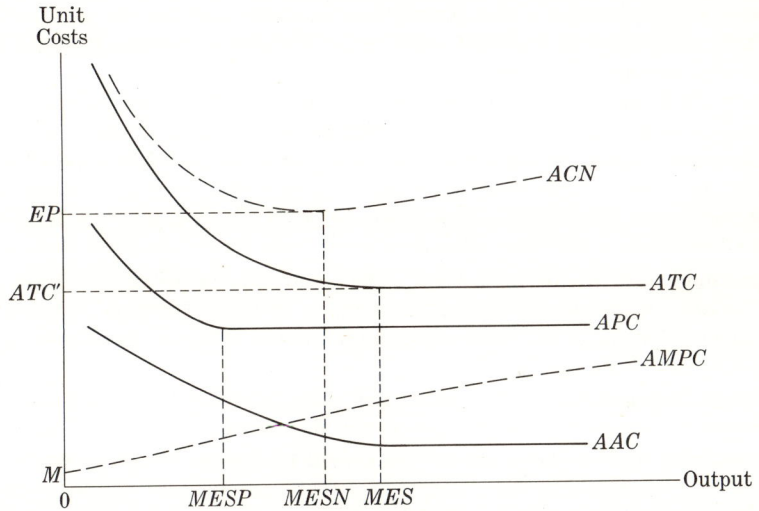

Figure 16.1

represents average production costs for established and prospective firms, and $MESP$ is minimum efficient scale in production. Curve AAC describes average advertising costs for existing firms as well as for new entrants after they have become established. It denotes unit advertising outlays which are required in order to maintain a firm's market position and to preserve a given volume of sales once it has been established. This will depend on both the total level of advertising

---

[12] The extent of discounts given to large advertisers is documented in *Federal Trade Commission vs. The Procter & Gamble Company,* Brief for the Federal Trade Commission in the Supreme Court of the United States (Dec. 1966), 12–13.

outlays and their distribution among established firms, and therefore, it describes prospective advertising costs for entrants only if existing firms do not react to any loss of market share. To the extent that they do respond, required advertising outlays will be higher. Curve ATC, the vertical sum of these two curves, represents average total costs for established firms.[13] MES denotes the minimum efficient scale in both production and advertising for an established firm with a given market share.

In addition, curve $AMPC$ describes average market penetration costs for new entrants. Penetration costs represent an investment in establishing a market position and therefore depend on the opportunity cost of capital as well as on total penetration expenditures.[14] This schedule therefore denotes the required rate of return on capital invested in market penetration times the total expenditure required to establish a given volume of sales, all divided by the number of units sold. The figure illustrates the case where average penetration costs rise throughout the relevant range of output. This assumes that the growing difficulty involved in winning over customers with stronger preferences for the products of established firms, reinforced by rising required rates of return as the absolute amount of capital required for penetration increases with the scale of entry, is not fully offset by economies of scale in advertising or by bandwagon effects for the new entrant's products.

Curve ACN represents average costs, including penetration costs, for new entrants, and $MESN$ is the most efficient scale for entry if the reactions of established producers are neglected. From this, it follows that EP is the *minimum* price at which entry will occur. If $MESN$ is a negligible fraction of the market, EP is the entry-inducing price. If, however, $MESN$ is a significant fraction of the market, entry is unlikely to occur even at price EP because the entrant will expect established producers to contest the encroachment of their market position through an increase in advertising outlays or by a reduction in price. The gap between EP and ATC' represents, therefore, the minimum price-cost margin which may induce entry.

This figure demonstrates, moreover, that the interaction between rising penetration costs and economies of scale at the firm level is important even if no allowance is made for the reactions of existing producers. If economies of scale in both production and in advertising were absent, the relevant price-cost margin would be simply M, which is less than EP-ATC'.

VARIABLES USED IN THE MULTIVARIATE ANALYSIS

In this section, we briefly define and discuss the rationale for the selection of each of the specific measures.

---

[13] For simplicity, we assume here that advertising constitutes the only form of selling expense.

[14] Penetration costs include extra advertising outlays which are required for entry. These outlays will represent total penetration costs if the price charged by the entrant is the same as that set by established producers. If the entrant is forced to set a price below that of existing firms, there are additional penetration costs which equal the price differential times the amount of output sold by the entrant at the lower price.

Profit Rates

The profit rate variable used is profits after taxes as a percentage of stockholders' equity,[15] averaged within each industry for firms with assets exceeding $500,000. This procedure avoids the difficulty, noted by Stigler, of profit withdrawals in the form of executive salaries in small and closely held corporations.[16] Profit rates are also averaged for the period 1954–1957, which covers a complete business cycle.

Although the profit rate on stockholders' equity is viewed as a more appropriate variable than the rate of return (including interest) on total assets,[17] we examined whether the empirical results would be sensitive to this decision. The simple correlation between the profit rate on stockholders' equity and the rate of return on total assets is 0.93. In addition, the correlation coefficients between each of these variables and the 1954 four-firm concentration ratio[18] are, respectively, 0.36 and 0.33. These results suggest that our empirical findings are unlikely to be sensitive to the choice of a specific profit rate variable.

Advertising

In light of the discussion in the preceding section, it is useful to examine the absolute volume of advertising expenditures by existing firms as well as the advertising-sales ratio. The latter variable probably provides a good indication of the absolute cost disadvantage of the new entrant at small scales of entry, but is likely to be a less accurate index of the economies of scale and absolute capital requirements effects of advertising.

We have, therefore, calculated two measures of advertising intensity: advertising outlays per dollar of sales for firms with assets greater than $500,000, and average advertising expenditures per firm among firms which account for 50 per cent of industry output.[19] Both advertising variables are averages for the years 1954 through 1957.

[15] This profit ratio variable was used originally in Joe S. Bain, "Relation of Profit Rates to Industry Concentration: American Manufacturing, 1936-1940," *Quarterly Journal of Economics* (Aug. 1951), 296–297, and Bain, *Barriers to New Competition*, 192.

[16] George J. Stigler, *Capital and Rates of Return in Manufacturing Industries* (Princeton University Press), 125–127.

[17] This is because firms presumably maximize profits, rather than the sum of profits plus interest payments. The rate of return on stockholders' equity will therefore be a more sensitive indicator of the extent of freedom from competitive constraints.

[18] In two cases out of 41, our industry classifications differed from those presented by Stigler. In both of these cases, "Screens and Venetian Blinds," and "Radio, T.V., and Phonograph," it appeared that Stigler had combined these industries with smaller, miscellaneous industries. In these calculations, therefore, we used data for the more aggregated industry to stand for its major component.

[19] The procedure used was to select successive asset size classes of firms until 50 per cent or more of industry sales was covered. The proportion of sales in the boundary size class required to reach this degree of coverage was used to determine the amount of advertising and the number of firms from that size class included in both the numerator and denominator of the measure of advertising per firm. For some industries, the largest size class accounted for more than 50 per cent of sales. In such cases, the measure is simply advertising per firm in the largest size class.

Seller Concentration

Concentration is a sufficiently prominent variable in the literature to warrant introducing it in three alternative formulations. First, a trichotomous classification based on Kaysen and Turner's classification of market groups is used.[20] Second, the average four-firm concentration ratios published by Stigler are introduced.[21] Finally, a dichotomous classification is constructed on the basis of Bain's finding that a critical point is reached when the eight-firm concentration ratio exceeds 70 per cent.[22]

Economies of Scale in Production

Economies of scale in production presumably exist primarily at the level of the plant rather than the firm. In the absence of better estimates for most of the industries in the sample, a measure is derived from the size distribution of plants within the relevant industries. Since cost minimization is an element of profit maximization, large multi-plant firms should operate plants which are sufficiently large to realize available scale economies. Where demand is not a limiting factor, moreover, competition among firms should lead directly to plants which equal or exceed minimum efficient scale.[23] At the same time, however, small plants may exist. These may have been built in an earlier period, before demand had expanded or a technology which required large scale had been developed, or they may result from the entry of small firms. They may also exist in pockets of the market which are geographically segmented or may specialize in narrow product lines which are not representative of the industry generally. It is therefore important to select a measure which is insensitive to the entry of single-plant firms of sub-optimal scale.

The measure used is based on average plant size among the largest plants accounting for 50 per cent of industry output. This average plant size is divided by total output in the relevant market to obtain the scale economies variable used in the regression analyses.[24]

A test of the reliability of this variable can be made by comparing minimum efficient scale as a percentage of industry output with Bain's estimates. Not only did Bain concentrate on a smaller number of industries, but also he used varied forms of information. Therefore, his estimates can be considered a benchmark against which to appraise various methods of estimating the extent of scale economies. We examine both the method described above and an alternative method, the Survival Technique, as used by Weiss.[25]

[20] Carl Kaysen and Donald F. Turner, *Antitrust Policy*, 27.
[21] Stigler, *op. cit.*, 214–215.
[22] Bain, "Relation of Profit Rates to Industry Concentration," 314.
[23] Since the bulk of the evidence suggests that cost curves in manufacturing are "L shaped" rather than "U shaped," plants which exceed minimal efficient scale will typically be efficient plants. See J. Johnston, *Statistical Cost Analysis* (New York: McGraw-Hill, 1960), 44–168.
[24] An alternative measure based on average plant size among the largest plants accounting for 70 per cent of output was also constructed. This variable was highly correlated with the variable used.
[25] See Leonard Weiss, "The Survival Technique and the Extent of Suboptimal Capacity," *Journal of Political Economy* (June 1964), 246–261.

Of the 20 industries examined by Bain, data on the size distribution of plants are available for 19. Across those industries, the correlation coefficient between Bain's estimates and those derived from the method proposed above is 0.89.[26] Estimates based on the Survival Technique are available for 13 of the industries studied by Bain, and the correlation between these estimates and those presented by Bain is 0.66. When the comparison is limited to these same 13 industries, the correlation coefficient between estimates derived from the size distribution of establishments and those published by Bain is 0.86. The method proposed above is more consistent with Bain's estimates than those computed from the Survival Technique,[27] and it will therefore be used in the succeeding analysis.[28]

Absolute Capital Requirements

This amount of capital required for entry at the scale of a single efficient plant is based upon the above estimates of economies of scale. The average output level of plants at estimated minimum efficient scale is multiplied by the ratio of total assets to gross sales for the industry.[29]

The Rate of Growth of Demand

The rate of growth of demand is measured by the rate of growth of sales between 1947 and 1957.[30] A period of this length was chosen in order to emphasize the long-run effects of the growth of demand, and the terminal years selected were both years of nearly full employment for the economy as a whole.

Composite Variable Representing Technical Entry Barriers and Advertising

Industries were classified into three groups on the basis of the two variables which measure technical entry barriers (economies of scale and absolute capital requirements). Dummy variables identifying industries with high and moderate technical entry barriers were used in some regression models.[31]

---

[26] In these calculations, Bain's estimates of minimum efficient scale for the Steel Industry refer to "Steel Works and Rolling Mills," while for the Copper Industry, they refer to "Primary Copper."

[27] In addition, the survivor technique has the great disadvantage of frequently yielding indeterminate results. See Weiss, *op. cit.*, 258–259.

[28] Ideally, some account should be taken of the slope of the average cost function below minimal efficient scale. The variable used in this paper, in contrast to the estimates developed by Bain, ignores this aspect of economies of scale.

[29] This measure is likely on the average to understate capital requirements. The book value of total assets will normally be less than their replacement cost, as a result of inflation in preceding years. In addition, a new firm is likely to have higher input costs while it is learning the production and distribution techniques required in the market.

[30] The ideal measure, of course, would be the rate at which the demand curve shifted over time. The rate of growth of sales is an exact measure only if the price elasticity of demand is unity or if prices did not change over the period.

[31] High technical entry barriers are assumed to exist if either the scale of an efficient plant exceeded ten per cent of the market or the capital required for efficient entry equalled at least $50 million. In addition, if scale economies fell between six and 9.9 per cent *and* if capital requirements amounted to more than $25 million, the same

Similarly, industries were classified into three groups on the basis of the two advertising variables. Dummy variables identifying industries with high and moderate advertising expenditures were also used as an alternative measure of advertising intensity in some equations.[32]

Local Market Dummy Variable

In some of the regression equations, a dummy variable was introduced to identify the three local market industries.

THE SAMPLE OF INDUSTRIES

For the reasons presented above, the empirical analysis is confined to consumer goods industries.[33] Of the 41 industries included in the analysis, 29 produced non-durable consumer goods, and the remaining 12 produced consumer durables. In size, the industries ranged from motor vehicles with average sales of over $20 billion per year to hats with average sales of only $122 million per year. Spurious size effects are absent, however, since the dependent variable is expressed in ratio form. The core of the analysis is based upon unweighted interindustry regressions. However, as subsequent tests indicate that heteroscedasticity is present, weighted regressions are also estimated.

Three of the industries—soft drinks, bakery products, and dairy products—sell in local markets, and this factor influences the appropriate measures of both concentration and scale economies. Two techniques are used to handle this problem:

a) Economies of scale are estimated in relation to the typical local market, and the Kaysen and Turner concentration classifications, which take into account the local market character of these industries, are used.

b) In some equations, national concentration ratios are introduced along with a dummy variable which identifies the local market character of these three industries.

One interesting characteristic of the underlying data is that the distribution of advertising-sales ratios across the 41 industries is highly skewed. Twenty-five of

---

classification is designated. Low technical barriers exist when either scale economies amounted to less than three per cent and capital requirements are less than $25 million *or* when the former was less than six per cent but the latter sum was under $10 million. Moderate technical barriers are assumed in all other cases.

[32] High barriers are assumed either when the advertising-sales ratio exceeded eight per cent or when advertising expenditures among leading firms averaged more than $20 million. The same classification is given to industries where the average ratio fell between four and eight per cent *and* average annual expenditures amounted to between $5 and $20 million. Low barriers exist when the advertising sales ratio was less than two per cent and average expenditures less than $5 million *or* when the ratio lay between two and four per cent and expenditures did not exceed $1 million per firm. In other cases, moderate advertising barriers are assumed to exist.

[33] The Petroleum industry is excluded because of the difficulty of obtaining profit data comparable to other industries in view of the special tax treatment of that industry.

the industries have ratios below three per cent while eight have ratios between three and six per cent and only six have ratios which exceed six per cent. In the latter group, perfumes have an advertising-sales ratio of 15 per cent, cereals and drugs ten per cent each, soap nine per cent, malt liquor seven per cent, and soft drinks slightly over six per cent. Notable industries in the intermediate group include cigarettes and wines with ratios of about five per cent each.

Although advertising per firm is positively correlated with advertising per dollar of sales, the positions of two important industries change radically depending on which variable is used to measure advertising intensity. While tires and tubes and motor vehicles have quite low advertising-sales ratios, both are among the small group of industries with high or very high average advertising outlays per firm among the leading firms. As a result, tires and tubes and motor vehicles are classified respectively as industries with moderate and high overall advertising barriers.

MAJOR EMPIRICAL RESULTS

The simple correlation coefficients between profit rates and each explanatory variable are presented in Table 16.1. All of the coefficients have the expected sign and all are statistically significant in at least one functional form. Moreover, the logarithmic relationship appears appropriate in the case of the growth of demand variable, while the opposite is the case with regard to the advertising-sales ratio. As the latter variable is already expressed as a percentage, it is measured in units comparable to the dependent variable.

Table 16.1

SIMPLE CORRELATION COEFFICIENTS—PROFIT RATES AND VARIOUS DIMENSIONS OF MARKET STRUCTURE

MARKET STRUCTURE VARIABLES	CORRELATION WITH PROFIT RATES	
	NATURAL UNITS*	LOGARITHM†
Growth of Demand	0.17	0.42
Capital Requirements	0.43§	0.57§
Economies of Scale	0.25	0.37§
Advertising-Sales Ratio	0.42§	0.27‡
Advertising per Firm	0.43§	0.50§
Concentration Ratio (4 firms)	0.36‡	0.35‡

* The units of measurement are described in the text above.
† In computing these coefficients, the structural dimension is measured in logarithms although the profit rate is measured in natural units.
‡ Indicates coefficient is statistically significant at the 95 per cent level.
§ Indicates coefficient is statistically significant at the 99 per cent level.
Tests of significance are made on the basis of one-tailed t tests.

The correlation between profit rates and concentration in Table 16.1 is based on a continuous four-firm concentration ratio. The relationship between these two variables was also examined in terms of discrete groupings. Industries were divided according to both the three-way classification scheme proposed by Kaysen and Turner, and a two-way classification depending on whether the eight-firm concentration ratio exceeded or was less than 70 per cent. The following results are obtained:

	NUMBER OF INDUSTRIES	AVERAGE PROFIT RATES
Kaysen and Turner Trichotomy		
Type I Oligopolies	13	8.4
Type II Oligopolies	14	9.2
Unconcentrated	14	6.3
Dichotomy Based on Eight-Firm Concentration Ratio at 70 per cent		
Concentrated	8	10.0
Unconcentrated	33	7.5
All Industries	41	7.9

While the distinction between Type I and Type II Oligopolies seems, on the average, unimportant, there do appear to be substantial differences in profits between concentrated and unconcentrated industries. These differences are important in both classification schemes.

The core of the empirical work is the multiple regression equations which relate profit rates to various combinations of the explanatory variables. A set of linear equations is presented in Table 16.2. As may be observed, the advertising-sales ratio and the measure of capital requirements appear to be the most important explanatory factors. Their regression coefficients are generally significant even when all other variables are included. The variable describing economies of scale seems from these results to be quite weak, although it has the expected sign in all cases. The advertising per firm coefficient is significant if the advertising-sales ratio is not included. Where both are included, it tends to be insignificant. Advertising outlays per firms are correlated with absolute capital requirements (the simple correlation coefficient between these variables is 0.40) and this variable is not as statistically important in conjunction with the latter as is the advertising-sales ratio.

In none of the equations do the estimated coefficients of the concentration dummy variables exceed their standard errors. In addition, the coefficient for Type I Oligopolies has a negative sign throughout, which does not coincide with a priori expectations. While the impact of concentration is examined at greater length below, the linear results suggest that the partial effect of this variable may be relatively unimportant when it is introduced in conjunction with variables reflecting product differentiation, the height of technical entry barriers, and the rate of growth of demand.

In an alternative formulation, four dummy variables were defined to represent high and moderate technical entry barriers and high and moderate advertising intensities, and these were introduced in place of the advertising, economies of scale, and absolute capital requirements variables. The results are presented in Table 16.3. The dummy variables designed to measure the influence of technical barriers are not statistically significant, and in the second equation, the estimated

Table 16.2

MULTIPLE REGRESSION EQUATIONS EXPLAINING PROFIT RATES—LINEAR RESULTS

	INTERCEPT	ADVERTISING-SALES RATIO	ADVERTISING PER FIRM	ECONOMIES OF SCALE	ABSOLUTE CAPITAL REQUIREMENTS	GROWTH OF DEMAND	CONCENTRATION CLASSES*		R^2	CORRECTED R^2
							TYPE I	TYPE II		
1)	0.049	0.424† (2.4)	0.00000059 (1.1)	0.113 (0.8)	0.000281‡ (3.0)	0.0014 (0.6)	−0.0158 (1.0)	0.0084 (0.6)	0.47‡	0.34‡
2)	0.052	0.296 (1.6)	0.00000114† (2.0)	0.113 (0.7)	—	0.0018 (0.7)	−0.0058 (0.3)	0.0115 (0.8)	0.32†	0.19†
3)	0.051	0.437‡ (2.5)	0.00000060 (1.1)	—	0.000282‡ (3.0)	0.0012 (0.5)	−0.0091 (0.7)	0.0126 (1.0)	0.46‡	0.35‡
4)	0.048	0.499‡ (3.1)	—	0.116 (0.8)	0.000315‡ (3.5)	0.0016 (0.7)	−0.0117 (0.7)	0.0085 (0.6)	0.45‡	0.34‡
5)	0.058	—	0.00000112† (2.1)	0.145 (0.9)	0.000227† (2.3)	0.0012 (0.5)	−0.0147 (0.9)	0.0146 (1.0)	0.38‡	0.25‡

* Based on Kaysen and Turner Groupings.
Figures in parentheses are t values. The statistical significance of the regression coefficients is tested by means of one-tailed t test and of the multiple correlation coefficients by means of the F-ratio test.
† Indicates coefficient is statistically significant at the 95 per cent level.
‡ Indicates coefficient is statistically significant at the 99 per cent level.

Table 16.3

MULTIPLE REGRESSION EQUATIONS CONTAINING COMPOSITE VARIABLES

	INTERCEPT	ADVERTISING BARRIERS		TECHNICAL ENTRY BARRIERS		CONCENTRATION*		GROWTH OF DEMAND (LOGS)	R^2	CORRECTED R^2
		HIGH	MODERATE	HIGH	MODERATE	TYPE I	TYPE II			
1)	0.056	0.0552§ (3.3)	0.0080 (0.6)	0.0154 (0.9)	0.0090 (0.5)	−0.0132 (0.7)	−0.00085 (0.05)	0.020‡ (1.9)	0.46§	0.33§

	INTERCEPT	ADVERTISING BARRIERS		TECHNICAL ENTRY BARRIERS		CONCENTRATION RATIO†	REGIONAL INDUSTRY DUMMY VARIABLE	GROWTH OF DEMAND (LOGS)	R^2	CORRECTED R^2
		HIGH	MODERATE	HIGH	MODERATE					
2)	0.044	0.0403‡ (2.3)	−0.0049 (0.3)	−0.0150 (0.8)	−0.0013 (0.1)	0.000596 (1.4)	0.0311 (1.4)	0.024‡ (2.4)	0.48§	0.36§

* Based on Kaysen and Turner Groupings.
† Four-firm concentration ratio.
Figures in parentheses are t values. The statistical significance of the regression coefficients is tested by means of one-tailed t test and of the multiple correlation coefficients by means of the F-ratio test.
‡ Indicates coefficient is statistically significant at the 95 per cent level.
§ Indicates coefficient is statistically significant at the 99 per cent level.

coefficient for industries with high technical barriers is less than the coefficient for industries with moderate barriers. This result reflects in part the correlation between the high technical barrier dummy variable and concentration. The correlation coefficient between the dummy variable for high technical barriers and the Type I concentration dummy variable is 0.53. When the four-firm concentration ratio is used, this coefficient rises to 0.68. This collinearity obscures the separate effects of concentration and technical entry barriers.

To consider further the impact of concentration, the continuous concentration ratio was introduced into the analysis. As this variable is available only on a national basis, a dummy variable was also introduced to identify industries which sell in local rather than in national markets.[34] It is interesting that the continuous variable appears to have a stronger impact on profits than do the concentration dummy variables. Both the coefficient for concentration and for the local market dummy variable are significant at the 90 per cent level.

In contrast to the weak effect of composite technical barriers, the composite advertising variable has a strong effect. In both equations, the high advertising variable is statistically significant and the coefficient appears relatively stable. In addition, the growth of demand variable becomes significant when introduced in logarithmic form.

Additional sets of regression equations are presented in Tables 16.4 and 16.5. In both sets, capital requirements are introduced in logarithmic form and the estimated coefficients are generally significant. However, some degree of collinearity exists between the measures of capital requirements and scale economies. When both variables are introduced into the equations, the variance of the estimates increases, and in some cases, the capital requirements coefficient becomes statistically insignificant.

In Table 16.4, the advertising-sales ratio is used to measure the entry barriers created by high advertising expenditures, while in Table 16.5, the dummy variable representing high advertising barriers is introduced. Both advertising variables are statistically significant in all of the equations presented, and the estimated coefficients of both variables are very stable. The dummy variable for high advertising barriers appears to be somewhat stronger than the advertising-sales ratio. However, the coefficients of the other structural variables included in these equations are not sensitive to the particular advertising variable used.

In both Tables 16.4 and 16.5, a dummy variable identifying industries with eight-firm concentration ratios which exceed 70 per cent was introduced in order to examine the effect of this aspect of market structure in yet another specification. The coefficients, however, remain smaller than their standard errors.

The regional industry dummy variable was also introduced into the equations in both tables. In all cases, its estimated parameters are significant at the 90 per cent level, and reach the 95 per cent level in Table 16.5. While this variable was used originally to correct for the use of concentration ratios calculated on a national basis, it appears to have an independent effect which does not depend on the presence of the other variable. It is useful, therefore, to compare the structural features of the three local market industries included in our sample

---

[34] These market characteristics had already been accounted for in the Kaysen and Turner groupings.

294 PRODUCT DIFFERENTIATION ACTIVITIES

Table 16.4

MULTIPLE REGRESSION EQUATIONS EXPLAINING PROFITS RATES—MAJOR FINDINGS WITH ADVERTISING-SALES RATIO

	INTERCEPT	ADVERTISING-SALES RATIO	CAPITAL REQUIREMENTS (LOGS)	ECONOMIES OF SCALE (LOGS)	GROWTH OF DEMAND (LOGS)	CONCENTRATION CLASS*	REGIONAL INDUSTRY DUMMY VARIABLE	R^2	CORRECTED R^2
1)	0.042	0.362† (2.4)	0.0097‡ (3.2)	—	0.016 (1.6)	—	—	0.46‡	0.40‡
2)	0.042	0.362† (2.3)	0.0096‡ (2.5)	0.000067 (0.01)	0.016 (1.6)	—	—	0.46‡	0.38‡
3)	0.039	0.343† (2.3)	0.0105‡ (2.8)	—	0.015 (1.4)	0.0043 (0.3)	0.0278 (1.5)	0.49‡	0.40‡
4)	0.038	0.341† (2.3)	0.0111‡ (3.6)	—	0.014 (1.4)	—	0.0280 (1.6)	0.49‡	0.42‡

* An industry is concentrated if the eight-firm concentration ratio equals or exceeds 70 per cent; otherwise it is unconcentrated.
Figures in parentheses are t values. The statistical significance of the regression coefficients is tested by means of one-tailed t test and of the multiple correlation coefficients by means of the F-ratio test.
† Indicates coefficient is statistically significant at the 95 per cent level.
‡ Indicates coefficient is statistically significant at the 99 per cent level.

Table 16.5

MULTIPLE REGRESSION EQUATIONS EXPLAINING PROFIT RATES—MAJOR FINDINGS WITH HIGH ADVERTISING BARRIER

	INTERCEPT	HIGH ADVERTISING BARRIER	CAPITAL REQUIREMENTS (LOGS)	ECONOMIES OF SCALE (LOGS)	GROWTH OF DEMAND (LOGS)	CONCENTRATION CLASS*	REGIONAL INDUSTRY DUMMY VARIABLE	R^2	CORRECTED R^2
1)	0.053	0.0379‡ (2.8)	0.0066† (2.0)	—	0.018† (1.9)	—	—	0.48‡	0.42‡
2)	0.069	0.0388‡ (2.8)	0.0047 (1.1)	0.0038 (0.7)	0.019† (2.0)	—	—	0.49‡	0.42‡
3)	0.048	0.0395‡ (2.9)	0.0089‡ (2.4)	—	0.015 (1.5)	−0.0063 (0.5)	0.0318† (1.8)	0.53‡	0.45‡
4)	0.048	0.0379‡ (2.9)	0.0082‡ (2.5)	—	0.016† (1.7)	—	0.0316† (1.8)	0.52‡	0.46‡

* An industry is concentrated if the eight-firm concentration ratio equals or exceeds 70 per cent; otherwise it is unconcentrated. Figures in parentheses are t values. The statistical significance of the regression coefficients is tested by means of one-tailed t test and of the multiple correlation coefficients by means of the F-ratio test.
† Indicates coefficient is statistically significant at the 95 per cent level.
‡ Indicates coefficient is statistically significant at the 99 per cent level.

Table 16.6

LOCAL AND REGIONAL INDUSTRY CHARACTERISTICS

INDUSTRY	CONCENTRATION CLASS*	ADVERTISING–SALES RATIO (%)	ADVERTISING PER FIRM (MILLIONS OF DOLLARS)	CAPITAL REQUIREMENTS (MILLIONS OF DOLLARS)	ECONOMIES OF SCALE (%)	GROWTH OF DEMAND (RATIO)	PROFIT RATE (%)
Soft Drinks	Type I	6.2	0.26	0.75	8.2	1.98	10.0
Dairy	Type II	2.2	15.12	2.09	14.2	1.16	7.9
Bakery	Type II	2.9	1.97	2.57	8.3	1.69	9.3
Average of Three Industries		3.8	5.78	1.80	10.2	1.61	9.1
All Industries		3.3	6.03	24.32	4.7	1.83	7.9

* Kaysen and Turner groupings.

with the others. Relevant data are presented in Table 16.6. The scale economy variable is the most sensitive to this industry characteristic. As would be expected, these industries, on the average, have much higher estimates of the ratio of minimum efficient scale to market than do the national industries. We should expect, therefore, that the local market dummy variable represents the increased importance of economies of scale as well as the higher concentration levels in local markets.

The multiple correlation coefficients for these equations are always statistically significant. The included variables typically account for about half of the total variation in industry profit rates.

THE PROBLEM OF MULTICOLLINEARITY

As was noted above, a number of the explanatory variables included in the analysis are collinear to some extent. While the simple correlations between the advertising-sales ratio and the other independent variables are typically low,[35] it is useful to examine the sensitivity of the estimated coefficients for this variable to changes in the specifications of the regression equations. The results are presented in Table 16.7. The estimated coefficients are reasonably stable, ranging from 0.30 to 0.52. In addition, seven of the 15 coefficients presented are significant at the 99 per cent level, seven at the 95 per cent level, and the remaining coefficient at the 90 per cent level.

The stability of the estimated coefficient for the dummy variable denoting high advertising barriers is also tabulated. These coefficients appear to be insensitive to changes in the specifications of the equations. They lie between 0.038 and 0.050. Six of the seven coefficients presented are significant at the 99 per cent level and the remaining one at the 95 per cent level. The estimated effect of either the advertising-sales ratio or the high advertising dummy therefore does not appear to be affected by which of the other variables are included in the equations.

While there may be other variables which affect the estimated relationships between advertising and profits, the importance of both advertising variables is relatively insensitive to changes in specification of the variables and the models examined in this paper.[36]

Significant correlations also exist between capital requirements, economies of scale, and concentration. This is not surprising, for one should expect the first two variables to have some effect on the latter. At the same time, however, concentration is influenced by other factors, such as the past record of merger activity in the industry. To examine the extent to which concentration is

[35] The simple correlation coefficients between the advertising-sales ratio and other structural variables are as follows: the log of economies of scale, 0.27; the log of capital requirements, 0.21; the log of growth of demand, 0.40; and the four-firm concentration ratio, 0.10.

[36] This result, however, does not apply to average advertising expenditures per firm, which is more strongly correlated with the other explanatory factors. As a result, its statistical significance in regression analysis appears to depend on which of the other variables are included in the estimating equation.

Table 16.7

SENSITIVITY OF REGRESSION COEFFICIENTS FOR ADVERTISING VARIABLES TO CHANGES IN SPECIFICATION OF REGRESSION EQUATIONS

ESTIMATED COEFFICIENT	VALUE OF t	CONCENTRATION	A ADVERTISING-SALES RATIO				
			REGIONAL INDUSTRY DUMMY	CAPITAL REQUIREMENTS	SCALE ECONOMIES	GROWTH OF DEMAND	ADVERTISING PER FIRM
0.42	2.27	I, II					
0.30	1.61	I, II					
0.42	2.40	I, II					N
0.43	2.50	I, II					N
0.48	2.75			N			
0.52	3.24			N	N		
0.50	2.92		N	N	N	N	N
0.34	2.21	I		L	N	L	
0.35	2.29	I		L	N	L	
0.49	3.28			N	N	L	
0.41	2.41		N	N	N	L	
0.40	2.54	N	N		N	L	
0.46	3.02	N	N		N	L	N
0.36	2.43					L	
0.33	2.19	N	N			L	

B DUMMY VARIABLES FOR HIGH ADVERTISING BARRIERS—OTHER VARIABLES INCLUDED

ESTIMATED COEFFICIENT	VALUE OF t	CONCENTRATION	REGIONAL INDUSTRY DUMMY	CAPITAL REQUIREMENTS	ECONOMIES OF SCALE	GROWTH OF DEMAND	TECHNICAL BARRIERS	MODERATE ADVERTISING BARRIER
0.040	2.28	N	N			L	H, M	M
0.049	3.67	I, II				L	H, M	M
0.050	3.25	I, II	N			L		
0.045	3.39	N	N			L		
0.038	2.80			L	L	L		
0.039	2.83			L		L		
0.038	2.89	N	N	L		L		

N — Variable in natural units.
L — Variable in logarithms.
I and II denote Kaysen and Turner concentration classes.
H and M denote high and moderate dummy variables.

Table 16.8

MULTIPLE REGRESSION ANALYSIS—CONCENTRATION AND TECHNICAL ENTRY BARRIERS

CONCENTRATION*	INTERCEPT	CAPITAL REQUIREMENTS (LOGS)	ECONOMIES OF SCALE (LOGS)	REGIONAL INDUSTRY DUMMY VARIABLE	R^2	CORRECTED R^2
1) Natural units	49.9	7.08† (3.9)	6.91† (2.6)	−11.2 (1.2)	0.71†	0.68†
2) Logarithms	3.85	0.244† (5.1)	0.238† (3.4)	−0.294 (1.2)	0.81†	0.79†

* Four-firm Concentration Ratios.
Figures in parentheses are t values. The statistical significance of the regression coefficients is tested by means of one-tailed t test and of the multiple correlation coefficients by means of the F-ratio test.
† Indicates coefficient is statistically significant at the 99 per cent level.

explained by scale economies and capital requirements, two multiple regression equations were fitted. The results, which are striking, appear in Table 16.8.

Absolute capital requirements, scale economies, and the local market dummy variable[37] together account for a substantial share in the variation in national concentration ratios. In logarithmic form, over 80 per cent of the variation is explained by these variables. What is surprising is the small share of variation left to be accounted for by other factors. With this high a degree of inter-correlation, it is understandable that the estimated coefficients for concentration are not statistically significant. The role of concentration appears closely linked to that of technical entry barriers and there is little remaining influence which is evident.[38]

HETEROSCEDASTICITY AND WEIGHTED REGRESSIONS

An examination of the residuals from a leading equation (number 4 in Table 16.5) revealed that heteroscedasticity is present, as small industries typically have large residuals. There are two possible reasons for this phenomenon. The smaller industries may tend to have fewer firms, so that the variance of average profit rates is larger. The smaller industries may also have smaller firms. Previous studies have indicated that the variance of profit rates among small firms is greater than among larger firms,[39] and this would also account for a larger variance for smaller industries.

To determine an appropriate weighting scheme, an empirical approach was adopted. The variance of the residuals was calculated for successive quartiles in the distribution of industry sales. From this tabulation, it was clear that the use of industry sales is inappropriate as a weighting variable as it would give too much emphasis to the largest industries. The square root of sales, however, is nearly proportional to the variance of the residuals, and was therefore chosen as the weighting variable.

The weighted regressions were fitted both for all industries, and for all industries except motor vehicles, as this industry is an outlying observation with respect to some of the variables, including the weighting variable. The results appear in Tables 16.9 and 16.10. As is clear, the R^2 of each of the weighted regressions is

[37] The regional industry dummy variable was included because the concentration ratios are constructed on a national basis. The negative sign on the coefficient represents simply the downward bias of the national ratios in those industries.

[38] One should be wary of drawing any policy conclusion on the basis of this equation. Merger activity may be highly correlated with entry barriers. Furthermore, there is some element of spurious correlation between the scale economies measure and concentration. The scale economies measure used here is 0.5 times the reciprocal of the number of the largest plants required to account for one-half of industry output. It is, therefore, related to plant concentration. Since plant concentration and firm concentration may be expected to be correlated even in the absence of variations in relative scale economies, some spurious correlation exists between concentration and relative scale economies. (The authors are indebted to Joe S. Bain for the elaboration of this point.)

[39] Sydney S. Alexander, "The Effect of Size of Manufacturing Corporation on the Distribution of the Rate of Return," *The Review of Economics and Statistics*, XXXI (Aug. 1949), 229–235.

302 PRODUCT DIFFERENTIATION ACTIVITIES

Table 16.9

WEIGHTED REGRESSIONS WITH ADVERTISING-SALES RATIO

		INTERCEPT	HIGH ADVERTISING-SALES RATIO	CAPITAL REQUIRE-MENTS (LOGS)	ECONOMIES OF SCALE (LOGS)	GROWTH OF DEMAND (LOGS)	CONCEN-TRATION RATIO	REGIONAL INDUSTRY DUMMY VARIABLE	R^2	CORRECTED R^2
1)	a All Industries	0.040	0.29* (1.9)	0.013† (4.8)	—	0.0084 (1.0)	—	0.028* (1.9)	0.76†	0.72†
	b Motor Vehicles Excluded	0.045	0.44† (3.1)	0.0077* (2.4)	—	0.0096 (1.3)	—	0.020 (1.4)	0.67†	0.62†
2)	a All Industries	0.066	0.28* (1.8)	0.010† (3.1)	0.0046 (0.9)	0.0096 (1.1)	—	—	0.75†	0.71†
	b Motor Vehicles Excluded	0.074	0.42† (2.8)	0.0040 (1.2)	0.0052 (1.2)	0.011 (1.4)	—	—	0.67†	0.62†
3)	a All Industries	0.040	0.29* (1.9)	0.014* (2.4)	—	0.0081 (0.9)	−0.00003 (0.08)	0.028* (1.8)	0.76†	0.72†
	b Motor Vehicles Excluded	0.047	0.43† (2.9)	0.0090 (1.6)	—	0.0088 (1.1)	−0.00011 (0.3)	0.021 (1.4)	0.67†	0.61†

* Indicates coefficient is statistically significant at the 95 per cent level.
† Indicates coefficient is statistically significant at the 99 per cent level.
Figures in parentheses are t values.

Table 16.10

WEIGHTED REGRESSIONS WITH HIGH ADVERTISING BARRIER

	INTERCEPT	HIGH ADVERTISING BARRIER	CAPITAL REQUIRE-MENTS (LOGS)	ECONOMIES OF SCALE (LOGS)	GROWTH OF DEMAND (LOGS)	CONCEN-TRATION RATIO	REGIONAL INDUSTRY DUMMY VARIABLE	R^2	CORRECTED R^2
1) a All Industries	0.052	0.035† (2.9)	0.0080† (2.5)	—	0.012 (1.5)	—	0.027* (1.9)	0.78†	0.75†
b Motor Vehicles Excluded	0.055	0.032† (2.7)	0.0064* (1.8)	—	0.012 (1.5)	—	0.025 (1.7)	0.65†	0.59†
2) a All Industries	0.090	0.037† (3.1)	0.0034 (1.0)	0.0073* (1.7)	0.013 (1.6)	—	—	0.78†	0.75†
b Motor Vehicles Excluded	0.097	0.032† (2.7)	0.0010 (0.3)	0.0080* (1.9)	0.014* (1.8)	—	—	0.65†	0.60†
3) a All Industries	0.053	0.035† (2.9)	0.0093 (1.6)	—	0.011 (1.3)	−0.00010 (0.3)	0.028* (1.9)	0.78†	0.75†
b Motor Vehicles Excluded	0.057	0.031† (2.4)	0.0085 (1.5)	—	0.011 (1.3)	−0.00016 (0.4)	0.027* (1.8)	0.65†	0.58†

* Indicates coefficient is statistically significant at the 95 per cent level.
† Indicates coefficient is statistically significant at the 99 per cent level.
Figures in parentheses are t values.

considerably higher than the R^2 of its unweighted counterpart. This is to be expected, since the weighting procedure deliberately emphasizes industries with smaller residuals and the R^2 measures the proportion of the weighted variance of the dependent variable explained by the regression equation. Another way of looking at this is that weighting essentially involves multiplying the equation by the root of the weights (in this case by the fourth root of sales) and proceeding by ordinary least squares. The R^2 indicates the success at predicting profit rates multiplied by the fourth root of sales.[40]

The results are impressive. About 75 per cent of the weighted variance across all industries is accounted for by these equations and about 65 per cent of the weighted variance is explained when the outlying auto industry is excluded.

The high advertising barrier dummy variable and the advertising-sales ratio variable are introduced alternatively. The former is significant at the 99 per cent level in all equations, the latter at the 95 per cent level when the auto industry is included, at the 99 per cent level otherwise. The collinearity between capital requirements, economies of scale and concentration is again evident, but in contrast to the unweighted regressions, the economies of scale variable is sometimes significant when introduced alongside capital requirements (and the latter variable is sometimes insignificant).

These results, moreover, provide additional evidence of the stability of the coefficients for these two advertising variables. They also point to the joint significance of technical barriers to entry and of concentration, but the collinearity among these variables prevents precise measurement of the separate effects of each of these variables.

THE PROBLEM OF CAUSALITY

We have found that the inter-industry variation in profit rates can be explained quite well by a model incorporating the rate of growth of demand, some measure of advertising intensity, and variables reflecting the importance of concentration and technical barriers to entry. The relationship between profits and either of the advertising variables introduced into the equations is quite robust. Throughout this paper, we have assumed that the direction of causality is from the independent variables to profit rates. Could the reverse be the case?

A plausible case can be made that a significant feedback exists from profits to advertising expenditures, since advertising reflects the discretionary behavior of firms as well as the extent of product differentiation. Indeed, we should not be surprised if a time-series analysis, which emphasizes short-run effects, revealed that changes in profits preceded, rather than followed, changes in advertising expenditures.

[40] It is important to note that the increase in R^2 is no indication that the weighting used is the correct one. Indeed, a very high R^2 can be obtained by weighting with industry sales, which is clearly inappropriate. A subsequent test, moreover, was made on the extent of heteroscedasticity in the weighted regressions. The residuals from equation 1a in table 10 were calculated and the successive variances of these residuals were compared with the mean root sales in the relevant quartile. The fact that the two variables were nearly proportional provides some confirmation of the use of the square root of sales as the weighting variable.

There are a number of factors, however, which suggest that the causality of the observed relationships runs largely from advertising expenditures to profits. A cross-sectional study tends to emphasize the long-run differences between industries, and this in turn is more likely to reflect the structural rather than the behavioral aspects of advertising. Profit levels cannot influence those market and product characteristics which permit product differentiation via advertising. Firms with high profit rates will not have higher *optimum* advertising expenditures than firms with low profit rates in the same market situation. The pursuit of profits will hence limit the extent to which profits will be "spent" on advertising, especially over a period of several years.

In addition, if high profits lead to high advertising expenditures, we should expect that industries which have high profits for reasons other than product differentiation (e.g., concentration or technical entry barriers) would tend to have high advertising expenditures as well. Yet, as we noted above, advertising is only weakly correlated with the other dimensions of market structure.

CONCLUDING COMMENTS

On the basis of these empirical findings, it is evident that for industries where products are differentiable, investment in advertising is a highly profitable activity. Industries with high advertising outlays earn, on average, at a profit rate which exceeds that of other industries by nearly four percentage points. This differential represents a 50 per cent increase in profit rates. It is likely, moreover, that much of this profit rate differential is accounted for by the entry barriers created by advertising expenditures and by the resulting achievement of market power.

We note also the significant joint impact on profit rates of concentration and the entry barriers created by scale economies and high capital requirements. Although the composite effect of these factors is clearly important, a more precise indication of the distinct effect of any of these variables is hazardous because of the high degree of collinearity. As would be expected, the rate of growth of demand has an important positive impact on profits. Models which incorporate these variables fit the underlying data reasonably well, accounting for approximately 50 per cent of the variation in industry profit rates.

These empirical results suggest that factors which promote product differentiation may be as important as those which influence the size distribution of firms in terms of their effect upon the achievement of market power. Current policies which tend to emphasize the role played by concentration may need to be supplemented by those concerned directly with the nature and extent of product differentiation. Policies dealing with these matters would be an important component in a general policy designed to promote competition.

Appendix I to Reading 16

DATA SOURCES AND TECHNICAL ADJUSTMENTS

The industry data used are reported at or aggregated to the level of I.R.S. "minor industries," which are roughly comparable to S.I.C. three-digit industry groups. The source for each variable is listed in Table 16.11.

The sample was chosen originally to gain complete coverage of all consumer goods industries. All "miscellaneous" industries were eliminated, however, because of the obvious conceptual problems. In addition, three other industries were dropped from the sample: newspapers, while technically a manufacturing industry was considered to have sufficient "service" elements to make its inclusion inappropriate; petroleum refining, because of the unusual statistical problems which result from the tax treatment of mineral depletion; and motor vehicle parts, because of the lack of comparable Census data. Average profit rates and advertising-sales ratios for the remaining 41 industries are presented in Table 16.12.

The variables are defined and explained in the text. The calculation of the technical entry barrier variables and the rate of growth of demand involved using both Census and I.R.S. data. The various specific adjustments made to reconcile data drawn from these two sources and reported at different levels of aggregation are described in the next two sections.

Technical Barriers to Entry

These variables are based on data from the 1954 *Census of Manufactures*. To carry out these computations, it is necessary to relate industries as defined by

Table 16.11

SOURCES OF DATA

VARIABLE	SOURCE
1) Profit Rate	*Internal Revenue Service Source Book of Statistics of Income.* Average values for 1954–1957.
2) Advertising	*Internal Revenue Service Source Book of Statistics of Income.* Average values for 1954–1957.

3) Concentration
  a Trichotomous and dichotomous classifications
  b Continuous four-firm ratio
	Carl Kaysen and Donald F. Turner, *Antitrust Policy*, statistical appendix.
	George J. Stigler, *Capital and Rates of Return in Manufacturing Industries*, 206–215.

4) Economies of scale relative to market	1954 *Census of Manufactures.*
5) Absolute capital requirements	1954 *Census of Manufactures* and *Internal Revenue Service Source Book of Statistics of Income.*
6) Rate of growth of demand	*Internal Revenue Service Source Book of Statistics of Income.*
7) Local market dummy variables	Carl Kaysen and Donald F. Turner, *Antitrust Policy*, statistical appendix.

the Census Bureau to those of the Internal Revenue Service. This is done on the basis suggested by the Census Link Project.[41]

Within S.I.C. four-digit industries, average plant size among the largest plants which account for 50 per cent of industry output is used as the estimate of minimum efficient plant scale (MES). Data on shipments are used in all cases where available. In the few remaining cases, the calculations are based on value added. When the ratios of MES to industry output are obtained, the average percentage among component four-digit industries within the relevant I.R.S. industry is calculated, using shipments as weights where available and value added as weights elsewhere.

In determining the capital requirements variable, the scale of an efficient plant is measured in most instances by the value of the shipments but in a few by value added. In the latter cases, these figures are multiplied by the ratio of shipments to value added for the same four-digit industry but in a later year.

When estimates of MES measured in shipments for all four-digit industries are obtained, these are averaged, using value added as weights, to derive the value in the larger I.R.S. industry. These averages are then multiplied by the appropriate assets-sales ratio for the I.R.S. industry, and the resulting figures used to represent the level of capital required for efficient entry.

In the case of the motor vehicle industry, Census data are unavailable. Bain's

---

[41] Bureau of the Census, *Enterprise Statistics* (1958), Part 3.

Table 16.12

AVERAGE PROFIT RATES AND ADVERTISING-SALES RATIOS IN FORTY-ONE CONSUMER GOODS INDUSTRIES, 1954-1957

		PROFIT RATE (%)	ADVERTISING SALES RATIO (%)
1)	Soft Drink	10.0	6.2
2)	Malt Liquors	7.2	6.8
3)	Wines	7.3	5.2
4)	Distilled Liquors	5.0	2.1
5)	Meat	4.6	0.6
6)	Dairy	7.9	2.2
7)	Canning	6.4	2.9
8)	Grain Mill Products	7.0	1.9
9)	Cereals	14.8	10.3
10)	Bakery Products	9.3	2.9
11)	Sugar	5.8	0.2
12)	Confectionary	10.6	3.5
13)	Cigars	5.3	2.6
14)	Cigarettes	11.5	4.8
15)	Knit Goods	3.8	1.3
16)	Carpets	4.5	2.0
17)	Hats	1.6	2.2
18)	Men's Clothing	5.9	1.2
19)	Women's Clothing	6.1	1.8
20)	Millinery	−1.3	0.8
21)	Furs	5.7	1.0
22)	Furniture	9.7	1.5
23)	Screens and Venetian Blinds	9.3	1.6
24)	Periodicals	11.7	0.2
25)	Books	10.1	2.4
26)	Drugs	14.0	9.9
27)	Soaps	11.7	9.2
28)	Paints	9.9	1.5
29)	Perfumes	13.5	15.3
30)	Tires and Tubes	10.2	1.4
31)	Footwear	7.6	1.5
32)	Hand Tools	11.4	4.2
33)	Household and Service Machinery (not electrical)	7.3	1.9
34)	Electrical Appliances	10.3	3.5
35)	Radio, T.V., and Phonograph	8.8	2.2
36)	Motorcycles and Bicycles	5.2	1.1
37)	Motor Vehicles	15.5	0.6
38)	Instruments	12.0	2.0
39)	Clocks and Watches	1.9	5.6
40)	Jewelry (Precious Metal)	5.3	3.2
41)	Costume Jewelry	1.4	4.0

estimates for this industry are therefore used for both the extent of scale economies and the level of capital requirements.

For the three regional industries—soft drinks, dairy products, and bakery products—it is assumed that the appropriate market is the typical large metropolitan area. Output data are not available for four-digit industries by standard metropolitan area. Consequently, value added data for larger three-digit groupings are used. Average value added in large metropolitan areas for the three-digit industry[42] is multiplied by the ratio of total national shipments in the relevant four-digit industry to total value added in the associated three-digit industry to obtain the estimate of four-digit industry shipments within the typical local market. This figure is then used as the denominator in the estimate of M.E.S. to market for the four-digit industry.[43] Where necessary, the resulting estimates are aggregated to the I.R.S. minor industry level as described above.

Rate of Growth of Demand

This variable is the ratio of I.R.S. gross sales in 1957 to that in 1947. In a few cases, however, I.R.S. data are not available for both years and alternative procedures are used.

In 1947, the I.R.S. industries "Cigars" and "Cigarettes" are aggregated as "Tobacco Manufactures." To disaggregate the reported figure for gross sales, Census data on value of shipments (excise taxes excluded) for 1947 were examined. The ratio of shipments in "Cigars" to total tobacco manufacturing is multiplied by I.R.S. gross sales for tobacco manufactures, and the resulting product used to denote gross sales in "Cigars." Gross sales in "Cigarettes" is obtained residually.

I.R.S. data for "Screens and Venetian Blinds," in 1947, are included in "Miscellaneous Furniture." As a result, Census value added data for both 1947 and 1957 are used. Similar data problems exist in the case of "Drugs," "Perfumes," "Instruments," and "Costume Jewelry." In all of these instances Census data in 1947 and 1957 are used. With regard to "Perfumes" and "Costume Jewelry," information on value of shipments is available in both years and is therefore used, while value added data are used in the other cases.

Concentration

The classification of industries into Kaysen and Turner concentration classes is based on data for 1954, and their definitions are used in most cases. Where I.R.S. minor industries include a number of Kaysen and Turner markets, weighted averages based on value of shipments are used to determine the appropriate classifications.

Further adjustments are made to account for the local market character of three industries: soft drinks, dairy products, and bakery products. In addition, the soap industry falls just below the boundary between Type I and Type II

[42] Output data were available for 56 standard metropolitan areas for the beverage industry (S.I.C. 208); 59 such areas for bakery products (S.I.C. 205); and 61 such areas for dairy products (S.I.C. 202).

[43] These corrections were made for the following subindustries: S.I.C. 2081—bottled soft drinks: S.I.C. 2021—creamery butter; S.I.C. 2027—fluid milk and other products; S.I.C. 2051—bread and related products.

Oligopolies. Since the same major firms are dominant in the important product lines, the industry is reclassified as a Type I Oligopoly. The radio and television industry falls just above the same boundary. It is classified as a Type II Oligopoly since the largest single subindustry falls into that category. For appliances, the Kaysen and Turner definition differed substantially from that used by the Internal Revenue Service. After an appropriate adjustment the concentration data indicated that this industry is a Type II Oligopoly.

The classification of industries according to whether the eight-firm concentration ratio exceeded or fell short of the 70 per cent level is based on the concentration ratios presented by Kaysen and Turner.

17

The Firm's Decision Process: An Econometric Investigation*

Dennis C. Mueller

This article adds to an already long list of econometric studies of firm behavior. Its emphasis is upon the complexity of this behavior, and upon the eventual need for attempting to explain this behavior with models of corresponding complexity. It differs from much of the previous work on firm behavior in that it stresses the inherent simultaneity of many of the firm's decisions, and asserts that a complete understanding of this decision process can be obtained only by explicitly accounting for the numerous interactions which are a result of this simultaneity. Similarly, in formulating policy recommendations one must be aware of these interactions, not only in order to avoid undesirable side effects which might stem from a given policy, but also to be certain that these interactions do not actually result in a negation of a policy's primary goal.

The more forces a model takes into account, the more difficult full comprehension of the mechanisms depicted in the model becomes, and the more arduous is the task of estimation. Still, it is felt that these are costs which at some time

Reprinted by permission from Dennis C. Mueller, *The Quarterly Journal of Economics*, February 1967, Cambridge, Mass.: Harvard University Press, Copyright 1967, by the President and Fellows of Harvard College.

*The work on this paper was supported in part by the Ford Foundation grant to the Inter-University Program on the Micro-Economics of Technological Change and Economic Growth. The paper has benefited from comments on earlier drafts by my dissertation advisors Professors Jesse Markham and Stephen Goldfeld. Professor John Meyer has provided a number of additional suggestions which have improved greatly the content of the paper. The estimates of the model were made using a computer program written by Mr. Edward Pearsall.

must be incurred, for there are limits to the amount of information which can be obtained about a subject through the use of simple approximations. What is more important, no information about the location of these limits can be obtained unless we occasionally are able to penetrate deep enough to glimpse the entire structure we wish to understand.

A GENERAL FORMULATION OF THE MODEL

The Direct Statement of the Model

The allocation of the flow-of-funds to a firm may be viewed as a stepwise process in which some uses receive very high priority and others are determined almost as a residual. Expenditures which tend to meet a given set of firm objectives and are to some extent substitutes for one another will be given equal priority and will be determined by weighing one against the others.

An econometric model which sought to explain decisions having equal claim to a firm's funds might be formulated as follows:
Letting $n_1, n_2, \ldots n_r$ represent the endogenous variables and $x_1, x_2, \ldots x_s$, the set of predetermined variables, then

$$\begin{aligned} n_1 &= f_1(n_2, n_3, \ldots n_r, X_1) + \mu_1, \\ n_2 &= f_2(n_1, n_3, \ldots n_r, X_2) + \mu_2, \\ & \cdots \\ n_r &= f_r(n_1, n_2, \ldots n_{r-1}, X_r) + \mu_r \end{aligned} \quad (17.1)$$

is the stochastic representation of the model, where the X_j are subsets of the set of all x_j. That is, each dependent variable at a given level of priority is a function of *all* other decision variables at that level and *some* of the predetermined variables. The set of predetermined variables may include decision variables of higher priority, lagged dependent variables at this level of priority, or variables completely exogenous to the system. If one is willing to make a number of assumptions regarding the form of the functional relationships, the process which generates the error terms, etc., in (17.1), the model can be estimated using one of a number of statistical techniques. Preferably direct-least-squares will not be employed, for this procedure ignores the simultaneity we wish to emphasize. Instead one of the methods of estimation which explicitly allows for this simultaneity should be employed.[1]

An Optimization Model

In writing each equation the researcher makes explicit assumptions only regarding the variables the entrepreneur considers relevant for each decision and not about the motives behind these decisions. One's preconceptions regarding the goals of the firm are often implicitly introduced via the selection of the predetermined variables to be included in each question. Still, some equations will be consistent with a variety of assumptions about the goals of entrepreneurs. By stressing decision variables rather than motives, the approach is general in the

---

[1] J. Johnston, *Econometric Methods* (New York: McGraw-Hill, 1960), chap. 9.

sense that a model may be reconcilable with a number of hypotheses regarding the goals of the firm.

One might prefer to introduce assumptions concerning entrepreneurial goals explicitly by defining an objective function. Corresponding to (17.1) there would then be an objective function O, such that

$$O = O(n_1, n_2, \ldots n_r, x_1, x_2, \ldots x_s).$$

If O is maximized with respect to the n_j, a set of r equations is obtained which can be solved for each of the r dependent variables. Unless a rather complex functional relationship is hypothesized for O, each dependent variable will be a function of *all* predetermined variables and none of the other dependent variables. If a linear relationship is assumed the system (17.2) results. Making the usual

$$n_1 = a_1 x_1 + b_1 x_2 + \ldots w_1 x_5 + v_1,$$
$$\ldots \ldots \ldots \ldots \ldots \ldots$$
$$n_r = a_r x_1 + b_r x_2 + \ldots w_r x_5 + v_r$$

(17.2)

assumptions concerning the error terms and the x_j, the direct-least-squares estimates of this system will be maximum likelihood estimates. Formulating the problem explicitly as one of maximization has apparently eased the computational burden. While with (17.1) a sophisticated simultaneous estimating technique was required, with (17.2) it appears direct-least-squares will suffice.

The simplification of the computational task has not been without some cost. The decisions, over which predetermined variables should be included in each of the equations of (17.1), will have been made on the basis of a priori knowledge of firm behavior. The performance of (17.1) can be evaluated both on the basis of the usual statistical tests, and upon the amount of agreement between the estimated and predicted values of the structural coefficients. With (17.2) the latter test is not possible. The coefficient of a predetermined variable in (17.2) is a measure of the net impact of this variable upon the equation's dependent variable, after account has been taken of all the interactions of the system of equations. This is a direct result of having derived the system (17.2), by first solving algebraically the set of equations which resulted from the optimization of O. For small systems one may be able to make predictions concerning the signs and magnitudes of the coefficients of (17.2). For complex models this procedure is hazardous.

That (17.2) makes less use of one's a priori knowledge of firm behavior than (17.1) is not surprising, for (17.2) is the reduced form equivalent of (17.1). Indeed, a possible method for estimating (17.1) is first to estimate (17.2) using direct-least-squares and use the resulting estimates to solve for the coefficients of (17.1). But here again one's predictions about various coefficients could not be confirmed until after such a substitution had taken place. This procedure for estimating (17.1) has the least to recommend it of all the simultaneous equation techniques, and in fact only results in unambiguous estimates of the coefficients of (17.1), when each of the equations in that system is exactly identified. We conclude that the results from empirical work can be best employed as a check upon the reasonableness of one's preconceptions regarding firm behavior, and as a means of making further inferences about this behavior, if one concentrates upon a model analogous to (17.1).[2]

THE CHOICE OF DEPENDENT VARIABLES

Later sections of this article present the results for a model which focuses upon four decisions of the firm: capital investment, research and development (R & D), advertising, and dividend payments. The firm's decision concerning any one of these variables is assumed to be made while it considers the other three.

In what follows we assume the firm acts implicitly so as to maximize the present net worth of its stockholders. It may use its funds to pay out dividends, or employ them in some combination of the three competitive strategies included in the model. The trade-off between dividend payments and the strategy variables will depend upon: (1) the time-preference schedule of the firm's stockholders, (2) the extent to which the market reflects increases in expenditure on the strategies in increases in the value of equity shares, and (3) the expected returns from the three strategies. For example, a particularly attractive R & D opportunity should lead to: an increase in R & D, a reduction in dividend payments, the anticipation of a future rise in dividends, and an increase in the current value of a firm's stock.

Capital investment, R & D, and advertising are often alternative means to a similar end. When deciding between a marginal increase in capital investment and an increase in R & D, the firm may be weighing a change to a known but as yet unadopted process against trying to develop a process superior to anything currently available. Similarly, when it determines its R & D and advertising budgets, the firm may compare the opportunities for creating a new image for an old product with those of inventing an entirely new product.

Over a period of years, the firm can rely upon three sources of funds to finance these outlays: profits, depreciation and equity issues. Since the third of these has been a limited source of funds for firms in recent years,[3] we feel justi-

---

[2] W. H. Locke Anderson maximizes an objective function subject to a balance-sheet constraint which equates the sources and uses of funds for the firm. It should be noted that whether one chooses to think of the firm as operating within a balance-sheet constraint or not in no way affects the arguments in favor of estimating (17.1) as opposed to (17.2). The system of equations (17.1) easily can be modified to take into account such an identity by replacing one of the equations in the system by the identity. See *Corporate Finance and Fixed Investment* (Boston: Graduate School of Business Administration, Harvard University, 1964), chaps. 3 and 4.

A balance-sheet constraint only seems appropriate for decisions of the lowest priority and, therefore, will be ignored in the model presented below.

[3] *Ibid.*, p. 25. An additional reason for not including equity issues in the model is because of the problem of determining the direction of causality. This is also the problem with using long-term debt as a predetermined variable as Anderson does. That is, equity and debt are better treated as dependent variables in a model which focuses on lower priority decisions than as independent variables in our model. This is consistent with Anderson's work in chap. 4. In chap. 5 Anderson argues from aggregate time series data that increasing risk has a negative effect upon investment. His results conflict with those of John R. Meyer and Robert R. Glauber, *Investment Decisions, Economic Forecasting, and Public Policy* (Boston: Harvard

fied in concentrating on the two flows, profits and depreciation. Profits are returns from past expenditures on one of the three competitive strategies: investment, R & D, or advertising. They may be re-employed in these same activities, or distributed to stockholders in the form of dividend payments. Depreciation is a rebate upon specific past expenditure decisions, investments in capital equipment. It can be reinvested in capital equipment, used to finance R & D and advertising, or paid out as dividends. In short, the firm is envisaged as acting in a completely fluid manner, receiving funds as profits and depreciation, employing them either by investing in one of the three competitive strategies examined here, or paying them out as dividends. Its decisions are motivated by the desire to maximize stockholder net worth and are made by simultaneously weighing the effects of one choice versus those of the others.

In order to conserve space we shall not present a priori justifications for the inclusion of each predetermined variable in the four equations. Each dependent variable is assumed to be a function of the other three dependent variables and a group of the predetermined variables. While predictions were made concerning the signs of the predetermined variables in each equation, no attempt was made to penetrate the maze of interactions in the model and predict the signs of the right-hand-side dependent variables. Their inclusion in an equation will be justified on statistical grounds alone. Despite the absence of any small-sample theoretical support for such an action, the t, R, and F statistics will be calculated and interpreted in a manner similar to that usually followed using their direct-least-squares analogues. Partial justification for this can be obtained from John Cragg's work with Monte Carlo experiments.[4]

Table 17.1 lists the codetermined and predetermined variables employed in the model. In order to avoid the problem of heteroscedasticity, all variables, except the industry index variables, will be deflated by sales. This procedure was justified using a test of homoscedasticity recently developed by Goldfeld and Quandt.[5]

Table 17.1

VARIABLE DEFINITIONS

RD	Firm R & D outlays	G	Ten-year change in sales
I	Gross capital investment	TRD	Total R & D undertaken during a previous one-year period
A	Advertising		
D	Cash dividend payments	IRD	Industry R & D/industry sales
S	Sales	IAS	Industry assets/industry sales
P	Profits before taxes	IA	Industry advertising/industry sales
DP	Depreciation plus depletion	dS	One-year change in sales

Graduate School of Business Administration, Harvard University, 1964), pp. 88–91. Our sample resembles more closely that of Meyer and Glauber than that of Anderson and we have not tested, therefore, this particular hypothesis.

[4] J. G. Cragg, "Small-Sample Properties of Various Simultaneous-Equation Estimators: The Results of Some Monte-Carlo Experiments," Princeton Econometric Research Program, Research Memorandum no. 68, Oct. 1964, pp. 81–94 and 183–84.

[5] Stephen M. Goldfeld and Richard E. Quandt, "Some Tests for Homoscedasticity," *Journal of the American Statistical Association*, LX (June 1965).

Using their nonparametric test one cannot reject the hypothesis that the four equations in their deflated forms have homogeneous residuals for 1960. The intercepts of the equations will be interpreted as the coefficients of the sales variable.[6]

The sample consists of observations on sixty-seven firms for the four years 1957–60.[7] The model was estimated for each of the four years using the direct-least-squares, two-stage-least-squares, unbiased K-class, and limited-information procedures.[8] The estimates from the three consistent K-class procedures were bunched rather closely and often showed sharp differences in contrast to the estimates from direct-least-squares. Unfortunately, it does not appear that this result alone can be relied upon as evidence that these estimates are closer to the true values than the direct-least-squares estimates. Cragg's work indicates that this same type of bunching occurs, even when the direct-least-squares estimates possess the smaller bias.[9] Our emphasis upon the estimates obtained from the consistent K-class techniques will be justified, therefore, by their superior statistical properties and their generally superior performance in Monte Carlo studies.[10] Because of the closeness of the three consistent K-class estimates only the results obtained using the two-stage technique will be presented (Table 17.2). These results may be compared for 1960 with those obtained using direct-least-squares, which are presented in the same table. Hereafter, all references are to the two-stage estimates.

THE CAPITAL INVESTMENT EQUATION

Some Preliminary Considerations

Of the four outlays examined in the model, capital investment has received by far the most attention in the literature. Indeed, an adequate review of past efforts in this area does not seem feasible within the confines of this study.[11] In place of such a review, we shall justify our equation by first sketching the firm invest-

---

[6] Ideally, an index of interindustry differences which is not already deflated by sales should be employed, e.g., in the R & D equation, average firm R & D. This would allow us to employ the Goldfeld and Quandt test to both the ratio and the nonratio forms of the equations. Not possessing such a variable we have chosen industry R & D as a percentage of sales as a substitute. The use of variables of this form precludes the formation of nonratio models by multiplying each variable by sales in the deflated investment, R & D, and advertising equations. When their test was applied to the deflated and undeflated forms of the dividends equation, the latter was heteroscedastic at the 1 per cent level of significance and the former was not (8 versus 4 residual peaks). For a complete discussion of these variables see Table 17.1, and Appendix I.

[7] The sample is discussed fully in Appendix I.

[8] Johnston, *op. cit.*, Chap. 9.

[9] *Op. cit.*, Appendix D, Table C–1.

[10] *Ibid.*, and Johnston, *op. cit.*, Chap. 10.

[11] Robert Eisner and Robert H. Strotz have tackled the job in "Determinants of Business Investment," in Commission on Money and Credit, *Impacts of Monetary Policy* (Englewood Cliffs, N.J.: Prentice-Hall, 1963).

ment process as we see it, and secondly by rejecting two alternative formulations often employed.

A firm may invest in new capital equipment for the purpose of adopting presently known production processes, which it previously did not employ (these may be the result of past R & D), or it may reinvest in the same processes it has utilized in the past. A newly adopted process may produce an entirely new product, or it may produce at a lower cost a product currently marketed by the firm. A large portion of a firm's capital expenditure is to replace wornout plant and equipment, and is necessary for the firm's very survival. To some extent this fraction of a firm's investment differs from its expenditures on R & D and advertising, in that it is more of a necessity and involves less uncertainty. This point should not be overemphasized, however. Capital investment also involves uncertainty, and R & D and advertising expenditures are in part necessary in order for a firm to maintain its market position.

Our use of cross-section data requires that we interpret the estimated regression coefficients as long-run elasticities.[12] The firm is envisaged as relying upon the flows of profits and depreciation, in the long run, in order to finance its investment. These variables each serve a dual role in the equation. Profits represent both a flow-of-funds and a possible indication of future returns. To the extent the firm relates present profits to past capital expenditures, it may use them as a measure of future returns from similar investments. Depreciation is both a flow-of-funds and an index of replacement needs. Whether the firm decides to reinvest these funds in capital equipment will depend upon the comparative advantage this strategy has over the others. In periods of peak demand this advantage is likely to be great and the firm will reinvest in the same processes in an effort to meet current orders. In periods of low demand it may prefer to divert some of these funds into increasing present and future demand through advertising and R & D.

Zvi Griliches has argued that any equation which is used to explain investment should have as one of its explanatory variables a present or past value of the firm's capital stock.[13] This type of hypothesis envisages the firm as seeking a desired capital stock (K^*), and a negative coefficient is predicted for the present stock of capital variable. The higher this present stock is, the smaller the investment needed to reach the desired level, K^*. In a cross-section model, the present stock of capital will act as an index of the capital-intensiveness of the firm relative to the other firms in the sample and not as a measure of its present level of capital relative to some ideal quantity. The coefficient of this variable will not be negative as predicted, and therefore, it does not seem justifiable to include present capital stock as an independent variable in cross-section models. In our model, depreciation acts as an index of the capital-intensiveness of the firm and the predicted sign for its coefficient is positive.

[12] Edwin Kuh, *Capital Stock Growth: A Micro-Econometric Approach* (Amsterdam: North Holland, 1963), p. 182.
[13] "Capital Stock in Investment Functions: Some Problems of Concept and Measurement," in Carl F. Christ and others, *Measurement in Economics* (Stanford: Stanford University, 1963).

Table 17.2

REGRESSION ANALYSIS RESULTS

YEAR	METHOD				RIGHT-HAND SIDE VARIABLES					F	R
I =	RD	RD	A	TRD	IAS	dS	P_{t-1}	DP_{t-1}			
1960	DLS	−.404	−.290	.294	.489	.110	.071	1.221		75.54	.95
		1.22	1.77	1.31	3.69	2.66	1.01	6.98			
1960	TSLS	−.905	−.421	.566	.500	.101	.136	1.180		70.64	.95
		.61	.72	.76	2.62	1.45	.83	6.17			
1959	TSLS	−1.648	−.062	.756	.302	−.021	.257	1.271		57.11	.93
		2.00	.18	2.19	1.73	.53	1.87	6.77			
1958	TSLS	−1.045	−.121	.407	.613	.042	.212	.631		57.92	.93
		1.73	.46	1.84	3.90	1.64	2.16	3.66			
1957	TSLS	−1.912	−.508	.723	.689	.142	.225	1.329		69.34	.95
		2.26	1.52	3.02	3.61	2.65	1.74	5.63			
RD =	I	I	A	D	IRD	G	P_{t-1}	DP_{t-1}	S	F	R
1960	DLS	−.035	.051	−.125	.697	.0021	.138	.127	−.011	11.08	.75
		.63	.63	1.02	5.76	.94	3.02	1.15	1.99		
1960	TSLS	−.056	.170	−.151	.660	.0023	.149	.180	−.012	10.22	.77
		.55	1.22	1.07	5.21	1.02	2.93	1.16	1.80		
1959	TSLS	−.055	.178	−.258	.581	.0025	.213	.240	−.013	15.02	.79
		.44	1.42	1.87	5.46	1.28	4.09	1.43	2.28		
1958	TSLS	−.161	.021	−.054	.603	.0019	.125	.247	−.0066	10.93	.75
		2.07	.19	.35	5.19	.91	2.26	2.43	1.29		
1957	TSLS	−.041	.098	−.301	.467	.0017	.198	.186	−.0095	10.21	.76
		.73	.99	2.32	4.67	.96	4.17	1.73	1.98		

THE FIRM'S DECISION PROCESS: AN ECONOMETRIC INVESTIGATION 319

A =	I	D	G	IA	S	F	R
1960 DLS	.028	−.272	−.0013	.669	.0089	10.21	.63
	.49	2.33	.45	5.71	1.54		
1960 TSLS	.099	−.383	−.0014	.753	.0059	9.55	.65
	1.23	2.81	.47	5.68	.89		
1959 TSLS	.048	−.293	−.0011	.666	.0084	10.04	.61
	.52	1.97	.38	5.05	1.38		
1958 TSLS	.087	−.367	−.0013	.716	.0081	8.66	.59
	.87	2.29	.39	5.48	1.11		
1957 TSLS	.083	−.410	−.0027	.773	.0090	8.88	.64
	1.10	2.52	.82	5.64	1.32		

D =	RD	P	D_{t-1}			F	R
1960 DLS	.072	.042	.837			1702.28	.99
	2.45	3.63	26.48				
1960 TSLS	.075	.041	.836			1702.04	.99
	2.23	3.57	26.28				
1959 TSLS	.076	.033	1.007			507.69	.98
	.89	1.20	13.64				
1958 TSLS	−.067	.106	.731			1225.55	.99
	1.23	5.55	18.90				
1957 TSLS	.072	.030	.973			732.85	.99
	.80	.86	12.27				

Notes: TSLS = Two-stage-least-squares. DLS = Direct-least-squares. Values below regression coefficients are t values. Coefficients for sales variables are intercepts of ratio equations.

The stock adjustment model also can be used to justify including lagged investment in the equation. More generally one can follow Koyck and assume that

$$I_t = aS_t + \sum_{i=1}^{n} \lambda^i S_{t-1} \cong aS_t + I_{t-1}, \quad (17.3)$$

because

$$I_{t-1} \cong \sum_{i=1}^{n} \lambda^i S_{t-1}.^{14} \quad (17.4)$$

Alternatively, one can assume that a given investment flow is desired. If I_t^* is current desired investment, and b the one-period reaction coefficient, then one might hypothesize a function of the form

$$I_t - I_{t-1} = b(I_t^* - I_{t-1}). \quad (17.5)$$

If I_t^* is dependent upon S_t, an equation analogous to (17.3) results.

Similar demonstrations would justify the inclusion of lagged dependent variables in all of the equations of the model. In a cross-section model (particularly with a sample which is as heterogeneous as ours is), the performance of a lagged dependent variable will approach the spectacular. This performance may be out of proportion with that of the theory which it represents, for the variable may act as a surrogate for a number of separate influences upon firm behavior. This characteristic of lagged dependent variables introduces a number of problems in interpretation. The distributed lag variable conceivably might be any one of the variables in the equation which has a positive coefficient, it may be a combination of these variables, or even an excluded variable. The same problems of interpretation are present when one attempts to specify the determinants of I^*. When deciding whether or not to include a lagged dependent variable in an equation, the analyst is faced, therefore, with a dilemma. To include the variable is to risk misinterpreting the results, usually in favor of whatever hypothesis is being tested. If the variable is not included, the equation may be misspecified and the estimated regression coefficients are likely to be biased.[15] The choice should rest upon the analyst's confidence regarding the theory which justifies including the lagged variable. If he is certain about his theory and believes the parameter estimates can be interpreted without ambiguity, then the lagged variable approach is appropriate. In situations where some doubt exists regarding the true underlying structural relations, it is felt a little bias should be incurred in an effort to avoid misinterpreting the results. Using these criteria, we have rejected the lagged dependent variable approach for all but the dividends equation.[16]

In place of an investment equation which includes lagged investment as a predetermined variable, we have chosen one which has depreciation as its most important explanatory variable. Our use of depreciation should not be thought of as

---

[14] Leendert Marinus Koyck. *Distributed Lags and Investment Analysis* (Amsterdam: North Holland, 1954).

[15] Yehuda Grunfeld, "The Interpretation of Cross-Section Estimates in a Dynamic Model," *Econometrica*, vol. 29 (July 1961).

[16] Meyer and Glauber seem to find that lagged investment represents variables other than those they hypothesized, *op. cit.,* p. 134.

part of a rigid stock adjustment model, however. Depreciation is thought of as a measure of the flow-of-funds over time the firm *could* reinvest without implying that they will be so employed. If depreciation were also an accurate measure of the annual deterioration in plant and equipment, one would expect that in years of normal business activity this entire flow would be reinvested, i.e., a regression coefficient for depreciation of about one. In years of greater or less activity coefficients which were correspondingly greater or smaller would be anticipated. In years of expansion the increased incentives to invest should be proportional to the firm's capital stock and therefore to depreciation. In recession years, one expects that other expenditure outlets will have a comparative advantage over investment. This should result in a shifting of depreciation funds out of investment and into these other activities. Depreciation is not, of course, a perfect index of capital deterioration. On the other hand, it is not entirely unrelated to the size and durability of a firm's capital stock. This suggests that we can still look for a cyclical variation in the magnitude of the depreciation coefficient, as described above, but that its expected value in normal years may not be one.

The Empirical Results

In Table 17.2, we find that the depreciation variable has positive and significant coefficients for all four of the sample years. The coefficients exceed one for every year except 1958. In years when the pressure from demand is weak, depreciation funds appear to be channeled into activities promising higher returns than current investment. A glance at the results for the R & D equation suggests a possible recipient of these funds. The coefficient of depreciation in that equation has its highest and most significant value in 1958. These findings are in agreement with the dual interpretation given the depreciation variable above. The extent to which a firm chooses to use the available flow-of-funds from depreciation to restore the previous period's capital stock depends upon the comparative advantage this alternative has over others at the firm's disposal. The results for the investment and R & D equations viewed together stress the flexibility the firm has in allocating the funds at its disposal among their many potential uses. The coefficients of the profits variable are positive for all four years and of relatively close magnitudes. This consistent behavior argues in favor of its retention as an explanatory variable in the equation. Of the four coefficients the one for the recession year, 1958, has the highest t value. This is consistent with the Meyer and Kuh findings[17] and suggests, in accordance with their theory, that the liquidity component of the profits variable may be more important in explaining investment than are firm expectations.

The results for the change in sales variable are extremely interesting. Its coefficients are positive for all years except 1959. Meyer and Glauber interpret this variable as a surrogate for capacity utilization.[18] They anticipate a positive relationship between this variable and investment in years of high business activity. The most expansionary years in our sample are 1957 and 1959, and the change in sales variable receives respectively its highest and lowest coefficients

---

[17] John R. Meyer and Edwin Kuh, *The Investment Decision* (Cambridge: Harvard University Press, 1957), pp. 117–20.
[18] *Op. cit.*, p. 95.

for these two years, the latter being of the wrong sign. These results suggest that the variable should be interpreted in some way other than as a measure of capacity utilization in our model. For the years under examination here, a change in sales variable constitutes a poor measure of utilized capacity. The year 1957 followed two years of very high economic activity. Firms having high increases in sales in 1957 are likely to be closer to (further above) full capacity than are firms experiencing relatively high increases in 1959, a year following a recession. The same argument may be applied to explain the high coefficient for 1960. The change in sales variable would seem to be better interpreted as a measure of expectations than as an index of capacity. Firms which continue to experience relatively strong sales growth in nonpeak years may be very optimistic about the future. Conversely, firms experiencing high sales growth in years of greater than average economic expansion may realize that this is a transitory phenomenon and not base their expectations upon this increase in sales. We conclude that, in our model, the change in sales variable acts chiefly as a measure of expectations, not capacity, and that it measures expectations most accurately in years of normal economic expansion.[19]

R & D is expected to induce future investment, both by making current production processes obsolete and by creating a need for new techniques to produce new products. The coefficient for lagged total R & D is positive for all four sample years, and significant for two. Its magnitudes seem extremely large, e.g., in the 1960 equation the coefficient indicates that for every dollar spent on total R & D in 1956, 57 cents in investment is induced in 1960. Even assuming some of this apparent causal relationship is spurious and attributable to interfirm differences not accounted for by the industry index variable, our results suggest that R & D can be highly influential in inducing future investment.

The industry index variables have high coefficients and t values for all four years, indicating, not surprisingly, that significant interindustry differences exist to account for interfirm differences in capital investment.

The equations as presented do not contain intercepts. When intercepts are included, they are small and insignificant. Since in our ratio model the intercept represents the coefficient of sales, this result indicates that sales do not play an important part in explaining investment in our equation. Sales are interpreted usually as a measure of a firm's expectations. Both change in sales and profits have been interpreted as measures of expectations in our model. The fact that

---

[19] Meyer and Glauber also suggest that change in sales may measure expectations, but are not able to distinguish this variable from their index of capacity statistically. They therefore lump the expectational and capacity elements of these variables into a single accelerator hypothesis. The difference in the composition of the two samples and in the years covered may explain most of the contrast in performance for the change in sales variable in our model and the Meyer and Glauber study. In this respect, it is interesting to note the agreement between our results and the findings and inferences of the Meyer and Kuh study, *op. cit.*, pp. 121–22.

An attempt was made to include a capacity variable similar to that employed in the Meyer and Kuh and Meyer and Glauber studies (Meyer and Glauber, *op. cit.*, pp. 39–42), but without success. Their capacity measure has the undesirable property, in light of our view of the firm, of incorporating the concept of a fixed optimal capital/output ratio.

these variables consistently possess the anticipated sign may explain why the sales variable does not. While these findings disagree with those of others,[20] they do seem more in accordance with what our theory predicts. Both profits and change in sales reflect more accurately a firm's goal of maximizing stockholder income than do current sales.

Of the three codetermined variables, only the original performance of the dividends variable was such as to warrant an assumption of a zero coefficient. Hence the equation was re-estimated omitting this variable.

THE R & D EQUATION

Investments in R & D have as their objectives new products or processes. Schumpeter viewed this competitive strategy as the most lethal of those at the firm's disposal.[21] Of the three considered here, its returns are the most uncertain and distant, and in this respect its appeal as a strategy is reduced.

In the R & D equation, depreciation's coefficient is positive for all years, but significant only for the year 1958, in which its t value exceeds even that for the profits variable. The increased strength of its impact upon R & D in the recession year, coupled with its low coefficient for that year in the investment equation, indicates that a shifting of resources from investment to R & D occurs in years when the returns on the former activity are low. The returns from R & D can be expected to increase relative to those from investment in recession years; first, because they are more distant and uncertain and less subject to cyclical phenomena and, second, because it is a more continuous process requiring gradual changes in personnel in order to achieve optimal performance.

The Meyer and Kuh thesis, that liquidity has its strongest impact upon firm expenditures in recession years, is supported by the behavior of both depreciation in the R & D equation and profits in the investment equation. If we accept their theory, on the basis of these two instances of support, then profits in the R & D equation must be regarded chiefly as a measure of expectations. The ranking of the magnitudes of the four positive coefficients corresponds identically to the ranking of the percentage changes in GNP for the four years. It appears that in peak years when expectations are most buoyant, high returns, to the extent they are attributed to past R & D, have their strongest impact upon firm decision-making. The increased importance of profits as an explanatory variable in years of high economic activity suggests both, that past R & D outlays are reinforced by pesent profits, and that firms expect future returns to be similarly affected.[22]

[20] Kuh finds, for example, that sales are superior to profits as an explanatory variable in his investment equations, *op. cit.*, pp. 208–20. He observes, also, that the profits formulation of the model is aided when this variable is lagged and the equation deflated, *ibid*. The particular formulation of the model employed here is, therefore, perhaps conducive to the finding of a positive coefficient for profits.

[21] Joseph A. Schumpeter, *Capitalism, Socialism and Democracy* (3d ed.; New York: Harper and Row, 1950), Chap. 7.

[22] Jora R. Minasian's work with time series data argues in favor of an expectational role for the profits variable, also. He found a causal chain running from R & D to productivity, and from productivity to profits. He rejected a hypothesis assigning a liquidity role to profits. "The Economics of Research and Development," in National Bureau of Economic Research, *The Rate and Direction of Inventive Activity* (Princeton: Princeton University, 1962).

The importance of R & D as a competitive strategy must rest in large part upon the technological foundation and opportunities available to the firm. These vary greatly from one industry to another, and it is not surprising to find the industry index of R & D intensity the most important explanatory variable in the equation. In part, the strongly positive coefficient for this variable, and its analogue in the advertising equation, may measure a firm's response to similar outlays by its competitors. In this respect the industry index variables assume dual roles: (1) as measures of interindustry technological differences, and (2) as measures of intraindustry competition using identical strategies.[23]

Somewhat surprisingly the sales coefficient (intercept) is negative for all four years. One expects that larger firms will undertake more R & D: (1) because they can command more resources and possess more confidence over their future and are for these reasons in a better position to assume the uncertainties which accompany this activity,[24] and (2) because they have a greater economic incentive to do so, a given expenditure resulting in a greater gain for the large firm than for the small.[25] Simple correlation coefficients between undeflated firm R & D outlays and sales are positive. The negative intercepts are a result, therefore, of having included in the equation other positively correlated variables which offer a better explanation of the variance in firm R & D than sales. In the long run, firms can be expected to be extremely reluctant to finance uncertain R & D by borrowing. Sales, while possibly a good measure of a firm's capacity to raise funds from outside sources, are obviously inferior to both profits and depreciation as a measure of its command over internal funds. Similarly, profits, in their role as a measure of expectations, can better test a demand-pull hypothesis than sales. We conclude that the negative coefficients for sales should be interpreted not as refutation of the importance of uncertainty and demand-pull factors upon R & D, but merely as indicative of the inferiority of sales relative to other variables in the equation as a test of these hypotheses. The intercepts can be interpreted, also, as inconsistent with the assertion that size alone is necessary to induce R & D.[26] Indeed, weight is added to the arguments presented by skeptics of this thesis.[27]

[23] The inclusion of these variables is an attempt to remove some of the heterogeneity inherent in the sample without appealing to the costly (in terms of degrees of freedom) dummy variable procedure. Two studies which employ the latter technique also have found that interindustry differences explain a large fraction of the variance in firm R & D activity. See, Frederic M. Scherer, "Firm Size, Market Structure, Opportunity, and the Output of Patented Inventions," *American Economic Review*, LV (Dec. 1965); and Marshall Hall, "The Determinants of Investment Variation in Research and Development," *IEEE Transactions on Engineering Management*, vol. EM–11 (March 1964).

[24] D. E. Lilienthal, *Big Business: A New Era* (New York: Harper, 1952), Chap. 6; Henry H. Villard, "Competition, Oligopoly, and Research," *Journal of Political Economy*, LXVI (Dec. 1958).

[25] See Jacob Schmookler's papers with Oswald Brownlee, "Determinants of Inventive Activity," *American Economic Review*, LII (May 1962), and Zvi Griliches, "Inventing and Maximizing," *American Economic Review*, LIII (Sept. 1963); and for a recent test of the demand-pull hypothesis using sales, Scherer's paper, *op. cit.*

[26] Lilienthal, *op. cit.*

[27] Jacob Schmookler, "Bigness, Fewness and Research," *Journal of Political Economy*, LXVII (Dec. 1959).

The faster a firm's sales are increasing, the more confidence it will have about its ability to secure the benefits from uncertain R & D projects, and the more patience it can afford to show in waiting for these benefits. The faster a firm's sales are growing, the greater the economic advantage it receives from a given cost-reducing invention. The ten-year growth variable may be expected, therefore, to have a positive coefficient in the R & D equation, on the basis of both uncertainty and demand-pull hypotheses. It also may contribute to the poor behavior of sales as a test of these hypotheses in the equation. If present growth is a result of past R & D,[28] then the positive coefficient for growth may indicate merely a positive correlation between present and past R & D. If this is the case, the variable may serve as a measure of a firm's expectations. Firms continue to invest in R & D in the same relative proportions as they did in the past, because their previous R & D outlays have been reinforced by the growth in their sales.

The reader should note, also, the R & D equation's sensitivity to cyclical conditions. Six of the eight regression coefficients achieve an extreme value in the recession year, 1958.

Investment and dividends appear to have negative coefficients in the equation, and advertising the reverse.

THE ADVERTISING EQUATION

Advertising is a strategy for shifting the demand schedule of a product without changing its physical characteristics. Its impact is more rapid than R & D and for this reason probably involves less uncertainty. Like R & D it can be a strategy for achieving dominance over a market. Unlike R & D, this domination is liable to be temporary and is more susceptible to counterattacks by competitors.[29] In general, advertising probably involves more uncertainty and quicker payoffs than capital investment, although this may vary among industries.

Neither profits nor depreciation exhibited any influence upon firm advertising outlays. This suggests that firms regard advertising more as a necessary business expense than as an investment. The lack of any positive relationship between profits and advertising leads us to reject a causal chain running from past advertising to present profits, and in turn from these profits to present advertising.

The equation is dominated by the industry index variable. As with R & D, this variable may be thought of as serving two purposes: (1) measuring interindustry differences which are a direct result of the characteristics of the products sold, and (2) measuring firm responses to changes in advertising by other firms in the industry. In light of the absence of any positive relationship between the two flow-of-funds variables and advertising, the latter purpose takes on added importance. For, to the extent the industry index measures the second phenomenon, the results suggest that firms consider advertising a business expense,

[28] It is doubtful whether the immediate postwar growth is a result of previous R & D. Some of the growth later in the ten-year period may be, however.

[29] The toothpaste industry, since the advent of Crest, provides an interesting case study of the moves and countermoves of oligopolists using the advertising strategy "Colgate's 3-month, $3,751,000 Campaign Hikes Share 1.5%," *Advertising Age*, XXXIV (Aug. 26, 1963); "Toothpaste Tempest," *Chemical Week*, XCV (Aug. 22, 1964); "Look Ma, No Cavities," *Barron's*, XLV (Jan. 4, 1965).

the amount of which is dependent partly upon the advertising of their competitors.

The intercepts were positive for all four years. It was not surprising to find that firms which sell more, advertise more. Indeed, what was surprising was not to find analogous relationships in the previous two equations. The reason given for not observing the positive relationship in those two equations was the presence of the profits and depreciation variables in each equation. These variables exhibit no influence upon advertising, and we are left with a scale effect which is captured by sales.[30]

A positive coefficient was predicted for the ten-year growth variable in the R & D equation, by arguing that a rapidly expanding firm is in a better position to wait for R & D's distant and uncertain payoffs. Turning the argument around, the slowly expanding firm, feeling much more concerned about the future, may place heavier reliance on advertising with its more rapid and predictable returns. The four negative coefficients for the ten-year growth variable support this interpretation. The variable will be retained in the equation, because of this consistent agreement between the observed and predicted signs for the coefficients, and despite the fact that none of them is significant.

The investment and dividends variables possessed coefficients of the same sign for all four years and were retained in the equation. The R & D variable's coefficients were erratic in sign for the four years and it was excluded from the equation. The reader is reminded that it is because of the simultaneous nature of our model that no predictions, and hence no discussion, for these variables are given and their inclusion in an equation is justified on statistical criteria alone.

THE DIVIDENDS EQUATION

In the section entitled "The Capital Investment Equation" two justifications for including a lagged dependent variable in an equation were presented. An analogue to equation (17.5) is Lintner's dividend behavior hypothesis.[31] For the purposes of our model, Lintner's equation will be modified by including the three codetermined strategies and deflating all variables by sales.[32]

---

[30] Lester G. Telser has recently discussed the pros and cons of expecting increasing returns to scale from advertising, "Advertising and Competition," *Journal of Political Economy*, LXXII (Dec. 1964), 537–62.

There is one difficulty with including sales in the advertising equation which is not present with the other equations. Advertising's impact upon sales may be rapid enough to result in a feedback effect. It is felt, however, that the overriding causal flow is from right to left and that any feedback will not introduce serious bias into the estimates.

[31] John Lintner, "Distribution of Incomes of Corporations Among Dividends, Retained Earnings and Taxes," *American Economic Review*, XLVI (May 1956).

[32] A word is in order concerning the use of lagged and unlagged predetermined variables. In the investment and R & D equations lagged profits and depreciation were employed because of their superior statistical performance in comparison with the unlagged variables and in order to avoid biases which would accompany the use of the unlagged variables (e.g., since R & D can be expensed, a negative bias is introduced when profits are included in this equation). Others have observed the

A lagged dependent variable formulation of the equation has been employed for two reasons. First, the equation as hypothesized by Lintner is entirely consistent with a model which assumes that firms finance investment and similar competing outlays out of retained earnings.[33] Secondly, the chance of misinterpreting the actual behavior represented by the empirical results is much smaller than for the other equations in the model. We join with Kuh in believing that Lintner's hypothesis "stand(s) among the more thoroughly founded behavioral hypotheses in the area of business behavior." [34]

The results for the four years are completely dominated by the lagged dividends variable. A positive relationship is evident between the magnitude of its coefficient and the level of overall economic activity. This produces the rather disturbing result, that the reaction coefficients are about zero for both the years 1959 and 1957. It should be noted that this poor theoretical performance of the equation in these years is matched by a comparatively poor statistical performance. On the basis of both the t values of the lagged dividends variable and the F values of the equation, the estimates obtained for the years 1959 and 1957 are inferior to those for the other two years. The results for these latter years will be used, therefore, in a comparison with those of Lintner and Kuh.

Lintner, using time series data from 1918 to 1941, obtained values for b, the reaction coefficient, ranging from .21 to .30, and for a, the payout ratio, from .37 to .25.[35] Kuh obtained estimates of .50 and .22, respectively.[36] Our figures yield reaction coefficients (b) of .16 and .27, and payout ratios (a) of .26 and .39 for the years 1960 and 1958 respectively. Our results resemble those of Lintner more closely than those of Kuh. It is difficult to discern why this is so. Perhaps the answer lies in the fact that our sample, like Lintner's, is representative of the entire population of manufacturing firms, while Kuh's estimates are actually the median values of a group of individual industry estimates.

Lintner's hypothesis is an attempt to explain dividend behavior in the long run. Because we regard the coefficients obtained using cross-section data as estimates of long-run structural parameters, it is encouraging to see how closely our estimates correspond to Lintner's. While it is obvious that great care must be taken to assure that estimates are chosen which are truly representative of firm behavior, it appears that given a sufficient number of years of observations (and this number certainly exceeds 4), accurate representations of firm behavior can be obtained using cross-section data.

The only strategy whose performance warranted its inclusion in the equation

---

statistical superiority of the lagged variables, also, e.g., Meyer and Glauber, *op. cit.*, p. 80; and Kuh, *op. cit.*, p. 211.
The use of current profits in the dividends equation was justified on theoretical grounds and by the superior statistical properties it exhibited.

[33] Kuh, *op. cit.*, pp. 16–26.

[34] *Ibid.*, p. 17. If one prefers to think in terms of a distributed lag model, the possibility of misinterpretation is still small, the most probable choice of a distributed lag variable being profits.

[35] *Op. cit.*, p. 109. Both Lintner's and Kuh's coefficients for the profits variables have been divided by 2 to make their work using after-tax profits comparable to ours using the before-tax figures.

[36] *Op. cit.*, p. 310.

was R & D. Its coefficients for 1957, 1959, and 1960 were remarkably close together. There is a reversal of signs in 1958, which is consistent with the peculiar cyclical behavior of R & D already noted in the discussion of that equation.

Because of this rather weak performance by the strategy variables in the dividends equation, it has been suggested that a recursive formulation of the model might be superior to the one employed here, i.e., that dividends have prior claim to a firm's funds over investment, R & D, and advertising. While the writer does believe that few firm decisions have identical claims on a firm's funds, he still feels justified in including dividends as a variable that is codetermined with investment, R & D, and advertising because: (1) The extreme heterogeneity in the sample results in the domination of the equation by the lagged dividends variable; with a more homogeneous sample of firms, more of the variation in dividend payments probably would be explained by the other codetermined variables. (2) To deny dividends a place in this model would be equivalent to arguing that dividends are never adjusted in light of the profitability of alternative expenditure opportunities. The writer finds this argument intuitively objectionable, particularly with regard to R & D—the only codetermined variable whose statistical performance appeared to warrant its retention in the equation.

The equation was estimated without an intercept. This assumes, ignoring the impact of the codetermined variables, that $D_t = D_{t-1}$, if $D_t^* = D_{t-1}$. When the equation was estimated with intercepts their t values ranged from -2.59 to 0.09.

AN APPRAISAL OF THE MODEL

Of the four decisions examined in the study, advertising has proved the most enigmatic. The coefficients of multiple correlation for its equation are the lowest of any equation in the model. The absence of any correlation between advertising and either of the liquidity variables, profits and depreciation, leads us to conclude that firms regard advertising chiefly as a necessary business expense determined by the nature of their products, the advertising of their competitors, and the size of their operations.

In contrast with advertising, the dividends equation, borrowed from Lintner, is quite successful. Not only are all of the R's high, but the estimates of the reaction coefficients are close to those obtained by Lintner. It is apparent, however, that observations for a number of years would be required in order to select the appropriate set of estimates for a prediction model.

In addition to the fact that some of our results support those of the Meyer and Kuh and Meyer and Glauber studies, we feel our entire approach is in the same "eclectic" spirit[37] of these earlier studies. For this reason some comparisons between our work and theirs will be made in the discussion of the investment and R & D equations.

Throughout the paper, the dual roles played by some of the predetermined variables have been emphasized. This interpretation was given originally to the

[37] Meyer and Glauber, op. cit., pp. 3–7.

profits and depreciation variables. When the investment and R & D equations are viewed together, however, there is evidence that one component of a variable often dominates the other. In the R & D equation, depreciation can act only as a measure of a liquidity flow. The increased importance of this variable as an explanation of R & D in 1958, as evidenced by its high t value for that year, agrees with the Meyer and Kuh thesis that liquidity flows play their most important role in determining firm expenditure decisions during periods of recession. If one continues to think in terms of the Meyer and Kuh theory, then profits appear to represent mainly a flow of liquidity in the investment equation, for here also the t value for the variable's coefficient is highest in 1958. In the R & D equation, on the other hand, the variable's behavior is reversed. The coefficients of profits in the R & D equation vary directly with the level of overall business activity. If liquidity considerations are most important in recession years, then profits must measure something besides liquidity in the R & D equation. We regard this cyclical behavior of the profits' coefficients as consistent with an interpretation of the variable as a measure of expectations. In years of strong economic activity, firms are encouraged to spend heavily upon R & D as a result of present profit levels, which they probably attribute largely to past R & D expenditures.

In contrast with the findings of the Meyer and Kuh and Meyer and Glauber studies, the liquidity component of depreciation is not dominant in the investment equation. The variable exhibits its smallest amount of explanatory power in this equation for 1958, where both its regression coefficient and t value are roughly half of their respective magnitudes for other years. The Meyer and Kuh and Meyer and Glauber samples do not contain as much interfirm variation in capital stock as the sample employed in this study; hence, they feel justified in regarding depreciation as a measure of a cash flow. It is obvious that for our sample the variable measures both capital deterioration and liquidity.

The results for the profits and depreciation variables alone make evident the need for examining more than one facet of a firm's behavior at a time, in order to gain an understanding of this behavior. The performance of these two variables in the R & D and investment equations distinctly argues for a theory of the firm, based on the profits maximization assumption, which stresses the importance of internal funds. In years of economic expansion, the marginal returns on investment are high and firms reinvest their entire depreciation allowances. They spend on R & D during these years to the extent that returns therefrom are comparable with those from investment. Firms, which experience high profits from past R & D, probably allocate proportionally larger amounts to this activity, on the assumption that these outlays will continue to prove profitable. In years of recession, the returns on investment are lower than normal, and depreciation funds, which ordinarily are reinvested, are diverted into R & D, from which returns increase relative to investment returns during these years.

Meyer and Glauber prefer to use a "residual cash throw-off" variable equal to profits plus depreciation less dividend payments, rather than consider the separate effects of these three variables.[38] Their decision not to separate profits from depreciation is made because of the marked reduction in

[38] *Ibid.*, pp. 109–17.

the explanatory power of the latter, once lagged investment is introduced into the equation. That lagged investment detracts from, and surpasses, the explanatory power of depreciation is not surprising. Depreciation measures but two forces upon firm investment decisions. A high correlation can be expected between the forces which determined last year's investment and the one's which determine this year's. Lagged investment will measure, therefore, roughly the same forces which are included in depreciation *plus all others* which affect current investment. The problem with lagged investment, as mentioned above, is to identify these additional forces and determine their relative importance in explaining this year's investment. In short, while lagged investment has more *statistical* explanatory power, depreciation has more *behavioral* explanatory power. We feel more understanding of firm behavior is gained by omitting lagged investment, separating the effects of profits and depreciation, and trying to explain rather than assume dividend payment policy.

More emphasis has been placed upon expectations here than in the Meyer and Kuh and Meyer and Glauber studies. The interpretation of the one-year change in sales variable as a measure of capacity has been rejected, due largely to its negative coefficient in the boom year 1959, and it along with profits and the ten-year change in sales variable have been assumed to reflect, in part, the operations of expectations upon firm decisions. Greater than average increases in sales during years of normal or below normal economic activity appear to encourage firms to increase their capital investment in anticipation of future growth in sales. Here again it should be noted that the contrast between the results reported here and those in the Meyer and Glauber study may be due to differences in sample composition.

We are forced to reject the hypothesis that sales have a positive influence on either investment or R & D. Indeed, the variable is retained in the latter equation because it consistently and once significantly exhibits the opposite impact, suggesting that, *ceteris paribus*, size acts as a deterrent to inventive activity. Once again the findings for this variable are best explained after viewing the entire model. Profits and depreciation measure the same phenomena sales are often thought to represent, i.e., expectations and command over economic resources. In the investment and R & D equations they consistently have positive and often highly significant coefficients. By including them in these equations along with sales, we have effectively usurped the power of sales to affect R & D and investment positively. Consistent with these findings, in the advertising equation, where profits and depreciation exhibit no correlation with the dependent variable, the sales variable has a positive coefficient for all four years. The superiority of profits and depreciation over sales in the R & D and investment equations is consistent with both our emphasis on the importance of internal funds for these decisions and our view of the firm as a profits-maximizer.

To summarize the comparison of our work with that of Meyer and Kuh and Meyer and Glauber, we find ourselves in agreement with the general approach of these works, differing only with regard to some of the particulars of the structural model which "best" explains firm behavior. In part these differences can be attributed to the greater heterogeneity of the present sample and the differences in the time periods investigated.

The model has explained its four decision variables with mixed success. The coefficients of multiple correlation range from around 0.63 for the advertising equation to near perfect figures of 0.99 for the dividends equation. An additional point in the model's favor, however, is its performance when viewed over the entire four-year period. We were able to obtain insights to firm decision-making by examining the behavior of the four equations over the cycle, which could not have been inferred from the results for any one equation.

It should be noted that it was more important for our conclusions that the equations be viewed simultaneously than that they be estimated using a technique which eliminates Haavelmo bias. The conclusions for the profits, depreciation and change in sales variables, for example, are the same regardless of whether direct-least-squares or a consistent K-class technique is used.[39] Indeed, these conclusions are unchanged when each dependent variable is simply regressed on its respective set of predetermined variables. Hence virtually all of our most interesting observations are unchanged by a more recursive formulation of the model. The simultaneous equation approach has been stressed, because it is the most appealing intuitively and has been supported by the results. The consistent K-class estimating techniques have been emphasized because of their statistical superiority given the underlying structure of the hypothesized model.

POLICY IMPLICATIONS OF THE RESULTS

Problems Raised by the Dual Variables

Table 17.3 presents the coefficients of the reduced form equivalent of the model, which were obtained from Table 17.2 using the estimates for 1960. It was felt that 1960 was the year for which the results might be best characterized as "normal." Each dependent variable is written as a function of all the predetermined variables in the model. The net marginal effect of a change in one of the predetermined variables upon each of the four dependent variables can be observed by moving down the column representing the predetermined variable.

Unfortunately, the effects of different policies on the predetermined variables are not always easy to predict. This is due partly to the dual interpretation given to many of these variables. Unless a policy affects all of the components of a predetermined variable in the same proportions as measure their impact upon a dependent variable, the former's coefficient will not represent the marginal effect upon the latter of a change in the policy. The seriousness of this problem for the policymaker naturally depends upon: (1) the relative importance of each component of the variable, and (2) the asymmetry of a given policy's effects upon the components of a variable. Regarding the first, most analysts glean from their results enough confidence to assert that a given variable represents a flow-of-funds, expectations or some other single phenomenon. Our results also suggest that a particular component of a variable may be more important in one equation than in others. It is doubted, however, that in most instances the estimated parameters measure a single force upon the regressor. The second point varies in importance for each variable. For example, a

---

[39] For years other than 1960, the differences between the direct-least-squares and consistent K-class estimates were sometimes more pronounced than those appearing in Table 17.2.

Table 17.3
REDUCED FORM COEFFICIENTS FOR 1960

S	TRD	IAS	IA	G	dS	P_t	P_{t-1}	DP_{t-1}	D_{t-1}	IRD
					Investment					
.0465	.2086	.4377	.4628	−.0002	.1191	.0120	.0915	1.1181	.2431	.1936
					R & D					
−.0190	.0152	.0318	−.0938	.0025	.0087	.0044	.1544	.2603	.0886	.6700
					Advertising					
.0548	−.0212	−.0444	.7098	−.0015	−.0121	.0145	−.0135	−.1185	.2934	−.0384
					Dividends					
.0014	−.0011	−.0024	.0070	−.0002	−.0006	.0410	−.0116	−.0195	.8298	−.0501

change in the tax code regarding depreciation will alter the relationship between the actual deterioration in plant and equipment and the figure reported by firms. The coefficient of depreciation in the investment equation, but not the R & D equation, therefore, is not independent of changes in the tax statutes. Because of these difficulties, the following policy discussion should be regarded as suggestive rather than demonstrative.

Some Policy Implications

Consider the effects of an expansionary cut in the personal income tax rate. Both the expectations and liquidity components of the predetermined variables should be affected by this policy. The coefficients of current profits indicate an initial increase in all four outlays. Dividend payments receive the largest increase and R & D the smallest. The coefficients for lagged profits imply that later adjustments by the firm result in substantial increases in R & D and capital investment, an actual reduction in advertising (probably in response to the increased profitability of the competing R & D activity), and another slight increase in dividend payments.[40] The increase in expectations measured by the one-year change in sales variable will result in increases in R & D and investment and decreases in advertising and dividends. The coefficients for lagged depreciation imply a future expansion in investment and R & D in response to the increase in capital replacement needs and flow of depreciation funds induced by increases in current investment. Advertising and dividends will be cut in response to these needs (the latter only trivially). Finally, the coefficients of TRD, our measure of past R & D, imply a substantial stimulus to future investment as a result of present increases in R & D.

The implications of other policy changes can be derived from Table 17.3 in a similar manner. Some particularly interesting observations can be obtained from a closer examination of the coefficients of the industry R & D and advertising variables. R & D and advertising resemble one another in that the successful use of either can result in a firm's domination of a market. If the market structure warrants heavy expenditures for the promotion of a firm's current line of products, it also probably will warrant a heavy investment in the improvement of these products. Similarly, the invention of a new product usually will be followed by an increase in advertising to promote this product. Hence, it is not surprising to find a positive correlation between R & D and advertising in the long run.[41]

In the short run, R & D and advertising are in direct competition for the flow-of-funds available to the firm. Hence, one might expect a temporary cutback in one in response to an increase in a predetermined variable which stimulated the

---

[40] In order to calculate the *net* impact of lagged profits on dividend payments, its coefficient must be added to the product of the lagged dividends' and current profits' coefficients. The reader should recall, also, that to get the after-tax coefficients of profits all figures should be multiplied roughly by a factor of 2.

[41] We interpret cross-section correlations as "long-run correlations." In 1960 the simple correlation between firm R & D and advertising was 0.13 and between industry R & D and advertising 0.44. For further evidence of a positive correlation between R & D and advertising, see National Science Foundation, *Industrial R & D Funds in Relation to Other Economic Variables* (NSF 64-25; Washington, 1964), pp. 41-43.

other. This is what is observed when one examines the coefficients for the industry R & D and advertising variables. In part, the coefficients of these variables measure a firm's response to an increase in expenditures by its competitors. An increase in R & D by a firm's competitors results in an increase in its own R & D and a reduction in its advertising. Analogously, if industry advertising goes up the firm increases its advertising and cuts its R & D. These are very interesting findings. They indicate that while long-run competitive pressures result in a high allocation of funds to R & D and advertising, the short-run response of a firm to an intensification of a specific form of competition—say advertising—is a withdrawal of funds from the competing strategy—R & D.[42]

These findings have most provocative policy implications. Assume the government initiates a matching grant policy to encourage industrial R & D. Assuming the policy does result in some increase in R & D expenditures, there will be two incentives for a firm to increase its R & D; the lure of the matching grant, and the impetus of increased R & D outlays by some of its competitors. Some of the funds used to finance the increase in R & D would come from advertising budgets. A doubly reinforcing way to finance this grant program even might be to levy a tax on advertising.

CONCLUSION

We have attempted to place sufficient emphasis upon the important findings of the study so that no detailed review is necessary. We have had three major goals in this undertaking: (1) to outline a general econometric approach to the analysis of firm behavior which takes explicit account of the complex interactions which characterize this behavior, (2) to illustrate this approach by estimating a model which explains a specific set of firm decisions, and (3) to demonstrate the possible usefulness of such models to both students of firm behavior and those interested in policy issues.

[42] The implications of these two industry index variables are the same for all four years.

Appendix I to Reading 17

The sample consists of 67 firms selected on a cross-section basis from a population which corresponded roughly to all manufacturing firms. It is part of a larger sample of 150 firms which responded to a request for R & D data in the form of a questionnaire resembling closely those used by the National Science Foundation.[43] The definitions appropriate for our R & D variables are, therefore, those of the NSF.[44] Much has been said of the difficulties inherent in defining inventive activity,[45] and a review of this controversy would take up too much space to be appropriately included here. Let us only say in defense of our use of figures reported according to NSF definitions that: (1) these definitions have been employed virtually without change by the NSF since 1956, resulting in concepts which are as consistent over time as any possible alternatives; (2) the NSF's employment of 100 per cent sampling procedures among large firms of each industry assures the researcher that these figures have been recorded annually using the desired set of definitions, by all firms in the sample; (3) the fact that these figures were reported initially in response to a government survey which promised not to reveal the identity of any individual firm should result in

---

[43] National Science Foundation, *Funds for Research and Development in Industry, 1959* (Washington, 1962), pp. 93–96.

[44] *Ibid.*, p. 97.

[45] S. Kuznets, "Inventive Activity: Problems of Definition and Measurement," and comment by Jacob Schmookler; also B. S. Sanders, "Some Difficulties in Measuring Inventive Activity," both in National Bureau of Economic Research, *The Rate and Direction of Inventive Activity, op. cit.*

figures compiled as conscientiously as one can hope for, and minimize any "status bias" appearing in the figures reported to stockholders; and (4) the use of expenditure input figures seems more appropriate in a model which also attempts to explain investment, advertising, and dividend payments, than the alternatives of R & D employment, significant inventions, patents, etc. The R & D figure used as a dependent variable in the model was that reported by the firm as having been conducted in their own laboratories and financed by themselves. The figure

Table 17.4

DISTRIBUTION OF SAMPLE AMONG NSF INDUSTRIES ACCORDING TO FIRM R & D

INDUSTRY NUMBER	INDUSTRY NAME	NUMBER OF FIRMS
1.	Atomic Energy Devices	0
2.	Food and Kindred Products	6
3.	Industrial Inorganic and Organic Chemicals	9
4.	Plastics Materials, Synthetic Resins, Rubber, etc.	5
5.	Drugs	7
6.	Agricultural Chemicals	0
7.	All Other Chemicals	3
8.	Petroleum Refining and Extraction	9
9.	Rubber and Miscellaneous Plastics Products	4
10.	Stone, Clay, and Glass Products	4
11.	Primary Ferrous Products	3
12.	Primary and Secondary Nonferrous Metals	0
13.	Fabricated Metal Products	2
14.	Engines and Turbines	1
15.	Farm Machinery and Equipment	3
16.	Constructions, Mining, and Materials Handling Machinery	3
17.	Metalworking Machinery and Equipment	2
18.	Office, Computing, and Accounting Machinery	2
19.	Other Machinery, Except Electrical	5
20.	Electric Transmission and Distribution Equipment	0
21.	Electrical Industrial Apparatus	0
22.	Electronic Components and Accessories, etc.	6
23.	Other Electrical Machinery Equipment and Supplies	1
24.	Guided Missiles	1
25.	Aircraft and Parts	1
26.	Motor Vehicles and Equipment	5
27.	Other Transportation Equipment	0
28.	Professional and Scientific Equipment, etc.	0
29.	Optical, Surgical and Photographic Instruments, etc.	0
30.	Other Ordinance, Except Guided Missiles	1
31.	Other	10

Source: Industries defined in National Science Foundation, *Funds for Research and Development in Industry 1959* (Washington, 1962), p. 99.
Note: Firms were assumed to be in an industry if at least 25 per cent of their R & D for any of the four sample years was reported in that industry.

used as a predetermined variable in the investment equation was the total amount of R & D undertaken by the firm regardless of the financial source. Almost all of the noncompany financed R & D was government contract work. If the figure for 1956 was not available that for 1957 was substituted. The sample was somewhat biased against heavy government contract work both by the initial sampling selection process and by eliminating any firms for which more than 50 per cent of their R & D was financed by outside sources. It was hoped that this would make our conclusions more applicable to nondefense than to defense oriented R & D. In order to take advantage of the NSF's 100 per cent sampling practice among large firms an additional large firm bias was introduced into the original sampling list. Otherwise it was felt that a reasonably good cross-sectional representation of manufacturing firms was obtained with no pronounced biases in favor of firms which undertake a large amount of R & D, advertising, etc. Table 17.4 groups the firms according to NSF industry definitions.

Advertising expenditure figures refer to outlays for advertising within the major media as reported in *Printer's Ink*.[46] The few firms which did not undertake a sufficient amount of advertising to be included in this survey were given expenditure figures of $500,000.

All other figures referring to individual firm variables were taken either from *Moody's, Standard and Poor's Industry Surveys* or directly from company reports. Investment figures refer to gross capital investment. Depreciation equals depreciation plus depletion. Profits are operating income before taxes. While this variable is less appropriate for a flow-of-funds hypothesis than the after-tax variable, it is thought to be more so for an expectations hypothesis. The correlation between the two is high enough to produce only a trivial statistical difference regardless of which is used. Dividends are cash dividend payments to common stockholders.

So little variation in the industry index variables was present that they were not changed from year to year. The index in the investment equation is gross depreciable assets divided by business receipts.[47] The R & D industry index is company-financed R & D as a percentage of sales for 1959 using NSF industry definition.[48] The industry index for the advertising equation is advertising as a percentage of industry sales.[49]

The 150 firms responding to the R & D questionnaire were the starting point of the sample. The firms were asked to report their R & D figures for 1956–63. All 150 did so for 1963, and only 40 for 1956, with a gradually diminishing number of firms reporting figures for each year in between. In order to have a homogeneous sample, only firms which reported figures for 1957 and the three subsequent years were included in the sample. This greatly reduced the number of usable observations. The *Printer's Ink* figures on advertising are available only through 1960; hence observations for the three most recent years had to be ignored. In general firms were excluded from the analysis because of: (1) failure

[46] *Printer's Ink Advertiser's Guide to Marketing 1961*, pp. 345–70.
[47] Industry definitions conform to SIC two-digit industry definitions. See, U.S. Internal Revenue Service, *Statistics of Income, 1959–60*.
[48] *Funds for Research and Development in Industry, 1959*, op. cit., Table A-22, p. 74.
[49] *Advertising Age*, XXX (Aug. 27, 1962), 201–2.

to report all necessary data for any one year, (2) ten-year growth in sales in excess of 500 per cent (it should be noted that the same growth period 1947–56 was used for all four years to avoid the vagaries brought about by business cycle phenomena), (3) non-company-financed R & D in excess of 50 per cent, and (4) mergers for which no data adjustments were possible.

18
A Dissenting View of Duopoly and Spatial Competition[1]

Nicos E. Devletoglou

The process of competitive product-differentiation has a threefold foundation. A firm in competition aspires to maximum profits by seeking an efficient combination of three economic variables: adjustments over *space*, and changes in both *quality* and *price* of product. Unlike price analysis, however, the theory of locaion or of quality under conditions of imperfect competition has never been a *cause célèbre*.[2] Significantly, too, over the years economists have suffered a grow-

Reprinted from *Economica*, May 1965, pp. 140-160 by permission of the author and publisher.

[1] An earlier version of this paper was presented to Lord Robbins' Seminar at the London School of Economics in 1964. The author has profited from the Seminar's attention and suggestions. Professor R. G. D. Allen's comments, on a different occasion, have also been helpful.

[2] Except for two articles written on the subject several decades ago, spatial competition, in the present context, cannot be said to have attracted to date more attention than has been afforded to it by the occasional deferential references to Professor Hotelling's views on "centre-clustering", in "Stability in Competition", *Economic Journal*, March 1929. See in this connection A. P. Lerner and H. W. Singer, "Some Notes on Duopoly and Spatial Competition", *Journal of Political Economy*, April 1937; A. Smithies, "Optimum Location in Spatial Competition", *Journal of Political Economy*, June 1941; and E. H. Chamberlin, *The Theory of Monopolistic Competition*, eighth edition, Cambridge, Mass., 1962, pp. 260-65. For spatial theory in political science, where the notion of centre-clustering again features prominently, see D. E. Stokes, "Spatial Models of Party Organization", *American Political Science Review*, June 1963.

For some background literature, however, the reader may also wish to consult E. Schneider, "Bemerkungen zu einer Theorie der Raumwirtschaft", *Econometrica*,

ing tendency to regard the concepts of "price competition" and "competition" as synonymous. As a result, the term "spatial competition" is gradually disappearing from our vocabulary, though sporadically one still encounters it in the classroom and in print. But if this anomaly persists, an undesirable imbalance in microeconomic theory may become entrenched. A change in emphasis, therefore, is mandatory. Accordingly, my primary concern in this essay is to stimulate thought and discussion on so deserving a topic, chiefly by presenting the reader with a fresh pattern of analysis. The new analytical apparatus, leading to some interesting conclusions, is introduced below in a manner also suitable for the study of competition in quality.

We open the discussion with a quotation from Professor Chamberlin's summary endorsement of the prevailing views on spatial competition between two sellers. The reference is a convenient one. It contains both a clear statement of, and a typically faithful attachment to, a veteran thesis, in turn the principal target against which this article is directed:

> The fundamental question is whether sellers (of the same commodity) will tend to concentrate at one point or to disperse over the area so as to give a maximum of convenience to the buyers. Let us begin by assuming the buyers to be uniformly distributed; and the problem will be simplified (without affecting the nature of the conclusions) by considering them as distributed along a line instead of over an area. *It has been shown by Professor Hotelling that, where buyers are distributed along such a line, and where there are but two sellers, these latter will, contrary to expectations, locate as close to each other as possible, instead of at the quartile points of the line where convenience to the buyers would be a maximum.* . . . The final equilibrium point may, in fact, be defined with precision. It would be located at the centre of the line, since, if it were elsewhere, the seller whose market were smaller would move to the other side of his rival, and such moves would continue until both were established at the mid-point. This is a conclusion of great importance.[3]

January, 1935; W. Lewis, "Competition in Retail Trade", *Economica*, November 1945; E. M. Hoover, *The Location of Economic Activity*, New York, 1948; S. Enke, "Equilibrium among Spatially Separated Markets", *Econometrica*, January 1951; P. A. Samuelson, "Spatial Price Equilibrium and Linear Programming," *American Economic Review*, June 1952; A. Loesch, *The Economics of Location*, New Haven, 1954; Stefan Valavanis, "Loesch on Location", *American Economic Review*, September 1955; W. Isard, *Location and Space-Economy*, New York, 1956; M. L. Greenhut, *Plant Location in Theory and Practice*, Chapel Hill, 1956, and *Microeconomics and the Space Economy*, Chicago, 1963; E. W. Smykay and others, *Physical Distribution Management*, New York, 1961; V. L. Smith, "Minimization of Economic Rent in Spatial Price Equilibrium", *Review of Economic Studies*, February 1963; E. S. Mills and M. R. Lav, "A Model of Market Areas with Free Entry", *Journal of Political Economy*, June 1964; and T. Takayama and G. G. Judge, "Equilibrium among Spatially Separated Markets: A Reformulation", *Econometrica*, October 1964.

[3] *Op. cit.*, p. 260, my italics. Chamberlin goes on next to disagree with the Hotelling thesis under conditions of triopoly. Where three sellers make up the market, he argues in favour of definitive dispersion, contesting Hotelling's explicit belief that centre-clustering recurs. Neither solution, however, is satisfactory because, under

An operational mechanism capable of questioning the significance of the Hotelling thesis on duopoly, and establishing an alternative formulation of the equilibrium process, is set forth here. The analytical background required for this purpose is developed in the second and third sections. It is then put into use in the fourth section, where a concise statement of the proposed thesis is presented. We shall thus be enabled to demonstrate in a novel manner why competition over space between duopolists may well discourage centre-clustering—and produce instead results shown to favour community convenience, even where we have product standardization. In the first and last sections we discuss assumptions and conclusions, respectively.

Basically, I dispense with the customary assumption of a linear market, or "highway" restriction; and, generalizing the interpretation of the competitive plane, conclude that centre-clustering cannot be said to imply a stable location equilibrium. The various other assumptions employed also contribute to a more realistic setting, and allow us to discount best the allegedly inherent tendency in spatial competition for contestants to cluster at the centre. This is particularly so with the negatively-sloping demand curve postulated here, an approach in distinct contrast to Professor Hotelling's addiction to an infinitely inelastic flow of demand. Briefly, the familiar argument that maximization of each competitor's "hinterland" is the firm's main objective, leading to general equilibrium at the centre, will prove untenable. Equally problematic will emerge Professor Smithies' variation of the same argument, or that equilibrium at the centre is stable "if one assumes that each competitor sells only in his own hinterland and does not attempt to invade the hinterland of his rivals".[4] As it is not difficult for the reader, however, to familiarize himself with the limited literature, I prefer not to expatiate on it in this article. Finally, the method in this study is abstract rather than empirical. Field-work and further research, along the new lines suggested below, are required to test the significance of our purely theoretical contribution.

ASSUMPTIONS

(1) We imagine any delimited *area* populated by evenly scattered and perfectly (i.e. linearly) mobile consumer units.

(2) Consumers behave consistently, enjoy adequate knowledge, and minimize travelling distance (transport costs) subject to some *minimum sensibile* constraint of indifference. Quite simply, the principle put forth is that some positive minimum, however small or large, exists for the consumer where the difference in distance between patronizing one store rather than the other can be axiomatized as inconsequential, and thus too weak a criterion for practical choice or revealed preference. The consumer's postulated apathy toward applying the traditional economic calculus "to the

---

their particular assumptions, fluctuations between the two extremes are most likely to occur. This is recognized by R. G. Lipsey, *An Introduction to Positive Economics*, 1963, pp. 252–6. Unfortunately, Lipsey's analysis is in agreement with the accepted view, questioned in this essay, that clustering at the centre is inevitable in a duopolistic market.

[4] Smithies, *loc. cit.*, p. 434.

letter" beyond a given stage may be conveniently interpreted as the effect of discontinuities in utility functions.[5]

(3) Consumers within what I define below as the "doubtful area", or region of uncertainty, are subject to a "fashion effect". Further, the probability of mass imitation is said to rise the greater that area. The likelihood of serious inventory difficulties, as we show below, prescribes the adoption of this assumption, in so far as an even division at all times of the total market between the two sellers is ruled out. Nor would an even division of the total clientele in the *long run* be a consolation. It is essential, we see, to cover against the eventuality of an explicit economic need to have a steady stream of customers over a shorter period of time.

(4) Consumers as a whole optimally frequent a seller only where the latter is "best" located. In spatial competition a store's better proximity to the consumer is the equivalent of a price-cut in price competition.

(5) Transport costs vary in direct proportion to travelling distance; or, more generally, distance is measured in terms of cost of transport.

(6) We have only two firms. They sell at common prices an identical commodity whose price elasticity of demand is negative and finite, and whose income elasticity of demand is positive and finite.

(7) Prices and everything else but location "remain equal": firms vary sales only by varying their location, and are symmetrically mobile along a given axis. Symmetry, to begin with, is introduced in order to avoid an otherwise serious diagrammatical predicament. More basically, of course, symmetry is essential because only such a process of adjustment allows for full maximization of profits, *as long as both firms are taken to be mobile*. Asymmetrical reciprocation is of necessity inferior to symmetrical reactions to the moves of one's competitor. As will become clear from the new pattern of analysis, asymmetrical adjustment is tantamount to near-instantaneous symmetrical clustering at the centre, where a smaller total market obtains, and inventory difficulties, together with the doubtful area, generally reach a maximum. Nor does the suspension of symmetry, however, alter the conclusions of this study. Such a move, on the other hand, would amount to a blemish in the economics of our model—except where one of

---

[5] For example, to put it differently, let a consumer have to travel ten miles to go to one store, or ten miles but one step, as it were, to go to the other. Next, let the *difference* in distance travelled be measured along the x-axis, and consumer disutility along the y-axis. Our postulate explains that an upward-sloping disutility curve results, cutting the x-axis at some *positive* interval, equal to the prevailing *minimum sensibile* (or one step in this case), where this *minimum* remains permanently constrained away from nought. The attraction of the new principle, it will be seen, lies primarily in its ability to "humanize" the analysis considerably. Inasmuch as knowledge is normally imperfect, we have formalized, in essence, the reasonable notion that checking a pile of, say, pennies to establish whether one possesses 10,000 or 9,999 coins is confirmed nonsense for most human beings. In addition, we understand that random factors outside the system will also qualify the *minimum sensibile*. Lastly, it is necessary to note here that our model will continue to function smoothly as long as the *minimum sensibile* is *any* positive number, and even if the *minimum* under consideration should ever become an exceedingly small number.

the two firms, the new entrant, is free to seek a spatial optimum on the assumption that the other is permanently assigned to a fixed location. Thus, in sole harmony with the analytic style of previous models, we recognize as feasible the ability of both firms to readjust their locations freely. In this respect the device of the highly mobile "ice-cream stand" proves an excellent windfall. But the reader may also note that an efficient decision-making unit normally makes it its business nowadays to enjoy a constant flow of adequate knowledge about pending moves of competitors.

(8) Profits and sales are linearly related, and marginal revenue is equated to constant marginal cost (the latter long-term for simplicity). Buyers alone bear the cost of transport.

(9) With no external economies, and under conditions of market homogeneity, no groups of consumers need be wooed differentially, and product standardization is complete.

(10) Sellers maximize profits considering both a maximum share of the market, and maximum total sales for the industry. I elaborate briefly on this assumption because it is central to the development of the general argument. Any competitive firm, as we know, has three ways open to it for increasing its sales and profits: (a) securing a larger share of a given market; (b) maintaining that share, and endeavouring to enlarge instead the market in the aggregate in order to increase total sales; or (c) aiming at some combination of both. To reach a solution of centre-clustering, therefore, the analysis would have to be based, among other things, on the unnecessarily restrictive assumption that total sales are always fixed—and the two competing firms then said to be intent on enlarging their share of a given, non-expandable, market in order to increase profits. Such an approach, however, is unrealistic because total sales, and hence the firms' profits, vary significantly depending upon the locations chosen by the two firms. Indeed, there will always be some locations which minimize transport costs for the community as a whole, and thus make possible increases in total sales for the industry by exploiting released purchasing power. Hence, the income elasticity of demand is given due attention here.[6]

THE DOUBTFUL AREA

The "Minimum Sensibile" and the Hyperbolic Boundaries

We let the larger of the two circles, or the discontinuous lines forming a rectangle, in Figure 18.1, denote some delimited space defining the extent of the

---

[6] It is not difficult to perceive that, given a clustered equilibrium anywhere on the plane, by removing one of the two stores to any other (dispersed) position we are necessarily lowering the average distance travelled for the community as a whole. We discuss this basic principle below and show that *minimum* average transport costs are reached through optimal dispersion. In fact, tracing the implications of this obvious deduction, we conclude that maximum disposable income for the community must be maximally conducive to maximum profits and sales. Yet both in Chamberlin (*op. cit.*, p. 260) and in Smithies (*loc. cit.*, p. 432) concern over the distance travelled by the community is incidental. Neither author has appreciated sufficiently the significance of the "gravitational" properties of the average distance minima.

market or town under consideration. Ignoring the *minimum sensibile*, or allowing it for the moment to be zero, if we consider a consumer located, say, at (X_b, Y_b) it is clear that he would choose in favour of store B. He travels least to get to B, and gets standard service there. Similarly (X_a, Y_a) prefers store A. Hence, the

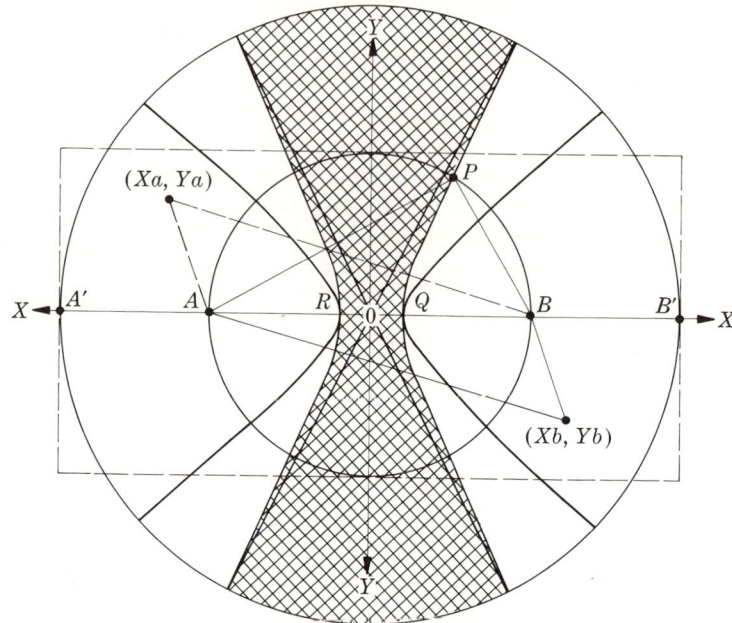

Figure 18.1

reasonable conjecture that consumer units located to the right of the $(\pm)$ y-axis are likely to prefer B; just as consumer units located to the left thereof must prefer A. Only those consumers remain undecided who live on the y-axis. Clearly, too, this division obtains regardless of the particular (symmetrical) locations assumed by the two firms.

As soon as we introduce into the picture the *minimum sensibile*, however, or constrain it away from nought, the pattern of the distribution of patronage becomes much less obvious. We gather at once that A and B will not be inclined to locate themselves anywhere at random. The central question we thus pose is: If the two stores are assumed to move symmetrically along a given axis, what direction will spatial competition between them take, and what are the main welfare implications?

We take as given the location of two stores A and B (where $OQ = a$, and $OB = t$), distance $2t$ apart, so that we have $A(-t, O)$ and $B(t, O)$. Next, we assume $2a$ to be the *minimum sensibile*, or the consumer's critical difference of distances for preference between A and B (i.e., if $BP - AP > 2a$, consumer at P goes to store A; if $AP - BP > 2a$, he goes to store B; and if $AP - BP \leqslant 2a$, there is no preference). It then follows that the locus of points P dividing the no-preference region from the preference region will be given by a fixed hyperbola —in turn, a result of unique significance for the kinetics of our model. Essentially, the discovery means that some area of uncertainty or indifference must exist, descriptively called "doubtful", and that *at any given time its form and extent depends upon the actual degree of dispersion undertaken by the two sellers.* Better still, we understand that the boundaries of this area are defined throughout by sets of confocal hyperbolæ whose behaviour is governed consistently by the spatial adjustment of the two foci (or two sellers) in the system. Considering Figure 18.1, therefore, our no-preference region is defined by the expression, $PA - PB = 2a$, which immediately gives (where $t > a$) the pure hyperbola.[7]

$$[x^2/a^2 - y^2/(t^2-a^2)] = 1, \text{ with asymptotes } y = \pm \sqrt{(t^2 - a^2)/a^2}\, x.$$

Hence, we have the mechanism yielding our shaded or doubtful area, pictured

[7] Where $PA^2 = (t + x)^2 + y^2$; $PB^2 = (t - x)^2 + y^2$; and $PA^2 - PB^2 = 4tx$, our no-preference region is defined by: $|PA - PB| = 2a$. We then have

$$PA^2 = PB^2 \pm 4aPB + 4a^2$$
$$PA^2 - PB^2 - 4a^2 = \pm 4aPB$$
$$(PA^2 - PB^2 - 4a^2)^2 = 16a^2 PB^2$$
$$(4tx - 4a^2)^2 = 16a^2[(t - x)^2 + y^2]$$
$$(t^2x^2 - 2a^2tx + a^4) = a^2(t^2 - 2tx + x^2 + y^2)$$
$$(t^2 - a^2)x^2 - a^2y^2 = a^2(t^2 - a^2),$$

thus giving the *pure hyperbola* $[x^2/a^2 - y^2/(t^2 - a^2)] = 1$.

The reader will note that it has been found necessary, mostly for achieving clarity of exposition, to simplify matters and take in this model the *minimum sensibile* as a fixed positive number regardless of distance travelled, and identical for all consumers. Relaxation of this postulate, whether in the direction of introducing (*a*) a uniformly or otherwise varying relationship to distance travelled by the consumer; and/or (*b*) varying evaluations *per capita*, and in turn independent of distance travelled, would seriously complicate the analysis—to little, if any, advantage. Although the implications of the model would persist, the distinction between our two contrasting regions would no longer be as clear-cut. For example, let us take the *minimum sensibile* as a number independent of distance travelled, but varying *per capita*. We could then go on and consider the straightforward supposition that the lower bound of some random variable v' has a probability density over the population, and denote by v the expected (or true average) lower bound. For an estimate of v, and equally simply, we might then use the sample mean (or median, mode, etc.):

$$\bar{v} = \frac{i = 1 \overset{n}{\Sigma} v'i}{n}, \quad [v'i]i = 1, \ldots n$$

applying a set of n random observations on v'. Indeed, our estimator would become yet more efficient in various ways, such as by stratifying the population (say by distance from centre, possibly sub-divided into concentric circles), and using the stratified mean as our estimate of v. Whatever our results, however, we would always find it most perplexing to present them diagrammatically. For the distinction between the doubtful area and the rest of the plane then becomes difficult, as some consumers shown within the area of uncertainty would really lie outside it, and *vice versa*. It has been found best, therefore, to introduce the principle of the *minimum sensibile* as was done above, and thus convey the message of the study both simply and more effectively.

as a "hyperbolic fan", and engulfing the set of all those consumer units said to be indifferent between patronizing either one of the two stores. Hence, too, we have the asymptotic properties of the system, shown below, which define the "beam" or particular "opening" assumed at any one time by the doubtful area.[8] The spatial adjustment of the two competing firms is necessarily causal, therefore, and accounts for the behaviour of all possible "duets" of hyperbolæ in the map.

The Basic Kinetic Concept

In order to clarify the significance of what has been introduced so far, we continue with the suggestion that the parameters a and t can be changed in a variety of interesting ways. Naturally, we assume here a fixed (consumers' pattern of discrimination), with t (the distance separating the two sellers) increasing as the two stores move apart.[9] Where such a relationship obtains, the slope of the asymptotes, $\pm \sqrt{(t^2 - a^2)/a^2}$, rises inevitably: thus indicating that the system of asymptotes, and hence the doubtful area, closes up via progressive store-dispersion, and *vice versa*. The construction is fundamental. It endows our competitive plane with a set of hyperbolæ, always through fixed R and Q, becoming *flatter* (steeper asymptotes) as t *rises*, or as the two firms disperse. Conversely, it confirms that *through progressive falls in the value of t the doubtful area opens up until it reaches its maximum with centre-clustering, or where the two foci degenerate to one focal point.*

With *one* focal point, the entire region which society occupies becomes doubtful. As the two foci close in toward the centre, the increasingly more curved branches of the new hyperbolæ which emerge reveal the actual pattern pursued by the spreading uncertainty. It is essential, however, to understand that the entire area becomes doubtful at an even earlier stage. This is because *complete* uncertainty is also generated where we have *insufficient* dispersion. Clearly, given the *minimum sensibile* preference constraint, $2a$ (or RQ), it follows that as soon as the two foci come to lie exactly on positions R and Q, respectively, the whole

[8] Given any degree of store dispersion, our doubtful area consists of the *whole* shaded segment lying between the branches of the appropriate two quadratics, and *not* only of that encompassed by the two straight line asymptotes from the origin, O, to the relevant two curves. The properties of hyperbolæ disallow tangents, as points of tangency with straight lines through the centre are reached invariably at infinity. This is important. The reader is reminded further that confocal hyperbolæ consider the distance between two foci as regarded from any (third) point on and along them. We know that in Figure 18.1 the difference between distances AP and BP is necessarily constant for any point P on the hyperbola in question. This simple mathematical property is the cornerstone of the mechanics of our model.

[9] Two other cases would be: (1) a and t increase in proportion, with $t = \lambda a$, where λ is fixed. Then $y = \pm \sqrt{\lambda^2 - 1}\ x$ gives the relevant sets of asymptotes, with slopes fixed as $\pm \sqrt{\lambda^2 - 1}$. A system of hyperbolæ of fixed asymptotes and of a generally steep nature emerges, therefore, as the two firms disperse progressively, cutting the x-axis at increasingly greater intervals (and *not* passing only through fixed R and Q). It should then be as though "stretching" the map would "straighten" all hyperbolæ, whilst letting it shrink would cause the opposite to occur. (2) t fixed (stores in given positions) and a increases (increasing lack of discrimination by consumers). We then have a system of confocal hyperbolæ for boundary regions, such that all curves move outwards with flatter asymptotes as a increases.

region emerges as totally doubtful. The branches of the "hyperbolic fan" are again perfectly collapsed along (featured asymptotic to) the x-axis: and the difference in distance between patronizing either one of the two sellers becomes equal to, or less than, the *minimum sensibile* for every consumer in the market.

Conversely, the farther away from the centre, the more the doubtful area is being eliminated, and the better each store is assured of gaining its maximum share, or one-half, of the market. For any consumer the difference in distance between going to A or to B is thus accentuated, a conclusion again dictated by the system's asymptotic properties. In the limit (i.e., extreme bi-polar outskirts of the town with respect to the x-axis), the doubtful area is reduced to its minimum. As the consumer has been assumed indifferent between the two sellers if the difference in distance in patronizing either one should be equal to, or less than, $2a$ (or RQ), consumer choice automatically proves easier where the two firms disperse. The difference between going to either firm becomes more pronounced in this manner alone. At some extreme outskirt positions A' and B', therefore, we expect the doubtful area to reach its minimum. Represented geometrically, that minimum is given by a rectangle. The region of uncertainty is then encompassed by two confocal hyperbolæ emerging through R and Q, with A' and B' as their focal points, and their branches asymptotic to straight vertical lines through R and Q, respectively. Of course, we may or may not want to assume that consumers live on the ($\pm$) y-axis.

Individual and Aggregate Uncertainty

We conclude this section with the explanation that we choose to understand by the shaded area a region of uncertainty not only on the basis of *individual* consumer uncertainty of choice, but, in addition, in terms of *aggregate* consumer uncertainty of choice. This surface is taken to quantify uncertainty, from the viewpoint of the two stores, as far as everyone enveloped by it is concerned. Uncertainty continues to persist, in short, notwithstanding the possible contention that if taken as a whole (and, therefore, if believed to involve large enough numbers of consumers) the no-preference region might divide evenly (split automatically into one-half for each) between the two stores in question. Anticipating the arguments presented in the second part of the fourth section, below, at least two reasons come to mind why we may consider it as singularly unlikely that the said probability distribution must follow, or that it ever should apply in this context.

First, marketing experience of revealed preference patterns could be invoked, and would probably confirm, that where some initial wave of customers choose, at random or otherwise, to patronize any one store in particular, the possibility arises that a *fashion* or *imitation effect* then comes into operation, and patronage quickly snowballs. Worse yet, however, even if the equal division were at all likely to occur, it might well extend over an uneconomic time-period, or one causing serious inventory anomalies to the firms. This is discussed in the fourth section. An equal division of the total clientele between the two stores in the *long run* cannot be of much use to the firm with an interest in enjoying a steady stream of customers over a shorter period of time. And there are many examples of such cases in the real world. I am prompted to underline, therefore, the possibility of sudden and random mass "walk-outs" in some *one* direction—as long as the doubtful area remains large. Hence, I postulate a pivotal rôle for the uncertainty-per-individual factor, and later emphasize the serious concern which this factor creates in the aggregate for the two sellers. The economist's intuition, in fact, would seem to suggest (the existing "standardization" assumption notwithstanding) that our doubtful area probably breeds such band-wagon phenomena; and that the latter become, in turn, the rule rather than the exception the larger that area of uncertainty.

Second, again invoking market experience, it appears no less useful to suggest that even where the equal division takes place in a manner satisfying our foregoing reservations, the result may still prove inadequate. For the two sellers, as I postulate further, are not interested only arithmetically in some given share of the market—or regardless, that is, of their clientele's composition per unit-time and unit-space. They display instead a market preference for serving consistently the same, or some very moderately varying, mix of the total consumer force to which they cater. Inasmuch, therefore, as each new (and, at best, only remotely equal) division of the market between the two contestants consists necessarily of a different set of customers, the result will always prove disagreeable to our firms. Both psychological and technical considerations are relevant here, and especially where product maintenance or servicing is concerned. Hence, our twofold assumption remains throughout that (a) the doubtful area portrays the uncertainty obtaining with respect both to individual consumers taken separately and/or all consumers taken as a whole; and, by implication, that (b) the two firms are anxious to keep that area at some optimum minimum, as we see below in the fourth section.

THE AVERAGE DISTANCE MINIMA AND NEW ENTRY

From the discussion in the preceding pages it cannot reasonably be deduced that the two firms will enjoy any real advantage by moving off to the extreme outskirts of the x-axis. This observation holds even though we may have shown that the doubtful area can be reduced progressively to its rectangular minimum in this manner. Bi-polarity will generally prove uneconomical, and dispersion may be expected to cease, therefore, at some earlier stage, as will be shown in the remainder of the study.

Average Distance Minima

We begin with the essential observation that some symmetrical positions, duly dispersed (rather than clustered at the centre, or at R and Q), do exist, fixed at approximately A and B in our main diagram, *where average distance travelled is at a minimum*. This important constraint is certainly obvious to the eye, but not as easy to prove mathematically. Its validity was established formally with the Monte Carlo method of random simulation—and irrespective, of course, of the *minimum sensibile*. The exercise was performed on the London University "Mercury" computer, and confirmed the notion that for any market area some *dispersed* symmetrical positions will always minimize average distance travelled. A value of approximately 0·4 times the radius was obtained for each semi-circular market. In the alternative case of a rectangular market area, and one consisting of two square regions, minimum average distance travelled occurs at approximately the centre of each regional square.

It will be of interest to the reader to trace this useful conclusion in another way. Taking first the case of a circular market area, we let S be the average distance walked, evaluated for a quadrant of a circle of radius r, over a uniform distribution of population. We thus write:

$$S = \int_0^r \int_0^{r^2-y^2} \sqrt{(x-m)^2 + y^2}(dxdy).$$

And we then solve for the minimum by putting $\partial S/\partial m = 0$:

$$-1/2\{r\sqrt{r^2 + (r-m)^2} + (r-m)^2 \log[\sqrt{r^2/(r^2-m^2)} + r/(r-m)]$$
$$-r\sqrt{(r^2m^2)} - m^2 \log[\sqrt{r^2/m^2 + 1} + r/m]\} = 0.$$

Using Newton's Approximation, the value which satisfies this equation is $m \cong 0\cdot 42 \times r$.

Further, in the case of a rectangular market area, we consider (Figure 18.2) the top right-hand quarter of a rectangle, diagram below, and consider next moving from the centre of line EF, b, to b'. It follows that Area C is indifferent about the move. Area B loses as much as Area D gains, and *vice versa:* i.e. $(B + D)$ is indifferent about the move. If, and only if, b is the mid-point for a move of any magnitude in either direction will there be an Area A which suffers a net loss. If b' is to the right of b, A will be to the left, and *vice versa*. Hence, b, the midpoint, is the optimal point.

Given, therefore, the existence of our average distance minima, we shall be led to infer below that the two stores do not disperse maximally. Bi-polarity emerges almost as disadvantageous as centre-clustering—although average distance travelled is at its maximum with centre-clustering.[10] But this decisive consideration

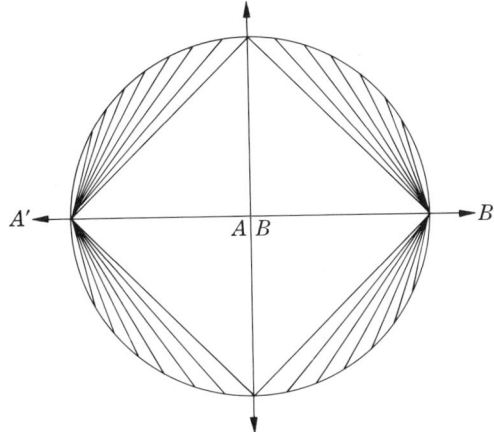

[10] Extreme dispersion is less undesirable than centre-clustering. For any area the average distance travelled by the consumer will be greater where the two firms are clustered rather than maximally dispersed. Our diagram is self-explanatory, where any given market area is imagined to be inhabited by a series of, say, concentric "population rings", each n distance apart and populated identically. If the two firms cluster at the centre, the entire diagram, illustrating any one such "ring", becomes completely covered with straight lines from the circle's periphery to the centre, depicting accordingly total distance travelled as per the population ring in question. On the other hand, it is equally clear that extreme dispersion is responsible or the rectangular portion "saved", or left intact in the diagram.

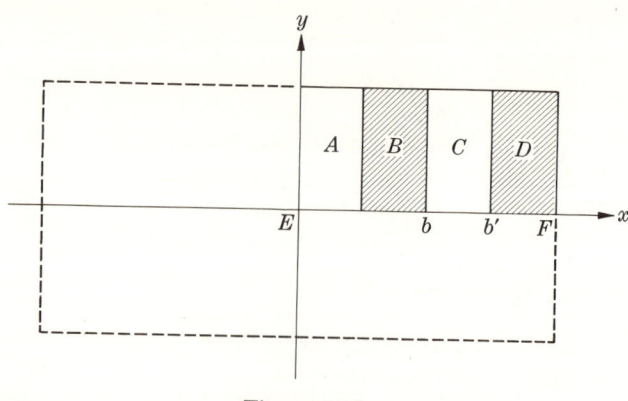

Figure 18.2

figures more prominently in the next section, where the two sellers end up efficiently located under the gravitational pull of the two average distance minima.

New Entry

Extreme symmetrical dispersion, however, is always undesirable on a further argument. The explanation which follows holds notwithstanding (*a*) the consideration that *two* nuclei of maximum satisfaction for the "neighbouring lucky few" (as opposed to one nucleus in the case of centre-clustering) are created through *any* dispersed positions; and/or (*b*) the possible claim that as long as they each retain half of a (smaller) market, the two sellers may just as well disregard the implications of a poorly served consumer force. The overriding argument here is obvious: namely, that the probability of new entry is also maximized where dispersion is allowed to approach its maximum. For the likelihood of some store C entering the market cannot be negligible where a huge spatial gap is encouraged between the two firms. (The same consideration pertains to the clustered position, due to the exaggerated "spatial availability" that such a location also implies.) Therefore, even though the doubtful area can be reduced to its minimum by persistent symmetrical dispersion, we already anticipate with reasonable certainty that the competing duopolists will tend to settle in the vicinity of the two average distance minima. The argument is finalized in the section which follows.

CENTRE-CLUSTERING VS. DISPERSION

We have now developed the various principles essential for the operation of our model. We begin, therefore, this section with a brief analytical statement of the proposed thesis. As different results obtain, however, depending upon whether or not we introduce inventory costs into the picture, the first half of the section is divided into two parts, the first excluding and the second including these costs. The sub-section including inventory costs should be understood as providing a supplement mainly to 2(i), 2(iii), 3(i) and 3(iii), below. Together with considerations relating to the average distance minima and new entry, the inventory-costs argument contributes heavily to the defence of the thesis against centre-clustering. Also, in both of these two broad parts we deal in terms of three relevant cases: government control, collusion and competition. In each case we list briefly the sets of factors conducive to centre-clustering, dispersion and bi-polarity. The section ends with a descriptive (mathematical) presentation of the solution mechanism. Equilibrium, we find, is generally reached at some dispersed positions, such as A and B in Figure 18.1, rather than at the centre. An explicit solution, however, is not advanced. Specific results will naturally vary widely depending upon the particular properties ascribed to the chosen constraints on the firms' utility functions.[11]

The Analysis: Inventory Costs Excluded

1. Government Control

Locations can be easily dictated in whatever fashion the authorities see fit. As such, therefore, this case is of no especial interest.

2. Collusion

Centre-Clustering

(i) The solution of centre-clustering may be sought through disregard of (a) the total-sales-for-industry component of profit-maximization; and (b) the notion, even where shares are fixed, that the complete uncertainty implied by maximization of each firm's hinterland can be disadvantageous, inasmuch as centre-clustering always drives the doubtful area to an automatic maximum.[12]

Dispersion

(ii) Where shares are *fixed* (and whatever the division undertaken there can be no adverse effects to the model), dispersion is naturally pursued to increase total sales for the industry. The average distance minima will be approached, therefore, subject to (a) the income elasticity of demand; (b) the price elasticity of demand; and (c) the possible higher frequency of patronage.[13] (iii) Dispersion up to, and possibly beyond, the average distance minima will also be initiated on

---

[11] The actual shape of the market is also relevant here. For instance, a "tall" rectangular market (height much greater than width) would hardly induce the same degree of store dispersion as a "long" rectangular market (width much greater then height). Such matters, however, are not explored here. Together with a set of comprehensive quantitative tests, they would provide ample material for a further study. (See Conclusion.)

[12] Far from being a theoretical caprice, our *minimum sensibile* threshold is a fundamental concept. Elegantly reflecting the functional rationality of human beings (or, alternatively, formalizing consumer "irrationality"), it warns that the maximization of each firm's hinterland can be a very undesirable practice. For better or worse, in short, men are not robots in this theoretical construction.

[13] The observation implies that total *visits* to the stores reach a maximum in the vicinity of the average distance minima. For we suspect that one does not normally get into the "habit" of travelling many miles to reach, of all things, a store. Whereas if a store is least inconveniently located the probability that the average customer will develop a *taste* for maximum visits naturally becomes greater.

the basis of evaluating the behaviour of the consumer force enveloped by the doubtful area. The firms then consider (a) the "fashion effect"—where unfavourable mass imitation will be more likely the greater the area of indifference; and/or (b) the same-mix-of-clientele consideration. For psychological or technical reasons, and depending largely upon the type of product sold, a firm may be interested in the same share of a given body of customers, but also in an extended market. (iv) Further, the probability of new entry is highest with centre-clustering as "spatial availability" for new sellers is thereby maximized, both topographically and by way of the consequent bad service (highest transport costs for the community). Hence, an additional tendency to disperse exists, always subject to the consideration that extreme dispersion, or bi-polarity, can also be disadvantageous. (v) The final incentive to reject centre-clustering and proceed to disperse is twofold, and will come through (a) the realization that centre-clustering becomes conspicuously open to possible anti-trust sanctions since it maximizes public inconvenience [the same would apply to extreme dispersion in 2(iii)]; and (b) the apprehension that certain costs (rents, etc.) are usually highest in the immediate vicinity of the "city centre", whilst prices offered to the consumer might have to be reduced to compensate for the rise in average distance travelled.

Bi-polarity

(vi) Extreme dispersion is rendered possible by 2(i), 2(iii), 2(v)b; but is incompatible with 2(ii), 2(iv), 2(v)a.

3. Competition

Centre-Clustering

(i) Equilibrium at the centre is again unsatisfactory because it carries no guarantee of the maximization of profits. A possible, but improbable, maximization of each firm's *share* of the market is coupled with an unwise disregard of the total-sales consideration. In addition, the highly dangerous maximization of the doubtful area persists of necessity.

Dispersion

(ii) The possibility is always present that profits may increase through increasing total sales for the industry. The realized degree of dispersion, however, depends upon whether profits would be greater through (a) higher total sales [with the three relevant variables accordingly operative, above 2(ii)], accompanied by a *possible* decline in the share, than they would be (b) by accepting whatever share obtains and foregoing the greater total of industry sales. (iii) The clustered position holds our doubtful area at its maximum, and a further tendency to disperse will depend, therefore, upon the extent of pressure coming from the two relevant variables here, as in 2(iii). (iv) Considerations of new entry will be the same as above, 2(iv). (v) Finally, dispersion may occur in order (a) to avoid maximal inconvenience to the public, and thus various possibly undesirable consequences of government intervention; and (b) to keep low certain costs such as rents, as in 2(v).

Bi-polarity

(iv) Extreme dispersion is rendered possible by 3(i), 3(iii) and 3(v)b; but is incompatible with 3(ii), 3(iv), 3(v)a.

The Analysis: Inventory Costs Included

The inventory-costs argument, here set forth briefly, is vital. It affords several interesting considerations relating to the significance of the extent of the doubtful area. Inventory costs constitute the most important reason, perhaps, why the firms will be interested in keeping the doubtful area to some optimum low level.

1. Government Control

Intervention could keep costs to a minimum by specifying which half of the consumer force enclosed in the area of uncertainty should continue to buy from one firm or the other.

2. Collusion

The cartel, on the other hand, cannot specify which individuals are to buy from which firm. Thus if, beyond the inventory period, fewer than half buy from one firm, the problem arises that although the costs of *total* inventory remain constant, the firms are faced with the cost of moving goods between themselves. We then perceive (i) a *centripetal* force, viz. the closer together the two firms, the lower the cost of transport between them; (ii) a *centrifugal* force, viz. the closer together the two firms, the larger the doubtful area: and the greater, therefore, the possibilities of sales switching outside the inventory period—and hence the greater the probability of given quantities of goods having to be sent from one firm to the other. Lastly, (iii) we bear in mind that total sales may become lower (income effects, etc.) as the two firms move outward and beyond the average distance minima.

It thus follows that according as the consideration in (i) exceeds the considerations in (ii) and (iii), the two firms locate closer together than in the original (non-inventory) optimal positions, and conversely.

3. Competition

As the firms do not co-operate, consideration 2(i) above is excluded. We write, therefore: (i) if, beyond the inventory period, fewer than half the total clientele in the doubtful area buy from one firm—and although over the "year" each firm may expect with confidence its maximum share, or half of the total—an outward movement of the two firms reduces their inventory costs. (ii) Again, however, an outward movement beyond the average distance minima may lower total sales and profits.

Thus if (i) is more significant than (ii), some outward movement, and one possibly persisting even beyond the optimal locations required socially, will yield the true equilibrium; whereas if, on the other hand, (i) is equal to or less than (ii), the two firms may well locate precisely at the two average distance minima, respectively.

The Analysis: Circular Distribution of Equilibria

In this final part of the section we begin with the solution of our problem in two-dimensional diagrammatical form, and conclude with a very brief, but more general, algebraic statement. The latter formulation will include the three variables which have been found to be the main relevant factors (doubtful area, average distance travelled by the community, and new entry). The reader can easily add more detail, however, on the basis of the simple framework which has been set out in this article.

1. The Geometric Representation

To start with, we visualize a situation where the two firms taken to be, say, maximally apart at A' and B' respectively (in Figure 18.1), proceed to discriminate in favour of positions closer to the two average distance minima. Both firms choose to operate on the basis of some "swap" rate between magnitudes relating to the doubtful area, the average distance travelled by consumers, and considerations of new entry. Each alternative position is evaluated in terms of the different degrees of utility which it is thought to yield. Clearly, by moving away from the extreme outskirt positions and toward A and B (by assumption at no extra cost), profits and sales are bound to be increasing. More people have to travel less, the doubtful area increases insignificantly at first, and the threat of new entry is reduced. Approaching, therefore, the two average distance minima, an optimal limit is to be sought, and a determinate solution found. It will lie where the two sellers best balance the threat of new entry with the position of having the greatest number of well-served customers (i.e. customers required to travel least), and also with the largest increase in the doubtful area which they see fit to tolerate. There, of course, profits reach their maximum. If for any reason, however, calculations prove to be erroneous, and the two firms overshoot the (spatial) optima, the tendency to converge unduly toward the centre can soon be corrected. Progressive dispersal "backwards" will then continue until profits are restored to their maximum.

Restating the matter from the opposite starting-point, in order to express the solution in diagrammatic form, let C and D (in Figure 18.3) stand for the certainty (*not* doubtful) area and for the average distance travelled by consumers, respectively. Thus the object of the firms is to maximize the internally-constrained function U where $U = U(C, D)$ with $\partial U/\partial C = 0$, $\partial U/\partial D = 0$, and where

$$\partial^2 U/\partial C^2 < 0 \begin{vmatrix} \partial^2 U/\partial C & \partial U/\partial C \partial D \\ \partial U/\partial C \partial D & \partial^2 U/\partial D \end{vmatrix} > 0.$$

Upward-rising indifference curves emerge where C and D are measured on the x-axis and y-axis, respectively, and where these two variables are functions of the analogous positions of the two firms on the x-axis. Utility is expressed along the invisible (third) axis looking straight into one's eye as one looks at the origin, O. It is equally clear that for any symmetrical locations of the two firms some area of certainty (which may be zero) obtains together with some average distance (which cannot be zero) travelled by the consumers. But we know that as the two focal points disperse along the x-axis, and away from the centre, the certainty area automatically increases; whereas, on the contrary, the average distance travelled by consumers begins to fall. We know, too, that this distance reaches its minimum at some positions A and B (in Figure 18.1), beyond which points it tends to rise. Hence, we have our TT' curve, which illustrates this simple relationship between C and D, and affords the relevant tangential solution, E, with the self-explanatory co-ordinates OC' and OD'. It is noteworthy, next, that equilibrium E lies to the right of the minimum point on the TT' curve, thus indicating that segment AB (and, therefore, any other relatively more "clustered" position) is incompatible with the equilibrium solution.

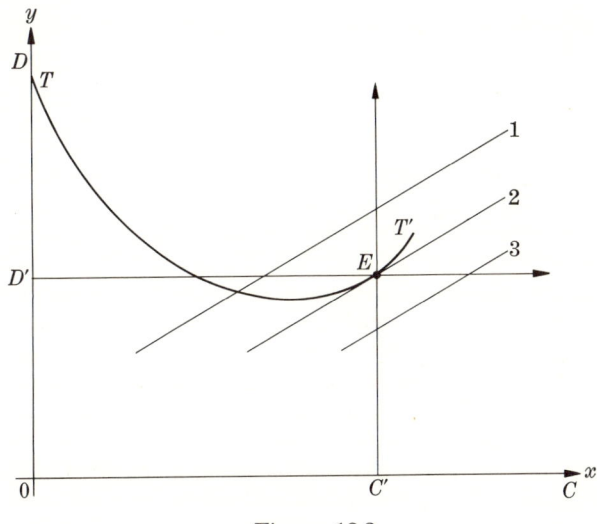

Figure 18.3

Two (symmetrical) equilibrium locations are implied, therefore, well away from the maximally doubtful centre, and converging toward the segregated positions which community convenience requires, or the well-known points A and B (in Figure 18.1). The gravitational pull of these quartile points cannot but be decisive. Of course, actual locations assumed would probably vary with each duopoly case, as utility is maximized by the two firms in accordance with a subjectively given pattern of evaluating the pertinent variables. It should be clear, too, that as the market is not linear, but defined instead by any given area (circular or other), there will be many possible alternative (pairs of) equilibria to the ones in fact attained by any one realized process of competitive behaviour. Each point on every such pair invariably will be a symmetric "reflection" of the other. Also, all pairs would lie on the small circle in Figure 18.1, with radius approximately OB. Orientation and length, respectively, of the radius-axis will depend upon the direction of competition over space, and the particular weights assigned by the duopolists to the several variables under consideration. Further, any one pair of these possible equilibria will be found to lie always on the same one set (duet) of confocal curves. Finally, as was implied earlier, the location segments actually contested would probably be AA' for the firm on the left of the y-axis, and BB' for its opposite.

2. The Algebraic Representation

To conclude, we sketch a somewhat more general expression of the solution. Equilibrium is reached where the symmetrically mobile duopolists maximize utility in accordance with a subjectively-given pattern of weighing three pertinent variables. Writing C for the certainty area, D for the average distance travelled by consumers, and E for the probability of new entry, optimum utility obtains by maximizing the internally-constrained function $U = U(C, D, E)$ subject to the condition:

(1) $\partial U/\partial C = \partial U/\partial D = \partial U/\partial E = 0$

(2) $b < 0$ (3) $\begin{vmatrix} b & g \\ g & c \end{vmatrix} > 0$ (4) $\begin{vmatrix} b & g & f \\ g & c & e \\ f & e & d \end{vmatrix} < 0$

where b, c, d, e, f, g denote, respectively $\partial^2 U/\partial C^2$, $\partial^2 U/\partial D^2$, $\partial^2 U/\partial E^2$, $\partial^2 U/\partial C \partial D$, $\partial^2 U/\partial C \partial E$, $\partial^2 U/\partial D \partial E$.

At this point the reader will agree that it is not difficult to dispense altogether (by definition) with the case of centre-clustering. In other words, one may simply constrain the position of maximum utility to be necessarily away from the centre. Any credible reason could prompt this action—always depending, as has been said, upon the subjective views of the two units in competition. For example, a realistic constraint might be $D < D_0$, where D_0 denotes the average distance travelled if the duopolists are clustered in the "city centre". Alternatively, the existence of the *minimum sensibile* may be said to imply another highly operational constraint in this connection. Thus, as in Figure 18.1, the location segments actually contested lie outside OR and OQ for our two respective firms.

CONCLUSION

The reader will now appreciate the limitations of the thesis of centre-clustering. For if, and only if, we are willing (a) to ignore the significance of varying total sales for the industry as the two firms change their locations, (b) to postulate price and income elasticities of demand to be zero, (c) to hold, in addition, that discontinuous utility functions for the consumer are a distinct impossibility, or that the concept of the *minimum sensibile* is a casual embellishment, and (d) to axiomatize that each seller contemplates alternative locations on the assumption that the other is incapable of adjusting symmetrically, is it at all likely that the two sellers would converge toward, and ultimately cluster at, the centre. But if we reflect on what has gone before, all this adds up to a rather long list of uneasy concessions to have to make. Clearly, if the duopolists converge unduly toward the centre, each would be able, at best, to count on the possible patronage of everyone in general, and hence of no one in particular. Inadequately dispersed, neither seller can rest at all assured of enjoying one-half of the total clientele at minimum cost. Worse still, in its dual rôle of consumer and administrator, the community would probably resent articulately the "solution". The theoretical conclusion is submitted, therefore, that in the *absence* of an uneven distribution of the population (which is normally directly responsible for the clustering that we observe in the world around us), the spatial equilibrium between two sellers of the same commodity is a dispersed one. Of course, the location problem does not arise in the same light where we have product differentiation. For then a firm may well operate under the assumption that its "addicts" will always seek to patronize it.

It follows, too, that where one of the two sellers is permanently established anywhere in a given market (and where, therefore, symmetrical reciprocation does not obtain), the potential new entrant will not choose to locate of necessity as closely as possible to the original firm. Evidently, for any given market configuration it is possible to compute "expected market share", "expected sales for the industry", and "expected sales for each firm". If we then take one firm to have a fixed location in the market, we can easily obtain the optimum position of the other (mobile) firm, such that the above economic variables be maximized, and where (*a*) the dimensions of, say, a rectangular market, (*b*) the distance of the fixed firm from a given boundary of the market, and (*c*) the *minimum sensible* are parameters. The maximum is thus found by a series of calculations where the distance between the two firms is a variable. And, as one may subsequently wish to show in a more heuristic study, store dispersion shall prevail once again. Basically, however, it is the *minimum sensibile* constraint on consumer utility maximization that we shall always recognize as the critical element in any dispersion solution. In fact, one might consider further that, if adequately generalized, this useful concept would enable us to rid current consumer behaviour theory of much of its ancient cumbersomeness. As such, the *minimum sensibile* only serves to formalize the common secret, amongst those of us who normally glance at the world in which we live, that we are on the whole too clever to worry about petty differentials in our affairs; or, to put it differently, that most people view as an onerous burden the psychic and material cost attached to behaving like perfect economic robots. Finally, it is imperative to stress that our "hyperbolic fan" mechanism will still be operative, and its consequences felt, as we have shown in this article, even where we assign to the *minimum sensibile* an exceedingly small value.

I conclude with a somewhat philosophical parenthesis. For if it can be said that the majority of "truths" in theoretical economics are generally sad creatures because, unlike the wise economist, they are afraid to die, the modest conclusion of this theoretical essay should be classed among the few joyful exceptions. I elaborate briefly.

The *raison d'être* of all sound theory, in economics as elsewhere, is threefold. (1) A theoretical apparatus helps us to understand and explain *observed* phenomena, which are either felt to be immediately relevant to some aspect of our welfare, or simply interesting and curious enough to merit, pedagogically or otherwise, our scientific attention. (2) A theoretical construction assists us to understand and predict or forecast "behaviour" as yet *unobserved* or possibly altogether unrevealed. Here, too, the reasons are the same as before. (3) In the last analysis, however, all reputable theories are found to prepare the ground for the ascent of their superior successors. But this truth, whose essence is beyond dispute historically, has never been popular amongst economists. Instead, over the years, and as our science has become progressively more analytical, the historian of economics has often encountered some of the profession's chief exponents unduly lamenting the passing of various favourite systems; or, worse still, emerging with the futile impression that permanently valid new ones ("changes") had become at last squarely established. Invariably, it has been a wrong approach, yet one that has frequented theoretical economics with disquieting persistence. Recently, things have improved considerably. Almost everyone nowadays takes the view that the first two objects which I have given above are realistic. Unfortunately, the same cannot be said of the third. In so far, therefore, as I classify this theoretical essay roughly under the second sub-division, and whilst I subscribe thoroughly to the third, I may ask the sympathetic reader (whether empirically or theoretically inclined, or both) to consider himself as having just acquired a fairly reasonable task to perform.

PART V

FIRMS' BEHAVIOR AND PUBLIC POLICY

The production decisions of individual firms determine what is produced by the economy's stock of productive resources and the way in which these resources are combined in production. The satisfaction derived by members of the community from the use of the economy's productive resources is influenced by the manner in which the resources are allocated among different kinds of output and the methods used to produce those outputs. The welfare of the community cannot be said to be maximized, if it is possible, by changing the existing resource allocation to increase the satisfaction of some members of the community without thereby reducing the satisfaction of any other members. A situation in which no further improvements of this kind are possible is termed a "Pareto optimum."

Economic analysis indicates that resource allocation in an economy will not be Pareto optimal if an industry's selling or buying behavior corresponds to that of a monopolist. Like all conclusions in economic analysis, this proposition is based upon a number of assumptions. Two of these are that (1) all firms in the economy pursue the goal of profit maximization, and (2) that there is no monopoly in any other sector of the economy. If firms pursue objectives other than profit maximization, or if there is a constraint which prevents the elimination of monopoly in other sectors of the economy, monopolistic behavior in a particular industry is compatible with resource allocation, which maximizes the welfare of the community. Despite these qualifications—and although public policies affecting industrial behavior may be intended to increase the welfare of the community by influencing other relevant factors in addition to resource allocation—underlying the application of much public policy, there is a presumption that monopolistic behavior leads to a misallocation of resources.

A group of independent firms may determine price and output policies as if the industry which they form were a monopoly. There is, in general, a presumption that agreements between independent firms with respect to prices, quantities, or markets served are against the public interest. In the United States, for example, price agreements are illegal per se. In Great Britain a slightly different approach is adopted; price agreements are presumed to be against the public interest unless the parties to the agreement can demonstrate the contrary to the satisfaction of the Restrictive Practices Court.

The five articles comprising Part V deal with public policy toward other features of firms' behavior. For example, instead of agreeing on prices or other terms, independent firms may agree to notify each other of prices and conditions of sale and changes therein, or to supply other information, such as cost and turnover data. Knowledge of how information agreements affect the behavior of firms who are parties to them is indispensable for purposes of formulating public policies governing such agreements. The article by O. P. O'Brien and D. Swann examines the effect of price information agreements on behavior; the authors emphasize the fact that the exchange of information can affect behavior even though there is no collusion in policy-making between the parties to the information agreement. The mere fact of dissemination may affect behavior; all that is necessary for behavior to be altered is that the information agreement change individual firms' expectations about rivals' reactions.

Turning next to merger policy, a number of countries have adopted public policy measures which restrict mergers between formerly independent firms in certain circumstances. The economic rationale underlying merger policy is that mergers may change some aspect of firms' behavior, and that this may adversely affect resource allocation and welfare in the economy. For example, a merger between two firms selling in the same market reduces the number of firms in that market, and a smaller number of firms may, in certain circumstances, make these firms more aware of their interdependence and, therefore, lead to more monopolistic pricing behavior.

Mergers have been defended by a number of arguments. Behavior need not necessarily be changed materially by merger. Alternatively, even if behavior is altered, the change need not be an adverse one from the point of view of achieving a welfare maximizing resource allocation. A prominent defense of merger, for example, is the argument that it may increase efficiency and reduce the cost of producing an industry's output by permitting scale economies to be reaped. In this case, increased technical efficiency depends on larger scales of output being produced in individual firms and involves a reduction in the number of independent decision-makers in the industry. A slightly different argument is advanced by H. G. Manne, who claims that the threat of merger promotes efficiency by compelling managers to make maximum feasible profits in order to avoid takeover and loss of control. Even in the absence of economies of scale the cost of an industry's output can be reduced if there are differences in the unit cost of producing comparable scales of output in different firms due to a failure of some managements to minimize costs. Where the threat of takeover alone is not sufficient to secure efficiency, and merger occurs, increased efficiency can be achieved without a reduction in the number of independent firms producing the product, if takeover is initiated by management previously operating in an unrelated market. Higher profits may be anticipated as a result of merger, not because of increased efficiency and lower costs in the firms taken over but because of higher revenues resulting from more monopolistic pricing. Therefore, as Manne points out, a problem confronting the public policy-maker is that of devising methods for distinguishing mergers motivated by a quest for monopoly profits from those merely trying to establish efficient management in poorly run companies.

While public policy toward pricing behavior is based, at least in part, on conclusions derived from economic analysis, the same cannot be said of policy toward advertising. The current body of economic analysis provides no clear guidelines for public policy in the case of advertising. Advertising is frequently treated with hostility by laymen and economists alike, and the opinion that advertising expenditures are "too high" in some industries is often heard. Antipathy toward advertising stems largely from a comparative neglect, existing until relatively recently in economic analysis, of the benefits of advertising from the point of view of buyers of advertised products as opposed to the benefits to sellers of these products. Traditionally, it was assumed in economic analysis that buyers are fully informed about the nature of all products available and the terms at which they are offered. This is not a valid description of the real world, where information about available products is not a free good automatically available to anyone and everyone. In the absence of advertising, buyers must acquire information in other ways, or make decisions without it. In certain circumstances this may be more costly, from the buyers' point of view, than the cost of resources devoted to advertising, which must be recouped in the prices of advertised products.

The articles by G. J. Stigler and H. G. Johnson both emphasize the possible benefits of advertising to buyers of advertised products. Even if high advertising and high profit margins are associated, as the article by Comanor and Wilson in Part IV suggests, it does not necessarily follow that policies which restrict advertising on grounds of reducing profit margins will increase the welfare of the community. Advertising activities provide information about goods and services which can be produced with the existing stock of technological knowledge, capital equipment, and labor. From the point of view of buyers of advertised products, this information may in certain circumstances be more valuable than alternative uses of the resources devoted to advertising.

Public policy may also be concerned with research & development activities, which add to the stock of technological knowledge and may result in new and improved products and processes. If firms base their R&D decisions on an expected return which underestimates the total benefits of the resulting new knowledge to the community, R&D levels in the economy may, in the absence of public policy measures, be lower than desirable from the point of view of maximizing the welfare of the community. In the final article, K. J. Arrow discusses some of the public policy problems associated with the production and dissemination of new knowledge and the relationship between market structure and these activities.

Before concluding, it is appropriate to point out that although the selections in this volume demonstrate that much has been accomplished recently in the field of industrial organization, a great deal of research remains to be done. Considerable scope still exists for broadening our understanding of the determinants of firms' pricing behavior. For example, in its present state, economic theory is still inadequate for purposes of predicting with reasonable accuracy the effect of oligopoly, vertical integration, and conglomerate merger on price and output levels.

The current state of economic theory concerning the determinants of advertising, product policies, and research and development activities is a good deal less satisfactory than theory concerning the determinants of pricing behavior. Despite research along the lines indicated in the article by Dennis Mueller in Part IV, much work remains to be done on the development of a broader and empirically relevant theory of the firm, encompassing the relationship between different features of a firm's behavior. Development of such a theory is essential in order to permit one to predict the effect of any particular public policy measure on all dimensions of a firm's behavior. This, in turn, is a necessary step toward avoiding undesirable side effects, on other features of behavior, of public policies designed to affect individual features of firms' activities.

The implications of alternative objectives for the behavior of firms is also a potential area for further study and refinement of existing knowledge. Although profit maximization may provide an adequate description of behavior for purposes of predicting the sign of changes in firms' policy-variables in response to changes in the firms' environment, it may not always be adequate when one is interested in the actual levels and characteristics of firms' activities themselves.

Finally, even if the determinants of, and the relationship between, all characteristics of a firm's behavior were known, the application of public policy requires standards against which existing behavior, or changes in behavior, can be compared. Unfortunately, we lack standards for judging most aspects of firms' behavior. Although the nature of ideal pricing performance, from the point of view of maximizing the aggregate welfare of the community, has been extensively investigated and is now fairly well defined, other types of ideal performance have not yet been satisfactorily defined. In the current state of knowledge, there is no way of knowing whether the level of R&D activities undertaken by firms in particular industries constitutes good or bad performance in a given situation. Similarly, an empirically applicable distinction between desirable and either excessive or deficient levels of advertising activity is not yet available. The lack of standards in these dimensions of firms' behavior is perhaps the greatest obstacle to the development of logically consistent public policy measures.

Even if it were possible to predict the effect of a particular measure on all the different dimensions of firms' behavior, there would still be no way, in the current state of knowledge, to judge whether the effects, on other dimensions of behavior, of measures to improve pricing performance are good or bad. Therefore, there is no way of knowing whether the measures which improve pricing performance are themselves, on balance, desirable or undesirable from the point of view of the welfare of the community.

19
Information Agreements— A Problem in Search of a Policy

D. P. O'Brien and D. Swann

INTRODUCTION

The Restrictive Trade Practices Act of 1956 was expected to bring about a significant increase in competition, and it is certainly true that a large number of agreements have been abandoned, a result which is satisfactorily consistent with the philosophy underlying the Act. By 30th June 1963, the end of the period covered in the latest report of the Registrar of Restrictive Practices, "the total number of agreements which had been terminated by act of the parties or effluxion of time or from which all registrable restrictions had been removed by virtue of an Order of the Court or by act of the parties was 1,610."[1] It has however been widely observed that the abandonment of these agreements has not resulted in any great increase in competition.[2]

Faced with the necessity or advisability of abandoning an agreement, there are several possibilities open to the firms involved. One such possibility is to reduce the number of firms through mergers. This has the effect of changing the com-

Reprinted from *The Manchester School of Economics and Social Studies*, September 1966, pp. 285-306 by permission of the authors and publishers.

[1] Registrar of Restrictive Trading Agreements, *Report for the period 1st July, 1961 to 30th June, 1963*, Cmnd. 2246, p. 10.
[2] See for instance J. B. Heath, "Freer Prices—What Progress?" *The Banker*, vol. 110, 1960, pp. 107-11; J. B. Heath, "Restrictive Practices and After," *Manchester School*, vol. 29, 1961, pp. 173-202; and D. L. MacLachlan and D. Swann, "Next Steps in Monopoly Policy," *Scottish Journal of Political Economy*, vol. XI, 1965, pp. 136-50.

petitive structure of the industry by reducing a large number case to a small number or oligopolistic case, where price leadership may most easily emerge. This has been the path followed to some extent in Lancashire after the Yarn Spinners' agreement was condemned in 1959,[3] and elsewhere. For instance the Registrar has drawn attention to a case in which a price agreement concerning a "major electrical component" was abandoned in 1959 before reference to the Court. Thereafter there was a severe bout of price cutting, prices in several companies being said to be below cost. Mergers subsequently took place leaving 11 firms in business. Subsequently one firm raised prices to restore part of the cuts made previously and the rest followed suit.[4] Alternatively, one firm might emerge as price leader without mergers taking place. Another, rather more popular choice has been to formulate an agreement which does not appear to come within the scope of the 1956 Act. These agreements fall into three types; all of them were mentioned in the White Paper on Monopolies, Mergers and Restrictive Practices[5] of 1964, but none of them was dealt with in the subsequent Act.[6] The first type of agreement is known as a "Bilateral Agreement". In this the Act is circumvented by a trade association entering into a separate agreement with each of its members, only one member accepting a registrable restriction. The Act, covering only agreements in which two or more parties accept restrictions is therefore evaded. There are also agreements which merely reformulate a condemned one but which, for technical reasons, are not "to the like effect" as the former, and can be operated until they in turn come before the Court. These however do not seem to be sufficiently widespread to constitute major evasions of the 1956 Act (although this alone would not justify the absence of legislation respecting them). But the third type of agreement which has generally not been held to come within the scope of the Act and which certainly *does* seem to be a major problem is the Open Price or Information Agreement. In such agreements a number of firms agree to notify each other, through a central secretariat, of prices and conditions of sale and changes therein, and often agree to supply other relevant data such as costs and turnover. It has generally been thought that such systems did not fall within the ambit of the 1956 Act since it would be impossible to prove the existence of an agreement or meeting of minds. Firm A might notify Firm B of its prices but Firm B could not be said to be necessarily influenced by that fact. Even if Firm B adopted Firm A's prices, it could plead that it had independently decided that such a price was commercially justified. Although no precise information is available as to the extent of these agreements[7] there appears to be fairly widespread consciousness of their importance, and the most

---

[3] 26th January, 1959, L.R.1. R.P.118. Initially, in this case, the competitive effects which would normally have followed on the judgement were, at least in part, supplanted by the operation of the Government re-organisation scheme. This however can hardly be regarded as a likely general consequence of unfavourable judgements.

[4] Registrar of Restrictive Trading Agreements, "Developments under the United Kingdom's Restrictive Trade Practices Act" (Summary of a paper read before the American Bar Association), 1960.

[5] Cmnd. 2299, pp. 5–6.

[6] Monopolies and Mergers Act 1965, Eliz. II, 13 and 14. c.50.

[7] See J. B. Heath, *Manchester School loc. cit.*, pp. 184–5 on the incidence of these agreements in the sample dealt with there.

prominent investigator of the impact of the 1956 Act has gone so far as to say that "it is already clear that by far the most *significant* change [following the 1956 Act] has been the substitution—so far to only a limited extent—of non-registrable agreements to exchange information, principally about prices".[8] The Registrar has also commented on these agreements stating in his second report: "Not infrequently on the ending of a price agreement the parties enter into an information agreement under which they send to their trade association or to a central agency their price lists or the prices at which they have entered into contracts. . . . Information agreements are considered under two heads; first as arrangements tending to hinder the revival of competition in industries in which there have been price agreements or other restrictive agreements for substantial periods; secondly as a framework within which, consciously or unconsciously, there may arise understandings about prices, allocation of contracts and so on."[9]

ECONOMIC IMPLICATIONS

Such agreements may be divided into two main types; those in which notification is given *prior* to the change in price and those in which notification is only given *after* the change has taken place. It is possible however to make further distinctions which are highly relevant to an analysis of the impact of such agreements upon market behaviour. Thus information agreements may require the association of firms' names with the data on prices and turnover; on the other hand such data may be supplied anonymously. Then again data on prices and costs may be specified in the form of actual levels over a period, or merely in the form of an average or range of fluctuation.

It would seem that the temporal distinction is relevant to the analysis. An agreement which requires notification of price changes before they occur (referred to henceforth as a "prenotification agreement") gives the most obvious opportunities for pressure to be brought to bear on a price changer *before* he has actually disturbed the market situation. It was presumably this type that the Registrar had chiefly in mind when he wrote that "If a measure of competition considered undesirable by the majority should emerge, the price information agreement provides both the material and the forum for the persuasion of the minority".[10] The second type ("post-notification agreement") reduces a large number to a small number case,[11] by perfecting the flow of information, but does not make the application of pressure so easy. Nevertheless a fear of social obloquy may deter a price changer even in the second case. (It would in our opinion be a great mistake to underrate the importance of this factor. There is clearly in many

[8] J. B. Heath, "Some Economic Consequence [of Restrictive Practices Legislation]," *Economic Journal*, vol. LXX, 1960, pp. 474–84, p. 474.
[9] Registrar of Restrictive Trading Agreements, *Report for the period 1st January, 1960 to 30th June, 1961*, Cmnd. 1603, pp. 3–4. See also the *Report for the period 1st July, 1961 to 30th June, 1963*, p. 4.
[10] *Report* (1960–1) p. 4.
[11] That this point is not widely understood is made clear by a recent analysis in which this effect does not appear to be envisaged and in which the distinction between pre- and post-notification agreements also seems to be overlooked—see A. Hunter, *Competition and the Law*, London, 1966, pp. 169–71.

industries an *esprit de corps* which is built up within the trade association and anyone who disturbs the market situation is bound to feel, or be made to feel, uncomfortable.[12] In the United States there is evidence in the case of open price agreements of members being "put on the carpet" and being subjected to searching questions about their conduct[13]). But although the second type would appear to give more scope to the would-be price changer, it is unfortunately the case that a post-notification agreement is unlikely to remain in that form for long—and in the Galvanised Tank Case to be discussed below, an arrangement which was nominally of the post-notification type was operated as a pre-notification agreement.

There are of course disadvantages to these agreements other than the opportunity for exercising pressure on firms. Most obviously perhaps there is the danger of a pre-notification agreement providing a temptation and a forum to move on to explicit (though secret) collusion. Secondly, a form of "gentleman's" agreement may arise, whereby one firm notifies the others, through the secretariat, of an intended price change, in the full expectation that the others will infer from the notification a course of action which will ensure the continued damping of competition. Thirdly, it has been observed that information agreements lead to product standardisation.[14] This last has a number of advantages: it can bring about longer production runs, reduced stockholdings, reduction in design and selling costs, and, by removing product differentiation it increases the elasticity of the firm's average revenue curve, thus reducing its market power. But on the other hand it may not only make the maintenance of uniform prices easier, but also act as a bar to product innovation.

But the opportunities provided by such an agreement for opposing price competition are the most obvious and striking. Any incentive to take advantage of a potentially more favourable cost situation, perhaps arising from a possible method change, will quite conceivably be stifled. If a price cutter can be identified straight away, and if he knows that he will gain nothing from this because his prices will be quickly, possibly immediately, matched by his competitors, then there is no incentive to him to cut prices. "Perfecting of the game" would seem here to have positive disadvantages, since in the absence of perfect information, the price cutter is able to operate to his own advantage until such time as his prices become known to his competitors. It is by no means inconceivable that customers may get to know of his lower prices sufficiently long before his competitors that for a time he will be able to reap the rewards of his strategy, and/or of his technical innovation which allows him to offer lower prices. It seems likely that eventually there will be competitive imitation but some of the custom attracted during the period in which the price cutter's prices are lower than those of his competitors may remain permanently with him. A number of reasons for this can be adduced. Firstly his original price cut may earn for him some extra goodwill on the part of customers who may elect to stay with him and they may continue to patronise him because of resentment at the restrictive attitude of his

[12] See R. Hall and C. J. Hitch, "Price Theory and Business Behaviour" in T. Wilson and P. W. S. Andrews (Eds.), *Oxford Studies in the Price Mechanism*, Oxford, 1951, p. 118.

[13] See A. D. Neale, *The Antitrust Laws of the U.S.A.*, Cambridge, 1960, p. 45.

[14] See A. R. Burns, *The Decline of Competition*, New York, 1936, p. 498.

competitors. Secondly an open price agreement leading to price uniformity, like a price-fixing agreement, may prove a method of restricting knowledge since customers, in the belief that prices are uniform, will not search for alternative sources of supply which might in fact prove to meet their needs more satisfactorily. Allied with this is the point that a price cut may be a means of attracting custom to a newly differentiated product. The fore-going should not be taken as implying any final welfare judgement; it is merely argued that an information agreement, even when operated honourably, can stifle the incentive to cut prices or to introduce technical innovations.

The important point here is the existence of a time lag before competitors receive information about the existence of a price cut, the degree of the price cut, who is making it, where it is being made and so forth. The significance of a time lag before a competitive riposte occurs is considerable. Schumpeter was concerned with a somewhat similar point when he developed the idea that monopoly is conducive to economic progress. This was not an unqualified commendation of monopoly but a suggestion that a nice blend of temporary monopoly followed by competitive imitation was the best system for encouraging innovation.[15]

Continuing the argument about the relationship between innovation and information, the possibility exists that a firm might introduce new methods in order to earn very large profits at existing prices without disturbing the market structure. However, this is of little benefit to the consumer, since it merely ensures the acquisition of a surplus by the producer, and as under many information agreements, data about costs is supplied, competitors may soon be able to copy such innovations. In this case any subsequent inflation of costs may be absorbed thus eroding the large profits being made by all the parties to the agreement and the innovating firm will cease to gain the advantages of its innovation; whereas, were it the only firm to innovate, a rise in costs would tend to lead to a general rise in prices and it would continue to make large profits. Provided the time lag existed the firm would have an incentive to innovate. (It would however be desirable that the innovation should eventually be copied.) A further consideration is that a new method may require a scale of operations greater than the firm's current market share. In the absence of an information agreement the firm wishing to innovate might be able to achieve such a scale by price-cutting, but in the presence of an agreement every price cut is likely to be matched.

So far we have concentrated upon the disincentive to price cutting. But it is also clear that open price agreements provide an excellent medium for bringing about a general rise in prices when costs rise[16] or even in the absence of such a change. Without such an agreement an individual firm may fear that its competitors will not match an increase. Because of this a firm may expect the elasticity of its average revenue curve to be greater than one above the prevailing price.[17] If an agreement exists a rise in price will be matched and each producer will tend

[15] J. A. Schumpeter, *The Theory of Economic Development*, Cambridge, Massachusetts, 1936, especially chs. 2 and 4; and *Capitalism, Socialism and Democracy*, London, 1947, ch. 8.

[16] Thus reducing the pressure on firms to rationalise their processes when faced with cost increases.

[17] Even if competitors do eventually follow the price increase, business lost by the initiator of the price change may very well never be fully recovered.

to believe demand conditions to be conducive to a price rise. It seems to us that under inflationary conditions the open price agreement is just the kind of flexible instrument which businessmen need to keep pace with frequent changes in costs stemming from rises in wages, raw material prices and so forth. A price change can be notified quickly and followed immediately. There is no time lag, during which profits are eroded, which a more formal machinery of price fixing might require. The time lags implicit in more formal arrangements might indeed make the position of relatively high cost producers quite uncomfortable.

Recent thought on decisions relating to investment in a competitive framework would suggest further considerations. G. B. Richardson[18] for example has suggested that following an increase in demand for a particular product, the kind of information supplied under an information agreement may assist the simultaneous and harmonious planning of investment by a number of firms, each being aware of the others' intentions. Richardson indicates that if, under the stimulus of a demand increase, the investment decisions were made simultaneously and in isolation, the distinct possibility exists that overinvestment would result. While not disputing the validity of this argument, it seems to us that the likelihood that in the real world expansion plans will be undertaken simultaneously is somewhat remote. Many factors may lead to the staggering of an investment response, even when the stimulating increase in demand is immediately apparent to all producers, and such staggering would enable an alternative step by step approach (which Richardson also envisages) to a new equilibrium to be achieved. A number of possible factors could lead to a staggered response; some firms may at a particular point in time be liquid whereas others may not, some firms may be able to tap the capital market whilst others may not and will therefore have to accumulate funds out of earnings, some firms will respond more rapidly to changes than others and so forth.

A number of further observations are suggested by this analysis. Firstly, an information agreement by perfecting the flow of information and disseminating knowledge of profitable investment opportunities, may itself reduce the temporal spacing of investments. This may occur because of the actual information supplied under the agreement and in the course of any market discussions which may take place within the group, and may also be consequent upon a reduction in uncertainty which may help to overcome entrepreneurial inertia. The information agreement under these circumstances while helping to remove the danger of over investment has an element of self-justification, for by improving knowledge in the first instance it creates conditions which might lead to over-investment. Secondly, we have argued earlier that information agreements can lead, via an unwillingness to disturb the market, to a uniform price which, other things being equal, implies a uniformity of market shares. This in turn is likely to react on investment decisions by requiring that each firm's expansion plans should not disturb the *status quo*. This may act as a deterrent to the relative expansion of the more efficient and to the achievement of economies of scale. This is not of

[18] See G. B. Richardson, *Information and Investment*, London, 1960, and "The Theory of Restrictive Practices," *Oxford Economic Papers*, N.S. vol. XVII, no. 3, November 1965, pp. 432–49. See also J. B. Heath, *Economic Journal, loc. cit.*, p. 476 and references there cited.

course inevitable but, as Richardson himself observes, it is a potentiality which should be taken into account. Thirdly, where there is a need for co-ordination of investment, as is likely to be the case where investments may be large, durable and simultaneous, it is still questionable whether the information agreement is the best medium for achieving co-ordination. Some alternative machinery may be necessary in which a representative of the public interest can be present.

Of course none of these arguments is conclusive; but it seems reasonable to argue that there is a strong possibility that an open price agreement may have at least some of the ill-effects envisaged. That is all that will be required by the argument below.

Nevertheless there are possible advantages. For instance it has been argued by the Galvanised Tank Manufacturers,[19] that such an agreement is necessary to avoid "phantom competition"—the quoting by customers of other suppliers' prices at lower levels than the true ones. But it can be argued that only a very limited amount of information is needed to overcome this problem—checking with a central secretariat on the range of prices, whenever phantom competition is suspected, would involve none of the detailed circulation of information including complete price lists, which is usual in an information agreement. Prices could be quoted anonymously in such a case, merely a range being given. Nevertheless it may be questioned whether this will prove sufficient to deal with the problem— the answer seems to be that it may or may not, depending on circumstances. For example, if a customer represents to firm x that firm y is offering a price 10 per cent below that of firm x, checking with the central secretariat may reveal that the maximum deviation below x's price at this point in time is 5 per cent. The customer's claim could then be regarded as bogus. But if price deviations of up to 10 per cent are reported then there is no way of ascertaining whether the customer's claim is genuine or not. The 10 per cent reduction may be being made by firm y but it may be being made by firm z in another segment, geographical or otherwise, of the market. In the latter case offers made by firm z would hardly be relevant to firm x and could indeed be regarded as phantom competition as far as it was concerned. The central secretariat could of course provide data on a geographical or other basis which would go some way towards dealing with this problem, but there is a danger that if this were pressed too far it would become easier to identify which firm was making a price offer and this would tend to be anti-competitive in effect. Secondly it is arguable that other firms' prices are less relevant to the price to be charged, than a particular firm's own cost situation. The latter is not however an unambiguous guide. In multi-product firms there will always be an element of arbitrariness in the apportionment of overheads between different products. A figure for average total cost will then contain some element of judgement. The problem would be less marked if the order were a single non-repeating one for the firm would then refer to average direct cost (assuming marginal cost to have no operational significance). However, even in this case, it would presumably wish to make some contribution to overheads. Its direct costs will then provide some guide but little more.

It is also claimed that Open Price Agreements reduce the level of uncertainty.

[19] L.R. 5 R.P. 325.

As an isolated proposition this seems undeniable. But the consequence of such a reduction in uncertainty need not be unambiguously beneficial. It is true that under normal circumstances a reduction in uncertainty (arising for instance from a stabilisation of consumer preferences) should help to tip the balance between efficiency and adaptability of plant in favour of the former, allowing entrepreneurs to invest, for example, in highly efficient specialised machine tools rather than in less efficient but more adaptable general purpose ones.[20] But where the reduction in uncertainty is brought about by the introduction of an open price agreement, the beneficial tendency may, to some extent at least, be counteracted —it has been argued above that such an agreement is likely to lead to a stabilisation of market shares, which implies difficulties for an entrepreneur who may wish to attain a more efficient scale of production.

Finally, it has been suggested that information agreements will help to avoid the misdirection of competitive effort.[21] In so far as such agreements remove the necessity for extensive entrepreneurial speculation about rivals' strategies, and enable entrepreneurial resources to be concentrated more upon improvements of products and methods of production, this will be advantageous. On the other hand it is arguable that a feeling of uncertainty may well help to produce in the entrepreneur, a more critical attitude towards methods and costs.

If possible disadvantages are admitted to exist, then it seems reasonable to argue that some policy for dealing with the phenomena of information agreements should be developed. The case for this would seem to be strengthened by the inadequacies of the claimed advantages.

UNITED STATES EXPERIENCE

First of all it should be noted that although the United States has a tradition of *per se* condemnation of price agreements, the circulation of prices does not seem to be condemned *per se* in the United States. The American approach is rather one of attempting to discover whether collusion actually exists with respect to the prices charged.

In a number of cases the antitrust authorities have been able to obtain a verdict against information agreements. Thus in the case of the *American Column and Lumber Company v. United States*, members of the trade association in question were required to let the secretary have daily reports of sales and deliveries and monthly reports of production and stocks. They also had to file price lists every month and inspectors were employed to check on the grades of timber offered at stated prices. The secretary in turn sent out periodical reports showing sales made at particular prices together with summaries of price lists. But in addition to this there was evidence of periodic meetings to discuss price and output policy. Also at the meetings it appeared that members were encouraged to adjust their policy so as to keep the industry profitable. Although a specific agreement to fix prices was not proved the Court concluded that the behaviour of the parties to the arrangement was that of

---

[20] See G. B. Richardson, *Information and Investment*, pp. 152–3.
[21] See Heath, *Economic Journal, loc. cit.*, pp. 479–80 and Richardson, *Oxford Economic Papers, loc. cit.*, pp. 447–8.

men united in an agreement express or implied, to act together and pursue a common purpose under a common guide.[22]

In the case of the *United States v. American Linseed Oil Company* a similar scheme was operated. There was however particularly strong evidence of action to keep members in line. Regular compulsory meetings were held and individuals were put on the carpet and subjected to intensive questioning as to their behaviour. Again the antitrust authorities won.

They were also successful in the case of *The Sugar Institute v. United States*. Here the Institute circulated statistics of production, stocks and deliveries. The Institute also administered a "Code of Ethics" one of whose conditions involved an agreement that parties would adhere to their published prices and it was this the Supreme Court objected to. Also important in deciding the case was the change in market conditions after the formation of the Institute. Price changes became less frequent, profit margins increased despite considerable excess capacity and the price of refined sugar followed changes in the price of raw sugar significantly less closely.

Not all the cases brought by the antitrust authorities have been so successful. In the case of *Maple Flooring Manufacturers' Association v. United States*, the association circulated data on costs, prices, sales and stocks. Meetings were held to discuss the industry's problems, although apparently after the Linseed Oil Case no discussions about prices took place. The Supreme Court did not however condemn the arrangement since prices were not uniform and lower than those of outsiders. Again in the case of the *Tag Manufacturers' Institute v. Federal Trade Commission* there was an elaborate scheme for notifying price lists but there was no agreement to adhere to list prices and there was evidence of substantial selling below list prices. The case failed.

In the case of the Vitrified China Association, the association had employed accountants to draw up an average figure for various elements of manufacturing costs and the members of the association had adopted a basic list of prices but because of deviations in various supplements to the basic price lists there was no uniformity of final price to the consumer and therefore no antitrust offence was deemed to exist.

What conclusions can be drawn from this experience? On the enforcement side we should note that, although there is no registration, very significant powers of investigation exist. As for the case decisions themselves, they afford no clear guide to policy in the United Kingdom. In the first place, since it appears that in this field there are no decisions in cases of pure price uniformity and nothing more, it is impossible to know whether or not the United States antitrust authorities would or would not be prepared to infer collusion merely in the light of simultaneous and equal price changes and in the absence of any supporting evidence of collusion or pressure. In the cases in which the Federal authorities have succeeded, in addition to price uniformity there have been other factors which they have been able to make use of. In the Sugar Institute case there was an express agreement not to deviate from published prices. In other cases there has been evidence of meetings to discuss price or output policy, pressure has been

[22] Quoted in A. D. Neale *op. cit.* p. 45; pp. 42–53 contain an excellent summary of this and the other cases referred to.

placed upon firms which have deviated and exhortations and guidance to maintain profitability have been employed. Also important in the Sugar Institute case was the reduced flexibility of prices and increased profit margins despite substantial excess capacity. In short, in reaching a decision against an information agreement, the antitrust authorities have sought evidence going beyond mere uniformity of prices. Supplementary evidence has been produced which in direction and extent was such that a reasonable man could not but infer the existence of collusion.

Secondly, the decisions throw little if any systematic light upon the possibility that certain forms of information agreement may be less innocuous than others.

There are two further observations which seem worthy of mention. One is that United States experience does provide examples of the kind of supporting evidence to look for in building up a case of collusion, if mere uniformity in itself is held by the courts or legislature to be insufficient evidence. The second observation, which springs out of the first, is that in the United States the cases have been dealt with in their totality—that is to say, the uniformity of prices springing out of the information agreement and the additional evidence have been considered simultaneously in reaching a verdict. We shall return to this point later in discussing British experience.

BRITISH EXPERIENCE

The British position was recently brought into prominence by the Galvanised Tank Case. It should be noted that although information agreements have possible disadvantages, there is no explicit legislative provision in the United Kingdom for dealing with them. The 1956 Act appears to say nothing about them and indeed, as already seen, a number of firms substituted them for agreements which were either actually condemned, or expected to be condemned. However it seems that there may be an implicit provision in the 1956 Act; for in the Basic Slag case[23] the meaning of the word "arrangement" in Section 6(3) of the 1956 Act was significantly extended. The report of that case is worth quoting as indicative of how far British legislation could conceivably have its effects extended. Diplock L. J. in his judgement stated that:

> " 'Arrangement' . . . involves a meeting of minds because under section 6(1) it has to be an arrangement 'between two or more persons', and since it must be an arrangement 'under which restrictions are accepted by two or more parties' it involves mutuality in that each party, assuming he is a reasonable and conscientious man, would regard himself as being in some degree under a duty, whether moral or legal, to conduct himself in a particular way as the case may be, at any rate so long as the other party or parties conducted themselves in the way contemplated by the arrangement.
>
> "No necessary or useful purpose would be served by attempting an expanded and comprehensive definition of the word 'arrangement' in section 6(3) of the Act. . . . it is sufficient to constitute an arrangement between

[23] L.R. 4 R.P. pp. 116–56.

A and B, if (1) A makes a representation as to his future conduct with the expectation and intention that such conduct on his part will operate as an inducement to B to act in a particular way, (2) such representation is communicated to B, who has knowledge that A so expected and intended, and (3) such representation or A's conduct in fulfilment of it operates as an inducement, whether among other inducements or not, to B to act in that particular way."[24]

The effect of this pronouncement was to widen considerably the scope of the 1956 Act; it was against this background that the Restrictive Practices Court came to consider the remarkable case of the *Galvanised Tank Manufacturers' Association's Agreement*.[25]

The Association had originally abandoned their registered agreement without defending it and had given the usual undertaking not to operate it or one to the like effect. This had occurred between July and September 1959. The agreement laid down that the members would not supply in the United Kingdom galvanised open-top cisterns, hot water tanks and cylinders including domestic water tanks used in houses except at prices and terms and conditions of sale (including discounts) agreed at general meetings of the Association. Earlier however, in May of that year, the members had entered into a new agreement for the submission of information on costs, sales and prices. "Although clause 3 of the notification agreement contemplated that members would give notice of changes in their prices and terms after the making of such changes, it was the consistent practice of the members in operating the agreement to give advance notification of their proposed changes in prices and terms to the secretaries of the association, and through them to the other members of the association, before such changes were actually made and in anticipation of their making".[26] The collection and dissemination of data on sales by product is particularly interesting. This was quite possibly a safeguard against undercutting since it would be suspicious if a member's sales increased out of line with those of other members serving the same market.

From the time of this agreement until the proceedings in 1965 in the Restrictive Practices Court respecting it (a period of six years), all the members of the association kept identical price lists (with the exception of a short-lived deviation by one firm) despite the fact that prices changed on no less than eleven occasions. Members changed their prices at virtually the same time. Their behaviour was drawn to the Registrar's attention by their customers. The Association was charged with contempt, and, luckily for the Registrar, admitted explicit collusion in two cases. However, there were four other occasions on which the Registrar asserted that collusion had taken place, and he asked the Court to infer this from the market behaviour of the firms i.e. from the consistent equality of their prices. He appeared to state through Counsel that he had no complaint against a post-notification agreement as such, but he objected to a post-notification agreement being converted to a pre-notification one. The Court was asked to infer from

---

[24] L.R. 4 R.P. 154–5.
[25] L.R. 5 R.P. 315–50.
[26] *Ibid.,* p. 319.

the identical price changes that these had resulted from an arrangement which was "to the like effect" of that abandoned, and that the pre-notification agreement, as operated, constituted such an arrangement and was indeed registrable.

In the face of this very important case the Court failed to come to any clear cut decision. For the two admitted cases of collusion the firms concerned were fined a total of £100,000. But the Court, while not actually finding the firms guilty of contempt in the other five cases, virtually refused to decide whether this could be a ground of contempt without supporting evidence or an admission, while issuing a stern warning.

> "The registrar submitted, further, that, even in the absence of what we may call express collusion in each of these five instances the court ought to hold that there was an arrangement, involving a breach of the companies' undertakings, arising out of the manner of operation of the notification agreement [as a pre-notification agreement]. The companies submitted . . . that this was not so. We do not think it necessary or desirable to deal with this matter on this motion, and we shall, therefore, proceed on the basis that no breach of undertaking—no 'arrangement to the like effect'— has been made out in connection with the changes of price or other terms which were brought about on any of these five occasions. *We treat that matter in this way, principally because it may not formerly have been realised, by these companies or their advisers, as indeed by many others, how wide the meaning of 'arrangement' may be.*[27] Therefore, in those special circumstances—*which would by no means necessarily be of equal force or relevance in the future*—the breach of undertakings involved, if the registrar's submission based on the Basic Slag case be right, would be relatively less grave compared with the seriousness of the admitted contempts. *We do not decide one way or the other whether the registrar's submission is right in relation to the facts before us.*
>
> "Having said this, we wish to give warning. . . . It is abundantly apparent . . . that those who, having been placed under an injunction or having given an undertaking such as here, thereafter exchange information of their intentions on matters such as prices, or partake in discussions, formal or informal, with their competitors on such matters, may be in real peril of . . . having passed easily and quickly from that which may be legitimate into actions which constitute a grave contempt." [28]

CONCLUDING OBSERVATIONS

Yet this leaves policy towards these agreements in the most uncertain state. There is no guidance on the Registrar's interesting and somewhat surprising view that pre-notification agreements are registrable. Nor is there any guidance as to which amongst the many possible forms of pre-notification agreement is likely to be condemned. A number of separate points may be noted.

[27] Authors' italics here and below.
[28] L.R. 5 R.P. 344–5. It will be noted that the judgment refers to five further cases whereas the Registrar relied on only four. The fifth case was not relied on by the Registrar because he possessed only one circular relating to the price change.

Firstly, the Registrar took the vital step of bringing this agreement before the court. This was in itself a significant departure for which there would seem to be no provision in the Act of 1956. It implies a need on the part of the Registrar for powers of investigation and enforcement which it is by no means clear that he as yet possesses. Such powers are clearly necessary for the regulation of information agreements. We discuss this further below.

Secondly, the opportunity for him to do this was provided by customers of the association who drew his attention to the price circulars. Clearly this is something which cannot be depended upon in future. As the Registrar's counsel said in his first submission "Customers are naturally reluctant to give evidence for fear of prejudicing their commercial position". The need for gathering of evidence under these circumstances again underlines the necessity for the Registrar to have power to enable him to do so.[29]

Thirdly, the philosophy underlying the Registrar's action is not at all clear. It has been argued above that even a post-notification agreement can have harmful effects. Yet the Registrar does not appear to object to these though he objects to pre-notification agreements. Since it is difficult to object to one and not the other, and since the Court has failed to give guidance on the necessity for registration of pre-notification agreements, the British position can hardly be regarded as satisfactory.

Fourthly, the Court has failed to rule on the submission that collusion may be inferred from market behaviour, and that to regard the equality of prices as a coincidence would "offend credulity".[30] Such a course would be a significant departure from previous British practice, but would seem to be able to follow from the wide meaning attached to the word "arrangement". It may be that the Court's warning implies a readiness to infer collusion in future; but this point certainly needs clarification.

Fifthly, if it is necessary, in order to sustain a charge of collusion that evidence in addition to mere parallelism of prices is required, then difficult problems may arise. On this occasion the companies involved admitted that they were guilty on two occasions; but had they not done so, it is extremely difficult to see, given the Court's equivocal attitude on the other five cases, whether any charge could have been made to bear enough weight.

Sixthly, it is perhaps worth observing, partly as a matter of comparison and partly as a possible suggestion for future treatment, that had the case occurred in the United States it would in all probability have been struck down. On the basis of the criteria discussed above, simultaneous and uniform changes in prices and the apparent lack of off-list selling, together with the past history of collusion and the two definite instances when agreements were proved to exist, would surely have been sufficient to ensure that the open price agreement was struck down. We emphasised earlier that in the United States the matter would have been judged as a whole—in this case the British court failed to do this and preferred to deal specifically with *only* that part of the case in which collusion was

---

[29] For a recent recognition of the need for greater powers of enforcement see N. H. Leyland, "Competition in the Court," *Oxford Economic Papers loc. cit.,* pp. 461–7.

[30] L.R. 5 R.P. p. 347.

admitted. Had the four or five cases on which the Court failed to decide been dealt with by themselves in the United States there seems no clear indication of what would have been the result.

Finally, in dealing with information agreements there is a temptation to take the view that the mere dissemination of information is not itself dangerous. What is dangerous is the possibility that collusion arises out of the system. Firm A informs Firm B of its increase in price in the knowledge and expectation that Firm B will follow. Therefore it is collusion which must be proved. But as we pointed out earlier the mere fact that price changes and changers are known about may act as a discouragement to price cutting and competition. Collusion is not necessary in order that competition be stifled. (It is true that there was in the first instance an agreement to circulate information but this is different from the collusion which subsequently develops out of a circulation of information.) We are here raising questions about the whole process of merely circulating information. These are deep and unchartered waters indeed but their exploration is necessary if our antitrust policy is to be fully comprehensive.

If it transpires that the Court is not prepared to infer collusion from market behaviour, particularly when this is supported by other evidence, then it seems inescapable that the legislature will have to deal explicitly with the problem.[31] What approaches can be envisaged? Perhaps most obviously these agreements could be objected to *per se*. Such an approach would however appear to be too sweeping. In the first place on grounds of consistency it would hardly be logical to apply such treatment to these arrangements whilst more explicitly collusive agreements were only deemed contrary to the public interest and even exemptable. Secondly, such a sweeping condemnation seems on the whole undesirable unless it can be established on *a priori* grounds that no possible good can ever come of such an agreement, or that any possible good can never outweigh any harm arising. The second alternative is to make these agreements registrable. This was the view of J. B. Heath[32] and the Conservative White Paper of 1964.[33] Heath suggested specifying a permissible type of agreement, more limited in scope than the information agreement currently operated in the United Kingdom. Only this type would be allowed. Unfortunately experience would tend to suggest that an apparently innocuous agreement can grow into one that is thoroughly objectionable. To ensure that this did not occur would require a machinery of investigation which it seems doubtful whether the Registrar as yet possesses. That is to say, although the Registrar has the power under Section 14 of the 1956 Act to require that agreements should be registered, it is first of all necessary that the agreement should be located. It would be no easy matter without powerful machinery of enforcement to police information agreements in order to detect those which strayed from the paths of legality.

---

[31] A recent statement by the Registrar seems to indicate that the latter is the most probable outcome—see R. L. Sich, "Evidence of Detriment caused by Restrictive Training Agreements," *Oxford Economic Papers loc. cit.*, p. 353. But it is possible that this is a statement of the position before the Galvanised Tank Case.

[32] *Economic Journal, loc. cit.*

[33] *Monopolies, Mergers and Restrictive Practice*, Cmnd. 2299.

The 1964 White Paper in advocating registration contained the following statement ". . . the Government are not prepared to see the intention of the 1956 Act undermined by agreements or arrangements for the exchange of information the purpose and effect of which is to limit competition. They therefore propose to bring information agreements within the scope of the 1956 Act, and thus to make them registrable and subject ultimately to consideration by the Court." Unfortunately there has been no provision for this in the legislation following the White Paper; and in any case the White Paper had begged the question of investigatory powers by stating that only those agreements which the Board of Trade considered to need registration, should be registered. How the Board of Trade was envisaged to make its selection was not made clear. The White Paper also suggested the need for a new gateway for information agreements, that is to say they could plead that the agreement was not contrary to the public interest because it did not restrict or deter competition. This is certainly one possible approach; and in addition those agreements which are registered (or if not registered are located by the enforcement machinery) which give rise to collusion are in practice the like effect of the type of agreement normally dealt with by the 1956 Act and can be treated in the same way. Another problem following from wholesale registration of information agreements is that either the Registrar has to be given power to bring *only* those agreements which he believes to restrict competition before the Court, or alternatively the Court will have a greatly increased volume of work thrust upon it. For the first case the Registrar would be effectively called upon to act as a preliminary judge and court; and the Court itself would be debarred from examining some agreements to which there might conceivably be objection. In the second case, though the possibility must be admitted to exist, the same problem was raised in relation to the 1956 Act's operation; but early adverse decisions led to widespread abandonment of agreements.

In the light of all that has gone before we would like to make the following suggestions. Firstly, that *all* information agreements, whether pre-notification or post-notification, should be registered; and it will be for the Court, not the Board of Trade or the Registrar alone, to decide upon their effect.

Secondly, although the Registrar has the power to call for information once a case has been set in motion, it would appear that greater powers are required to enable the Registrar to obtain the information necessary in order to establish that a case exists. Where an information agreement has been registered, the Registrar needs details of commercial behaviour in order to provide the basis of an examination before the Court. Where registration has been evaded the problem would be all the greater.

Thirdly, as we have indicated earlier, the mere dissemination of information may hinder competition quite apart from any collusion which may arise. There are two possible approaches to this problem. One would be to limit this effect by requiring that all information agreements conform to certain requirements. For example criteria could be laid down which included such things as anonymity of all firms supplying data (and the omission of turnover figures from data where these would identify the firms) and the requirement that all notification of price changes should be after the change. Alternatively, if this is thought to be too radical a departure, then at least in the judging of these agreements in relation to the public interest, any detriment to be outweighed might be regarded as being greater where such criteria were not satisfied. Either arrangement would help to remove some of the most objectionable features of the agreements, and together with registration and explicit powers of investigation should help to provide the stimulus to competition which the 1956 Act has so clearly failed to do.

20
Mergers and the Market for Corporate Control[1]

Henry G. Manne

In recent years many of the traditional economic justifications of our antitrust laws have been seriously questioned. A new sophistication has developed, and economic activities frequently held illegal by the courts are now thought by many to be consistent with our antitrust goals. The rules against tie-ins, vertical mergers, predatory competition, among others, have to a greater or lesser degree had their theoretical foundations considerably weakened. Recently even cartels, the most venerable victim of American antitrust laws, have found their near champion.[2]

One practice, however, remains generally condemned in both the economic literature and the most recent Supreme Court rulings. Mergers among competitors would seem to have no important saving grace. The position has gained considerable legal currency that any merger between competing firms is at least suspect and perhaps per se illegal. The latter result seems especially likely when

Reprinted from *Journal of Political Economy* (April 1965), by permission of The University of Chicago Press. Copyright, 1965, pp. 110–120.

[1] Helpful criticisms and suggestions on this article by Professors Armen A. Alchian, Joseph Aschheim, Donald Dewey, and Joseph P. McKenna are gratefully acknowledged.

A companion article to this one by the same author, entitled "Some Theoretical Aspects of Share Voting," appears in *Columbia Law Review*, LXIV (1964), 1427–45. That article analyzes the strategies available to shareholders when different techniques for taking over control of a corporation are used.

[2] Donald Dewey, "The Economic Theory of Anti-Trust: Science or Religion?" *Virginia Law Review*, L (1964), 413–34. This article also contains references to the other iconoclastic literature (pp. 426–27).

one of the combining firms already occupies a substantial position in the relevant market. Antitrust problems in the merger field seem more and more to be confined to discussions of relevant product and geographic markets and perhaps to the issue of quantitative substantiality.[3]

Presumably there is still a so-called failing-company defense to an illegal merger charge. The announced justification for this doctrine was that, if indeed the merged company was failing, then it was not actually a competitor in the industry.[4] But there are strong suggestions that even that defense may be unavailable when a large corporation is making the acquisition, or when there is any chance of absorption by a non-competing firm, or when the acquired company has not "failed" enough.[5]

There is general agreement among economists that the courts' approach to horizontal mergers is correct.[6] Professor Donald Dewey, who appears slightly regretful about the severe treatment of mergers by our courts and administrative agencies, concedes that no important economies can be attained through a merger

[3] Among the recent articles and cases bearing out this conclusion are the following: Donald Dewey, *op. cit.*; Richard E. Day, "Conglomerate Mergers and the 'Curse of Bigness,'" *North Carolina Law Review*, XLII (1964), 511–66; James A. Rahl, "Current Anti-Trust Developments in the Merger Field," *Anti-Trust Bulletin*, VIII (1963), 493–515; United States v. El Paso Natural Gas Company, 376 U.S. 651 (1964); and United States v. First National Bank and Trust Company of Lexington, 376 U.S. 665 (1964).

[4] International Shoe Company v. Federal Trade Commission, 280 U.S. 291, 294 (1929); but see Derek C. Bok, "Section 7 of the Clayton Act and the Merging of Law and Economics," *Harvard Law Review*, LXXIV (1960), 226–335, esp. p. 340, where concern for the interests in the failing company is argued to be the most likely reason for the doctrine.

[5] Derek C. Bok, *op. cit.*, pp. 339–47; and see cases cited in anonymous comment, "An Updating of the 'Failing Company' Doctrine in the Amended Section 7 Setting," *Michigan Law Review*, LXI (1963), 566–83.

There is also a "solely for investment" defense to Clayton Act charges. This appears as an explicit proviso in the third paragraph of Section 7, 15 U.S.C.A. sec. 18 (1962). But the famous du Pont-G. M. case, United States v. E. I. Du Pont de Nemours and Company, 353 U.S. 586 (1957), seems to have very substantially weakened the force of this proviso. Also see Swift and Co. v. F.T.C., 8 Fed. 2d 595, 599, reversed on other grounds, 272 U.S. 554 (1925), where it is stated: "It would be difficult to conceive of any case where one corporation purchased all the stock of its competitor solely for investment. Such a case would be a rare one."

There was once thought to be an illegal purpose requirement for convictions under the Sherman Act. See Eugene V. Rostow, "Monopoly under the Sherman Act: Power or Purpose?" *Illinois Law Review*, XLIII (1949), 745–92. But recent Supreme Court decisions in the merger field have left little vitality to that notion. Cf. United States v. First National Bank and Trust Company of Lexington, 376 U.S. 665, 669 (1964).

[6] See George J. Stigler, "Mergers and Preventive Anti-Trust Policy," *Pennsylvania Law Review*, CIV (1955), 176–84 (Stigler too recognizes the possibility that some mergers may increase competition, but he finds it "most uncommon" [p. 181]); M. A. Adelman, "The Anti-Merger Act, 1950–60," *American Economic Review*, LI (May, 1961), 236–54 ("The horizontal elements of mergers . . . have been treated severely and—if maintaining competition is the object—rationally" [p. 238]).

which cannot be gained either by internal growth or, at worst, by a cartel, if that were legal. But Dewey is certainly not as severe in his personal indictment of horizontal mergers as most other economists. He has argued that most mergers "have virtually nothing to do with either the creation of market power or the realization of scale economies. They are merely a civilized alternative to bankruptcy or the voluntary liquidation that transfers assets from falling to rising firms." [7]

Consistent with his alternative-to-bankruptcy explanation of mergers, Dewey points out that, "[i]f the capital market were perfect and a merger conferred no monopoly power, a rising firm would be indifferent between the two forms of expansion." [8] Thus a rapidly expanding industry with a relatively short life cycle of its firms would be characterized by substantial external growth of successful firms. Mergers then would "most commonly indicate not the decline of competition but its undoubted vigor." [9]

Dewey's argument is, however, only a partial redemption of mergers, since a great many have occurred in industries in which the life cycle of firms is not as short as in the southern textile industry, which he mentions as his example. Further, Dewey's defense of mergers seems to be limited to those cases in which bankruptcy or liquidation is imminent. But, if a merger can be justified at this stage of the firm's life, presumably it is also desirable before bankruptcy becomes imminent in order to avoid that eventuality. If, as Dewey suggests, mergers actually are superior to bankruptcy as a method of "shifting assets from falling to rising firms," and if mergers were completely legal, we should anticipate relatively few actual bankruptcy proceedings in any industry which was not itself contracting. The function so wastefully performed by bankruptcies and liquidations would be economically performed by mergers at a much earlier stage of the firm's life.

THE CORPORATE-CONTROL MARKET

The conventional approach to a merger problem takes corporations merely as decision-making units or firms within the classical market framework. This ap-

[7] "Mergers and Cartels: Some Reservations about Policy," *Market Economic Review*, LI (May, 1961), 257. Dewey analyzed four relatively unimportant cases of scale economies that can be realized only through a consolidation, but he concluded, in substantial agreement with Stigler and Adelman, "that the present experiment discouraging growth by mergers should be continued" with a ban in any industry not generally considered a good example of workable competition (p. 261).

Jesse W. Markham has remarked that some mergers are the "means by which some entrepreneurs make their exit from the industry, selling their undepreciated assets to other entrepreneurs. . . . Since 1930 most mergers appear to have been of the ordinary business variety in that they had neither monopoly nor promotional gains as their objective" ("Survey of the Evidence and Findings on Mergers," in *Business Concentration and Price Policy* [New York: National Bureau of Economic Research, 1955], p. 181). He concluded that "while some mergers impair a competitive enterprise system, others may be an integral part of it" (p. 182).

[8] "Mergers and Cartels . . . ," *op. cit.*, p. 257.

[9] *Ibid.*

proach dictates a ban on many horizontal mergers almost by definition. The basic proposition advanced in this paper is that the control of corporations may constitute a valuable asset; that this asset exists independent of any interest in either economies of scale or monopoly profits; that an active market for corporate control exists; and that a great many mergers are probably the result of the successful workings of this special market.

Basically this paper will constitute an introduction to a study of the market for corporation control. The emphasis will be placed on the antitrust implications of this market, but the analysis to follow has important implications for a variety of economic questions. Perhaps the most important implications are those for the alleged separation of ownership and control in large corporations. So long as we are unable to discern any control relationship between small shareholders and corporate management, the thrust of Berle and Means's famous phrase remains strong. But, as will be explained below, the market for corporate control gives to these shareholders both power and protection commensurate with their interest in corporate affairs.

A fundamental premise underlying the market for corporate control is the existence of a high positive correlation between corporate managerial efficiency and the market price of shares of that company.[10] As an existing company is poorly managed—in the sense of not making as great a return for the shareholders as could be accomplished under other feasible managements—the market price of the shares declines relative to the shares of other companies in the same industry or relative to the market as a whole. This phenomenon has a dual importance for the market for corporate control.

In the first place, a lower share price facilitates any effort to take over high-

---

[10] The claim of a positive correlation between managerial efficiency and the market price of shares would seem at first blush to raise an empirical question. In fact, however, the concept of corporate managerial efficiency, with its overtones of an entrepreneurial function, is one for which there are no objective standards. But there are compelling reasons, apart from empirical data, for believing that this correlation exists. Insiders, those who have the most reliable information about corporate affairs, are strongly motived financially to perform a kind of arbitrage function for their company's stock. That is, given their sense of what constitutes efficient management, they will cause share prices to rise or decline in accordance with that standard.

The contention is often made that stock-market prices are not accurate gauges, since far more trades take place without reliable information than with it. But there is reason to believe that intelligence rather than ignorance ultimately determines the course of individual share prices. Stock-market decisions tend to be of the one-out-of-two-alternatives variety, such as buy or not buy, hold or sell, or put or call. To the extent that decisions on these questions are made by shareholders or potential shareholders operating without reliable information, over a period of time the decisions will tend to be randomly distributed and the effect will therefore be neutral. Decisions made by those with higher degrees of certainty will to that extent not meet a canceling effect since they will not be made on a random basis. Over some period of time it would seem that the average market price of a company's shares must be the "correct" one.

paying managerial positions. The compensation from these positions may take the usual forms of salary, bonuses, pensions, expense accounts, and stock options. Perhaps more important, it may take the form of information useful in trading in the company's shares; or, if that is illegal, information may be exchanged and the trading done in other companies' shares. But it is extremely doubtful that the full compensation recoverable by executives for managing their corporations explains more than a small fraction of outsider[11] attempts to take over control. Take-overs of corporations are too expensive generally to make the "purchase" of management compensation an attractive proposition.[12]

It is far more likely that a second kind of reward provides the primary motivation for most take-over attempts. The market price of shares does more than measure the price at which the normal compensation of executives can be "sold" to new individuals. Share price, or that part reflecting managerial efficiency, also measures the potential capital gain inherent in the corporate stock. The lower the stock price, relative to what it could be with more efficient management, the more attractive the take-over becomes to those who believe that they can manage the company more efficiently. And the potential return from the successful take-over and revitalization of a poorly run company can be enormous.[13]

Additional leverage in this operation can be obtained by borrowing the funds with which the shares are purchased, although American commercial banks are generally forbidden to lend money for this purpose. A comparable advantage can be had from using other shares rather than cash as the exchange medium. Given the fact of special tax treatment for capital gains, we can see how this mechanism for taking over control of badly run corporations is one of the most important "get-rich-quick" opportunities in our economy today.

But the greatest benefits of the take-over scheme probably inure to those least conscious of it. Apart from the stock market, we have no objective standard of managerial efficiency. Courts, as indicated by the so-called business-judgment rule, are loath to second-guess business decisions or remove directors from office. Only the take-over scheme provides some assurance of competitive efficiency among corporate managers and thereby affords strong protection to the interests of vast numbers of small, non-controlling shareholders. Compared to this mechanism, the efforts of the SEC and the courts to protect shareholders through the development of a fiduciary duty concept and the shareholder's derivative suit seem small indeed. It is true that sales by dissatisfied shareholders are necessary to trigger the mechanism and that these shareholders may suffer considerable

[11] "Outsider" here refers to anyone not presently controlling the affairs of the corporation, even though it may include one or more individuals on the corporation's board of directors.

[12] To the extent that executive compensation increases with higher share prices, the take-over is most attractive at the time when it is also most expensive. Indeed, the danger of a take-over may account for managers' voluntarily decreasing their compensation when the company's share price is down.

[13] The clearest modern illustration is probably furnished by Louis Wolfson's successful venture into Montgomery Ward. For details of this and other large stock price gains associated with corporation "raids" see David Karr, *Fight for Control* (New York: Ballantine Books, 1956).

losses. On the other hand, even greater capital losses are prevented by the existence of a competitive market for corporate control.[14]

There are several mechanisms for taking over the control of corporations. The three basic techniques are the proxy fight, direct purchase of shares, and the merger. The costs, practical difficulties, and legal consequences of these approaches vary widely. The selection of one or another or some combination of these techniques frequently represents a difficult strategy decision. An attempt will be made in this paper to analyze some of the considerations involved in a selection of one device over another.

PROXY FIGHTS

The most dramatic and publicized of the take-over devices is the proxy fight; it is also the most expensive, the most uncertain, and the least used of the various techniques. Indeed it is somewhat difficult to describe the necessary conditions under which a proxy fight rather than some other take-over form will be indicated. At first blush, the proxy fight appears to be inexpensive since one does not have to own a large number of shares (or for that matter any shares) in order to wage a fight. But this fact is most relevant when the take-over is for the purpose of gaining the incumbents' compensation. If the outsider wants capital gains, he will be interested in owning more, not fewer, shares. This suggests that proxy fights will be relatively more often used when the issue is not one of management policies but of distribution of insiders' compensation.[15]

Even as a device for settling internal power struggles, actual proxy fights constitute only a small percentage of threatened fights.[16] The parties will generally prefer to negotiate a settlement in accordance with their respective strengths than incur the costs of soliciting proxies. The more reliable the information about relative strengths available, the more will settlement be likely to occur. This suggests that proxy fights will be relatively more common when there is widespread dis-

[14] Unfortunately the suppression of this market would be the consequence of proposals made by several writers in the field. For a review and a criticism of this literature see Henry G. Manne, "The 'Higher Criticism' of the Modern Corporation," *Columbia Law Review*, LXII (1962), 399–432. For another defense of this market see Harry G. Johnson, *The Canadian Quandary* (Toronto: McGraw-Hill Book Co., 1963), pp. xvii–xviii.

[15] The courts draw a similar distinction for purposes of determining when contestants in a proxy fight may recover their expenses from the corporate treasury. Generally they may recover if the contest is found to be one of policy rather than a "purely personal power contest" (Rosenfeld v. Fairchild Engine & Airplane Corp., 309 N.Y. 168, 129 N.E. 2d 291 [1955]). It does not seem to be too difficult, however, to establish the existence of a "policy" controversy to the court's satisfaction.

[16] In the SEC's fiscal year 1962 seventeen companies were involved in proxy contests, while a total of 253 persons, both management and non-management, filed statements as participants. The respective figures for 1961 were thirty-two proxy contests and 463 participant filings. Many non-management filings are multiple; that is, several people are involved in the same fight. But no breakdown beyond the total number of participants is available. Therefore, it is impossible to prove the point made in the text from published data. See *27th and 28th Annual Reports* (Washington: Securities and Exchange Commission, 1961 and 1962).

tribution of the company's shares than when there are relatively large holdings.

In a number of cases the outsider would probably like to own more shares and take over control without waging or threatening a proxy fight. But if he is unable to accumulate sufficient capital to purchase control directly, he may settle for half a loaf. In effect he indicates his willingness to share the capital-gain potential with all other shareholders in exchange for enough of their votes to put him into control.

When a proxy fight is announced, the shares tend to rise in price, reflecting a rise in both the market value of the vote and the discounted value of potential gain in the underlying share interest if the outsider wins.[17] Other outsiders will find it in their interest to retain their shares or purchase shares, to vote for the outsider seeking control, and to share in the capital appreciation. It may be cheaper to elicit the support of these voters through expenditures on persuasion than through outright purchase of the shares. But to the outsider seeking control, every voter represents another person with whom he must share the potential gain resulting from his more efficient management. These voters are analogous to, or substitutes for, the capital or credit with which the outsider would otherwise purchase control directly.

Proxy-fight expenses have always included direct expenses of mailings, advertising, telephone calls, and visits to large shareholders. But since the Securities Exchange Act of 1934, the cost of waging a proxy fight has probably increased substantially. Prior to the act, the proxy system operated largely through broker intermediaries acting as full agents for the beneficial owners of the shares. To the brokers was delegated not merely the ministerial job of voting but the more important responsibility of deciding how to vote. That practice has been largely replaced because of the SEC philosophy that the proxy system should duplicate actual meetings of shareholders as closely as possible. Thus, today, "giving a proxy" is really tantamount to voting. And, since the shareholder himself is voting, it is also felt that he should be fully and truthfully informed about all aspects of the corporation's affairs. This has tremendously increased the cost of soliciting proxies. But while the incumbents finance the bulk of their proxy solicitation expenses from corporate funds, the outsider will have this advantage only if he wins.[18]

---

[17] See Henry G. Manne, *op. cit.*, pp. 410–13. It is possible, of course, for the vote price to be rising while the market value of the underlying investment interest is declining, though this would seem to be uncommon.

[18] The SEC rules on proxy solicitations have aided the insiders in unexpected and curious ways. Outsiders in a proxy fight are not privy to the particulars of corporate information as are the insiders, so they must frequently "guess" why the company is not doing as well as it should. These "guesses" will take the form of broad accusations and innuendoes directed at the incumbents. Outsiders would like the opportunity to include in their proxy solicitation such general statements as "the incumbents are wasting corporate assets"; "the incumbents are paying themselves fraudulently high salaries"; or "the officers of the company have been negligent in failing to acquire new opportunities for the corporation." The SEC generally refuses to allow such statements to be mailed to shareholders unless the insurgents can prove the truthfulness of the allegations. Frequently there is no way the insurgents can find that proof, short of discovery proceedings in a suit, though they might in all good faith suspect

DIRECT PURCHASE OF SHARES

The second mechanism for taking over control of a corporation is the direct purchase of the requisite number of shares of the corporations. There are several techniques that may be used in the direct purchase of shares. The most obvious is outright purchase on the open market of the requisite percentage of shares.[19] The outsider might also try to buy the shares from large individual owners, thus preserving secrecy and allowing negotiation on price. Finally, he may make a bid for tenders, that is, a request that shareholders make an offer to sell their shares to him at a certain price, usually above the market. This last form of direct purchase is most apposite when the shares are widely held and there is a chance of a fast increase in market price if the news spreads that there is a heavy buyer in the market for the company's shares. A tender bid is usually stated to be effective only if a minimum percentage of shares is offered at the announced price. Also, the bid will ordinarily be for less than 100 per cent of the shares in order to avoid the problem of many individual shareholders trying to be the sole holdout. In practice, private negotiation for large blocks of shares may be combined with either open-market purchases or a tender bid.

There are few serious legal problems with any of the direct purchase techniques. In fact, about the only one which has arisen with any regularity in recent years results from Professor Adolf A. Berle's contention that control is a corporate asset.[20] The implication of this notion is that any premium received by

---

the facts alleged. Therefore, the practice has developed of filing shareholder derivative suits when a proxy fight is decided upon. Then the solicitation materials may legally say, "A shareholder's derivative suit is presently pending in the Federal District Court for the Southern District of New York charging the officers and directors with waste of corporate assets"; or "a suit to force the officers to pay back part of their salaries has been filed by a shareholder in Delaware"; etc.

Not only has the Securities Exchange Act increased the cost of waging a proxy fight because of the additional materials that must be cleared through the SEC, but it has also increased uncertainty because of the panoply of SEC regulations. For instance, the Chicago and North Western Railroad's successful fight against the Union Pacific's first bid for control of the Rock Island Railroad was recently voided on the grounds, among others, that unsolicited advice by a broker to his customer advising acceptance of the C. & N.W.'s offer constituted an illegal solicitation of proxies (Union Pacific Railroad Company v. Chicago and North Western Railway Company, 226 F. Supp. 400 [N.D., Ill., 1964]).

[19] This percentage may range from less than 51 per cent if the purchaser is only interested in establishing a foundation for a proxy fight; to 51 per cent when only simple control is desired; to 66⅔ or 75 per cent, when state law requires that percentage for approval of a merger or reorganization; to 80 per cent, the figure required for consolidation of income statements under the Internal Revenue Code as well as for tax-free reorganizations; to 90 per cent, the figure required for simplified mergers of subsidiaries into parent companies in Delaware (95 per cent in New York); or 100 per cent if no minority interests are wanted.

[20] Adolf A. Berle and Gardiner C. Means, *The Modern Corporation and Private Property* (New York: MacMillan Co., 1933), p. 244; Adolf A. Berle, " 'Control' in Corporate Law," *Columbia Law Review*, LVIII (1958), 1212–25, esp. 1221.

an individual for a sale of control belongs in equity to all of the shareholders. As a general proposition, the courts have refused to follow this thesis; and there are numerous judicial statements to the effect that one may claim a premium for control.[21]

A number of legal writers, following Berle, continue to press for a rule of equality in share purchase price when an outsider buys control in a corporation.[22] The economic results of such a rule could be most unfortunate. Many holders of control blocks of shares would refuse to sell at a share price which did not pay them a premium at least sufficient to compensate them for the loss of net values presently being received from their position in the corporation. If all non-controlling shareholders must accordingly be paid a premium over the market price of their shares, then in a substantial number of cases the purchaser will not conclude the bargain. This further suggests that, if control is securely held in one block, the "market price" of traded shares is the price for an underlying share interest without an aliquot portion of control. That is, if one person owns 51 per cent of the shares of a company, nothing will be paid for the vote attached to the other shares,[23] no matter how actively the shares may be traded on the market. The less securely control is held in one block, the more likely are non-controlling shareholders to participate in the "premium," and the less will an outsider be willing to pay one shareholder for control. Both proxy fights and competitive tender bids are more likely to occur under these conditions, since each of them gives shareholders the power to sell their votes at a premium.

[21] The difficult cases have been those in which control carried with it peculiar advantages not normally assumed to be part of the standard compensation of corporate managers. The problem is illustrated by the now classic case of Perlman v. Feldmann, 219 F. 2d 172 (2d Cir., 1955), in which only a controlling block of shares was purchased, but at a price reflecting the value of the right to allocate the company's steel production to the purchaser at a time when quasi-official price controls existed. The court found the control seller liable to the other shareholders for a part of the premium received over the normal market price of the shares. The most convincing factor, not emphasized by the court, was that the company had probably been receiving a full free-market price for its steel, with the difference over the controlled price taken in the form of interest-free loans and guaranteed future orders. Indications were that the new controllers would sell to themselves at the "quasi-legal" price and discontinue these other valuable practices. Thus the premium paid for the control block of shares was given partly in exchange for a right more appropriately thought of as belonging equally to each share than to the control group. That is, if a "gray-market" profit was to be made, it should go to all the shareholders. The court was explicit, however, that the seller could retain that part of the premium received for control not covering the power to allocate steel.

[22] Richard W. Jennings, "Trading in Corporate Control," *California Law Review*, XLIV (1956), 1–39; and Noyes Leech, "Transactions in Corporate Control," *University of Pennsylvania Law Review*, CIV (1956), 725–839. For a sharply opposing viewpoint see Wilbur G. Katz, "The Sale of Corporate Control," *Chicago Bar Record*, XXXVIII (1957), 376–80; also Alfred Hill, "The Sale of Controlling Shares," *Harvard Law Review*, LXX (1957), 986–1039.

[23] This holds true only to the extent that 51 per cent is the relevant majority. If a higher percentage is necessary for some purpose, minority votes will have some value so long as the requisite percentage is not already controlled.

MERGERS

The third major mechanism for taking over control of the corporation is the merger. Here, by definition, the acquiring concern will be a corporation and not an individual, and the medium of exchange used to buy control will typically be shares of the acquiring company rather than cash. Another major difference between the merger and other take-over forms is that, almost without exception, a merger requires the explicit approval of those already in control of the corporation.[24] And most statutes require more than a simple majority vote by shareholders to effectuate a merger. If the merger occurs after an acquisition of shares in a tender bid, then the tender bid and not the merger is the actual mechanism for changing control.

The requirements of management's approval for a merger generates some peculiar results. Generally speaking, managers' incentives and interests coincide with those of their shareholders in every particular except one: they have no incentive, as managers, to buy management services for the company at the lowest possible price.[25] Even if the market for corporate control is working perfectly, so long as the cost to the corporation of the incumbent managers' inefficiency is below the cost to an outsider of taking over control, the insiders will remain secure in the positions with protected high salaries.[26]

In the case of tender bids, as we have seen, a premium for control may be paid; and in the proxy fight situation, in one sense at least, the premium is paid in the form of expenditures necessary to persuade shareholders to vote a certain way. But the merger has considerable cost advantages over the other two forms of take-over, not the least being the ability to use shares rather than cash as the purchasing medium.

The shareholders should ordinarily be willing to accept any offer of a tax-free exchange of new marketable shares worth more than their old shares. But the managers are in a position to claim almost the full market value of control, since they have it in their power to block the merger by voting against it.[27] When we find incumbents recommending a control change, it is generally safe to assume that some side payment is occurring.

[24] There is a slight possibility that outsiders might be able to force a merger vote by shareholders under the Securities Exchange Act's "Stockholder's Proposal" Rule, although the SEC seems to take the position that such a proposal may only be advisory, not mandatory, on the board, if passed. See Louis Loss, *Securities Regulation* (Boston: Little, Brown & Co., 1961), p. 908.

[25] To the extent that the same individuals are also shareholders, their motivation will reflect a conflict. If their ownership interest is great enough, they may sacrifice the emoluments of management in order to improve their position as shareholders. The decision will simply reflect the greater of the two conflicting interests.

[26] This may furnish some proof for the notion that executive compensation is a function of size. If the cost of taking over control is a function of the number of shareholders, as it certainly is in the case of proxy fights, it is likely that managers may be able to claim larger compensation to the extent of the higher cost to outsiders of buying control.

[27] The greater the shareholdings of management, the more likely they are to approve a merger offer with little or no side payment.

Side payments are often not simple transactions at law because of the rule that directors and officers may not sell their positions shorn of the share interest necessary to insure a transfer of control.[28] The most obvious kind of side payment to managers is a position within the new structure either paying a salary or making them privy to valuable market information.[29] This arrangement, easily established with mergers, can look like normal business expediency, since the argument can always be made that the old management provides continuity and a link with the past experience of the corporation.

There is still another very important reason why mergers may be more desirable than proxy fights or take-over bids as a way of operating in the corporate-control market. This is a market in which reliable information about valuable opportunities will be extremely difficult to discover. For reasons already mentioned, the corporate insiders will generally have no incentive to advertise this kind of information. Blatant cases will, of course, be evident from casual observation of industrial affairs and the stock market.[30]

The great problem in the corporate-control market is finding reliable information about new opportunities. There have generally been a few individual operators in this market, and perhaps they have found the more obvious cases of bad management. But to guarantee effective competition in the market for corporate control, it seems clear that corporations must be allowed to function therein. Managers of a competing firm, unlike free-wheeling individual participants in the market for corporate control, almost automatically know a great deal of the kind of information crucial to a take-over decision. Careful analysis of cost conditions in their own firm and the market price of shares of other corporations in the same industry will provide information that can be relied upon with some degree of confidence.

Since, in a world of uncertainty, profitable transactions will be entered into more often by those whose information is relatively more reliable,[31] it should not surprise us that mergers within the same industry have been a principal form of changing corporate control. Reliable information is often available to suppliers

[28] Essex Universal Corp. v. Yates 305 F.2d (2d Cir., 1962).
[29] See, e.g., Smith v. The Good Music Station, 129 A.2d 242 (Del. Ch. 1957), and Borak v. J. I. Case Co., 317 Fed. 2d 838, at 844 (7th Cir., 1963), aff'd 377 U.S. 426 (1964). There are no reported cases of differential numbers of shares being offered controlling and non-controlling shareholders in a merger. Such an arrangement may be illegal under state statutes, and it is not likely to receive the high-majority-share vote required for most mergers.
[30] The most obvious example is that of a corporation whose total assets in liquidation would be worth more than the aggregate market value of all of its shares. This situation can continue to exist only because no individual shareholder believes there is any way of claiming the premium, since the managers will take no step toward liquidation and there is no indication that the corporation will not continue to be badly run. Perhaps the classic case of this sort was the take-over by Louis Wolfson of the Capital Transit Corporation. For this and other examples see Karr, *op. cit.*, p. 150.
[31] Cf. H. B. Malmgren, "Information, Expectations, and the Theory of the Firm," *Quarterly Journal of Economics*, LXXIX (1961), 399–421; and George J. Stigler, "The Economics of Information," *Journal of Political Economy*, LXIX (1961), 213–25.

and customers as well. Thus many vertical mergers may be of the control takeover variety rather than of the "foreclosure of competitors" or scale-economies type. Undoubtedly many more mergers, both horizontal and vertical, would have occurred but for our antitrust laws. The managers of corporations have considerable incentive to exploit such opportunities for their corporation, just as they are motivated to find any good new investment opportunity. And there are both legal and practical barriers to the individuals' utilizing such opportunities for themselves.

CONCLUSIONS

Mergers seem in many instances to be the most efficient of the three devices for corporate take-overs. Consequently, they are of considerable importance for the protection of individual non-controlling shareholders and are desirable from a general welfare-economics point of view. Certainly they are more desirable than the increased number of bankruptcies that would undoubtedly ensue if this avenue of taking over control were totally closed.

This is not to suggest that the antitrust norm of competition in the product market need be entirely sacrificed to the norm of competition in the market for corporate control. Rather it points up some of the serious problems with current antitrust doctrine. The market for corporate control implies a number of important advantages which must be compared to those existing in present antitrust enforcement. Among the advantages of the former, as we have seen, are a lessening of wasteful bankruptcy proceedings, more efficient management of corporations, the protection afforded non-controlling corporate investors, increased mobility of capital, and generally a more efficient allocation of resources.

The greatest difficulty in assessing the proper role for the market for corporate control comes in the area of horizontal mergers, where, as previously indicated, this market may operate most effectively.[32] It may be that, so long as entry into an industry is kept open, there is no reason at all for rules against mergers, at least short of a monopolization charge under Section 2 of the Sherman Act. It is extremely unlikely, however, that Congress or the courts would ever adopt such a rule.

Far more likely is an *ad hoc* recognition of the importance of the market for corporate control in individual cases.[33] Courts or agencies might begin to look at such factors as the average life cycle of firms in the industry, the amount of total new investment in the industry, the condition of the acquired firms in terms of both financial and managerial strength, the number of bankruptcies in the industry, and the amount of proxy-fight and tender-bid activity. These factors would then have to be weighed on the scales with the more traditional

---

[32] The case for a free market in corporate control as between supplier and customer firms seems quite strong, since the arguments in favor of present anti-merger policy are perhaps weakest there. See Robert Bork, "Vertical Integration and the Sherman Act: The Legal History of an Economic Misconception," *University of Chicago Law Review*, XXII (1954), 157–201.

[33] This might be done either through the resurrection of the "business-purpose" doctrine or, in Clayton Act cases, by beefing up the "solely-for-investment" proviso. See n. 5. above.

approach in terms of number of firms in the industry, concentration ratios, size of the acquiring firm, and its acquisitions history. But no longer does the tendency to hold most mergers illegal per se seem justified.

One real problem will be in devising statistical methods for distinguishing mergers motivated by a quest for monopoly profit from those merely trying to establish more efficient management in poorly run companies. But if the theoretical aspects of these transactions are well enough understood, this should not be insuperable. There may be different effects on the prices of shares depending on the motive behind the merger. In the normal merger for acquisition of control, something will be paid by the acquiring company for the control opportunity. Since this factor does not figure largely in the market price of even badly run companies until the possibility of a takeover is known, the exchange ratio in the merger will appear to be too favorable to the acquired company, judged by the relative premerger announcement prices. The price of the shares of the acquiring company in such a merger should then tend to decrease and those of the acquired company to increase upon the announcement of the merger. If, on the other hand, the merger is motivated by a quest for market power, or by economies of scale available to both corporations, then the price of stock of each company should increase on the announcement of the merger terms. The first of these two results conforms to what seems most frequently to occur when mergers are announced, though no data are presently available on this subject.[34] The study of the economics of the market for corporate control is still in its infancy.

[34] A study of the effect of mergers on stock prices has been completed by the staff of the Subcommittee on Anti-Trust and Monopoly of the Senate Judiciary Committee. That study was unavailable at the time of writing this article.

Another possible approach to proof in this area is to determine if actual changes in the management personnel ultimately follow the merger. In mergers for market power, there is little reason to believe that this will occur very quickly; whereas, if the position is in the nature of a side payment, as it would be if the merger was motivated more by the control potential, we might anticipate somewhat earlier efforts to "ease out" the old managers of the acquired company.

21

The Economics of Information[1]

George J. Stigler

One should hardly have to tell academicians that information is a valuable resource: knowledge *is* power. And yet it occupies a slum dwelling in the town of economics. Mostly it is ignored: the best technology is assumed to be known; the relationship of commodities to consumer preferences is a datum. And one of the information-producing industries, advertising, is treated with a hostility that economists normally reserve for tariffs or monopolists.

There are a great many problems in economics for which this neglect of ignorance is no doubt permissible or even desirable. But there are some for which this is not true, and I hope to show that some important aspects of economic organization take on a new meaning when they are considered from the viewpoint of the search for information. In the present paper I shall attempt to analyze systematically one important problem of information—the ascertainment of market price.

THE NATURE OF SEARCH

Prices change with varying frequency in all markets, and, unless a market is completely centralized, no one will know all the prices which various sellers (or buyers) quote at any given time. A buyer (or seller) who wishes to ascertain the most favorable price must canvass various sellers (or buyers)—a phenomenon I shall term "search."

Reprinted from *Journal of Political Economy* (June 1961), by permission of The University of Chicago Press. Copyright, 1961, pp. 213–225.

[1] I have benefited from comments of Gary Becker, Milton Friedman, Zvi Griliches, Harry Johnson, Robert Solow, and Lester Telser.

The amount of dispersion of asking prices of sellers is a problem to be discussed later, but it is important to emphasize immediately the fact that dispersion is ubiquitous even for homogeneous goods. Two examples of asking prices, of consumer and producer goods respectively, are displayed in Table 21.1. The

Table 21.1

ASKING PRICES FOR TWO COMMODITIES

A. CHEVROLETS, CHICAGO, FEBRUARY, 1959*

PRICE (DOLLARS)	NO. OF DEALERS
2,350–2,400	4
2,400–2,450	11
2,450–2,500	8
2,500–2,550	4

B. ANTHRACITE COAL, DELIVERED (WASHINGTON, D.C.), APRIL, 1953†

PRICE PER TON (DOLLARS)	NO. OF BIDS
15.00–15.50	2
15.50–16.00	2
16.00–16.50	2
16.50–17.00	3
17.00–18.00	1
18.00–19.00	4

* Allen F. Jung, "Price Variations Among Automobile Dealers in Metropolitan Chicago," *Journal of Business*, XXXIII (January, 1960), 31–42.
† Supplied by John Flueck

automobile prices (for an identical model) were those quoted with an average amount of "higgling": their average was $2,436, their range from $2,350 to $2,515, and their standard deviation $42. The prices for anthracite coal were bids for federal government purchases and had a mean of $16.90 per ton, a range from $15.46 to $18.92, and a standard deviation of $1.15. In both cases the range of prices was significant on almost any criterion.

Price dispersion is a manifestation—and, indeed, it is the measure—of ignorance in the market. Dispersion is a biased measure of ignorance because there is never absolute homogeneity in the commodity if we include the terms of sale within the concept of the commodity. Thus, some automobile dealers might perform more service, or carry a larger range of varieties in stock, and a portion of the observed dispersion is presumably attributable to such differences. But it would be metaphysical, and fruitless, to assert that all dispersion is due to heterogeneity.

At any time, then, there will be a frequency distribution of the prices quoted by sellers. Any buyer seeking the commodity would pay whatever price is asked by the seller whom he happened to canvass, if he were content to buy from the first seller. But, if the dispersion of price quotations of sellers is at all large (relative to the cost of search), it will pay, on average, to canvass several sellers. Consider the following primitive example: let sellers be equally divided between asking prices of $2 and $3. Then the distribution of minimum prices, as search is lengthened, is shown in Table 21.2. The buyer who canvasses two sellers instead of one has an expected saving of 25 cents per unit, etc.

Table 21.2

DISTRIBUTION OF HYPOTHETICAL MINIMUM PRICES
BY NUMBERS OF BIDS CANVASSED

NUMBER OF PRICES CANVASSED	PROBABILITY OF MINIMUM PRICE OF		EXPECTED MINIMUM PRICE
	$2.00	$3.00	
1	.5	.5	$2.50
2	.75	.25	2.25
3	.875	.125	2.125
4	.9375	.0625	2.0625
∞	1.0	0	2.00

The frequency distributions of asking (and offering) prices have not been studied sufficiently to support any hypothesis as to their nature. Asking prices are probably skewed to the right, as a rule, because the seller of reproducible goods will have some minimum but no maximum limit on the price he can accept. If the distribution of asking prices is normal, the distributions of minimum prices encountered in searches of one, two, and three sellers will be those displayed in Figure 21.1. If the distribution is rectangular, the corresponding distributions would be those shown in Panel B. The latter assumption does not receive strong support from the evidence, but it will be used for a time because of its algebraic simplicity.

In fact, if sellers' asking prices (p) are uniformly distributed between zero and one, it can be shown that:[2] (1) The distribution of minimum prices with n searches is

[2] If $F(p)$ is the cumulative-frequency function of p, the probability that the minimum of n observations will be greater than p is

$$[1 - F(p)]^n = \left[\int^1 dx\right]^n.$$

$$n(1 - p)^{n-1}, \tag{21.1}$$

(2) the average minimum price is

$$\frac{1}{n+1},$$

and (3) the variance of the average minimum price is

$$\frac{n}{(n+1)^2(n+2)}.$$

Whatever the precise distribution of prices, it is certain that increased search will yield diminishing returns as measured by the expected reduction in the minimum asking price. This is obviously true of the rectangular distribution, with an expected minimum price of $1/(n+1)$ with n searches, and also of the normal distributions.[3] In fact, if a distribution of asking prices did not display this property, it would be an unstable distribution for reasons that will soon be apparent.[4]

For any buyer the expected savings from an additional unit of search will be approximately the quantity (q) he wishes to purchase times the expected reduction in price as a result of the search,[5] or

[3] The expected minimum prices with a normal distribution of mean M and standard deviation σ are

SEARCH	EXPECTED MINIMUM PRICE
1	M
2	$M - .564\sigma$
3	$M - .846\sigma$
4	$M - 1.029\sigma$
5	$M - 1.163\sigma$
6	$M - 1.267\sigma$
7	$M - 1.352\sigma$
8	$M - 1.423\sigma$
9	$M - 1.485\sigma$
10	$M - 1.539\sigma$

[4] Robert Solow has pointed out that the expected value of the minimum of a random sample of n observations,

$$E(n) = n \int_0^\infty p(1 - F)^{n-1} F' \, dp,$$

is a decreasing function of n, and

$$[E(n + 2) - E(n + 1)] - [E(n + 1) - E(n)]$$

is positive so the minimum decreases at a decreasing rate. The proofs involve the fact that the density function for the rth observation from the maximum in a sample of n is

$$n \binom{n-1}{r-1} F^{n-r}(1 - F)^{r-1} F' \, dp.$$

[5] The precise savings will be (a) the reduction in price times the quantity which would be purchased at the higher price—the expression in the text—*plus* (b) the average saving on the additional purchases induced by the lower price. I neglect this quantity, which will generally be of a smaller order of magnitude.

$$q \left| \frac{\partial_{\min}}{\partial_n} \right|. \tag{21.2}$$

The expected saving from given search will be greater, the greater the dispersion of prices. The saving will also obviously be greater, the greater the expenditure

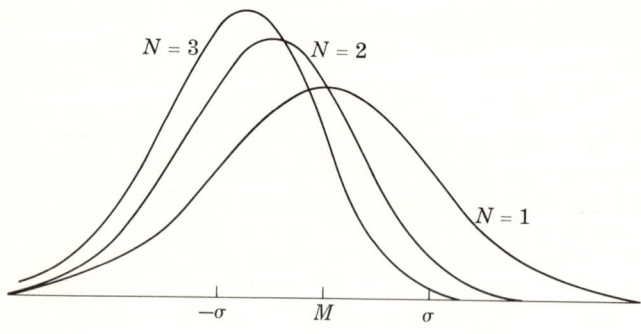

A. Normal Distribution

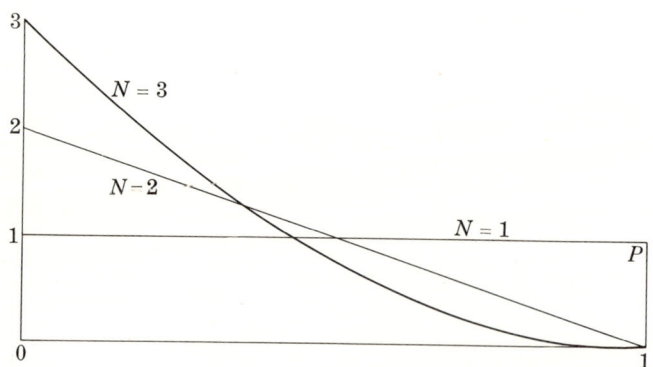

B. Uniform Distribution

Figure 21.1

on the commodity. Let us defer for a time the problem of the time period to which the expenditure refers, and hence the amount of expenditure, by considering the purchase of an indivisible, infrequently purchased good—say, a used automobile.

The cost of search, for a consumer, may be taken as approximately proportional to the number of (identified) sellers approached, for the chief cost is time. This cost need not be equal for all consumers, of course: aside from differences in tastes, time will be more valuable to a person with a larger income. If the cost of search is equated to its expected marginal return, the optimum amount of search will be found.[6]

---

[6] Buyers often pool their knowledge and thus reduce the effective cost of search; a few remarks are made on this method below.

Of course, the sellers can also engage in search and, in the case of unique items, will occasionally do so in the literal fashion that buyers do. In this—empirically unimportant—case, the optimum amount of search will be such that the marginal cost of search equals the expected increase in receipts, strictly parallel to the analysis for buyers.

With unique goods the efficiency of personal search for either buyers or sellers is extremely low, because the identity of potential sellers is not known—the cost of search must be divided by the fraction of potential buyers (or sellers) in the population which is being searched. If I plan to sell a used car and engage in personal search, less than one family in a random selection of one hundred families is a potential buyer of even a popular model within the next month. As a result, the cost of search is increased more than one hundredfold per price quotation.

The costs of search are so great under these conditions that there is powerful inducement to localize transactions as a device for identifying potential buyers and sellers. The medieval markets commonly increased their efficiency in this respect by prohibiting the purchase or sale of the designated commodities within a given radius of the market or on nonmarket days. The market tolls that were frequently levied on sellers (even in the absence of effective restrictions on non-market transactions) were clear evidence of the value of access to the localized markets.

Advertising is, of course, the obvious modern method of identifying buyers and sellers: the *classified* advertisements in particular form a meeting place for potential buyers and sellers. The identification of buyers and sellers reduces drastically the cost of search. But advertising has its own limitations: advertising itself is an expense, and one essentially independent of the value of the item advertised. The advertising of goods which have few potential buyers relative to the circulation of the advertising medium is especially expensive. We shall temporarily put advertising aside and consider an alternative.

The alternative solution is the development of specialized traders whose chief service, indeed, is implicitly to provide a meeting place for potential buyers and sellers. A used-car dealer, turning over a thousand cars a year, and presumably encountering three or five thousand each of buying and selling bids, provides a substantial centralization of trading activity. Let us consider these dealer markets, which we shall assume to be competitive in the sense of there being many independent dealers.

Each dealer faces a distribution of (for example) buyers' bids and can vary his selling prices with a corresponding effect upon purchases. Even in the markets for divisible (and hence non-unique) goods there will be some scope for higgling (discrimination) in each individual transaction: the buyer has a maximum price given by the lowest price he encounters among the dealers he has searched (or plans to search), but no minimum price. But let us put this range of indeterminacy aside, perhaps by assuming that the dealer finds discrimination too expensive,[7] and inquire how the demand curve facing a dealer is determined.

Each dealer sets a selling price, p, and makes sales to all buyers for whom this is the minimum price. With a uniform distribution of asking prices by

[7] This is the typical state of affairs in retailing except for consumer durable goods.

dealers, the number of buyers of a total of N_b possible buyers who will purchase from him is

$$N_i = KN_b n(1 - p)^{n-1}, \qquad (21.3)$$

where K is a constant.[8] The number of buyers from a dealer increase as his price is reduced, and at an increasing rate.[9] Moreover, with the uniform distribution of asking prices, the number of buyers increases with increased search if the price is below the reciprocal of the amount of search.[10] We should generally expect the high-price sellers to be small-volume sellers.

The stability of any distribution of asking prices of dealers will depend upon the costs of dealers. If there are constant returns to scale, the condition of equal rates of return dictates that the difference between a dealer's buying and selling prices be a constant. This condition cannot in general be met: any dealer can buy low, and sell high, provided he is content with a small volume of transactions, and he will then be earning more than costs (including a competitive rate of return). No other dealer can eliminate this non-competitive rate of profit, although by making the same price bids he can share the volume of business, or by asking lower prices he can increase the rewards to search and hence increase the amount of search.

With economies of scale, the competition of dealers will eliminate the profitability of quoting very high selling and very low buying prices and will render impossible some of the extreme price bids. On this score, the greater the decrease in average cost with volume, the smaller will be the dispersion of prices.[11] Many distributions of prices will be inconsistent with any possible cost conditions of dealers,[12] and it is not evident that strict equalities of rates of return for dealers are generally possible.

[8] Since $n(1 - p)^{n-1}$ is a density function, we must multiply it by a dp which represents the range of prices between adjacent price quotations. In addition, if two or more sellers quote an identical price, they will share the sales, so $K = dp/r$, where r is the number of firms quoting price p.

[9] For

$$\frac{\partial N_i}{\partial p} = -\frac{(n-1)N_i}{(1-p)} < 0,$$

and

$$\frac{\partial^2 N_i}{\partial p^2} = \frac{(n-1)(n-2)N_i}{(1-p)^2} > 0$$

if $n > 2$.

[10] Let

$$\log N_i = \log K + \log N_b + \log n + (n-1)\log(1-p).$$

Then

$$\frac{1}{N_i}\frac{\partial N_i}{\partial n} = \frac{1}{n} + \log(1-p) = \frac{1}{n} - p,$$

approximately.

[11] This argument assumes that dealers will discover unusually profitable bids, given the buyers' search, which is, of course, only partly true: there is also a problem of dealers' search with respect to prices.

[12] With the rectangular distribution of asking prices, if each buyer purchases the same number of units, the elasticity of demand falls continuously with price, so that, if average cost equaled price at every rate of sales (with one seller at each price), marginal costs would have to be negative at large outputs. But, of course, the number of sellers can be less at lower prices.

If economies of scale in dealing lead to a smaller dispersion of asking prices than do constant costs of dealing, similarly greater amounts of search will lead to a smaller dispersion of observed selling prices by reducing the number of purchasers who will pay high prices. Let us consider more closely the determinants of search.

Determinants of Search

The equation defining optimum search is unambiguous only if a unique purchase is being made—a house, a particular used book, etc. If purchases are repetitive, the volume of purchases based upon the search must be considered.

If the correlation of asking prices of dealers in successive time periods is perfect (and positive!), the initial search is the only one that need be undertaken. In this case the expected savings of search will be the present value of the discounted savings on all future purchases, the future savings extending over the life of the buyer or seller (whichever is shorter).[13] On the other hand, if asking prices are uncorrelated in successive time periods, the savings from search will pertain only to that period,[14] and search in each period is independent of previous experience. If the correlation of successive prices is positive, customer search will be larger in the initial period than in subsequent periods.[15]

The correlation of successive asking prices of sellers is usually positive in the handful of cases I have examined. The rank correlation of anthracite price bids (Table 21.1) in 1953 with those in 1954 was .68 for eight bidders; that for Chevrolet dealers in Chicago February and August of 1959 was .33 for twenty-nine dealers—but, on the other hand, it was zero for Ford dealers for the same dates. Most observed correlations will, of course, be positive because of stable differ-

[13] Let the expected minimum price be $p_1 = f(n)_1$ in period 1 (with $f' < 0$) and let the expected minimum price in period 2, with r a measure of the correlation between sellers' successive prices, be

$$p_2 = \left(\frac{p_1}{f(n_2)}\right)^r f(n_2).$$

If the cost of search is λ per unit, total expenditures for a fixed quantity of purchases (Q) per unit of time are, neglecting interest,

$$E = Q(p_1 + p_2) + \lambda(n_1 + n_2).$$

Expenditures are a minimum when

$$\frac{\partial E}{\partial n_1} = Qf'(n_1) + Qr[f(n_1)]^{r-1} \times [f(n_2)]^{1-r} f'(n_1) + \lambda = 0$$

and

$$\frac{\partial E}{\partial n_2} = (1-r)Q[f(n_1)]^r \times [f(n_2)]^{-r} f'(n_2) + \lambda = 0.$$

If $r = 1$, $n_2 = 0$, and n_1 is determined by $Qf'(n_1) = -\lambda/2$, the cost of search is effectively halved.

[14] See n. 13; if $r = 0$, $n_1 = n_2$.

[15] Let $f(n) = e^{-n}$. Then, in the notation of our previous footnotes,

$$n_1 - n_2 = \frac{2r}{1-r},$$

approximately.

ences in the products or services, but our analysis is restricted to conditions of homogeneity.

As a rule, positive correlations should exist with homogeneous products. The amount of search will vary among individuals because of differences in their expenditures on a commodity or differences in cost of search. A seller who wishes to obtain the continued patronage of those buyers who value the gains of search more highly or have lower costs of search must see to it that he is quoting relatively low prices. In fact, goodwill may be defined as continued patronage by customers without continued search (that is, no more than occasional verification).

A positive correlation of successive asking prices justifies the widely held view that inexperienced buyers (tourists) pay higher prices in the market than do experienced buyers.[16] The former have no accumulated knowledge of asking prices, and even with an optimum amount of search they will pay higher prices on average. Since the variance of the expected minimum price decreases with additional search, the prices paid by inexperienced buyers will also have a larger variance.

If a buyer enters a wholly new market, he will have no idea of the dispersion of prices and hence no idea of the rational amount of search he should make. In such cases the dispersion will presumably be estimated by some sort of sequential process, and this approach would open up a set of problems I must leave for others to explore. But, in general, one approaches a market with some general knowledge of the amount of dispersion, for dispersion itself is a function of the average amount of search, and this in turn is a function of the nature of the commodity:

1. The larger the fraction of the buyer's expenditures on the commodity, the greater the savings from search and hence the greater the amount of search.
2. The larger the fraction of repetitive (experienced) buyers in the market, the greater the effective amount of search (with positive correlation of successive prices).
3. The larger the fraction of repetitive sellers, the higher the correlation between successive prices, and hence, by condition (2), the larger the amount of accumulated search.[17]
4. The cost of search will be larger, the larger the geographical size of the market.

An increase in the number of buyers has an uncertain effect upon the dispersion of asking prices. The sheer increase in numbers will lead to an increase in the number of dealers and, *ceteris paribus*, to a larger range of asking prices. But, quite aside from advertising, the phenomenon of pooling information will increase. Information is pooled when two buyers compare prices: if each buyer

---

[16] For that matter, a negative correlation would have the same effects.

[17] If the number of sellers (s) and the asking-price distributions are the same in two periods, but k are new sellers, the average period-1 buyer will have lost proportion k/s of his period-1 search.

canvasses s sellers, by combining they effectively canvass $2s$ sellers, duplications aside.[18] Consumers compare prices of some commodities (for example, liquor) much more often than of others (for example, chewing gum)—in fact, pooling can be looked upon as a cheaper (and less reliable) form of search.

SOURCES OF DISPERSION

One source of dispersion is simply the cost to dealers of ascertaining rivals' asking prices, but even if this cost were zero the dispersion of prices would not vanish. The more important limitation is provided by buyers' search, and, if the conditions and participants in the market were fixed in perpetuity, prices would immediately approach uniformity. Only those differences could persist which did not remunerate additional search. The condition for optimum search would be (with perfect correlation of successive prices):

$$q \left| \frac{\partial p}{\partial n} \right| = i \times \text{marginal cost of search,}$$

where i is the interest rate. If an additional search costs \$1, and the interest rate is 5 per cent, the expected reduction in price with one more search would at equilibrium be equal to \$0.05/q—a quantity which would often be smaller than the smallest unit of currency. But, indivisibilities aside, it would normally be unprofitable for buyers or sellers to eliminate all dispersion.

The maintenance of appreciable dispersion of prices arises chiefly out of the fact that knowledge becomes obsolete. The conditions of supply and demand, and therefore the distribution of asking prices, change over time. There is no method by which buyers or sellers can ascertain the new average price in the market appropriate to the new conditions except by search. Sellers cannot maintain perfect correlation of successive prices, even if they wish to do so, because of the costs of search. Buyers accordingly cannot make the amount of investment in search that perfect correlation of prices would justify. The greater the instability of supply and/or demand conditions, therefore, the greater the dispersion of prices will be.

In addition, there is a component of ignorance due to the changing identity of buyers and sellers. There is a flow of new buyers and sellers in every market, and they are at least initially uninformed on prices and by their presence make the information of experienced buyers and sellers somewhat obsolete.

The amount of dispersion will also vary with one other characteristic which is of special interest: the size (in terms of both dollars and number of traders) of the market. As the market grows in these dimensions, there will appear a set of firms which specialize in collecting and selling information. They may take the form of trade journals or specialized brokers. Since the cost of collection of information is (approximately) independent of its use (although the cost of dissemination is not), there is a strong tendency toward monopoly in the provision of information: in general, there will be a "standard" source for trade information.

[18] Duplications will occur more often than random processes would suggest, because pooling is more likely between buyers of similar location, tastes, etc.

ADVERTISING

Advertising is, among other things, a method of providing potential buyers with knowledge of the identity of sellers. It is clearly an immensely powerful instrument for the elimination of ignorance—comparable in force to the use of the book instead of the oral discourse to communicate knowledge. A small $5 advertisement in a metropolitan newspaper reaches (in the sense of being read) perhaps 25,000 readers, or fifty readers per penny, and, even if only a tiny fraction are potential buyers (or sellers), the economy they achieve in search, as compared with uninstructed solicitation, may be overwhelming.

Let us begin with advertisements designed only to identify sellers; the identification of buyers will not be treated explicitly, and the advertising of price will be discussed later. The identification of sellers is necessary because the identity of sellers changes over time, but much more because of the turnover of buyers. In every consumer market there will be a stream of new buyers (resulting from immigration or the attainment of financial maturity) requiring knowledge of sellers, and, in addition, it will be necessary to refresh the knowledge of infrequent buyers.

Suppose, what is no doubt too simple, that a given advertisement of size a will inform c per cent of the potential buyers in a given period, so $c = g(a)$.[19] This contact function will presumably show diminishing returns, at least beyond a certain size of advertisement. A certain fraction, b, of potential customers will be "born" (and "die") in a stable population, where "death" includes not only departure from the market but forgetting the seller. The value of b will obviously vary with the nature of the commodity; for example, it will be large for commodities which are seldom purchased (like a house). In a first period of advertising (at a given rate) the number of potential customers reached will be cN, if N is the total number of potential customers. In the second period $cN(1-b)$ of these potential customers will still be informed, cbN new potential customers will be informed, and

$$c[(1-b)n - cN(1-b)]$$

old potential customers will be reached for the first time, or a total of

$$cN[1 + (1-b)(1-c)].$$

This generalizes, for k periods, to

$$cN[1 + (1-b)(1-c) + \ldots + (1-b)^{k-1}(1-c)^{k-1}],$$

and, if k is large, this approaches

$$\frac{cN}{1-(1-c)(1-b)} = \lambda N. \qquad (21.4)$$

The proportion (λ) of potential buyers informed of the advertiser's identity thus depends upon c and b.

[19] The effectiveness of the advertisement is also a function of the skill with which it is done and of the fraction of potential buyers who read the medium, but such elaborations are put aside.

If each of r sellers advertises the same amount, λ is the probability that any one seller will inform any buyer. The distribution of N potential buyers by the numbers of contacts achieved by r sellers is given by the binomial distribution:

$$N(\lambda + [1 - \lambda])^r,$$

with, for example,

$$\frac{Nr!}{m!(r-m)!} \lambda^m (1-\lambda)^{r-m}$$

buyers being informed of exactly m sellers' identities. The number of sellers known to a buyer ranges from zero to r, with an average of $r\lambda$ sellers and a variance of $r\lambda(1-\lambda)$.[20]

The amount of relevant information in the market, even in this simple model, is not easy to summarize in a single measure—a difficulty common to frequency distributions. If all buyers wished to search s sellers, all buyers knowing less than s sellers would have inadequate information, and all who knew more than s sellers would have redundant information, although the redundant information would not be worthless.[21] Since the value of information is the amount by which it reduces the expected cost to the buyer of his purchases, if these expected reductions are $\Delta C_1, \Delta C_2, \ldots$, for searches of 1, 2, $\ldots$, the value of the information to buyers is approximately

$$\sum_{m=1}^{r} \frac{r!}{m!(r-m)!} \lambda^m (1-\lambda)^{r-m} \Delta C_m.$$

The information possessed by buyers, however, is not simply a matter of chance; those buyers who spend more on the commodity, or who search more for a given expenditure, will also search more for advertisements. The buyers with more information will, on average, make more extensive searches, so the value of information will be greater than this last formula indicates.

We may pause to discuss the fact that advertising in, say, a newspaper is normally "paid" for by the seller. On our analysis, the advertising is valuable to the buyer, and he would be willing to pay more for a paper with advertisements than for one without. The difficulty with having the sellers insert advertisements "free" and having the buyer pay for them directly is that it would be difficult to ration space on this basis: the seller would have an incentive to supply an amount of information (or information of a type) the buyer did not wish, and, since numerous advertisements are supplied jointly, the buyer could not register clearly his preferences regarding advertising. (Catalogues, however, are often sold to buyers.) Charging the seller for the advertisements creates an incentive for him to supply to the buyer only the information which is desired.

It is commonly complained that advertising is jointly supplied with the commodity in the sense that the buyer must pay for both even though he wishes only the latter. The alternative of selling the advertising separately

[20] This approach has both similarities and contrasts to that published by S. A. Ozga, "Imperfect Markets through Lack of Knowledge," *Quarterly Journal of Economics*, LXXIV (February, 1960), 29–52.

[21] The larger the number of sellers known, the larger is the range of prices among the sellers and the lower the expected minimum price after s searches. But this effect will normally be small.

from the commodity, however, would require that the advertising of various sellers (of various commodities) would be supplied jointly: the economies of disseminating information in a general-purpose periodical are so great that some form of jointness is inescapable. But the common complaint is much exaggerated: the buyer who wishes can search out the seller who advertises little (but, of course, enough to be discoverable), and the latter can sell at prices lower by the savings on advertising.

These remarks seem most appropriate to newspaper advertisements of the "classified" variety; what of the spectacular television show or the weekly comedian? We are not equipped to discuss advertising in general because the problem of quality has been (and will continue to be) evaded by the assumption of homogeneous goods. Even within our narrower framework, however, the use of entertainment to attract buyers to information is a comprehensible phenomenon. The assimilation of information is not an easy or pleasant task for most people, and they may well be willing to pay more for the information when supplied in an enjoyable form. In principle, this complementary demand for information and entertainment is exactly analogous to the complementary demand of consumers for commodities and delivery service or air-conditioned stores. One might find a paradox in the simultaneous complaints of some people that advertising is too elaborate and school *houses* too shoddy.

A monopolist will advertise (and price the product) so as to maximize his profits,

$$\pi = Npq\lambda - \phi(N\lambda q) - ap_a,$$

where $p = f(q)$ is the demand curve of the individual buyer, $\phi(Nq\lambda)$ is production costs other than advertising, and ap_a is advertising expenditures. The maximum profit conditions are

$$\frac{\partial \pi}{\partial q} = N\lambda \left(p + q \frac{\partial p}{\partial q} \right) - \phi' N\lambda = 0 \qquad (21.5)$$

and

$$\frac{\partial \pi}{\partial a} = Npq \frac{\partial \lambda}{\partial a} - \phi' Nq \frac{\partial \lambda}{\partial a} - p_a = 0. \qquad (21.6)$$

Equation (21.5) states the usual marginal cost-marginal revenue equality, and equation (21.6) states the quality of (price − marginal cost) with the marginal cost $[p_a/Nq(\partial\lambda/\partial a)]$ of advertising.[22]

With the Cournot spring (where production costs $\phi = 0$) the monopolist advertises up to the point where price equals the marginal cost of informing a buyer: the monopolist will not (cannot) exploit ignorance as he exploits desire. The monopolist will advertise more, the higher the "death" rate (b), unless it is

---

[22] The marginal revenue from advertising expenditure,

$$\frac{Npq}{p_a} \frac{\partial \lambda}{\partial a},$$

equals the absolute value of the elasticity of demand by equations (21.5) and (21.6); see R. Dorfman and P. O. Steiner, "Optimal Advertising and Optimal Quality," *American Economic Review*, XLIV (1954), 826.

very high relative to the "contact" rate (c).[23] The monopolistic situation does not invite comparison with competition because an essential feature—the value of search in the face of price dispersion—is absent.

A highly simplified analysis of advertising by the competitive firm is presented in the Appendix. On the assumption that all firms are identical and that all buyers have identical demand curves and search equal amounts, we obtain the maximum-profit equation:

$$\text{Production cost} = p\left(1 + \frac{1}{\eta_{qp} + \eta_{Kp}}\right), \qquad (21.7)$$

where η_{qp} is the elasticity of a buyer's demand curve and η_{Kp}, is the elasticity of the fraction of buyers purchasing from the seller with respect to his price. The latter elasticity will be of the order of magnitude of the number of searches made by a buyer. With a uniform distribution of asking prices, increased search will lead to increased advertising by low-price sellers and reduced advertising by high-price sellers. The amount of advertising by a firm decreases as the number of firms increases.

Price advertising has a decisive influence on the dispersion of prices. Search now becomes extremely economical, and the question arises why, in the absence of differences in quality of products, the dispersion does not vanish. And the answer is simply that, if prices are advertised by a large portion of the sellers, the price differences diminish sharply. That they do not wholly vanish (in a given market) is due simply to the fact that no combination of advertising media reaches all potential buyers within the available time.

Assuming, as we do, that all sellers are equally convenient in location, must we say that some buyers are perverse in not reading the advertisements? Obviously not, for the cost of keeping currently informed about all articles which an individual purchases would be prohibitive. A typical household probably buys several hundred different items a month, and, if, on average, their prices change (in some outlets) only once a month, the number of advertisements (by at least several sellers) which must be read is forbiddingly large.

The seller's problem is even greater: he may sell two thousand items (a modest number for a grocery or hardware store), and to advertise each on the occasion of a price change—and frequently enough thereafter to remind buyers of his price—would be impossibly expensive. To keep the buyers in a market informed on the current prices of all items of consumption would involve perhaps a thousandfold increase of newspaper advertising.

From the manufacturer's viewpoint, uncertainty concerning his price is clearly disadvantageous. The cost of search is a cost of purchase, and consumption will therefore be smaller, the greater the dispersion of prices and the greater the optimum amount of search. This is presumably one reason (but, I conjecture, a very minor one) why uniform prices are set by sellers of nationally advertised brands: if they have eliminated price variation, they have reduced the cost of the com-

---

[23] Differentiating equation (21.6) with respect to b, we find that $\partial a/\partial b$ is positive or negative according as

$$b \lessgtr \frac{c}{1-c}.$$

If $c \geq \frac{1}{2}$, the derivative must be positive.

modity (including search) to the buyer, even if the dealers' margins average somewhat more than they otherwise would.

The effect of advertising prices, then, is equivalent to that of the introduction of a very large amount of search by a large portion of the potential buyers. It follows from our discussion in the first section that the dispersion of asking prices will be much reduced. Since advertising of prices will be devoted to products for which the marginal value of search is high, it will tend to reduce dispersion most in commodities with large aggregate expenditures.

CONCLUSIONS

The identification of sellers and the discovery of their prices are only one sample of the vast role of the search for information in economic life. Similiar problems exist in the detection of profitable fields for investment and in the worker's choice of industry, location, and job. The search for knowledge on the quality of goods, which has been studiously avoided in this paper, is perhaps no more important but, certainly, analytically more difficult. Quality has not yet been successfully specified by economics, and this elusiveness extends to all problems in which it enters.

Some forms of economic organization may be explicable chiefly as devices for eliminating uncertainties in quality. The department store, as Milton Friedman has suggested to me, may be viewed as an institution which searches for the superior qualities of goods and guarantees that they are good quality. "Reputation" is a word which denotes the persistence of quality, and reputation commands a price (or exacts a penalty) because it economizes on search. When economists deplore the reliance of the consumer on reputation—although they choose the articles they read (and their colleagues) in good part on this basis—they implicitly assume that the consumer has a large laboratory, ready to deliver current information quickly and gratuitously.

Ignorance is like subzero weather: by a sufficient expenditure its effects upon people can be kept within tolerable or even comfortable bounds, but it would be wholly uneconomic entirely to eliminate all its effects. And, just as an analysis of man's shelter and apparel would be somewhat incomplete if cold weather is ignored, so also our understanding of economic life will be incomplete if we do not systematically take account of the cold winds of ignorance.

Appendix I to Reading 21

Under competition, the amount of advertising by any one seller (i) can be determined as follows. Each buyer will engage in an amount s of search, which is determined by the factors discussed above in the first section. He will on average know

$$(r - 1)\lambda + \lambda_i$$

sellers, where λ_i is defined by equation (21.4) for seller i. Hence,

$$\frac{\lambda_i}{(r - 1)\lambda + \lambda_i}$$

per cent of buyers who know seller i will canvass him on one search, and

$$\left(1 - \frac{\lambda_i}{(r - 1)\lambda + \lambda_i}\right)^s$$

per cent of the buyers who know i will not canvass him in s searches,

$$s \leq (r - 1)\lambda + \lambda_i.$$

Therefore, of the buyers who know i, the proportion who will canvass him at least once is[24]

$$1 - \left(1 - \frac{\lambda_i}{(r - 1)\lambda + \lambda_i}\right)^s.$$

[24] The formula errs slightly in allowing the multiple canvass of one seller by a buyer.

If we approximate

$$\frac{\lambda_i}{(r-1)\lambda + \lambda_i}$$

by

$$\frac{\lambda_i}{r\lambda}$$

and take only the first two terms of the binomial expansion, this becomes

$$\frac{s\lambda_i}{r\lambda}.$$

The receipts of any seller then become the product of (1) the number of buyers canvassing him,

$$\frac{s\lambda_i}{r\lambda}\lambda_i N = T_i,$$

(2) the fraction K of those canvassing him who buy from him, where K depends upon his relative price (and the amount of search and the number of rivals), and (3) sales to each customer, pq. If $\phi(T_i Kq)$ is production costs and ap_a advertising costs, profits are

$$\pi = T_i K pq - \phi(T_i Kq) - ap_a.$$

The conditions for maximum profits are

$$\frac{\partial \pi}{\partial p} = T_i\left(K\frac{\partial pq}{\partial p} + pq\frac{\partial K}{\partial p}\right) - T_i\phi'\left(K\frac{\partial q}{\partial p} + q\frac{\partial K}{\partial p}\right) = 0 \quad (21.8)$$

and

$$\frac{\partial \pi}{\partial a} = Kpq\frac{\partial T_i}{\partial a} - \phi' Kq\frac{\partial T_i}{\partial a} - p_a = 0. \quad (21.9)$$

The former equation can be rewritten in elasticities as

$$\phi' = p\left(1 + \frac{1}{\eta_{qp} + \eta_{Kp}}\right) \quad (21.8a)$$

Price exceeds marginal cost, not simply by $(-p/\eta_{qp})$ as with monopoly, but by the smaller amount

$$\frac{-p}{\eta_{qp} + \eta_{Kp}},$$

where η_{Kp} will generally be of the order of magnitude of the number of searches made by a buyer.[25] Equation (21.2) states the equality of the marginal revenue of advertising with its marginal cost. By differentiating equation (21.2) with respect to s and taking ϕ' as constant, it can be shown that increased search by buyers will lead to increased advertising by low-price sellers and reduced advertising by high-price sellers (with a uniform distribution of prices).[26]

[25] In the case of the uniform distribution, η_{Kp} is

$$\frac{-(s-1)p}{1-p}.$$

[26] The derivative $\partial a/\partial s$ has the sign of $(1 + \eta_{Ks})$, and this elasticity equals

$$1 + s\log[1-p]$$

with a uniform distribution of prices.

By the same method it may be shown that the amount of advertising by the firm will decrease as the number of rivals increases.[27] The aggregate amount of advertising by the industry may either increase or decrease with an increase in the number of firms, s, depending on the relationship between λ and a.

[27] By differentiation of equation (21.2) with respect to r one gets

$$r \frac{\partial a}{\partial r} \left\{ \lambda_i \frac{\partial^2 \lambda_i}{\partial a^2} + \left(\frac{\partial \lambda_i}{\partial a}\right)^2 \right\} = \lambda_i \frac{\partial \lambda_i}{\partial a} \left(1 - \frac{r}{K} \frac{\partial K}{\partial r}\right).$$

The term in brackets on the left side is negative by the stability condition; the right side is positive.

22
The Economics of Advertising

Harry G. Johnson

The report on the Economics of Advertising, prepared by the Economists Advisory Group on the commission of the Advertising Association, was completed in three months. The subject posed three special problems, as the authors state in their introduction: the intellectual difficulty of handling advertising in the framework of conventional price and production theory, the dearth of empirical material testing propositions about advertising, especially for Britain (their own two efforts at empirical research produced results too inconclusive to be worth reporting), and the problem of achieving objectivity. Given the difficulties and the time constraint, the Report is, on the whole, admirably comprehensive and reasonably objective. The main criticism that can be made of it is that it is unnecessarily (and self-consciously) difficult to read, partly because the Group has a propensity to advertise the difficulty of economics, partly because of the way in which the material has been organised, but largely because the Group has not digested and ruminated over the materials it has assembled sufficiently for an integrated view of the economic role of advertising to emerge. It should, in fairness, be added that to do better would have demanded an exceptional degree of intellectual creativity: the economic problem of advertising is one aspect of the economics of information, and until very recently economic theory has been built on the assumption that information is a free good.

The study begins with a discussion of the factual importance of advertising in the national economy. Here it makes the important point that the ratios of advertising expenditure to net national income, gross national product, or consumers'

Reprinted from *The Advertising Quarterly*, no. 13 (Autumn 1964), pp. 9–14, by permission of the Advertising Association, London and the author.

expenditure customarily used to measure the importance of advertising are meaningless, because advertising expenditure is a production input whereas the other magnitudes are outputs. After some complex reasoning about national accounting concepts, the study concludes that a reasonable measure might be the ratio of the cost of advertising directed at final buyers of goods (i.e. excluding trade and technical advertising and advertising promoting saving, and deducting the net contribution of advertising revenue to the earnings of the communications media) to total resources available (total domestic final expenditures plus value of export sales). On this basis, the study concludes that advertising expenditure 'is certainly no more than *1 per cent* of total resources available'.

This figure, or others derivable by similar reasoning, might be taken as a maximum measure of the 'waste' of productive resources that might be involved in advertising. But the study is quite wrong to conclude from this figure that advertising is quantitatively insignificant, to launch into a diatribe against those who believe that advertising is either a good thing or a bad thing, and to ask 'how so small a commitment of the community's resources can have such far-reaching effects, whether good or bad'. Almost every distinguishable economic activity is a small percentage of the aggregate; as to social significance, it is equally certain that the resources required to pay the costs of Parliament (salaries of M.P.s, election expenses, operating costs) are a fraction of 1 per cent of any relevant aggregate; but no one in his right mind would use this fact alone to suggest that what goes on in Parliament cannot be as important for national welfare as everyone else seems to think, or to conclude that it makes no real difference whether government is democratic or dictatorial, or which party is in power.

PRESS 'SUBSIDY'

The study is on sounder ground in pointing out that advertising is a small part of total selling costs, and in asking why advertising should be singled out for special attention. But it does not raise the question of the economic function of selling expenditure.

This chapter concludes with a useful discussion of the notion that advertising provides a subsidy to the press and television. It argues, correctly, that the net advertising revenue of the communications media is not a subsidy—a gift from one party to the other—but the outcome of a mutually advantageous commercial transaction, and also that if advertising is socially undesirable, it cannot be defended on the grounds that part of its ill-gotten gains support socially desirable communications activities.

Chapter 3 moves on to summarise the position of economic theory on the place of advertising in the theory of the firm. Here the study makes matters excessively difficult for the reader by appraising economic theory in terms of that theory's own standards, rather than by what emerges for the practical man. Theory has tried to introduce advertising (more generally, selling expenditures) as a factor that affects both costs and revenues; the question for theory is whether any predictions can be made about the effects of the presence of advertising on the prevalence of excess capacity in the industries using advertising, and the effects of changes in economic conditions on the amount of advertising expenditures and the price of the product. The answer is that no reliable predictions can be made; the results depend on the circumstances. This is a failure for theory, conceived as a means of making qualitative predictions from limited qualitative information; but its pragmatic implication is that none of the questions to which we should like to know the answers can be settled by *a priori* reasoning: for example, pure theory does not tell us either that firms that advertise will have higher production costs than they could have, or that advertising is associated with lower costs resulting from economies of scale. This is a very important point for public discussion of the economic effects of advertising; no one's hunches or logical argument, however appealing or plausible, can be accepted as plausible without detailed study of the facts.

EMPIRICAL TESTS

Chapter 4 moves on from the formal (static) theory of the firm to a summary of hypotheses about the relation between advertising, good will, and oligopoly produced by various experts in the economics of industry. Chapter 5 summarises the empirical tests that other economists have made of these hypotheses. The main findings (mostly the result of American research) are as follows: While the prices of advertised goods tend to be higher than those of non-advertised goods, the difference may be accounted for by better quality and greater consumer certainty about quality. The evidence does not confirm the prediction that more heavily advertised brands will have a more stable share of the market than less heavily advertised brands; on the contrary, heavy advertising is associated with high brand turnover, implying that advertising is a means of competition rather than a method of establishing a monopoly. The proposition that advertising promotes industrial concentration (an increase in the market share of the three or four largest firms) is not supported by the evidence on concentration, which suggests that more fundamental forces are at work. Heavy advertising expenditure may be either a barrier to the entry of new competitors, or a means by which new competitors can establish themselves. There is no evidence that business concentration yields higher rates of profit. 'The empirical evidence is then that advertising is neither a general barrier to entry into manufacturing industries nor have particular cases of restrictions been convincingly established.' Advertising intensity is not correlated with the size of firms.

The study argues, convincingly, that even if a connection between advertising and oligopoly could be proved, correct public policy should attack oligopoly rather than advertising; if the attack is on advertising, it should logically be applied to all selling expenditures, since advertising is only one method of selling; and that it has yet to be shown that governmental restriction of advertising or selling expenditure would in fact produce an improvement over present actuality. On the other hand, it disposes effectively of two arguments that advertisers and businessmen have typically resorted to in defence of advertising—that advertising promotes large-scale lower-cost production, and that businessmen try to minimise selling costs. Both arguments are shown to involve the 'fallacy of composition'. Advertising may increase the scale of individual firms without increasing the scale of the economy; firms may minimise their own costs, but costs for all firms may be higher than they need be because of oligopolistic competition implemented through advertising.

INFORMATION AS A 'GOOD'

Chapter 6 turns from the production to the consumption side of the economy, examining the role of advertising in the theory of demand. This chapter introduces the concept of information as an economically expensive and valuable good, which advertising supplies, and raises the relevant question of whether that information could be supplied more cheaply without reducing consumer satisfaction. The study rightly dismisses the common distinction between informative and persuasive advertising as non-operational metaphysics. It then argues that the fact that advertising information is provided 'free', as a joint product with the good advertised, does not mean that the amount of it provided is excessive, because the 'contract costs' involved in providing joint products separately may make it more efficient to provide them jointly. Instead, it argues that the fact that advertising information is designed by the sellers of goods, and biased both by self-interest and by the libel laws, implies a need for independent information services for consumers, which should be provided through some social subsidisation arrangement. This is a valid point, though the question of what is 'information' and what is 'persuasion' arises as well with independent information services as with advertising. Finally, the study deals briefly with the vexed question of whether advertising 'creates' wants or merely caters to the better satisfaction of existing wants. This too is a metaphysical question; and the report wisely settles for the principle that what matters is whether or not the consumer has a wide range of choice: if he has, it must be assumed that what he chooses is what he wants.

Chapter 7 deals with the relation between advertising and price competition. Here the study makes the strong point that there is no real reason for preferring price competition to other forms of competition. In a world of imperfect knowledge, uncertainty, and technical change, the consumer is interested not only in the prices of standard goods supplied by rival suppliers but about improvements in the technical characteristics of these goods, and about the reliability of their performance; and he may rationally be attracted more by improved quality or more certain performance than by a lower price of an ambiguously specified product. The study also points out that price competition is frequently a substitute for advertising and other forms of non-price competition, which keeps the latter types of competition in line, and that non-price competition may indirectly be price competition—as in the case of the advertisement of superior quality at the same price, or the use of coupons, 'economy sizes', and so forth, which reduce the real cost to the consumer per unit of standard quality product. On the other hand, the study rightly disputes the view of some apologists for advertising, that price competition is unimportant: consumers are sensitive to prices, and any restriction on price competition among firms is a restriction on consumer freedom and economic efficiency.

'NOT SUITABLE'?

In summary, the Report is a comprehensive presentation of the economics of advertising as it now stands. Where it leaves most to be desired—unfortunately, from the point of view of sequence of topics—is in the emphasis placed in Chapter 2 on the assumed connection between the resources devoted to advertising and the presumptive social significance of advertising, and in the emphasis given in Chapter 3 to the assumption that if theory cannot produce definite predictions it is therefore useless. Understanding of the economics of advertising by the general public would have been better promoted by recognition that some of the things economists talk to each other about are not suitable for airing in public. On the other hand, the study could have contributed much more to public education by emphasising that information is not a free good, but that instead the provision of it is a socially useful process; that advertising is only one among a variety of selling (or buying) techniques that can be employed; and that advertising as we know it represents an accommodation by market competition between the kind of informational messages that consumers would like to have and the kind of effective selling messages that producers find it most economical to communicate, given the technology of the communications industries.

The approach of politicians and the general public to advertising, like that of economic theory, is still dominated by the idea that everyone knows what he wants, and that efforts to inform him either that what he wants can be obtained cheaper or in better quality elsewhere, or that what he really wants is something different from what he thinks he wants—on the basis of obsolete knowledge of the available alternatives—must involve a waste of resources for the knowledgeable and victimisation of those who are too gullible to trust their own judgment of their needs. In other words, public opinion on advertising needs to catch up with two not very complex ideas: that information is important, worth spending resources on acquiring; and that advertising is both only one of many ways of providing information, and a way that exploits the possibilities of mass provision of information opened up by the technologies of printing and of radio and television broadcasting. These technologies are changing the nature of our society, in ways that have been explored by Marshall McLuhan; it is a grave mistake to blame advertising for the changes.

23

Economic Welfare and the Allocation of Resources for Invention

Kenneth J. Arrow

Invention is here interpreted broadly as the production of knowledge. From the viewpoint of welfare economics, the determination of optimal resource allocation for invention will depend on the technological characteristics of the invention process and the nature of the market for knowledge.

The classic question of welfare economics will be asked here: to what extent does perfect competition lead to an optimal allocation of resources? We know from years of patient refinement that competition insures the achievement of a Pareto optimum under certain hypotheses. The model usually assumes among other things, that (1) the utility functions of consumers and the transformation functions of producers are well-defined functions of the commodities in the economic system, and (2) the transformation functions do not display indivisibilities (more strictly, the transformation sets are convex). The second condition needs no comment. The first seems to be innocuous but in fact conceals two basic assumptions of the usual models. It prohibits uncertainty in the production relations and in the utility functions, and it requires that all the commodities relevant either to production or to the welfare of individuals be traded on the market. This

"Economic Welfare and the Allocation of Resources for Invention" by Kenneth J. Arrow from *The Rate and Direction of Inventive Activity* (Copyright © 1962 by National Bureau of Economic Research; published by Princeton University Press, 1962). Reprinted by permission of Princeton University Press.

Note: I have benefited greatly from the comments of my colleague, William Capron. I am also indebted to Richard R. Nelson, Edward Phelps, and Sidney Winter of The RAND Corporation for their helpful discussion.

will not be the case when a commodity for one reason or another cannot be made into private property.

We have then three of the classical reasons for the possible failure of perfect competition to achieve optimality in resource allocation: indivisibilities, inappropriability, and uncertainty. The first problem has been much studied in the literature under the heading of marginal-cost pricing and the second under that of divergence between social and private benefit (or cost), but the theory of optimal allocation of resources under uncertainty has had much less attention. I will summarize what formal theory exists and then point to the critical notion of information, which arises only in the context of uncertainty. The economic characteristics of information as a commodity and, in particular, of invention as a process for the production of information are next examined. It is shown that all three of the reasons given above for a failure of the competitive system to achieve an optimal resource allocation hold in the case of invention. On theoretical grounds a number of considerations are adduced as to the likely biases in the misallocation and the implications for economic organization.[1]

RESOURCE ALLOCATION UNDER UNCERTAINTY

The role of the competitive system in allocating uncertainty seems to have received little systematic attention.[2] I will first sketch an ideal economy in which the allocation problem can be solved by competition and then indicate some of the devices in the real world which approximate this solution.

Suppose for simplicity that uncertainty occurs only in production relations. Producers have to make a decision on inputs at the present moment, but the outputs are not completely predictable from the inputs. We may formally describe the outputs as determined by the inputs and a "state of nature" which is unknown to the producers. Let us define a "commodity-option" as a commodity in the ordinary sense labeled with a state of nature. This definition is analogous to the differentiation of a given physical commodity according to date in capital theory or according to place in location theory. The production of a given commodity under uncertainty can then be described as the production of a vector of commodity-options.

This description can be most easily exemplified by reference to agricultural production. The state of nature may be identified with the weather. Then, to

[1] For other analyses with similar points of view, see R. R. Nelson, "The Simple Economics of Basic Scientific Research," *Journal of Political Economy*, 1959, pp. 297–306; and C. J. Hitch, "The Character of Research and Development in a Competitive Economy," The RAND Corporation, p. 1297, May 1958.

[2] The first studies I am aware of are the papers of M. Allais and myself, both presented in 1952 to the Colloque International sur le Risque in Paris; see M. Allais, "Généralisation des théories de l'équilibre économique général et du rendement social au cas du risque," and K. J. Arrow, "Rôle des valeurs boursières pour la répartition la meilleure des risques," both in *Économétrie*, Colloques Internationaux du Centre National de la Recherche Scientifique, vol. XL, Paris, Centre National de la Recherche Scientifique, 1953. Allais' paper has also appeared in *Econometrica*, 1953, pp. 269–290. The theory has received a very elegant generalization by G. Debreu in *Theory of Values*, New York, Wiley, 1959, chap. VII.

any given set of inputs there corresponds a number of bushels of wheat if the rainfall is good and a different number if rainfall is bad. We can introduce intermediate conditions of rainfall in any number as alternative states of nature; we can increase the number of relevant variables which enter into the description of the state of nature, for example by adding temperature. By extension of this procedure, we can give a formal description of any kind of uncertainty in production.

Suppose—and this is the critical idealization of the economy—we have a market for all commodity-options. What is traded on each market are contracts in which the buyers pay an agreed sum and the sellers agree to deliver prescribed quantities of a given commodity *if* a certain state of nature prevails and nothing if that state of nature does not occur. For any given set of inputs, the firm knows its output under each state of nature and sells a corresponding quantity of commodity-options; its revenue is then completely determined. It may choose its inputs so as to maximize profits.

The income of consumers is derived from their sale of supplies, including labor, to firms and their receipt of profits, which are assumed completely distributed. They purchase commodity-options so as to maximize their expected utility given the budget restraint imposed by their incomes. An equilibrium is reached on all commodity-option markets, and this equilibrium has precisely the same Pareto-optimality properties as competitive equilibrium under certainty.

In particular, the markets for commodity-options in this ideal model serve the function of achieving an optimal allocation of risk bearing among the members of the economy. This allocation takes account of differences in both resources and tastes for risk bearing. Among other implications, risk bearing and production are separated economic functions. The use of inputs, including human talents, in their most productive mode is not inhibited by unwillingness or inability to bear risks by either firms or productive agents.

But the real economic system does not possess markets for commodity-options. To see what substitutes exist, let us first consider a model economy at the other extreme, in that no provisions for reallocating risk bearing exist. Each firm makes its input decisions; then outputs are produced as determined by the inputs and the state of nature. Prices are then set to clear the market. The prices that finally prevail will be a function of the state of nature.

The firm and its owners cannot relieve themselves of risk bearing in this model. Hence any unwillingness or inability to bear risks will give rise to a nonoptimal allocation of resources, in that there will be discrimination against risky enterprises as compared with the optimum. A preference for risk might give rise to misallocation in the opposite direction, but the limitations of financial resources are likely to make underinvestment in risky enterprises more likely than the opposite. The inability of individuals to buy protection against uncertainty similarly gives rise to a loss of welfare.

In fact, a number of institutional arrangements have arisen to mitigate the problem of assumption of risk. Suppose that each firm and individual in the economy could forecast perfectly what prices would be under each state of nature. Suppose further there were a lottery on the states of nature, so that before the state of nature is known any individual or firm may place bets. Then it can be seen that the effect from the viewpoint of any given individual or firm is the same as if there were markets for commodity-options of all types, since any commodity-option can be achieved by a combination of a bet on the appropriate state of nature and an intention to purchase or sell the commodity in question if the state of nature occurs.

References to lotteries and bets may smack of frivolity, but we need only think of insurance to appreciate that the shifting of risks through what are in effect bets on the state of nature is a highly significant phenomenon. If insurance were available against any conceivable event, it follows from the preceding discussion that optimal allocation would be achieved. Of course, insurance as customarily defined covers only a small range of events relevant to the economic world; much more important in shifting risks are securities, particularly common stocks and money. By shifting freely their proprietary interests among different firms, individuals can to a large extent bet on the different states of nature which favor firms differentially. This freedom to insure against many contingenices is enhanced by the alternatives of holding cash and going short.

Unfortunately, it is only too clear that the shifting of risks in the real world is incomplete. The great predominance of internal over external equity financing in industry is one illustration of the fact that securities do not completely fulfill their allocative role with respect to risks. There are a number of reasons why this should be so, but I will confine myself to one, of special significance with regard to invention. In insurance practice, reference is made to the moral factor as a limit to the possibilities of insurance. For example, a fire insurance policy cannot exceed in amount the value of the goods insured. From the purely actuarial standpoint, there is no reason for this limitation; the reason for the limit is that the insurance policy changes the incentives of the insured, in this case, creating an incentive for arson or at the very least for carelessness. The general principle is the difficulty of distinguishing between a state of nature and a decision by the insured. As a result, any insurance policy and in general any device for shifting risks can have the effect of dulling incentives. A fire insurance policy, even when limited in amount to the value of the goods covered, weakens the motivation for fire prevention. Thus, steps which improve the efficiency of the economy with respect to risk bearing may decrease its technical efficiency.

One device for mitigating the adverse incentive effects of insurance is coinsurance; the insurance extends only to part of the amount at risk for the insured. This device is used, for example, in coverage of medical risks. It clearly represents a compromise between incentive effects and allocation of risk bearing, sacrificing something in both directions.

Two exemplifications of the moral factor are of special relevance in regard to highly risky business activities, including invention. Success in such activities depends on an inextricable tangle of objective uncertainties and decisions of the entrepreneurs and is certainly uninsurable. On the other hand, such activities should be undertaken if the expected return exceeds the market rate of return, no matter what the variance is.[3] The existence of common stocks would seem to solve the allocation problem; any individual stockholder can reduce his risk by buying only a small part of the stock and diversifying his portfolio to achieve his

---

[3] The validity of this statement depends on some unstated assumptions, but the point to be made is unaffected by minor qualifications.

own preferred risk level. But then again the actual managers no longer receive the full reward of their decisions; the shifting of risks is again accompanied by a weakening of incentives to efficiency. Substitute motivations whether pecuniary, such as executive compensation and profit sharing, or nonpecuniary, such as prestige, may be found, but the dilemma of the moral factor can never be completely resolved.

A second example is the cost-plus contract in one of its various forms. When production costs on military items are highly uncertain, the military establishment will pay, not a fixed unit price, but the cost of production plus an amount which today is usually a fixed fee. Such a contract could be regarded as a combination of a fixed-price contract with an insurance against costs. The insurance premium could be regarded as the difference between the fixed price the government would be willing to pay and the fixed fee.

Cost-plus contracts are necessitated by the inability or unwillingness of firms to bear the risks. The government has superior risk bearing ability and so the burden is shifted to it. It is then enabled to buy from firms on the basis of their productive efficiency rather than their risk bearing ability, which may be only imperfectly correlated. But cost-plus contracts notoriously have their adverse allocative effects.[4]

This somewhat lengthy digression on the theory of risk bearing seemed necessitated by the paucity of literature on the subject. The main conclusions to be drawn are the following: (1) the economic system has devices for shifting risks, but they are limited and imperfect; hence, one would expect an underinvestment in risky activities; (2) it is undoubtedly worthwhile to enlarge the variety of such devices, but the moral factor creates a limit to their potential.

INFORMATION AS A COMMODITY

Uncertainty usually creates a still more subtle problem in resource allocation; information becomes a commodity. Suppose that in one part of the economic system an observation has been made whose outcome, if known, would affect anyone's estimates of the probabilities of the different states of nature. Such observations arise out of research but they also arise in the daily course of economic life as a by-product of other economic activities. An entrepreneur will automatically acquire a knowledge of demand and production conditions in his field which is available to others only with special effort. Information will frequently have an economic value, in the sense that anyone possessing the information can make greater profits than would otherwise be the case.

It might be expected that information will be traded in, and of course to a considerable extent this is the case, as is illustrated by the numerous economic institutions for transmission of information, such as newspapers. But in many instances, the problem of an optimal allocation is sharply raised. The cost of transmitting a given body of information is frequently very low. If it were zero, then optimal allocation would obviously call for unlimited distribution of the information

---

[4] These remarks are not intended as a complete evaluation of cost-plus contracts. In particular, there are, to a certain extent, other incentives which mitigate the adverse effects on efficiency.

without cost. In fact, a given piece of information is by definition an indivisible commodity, and the classical problems of allocation in the presence of indivisibilities appear here. The owner of the information should not extract the economic value which is there, if optimal allocation is to be achieved; but he is a monopolist, to some small extent and will seek to take advantage of this fact.

In the absence of special legal protection, the owner cannot, however, simply sell information on the open market. Any one purchaser can destroy the monopoly, since he can reproduce the information at little or no cost. Thus the only effective monopoly would be the use of the information by the original possessor. This, however, will not only be socially inefficient, but also may not be of much use to the owner of the information either, since he may not be able to exploit it as effectively as others.

With suitable legal measures, information may become an appropriable commodity. Then the monopoly power can indeed be exerted. However, no amount of legal protection can make a thoroughly appropriable commodity of something so intangible as information. The very use of the information in any productive way is bound to reveal it, at least in part. Mobility of personnel among firms provides a way of spreading information. Legally imposed property rights can provide only a partial barrier, since there are obviously enormous difficulties in defining in any sharp way an item of information and differentiating it from other similar sounding items.

The demand for information also has uncomfortable properties. In the first place, the use of information is certainly subject to indivisibilities; the use of information about production possibilities, for example, need not depend on the rate of production. In the second place, there is a fundamental paradox in the determination of demand for information; its value for the purchaser is not known until he has the information, but then he has in effect acquired it without cost. Of course, if the seller can retain property rights in the use of the information, this would be no problem, but given incomplete appropriability, the potential buyer will base his decision to purchase information on less than optimal criteria. He may act, for example, on the average value of information in that class as revealed by past experience. If any particular item of information has differing values for different economic agents, this procedure will lead both to a nonoptimal purchase of information at any given price and also to a nonoptimal allocation of the information purchased.

It should be made clear that from the standpoint of efficiently distributing an existing stock of information, the difficulties of appropriation are an advantage, provided there are no costs of transmitting information, since then optimal allocation calls for free distribution. The chief point made here is the difficulty of creating a market for information if one should be desired for any reason.

It follows from the preceding discussion that costs of transmitting information create allocative difficulties which would be absent otherwise. Information should be transmitted at marginal cost, but then the demand difficulties raised above will exist. From the viewpoint of optimal allocation, the purchasing industry will be faced with the problems created by indivisibilities; and we still leave unsolved the problem of the purchaser's inability to judge in advance the value of the information he buys. There is a strong case for centralized decision making under these circumstances.

INVENTION AS THE PRODUCTION OF INFORMATION

The central economic fact about the processes of invention and research is that they are devoted to the production of information. By the very definition of information, invention must be a risky process, in that the output (information obtained) can never be predicted perfectly from the inputs. We can now apply the discussion of the preceding two sections.

Since it is a risky process, there is bound to be some discrimination against investment in inventive and research activities. In this field, especially, the moral factor will weigh heavily against any kind of insurance or equivalent form of risk bearing. Insurance against failure to develop a desired new product or process would surely very greatly weaken the incentives to succeed. The only way, within the private enterprise system, to minimize this problem is the conduct of research by large corporations with many projects going on, each small in scale compared with the net revenue of the corporation. Then the corporation acts as its own insurance company. But clearly this is only an imperfect solution.

The deeper problems of misallocation arise from the nature of the product. As we have seen, information is a commodity with peculiar attributes, particularly embarrassing for the achievement of optimal allocation. In the first place, any information obtained, say a new method of production, should, from the welfare point of view, be available free of charge (apart from the cost of transmitting information). This insures optimal utilization of the information but of course provides no incentive for investment in research. In an ideal socialist economy, the reward for invention would be completely separated from any charge to the users of the information.[5] In a free enterprise economy, inventive activity is supported by using the invention to create property rights; precisely to the extent that it is successful, there is an underutilization of the information. The property rights may be in the information itself, through patents and similar legal devices, or in the intangible assets of the firm if the information is retained by the firm and used only to increase its profits.

The first problem, then, is that in a free enterprise economy the profitability of invention requires a nonoptimal allocation of resources. But it may still be asked whether or not the allocation of resources to inventive activity is optimal. The discussion of the preceding section makes it clear that we would not expect this to be so; that, in fact, a downward bias in the amount of resources devoted to inventive activity is very likely. Whatever the price, the demand for information is less than optimal for two reasons: (1) since the price is positive and not at its optimal value of zero, the demand is bound to be below the optimal; (2) as seen before, at any given price, the very nature of information will lead to a lower demand than would be optimal.

As already remarked, the inventor will in any case have considerable difficulty in appropriating the information produced. Patent laws would have to be unimaginably complex and subtle to permit such appropriation on a large scale. Suppose, as the result of elaborate tests, some metal is discovered to have a desirable property, say resistance to high heat. Then of course every use of the

[5] This separation exists in the Soviet Union, according to N. M. Kaplan and R. H. Moorsteen of The RAND Corporation (verbal communication).

metal for which this property is relevant would also use this information, and the user would be made to pay for it. But, even more, if another inventor is stimulated to examine chemically related metals for heat resistance, he is using the information already discovered and should pay for it in some measure; and any beneficiary of his discoveries should also pay. One would have to have elaborate distinctions of partial property rights of all degrees to make the system at all tolerable. In the interests of the possibility of enforcement, actual patent laws sharply restrict the range of appropriable information and thereby reduce the incentives to engage in inventive and research activities.

These last considerations bring into focus the interdependence of inventive activities, which reinforces the difficulties in achieving an optimal allocation of the results. Information is not only the product of inventive activity, it is also an input—in some sense, the major input apart from the talent of the inventor. The school of thought that emphasizes the determination of invention by the social climate as demonstrated by the simultaneity of inventions in effect emphasizes strongly the productive role of previous information in the creation of new information. While these interrelations do not create any new difficulties in principle, they intensify the previously established ones. To appropriate information for use as a basis for further research is much more difficult than to appropriate it for use in producing commodities; and the value of information for use in developing further information is much more conjectural than the value of its use in production and therefore much more likely to be underestimated. Consequently, if a price is charged for the information, the demand is even more likely to be suboptimal.

Thus basic research, the output of which is only used as an informational input into other inventive activities, is especially unlikely to be rewarded. In fact, it is likely to be of commercial value to the firm undertaking it only if other firms are prevented from using the information obtained. But such restriction on the transmittal of information will reduce the efficiency of inventive activity in general and will therefore reduce its quantity also. We may put the matter in terms of sequential decision making. The a priori probability distribution of the true state of nature is relatively flat to begin with. On the other hand, the successive a posteriori distributions after more and more studies have been conducted are more and more sharply peaked or concentrated in a more limited range, and we therefore have better and better information for deciding what the next step in research shall be. This implies that, at the beginning, the preferences among alternative possible lines of investigation are much less sharply defined than they are apt to be later on and suggests, at least, the importance of having a wide variety of studies to begin with, the less promising being gradually eliminated as information is accumulated.[6] At each stage the decisions about the next step should be based on all available information. This would require an unrestricted flow of information among different projects which is incompatible with the complete decentralization of an ideal free enterprise system. When the production of

---

[6] The importance of parallel research developments in the case of uncertainty has been especially stressed by Burton H. Klein; see his, "A Radical Proposal for R. and D.," *Fortune*, May 1958, p. 112 ff.; and Klein and W. H. Meckling, "Application of Operations Research to Development Decisions," *Operations Research*, 1958, pp. 352–363.

information is important, the classic economic case in which the price system replaces the detailed spread of information is no longer completely applicable.

To sum up, we expect a free enterprise economy to underinvest in invention and research (as compared with an ideal) because it is risky, because the product can be appropriated only to a limited extent, and because of increasing returns in use. This underinvestment will be greater for more basic research. Further, to the extent that a firm succeeds in engrossing the economic value of its inventive activity, there will be an underutilization of that information as compared with an ideal allocation.

COMPETITION, MONOPOLY, AND THE INCENTIVE TO INNOVATE

It may be useful to remark that an incentive to invent can exist even under perfect competition in the product markets though not, of course, in the "market" for the information contained in the invention. This is especially clear in the case of a cost reducing invention. Provided only that suitable royalty payments can be demanded, an inventor can profit without disturbing the competitive nature of the industry. The situation for a new product invention is not very different; by charging a suitable royalty to a competitive industry, the inventor can receive a return equal to the monopoly profits.

I will examine here the incentives to invent for monopolistic and competitive markets, that is, I will compare the potential profits from an invention with the costs. The difficulty of appropriating the information will be ignored; the remaining problem is that of indivisibility in use, an inherent property of information. A competitive situation here will mean one in which the industry produces under competitive conditions, while the inventor can set an arbitrary royalty for the use of his invention. In the monopolistic situation, it will be assumed that only the monopoly itself can invent. Thus a monopoly is understood here to mean barriers to entry; a situation of temporary monopoly, due perhaps to a previous innovation, which does not prevent the entrance of new firms with innovations of their own, is to be regarded as more nearly competitive than monopolistic for the purpose of this analysis. It will be argued that the incentive to invent is less under monopolistic than under competitive conditions but even in the latter case it will be less than is socially desirable.

We will assume constant costs both before and after the invention, the unit costs being c before the invention and $c' < c$ afterward. The competitive price before invention will therefore be c. Let the corresponding demand be x_c. If r is the level of unit royalties, the competitive price after the invention will be $c' + r$, but this cannot of course be higher than c, since firms are always free to produce with the old methods.

It is assumed that both the demand and the marginal revenue curves are decreasing. Let $R(x)$ be the marginal revenue curve. Then the monopoly output before invention, x_m, would be defined by the equation,

$$R(x_m) = c.$$

Similarly, the monopoly output after invention is defined by,

$$R(x'_m) = c'.$$

Let the monopoly prices corresponding to outputs x_m and x'_m, respectively, be p_m and p'_m. Finally, let P and P' be the monopolist's profits before and after invention, respectively.

What is the optimal royalty level for the inventor in the competitive case? Let us suppose that he calculates p'_m, the optimal monopoly price which would obtain in the postinvention situation. If the cost reduction is sufficiently drastic that $p'_m < c$, then his most profitable policy is to set r so that the competitive price is p'_m, i.e. let,

$$r = p'_m - c'.$$

In this case, the inventor's royalties are equal to the profits a monopolist would make under the same conditions, i.e. his incentive to invent will be P'.

Suppose, however, it turns out that $p'_m > c$. Since the sales price cannot exceed c, the inventor will set his royalties at,

$$r = c - c'.$$

The competitive price will then be c, and the sales will remain at x_c. The inventor's incentive will then be, $x_c(c - c')$.

The monopolist's incentive, on the other hand, is clearly $P' - P$. In the first of the two cases cited, the monopolist's incentive is obviously less than the inventor's incentive under competition, which is P', not $P' - P$. The preinvention monopoly power acts as a strong disincentive to further innovation.

The analysis is slightly more complicated in the second case. The monopolist's incentive, $P' - P$, is the change in revenue less the change in total cost of production, i.e.,

$$P' - P = \int_{x_m}^{x'_m} R(x)\,dx - c'x'_m + cx_m.$$

Since the marginal revenue $R(x)$ is diminishing, it must always be less than $R(x_m) = c$ as x increases from x_m to x'_m, so that,

$$\int_{x_m}^{x'_m} R(x)\,dx < c(x'_m - x_m),$$

and,

$$P' - P < c(x'_m - x_m) - c'x'_m + cx_m = (c - c')x'_m.$$

In the case being considered, the postinvention monopoly price, p'_m, is greater than c. Hence, with a declining demand curve, $x'_m < x_c$. The above inequality shows that the monopolist's incentive is always less than the cost reduction on the postinvention monopoly output, which in this case is, in turn, less than the competitive output (both before and after invention). Since the inventor's incentive under competition is the cost reduction on the competitive output, it will again always exceed the monopolist's incentive.

It can be shown that, if we consider differing values of c', the difference between the two incentives increases as c' decreases, reaching its maximum of P (preinvention monopoly profits) for c' sufficiently large for the first case to hold. The ratio of the incentive under competition to that under monopoly, on the other hand, though always greater than 1, decreases steadily with c'. For c' very close to c (i.e., very minor inventions), the ratio of the two incentives is approximately x_c/x_m, i.e., the ratio of monopoly to competitive output.[7]

The only ground for arguing that monopoly may create superior incentives to invent is that appropriability may be greater under monopoly than under competition. Whatever differences may exist in this direction must, of course, still be offset against the monopolist's disincentive created by his preinvention monopoly profits.

The incentive to invent in competitive circumstances may also be compared with the social benefit. It is necessary to distinguish between the realized social benefit and the potential social benefit, the latter being the benefit which would accrue under ideal conditions, which, in this case, means the sale of the product at postinvention cost, c'. Clearly, the potential social benefit always exceeds the realized social benefit. I will show that the realized social benefit, in turn, always equals or exceeds the competitive incentive to invent and, a fortiori, the monopolist's incentive.

Consider again the two cases discussed above. If the invention is sufficiently cost reducing so that $p'_m < c$, then there is a consumers' benefit, due to the lowering of price, which has not been appropriated by the inventor. If not, then the price is unchanged, so that the consumers' position is unchanged, and all benefits do go to the inventor. Since by assumption all the producers are making zero profits both before and after the invention, we see that the inventor obtains the entire realized social benefit of moderately cost reducing inventions but not

[7] To sketch the proof of these statements quickly, note that, as c' varies, P is a constant. Hence, from the formula for $P' - P$, we see that,

$$d(P' - P)/dc' = dP'/dc' = R(x'_m)(dx'_m/dc') - c'(dx'_m/dc') - x'_m = -x'_m,$$

since $R(x'_m) = c'$. Let $F(c')$ be the difference between the incentives to invent under competitive and under monopolistic conditions. In the case where $p'_m < c$, this difference is the constant P. Otherwise,

$$F(c') = x_c(c - c') - (P' - P),$$

so that

$$dF/dc' = x'_m - x_c.$$

For the case considered, we must have $x'_m < x_c$, as seen in the text. Hence, $dF/dc' \leq 0$, so that $F(c')$ increases as c' decreases.

Let $G(c')$ be the ratio of the incentive under competition to that under monopoly. If $p'_m < c$, then,

$$G(c') = P'/(P' - P),$$

which clearly decreases as c' decreases. For $p'_m > c$, we have,

$$G(c') = x_c(c - c')/(P' - P).$$

Then,

$$dG/dc' = [-(P' - P)x_c + x_c(c - c')x'_m]/(P' - P)^2.$$

Because of the upper bound for $P' - P$ established in the text, the numerator must be positive; the ratio decreases as c' decreases.

Finally, if we consider c' very close to c, $G(c')$ will be approximately equal to the ratio of the derivatives of the numerator and denominator (L'Hopital's rule), which is, x_c/x'_m, and which approaches x_c/x_m as c' approaches c.

of more radical inventions. Tentatively, this suggests a bias against major inventions, in the sense that an invention, part of whose cost could be paid for by lump-sum payments by consumers without making them worse off than before, may not be profitable at the maximum royalty payments that can be extracted by the inventor.

ALTERNATIVE FORMS OF ECONOMIC ORGANIZATION IN INVENTION

The previous discussion leads to the conclusion that for optimal allocation to invention it would be necessary for the government or some other agency not governed by profit-and-loss criteria to finance research and invention. In fact, of course, this has always happened to a certain extent. The bulk of basic research has been carried on outside the industrial system, in universities, in the government, and by private individuals. One must recognize here the importance of nonpecuniary incentives, both on the part of the investigators and on the part of the private individuals and governments that have supported research organizations and universities. In the latter, the complementarity between teaching and research is, from the point of view of the economy, something of a lucky accident. Research in some more applied fields, such as agriculture, medicine, and aeronautics, has consistently been regarded as an appropriate subject for government participation, and its role has been of great importance.

If the government and other nonprofit institutions are to compensate for the underallocation of resources to invention by private enterprise, two problems arise: how shall the amount of resources devoted to invention be determined, and how shall efficiency in their use by encouraged? These problems arise whenever the government finds it necessary to engage in economic activities because indivisibilities prevent the private economy from performing adequately (highways, bridges, reclamation projects, for example), but the determination of the relative magnitudes is even more difficult here. Formally, of course, resources should be devoted to invention until the expected marginal social benefit there equals the marginal social benefit in alternative uses, but in view of the presence of uncertainty, such calculations are even more difficult and tenuous than those for public works. Probably all that could be hoped for is the estimation of future rates of return from those in the past, with investment in invention being increased or decreased accordingly as some average rate of return over the past exceeded or fell short of the general rate of return. The difficulties of even ex post calculation of rates of return are formidable though possibly not insuperable.[8]

The problem of efficiency in the use of funds devoted to research is one that has been faced internally by firms in dealing with their own research departments. The rapid growth of military research and development has led to a large-scale development of contractual relations between producers and a buyer of invention and research. The problems encountered in assuring efficiency here are the same as those that would be met if the government were to enter upon

[8] For an encouraging study of this type, see Z. Griliches, "Research Costs and Social Returns: Hybrid Corn and Related Innovations," *Journal of Political Economy*, 1958, pp. 419–431.

the financing of invention and research in civilian fields. The form of economic relation is very different from that in the usual markets. Payment is independent of product; it is governed by costs, though the net reward (the fixed fee) is independent of both. This arrangement seems to fly in the face of the principles for encouraging efficiency, and doubtless it does lead to abuses, but closer examination shows both mitigating factors and some explanation of its inevitability. In the first place, the awarding of new contracts will depend in part on past performance, so that incentives for efficiency are not completely lacking. In the second place, the relation between the two parties to the contract is something closer than a purely market relation. It is more like the sale of professional services, where the seller contracts to supply not so much a specific result as his best judgment. (The demand for such services also arises from uncertainty and the value of information.) In the third place, payment by results would involve great risks for the inventor, risks against which, as we have seen, he could hedge only in part.

There is clear need for further study of alternative methods of compensation. For example, some part of the contractual payment might depend on the degree of success in invention. But a more serious problem is the decision as to which contracts to let. One would need to examine the motivation underlying government decision making in this area. Hitch has argued that there are biases in governmental allocation, particularly against risky invention processes, and an excessive centralization, though the latter could be remedied by better policies.[9]

One can go further. There is really no need for the firm to be the fundamental unit of organization in invention; there is plenty of reason to suppose that individual talents count for a good deal more than the firm as an organization. If provision is made for the rental of necessary equipment, a much wider variety of research contracts with individuals as well as firms and with varying modes of payment, including incentives, could be arranged. Still other forms of organization, such as research institutes financed by industries, the government, and private philanthropy, could be made to play an even livelier role than they now do.

[9] *Op. cit.*